AMERICA'S SECRET WAR AGAINST BOLSHEVISM

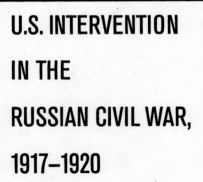

U.S. INTERVENTION

IN THE

RUSSIAN CIVIL WAR,

1917–1920

THE UNIVERSITY OF NORTH CAROLINA PRESS • CHAPEL HILL & LONDON

AMERICA'S SECRET WAR AGAINST BOLSHEVISM

DAVID S. FOGLESONG

The paper in this book meets the guidelines for permanence and
durability of the Committee on Production Guidelines for Book
Longevity of the Council on Library Resources.

Publication of this book has been supported by generous grants from the
L. J. Skaggs and Mary C. Skaggs Foundation and the Rutgers University
Research Council.

Library of Congress Cataloging-in-Publication Data

Foglesong, David S.

America's secret war against Bolshevism: U.S. intervention

in the Russian Civil War, 1917–1920/David S. Foglesong.

p. cm.

Includes bibliographical references (p.) and index.

ISBN 0-8078-2228-0 (cloth: alk. paper)

1. Soviet Union—History—Allied intervention, 1918–1920.

2. United States—Foreign relations—1913–1921. I. Title.

DK265.42.U5F64   1995

947.084′1—dc20   94-49528

CIP

99 98 97 96 95   5 4 3 2 1

THIS BOOK WAS DIGITALLY MANUFACTURED.

For RoseMary,

who ran the marathon with me

CONTENTS

A section of illustrations follows page 129.

ACKNOWLEDGMENTS

In the more than ten years that I worked on this book, many people helped me to complete the research, improve the writing, overcome obstacles, and carry through to the finish. I am glad to have an opportunity to give at least partial recognition to their invaluable assistance.

This project first took shape as a dissertation at the University of California, Berkeley. Diane Shaver Clemens offered constant moral support while guiding the dissertation to completion. Anthony Adamthwaite, Todd Foglesong, Linda Killen, Alan Lawrence, Victor Silverman, and Reggie Zelnik gave me the benefit of close readings and constructive criticism of dissertation chapters.

Several people generously assisted my research by providing access to materials in private collections. David Ray Thomson kindly gave me copies of letters his father, Consul Alfred Ray Thomson, wrote from Russia. Walt and Kay Hays graciously allowed me to examine their collection of the sermons of Rev. Walter G. Hays. I am especially grateful to Mary Wright Lampson, who sent me the diary her father, Joshua Butler Wright, kept as counselor of the American embassy in Petrograd in 1917, and who provided valuable insights about his views in numerous conversations and letters.

On research trips across the United States and to Russia I benefited from the assistance of many colleagues and archivists. In Moscow, Viktor Mal'kov, Genrikh Ioffe, Aleksandr Ushakov, and Aleksandr Volkov gave me helpful advice and generous aid with work in Russian archives. Of the many American archivists who facilitated my research, I am particularly indebted to Carol Leadenham of the Hoover Institution Archives, Martha Clevenger of the Missouri Historical Society, and Ben Primer and Nanci Young at the Seeley G. Mudd Manuscript Library in Princeton.

As I revised and expanded the manuscript, many friends and colleagues offered words of encouragement and provided helpful critiques of parts of the work in progress, including Michael Adas, Richard Debo, Carole Fink, Ziva Galili, Alice Kessler-Harris, John Long, Viktor Mal'kov, Norman Markowitz, Gail Owen, Ray Rocca, Norman Saul, Susan Schrepfer, and Gregg Wolper. I especially want to thank those who read the entire work and offered detailed suggestions for improvement: Lloyd Gardner, Robert Johnson, Warren Kimball, Dee Garrison, and William O'Neill. My editor, Lewis Bateman, showed amazing patience with a first-time author and gave me much needed advice about tightening the prose. My copyeditor, Eric Schramm, went through the manuscript with great care and corrected numerous lapses.

As scholarly specialists will quickly recognize, I have been deeply influenced by several previous studies of Wilsonian policy toward Russia, particularly the work of William Appleman Williams, N. Gordon Levin Jr., and Lloyd C. Gardner. Perhaps less obvious is my enormous debt to Arthur S. Link for his editing of *The Papers of Woodrow Wilson.* Without his indefatigable labor on that series, my own work would have been impossible.

For financial support I am grateful to the MacArthur Interdisciplinary Group for International Security Studies at Berkeley; the Berkeley-Stanford Program in Soviet Studies; the Mellon Foundation; the Kennan Institute for Advanced Russian Studies; the Department of History at the University of California, Berkeley; and the Department of History at Rutgers University.

My parents, Robert and Jane Foglesong, stood loyally behind me through a very long education. They set high standards and provided emotional and financial support to help me try to live up to them.

Above all I am grateful to my wife, RoseMary. She supported me through graduate school, 'helped with the research, gave encouragement about the writing, endured my absences, and tolerated my preoccupation. Her hard work, sacrifice, love, and devotion sustained me to the end.

NOTE ON DATES AND RUSSIAN TRANSLITERATION

Since this study focuses more on American policy than on events in Russia, all dates are given according to the Gregorian (New Style) calendar, although the Julian (Old Style) calendar was in use in Russia until February 1918. Hence, I refer to the revolutions of March and November, rather than February and October, 1917.

With regard to transliterations, exceptions have been made from the Library of Congress system where a different transliteration of a name has become conventional (Trotsky, rather than Trotskii), or where an individual had a consistent preference (Bakhmeteff, not Bakhmetev).

AMERICA'S SECRET WAR AGAINST BOLSHEVISM

INTRODUCTION

"Do you not know," Woodrow Wilson asked the citizens of Des Moines in September 1919, "that the world is all now one single whispering gallery?" The extension of the lines of commerce and the development of new methods of communication had drawn the peoples of the world close together in a global theater, thereby increasing the danger of contagion. "All the impulses of mankind," Wilson explained, "are thrown out upon the air and reach to the ends of the earth; quietly upon steamships, silently under the cover of the Postal Service, with the tongue of the wireless and the tongue of the telegraph, all the suggestions of disorder are spread through the world." Even America, despite its oceans of insulation, was vulnerable to the "propaganda of disorder and discontent and dissolution throughout the world." [1]

The global currents of trade and thought that made Bolshevism and other manifestations of "disorder" threats to American prosperity and tranquillity simultaneously inhibited American leaders' ability to intervene to preserve order. "The opinion of the world is everywhere wide awake," Wilson observed in December 1917. "No representative of any self-governed nation will dare disregard it." In modern conditions, particularly in a total war for which governments needed the cooperation of whole societies, even authoritarian regimes had to be attuned to the "very simple and unsophisticated standards of right and wrong" of the "plain people." This was especially true in the United States. As long as Americans believed that U.S. actions were motivated by "high principle," they would support overseas action with "zeal and enthusiasm." However, if they suspected U.S. policy served selfish ambitions or unprincipled objectives, the government would soon lose their support. [2]

Wilson had long been acutely conscious of the moral force of public opinion. In his 1912 campaign for the presidency, Wilson appealed to the muckraking spirit of the time, calling for a purifying publicity to cleanse government of the corruption that "thrives in secret places." "We are never so proper in our conduct," he commented, "as when everybody can look and see exactly what we are doing." In the following years Wilson extended the idea of moralizing publicity from domestic politics to foreign affairs. By 1916 he embraced a progressive vision of "a new and more wholesome diplomacy" that centered on repudiation of "secret counsels" and respect for the sovereign rights of all peoples. That peace position, combined with sweeping reform legislation, earned him crucial support from Progressives and Socialists for his reelection. As he led the United

States into the world war and witnessed the way Russian appeals for peace without annexations or indemnities echoed around the world in 1917, Wilson grew ever more keenly aware of the need to publicize the idealistic principles for which America was fighting. Wilson's espousal of a "new diplomacy" culminated in his Fourteen Points speech of January 1918. Responding to the Bolsheviks' peace proposals and their publication of the Allies' secret treaties, Wilson declared that "the day of conquest and aggrandizement is gone by," proclaimed that the world had to be made safe for peace-loving nations to determine their own institutions, and announced that in the future diplomacy should "proceed always frankly and in the public view."[3]

However, Wilson's championing of open diplomacy subject to popular control was only one side of his adaptation to statesmanship in the global "whispering gallery." Long before he became president, Wilson believed that the great issues of politics, especially the questions of peace and war, involved elements that would be visible only to the few— "the selected leaders of public opinion." Such leaders, he felt, should use "masterful qualities of mind or will" to get the assent of the people to their purposes. Wilson's deep conviction that enlightened statesmen would judge more wisely than the broad masses of the people led him to consider incomplete candor and perhaps even deliberate deception justified. According to his wily confidant, Colonel Edward House, shortly before Wilson entered the White House in 1913, he "said he thought lying was justified in some instances, particularly where it involved the honor of a woman," and also "where it related to matters of public policy." When House suggested that maintaining a tight-lipped silence was preferable to active dishonesty, Wilson said he would follow that advice in the future.[4]

House's recommendation of secrecy accorded with Wilson's disposition. In his long professorial career, Wilson had "loved quiet ways, and even seclusion," his physician recalled, and he "carried into public life this aversion to publicity." Many of Wilson's presidential advisors consequently found that he was "secretive of nature."[5] That temperamental inclination was reinforced by Wilson's perception that U.S. interests sometimes required actions abroad that the American people might not approve. In those cases, preserving public faith in the essential idealism of Wilsonian foreign policy required a high level of secrecy, tightly centralized presidential control, and ambiguous pronouncements.

The Wilsonian penchant for secrecy was evident from his first years in office, but it became especially pronounced in his second term. When Russian socialists challenged the expansionist war aims of the great powers and vied with Wilson for leadership of world opinion, he grew not only more sensitive to popular attitudes but also almost obsessively secretive and "autocratic."[6] Two months after the Bolsheviks took power, in December 1917, one assistant secretary of state complained, "Everything great and small must be referred to the President, who receives no one, listens to no one, seems to take no one's advice."[7] In July 1918, the liberal weekly the *Nation*, which had hailed Wilson's idealism earlier, commented that his evasiveness, particularly in his decision making about Russia, did not square with his "declarations against secret diplomacy." At the Paris Peace Conference in 1919, his liaison to the press, Ray Stannard Baker, was disturbed to discover that Wilson depended "on publicity for his support & his power — & yet dreads publicity." As Baker sensed, Wilson's secretiveness was not simply a product of his temperament but also a response to the challenge of stabilizing a world shaken by revolutionary turmoil.[8]

Wilsonian policies, then, cannot be understood simply or primarily in terms of Wilson's idealistic principles.[9] To comprehend the Wilsonian response to disorder, discontent, and dissolution, one must begin by recognizing the sharp discordance between Wilson's public addresses and his administration's secretive actions.

As they sought to lead the world from the violent competition of states and the chaos of revolution toward an orderly and peaceful community of nations, pressed from one side by Allied and Republican proponents of traditional power politics and from the other side by advocates of a radical democratization of international relations, Wilson and his advisors found it necessary to employ secretive and indirect methods of intervention. The era of total war and unprecedented public involvement in foreign relations brought not only the withering of the old aristocratic statecraft but also the seedtime for modern methods of covert action. As the chief of the German secret service observed, the Great War "first let loose on the world" the "modern Intelligence Service," whose covert activities subsequently fostered a condition of "'War in Peace.'" The old diplomacy was dying. Rising in its place, in America as well as in Europe, was not simply the "new diplomacy" but also the methods of "secret war."[10]

Wilson first began to develop his distinctive style of intervention as he faced a civil war in Mexico that disrupted that country's political and economic life, endangered American property and lives, and divided Americans between defenders of order and partisans of revolution. Wilson could and did send U.S. troops to intervene overtly and directly in Haiti and the Dominican Republic when those countries were afflicted by what he regarded as personal revolutions — seizures of power by selfish individuals. However, from early in his presidency Wilson repeatedly declared that the United States had no right to intervene against profound social revolutions that were expressions of deep and legitimate grievances by suffering peoples. Although Wilson ordered U.S. military forces to intervene at Veracruz in the spring of 1914 and dispatched the Pershing expedition much deeper into Mexico in 1916, his proclamation of the principle of self-determination and his concern about public opinion did constrain his policy toward Mexico. Those considerations reinforced his aversion to direct, aggressive intervention and increased his reliance upon less forceful, more secretive methods. Thus, while Wilson repeatedly declared his opposition to "intervention," his administration used diplomatic pressure, economic sanctions, and arms embargoes to oppose undesirable leaders and facilitated arms shipments to friendly "strong men" who promised to respect American interests and establish stable self-government.

The second major test of Wilson's approach to the intertwined problems of democracy, revolution, and intervention emerged when Bolsheviks overthrew the liberal Provisional Government of Russia in November 1917, threatened the Allied war effort by calling for immediate peace negotiations, and urged the oppressed peoples of the world to revolt against their rulers. Those challenges were compounded when the Bolsheviks dispersed the democratically elected Constituent Assembly, repudiated foreign loans, nationalized foreign assets, and signed a peace treaty that conceded enormous material and territorial gains to Imperial Germany. Soviet rule in Russia thus posed perplexing problems for American leaders: how to reorganize military resistance to the Central Powers in a country exhausted by war, how to promote self-determination without further splintering a fragmented empire, how to preserve Russian territorial integrity against both German and Japanese depredation, how to secure an "open door" for American trade and investment between the Baltic and the Pacific, and how to safeguard international stability in the face of Russian revolutionary propaganda.

The question of how Wilson and his advisors responded to these epic challenges has sparked heated controversy and spurred the creation of a rich historical literature. Since Wilson's speeches sometimes seemed to express friendship for Soviet Russia, many historians have argued that, like Colonel House, Wilson was sympathetic to or at least tolerant of Bolshevism,[11] while other scholars have concluded that Wilson's views were nearly identical to those of his vehemently anti-Bolshevik secretary of state, Robert Lansing.[12] The relationships between the three men and their attitudes toward revolutionary Russia were more complicated than the divergent scholarly approaches have recognized. Wilson greatly valued House's intimate friendship and political advice, particularly on questions of tactics. In contrast, he held Lansing at arm's length and disparaged his "wooden mind."[13] However, Wilson was, like Lansing, an orthodox Presbyterian, and their common religious and cultural heritage helped to shape similar responses to Bolshevism. Although Wilson's early attitudes toward Soviet Russia were more supple than Lansing's, he became increasingly stern and inflexible as the Bolsheviks defied predictions of their imminent demise and sought to incite revolution throughout the world. For both men, Bolshevism represented not only a threat to America's interest in a stable global order, but also a menace to American domestic unity and a challenge to their "Puritan" values. Men of their Calvinist temperament could not be content to coexist with an evil force obstructing the reformation of the world. Although Wilson declined Lansing's proposals for frank public condemnations of the Soviet regime that would have undercut the administration's support on the Left, he repeatedly agreed with his secretary of state on the need to assist opponents of the Bolshevik government.

From the Bolshevik Revolution to the end of the Russian Civil War, the United States sought to encourage and support anti-Bolshevik movements in a variety of secretive and semi-secret ways. Constrained by a declared commitment to the principle of self-determination and hemmed in by idealistic and later isolationist popular sentiments, Wilson and his advisors pursued methods of assisting anti-Bolshevik forces that evaded public scrutiny and avoided the need for congressional appropriations.

While refusing to establish diplomatic relations with Soviet Russia, the Wilson administration signaled its hope for a restoration of democracy in Russia by continuing to recognize the ambassador of the defunct Provisional Government as the legitimate representative of the Russian people. With Wilson's approval, State Department and Treasury officials worked to transmit covert financial aid through the British and French governments to anti-Bolshevik "strong men" in southern Russia. Under American supervision, the Russian embassy in Washington secretly used United States funds to send many shipments of war supplies to anti-Bolshevik armies, particularly in Siberia. Inside Soviet Russia, American diplomats and military attachés organized intelligence-gathering networks that maintained clandestine contact with foes of the Soviet regime, passed information to Allied and anti-Bolshevik forces, and conducted sabotage to obstruct Red Army operations. Although Wilson was reluctant to interfere openly and directly in Russia, in the summer of 1918 he finally sanctioned limited military expeditions to northern Russia and Siberia, which he declared would be helping Russians to restore self-government rather than intervening in their internal affairs. Through the American Relief Administration and the Red Cross, the United States provided food, clothing, and other "humanitarian" assistance in 1919 to buttress anti-Bolshevik governments in the Baltic region and to support the Russian Northwestern Army's campaign to capture Petrograd. Even after the last anti-Bolshevik armies were defeated in 1920, the United States maintained a moral embargo on trade with Soviet Russia that Wilson and his advisors hoped would hasten the inevitable demise of the Bolshevik regime.

Although Wilson and his aides insisted that the United States was not at war with Russia, they in fact fought a long undeclared war against Bolshevism. Since the administration declined to be candid with Congress and the American people about the support for anti-Bolshevik forces or the purposes of the military expeditions, it faced tight constraints on its ability to aid White armies and encountered mounting pressure to bring U.S. troops home. At some moments in 1918 and 1919 the limited and secretive support for opponents of the Bolsheviks seemed like it might be sufficient to help them topple the Soviet government. Ultimately, however, the Wilsonian resort to the methods of secret war failed to dislodge the Bolshevik regime, alienated idealistic liberals and socialists who had supported the Wilson administration, antagonized Bolsheviks, and embittered anti-Bolsheviks who resented meddling and inadequate assistance by irresolute Americans.

While most Americans had little knowledge of forms of U.S. intervention in Russia beyond the military expeditions to Archangel and Vladivostok, Soviet leaders had wider views of America's secret war against Bolshevism. The Soviet government received information from sympathizers in Western countries, captured agents of U.S. intelligence services in Russia, and acquired the correspondence of anti-Bolshevik diplomats. Hence, they knew that while "America did not officially take part in armed attacks against Russia . . . indirectly America all the time assisted White Guard attacks" with arms and other military supplies.[14] In one of the fuller Soviet indictments of American intervention, Ludwig Martens, the unrecognized Soviet representative in New York, declared that the U.S. government "has invaded the territory of Russia with its armed forces and has waged war upon the Russian people; its agents have engaged in plots and intrigues upon Russian soil against the Russian Soviet Government; it has maintained . . . a blockade which has resulted in great suffering to the Russian people; [and] it has given material encouragement and assistance to various counter-revolutionary bands in insurrection against the Russian Government."[15]

Despite their knowledge of covert as well as semi-overt forms of American intervention, Soviet leaders persistently differentiated the United States from other capitalist countries. Believing that American democracy and free enterprise made the United States the most likely place to break through the wall of foreign hostility, Soviet officials appealed to the liberal ideals of U.S. leaders, encouraged Americans to press for diplomatic relations between the two countries, restrained the punishment of Americans accused of espionage, tried to stimulate American protests against intervention, offered to accept responsibility for Russian debts, and dangled commercial privileges and investment opportunities in front of American manufacturers and financiers. Some of those tactics seemed at times to be working. However, Wilson's fleeting expression of interest in negotiations with Soviet leaders in early 1919 did not lead to the rapprochement they sought. Ultimately, Soviet officials had to reckon with a hardening of Wilson administration opposition into a grim determination to contain the menace of Bolshevism while waiting for its extinction.

During the long Cold War struggle, Soviet and American leaders often talked past one another when they referred to the early years of United States–Soviet relations. In September 1959, when Soviet Premier Nikita Khrushchev visited Hollywood, he declared that America's "armed intervention in Russia was the most unpleasant thing that ever occurred in the relations between our two countries . . . ; our troops have never set foot on American soil, while your troops have set foot on Soviet soil." [16] In contrast to Khrushchev, when President Richard Nixon flew to Moscow in May 1972, he proclaimed that there was no need for Americans and Soviets to be enemies, especially because they had "never fought one another in war" — a statement *Pravda* omitted when it printed Nixon's speech. [17] Twelve years later, after a new round of American-Soviet confrontation, Ronald Reagan seemed to borrow a page from Nixon, announcing "to the people of the Soviet Union" that "it's true that our governments have had serious differences. But our sons and daughters have never fought each other in war. And if we Americans have our way, they never will." [18] Reagan's perspective was not unusual. Only 14 percent of Americans surveyed in a 1985 *New York Times* poll "were aware that in 1918, the United States landed troops in northern and eastern Russia." [19]

Historians were not untouched by the political and ideological contest. During the Cold War, Soviet and American scholars waged a polemical war that revolved around blame for the origins of United States–Soviet antagonism. While Soviet writers commonly portrayed the United States as an eager participant in an imperialist crusade against Bolshevism, American historians often sought to refute charges that the United States tried to overthrow the Soviet regime. [20]

The ending of the Soviet-American rivalry has created opportunities for less combative scholarship and more balanced interpretations. To move beyond the polarized positions of the past it is vital to recognize that beside conventional diplomacy and military action there was another dimension of subversion and political warfare from the beginning of Soviet-American relations. While during the Cold War the historical debate on American intervention in Russia focused almost exclusively on the military expeditions to northern Russia and Siberia, it is crucial to develop a broader view of American policy by including the more secretive forms of American support for anti-Bolshevik movements. [21] Redefining "intervention" to embrace a wider scope of activity allows one to see the military expeditions not as peculiar departures from a policy of nonintervention but as two of the many limited and indirect methods by which the U.S. government attempted to influence the outcome of the Russian Civil War. The recent, partial opening of Russian archives to foreign historians has helped to reveal what Soviet leaders knew about the covert aid to anti-Bolshevik groups and how they reacted to American intelligence operations. It has also helped to show how Soviet officials struggled to end American intervention in Russia and establish diplomatic relations with Washington, even as they dispatched secret couriers with funds to support pro-Bolshevik organizations in the United States. As a result, it is now possible to see how from early on both Soviet Russia and the United States were waging "war in peace."

In the aftermath of the Cold War it is also essential to overcome the false dichotomies that have marked debates about the motivation and intensity of American intervention in Russia. While Soviet writers generally stressed capitalist fears that the Russian revolutionary example would lead to world revolution and Western authors often emphasized Allied pressure on Wilson for action to re-create an eastern front against Germany, a more inclusive view is needed. U.S. policy was influenced by a complex mix of factors, including strategic considerations, coalition politics, economic interests, and ideological commitments. These factors were often intertwined. Thus, American officials hoped that supporting anti-Bolshevik forces would obstruct German exploitation of Russian resources while at the same time creating a "nucleus" for the regeneration of a non-Bolshevik Russia. Promoting a strong, united, democratic Russia, U.S. officials believed, would simultaneously constrain future German and Japanese expansionism, enhance American access to Russian markets, and advance Wilson's hopes for reforming and stabilizing the international system.

While Soviet accounts typically depicted a determined, coordinated campaign to crush the Bolshevik regime and Western studies often presented Wilson's decisions to intervene as reluctant concessions to Allied badgering, a broader view of American intervention in Russia shows that it was more hesitant and less single-minded than Soviet writers usually allowed but at the same time more diverse and persistent than most American historians recognized. Although Wilson wavered and procrastinated about overt military intervention, he moved more quickly to intervene in secretive ways and expressed more consistent support for diplomatic and economic resistance to Bolshevism.

Wilson's uncertainty and his exclusion of advisors from full roles in policymaking led some to doubt whether there was a Russian policy.[22] The contradictions that struck many observers as signs of hypocrisy were often products of self-deception, confusion, and distraction. Yet Wilson's decisions were not completely incoherent. The president's inability to preserve complete control over all aspects of American policy meant that some forms of intervention were unauthorized initiatives by subordinates. Yet since Wilson made many of the key decisions in almost hermetic seclusion, America's secret war against Bolshevism cannot be explained as the sabotage of Wilsonian principles by reactionary underlings. Although the Wilsonian ship of state wobbled, drifted, and adjusted its sails to the political winds, it nonetheless held to an anti-Bolshevik course. While Wilson vacillated between doubts about the illiterate Russian masses' readiness for sober self-government and worries that supporting Russian "strong men" would lead to a restoration of the reactionary old order, he persistently tacked toward the distant shore of a democratic Russia. Although Wilson occasionally showed some interest in unofficial contacts with Soviet leaders, nothing they said persuaded him to accommodate Bolshevism, abandon anti-Bolshevik forces, or give up his faith that Russia was "democratic at heart." While trying to avoid actions that would blatantly contradict liberal democratic ideals, Wilson and other U.S. officials did everything they felt was practicable to accelerate the demise of Bolshevism and restore "ordered liberty" to the Russian people.

Although those efforts failed to achieve U.S. objectives in revolutionary Russia, Americans had pioneered secretive means of intervention, including propaganda, financing of counterrevolutionary forces, and covert action, which Wilson administration veterans would utilize during the later Cold War. The development of American covert methods in the era of demands for a "new diplomacy" would have lasting reverberations in American foreign policy.

At the height of the Cold War (to offer one illustration of a legacy discussed in chapter 5), veteran diplomat and intelligence agent Allen Dulles found that the global challenges to American leaders were much the same as those that Woodrow Wilson faced thirty years earlier. In a Woodrow Wilson Foundation broadcast on January 1, 1949, Dulles cited Wilson's warning at Des Moines in September 1919 about the spread of "the poison of disorder" in Europe, commenting that it "could just as well as have been said today." Wilson, Dulles recalled, had preached that Americans "could not have any narrow conception that the frontiers of our safety could be drawn on our Atlantic and Pacific seaboards," and he was pleased that Americans were coming to realize "that our frontiers are wherever free nations are standing against aggression." However, facing "a situation which is neither peace nor war," U.S. leadership required instruments beyond conventional diplomacy and military forces. On the same day as his Wilson Foundation broadcast, Dulles and two other consultants submitted their report to the National Security Council on how the Central Intelligence Agency should be reorganized for the Cold War struggle. Although Dulles did not mention the CIA in his Wilson Foundation broadcast, he had shown a special interest in enhancing the agency's capacity for covert intervention in the preceding year, and the necessity for covert action was implicit in his thinking about the Wilson legacy. "We need to put into our thinking and into our actions the essence of what Wilson taught us," the future CIA director declared. "We need to combine the practical measures he advocated with his high idealism."[23]

1

THE DEVELOPMENT OF A WILSONIAN STYLE OF INTERVENTION

My policy regarding Russia is very similar to my Mexican policy. I believe in letting them work out their own salvation, even though they wallow in anarchy for a while.
— Woodrow Wilson, October 1918

"I hold it as a fundamental principle," Woodrow Wilson declared in January 1915, "that every people has the right to determine its own form of government." Addressing a crowd in Indianapolis, Wilson insisted that it was none of his business and none of their business how the people of Mexico chose their leaders. "And, so far as my influence goes," Wilson vowed, "nobody shall interfere with them." [1]

No president has spoken more passionately and eloquently about the right of self-determination. Yet no president has intervened more often in foreign countries. Wilson directed the navy to seize Veracruz in 1914, ordered U.S. forces to occupy Haiti in 1915, commanded marines to pacify the Dominican Republic in 1916, sent soldiers deep into Mexico in the same year, and dispatched military expeditions to Vladivostok and

Archangel in 1918. Less blatantly, Wilson used diplomatic pressure, economic sanctions, arms embargoes, and arms shipments to influence political developments from Central America to Siberia and from the Caribbean to the Baltic.

In the face of those actions, how could Wilson believe that his policies were consistent with the principle of self-determination? Wilson's response to the tension between intervention and self-determination emerged gradually over several decades. While he expressed deep reservations in the 1890s about aggressive action in foreign lands, by the turn of the century he became convinced that America had a mission to promote orderly self-government around the world. If presidents took care to explain how intervention abroad was in harmony with American moral values and necessary to fulfill American ideals, he realized, it could unite rather than divide the country.

Wilson's approach evolved further in the first years of his presidency, when his perceptions of Mexican needs and American interests tempted him to intercede in insurgent Mexico. Encountering domestic and foreign criticism of both direct military invasion and inaction, Wilson and his advisors came to rely on covert action and limited, indirect methods that he insisted did not constitute "intervention." Thus, a distinctive Wilsonian style of intervention arose — one that embodied a combination of idealistic publicity, secrecy, and circumscribed operations.

Wilson neither drifted blindly into blunders in Mexico that converted him to strict nonintervention nor mastered the use of force with surgical precision. Rather, he developed a clear conception of methods beyond conventional diplomacy but short of outright war and repeatedly resorted to them, though they were often ineffective and sometimes escaped his control with damaging consequences. His policy regarding Russia would indeed be similar to his policy toward Mexico: American actions in Mexico between 1913 and 1917 marked the development of a persistent Wilsonian way of intervention that would be evident again in Russia from 1917 to 1920.[2]

Development of Wilson's Attitudes toward Intervention before 1913

During his career as a historian, Wilson repeatedly expressed repugnance at the use of military force for selfish purposes. In *Division and Reunion* (1893), Wilson condemned President Polk's unconstitutional "war of ruthless aggrandizement" against Mexico, which aggravated the sectional divisions that led to the Civil War. Eight years later, in *A History of the American People*, Wilson again chastised the "inexcusable aggression" upon a weak neighbor. While Wilson was not categorically opposed to war, when he became president "his shame as an American over the first Mexican war, and his resolution that there should never be another such predatory enterprise" fired fierce (though sporadic and not entirely successful) efforts to control the scope and objectives of military action.[3]

Like rapacious wars, intrigues by greedy private interests evoked scorn in Wilson. He frowned at the way American planters in the Hawaiian Islands conspired in 1893 to "get the government into their own hands," and he applauded when Democratic president Grover Cleveland, repudiating the "singular revolution," withdrew an annexation treaty from the Senate. In Wilson's view, America's foreign relations were then "generally simple enough to require little more" than a leader's "own natural apprehension of right and wrong to guide him."[4]

As America became more entangled in world affairs in the following years, Wilson learned that while his ideal statesman would answer above all to his own moral judgment, presidents also had to listen to the increasingly powerful voices of ordinary people. When Cleveland intervened in a boundary dispute between Britain and Venezuela in 1895, Wilson initially feared the American action would "bring about a deadly war between the two branches of the Eng[lish] race," and he maintained that Americans should not compromise their "dignity and self-respect" by assuming an anti-European "protectorate and dictatorship over South America" that would lead to "interference . . . in breach alike of international law and courtesy." Yet Wilson changed his mind after seeing the enthusiastic popular response to Cleveland's stand. Thrilled by the way Cleveland enlisted the support of Anglo-American public opinion, Wilson commended Cleveland's service as the "nearest friend" of Venezuela and lauded his "assertion of the Monroe doctrine in a new aspect, with a new dignity."[5]

Wilson received an even more striking lesson about how chivalrous action abroad could electrify Americans when the United States went to war in 1898, ostensibly to free Cubans from Spanish tyranny. Although Wilson suspected that politicians, sensational newspapers, and other "influences" were pursuing their own selfish interests, he became convinced of the righteousness of the Spanish-American War and rejoiced in the way it forged "a new sense of union," healing sectional divisions. "Intervention had come," he wrote at the turn of the century, "not for the material aggrandizement of the United States, but for the assertion of the right of the government to succor those who seemed hopelessly oppressed." While Wilson enumerated other objectives, including freeing American trade from the hindrances of the long Spanish-Cuban conflict, he stressed the saving grace of an altruistic spirit. "The consciences of the vast majority of us are void of offense," he declared in 1903. "We know that our pulses beat high in that war because we truly believed ourselves to be defending peoples who were trodden upon and degraded by corrupt and selfish governors."

Adopting the same attitude he would take toward Mexico and Russia later, Wilson vowed, "We kept faith with Cuba, and we mean, with God's help, to keep faith also with the people of the Philippine Islands, by serving them and ameliorating their condition, by showing them the way to liberty without plundering them or making them our tools for a selfish end."[6]

To Robert Lansing, then a Democratic activist in upstate New York, that kind of humanitarian rhetoric from the mouths of Republicans seemed "the twaddle of sentimentalists . . . only useful as an excuse to cover unjustifiable acts." Fifteen years before he soldiered in Wilson's campaign to make the world "safe for democracy," Lansing worried that Republican imperialists had set America on a course of global interventionism under the pretext of a "destiny to right the wrongs of the oppressed and succor the distressed." In a remarkable premonition of Wilsonian policy, Lansing asked: "The Republics of Central and South America are in a perennial state of revolution . . . ; why do we not commence some *humane* wars and give them *humane* government? If we adopt '*Only for the sake of Humanity*' as the United States motto, we shall find an endless field for our operations on this globe."[7]

While Lansing criticized Republicans for abandoning "the safe and conservative path" of nonentanglement laid out by George Washington, Wilson shared many of Theodore Roosevelt's expansionist views. Like Roosevelt, Wilson believed it was impossible for America to adhere to its traditional policy of "isolation," since the world was becoming "a single commercial community" and America's mission to open and transform Asia was part of "Providence." During TR's reign, Wilson began to call himself an "imperialist." With the closing of the western frontier Wilson believed that the United States had to be ready to use force to secure new frontiers overseas where businessmen could sell the surplus of manufactured goods. "The great East," he explained at the turn of the century, was "the market to which diplomacy, and if need be power, must make an open way."[8]

Yet Wilson was disquieted by the Rough Rider's high-handedness. Shortly after Roosevelt surreptitiously instigated a "revolution" in Panama in 1903, Wilson ventured an oblique criticism of those who "put a private interpretation upon international law," and worried that "if we keep on, like a big man who was bullying a little one," the United States would provoke a violent reaction from its "victim."[9] While Roosevelt was confident that the use of American might was invariably right and that by acting in their own interest Americans would be serving humanity, Wilson was more anxious to see American assertiveness redeemed by beneficent results and more sensitive to public perceptions. Facing rising ethical criticism of his foreign actions from Congress, the press, and an attentive public, even the stout TR began to doubt the fitness of democracies for administering empires. By the time Wilson entered the White House, growing tensions over foreign policy issues between labor and capital, pacifists and militarists, and isolationists and imperialists, combined with the cultural turmoil and moral upheaval of an increasingly urban, industrial, and multiethnic society, would make consideration of popular sentiment more important than ever.[10]

Major Influences on Wilsonian Policy toward Mexico

Busy introducing reforms as governor of New Jersey and launching a presidential campaign in 1911 and 1912, Wilson paid little attention to a revolution against the aged Mexican dictator Porfirio Díaz that was led by an American-educated liberal landowner, Francisco Madero. The principal impression Wilson recorded focused on the "disorders" in Mexico, a "wretched, unstable place." Colonel House had been giving Mexico more thought: in 1911 he envisioned a military occupation to "bring order out of chaos," break the Latin American "habit of revolutions without just cause," safeguard foreign property, and educate Mexicans "for the responsibilities of self-government." In January 1913, though, House suggested a much more modest plan, advising president-elect Wilson that Madero was an idealistic reformer who deserved America's sympathy and support. That idea became moot in February, shortly before Wilson entered the White House, when General Victoriano Huerta led a coup in which Madero was murdered.[11]

Worried that other Latin American adventurers would be emboldened to foment revolution with a Democratic administration in Washington, Wilson issued a statement that sternly warned against selfish seizures of power. He also used the occasion to outline policies that would protect American trade and investment abroad while pleasing the antimonopoly progressives who supported him at home. Seeking to distinguish his approach from the bruising "Big Stick" and degrading "Dollar Diplomacy" of his Republican predecessors, Wilson pledged "to cultivate the friendship and deserve the confidence" of Latin American republics. However, he stipulated that inter-American cooperation would be based on certain principles. Disapproving of "disorder, personal intrigue and defiance of constitutional rights," Wilson proclaimed that the United States would pursue the universal ideal of "orderly processes of just government." While Washington would prefer leaders "who protect private rights," it would not intercede in foreign countries on behalf of special interests. It would seek only mutually profitable trade between the United States and Latin America that would "interfere with the rights and liberties of neither."[12]

Wilson's principles did not lead toward a noninterventionist policy.

Whereas selfish British imperialism focused on preserving order and advancing trade, America had a higher calling, Wilson believed. Instead of merely "being a policeman in Mexico," Wilson informed a journalist, he wanted to lay secure foundations for liberty.[13] Mexicans would need a guiding hand along the road to democracy, Wilson and many of his advisors contended. Like Filipinos, Mexicans were childlike people who required tutoring from more mature Americans to make them fit for self-government. While some of Wilson's advisors and many Republican critics felt he was too hesitant to spank the unruly Mexicans, his paternalistic view of Mexicans disposed him to insist "that they shall take help when help is needed." [14]

Wilson suspected that Americans who owned large tracts of land and other property in Mexico were plotting to bring about intervention, and he dug in his heels against such intrigues.[15] However, he felt the U.S. government did have a duty "to protect American interests in the large sense" by facilitating the expansion of non-exploitative American commerce, creating secure environments for honest investors, and fighting against exclusionary concessions to foreign firms. Those objectives required a stable Mexican government that would respect foreign property and repay foreign loans. In pursuit of his political, economic, and humanitarian goals, Wilson would pressure, threaten, and even use force against Mexican leaders.[16]

His first step was to try to engineer the removal of Huerta. In May 1913 Wilson briefly toyed with the idea of recognizing Huerta if he would allow free elections and retire from office. However, the idea of granting recognition to a usurper ran against Wilson's grain. When the general defiantly clung to power, Wilson withheld diplomatic recognition in order to encourage Huerta's opponents to remove him.[17]

Moral and diplomatic pressure took time to work, and Wilson was impatient to end the turmoil in Mexico. Less than two months into his presidency he began considering military intervention. As House noted in May 1913, the two of them did not believe that "intervention and war would be as bad as his Cabinet thought." By August 1913, determined "to act as Mexico's nearest friend," Wilson felt that he was not "at liberty any longer to stand inactively by." [18]

The situation became even more intolerable in October, when Huerta arrested the Mexican Chamber of Deputies and a new British minister to Mexico seemed to dominate Huerta's dictatorship. Since Huerta's government was based on force and support from British diplomats and oil interests, in Wilson's view, American action to depose the regime would be in sympathy with Mexican self-determination rather than unjustified intervention. In anticipation of American intervention, House claimed, he advised Wilson "to sound a very high note" regarding America's un-selfish motives. At Mobile, Alabama, in late October, Wilson explained that he aimed to protect Latin American states from corruption by "con-cessions to foreign capitalists." "We must prove ourselves their friends and champions," Wilson proclaimed.[19]

Within days of the Mobile speech, Wilson considered declaring war against Mexico and sending troops to the northern states, if they con-sented, in order to protect foreign lives and property. He even drafted a war message to Congress. However, a British shift toward a more cooper-ative stance renewed Wilson's hopes to secure Huerta's departure with-out the use of force. In addition, the chairman of the Senate foreign re-lations committee, Augustus O. Bacon, advised Wilson that senators preferred methods other than armed intervention and that public expec-tations were against intervention. "We have so industriously preached non-intervention during the past three or four months," Bacon wrote, "that the idea has taken very deep root and it may be difficult to effect a change of views in this regard."[20]

While Wilson's espousal of the principles of nonintervention and self-determination did not keep him from considering military intervention and even war, it created public expectations that inhibited his use of force, affected the way he described his actions, and influenced his definition of "intervention." With widespread antipathy in America to monopolies and trusts, Wilson and his top advisors could not cooperate with such interests to bring peace and order to Mexico; they had to align themselves with Mexican popular aspirations. As Wilson confided in early 1914, he found it essential to "steer our own public opinion in the right path." The increas-ingly acute division between Americans who demanded aggressive action and those who opposed any use of force helped make the extreme courses of doing nothing or declaring war unpalatable and inclined the Wilson ad-ministration toward limited and secretive forms of intervention.[21]

Methods of Intervention in Mexico

After Wilson pulled back from declaring war on Mexico in November 1913 he contemplated other methods to secure an acceptable government in Mexico City, ranging from diplomatic pressure to arms shipments, a naval quarantine, and military occupation. As Secretary of State William Jen-nings Bryan explained, "The President feels it is his duty to force Huerta's retirement, peaceably if possible but forcibly if necessary[.] The steps which he has in mind are (A) withdrawing of diplomatic representatives (B) raising of embargo on arms shipped to Constitutionalists (C) Block-ading of ports (D) use of army."[22] Thus, by his eighth month in office

Wilson envisioned a series of measures beyond traditional diplomacy but short of direct warfare. In the next two years Wilson took each of those steps.

Moral Sanctions

"Recognition or non-recognition" were for Wilson "means of compulsion," tools to force Huerta from power and influence his successors. "The withdrawal of all moral and material support from without," Wilson wrote, "is the indispensible [sic] first step to a solution from within."[23] After Wilson resolved to remove Huerta, he secured guarantees from Huerta's main opponent, Venustiano Carranza, that he had not granted special concessions to foreign interests and that he would respect "American interests and property rights in Mexico."[24] Once Constitutionalist forces took control of Mexico City in the summer of 1914, Wilson used the possibility of diplomatic recognition and the threat of nonrecognition as carrots and sticks to induce Carranza and his rival Francisco (Pancho) Villa to heed American advice.[25]

Economic Sanctions

Granting or refusing to give diplomatic recognition also allowed the United States to exert economic pressure. Withholding this benediction from Huerta made it more difficult for him to secure foreign loans, leading his foreign minister to plead, "Intervene, do something, but don't strangle us financially." Further economic leverage was applied by assisting trade with parts of Mexico under the control of friendly leaders and obstructing commerce with areas held by unfriendly forces. At the height of a confrontation with Carranza in 1916, Wilson went further, ordering the navy to quarantine every major Mexican port and cut off all trade with Mexico.[26]

Arms Embargoes and Arms Shipments

During Wilson's first months in office, Huerta's government was able to receive weapons shipments from the United States, while shipments to his Constitutionalist adversaries were prohibited. In the fall of 1913, increasingly vexed by the Mexican dictator, Wilson threatened "to cut the government of Huerta off . . . from all outside aid or countenance," and to provide "active assistance" to the Constitutionalists. When Huerta persisted in ignoring American demands, Wilson's representatives encouraged relaxation of the embargo, and American customs inspectors increasingly turned their heads while arms were smuggled across the border to the Constitutionalists.[27] In January 1914, exasperated by Huerta and satisfied with Carranza's pledges of free elections and respect for American economic interests, Wilson decided to lift the embargo against the Constitutionalists in order to add impetus to their efforts to oust Huerta.[28]

To Colonel House, this was preferable to having U.S. troops "enter Mexico and put Huerta out by force," and he urged Wilson "to do what he could to settle the Mexican matter without intervention." Wilson agreed. "Settlement by civil war," he wrote, was better than having the United States "undertake to sweep Mexico with its armed forces from end to end."[29] In addition to risking American casualties, direct U.S. military intervention would contradict the Wilsonian commitment to self-determination. As the British ambassador in Washington commented, Wilson's pledges "to throw Huerta out" but "not to intervene" led him "to encourage and assist Villa." British officials often did not appreciate Wilsonian scruples about methods of intervention. Ambassador Spring Rice found it odd that the U.S. pledge "to be guided by the purest moral principle" led it to support Villa, "the most unconscionable ruffian ever known."[30]

Searching for "Strong Men" to "Restore Order"

Wilson embraced Villa for a time as "a sort of Robin Hood" who represented Mexico's poor agricultural population, but perhaps more important was his image of Villa as "the sword of the revolution," a warrior who could bring the civil war to an end, then yield to a political leader. The Wilson administration's quest for such a strongman passed through several stages. One of the leading counts in Wilson's indictment of Huerta was that he was "without force or means to establish order." After backing the Constitutionalists against Huerta, the Wilson administration came to see Carranza as both "difficult to deal with" and not "strong enough." By August 1914 Wilson considered Villa to be "the only man of force now in sight in Mexico." Later, Alvaro Obregón would replace Villa as "the man of the hour" in the eyes of Wilson and House. In each stage, Wilson hoped that restoration of order by a strongman would avoid the need for American military intervention.[31]

Limited Military Intervention

Although Wilson and many of his advisors worried that foreign military intervention "would unite against the invading party all the patriotism and all the energies of which the Mexicans were capable,"[32] Wilson eventually persuaded himself that the Mexican people would appreciate America's altruistic purposes and welcome friendly American forces. In April 1914, when Wilson ordered the navy to seize the customhouse at Veracruz to prevent a German ship from delivering arms to Huerta, he expected Mexicans to understand that he was only trying to help them remove an obnoxious dictator tied to foreign interests. On April 20, the day before marines and bluejackets went into action, Wilson avowed to Congress, "The people of Mexico are entitled to settle their own domestic affairs in their own way, and we sincerely respect their right." In language that anticipated his explanation of the military expeditions to Russia four years later, Wilson announced that the United States' "object would be only to restore to the people of the distracted republic the opportunity to set up again their own laws and their own government."[33]

Wilson was therefore shocked by the Mexican resistance at Veracruz, where hundreds were killed and wounded. Combined with heated denunciations by Carranza, anti-American protests throughout Latin America, and antiwar petitions from church groups, peace societies, and labor organizations in the United States, the bloodshed led Wilson to reign in military operations. Rejecting Secretary of War Lindley Garrison's recommendation that the United States prepare "to move to the interior" of Mexico, Wilson reiterated: "We shall have no right at any time to intervene in Mexico to determine the way in which the Mexicans are to settle their own affairs."[34]

While Wilson refused to have American troops occupy Mexico City as they had under President Polk, the United States continued to intervene in less direct ways. Wilson accepted an offer of mediation by Argentine, Brazilian, and Chilean diplomats as an alternative way to try to secure the elimination of Huerta. After Huerta finally left the country in July 1914, U.S. officers in Veracruz supervised the stockpiling of massive arms shipments that were turned over to Constitutionalists in November 1914 and proved crucial in their defeat of the Villistas. Once Washington recognized Carranza as the de facto ruler of Mexico in October 1915, it placed an embargo upon arms and ammunition going to Villa and other opponents of Carranza in northern Mexico.[35]

Villa's anger and suspicion about ties between Carranza and Washington spurred him to launch a March 1916 raid on Columbus, New Mexico, in which eighteen Americans were killed. With Americans outraged, Colonel House believed Wilson "was compelled to go into Mexico." Even as he ordered the U.S. Army to cross into Mexican territory to chase Villa, however, Wilson assured the American and Mexican peoples that this was "in no sense intended as an invasion of the republic or as an infringement of its sovereignty."[36]

Although Wilson later used the presence of the Pershing expedition in Mexico as leverage in negotiations with Carranza, he continued to assert that his altruistic motives and the limitations he imposed upon U.S. actions made them something other than "intervention." Even when American soldiers roaming deep inside Mexico blundered into a shootout that nearly precipitated war in June 1916, Wilson insisted privately that there would be no "intervention (that is the rearrangement and control of Mexico's domestic affairs by the U.S.)" if he could prevent it. Later that year, he explained publicly that "by intervention, I mean the use of the power of the United States to establish internal order there without the invitation of Mexico and determine the character and method of her political institutions." Hence, if Wilson could feel that he had some invitation to send troops, or that he was acting in sympathy with the revolutions (as he understood and defined them), or that he was countering some alien threat to native self-determination, he could avoid seeing any contradiction of his principles.[37]

Wilson's extreme definition of intervention suited his interests and soothed his conscience. However, to understand his polices it is important to define "intervention" more broadly, to include the variety of limited, indirect, and covert forms of intervention that the Wilson administration pioneered in response to the Mexican and Russian civil wars.[38]

Intelligence Gathering and Covert Action

While the U.S. Army and Navy intervened in overt ways, American officials employed agents to gather military intelligence and carry out covert actions. In 1914, Wilson's representative John Lind dispatched officers to inspect Huerta's installations and map potential theaters of operation, recommended assistance to Mexican "intelligence departments," proposed actions such as seizing Mexican gunboats, and commented that he was "not taking any nice distinctions of international law into consideration."[39] As the Mexican Civil War continued, the Bureau of Investigation and U.S. military intelligence supervised agents throughout the country who gathered information about ammunition factories, arms contracts, and other matters.[40] In 1916, Department of Justice officials and U.S. military intelligence officers prepared Japanese agents to infiltrate Villa's camp and poison his coffee. Top officials in Washington apparently did not authorize the failed assassination attempt, though Wilson had approved a recommendation that U.S. forces be "maintained indefinitely" in part of Chihuahua "as an incentive to Carranza forces to kill or capture Villa."[41]

Although Wilson had little or no advance knowledge of the most sensational covert actions conducted in Mexico, it was not merely coincidental that his presidency featured an increased reliance upon limited intervention and the methods of secret war. Wilson circumscribed American options with his declarations about the right of self-determination and his speeches forswearing aggressive military intervention. Within those limits, Wilson and lower ranking American officials who shared many of his goals but not all of his scruples initiated a variety of efforts to contain and alter the course of the Mexican Revolution.

While Lansing had criticized militant humanitarian globalism at the turn of the century, by 1917 he recognized that "conditions" were "driving the U.S. from its traditional policy of isolation" and commented that "an irresistable [sic] power" was forcing Americans on "against our will." Reviewing Wilsonian policy toward Central America and the Caribbean, the secretary of state noted that in its efforts to prevent revolutions for personal gain and stabilize constitutional governments, the administration came to rely heavily on nonrecognition and financial strangulation of unprincipled revolutionists. While this policy ran counter to strict application of international law, Lansing had come around to the view that a government "inspired by moral precepts and high motives" was justified in sitting in judgment on an "immoral" revolutionary regime that sought "to impose its will upon a vanquished people."[42]

Wilson learned much from experiences in Mexico about how difficult it could be to try to influence the path of foreign revolutions. However, those lessons did not keep Wilson and his advisors from intervening in Russia in many of the same ways.[43] Much as Wilson had passed sentence on Huerta, Wilson and Lansing would judge against the Bolsheviks when they seized power in Petrograd. Between 1917 and 1920 Wilson would again withhold diplomatic recognition from disreputable leaders, impede trade with the territory they controlled, and approve arms shipments to their opponents. In Russia, as in Mexico, Wilson would first fear that military intervention would provoke a nationalistic reaction but then be persuaded that limited expeditions by Americans would be welcomed. When military intervention seemed counterproductive, in Russia, as in Mexico, Wilson would pull back and consider negotiations, but later continue with other methods of intervention. In Russia, as in Mexico, Wilson would reject proposals to expand the scope of U.S. military operations and insist that the circumscribed U.S. actions did not constitute "intervention." Despite those distinctions he would once again be disappointed by the foreign response to American assistance and face criticism in America of actions that seemed to contradict his principles.

Although there were major differences between neighboring Mexico and distant Russia, Wilsonian responses to revolutions in the two countries displayed striking similarities. While Wilson emphasized that commerce linked Mexico very closely with the United States, he regarded Russia as "the remotest of European nations, . . . the one with which we have had the least connections in trade." Yet Wilson realized that Russia was part of an increasingly interdependent world economy and he would agree with more wild-eyed Americans that Russia, especially Siberia, offered important fields for American exports and investments that were jeopardized by political instability and radical socialist experiments.[44] In Russia, as in Mexico, Wilson and his advisors would seek assurances that the forces

they supported would promote stable conditions and open economic opportunities by holding democratic elections, repaying foreign debts, and
granting no special concessions to other foreign powers.[45] While American officials who compared Russia to Mexico often implied the need for
forceful intervention to impose order, Wilson showed greater patience and
more empathy with popular demands for equality and justice. Yet Wilson
shared with many of his advisors the assumption that the majority of the
Russian people were, like Mexicans, backward, ignorant, childlike, or,
as he repeatedly put it, "naive."[46] When liberals like Madero seemed
too weak to secure both reform and stability, in Russia as in Mexico Wilson, Lansing, and other U.S. officials would support "strong men" who
promised to restore the order necessary for future democratic development. While left-leaning writers such as John Reed and Max Eastman
praised Wilson's profound sympathy with Mexico's revolutionary masses,
they would find that there were limits to the elasticity of Wilsonian liberalism when Bolshevism posed a threat to world order that was much
broader than the regional challenge of Mexican economic nationalism. As
we shall see, Wilson's antipathy to Bolshevism would arise not only from a
determination to defend the capitalist system (as disillusioned socialists
like Eastman would suspect), but also from anger at how the Bolsheviks
undermined American unity and defied American values in ways Mexican
revolutionaries never did.[47]

2

THE ORIGINS OF AMERICAN ANTI-BOLSHEVISM

Woodrow Wilson sometimes seemed a warm friend of Soviet Russia. Addressing Congress in January 1918, Wilson appeared to praise the Soviet quest for peace with the Central Powers through negotiations that Russian representatives, "in the true spirit of modern democracy," insisted be open to the world. When the president assured "Russia" of "a sincere welcome into the society of free nations," some liberal journalists jumped to the conclusion that Wilson planned to recognize the Soviet government, which one supposed had "spiritual kinship" with Wilsonian ideals. At the Paris Peace Conference a year later, Wilson again seemed to extend his hand to the Bolshevik regime when he drafted a proclamation that the Associated Powers "recognise the revolution without reservation, and will in no way, and in no circumstances, aid or give countenance to any attempt at a counter-revolution." [1]

However, the only revolution Wilson recognized was the revolution against tsarism in March 1917. He never opened diplomatic relations with the Soviet government. He repeatedly authorized U.S. support for anti-Bolshevik forces in the Russian Civil War. And in September 1919, with a Red Scare raging across America, Wilson poured gasoline on the flames at many stops on a cross-country speaking tour. He warned that Bolshevism — "the poison of disorder, the poison of revolt, the poison of chaos" — had spread, and that some "of that poison has got in the veins of this free people." Wilson had welcomed the revolution against the Romanov autocracy as "wonderful and heartening," but the revolution that brought the Bolsheviks to power was evil. "That sort of revolution," Wilson warned, "means government by terror, government by force, not government by vote. It is the negation of everything that is American."[2]

How could Wilson seem friendly to the Soviet government as late as January 1919 yet denounce it so heatedly and categorically only eight months later? How could Wilson at times show a much more flexible understanding of the appeal of Bolshevism than conservatives such as Robert Lansing, yet ultimately be as rigid as Lansing in opposing the Bolshevik regime?

According to Ray Stannard Baker, a journalist who served as Wilson's press liaison at Paris, "the President's natural sympathies" were with a liberal, noninterventionist approach to Russia, but he was "carried away beyond his real convictions by undefined antipathies, shadowy fears, and the pressure of active partisans of intervention."[3] As Wilson's relations with Mexico showed, his convictions about intervention were more ambiguous than Baker's statement recognized. However, pursuing Baker's insight about the roles of "shadowy fears" and "partisans of intervention" leads to a more complex picture than one-dimensional images of Wilson either as an unequivocal foe of socialism and Bolshevism or as an advanced progressive who sympathetically understood the Bolshevik Revolution and consistently opposed foreign intervention in Russia.[4]

To understand the limits of Wilson's political sympathies and the origins of his views of Bolshevism one must begin by examining the swings in his ambivalent views of socialism and revolution in the decades before 1917. As detailed studies of Wilson's pre-presidential years have shown, being raised the son of a Presbyterian minister in the South during the Civil War and Reconstruction shaped his view of the world, spurring a powerful drive for order and contributing to his discomfort with radical change.[5] While Wilson could sympathize with popular struggles against injustice, he was as deeply disturbed by revolutionary disorder as more consistently conservative men.

In the late nineteenth century and the first decades of the twentieth, many of Wilson's peers became increasingly troubled by challenges to traditional American institutions and values from massive immigration, radical ideologies, religious skepticism, and changing moral standards. After the Bolshevik Revolution, guardians of "Puritan" traditions came to view "Bolshevism" as a composite of those domestic social and cultural challenges. While radicals in America embraced Soviet Russia as the embodiment of their hopes for a new society, defenders of Americanism urgently demanded intervention in Russia to safeguard the United States from the influence of the Russian revolutionary example and the menace of Bolshevik propaganda. Although Wilson was reluctant to authorize overt military intervention, he shared many of the fears of partisans of intervention. Their pressure and his anxieties did not by themselves determine the U.S. decisions to intervene, but the shadow of "Bolshevism" lurked in the background of the decisions and ultimately loomed over Wilson administration policy toward Soviet Russia.

This chapter does not present a comprehensive analysis of all the elements that figured in American hostility toward Soviet Russia. Perceptions of Bolsheviks as German agents, dismay at the Bolshevik setback to hopes for orderly democracy in Russia, displeasure at the Soviet repudiation of Russia's foreign debts, and other factors will be discussed in more depth in subsequent chapters. The focus here is on elucidating the ideological antipathies and inarticulate anxieties that exerted a broad influence on Wilsonian policy but can be missed in detailed examination of specific decisions.

The Development of Wilson's Views of Revolution and Socialism

The danger of revolution troubled Wilson from his days as a college student to the end of his life. In the summer of 1877, when railroad strikes sparked the first major labor uprising in America, the twenty-year-old Wilson commented on the "disorderly and chaotic condition of society," which called for men of "independent conviction" who would transcend narrow class interests. Widening his vision, Wilson observed in an essay on Prince Bismarck that few centuries had been "more fruitful in crisis, in revolutions and counter-revolutions . . . than our own." Identifying with Bismarck as a young country squire who rose to be a great statesman, Wilson projected some of his concerns about contemporary America onto his discussion of the revolutions of 1848, when "Prussia . . . found herself obliged to fight a domestic enemy in the shape of radicalism." Bismarck, Wilson wrote, "looked with deep apprehension at the alarming spread of revolutionary principles." [6]

Almost fifty years later, in the final article before his death, Wilson was still disturbed by external turmoil. "In these doubtful and anxious days," he reflected in 1923, "when all the world is at unrest . . . we should . . . attempt to assess the causes of distress and the most likely means of removing them." The ex-president argued that Christian reforms were needed to pave "the road that leads away from revolution." [7]

In the decades between those two essays, Wilson oscillated between the poles of order and reform. Although he personally had "little impatience with existing conditions," when corruption and injustice seemed to be breeding a revolution in the future he tended to emphasize the need for reforms to ameliorate social conditions. But when revolutionary turmoil seemed an imminent menace, he often stressed the need for order and discipline.[8]

Like many Christians in American colleges in the 1880s, Wilson sympathized with socialistic reforms that promised to control irresponsible, domineering corporations and show greater compassion for the poor and weak. As a graduate student and then visiting lecturer at Johns Hopkins in the mid-1880s, Wilson was attracted to the "saner socialistic writers." Seeing socialism as the ultimate extension of a community's right to govern its development, Wilson concluded that "in fundamental theory socialism and democracy are almost if not quite one and the same." In a democracy socialism need not be a revolutionary doctrine, he thought; society could grow into socialism.[9]

Even as he was drawn to mild conceptions of socialism, however, Wilson chided socialists as impractical sentimentalists and worried that implementing socialism would require absolute state power. In language that anticipated his reactions to the Bolshevik government, Wilson derided socialistic schemes that were "mistaken enough to provoke the laughter of children," and criticized extreme socialists as a "radically mistaken class of thinkers."[10]

Much as he distinguished between gradual socialistic reforms and radical socialist transformations, Wilson drew a line between democratic revolutions led by sober, God-fearing men and anarchic revolutions incited by impassioned demagogues. Like most Americans of his generation, Wilson implicitly and explicitly compared violent foreign tumults with images of an almost bloodless colonial revolution in America. There was "almost nothing in common between popular outbreaks such as took place in France at her great Revolution and the establishment of a government like our own," he declared in 1889. Whereas "Democracy in Europe . . . has acted always *in rebellion,* as a *destructive* force," Wilson stressed, "Democracy in America . . . has had . . . a truly organic growth. There was nothing revolutionary in its movements."[11] In the nineteenth century Americans were repeatedly disappointed when other peoples first seemed to be following the example of the American Revolution, then appeared to diverge from the American model and embark on more radical paths.[12] Yet most Americans, including Wilson, still assumed that foreign peoples should and eventually would follow Americans along the path of political evolution.[13]

In the last quarter of the nineteenth century, despite a rising fear of anarchists and socialists at home, many Americans sympathized with a revolutionary movement in Russia. Although Wilson believed Russian nihilists who tried to assassinate tsarist officials were disgracing the movement, even those "hideous outbreaks of violence," he commented in 1880, were "manifestations of a revolt against absolutism which has the germs of honorable patriotism in it." While Wilson differentiated between "revolutions" and "true political progress," he suggested that Russia was beginning to espouse "the cause of self-government and freedom." Thus, Wilson's writing in the 1880s partially foreshadowed his different responses to the two Russian revolutions of 1917: the March Revolution that he would see as a patriotic revolt against tsarist despotism and the Bolshevik Revolution that he would regret as a deviation from progress toward Russian self-government.[14]

In the 1890s, when Wilson rose in prominence as a professor at Princeton, he increasingly differentiated his practical liberalism from wrongheaded socialism. Democracy was "sometimes mistaken for a basis for socialism," he noted in 1895, but "political democracy is one thing, *economic* democracy another." In fact, socialism was the opposite of his approach to politics. "My ideal *reverses the order of the socialist*," he stressed. Whereas socialists wanted to start by reorganizing the state, Wilson believed "the work" had to begin with "*character*." While Wilson was troubled by the un-Christian selfishness of capitalism, his religious beliefs also influenced his thinking in the opposite direction: the "covetous" and "self-indulgent" nature of people, he felt, made radical social reform impractical. Impatient attempts to outstrip the natural pace of progress could even be catastrophic. "I should fear nothing better than utter destruction," Wilson warned, "from a revolution conceived and led in the scientific spirit."[15]

Alarmed by the depression and Populist agitation of the 1890s, Wilson turned toward a conservative emphasis on the need for "the best order" to prevent liberty from degenerating into "license and folly." An elite of gentlemen with "elevated ideals" was needed, he urged in 1894, to preserve "stability and righteousness against the petty and ineffectual turbulence of revolution." As Wilson swung toward this emphasis on order he expressed the pendular limits of his own sympathies in remarks about his favorite political thinker, Edmund Burke: "He pressed forward with the most ardent in all plans of just reform, but he held back with the most conservative from all propositions of radical change."[16]

That pattern was evident in the first decade of the twentieth century, when Wilson's concern about the rising tension "between the power of accumulated capital and the opportunities of the masses of the people" led him to the verge of endorsing socialism before he pulled back from the brink. In 1906, Wilson declared that "the Socialist motive is that of Christ himself," but then he quickly added that "the method is madness." In April of the same year Wilson vowed to "reject, as we would reject poison itself, the prescriptions of Socialism," which he distinguished from the Jeffersonian "creed of individualism."[17]

While rejecting socialism, Wilson worried that the backbone of American individualism, the enterprising middle class, was being squeezed between a business elite that dominated the government and an underprivileged working class. Those conditions, Wilson believed, were responsible for the doubling of the socialist vote in elections between 1900 and 1912, and they called for a peaceful revolution to rescue government from the clutches of special interests.[18] Such ideas inclined Wilson to speak more favorably of revolution after he left the presidency of Princeton University in 1910 to become governor of New Jersey. While in the 1890s Wilson had attacked "French revolutionary philosophy" as "radically evil" and un-American, in 1911 he lectured New Jersey legislators "that it was the American Revolution that bred the French Revolution," and argued that "the fires and blood of that terrible time" were necessary to remove an old regime that treated people like slaves rather than citizens.[19] As president, Wilson would cite similarly sympathetic views of the French revolt against feudalism to illustrate his compassion for the aspirations of Mexican peons and Russian peasants.[20] Yet revolutionary turmoil in Mexico and Russia stirred Wilson's anxiety about disorder, and he eventually returned to his older view of the French Revolution as he denounced Bolshevik terror.

Wilson's ambivalent attitudes toward socialism and revolution would place him between his two key foreign policy advisors, Robert Lansing and Edward House. While Wilson's sympathy for socialist ideals drew him close to House and other friends on the Left, his worries about anarchy and radical change gave him much in common with Lansing and others on the Right.

Lansing's Views of Socialism and Revolution

Born in 1864, eight years after Wilson, Robert Lansing was a descendant of a prominent Dutch family that came to the Hudson River valley in the seventeenth century. After graduating from Amherst College in 1886, "Bert" joined his father's law firm and became a leading figure in the New York Democratic Party. In 1890, he married the daughter of John Watson Foster, a respected authority on international law who introduced the use of military attachés to gather intelligence during his brief tenure as secretary of state (1892–93). Following in the footsteps of his father-in-law, Lansing became associate counsel in the Bering Sea Fur Seal case of 1892, and thereafter handled other important cases in international law.[21]

As a "Bourbon Democrat," dedicated to honest government by an established elite and determined to prevent unruly workers or farmers from upsetting traditional social and economic arrangements, Lansing took a dim view of revolutions. Amid the Populist agitation of the early 1890s, Lansing penned a historical essay that reflected his conservative views. In "Clubs of the French Revolution," he abhorred the Palais Royal Club as "a blasphemer of Liberty's sacred name, a nursery of riot and revolution." Appalled by the way the revolution that overthrew the Bourbon monarchy "set the lowest classes of society against the middle and higher classes," Lansing justified Thermidorian violence so the nation could "regain its health."[22]

Like France in the late eighteenth century, America at the end of the nineteenth century was troubled by class tensions. The educated middle class's traditional moral leadership of America was being jeopardized, Lansing felt, by the social ascendancy of new millionaires and by the despondency of poorer farmers and workers. In 1902 Lansing commented on such threats to the American way of life in a series of short political essays. The grasping, immoral practices of corporations were leading the people to "believe in government control" as "the only remedy," thereby "making converts to Socialism." If the "virus," or "*poison of Centralization*," was not purged from "the veins of our great body politic," Lansing cried, it would lead to Socialism, "the antithesis of Individualism."[23]

Lansing's views differed from Wilson's, but not as starkly as some historians have supposed. While Lansing was more reluctant than Wilson to see government regulation of capitalism, he recognized that reforms were necessary. Like Wilson he argued "that change must take place soberly and cautiously; the people must not be guided by demagogues, by extremists, by hasty counsel." Although Lansing showed less sympathy for socialist ideals than Wilson did, he resembled Wilson in the way his religious beliefs influenced his objections to socialism. To be successful socialism required absolutely honest leaders, Lansing held. Since dishonesty and corruption were part of human nature, socialist government would be "tyrannical and despotic." Only if Christianity redeemed humanity from its sinfulness could the "rosy dream" be practicable, Lansing concluded.[24]

Colonel House, Socialism, and Revolution

Edward M. House, an independently wealthy political operator from Texas, shared with Wilson and Lansing the basic assumption that reforms were needed to alleviate the abuses of capitalism. In *Philip Dru: Administrator* (1912), a novel that set out his political ideas, House foresaw an America in 1920 on the verge of "civil war." "Wealth had grown so strong," House wrote, "that the few were about to strangle the many, and among the great masses of the people, there was sullen and rebellious discontent." To avoid a revolution, House proposed unselfish action to alleviate inequality, exploitation, and other problems of "the system." After assisting Wilson's political campaign in 1912, House urged the president-elect to stress in his speeches that the "strong should help the weak, that the fortunate should aid the unfortunate, and that business should be conducted upon a higher and more humane plane." Although House was not conventionally religious like Wilson and Lansing, he suggested through Philip Dru that what he envisioned was bringing true Christianity to "a cruel, selfish and ignorant world." As House had Dru explain, he was not advocating the impractical "Socialism as dreamed of by Karl Marx." However, as he maintained contact with the Wilson administration's supporters on the Left from his New York apartment, House showed a sympathetic interest in the views of socialists.[25]

Dru's eagerness to promote dramatic change foreshadowed the way that House would be more tolerant of radicalism and disorder in Russia than Lansing and Wilson. While writing the novel House contemplated helping Russia, like France in 1789, to achieve deliverance from ignorance, hopelessness, and despotism. After the Russian people dethroned their despot in March 1917, House sometimes feared that "zealous friends of liberty [and] progress might go too fast," but he sympathized with the Russians' eagerness "to make peace and take up their new and important domestic problems." Unlike Lansing and Wilson, House would not show a visceral reaction against Bolshevism. His views of Soviet Russia would be driven by practical political and strategic considerations rather than moral principles and ideology.[26]

American policymakers' responses to the Russian revolutions were shaped not only by conscious political views and religious beliefs, but also by subconscious fears about their own society. Among the most important fears were white Protestant officials' concerns about Americans of other racial and ethnic backgrounds.

Racism, Nativism, and Anti-Semitism

Wilson's upbringing in the South in the Reconstruction era cast a shadow over his later progressivism and left a legacy of anxiety about African Americans. As a law student at the University of Virginia in 1880, he denounced the idea of granting what he considered an inferior race equality with whites or responsibility for political leadership. In later writings, Wilson justified the disfranchisement of "ignorant negroes" and described the Ku Klux Klan as an organization "to protect the southern country from some of the ugliest hazards of a time of revolution." Fearful that social intercourse between whites and blacks would lead to race mixing and the degradation of white nations, Wilson favored segregation. As president, despite pressure from liberal northerners, Wilson approved of the segregation of government departments. Privately he continued to tell stories that reflected his nagging fears, such as his anecdote that "a Princeton professor who did not believe in Democracy said the logic of a democracy would make a Negro woman President of the US."[27]

While Wilson and many Americans of his generation worried about African American insubordination, they saw another source of danger in the massive immigration from southern and eastern Europe that began in the late nineteenth century. In 1889, Wilson worried that "our own temperate blood, schooled to self-possession and to the measured conduct of self-government," was "yearly experiencing a partial corruption of foreign blood" that contained "the feverish habits of the restless old world." In 1896, Wilson compared the challenge of assimilating immigrants in America to the danger of having the "proletariat in the saddle" in Europe. After the turn of the century, Wilson continued to express concern about the admission into America of "multitudes of men of the lowest class" from Italy, Hungary, and Poland, and he fretted that "a miscellaneous immigration has poured social chaos."[28]

Wilson learned that airing such views in public was a political liability in 1910, when Republicans used his writings against him as he ran for the governorship of multi-ethnic New Jersey. To minimize the damage, he claimed to admire Poles and Italians, and declared that "America has always been proud to open her gates to everyone who loved liberty and sought opportunity." In his first term as president, Wilson maintained this posture and opposed immigration restriction legislation. Privately, after war broke out in Europe in 1914, Wilson confided to the British ambassador that "there was imminent danger of civil discord, the country was divided into groups which did not understand one another, which were of different origin and which might at any moment fly at each other's throats." The Americanization programs of the war years failed to alleviate Wilson's anxiety. During the 1916 campaign he returned to attacking hyphenated-Americans who had "poured the poison of disloyalty into the very arteries of our national life," and he vowed to crush "such creatures of passion, disloyalty, and anarchy."[29]

Among the immigrants who most worried U.S. leaders were the approximately two million Jews who had emigrated from Russia and eastern Europe. By the Wilson era, American nativists felt doubly threatened by these new immigrants: while the financial success of many Jewish Americans challenged Anglo-Saxon social preeminence, the involvement of Jews in growing labor unions and socialist parties posed a political threat. After

Bolsheviks seized power in Russia in 1917, those fears would merge with the widespread belief that most Bolsheviks were Jews to create the specter of a Jewish-Bolshevik conspiracy, which haunted many Wilson administration officials.[30]

Cultural Revolution vs. "Puritanism"

In addition to the problem of absorbing millions of immigrants, many white Protestant Americans believed the nation's health was endangered by other maladies. As America became a more urban, industrial, and secular society in the late nineteenth and early twentieth centuries, traditional religious faith, conventional moral standards, and Victorian sexual norms were increasingly undermined. While churches were rocked by the popularization of Darwinian theory, patriarchal family structures were shaken when women left home to work in modern offices and suffragettes demanded the right to vote. During the Wilson era, such changes combined to pose the danger of a "cultural revolution" against "Puritan" traditions and values.[31]

By the first years of the twentieth century, Lansing was so perturbed by challenges to the traditional American ethos that he penned a full jeremiad about the "National Menaces." "Puritanism and Independence," Lansing declared, "were the two pillars of the United States," and they were being threatened. "Agnosticism on the one hand is battering against Spirituality, while Socialism or its parent Nationalism is striving to overturn our Individualism. . . . Indifference to spiritual things, lack of respect for religion and creeds, are in evidence on every hand. . . . Lynchings, assassinations, immoralities, violations of marriage laws, easy divorces, . . . are fearful blots upon our national life." As an orthodox Presbyterian elder, Lansing had long looked to religion to ward off the threat of "riot and lawlessness." In 1903 he urged voters to return the Republic to its purity and reverence by electing men who were "not scoffers at religion" and who hated wickedness.[32]

Although Wilson did not bemoan America's moral and spiritual declension as the uptight Lansing did, Wilson was, like Lansing, an elder in the Presbyterian Church, and he shared some of Lansing's sentiments. In an early essay, Wilson argued that the "so-called 'harsh' Christianity of our fathers," mislabeled as "puritanism," was actually the "true Christianity in which alone rests safety and where salvation is sure."[33] While Wilson's religious orthodoxy became more relaxed over time, Calvinist tenets, particularly about election and salvation, continued to influence his worldview, undergirding his deep attachment to individualism. "The Puritan ingredient has colored all our national life," Wilson wrote in 1893. "We have gotten strength and persistency and some part of our steady moral purpose from it." After the turn of the century, Wilson joined others in poking fun at the asceticism of "the Puritan," but he praised the "Puritan" principles of order and "discipline that pulls in harness."[34]

Like Lansing, Wilson believed that virtuous leadership was essential to national salvation. He thought harsh, intractable "Puritan" statesmen like John Adams should soften their public personalities in order to retain power and keep the nation from taking reckless leaps. However, as president, Wilson himself suffered from being seen as cold, austere, and intransigent. Noting the common view that Wilson tended "in many things to 'lean backwards,' to be unnecessarily severe," his physician commented: "Perhaps so. Generations of Puritan ancestry engrave deep lines in a descendant." Wilson did not drink, did not smoke, had an unquestioning faith in a literal Presbyterianism, and opposed female suffrage until the war made it a necessary concession. To Bohemian social critics, the aloof president, whose yacht and car were both called *The Mayflower*, seemed the epitome of "the Puritan."[35] In an era of widespread social upheaval, Wilson's views of Bolshevism would be shaped not only by his liberal political principles, but also by his "Puritan" background and temperament.

In the 1910s Wilson moved far to the left in pursuit of reforms that would stabilize American society. By 1918 he had "started so actively on the liberal road" that he left House "rather in the rear." Late in that year he remarked that "liberalism must be more liberal than ever before; it must even be radical, if civilization is to escape the typhoon." Yet as Wilson worried about an impending "flood of ultra-radicalism," an undercurrent of fear pulled him in the opposite direction, back toward the "Puritan" principle of order. Both the liberal and conservative currents were affected by turbulence in Russia.[36]

The Enemy Within and the Enemy Without

As Wilson considered leading a divided nation to war in March 1917, the Russian Revolution cleansed the Allied camp of the taint of autocracy and made it easier to unify Americans around a democratic cause. However, soon after Congress declared war against Germany in April, calls for peace negotiations emanating from Petrograd clashed with the Wilson administration's effort to mobilize Americans behind a military crusade. Already in the spring of 1917, U.S. officials and prominent Americans outside the government began to regard Russian radicalism as a threat to American unity and internal stability, as well as to Allied victory.

In May 1917, Wilson's press secretary warned that the "contagious effects" of socialist peace propaganda "threaten soon to touch our own shores" and urged moves to contain the disease. Wilson agreed. In a Flag

Day address he declared that Germany's "sinister intrigue" for peace was being "no less actively conducted in this country than in Russia." Samuel Gompers, the leader of the American Federation of Labor (AFL), struck the same note when he accused Americans who supported Bolshevik peace proposals of being "the conscious or unconscious agents of the Kaiser in America." In collaboration with the Wilson administration, Gompers and the AFL formed the American Alliance for Labor and Democracy to combat pacifist and socialist groups such as the People's Council of America, which, Wilson was told in August, claimed "to be modeled along the lines of the Workmen's and Soldiers' organization in Russia."[37]

The danger from Bolshevik propaganda increased dramatically when the Bolsheviks captured the resources of the Russian state in November and proposed an immediate armistice to all belligerents. One day after V. I. Lenin issued his Decree on Peace, Gompers urged Wilson to address an AFL convention, arguing that "such a manifestation of solidarity of the people of the United States without regard to class or condition, particularly in view of the chaotic Russian situation[,] would have a wonderfully stabilizing influence." Like Gompers, Wilson worried that revolutionary propaganda and peace proposals from Russia could divide Americans. "Let us show ourselves Americans," Wilson implored the AFL delegates in Buffalo on November 12, 1917, "by showing that . . . we want to cooperate with all other classes and all other groups." While appealing for unity and praising Gompers as a man who knew "how to pull in harness," Wilson also issued a stern injunction about the need for order and obedience. Alluding to groups like the Industrial Workers of the World (IWW), Wilson warned that he would not tolerate strikes and other disruptive actions by organizations "whose object is anarchy and the destruction of law." He hoped Americans would understand the necessity of labor discipline during the war and would not be "as fatuous as the dreamers in Russia," who imagined they could enjoy peace in the shadow of Imperial Germany.[38]

Fears about the influence of Bolshevism prodded more vehement anti-Bolsheviks to press for action against the Soviet regime. By late November, former secretary of state Elihu Root was so disturbed by the way "Russian revolutionists" and IWW members were acting "as German agents" that he favored "instant and severe punishment" for radical and pro-German agitation. The danger, he told the British ambassador, "was in two forms, external and internal, and . . . the internal form was the more dangerous of the two." While sanctioning lynchings in America, Root urged the Wilson administration to provide financial support to anti-Bolshevik forces in Russia.[39]

Although Wilson's reaction was much less violent, like Root he saw connections between the external and internal threats. In a State of the Union Message on December 4, Wilson lamented that the Russian people had been poisoned by German falsehoods and warned that Kaiser Wilhelm's "sinister forces" had "corrupted the very thought and spirit" of many Americans as well. Lansing, who believed there were "many of the same type of people in this country as are guilty of Russia's crime," expressed similar disappointment that Russians had not resisted "the intrigues of German agents." In addition to negotiating for peace with Germany, the Bolsheviks were distributing propaganda that constituted a threat "to the principle of democracy and to a social order based on individual liberty." Lansing proposed to counter this menace by declaring that the United States would not recognize the Soviet government and by expressing the conviction that free elections, "uninfluenced by class-hatreds and unconstrained by class-despotism," would lead to "a strong and stable government founded on the principles of democracy."[40]

Wilson declined to issue such a public statement, which would have alienated Wilson administration supporters on the Left and played into the hands of German propagandists who stressed Allied hostility toward Soviet Russia. Although such a declaration was inexpedient, Wilson agreed with Lansing on the undesirability of granting diplomatic recognition to the Soviet government, and he shared Lansing's anger at Bolshevik propaganda. At a cabinet meeting on December 21, Wilson voiced his ire at the "impudence" of a telegram from Soviet Foreign Commissar L. D. Trotsky, which suggested that Soviet "consuls be given passports to America & other countries to propose the overturning of all governments not dominated by the working people." Secretary of War Newton Baker opposed publication of Trotsky's message because it "might encourage men of IWW type in America." Wilson concurred.[41]

Near the end of December, Wilson received an alarming memorandum from Lincoln Steffens, a muckraking journalist close to Colonel House. "The war is dividing men along the class line," Steffens warned. To avoid worsening the developing "class war" and increasing sympathy for "the I.W.W. and other radical labor groups," Steffens urged the president to "Stop the appearance of 'war on Labor.'"[42]

Although Wilson did not take that advice to halt domestic repression, he did continue to worry about domestic divisions, which Bolshevik propaganda could aggravate. In early January, 1918, the British ambassador reported that Wilson told him the Bolshevik appeal for peace "had not been without its effect" in Europe, and that "in the United States active agitation was proceeding." Wilson did not see any immediate danger in America. Yet he could not be silent in the face of Soviet propaganda: "if the appeal of the Bolsheviki was allowed to remain unanswered, if nothing were done to counteract it, the effect would be great and would increase."[43]

In February Wilson read a memorandum from Gompers and pro-war socialist William English Walling that accentuated the peril of Petrograd-inspired pacifism. The alarming growth of the international peace movement, Walling and Gompers argued, stemmed from "war weariness —accompanied by Utopian dreams fanned into new life by the Russian revolution." Walling and Gompers opposed any diplomatic recognition or display of friendliness toward the Soviet government, in part because "the continuing success of Bolshevism in Russia" was encouraging "the already dangerous pacifist movements" among workers in Europe, and in part because Lenin had "declared a world wide class war" against imperialist governments, including the United States. There was "a very grave danger," Gompers and Walling warned, that a revolutionary strike movement would develop in Italy and France and spread from there first to England and then to "Chicago, New York, San Francisco and our other foreign industrial centers." Thus, in addition to formulating an early version of the "domino theory," Gompers and Walling were conjuring the specter of urban immigrant radicalism that had haunted Wilson and Lansing for decades. On February 13, Wilson informed Lansing that the memorandum seemed "to speak an unusual amount of truth." Lansing agreed that Walling and Gompers showed a keen appreciation of the forces menacing the social order in Europe and potentially in America.[44]

Although House concurred with Wilson that they should "not allow the ignoble element to run away with the situation [in the rest of the world] as they had done in Russia," he did not share the indignation and alarm Wilson and Lansing felt at Bolshevik revolutionary propaganda. Taking a more pragmatic approach, he favored recognition of the Soviet government as a way to pull the Bolsheviks away from the Germans.[45]

Wilson and Lansing were moving in a different direction. The statement from Walling and Gompers reinforced their aversion to recognizing the Bolsheviks. In late February 1918, when the Soviet-German peace talks were broken off and Trotsky was exploring the possibility of military aid from the Allies and Americans, Wilson and Lansing also ruled out any military or financial support for the Bolsheviks. Principled opposition to Bolshevism precluded such "expedients."[46]

Despite his antipathy to the Bolsheviks, in the first half of 1918 Wilson resisted proposals for direct military intervention in Russia, in part because that would erode the difference between the "moral position" of America and the unprincipled policy of Germany.[47] However, as concern about internal and international disorder mounted, Wilson faced intensified pressure for action in Russia.

In May 1918, for example, Edgar Sisson, an agent for the Committee on Public Information, returned from Russia and circulated a call for intervention. "The military, naval and internal perils that threaten us increasingly each day that the present Russian situation continues" filled Sisson with "depression and alarm." He was appalled by "resolutions in favor of

Bolshevism adopted by conventions, [and] the unhampered spread of the tenets of violent re[v]olution by unhindered Bolsheviki papers." These threats could not "be dealt with adequately," Sisson argued, "unless we deal with the parent corruption."[48]

Wilson did not simply bow to such anxious lobbying. His decisions to send military expeditions to northern Russia and Siberia in the summer of 1918 were influenced by many other factors, including a desire to help Russians establish democratic governments, a need to conciliate his Allied partners, and concern about unrestrained Japanese expansionism. However, Wilson did share the fear about Bolshevik threats to American internal security expressed by partisans of intervention like Sisson. "The danger of conflagrations and revolutions menaces all organized states if the necessary precautions are not taken in time to assure the maintenance of order and the triumph of law," Wilson told French ambassador Jean Jules Jusserand in September 1918. According to Jusserand, Wilson alluded "to the demoralizing role of the I.W.W. and to the steps already taken to cut it short." In the same month Socialist Party leader Eugene Debs was sentenced to ten years in prison for violating the Espionage Act with a speech in which he criticized the war as a class war and declared, "Our hearts . . . are with the Bolsheviki of Russia." Despite the prosecution of such radicals Wilson worried in mid-October that "the spirit of the Bolsheviki is lurking everywhere." He expressed particular concern about "the foreign born population, such as the Italians."[49]

After Germany surrendered in November 1918, Wilson recoiled from further military intervention in Russia and shifted from portraying the Bolsheviks as German agents to viewing Bolshevism as an outgrowth of deep historical processes. Much as he had earlier compared the Mexican and French Revolutions, Wilson described the violent and chaotic state of Russia as a temporary phase through which the Russians, like the French, would have to pass.[50] In early 1919, influenced by academic experts and liberal advisors, Wilson came to the verge of understanding the social and economic bases of Bolshevism, describing it as a result of conflict between "labor and capital." Apparently trying to fit Bolshevism within his understanding of the sources of the Progressive reform movements, Wilson suggested that Bolshevism was part of a worldwide "feeling of revolt against the large vested interests" and said that it attracted sympathy among Americans because it appeared to offer a "regime of opportunity to the individual."[51] In much the same way that he had praised the motives and criticized the methods of socialists in previous decades, Wilson ventured that the "theory" of Bolshevism "had some advantages," though "an attempt was being made to accomplish it in the wrong way."[52]

Even in this most tolerant phase, however, Wilson had difficulty fathoming the depth of Russian class hatreds or the breadth of Russian skepticism about "bourgeois democracy." He sometimes implied that Bolshevism was primarily a reaction to corrupt or dishonest government. "The only thing that that ugly, poisonous thing called Bolshevism feeds on," Wilson told Democratic Party leaders in February 1919, "is the doubt of the man in the street of the essential integrity of the people he is depending on to do his governing." After observing Wilson at Paris in the first half of 1919, Ray Stannard Baker concluded that there were rigid boundaries to Wilson's sympathies and understanding: "With political revolution, up to the point of introducing democratic institutions of the type he knew and believed in, he was thoroughly in sympathy. With anything beyond and more radical—especially with social and economic revolution—he was just as thoroughly out of sympathy." While Wilson did understand Russian peasants' desire to hold their lands, other Americans in Paris shared Baker's impression of the constraints of Wilson's nineteenth-century political philosophy.[53]

As revolutions erupted across central Europe in the spring of 1919, Wilson backed away from half-hearted efforts to end hostilities with the Bolsheviks. While he withdrew U.S. troops from north Russia, he approved continued military assistance to anti-Bolshevik forces, authorized "humanitarian" aid to White armies, and favored the perpetuation of an effective blockade of Soviet Russia.

Those measures seemed insufficient to Americans like Colonel James Ruggles, who served in 1918 as military attaché in Soviet Russia. In August 1919 Ruggles warned from Archangel that "no government will be safe . . . as long as this Bolshevik Government exists which has repeatedly declared its intention to destroy all other Governments." Frightened by the Bolsheviks' "clever and very dangerous" propaganda, Ruggles urged: "It is far better to kill the head—here in Russia—than to run the risk of having to do it at home."[54] Elihu Root agreed, urging Americans to "fight Bolshevism at its centre, at its source." Ambassador David Francis, similarly, "advocated the eradication of Bolshevism in Russia," arguing that it was in America's "interest to exterminate it in the land of its birth." "All of the unrest throughout Europe and in this country," Francis explained, "can be traced back to this Bolshevik experiment in Russia."[55]

In August 1919 Lansing, who shared Francis's feelings though he could not accept the recommendation of direct military liquidation of Bolshevism, urged Wilson "to make a frank declaration against the Bolshevist doctrines which are certainly extending far beyond the confines of Russia." To buttress his appeal, Lansing sent the president memoranda prepared by DeWitt Poole, who had returned from serving as a diplomat in Russia. "The present startling spread of social and industrial unrest in the United States and throughout the world," Poole argued, made it important to repudiate the Bolsheviks. "That they can still carry on their work of destruction at home and their subversive propaganda abroad is due in part to the fact that final condemnation has not yet been passed upon them." Sowing the seeds for such a condemnation, Poole wrote that "healthy democratic currents" were "in danger of being poisoned" by Bolshevik propaganda; that the Bolsheviks were "a small coterie of men who are seeking to profit by the existing unrest"; and that they had inaugurated "a reign of terror" against "liberal elements" who could lead Russia "along modern democratic lines." For all these reasons, Poole pressed for a public excoriation of "the evil fatuity of Bolshevism."[56]

Wilson had deferred such a candid statement since December 1917. However, the German delegates' signing of the Versailles peace treaty in June 1919 and the progress of anti-Bolshevik armies in Russia seemed to lessen the danger that anti-Bolshevik pronouncements would cement Soviet-German ties. More importantly, there was a new incentive: dramatizing the menace of Bolshevism might help to rally support for the League of Nations. On August 14 Wilson informed Lansing that he might find an opportunity "to warn the country against Bolshevism in some way that may attract attention."[57]

On his speaking tour in September Wilson issued not just one proclamation but repeated denunciations of Bolshevism along the lines Poole had suggested. In Minnesota, for example, Wilson attacked the Bolsheviks as "a little handful of men" who had replaced "an old and distinguished and skillful autocracy" with "an amateur autocracy," and a "bloody terror." The language Wilson used marked a reversion to the political vocabulary he absorbed in the nineteenth century. In 1889, Wilson had compared revolutionary passions to "poisons"; in 1919 he cried that the "poison" of Bolshevism was "running through the veins of the world." In 1879, he had criticized Jacobins for being "more cruel than ever poor Louis XVI dared to be or wished to be"; in September 1919, he indicted the Bolsheviks for being "more cruel than the Czar himself."[58]

Nativism, Anti-Semitism, Racism, and Anti-Bolshevism

When Wilson denounced the Bolsheviks' "bloody terror" he aligned himself with conservative advisors such as Lansing, who regarded terror as the essence of both the French and Russian Revolutions and who embraced a Thermidorian restoration of order more eagerly than Wilson did.[59] Since Wilson had shown so much more flexibility than Lansing and had alarmed men like Poole by considering negotiations with the Bolsheviks earlier in 1919, what led him to turn toward their adamant, unbending anti-Bolshevik stance? What "shadowy fears" influenced Wilson's redefinition of Bolshevism?

One of the shadows was cast by the swarthy immigrant, who figured in many of Wilson's speeches in September 1919. Implicitly linking immigrants to the menace of Bolshevism in the "veins" of America, Wilson charged that "a hyphen" was "the most un-American thing in the world" and compared it to "a dagger" that immigrants were "ready to plunge into the vitals of this Republic." State Department officials responsible for implementing American policy toward Russia shared Wilson's fear of immigrant radicalism. Lansing, for example, believed that many of the newer immigrants were infected "with fanciful and vicious theories of social order," and had brought "to our shores the germs of sedition and revolution." Using images similar to Wilson's, Lansing cried, "The national life blood is being diluted and corrupted by this influx of immigrants" who were in many cases "secretly intent upon changing our institutions." Thus, despite their sharp personal and political differences, Lansing and Wilson both experienced the nativist anxiety that was the strongest source of the Red Scare hysteria.[60]

Jewish immigrants were linked to Bolshevism in a particularly virulent strain of nativism. In 1918, Russian monarchist military officers brought to the United States copies of "The Protocols of the Elders of Zion," which purported to lay out a Jewish plan for world domination through financial control, war, and revolution. The spurious documents circulated widely in Washington, where credulous State Department advisors and top military intelligence officials saw in them an explanation for the power of Jews and the menace of Bolshevism. Robert Lansing's secretary, Richard Crane, was particularly obsessed by the documents concerning the "Jewish aspiration for establishing world dominion by the overthrow of existing governments." Crane was convinced that Lenin was the only Bolshevik leader who was not a Jew, and he believed that many Bolsheviks had learned their politics on the East Side of New York City before returning to Russia. Lansing had feared since at least December 1917 that New York Jews were unreliable, and in 1919 he concluded that "a vigorous propaganda" in favor of Bolshevism was "largely in the hands of Jews."[61]

American representatives in and around Russia also spied a Jewish plot. The U.S. commissioner to the Baltic provinces, for example, insisted that "the Russian Revolution has largely been engineered by the Jews. Bolshevism is their great revenge." Herbert Hoover, head of the American Relief Administration, similarly struck by "the very large majority of Jews" in the leadership of "Communistic outbreaks," determined that "the plague of social arson" was "the penalty that the Gentile is paying for his injustice of the past."[62]

Although Wilson was less susceptible to anti-Semitism, he did worry about the loyalty of Jews, particularly "on the East Side of New York."[63] The president was also not immune to the epidemic of wild rumors about

Jewish connections to Bolshevik conspiracies. At a cabinet meeting in November 1918, "the President spoke of the Bolsheviki having decided upon a revolution in Germany, Hungary, and Switzerland, and that they had $10 million ready in Switzerland, besides more money in Swedish banks held by the Jews from Russia, ready for the campaign of propaganda."[64] Thus, while some government officials suspected that Wilson had succumbed to Jewish and Bolshevik influence, the president actually shared some his advisors' fears.[65]

Wilson also shared with Lansing and other members of his cabinet an anxiety about increasing African American militancy, which many Americans blamed on Bolshevik propaganda. In July 1918, Secretary of War Newton Baker advised Wilson that he was "much disturbed" by the situation "among the negroes," since "reports of the Military Intelligence Branch of the Army seem to indicate more unrest among them than in years." Later, military intelligence officers asserted that Soviet emissary Ludwig Martens "has been actively financing plans for an uprising among the negroes," and legislators and journalists made similar charges. Wilson did not often voice his deepest fears. However, sailing across the Atlantic in March 1919 his doctor heard him say that blacks in America had grown more demanding, that black soldiers in France had been placed on the same level as whites and it had "gone to their heads," and that "the American negro returning from abroad would be our greatest medium in conveying bolshevism to America."[66]

"Puritanism" vs. Bolshevism

Beyond the "shadowy fears" about immigrants and African Americans, there were other "undefined antipathies" that associated domestic sexual, moral, and religious turmoil with Russian radicalism. Soon after the March Revolution feminists urged Wilson to follow the Russian example of enfranchising women. Suffragettes demonstrating outside the White House angered the president and first lady by displaying a banner which announced to a visiting Russian mission that Wilson was "deceiving Russia" about America being a democracy, since many American women were denied the right to vote.[67]

After November 1917, Americans who favored equality for women and challenged traditional sex roles were increasingly labeled "Bolsheviki," while American diplomats in Europe envisioned "Bolshevism" as a compound of fanatical feminism and Jewish radicalism. Linking internal and external challenges in that way became a favorite tactic for defenders of the moral and social order. Thus, conservatives played on the common association of Bolshevism with free love as they advocated intervention in Russia. In 1918 Ambassador David Francis warned the State Department that

"Bolshevik success in Russia would be [a] menace to all orderly governments, ours not excepted, and would . . . impair the foundations of society
itself," in part because "it looks contemptuously on the sacredness of the
family." After returning to the United States in 1919, Francis helped to
spread this idea with sensational testimony before a Senate committee that
several Soviet provinces "have gone so far as to nationalize their women."
Like-minded Senators inserted reports of the alleged Soviet "nationalization of women" into the *Congressional Record* in support of arguments that
the United States should use force to restore order in Russia.[68]

"Bolshevism" also seemed to many to embody the menace of rising indifference or hostility to religion. In California, a Presbyterian minister
who had been close to Christian Socialism before 1917 warned in 1919
that the "radical atheism" of the "rabid Russian Bolshevists" was being
matched by anarchists in the United States. Religious newspapers printed
cartoons that graphically associated Bolshevism with "heresy" and "apos-
tasy," as well as immorality. While Presbyterians were of course not the
only religious group disturbed by "Bolshevism," conservative Presbyterians reacted with special intensity to a perceived threat to civilization.[69]

Thus, in many lurid ways, Bolshevism was implicated with a wide-
ranging challenge to the traditional religion, morality, and culture that
both critics and defenders characterized as "Puritanism."[70] After November 1917, Robert Lansing was quick to identify these domestic menaces
with Bolsheviks in Russia. "The one thing they are striving to bring
about," he concluded in December, "is the 'Social Revolution,' which will
sweep away national boundaries, racial distinctions and modern political,
religious and social institutions, and make the ignorant and incapable
mass of humanity dominant in the earth." Bolshevism, Lansing reemphasized in October 1918, was a threat to "life, property, family ties, personal
conduct, all the most sacred rights."[71] Reinforcing religious faith would
help to thwart international Bolshevism, Lansing believed. Near the
height of the Red Scare, Lansing advised Presbyterian leaders that the radicalism that threatened "the disruption of the present social order" called
for "a living aggressive Christianity to win in this supreme conflict and to
vanquish the evil ideas which now seem so potent in the world."[72]

Another American who linked the domestic social and cultural crisis to
the external menace of communism was David Prescott Barrows, a Berkeley professor who enlisted in the army in 1917. At the end of that year, dis-
gusted by the "widely spread contagion of life and morals" in America and
disturbed by the course of events in Russia, Barrows underwent a revival
of his "Puritan faith." Fired by this "renewed religious experience," Barrows scrawled a passionate tirade in his diary, encapsulating his worldview
in one vehement sentence: "If I have any enemies, if there are any with
whom I burn to contest for the mastery of the coming generation of men

and nations, it is with these people — Radical social reformers, Bolsheviki, luxury seeking Jews, Pacifists generally, writers and readers of *The Masses*, University teachers of lax moral standards, the idle [?] privileged classes everywhere — these are my enemies, and the enemies, in my belief, of the Lord God, of all needful authority, of all great efforts of statesmanship, of the ordered progress of the world and of the redemption of the dark and disordered countries of the world."[73] Assembling that cast of domestic devils and foreign enemies helped Barrows to purge enervating doubts and regain a strong sense of direction. Eager to take action "against the Bolsheviki," Barrows volunteered to inspect anti-Bolshevik forces in Manchuria in early 1918, and then became head of the intelligence section for the U.S. military expedition to Siberia. After returning from Siberia in 1919, Barrows launched a polemical war against the internal enemy, accusing Berkeley Socialists of being Bolshevists who had "repudiated the moral order" and wanted to establish governments based on "committees of propertyless workingmen." Barrows's experience thus illustrated the way Americans who felt threatened by radical social change used Bolshevism as a scapegoat to exorcise demons and revitalize "Puritan" traditions.[74]

Like Barrows and prominent members of the National Civic Federation who condemned the Bolshevik aim "to destroy the bulwarks of morality and social order," many of the most ardent and influential opponents of Bolshevism were of "Puritan" backgrounds.[75] George Kennan, whom Lansing respected as "the highest authority in America on Russia," was a descendant of Pilgrims and Puritans, and the religious training he received from his Presbyterian family was, he later recalled, "of the strictest and severest kind." As Kennan observed, he "began fighting . . . the Bolsheviki" in May 1917, and thereafter did whatever he could "to array our people and our Government against them." In letters to Lansing, Kennan argued that "under no circumstances should the United States recognize the Bolsheviki" or cooperate with them, in part "because their political and economic opinions and theories constitute a disrupting and destructive force which could demoralize any people and ruin any country."[76]

Although DeWitt Clinton Poole, the U.S. consul general in Moscow in 1918, was part of a younger generation, like Kennan he remembered a strict upbringing by a father who "came out of a very severe background," a "Puritan background." To Poole, the struggle with Bolshevism in Russia "very early presented itself in terms of relative morality or amorality as over against eternal moral values," and he became "emotionally and morally a deep enemy of the Bolsheviks." Outraged by the Bolshevik government's "barbarous oppression," Poole warned the Soviet foreign commissar in September 1918, "Your cause loiters on the verge of complete moral bankruptcy."[77]

The sternly judgmental Calvinist temperament contributed to the fervor of "Puritan" anti-Bolshevism. David Barrows, for example, believed the U.S. government should say to the Bolsheviks: "We will assail you on every possible side and we will not remit . . . until you go down, into the pit with every government that forgets God." "Puritanism" also spurred a missionary drive. In 1919, Barrows supported the League of Nations because he wanted "to see us committed to the task of stabilizing this world and giving justice to those afflicted peoples [in Siberia, Silesia, and Armenia] by the use of our military forces."[78]

While Woodrow Wilson was reluctant to endorse overt military intervention in Russia, much of the "Puritan" fire burned in him, and it helped fuel his opposition to Bolshevism. At Paris in April 1919, Ray Stannard Baker was struck by the thought that Wilson "would be terrible if he were evil. In him John Knox — Calvin — on too large a scale." The Calvinist in Wilson emerged even more forcefully later that year. As Wilson lashed out at domestic opponents of the League and the Bolshevik pariahs in September, he repeatedly declared that he was a descendant of Scottish Covenanters. Just as they stood "by their religious principles" he was determined "to see this job through no matter what influence of evil I must withstand." Bolshevism was repugnant not only to Wilson's religious principles, but also to his political ideals and his faith in capitalism, all of which combined in his "Puritan ethic." Wilson epitomized that deep sense of ideological antipathy when he declared in September 1919 that Bolshevism meant "the negation of everything that is American."[79]

Many Soviet actions had angered Wilson and his advisors. In addition to inciting workers in the West to overthrow their governments, Lenin and Trotsky formalized Russia's withdrawal from the war against the Central Powers, repudiated responsibility for loans to previous Russian governments, and nationalized foreign investments. However, American anti-Bolshevism was not simply or primarily a reaction to the acts of the Soviet regime.[80] Antipathy toward socialism and communism was deeply embedded in American political culture long before the Bolsheviks seized power in Petrograd. Years earlier, Americans had "heard all sorts of Bolshevik oratory" in U.S. cities, and conservatives, dreading the prospect of revolutionary change, had imagined the creation of a "Scarlet Empire."[81] After the Bolshevik Revolution, "Puritan" Americans' anxieties about social and cultural rebellion at home fused with their images of "Bolshevism," which they came to loathe as a total challenge to the American way of life and to their vision of the future of the world.

Americans disagreed about the best way to counter Bolshevism. Some favored direct military action, accompanied by straightforward declarations of holy war. Others, committed to sending as many soldiers as possible to France and worried about the political repercussions of overt intervention against Bolshevism, preferred subtler methods, including diplomatic ostracism of the Soviet regime, moral encouragement of Russian democrats, and financial support for anti-Bolshevik forces. Each of these indirect efforts was initiated by the Wilson administration in the first weeks after the Bolshevik Revolution, before Soviet economic policies were clearly enunciated, while many American firms were exempted from nationalization, and well before the Soviet government ratified the Brest-Litovsk peace treaty. While ideological antipathy to Bolshevism was not the sole determinant of the early decisions about relations with Soviet Russia, it figured in the first moves toward intervention in Russia and gradually became the dominant factor in U.S. policy.

3

KEEPING FAITH WITH RUSSIA

AMBASSADOR BORIS BAKHMETEFF
AND U.S. EFFORTS TO RESTORE "DEMOCRACY"

In an impromptu speech to wealthy Red Cross volunteers at the New York Metropolitan Opera House on May 18, 1918, Woodrow Wilson's thoughts spontaneously turned to Russia. Rejecting "insincere approaches" about peace from Germany as attempts to gain "a free hand, particularly in the East, to carry out purposes of conquest and exploitation," the president vowed: "I intend to stand by Russia as well as France." While someone shouted "God bless you!" Wilson swept the crowd up in his crusading zeal. Declaring that "the helpless and the friendless are the very ones that need friends and succor," he called for pride and determination in waging America's "unselfish war," its "fight for mankind."[1]

Like many of Wilson's pronouncements about Russia in the first year and a half after the Bolshevik Revolution, his Red Cross speech featured an inspired highmindedness, vague enough to permit a variety of interpretations. To some of the president's supporters on the Left, standing by Russia meant resisting Allied intervention as well as German imperialism in Soviet Russia. To Wilson's more conservative friends, standing by Russia entailed a military expedition, combined with economic relief, to rescue the country from Bolshevik and German domination.[2] Wilson himself interpreted the ambiguous phrase as a reflection of "the most intimate feeling for the sufferings of the ordinary man in Russia" and an expression of American altruism. "We cannot make anything out of our standing by Russia at this time," Wilson explained to Mexican editors in June 1918, "and yet the people of the United States rose to that suggestion as to no other that I made in that address."[3]

Through all the confusion and vacillation of Wilsonian policy toward revolutionary Russia, the most consistent manifestation of the desire to "stand by Russia" was U.S. support for Boris Bakhmeteff, the Russian ambassador sent to Washington after the tsarist government collapsed. In the summer of 1917, as the United States began providing financial support to bolster the new Provisional Government and back the Russian war effort, Bakhmeteff developed close relations with top Wilson administration officials, advising them on how to pursue the common goal of a fighting Russian democracy. Although the Kerensky regime fell in November 1917, the United States continued to recognize Bakhmeteff as ambassador. President Wilson and his key advisors agreed with the Russian embassy that the Bolsheviks did not represent the Russian people. To speed the restoration of "democracy," the administration arranged with Bakhmeteff for his embassy to become the most important conduit for covert American assistance to anti-Bolshevik armies in Russia. Although that aid did not produce a White victory in the Russian Civil War, the United States persisted in recognizing Bakhmeteff as a symbol of its hopes for a reunited, democratic Russia after the civil war ended. Thus, the Wilson administration's political and financial relationship with the Russian embassy, which has been neglected in many studies, must be considered in order to understand the origins of secretive American intervention in revolutionary Russia and the elements of continuity in U.S. policy from 1917 through 1920.[4]

At the end of the harsh winter of 1916–1917, staggered by military losses, stung by accusations of treason, undermined by deep divisions in Russian society, and unable to cope with a breakdown of transportation, the ancient Romanov autocracy disintegrated. In March 1917 bread shortages, strikes, and street demonstrations in Petrograd sparked a spontaneous revolution that the Russian police and army were unable and unwilling to extinguish. When Nicholas II abdicated, liberal and moderate socialist members of the tsarist Duma formed a Provisional Government to lead the country until elections for a Constituent Assembly could be held. This temporary regime's claims to legitimacy were tenuous, and its exercise of power was contingent upon the consent of the socialist-dominated Soviet of Workers' and Soldiers' Deputies.[5]

American diplomats in Petrograd were initially troubled by this unexpected turn of events. Joshua Butler Wright, counselor of the U.S. embassy, feared that the "disorders" might lead to "a socialist outbreak." Ambassador David Francis warned the State Department about "lawless demonstrations" and worried about the actions of "irresponsible soldiers."[6]

Francis and Wright were relieved when they found that Duma leaders were assuming power and making "strenuous efforts to preserve order." On March 14, Francis wired Washington that in contrast to the proclamations issued by the Soviet, which were "violent in tone and tended to alarm all law-abiding citizens," the ministers who formed a Provisional Government were "appealing to the reason and patriotism of the people" and taking steps to suppress anarchy.[7]

Comforted by the sense that political elites had taken command of the situation, Francis and other Americans delighted in what they saw as a marvelous triumph of democracy over autocracy. Requesting authority to recognize the Provisional Government, Francis breathlessly assured the State Department on March 18 that "this Revolution is the practical realization of that principle of government which we have championed and advocated, I mean consent by the governed." Before Francis's telegram reached Washington, Secretary of State Lansing urged Wilson to "encourage and strengthen the new democratic government of Russia." Agreeing that the United States "should aid in every way the advancement of democracy in Russia," Colonel House suggested that Wilson should "recognize the new Russian government as soon as England and France do so." Feeding the president's vanity, House intimated that Wilson's speeches had "accelerated democracy throughout the world" and were largely responsible for "the present outcome in Russia."[8]

Unaware of the extent of Russian war-weariness, U.S. officials fancied that "the purpose of the Revolution is primarily to strengthen the nation in the present war." Samuel Harper, one of America's few academic experts on Russia, contributed to the euphoric misunderstanding. On March 15, the University of Chicago professor advised the State Department that the aim of the revolution was "to create conditions that would make it possible for Russia to bring into force all her strength. Means therefore more effective prosecution of war and war until victory." Strongly influenced by conversations he had with liberal and conservative Duma leaders in 1916, Harper repeatedly insisted in the spring of 1917 that "the element that has engineered the revolution is not socialistic or anarchistic," and that "it was a purely political and not a social revolution."[9]

Harper's misleading views were solicited not only by the State Department, but also by wealthy men who advised the president informally on Russian policy. One of Harper's patrons was Charles R. Crane, the largest contributor to Wilson's re-election campaign, who declined Wilson's 1914 offer to be ambassador to Russia. Another magnate who sought Harper's guidance was Cyrus H. McCormick Jr., a powerful Princeton trustee and head of the International Harvester Company, which was very active in Russia. Influenced by Harper, these friends of Wilson stressed the sobriety and moderation of the revolution in Russia. McCormick found it reassuring that "this revolution seems (for the present at least) to be in the control of the conservative rather than the radical element." Crane, a long-time supporter of new foreign minister P. N. Miliukov, gushed that the Provisional Government's members were all "splendid administrators, and represent the new Russia." [10]

By March 20, Wilson concluded that "the revolution against the autocracy had been successful," and his administration expressed its enthusiasm by rushing to be first to recognize the new government. At a cabinet meeting on March 23, Wilson's personal identification with the Provisional Government was evident in an allusion to Miliukov, a former professor. The government "ought to be good," Wilson said with a smile, "because it has a professor at its head." [11]

As they anxiously contemplated taking a divided country into the war against Germany, Americans saw in Russia what they wanted to see. Wilsonian liberals needed to believe that entering the Great War was not just a selfish action in pursuit of American economic and strategic interests. Bloodshed had to be redeemed by a higher, unselfish purpose. The miraculous Russian Revolution of March 1917 provided that transfiguring justification. The *New York World*, edited by Frank Cobb, an ardent admirer of Woodrow Wilson, proclaimed that the war had become "a war of democracy against autocracy" whose "momentous conclusions . . . must transcend the terms of any possible treaty of peace." On March 25, a few days after Cobb interviewed Wilson about the war, the *World* urged Americans to "stand for a free Russia" and argued that the revolution in Petrograd removed "the last considerable honest doubt of our national duty in the world crisis." [12]

When Robert Lansing suggested on March 20 that "the revolution in Russia . . . had removed the one objection to affirming that the European War was a war between Democracy and Absolutism," Wilson at first demurred, but then warmed to the idea. [13] Addressing Congress on April 2, the president cited the "wonderful and heartening" events in Russia as he summoned America to a crusade to make the world "safe for democracy." In a reflection of the fact that his study of history rarely had encompassed the lands east of Germany, Wilson asserted that the "terrible" Romanov autocracy "was not in fact Russian in origin, character, or purpose," and proclaimed that "Russia was . . . always in fact democratic at heart." Now that the alien despotism had been shaken off, he enthused, "the great, generous Russian people" were adding their might to the forces that were fighting for freedom in the world.[14]

Like Wilson, many Americans convinced themselves that in one of the great, transcendent moments of history, patriotic Russians had deposed an incompetent, pro-German despotism in order to join the kindred Western democracies in a holy war. The revolution, it was widely believed, would not only reinvigorate Russia's fighting spirit, but also touch off revolts against the German and Austro-Hungarian autocracies.[15]

Such wishful thinking fostered an underestimation of the sacrifices America would have to make to defeat Germany and an illiberal attitude toward the Russian war effort. Immediately after Wilson delivered his war message to Congress, his advisors offered a credit to help the Provisional Government carry on the war. As Wilson explained on April 14, he made "a stipulation that the money lent should be spent upon the war." The president knew that "the position of Russia was very uncertain"; he recognized that the Russians might "find the war an intolerable evil and . . . desire to get an end of it on any reasonable terms." Yet that "would be a serious blow to the Allies," and he was "not prepared to finance Russia . . . in order that she might get out of the war." Richard Crane of the State Department was more blunt: "The stand by the people here," he reported, "is that if Russia should fall down we would be in the war up to our necks." By May 17 Secretary of the Treasury William G. McAdoo established a $100 million credit for the Provisional Government to purchase war supplies in the United States, in the hope that this would allow Russia both to continue the war and to secure "the blessings of self-government."[16]

The Wilson administration's faith in a regenerated democratic Russia was reinforced by the man the Provisional Government named as its ambassador to Washington. Boris A. Bakhmeteff was born in Tbilisi in 1880, became a professor at the Polytechnic Institute in St. Petersburg in 1905, and taught there until 1917. From 1915 to November 1916, he headed a Russian war industries purchasing mission to the United States. When the tsar abdicated, the liberal-minded Bakhmeteff became vice minister of commerce and industry in the Provisional Government. Like many members of the Constitutional Democratic (Kadet) Party, he aspired to an "above-party" position, viewing himself as less of a political figure than "a professional contributor to the constructive building of a new Russia." His experience on the 1915–16 mission led him to feel an affinity for the atmosphere of "practical idealism" in Wilsonian Washington and gave him an understanding of American institutions and people that he believed would be useful in representing Russia.[17] Bakhmeteff impressed Americans in Petrograd. In April 1917, Ambassador Francis predicted that Bakhmeteff would be a "most capable" diplomat, and in May Charles Crane praised him as "one of the foremost men of present-day Russia." [18]

Preceded by those recommendations, Bakhmeteff journeyed to Washington in June 1917 to replace the tsar's ambassador, who had been scorned by President Wilson because of his monarchist sympathies.[19] In contrast to his more conservative predecessor, Boris Bakhmeteff seemed to embody the liberal democratic spirit and pro-Ally military resolve that Wilson and his top diplomatic advisors championed in Russia.

From the beginning, Bakhmeteff showed a knack for saying what the Wilson administration and the American people wanted to hear. After greeting the new ambassador-designate, Third Assistant Secretary of State Breckinridge Long noted that "Bakhmetieff says Russia is strengthening daily and will not make separate peace." Similarly, Assistant Secretary of State William Phillips observed on June 21 that the Russian mission "made a good impression" at a White House dinner by being "eager to talk of the great offensive which is to be made by the Russians." [20]

Bakhmeteff promoted unwarranted optimism about the Russian war effort in newspaper interviews and addresses to wildly enthusiastic crowds as well. Ignoring demonstrations for peace in the streets of Petrograd, Bakhmeteff told the *New York Times* that "the war was one of the great fundamental indisputable things upon which all Russia was agreed." Even after German troops occupied Riga in September, Bakhmeteff insisted that "only 1 or 2 per cent of the army" was unreliable and vowed that "the Russian army is not crushed, and is not going to be crushed." [21]

The ambassador also won approval from American leaders and audiences by pandering to the popular notion that the Russian peasant commune had made democratic principles "a part of the very life of the Russian people." Paralleling Wilson's address to Congress on April 2, Bakhmeteff argued that the "idea of democracy" was not "new and strange" to Russians, but had been instilled "in the blood." The Slav, he insisted, was prepared to imitate and assimilate American ideas and practices. As a result, he told a cheering throng in Boston, "Russia, the great democracy of the East, will stand hand in hand with you, her eldest sister, this great democracy of the West, to uphold throughout the world the high ideals of humanity, liberty, and justice." [22]

When the new Russian ambassador formally presented his credentials at the White House on July 5, he sang a rhetorical duet with the president. Echoing themes from Wilson's declaration of war speech, Bakhmeteff stressed that the United States and Russia were joined in a "common struggle for freedom and lasting peace" and were "guided by the same unselfish aims, the same human and democratic principles." In harmony with Bakhmeteff, Wilson affirmed that the two governments and peoples were "actuated by the same lofty motives" and expressed his conviction that "the devoted people of Russia" would, by "overcoming disloyalty from within and intrigue from without, remain steadfast to the cause."[23]

Soon after Wilson and Bakhmeteff proclaimed the solidarity of their countries, news of the failure of the Russian offensive, violent clashes in the streets of Petrograd, and the resignations of ministers of the Provisional Government raised serious doubts among American officials about Russia's ability to overcome antiwar agitation and wage war vigorously. In the wake of the "July Days" demonstrations, Ambassador Francis told the Russian foreign minister that he would "recommend no further assistance until stable government formed which would prosecute war" and suppress lawlessness.[24]

Such American and Allied pressure aggravated the predicament of the Provisional Government by reinforcing the reluctance of its leaders to press for the negotiated peace Russians increasingly demanded. Already in May, the U.S. consul in Petrograd observed that "distrust of the Allies" and a "feeling of being forced to continue a distasteful and irksome war" posed "an imminent and tremendous danger." In the following months, "peasants in uniform" deserted in droves and many Russians impatient for an end to the war joined the Bolshevik Party. While Bakhmeteff recommended that Russia seek American support for "elucidation of the purposes of the war" at an Allied conference in order to ease the Provisional Government's domestic predicament, Foreign Minister M. I. Tereshchenko decided that Russia could not negotiate successfully from a position of humiliating weakness and postponed war aims discussions. "Staying in the war was perhaps a fatal mistake," Bakhmeteff later acknowledged, but like Tereshchenko and other Russian liberals he believed "it was the right thing to do."[25]

Bakhmeteff had hoped that emphasizing ideological sympathies and stressing that the United States needed to support a democratic Russia in order to have a strong role in Europe would win sufficient American aid to stabilize Russian domestic conditions. Now he faced the challenge of overcoming the uncertainty and reserve of American officials, which was delaying the establishment of further credits.[26]

Instead of demanding further audiences with the increasingly isolated Wilson, Bakhmeteff pursued a more tactful course. He followed House's advice "to press the proper officials rather than to take his troubles" to the president directly.[27] The Russian ambassador began meeting frequently with top State Department representatives, particularly Breckinridge Long and Counselor Frank Polk, with whom he established "very close and warm ties of friendship."[28]

While cultivating personal connections to officials who were responsible for the day-to-day supervision of American relations with Russia,

Bakhmeteff also opened and preserved lines of communication to Wilson's two key foreign policy advisors, House and Lansing, whose ideas about Russia increasingly diverged. Adapting quickly to the unconventional policy process of the Wilson administration, the ambassador realized that in 1917 the best way to reach the White House was often to travel to New York or Magnolia, Massachusetts, to see House. On his first visits to Magnolia, Bakhmeteff quickly developed friendly relations with the colonel in discussions of peace proposals and war aims. "I like Bachkmeteff [*sic*]," House noted on July 22. "He seemed sympathetic to my peace plans . . . and he assured me that the new Russia would stand side by side with the United States in the advancement of such a program." In August, after a long discussion of how to respond to an appeal for peace by the pope, House wrote warmly in his diary: "Bakhmetieff and I 'speak the same language.' He is a thorough-going liberal."[29]

Bakhmeteff confided to House that he found "no sympathy in Lansing," who did "not appear sympathetic or to have any real understanding of Russian liberal opinion."[30] While Colonel House was sensitive and tolerant toward the Russian desires for war aims revision and peace, Lansing showed less patience. In April 1917, Lansing was impressed by Bakhmeteff's predecessor's prediction that the Provisional Government would "not last and that Socialists may get upper hand and make peace with Germany." In May and June, Lansing received letters from Russian expert George Kennan, who criticized "the irresolute, not to say timid, policy of the Provisional Government," urged giving "no encouragement whatever" to the "dangerous" Soviet, and hoped that "the true Russian democracy" would "put down" the radical socialists. The moderate socialist A. F. Kerensky became minister of war and then prime minister in reorganizations of the Provisional Government in the spring and early summer of 1917. Partly because of Kennan's influence, Lansing was more pessimistic than House and Wilson about the ability of Kerensky to "suppress radicalism, and make society safe from lawlessness." By August 1917 he looked instead for "some dominant personality" to impose "order by arbitrary military power."[31]

Bakhmeteff waged a difficult struggle against such skepticism about Kerensky and the Provisional Government. As House reported to Wilson on July 23, Bakhmeteff warned that unless the Provisional Government received more American financial assistance it could not last, but with more money, he predicted, conditions would steadily improve and a stable democracy would be established. A month later, after Bakhmeteff reiterated his appeal, he was able to report a shift in American attitudes to a full desire to meet Russian needs.[32]

While Lansing and Wilson were disturbed by reports of "disloyalty and enemy-inspired propaganda" in Russia, they agreed with Bakhmeteff that it was important to maintain public optimism about Russia's "democracy" and eventual military victory. In an August 24 message to a state conference Kerensky convened in Moscow, Wilson expressed "confidence in the ultimate triumph of ideals of democracy and self-government against all enemies within and without," and gave "renewed assurance of every material and moral assistance" to the Provisional Government. The administration backed Wilson's words with a new $100 million credit to cover military contracts. Although Wilson did not explicitly identify Russia's "enemies within," it was significant that several months before the Bolsheviks seized power American policy was acquiring a simultaneously anti-German and anti-Bolshevik momentum that would carry over into 1918.[33]

In late August and early September, when American representatives in Russia hoped General Lavr Kornilov was moving to take control in Petrograd, the Russian embassy in Washington sided with Kerensky in the power struggle and rejoiced when the Kornilov revolt failed. As the authority of the Provisional Government deteriorated in the fall of 1917, however, Bakhmeteff came to share Lansing's belief in the necessity of a military crackdown. At Lansing's house on October 3, the Russian ambassador "said that he felt that bloodshed in Petrograd was almost impossible to prevent and that the radicals would have to be put down by force."[34]

While privately growing more pessimistic, Bakhmeteff still emphasized to Lansing that it was "extremely essential" for the Allies to banish distrust and "gain faith in the decision of Russia to continue their stand with the Allies in the coming fight with the foe despite all the difficulties and obstacles." Expressions of confidence and signs of cooperation, he said, "could be of the greatest moral and political value." The public pronouncements by Lansing and other administration officials accorded with this advice. As long as the Provisional Government clung to power, the secretary recognized the need to keep his doubts to himself and to "do all that we can to strengthen morally and materially the existing government."[35]

In mid-October, after Bakhmeteff applied for additional credits, the Treasury Department extended a further $50 million. By November, the administration had agreed to provide a total of $325 million in loans and credits, though it had actually transferred only $187,729,750 to the Provisional Government. This American assistance was much less than Russian officials requested and it was only a small fraction of the aid given to Britain and France, but it was the most anxious U.S. leaders felt they could do.[36]

Disturbed by reports of Russian demoralization and military inactivity, Washington privately reemphasized the conditionality of its assistance to the Provisional Government. On November 2, after newspaper reports that Prime Minister Kerensky said the burden of the war was on the rest of the Allies, Frank Polk and Assistant Secretary of the Treasury Russell Leffingwell discussed "whether we could continue to give Russia aid in view of Kerensky's interview." The next day Polk reiterated to Bakhmeteff that "it was very necessary we should be convinced that Russia intended to fight."[37]

Bakhmeteff did not need the reminder, as he was already working together with Lansing to restore the facade of optimism. Under the headline, "We Assist Russia; She Stays in War — Lansing Voices Full Faith," the *New York Times* reported on November 3 that "Russia is not out of the war. She is to make no separate peace. The Russian Embassy and the State Department made that clear today. The confidence of the United States Government in the Russian cause was emphasized by the action of the Treasury Department in placing an additional credit of $31,700,000 at Russia's disposal."

When news of the Bolshevik seizure of power in Petrograd reached the United States on November 8, Bakhmeteff was in Memphis on a speaking tour to arouse American enthusiasm for the Russian war effort. Informed of the upheaval in the Russian capital, Bakhmeteff stressed a distinction between the Russian people and the Soviet regime that would become a cardinal theme of American policy. "The spirit prevailing in Petrograd is not representative of the Russian spirit as a whole," he declared. That night, Bakhmeteff assured a large audience that the majority of Russians were still "heart and soul with the Kerensky government," argued that "the maximalist revolt was a revolt of a few against the many," and urged that the Bolsheviks "must be overthrown."[38]

In Washington, U.S. officials looked to Bakhmeteff and his staff for advice, and many shared his immediate reaction that the Soviet government had to be eliminated. "The Russian Embassy," William Phillips noted on November 8, "is of the opinion that . . . the Bolsheviki are not very strong throughout the country nor possessed of sufficient brains to form a Government. All believe, however, that bloodshed will occur in Petrograd." Through the following week, Phillips anxiously followed reports on Kerensky's efforts to gather "loyal troops" to retake the capital and remained hopeful that Kerensky was "getting the upper hand." The only "ray of hope" officials at the State Department saw was that the upheaval "might serve to get the extreme and dangerous radical views 'out of Russia's system,'" and that "an 'iron man' capable of getting order out of chaos" would emerge.[39]

While many watched for a military strongman, other officials had not yet abandoned hope that Kerensky would regain power. George Creel, chairman of Wilson's organization for war propaganda, the Committee on Public Information (CPI), confided on November 9 that "we are hoping that the disturbance is confined to Petrograd, and that Kerensky will reach

Moscow and rally the people for a finished fight." On the same day, Wilson told cabinet members he "thought we could not yet presume R[ussia] would fail." According to the *Washington Post*, Wilson had "not for a moment wavered in his faith in the greatness of the Russian people." Much as Wilson had separated the Russian people from the tsarist autocracy in April 1917, in November 1917 he began to differentiate between the true Russian people and radicals in Petrograd. The *New York American* reported that Wilson was clinging to the belief that Kerensky would return to power and predicted that the United States would support him "in an effort to overthrow the Maximalists." The *New York World*, similarly, learned that "the United States . . . will furnish Kerensky all the funds he may need to rehabilitate his Government and suppress the extreme radicals." Although Kerensky once again proved a disappointment, the newspapers correctly gauged the direction of U.S. policy when they anticipated American support for anti-Bolshevik movements.[40]

Even amid the optimism about Kerensky's last stand, Wilson and his aides expressed consternation about how to pursue the inherently contradictory goal of a belligerent Russian democracy. Wilson fretted on November 10, 1917, that "all sorts of work in Russia now is rendered extremely difficult because no one channel connects with any other, apparently." Bakhmeteff found his Washington contacts similarly gloomy about the disruption of the American financial relationship with Russia. U.S. credits had been linked directly to the Russian war effort, and the Soviet call for an immediate armistice dashed American hopes for renewed Russian military action against Germany.[41]

Immediately after the Bolsheviks seized power, the Wilson administration suspended financial credits and contracts for military supplies to Russia. As the *New York Times* explained on November 10, "the United States Government had decided to make no more payments to the Russian Government," in part because Treasury Department officials were "concerned as to . . . the ability of the de facto authority in Petrograd to meet its obligations to this country." If Kerensky or other anti-Bolshevik leaders succeeded in retaking the capital, however, financial assistance might resume: the Treasury Department was disposed "to continue advances as soon as the present chaos has given way to orderly administration provided that the authority established does not attempt to take Russia out of the war."[42]

The fall of the Provisional Government placed Bakhmeteff in an awkward position. While support for governments in exile would become common later in the century, in 1917 being an ambassador without a government was "unprecedented," as Bakhmeteff later recalled.[43] However, he found that he continued to share many views and aims with the Wilson administration. By stressing the common policies of nonrecognition of the Soviet government, friendship for the Russian people, and efforts toward a restoration of democracy, he succeeded in laying a foundation for continuing cooperation and financial relations with the administration.

Recognition of "Loyal Russia," Nonrecognition of the Bolsheviks

When he returned from Memphis to Washington on November 10, Bakhmeteff reiterated that the Bolsheviks were "in no way representative of the whole of Russia" and announced that the Russian embassy would refuse to accept the authority of the Soviet regime. This declaration harmonized with the Wilsonian policy of refusing to recognize morally repugnant regimes, which dated back to Wilson's disapproval of the Mexican dictator Huerta's seizure of power in 1913. Bakhmeteff's position was also in sympathy with the views of top officials at the State Department. On November 10, for example, Lansing indicated to the *New York Times* that "the United States would be in no haste to extend recognition" to the Bolsheviks.[44]

Bakhmeteff could take some comfort from Wilson's first public references to the Bolshevik regime. In Buffalo on November 12, the president reacted to the Soviet interest in peace negotiations with Germany by ominously warning, "Any body of free men that compounds with the present German government is compounding for its own destruction." After consulting at the State Department about how to interpret Wilson's remarks, Albert Fox of the *Washington Post* reported that "the President has good reason to know that Lenine [*sic*] and many of his followers are tools of Germany," that his mind was against the "dupes of Lenine," and that the United States would probably join Entente leaders in "sending sound advice and promise of practical support" to "loyal Russia." While Wilson's anti-Bolshevism was more ambiguous than that of his State Department advisors, his insinuation that the Bolshevik leaders were agents of German intrigue was an early sign that he would not recognize them.[45]

In the absence of a formal U.S. statement or direct private assurances, however, Bakhmeteff's diplomatic position remained unclear. For several days he endured this gloomy uncertainty, but then he moved aggressively to clarify his status and influence American policy toward Russia. Realizing that "Mr. Wilson and Mr. Lansing were not on very good terms, and no one knew whether Mr. Lansing *could* get an answer from the President," the ambassador decided to go around the secretary by calling George Creel.[46]

When Creel came to see Bakhmeteff, probably on the night of November 20–21, the ambassador stated that in Petrograd power "had been seized by a small group, obviously against the natural inclinations and desires of the people at large." Instead of allowing this turn of events to paralyze American-Russian relations, Bakhmeteff urged that Wilson should say that the Russian people were allies of America, but Americans did "not sympathize with the Bolshevik form of government nor with the way they seized power." Thus, Bakhmeteff suggested, the United States could help and cooperate with the people, "while no relations with the government were to be maintained."[47]

Bakhmeteff's suggestion accorded with Wilson's private sentiments. On November 13, the president had written a Florida congressman that he had "not lost faith in the Russian outcome by any means. Russia, like France in a past century, will no doubt have to go through deep waters but she will come out upon firm land on the other side and her great people . . . will . . . take their proper place in the world." Wilson and Bakhmeteff both saw the Bolshevik Revolution as a temporary setback that eventually would be overcome. Both also distinguished between the regime in control in Petrograd at that moment and the true, valiant Russian people.[48]

The ambassador's anxiety about his status soon eased. On the day after meeting Bakhmeteff, Creel called to say that "he had seen the President, had given him the complete message, and everything was all right."[49] Shortly thereafter, the State Department invited Bakhmeteff to call on the secretary. Meeting Lansing on November 24, Bakhmeteff stressed the temporary nature of the Bolshevik government and vowed to "continue in not recognizing a 'Bolsheviki' or any similar government which would break loyalty to Russia's Allies and lead the country to a non-participation in the War." Bakhmeteff also pledged to remain at his post in order to maintain responsibility for the financial commitments of "loyal Russia." While Lansing did not make any formal commitment, Bakhmeteff found him "quite sincere in his denunciation of Bolshevism." "After my conversation with Lansing," Bakhmeteff recalled, "our relations with the State Department continued as if, politically, nothing had happened."[50]

The ambassador followed up on the meeting by taking his story to the press. The next day the *New York Times* reported that Lansing gave Bakhmeteff to understand "that the Government would not deal with the Bolsheviki, but would have its transactions with Russia through the Ambassador alone." While no official statement was forthcoming, the *Times* added, it was known that "the Administration does not recognize the Bolsheviki, but does recognize the Ambassador."[51]

In the same weeks that the administration confirmed Bakhmeteff's diplomatic status, it made initial decisions to safeguard the economic ties between the U.S. government and the Russian embassy. Funds advanced by the United States to the Provisional Government that had not yet been expended were deposited at the National City Bank of New York. On November 14, Polk informed a bank officer that despite the "rebellion in Petrograd," the bank was "justified in going ahead" in making payments from those funds "on order of Embassy." While Polk authorized the bank to pay the interest on Provisional Government obligations, Wilson's advisors were divided about whether Bakhmeteff should be able to continue expending U.S. credits. As Polk noted on November 22, "Some have expressed doubt as to whether he is properly accredited representative." Colonel House, who believed there was "no responsible government within sight," counseled "making no more advances at present or permitting any further contracts for purchases." Ambassador Francis, on the other hand, was inclined to allow small additional advances "provided Bakhmeteff [is] still acting Ambassador and authorized to sign obligation."[52]

Without reaching a consensus or making a formal decision, the administration allowed the Russian embassy to continue to draw on the American credits previously extended. On November 22, Treasury Secretary McAdoo informed the State Department that the embassy had between $60 and $70 million on deposit at the National City Bank, and that the bank wanted to know whether it should continue to honor drafts by representatives of the Provisional Government.[53] The State Department evidently approved: on the same day Assistant Secretary of the Treasury Leffingwell requested the National City Bank to transfer funds totaling three million British pounds to the "account of the Russian Government" in London, probably to cover a joint British-American contract to manufacture rifles for the Provisional Government.[54]

Bakhmeteff raised the question of the financial relationship when he met with Lansing on November 24. U.S. credits had allowed the Provisional Government to sign contracts with American firms for locomotives, rifles, clothing, and other goods. Suspending these deals, Bakhmeteff told Lansing, "would ruin a lot of people, throw a lot of labor out of work, and would be extremely harmful to Russian-American relations." On the other hand, continuation of the contracts and the financial ties between the United States and the Provisional Government would assist the struggle against Bolshevism. With the cooperation of the administration, Bakhmeteff planned to "give support to all activities of individuals and institutions in Russia whose endeavors are directed to frustrating the rule of anti-national elements." After plying his diplomatic contacts for reactions to Bakhmeteff's ideas, a *New York Times* correspondent recorded his impression "that the State Department would reply favorably to Ambassador Bakhmeteff's communication and, while not committing the United States to assist him in his efforts to aid the elements hostile to the Maximalists, would not place any obstacles in the way of such aid."[55]

Lansing declined to give a direct response to Bakhmeteff's appeal for continuation of the Russian-American contracts, but suggested that the ambassador discuss the matter with Counselor Frank Polk.[56] On November 26, Polk told Bakhmeteff that no further credits would be extended, but that the funds already advanced could be used to pay for supplies for which the Provisional Government had contracted, as long as he was recognized as the legal Russian ambassador. In return for this continuing diplomatic recognition and financial cooperation, Polk asked for only one thing—that the embassy get American approval prior to requesting the bank to make payments on specific contracts. Bakhmeteff immediately accepted this condition. He agreed with Polk that each week the financial attaché of the Russian embassy, Serge Ughet, "would submit a list of the payments which we were intending to make . . . so that the Treasury would be informed." [57]

The details of the new arrangement were worked out in the following days. By December 5, Ughet and lawyers for the National City Bank concluded an agreement regarding disbursements. Subsequently, payments were made in accordance with the procedure Polk and Bakhmeteff had sketched. Ughet would submit a list of payments; the bank would telephone the Treasury and State Departments for approval; the administration would almost always authorize the disbursements; the bank would then release the requested funds and send Leffingwell a letter of confirmation. Thus, the U.S. government had full control over the funds in the embassy's accounts. As Polk later testified before Congress, "Since December 1917, . . . every payment of any size was made with the knowledge of this Government." [58]

For some in the administration, particularly at the Treasury Department, the main reason for allowing the Russian embassy to continue drawing on U.S. credits was to protect American companies from losses on contracts with the former Provisional Government. However, others realized early on that if the embassy were able to continue purchasing supplies, they could be sent to anti-Bolshevik forces in Russia who were loyal to the Allies. [59]

The White House shared the State Department's basic inclination against diplomatic relations with the Bolsheviks and its sympathy with the idea of supporting anti-Bolshevik Russians. At a cabinet meeting on November 27, the president read a speech by Trotsky, who made the insulting assertion that America intervened in the Great War when "the finance capitalists sent an ultimatum to Wilson" and "Wilson accepted the ultimatum." The president and cabinet decided that there would be "no answer now . . . , for any answer would imply recognition." Wilson was more favorably inclined toward Russians who, like Bakhmeteff, proclaimed their loyalty to the Allied cause. According to the notes of Navy Secretary Josephus Daniels, Wilson observed on November 30 that "Cossacks & others in S[outh] Russia would not follow T[rotsky] but declared for continuance of war, & had asked help and recognition." [60]

Beyond Trotsky's challenge to the unselfish image of the American military crusade, the Bolshevik seizure of power in Russia raised doubts about whether the war would in fact make the world "safe for democracy." The *New York World,* whose consistent support for the president led many to consider it "Mr. Wilson's Organ,"[61] commented on November 11: "Without a self-governing Russia that is sane and sound and ruled according to law and liberty there can be no durable peace in the world. The United States stands always ready to aid that kind of a Russia." Although the editors thought the Bolshevik regime was "certain to collapse," it clung to power week after week. However, like Wilson and his advisors, the *World* was determined to stand by a democratic Russia. "If the world is to be made safe for democracy," the paper editorialized on November 28, "a self-governing Russia must emerge from this Bolshevik welter, and that can come only with the help and encouragement of Great Britain, France, and the United States."

On November 30, the White House press secretary embodied similar thinking in suggestions for an address to Congress. "As for Russia," Joseph Tumulty advised Wilson, "it is timely to renew our faith in the ability of her people to right themselves. . . . Misguided extremists [or] tools of the enemy may be in control for a time but the people will soon expel them. We must be patient and seek in the best way we can to aid and stimulate those elements which are in truth seeking democracy." When Wilson delivered his speech on December 4, he expressed these ideas more indirectly, lamenting "the sad reverses which have recently marked the progress" of Russia "towards an ordered and stable government of free men," and insinuating that the Bolsheviks had come to power as a result of poisonous German propaganda.[62]

Although the president's hostility toward the Soviet leaders was reflected in such allusions, he declined to make a frank statement of his views. On December 4 Lansing presented Wilson with a draft declaration of a refusal to recognize the Bolshevik regime, based on the reasoning that, since Russia was by definition "overwhelmingly democratic in spirit and purpose" and loyal to the Allied cause, "it cannot be that the Bolshevik leaders represent the Russian people or express their true will." According to Lansing, Wilson "approved in principle" of that position, but "did not think that it was opportune to make a public declaration of this sort at the time."[63] The secretary was not as alert as Wilson and House were to the ramifications of a candid anti-Bolshevik proclamation, which would antagonize the Soviet regime, alienate its sympathizers in the West, and restrict the administration's freedom to maneuver.

While Wilson postponed a condemnation of the Bolsheviks, he sympathized with Lansing, Bakhmeteff, and others who proposed sending aid to pro-Ally Russians. Bakhmeteff developed his proposal in a ten-page confidential memorandum distributed throughout the administration in early

December. Reiterating his "emphatical distinction between the Russian people and its passing rulers of violence," Bakhmeteff urged the American government to provide aid to anti-Bolshevik forces in order "to actively assist the reconstruction of the Russian democracy." "Support has to be given to the sound and constructive forces which arise throughout the present chaos in Russia," he argued, "so as to enable them to vanquish the destructive and demoralizing activities of ext[r]emism backed by fraudulous German plans." Helping the opponents of the Bolsheviks would, according to Bakhmeteff, constrain the German war machine's access to Russian resources, block a German "commercial conquest," and revive the prospects of "the great aim of the Russian Revolution — the establishment on the East of Europe of a Great Unified Democratic State." [64]

The support Bakhmeteff envisioned was to include pro-Ally propaganda and economic aid to certain parts of Russia, where it would not "encourage disorderly factors," but would assist "the consolidating work of democratic elements of constructive character." Bakhmeteff specified several areas not under Bolshevik control: the Caucasus, south Russia, and Siberia. To implement this plan, the ambassador suggested that "a special committee, named by the Government . . . should be given disposal of the necessary funds, . . . should inherit the whole complex of orders actually executed or contemplated in behalf of the Russian Government," and "decide which orders would be suspended and which would go forward." [65]

Bakhmeteff's proposal was supported by members of the Root Mission Wilson had sent to Russia in the summer of 1917, including Samuel R. Bertron, a New York banker who worked for the Treasury Department. In a letter to Wilson on December 12, Bertron stated that he had "been in close touch with the Russian Ambassador," and that they had devised a "practical method" for assisting Russia. "Notwithstanding the demoralization of Russia," Bertron argued, "a large portion of the population is sound and can be utilized as a basis for the redemption of Russia, if not as a fighting force, in any event as a permanent great Democracy." Bertron noted that he had discussed the idea with veterans of the Root Mission, Lansing and McAdoo, "who concur." In response to Bertron's request for a meeting, the harried Wilson asked him to "discuss the whole matter" with Lansing "in order that the Secretary of State may advise me regarding its feasibility." [66]

According to historian George F. Kennan, Lansing was "distinctly cool to the suggestion," viewing it as an effort to take "control of policy toward Russia from the Department of State." When Wilson also proved unreceptive, Kennan asserts, "the matter was dropped." While it is true that responsibility was not transferred to a special committee, subsequent U.S. policy paralleled Bakhmeteff's recommendations in many respects. Within days, Lansing and Wilson authorized financial assistance to anti-

Bolshevik forces organizing in southern Russia. (See chapter 4.) Later, when Wilson approved American intervention in Siberia, propaganda and economic relief were important elements of his plans, and a new agency was designated to provide the economic relief.[67]

Apart from a temporary interruption of work on arms contracts in the middle of December, the financial arrangement between the Russian embassy, the State Department, and the Treasury Department developed along the lines Bakhmeteff, Polk, and Leffingwell had drawn.[68] On December 20, the National City Bank made several payments for the Russian embassy, including $325,000 to the Remington Company for rifles and $2,075,000 to J. P. Morgan in connection with a Westinghouse arms contract. While the disposition of such supplies had not been fully resolved, Bakhmeteff informed the Provisional Government's ambassador to France in late December, American officials were doing everything possible to safeguard Russian military orders that were of vital significance for the future of Russia.[69]

Two pledges were central to the financial relationship between the Russian embassy and the U.S. government. Bakhmeteff and leaders of White forces in Russia promised eventually to repay the U.S. funds advanced to them. In return, the Wilson administration remained true to its faith that with American assistance an orderly democracy could be restored in Russia.

While establishing a foundation for covert assistance to anti-Bolshevik forces, Bakhmeteff counseled the Wilson administration to avoid explicit denunciation of the Bolsheviks. In November and December, 1917, House consulted Bakhmeteff about the preparation of a major presidential address on war aims. The Soviet government's appeal to the Allies for an armistice could not "remain unanswered," Bakhmeteff advised House, "for any evasion on the part of the Allies in the matter of peace will simply strengthen the Bolsheviks and help them to create an atmosphere in Russia hostile to the Allies. Any formal protest against Lenin's policy or any threats will have the same effect; they will simply aggravate the situation and aid the Maximalists to go to extremes." Bakhmeteff's recommendation of a restatement of war aims without direct condemnation of the Bolsheviks appealed to House, who asked the Russian ambassador "to make a memorandum of the position he thought this country should take." On December 31, 1917, after meeting twice with Bakhmeteff, House recorded that he "had in mind to advise the President almost along the exact lines he [Bakhmeteff] urged upon me." When House met with Wilson to draft the speech, he read the president a sentence that he had prepared regarding Russia, which he "had submitted to the Russian Ambassador, who thoroughly approved." Wilson agreed with House that they should respond to the Soviet peace proposal with "the broadest and friendliest expressions of sympathy and a promise of more substantial help." George Creel was thinking along the same lines as Bakhmeteff. In late December he urged Wilson to make "some definite statement" of sympathy and desire to help, which would be addressed to "those portions of Russia . . . in possession of anti-German, anti-Lenine hordes. Such a statement would strengthen these forces even while cutting away Bolshevik supports."[70]

Wilson could not afford to be as explicit in public as Creel was in private. In addition to antagonizing the Bolsheviks, a direct, unambiguous promise of support to anti-Bolshevik Russians would disillusion left-leaning Americans and Europeans who sympathized with the Bolshevik peace initiative but might still be enlisted behind an idealistic war against Germany. As Wilson prepared his answer to the Bolsheviks' call for peace in the first week of January 1918, he therefore sought to find the high ground of idealistic principles and an altruistic sympathy for Russia that would mobilize further support for the war while counteracting Bolshevik agitation.

When Wilson delivered his Fourteen Points address on January 8, the ideas of Bakhmeteff, House, and Creel were incorporated in the ambiguous language of Point VI, which promised to help "Russia" obtain "an unhampered and unembarrassed opportunity for the independent determination of her own political development and national policy." Some sympathizers with the Soviet government read that as a statement of friendly sympathy to the Bolsheviks. However, Wilson's allusions to Bolshevik complicity with Germany in his addresses of November 12 and December 4, 1917, together with the aversion to recognition of Trotsky that he expressed on November 27, showed that he did not think of Bolshevik internationalists as representatives of an independent Russian nation. Instead of embracing the Soviet regime, Wilson was assuming the position of a trustee of Russia's independence and territorial integrity while trying to help Russia emerge from the deep waters of her revolutionary turmoil. In the preceding weeks Wilson had shown an interest in assisting pro-Ally elements in southern Russia; in the Fourteen Points speech he made an implicit offer to help patriotic Russians liberate Russia from domination by Germany and German agents. On January 3 Wilson had reminded the British ambassador that he earlier "made an appeal to the German people behind the back of the German government." In the Fourteen Points address he appealed in similar fashion to the Russian people over the heads of the Soviet leaders. The "Russian people," Wilson declared, "are prostrate . . . before the grim power of Germany. . . . And yet their soul is not subservient. . . . Whether their present leaders believe it or not, it is our heartfelt desire and hope that some way may be opened whereby we may be privileged to assist the people of Russia to attain their utmost hope of liberty and ordered peace." Bakhmeteff had stressed the distinction between the Russian people and their temporary leaders when House consulted him about the Fourteen Points address, and he was pleased that the speech was framed "exactly in these terms."[71]

For a time in January and early February 1918, when it seemed possible that the Soviet government might be encouraged or forced to reenter the war against Germany, Wilson appeared sympathetic to proposals to "establish . . . unofficial relations with the Bolscheviki [sic]."[72] This alarmed some foes of the Bolsheviks who exaggerated the influence of Wilson's liberal intellectual friends and underestimated the extent to which the president's moralistic backbone aligned him with his more conservative secretary of state. By mid-January even Bakhmeteff grew worried by misleading newspaper stories and rumors that the United States was going to recognize the Bolshevik government. When Bakhmeteff visited the State Department on January 14, however, Counselor Frank Polk told him there was nothing in the rumors, and Lansing gave the ambassador similar assurances the next day.[73]

On February 12, Colonel House was considering recommending to Wilson "that the United States should recognize the Bolshevic [sic] Government in Russia," and he thought that Wilson was thinking along the same line. However, Wilson had just read the Gompers-Walling memorandum, which argued against recognition of the Soviet regime because of its ideological menace, and he informed Lansing that this paper seemed "to furnish a very proper basis of the utmost caution" in U.S. policy.[74]

In late February, with the Brest-Litovsk peace talks broken off and the German army driving on the Russian capital, the French proposed joint material and financial assistance to the Soviet regime. Wilson and Lansing rejected the French idea as "out of the question." On February 23, Breckinridge Long told Lansing that if there was "confirmation of Russian military opposition to Germany," he would "recommend recognition of Balshivici [sic] and offering of material & military aid." Lansing opposed this recommendation, explaining that the Bolsheviks were "dangerous — more so than Germany," since they denied nationality and the right to own private property and had "threatened us with revolution." Long agreed but thought recognizing the Bolsheviks "might be wise" as a "war expedient." Lansing, who had a "long talk about it" with Wilson the preceding day, said the president "would not approve of expedients & could not recognize on principle." Wilson and Lansing wanted Russians to resume fighting against Germany, but their distrust and disdain for the Bolsheviks barred one way of achieving that goal.[75]

Three months after the Fourteen Points speech, Wilson again sent a message of sympathy for the Russian people over the heads of their leaders. On March 11, 1918, Frank Polk advised Wilson to address the note to the Russian people through the Congress of Soviets "so that Congress could not consider it an official communication and treat it contemptuously." Although the phrasing was ambiguous—House considered it "one of the most cleverly worded, three-sentenced messages extant"—the anti-Bolshevik thrust of the telegram was implicit in the conclusion that "the whole heart of the people of the United States is with the people of Russia in the attempt to free themselves forever from autocratic government and become the masters of their own life."[76]

In the spring of 1918, Bakhmeteff sought to buttress Wilson's faith that the Russian people were still "democratic at heart" by forwarding to the president pro-Ally resolutions by anti-Bolshevik Russian groups. One of these messages, from the Russian Colony of New York, assured Wilson that Russia was "still in her heart with the Allies" and wanted to rejoin the "Allied ranks . . . as a fighting power for liberty and democracy." In response, on May 8 the harried president took the time to effuse about the "great pleasure" he received from the resolutions, conveyed his "very profound appreciation" to the ambassador, and expressed his "continued and growing interest in doing everything that it is possible to do to manifest our sincere friendship for the great Russian people."[77]

As the Wilson administration moved toward intervention in north Russia and Siberia in June 1918, it demonstrated its support for Bakhmeteff by helping him to squelch a rival representative of the Russian people. On June 10, G. V. Lomonosov, a Menshevik professor whom the Provisional Government had dispatched to purchase railroad supplies in the United States, issued a press release that opposed intervention in Russia—predicting that foreign intervention would cause even enemies of the Soviet government to rally around it. The next day Lomonosov made similar statements at a pro-Bolshevik mass meeting in Madison Square Garden. Neither the Russian embassy nor the Wilson administration wanted to hear such views. Bakhmeteff immediately fired Lomonosov. When Lomonosov resisted, Bakhmeteff secured strong backing from the Departments of State and Justice, whose agents compelled Lomonosov to leave his office and turn over his records.[78]

In sharp contrast to Lomonosov, on the eve of Independence Day representatives of Russian political and religious organizations in the United States, probably encouraged by the Russian embassy, prepared an appeal to Wilson, the "last hope for Russia's regeneration," urging him to "hurry!" since "the very idea of democracy is perishing in Russia!" Although Wilson probably did not see that appeal, on July 4 he spoke in a sympathetic spirit, delivering an address at Mount Vernon that Bakhmeteff later considered the "climax" of the policy of distinguishing between the Russian people and the Bolshevik regime. "On the one hand," the president declared, "stand the peoples of the world,—not only the peoples actually engaged, but many others also who suffer under mastery but cannot act . . . — the people of stricken Russia still, among the rest, though they are for the moment unorganized and helpless. Opposed to them . . . stand an isolated, friendless group of governments . . . which fear their people and yet are for the time their sovereign lords." Although Bakhmeteff worried that American leaders' fear of "the specter" of Russian reactionaries would still delay intervention, by July 8 he was able to report that Wilson was finally translating his vague sympathy into concrete action. A week later, as Wilson approved the sending of U.S. troops to Russia, the president explained that that was "in the interest of what the Russian people themselves desire." Bakhmeteff's tireless efforts contributed to that view, and he was pleased by that application of the policy of standing by Russia. Since he had succeeded in preserving political and financial relations with the Wilson administration, as American soldiers moved toward Russia the Russian embassy in Washington was able to begin sending supplies to anti-Bolshevik forces in Siberia.[79]

Although Wilson and many of his advisors lost faith in leaders of the defunct Provisional Government because of their "blunder and ineptitude,"[80] State Department officials retained their high regard for Ambassador Bakhmeteff. After the Bolshevik Revolution, a common anti-Bolshevism cemented a bond between Lansing and Bakhmeteff. The secretary of state frequently cited Bakhmeteff's views, particularly in opposing the "breaking up" of Russia "into separate states."[81] In his memoirs, Lansing glowingly reviewed how Bakhmeteff "conducted himself and the affairs of his Embassy with tact and discretion, so that when he gave up the post . . . he retained the respect and good will of the numerous friends whom he had made during his career as ambassador." Frank Polk, similarly, told a former tsarist foreign minister that he "liked Bakhmeteff and that he had been an extremely useful representative for them."[82]

Such respect for Bakhmeteff helped him to secure his embassy's status despite the fact that the government he represented no longer existed. In April 1918, for example, when the British censor suppressed messages between Bakhmeteff and his counterpart in Paris, Lansing went to bat for Bakhmeteff, wiring the American embassy in London: "The Department has confidence in Russian Ambassador and grants him unrestricted cable privileges."[83] Near the end of 1918, Bakhmeteff asked Polk whether he could use his American-supported fund to travel to the Paris Peace Conference. Polk thought this "was a perfectly proper expenditure." As a result, the United States subsequently subsidized the lobbying in Paris by Bakhmeteff and other anti-Bolshevik Russians — an expense of $100,000.[84]

Although American advisors in France were annoyed by the uncompromising arrogance and reactionary views of other Russian representatives, they enjoyed working with Bakhmeteff, whom they found more practical and liberal. In fact, some Americans considered Bakhmeteff one of "the 'lions' attending the conference" at Paris. Besides meeting regularly with American officials such as Vance McCormick, head of the War Trade Board, Bakhmeteff lunched and dined with them. This gave him numerous opportunities to press his views on Western policy toward the Russian Civil War and to work with Wilson administration officials to aid anti-Bolshevik forces.[85]

To keep funds and supplies flowing to White armies, the administration postponed collections on government loans. In October 1918, for example, Polk and Treasury Department representatives "agreed that we would have to waive interest on our note in order to let the Russians have the money for their needs, as it would be all wrong to be helping Russia and at the same time taking all the Ambassador's money to pay interest."[86]

U.S. officials also helped the embassy keep Russia's private creditors at bay. In April 1919, citing "political considerations, together with our frequently announced purpose to render economic assistance to Russia," State and Treasury Department officials helped financial attaché Ughet to defer payment of $11 million on notes held by U.S. banks. In June 1919, Ughet assured American bankers who held $50 million in Russian bonds that although he could not then make the necessary payments, "the external obligations of the Russian Government issued prior to November, 1917, will be recognized." Supporting Ughet, Polk wrote the same banking group that "the people of America are most sympathetic with the Russian people and eagerly desire to see them work out for themselves a stable form of Government, and when that time comes the State Department will use its good offices to call [American] claims to the attention of that Government."[87]

With such support from the State Department, the Treasury Department, and the White House, the Russian embassy was able to send millions of dollars of supplies to White forces in the Russian Civil War, particularly those in Siberia under Admiral Kolchak. Two cases may serve to illustrate the complicated nature of the transactions.

On March 22, 1919, Acting Secretary of State Phillips relayed to the American mission in Paris a request from the Russian embassy to use $150,000 to purchase spare parts for about 40,000 rifles. "I recommend approval," Phillips wrote, "unless you see objection to using Russian funds at this time for further military assistance to anti-Bolshevik forces in Siberia." The initial response from Paris, where Wilson, Lansing, and House were attending the peace conference, was to reserve judgment, pending "developments in general Russian situation," and to seek the opinion of General William S. Graves, head of the American expedition to Siberia. At that point, William C. Bullitt had just returned to France from a mission to Moscow, and some State Department aides wondered whether "Bolshevik recognition" might be "under favorable consideration" in Paris. However, after General Graves sent his approval, the American mission in Paris authorized "the purchase and shipment by the Russian Embassy of the spare parts for Russian rifles."[88]

While waiting for that decision, Ughet informed Polk that there was an urgent larger need for rifles in Siberia and he requested credit to allow the Russian embassy to ship more than 250,000 rifles then held by the War Department. The embassy or the government of Admiral Kolchak in Siberia "would be able to guarantee remuneration" later, Ughet pledged. Polk suggested that this "arrangement seems desirable," but he had to wait several weeks for a response, since even requests involving relatively small sums of money were referred to the highest levels of the U.S. government. President Wilson wanted "to withhold his decision," Polk learned on June 3, until he and the Allied leaders received pledges from Kolchak that he would pay Russia's debts, hold free elections, and not restore the tsarist regime. After Kolchak gave the required assurances, the American mission in Paris wired Polk that there was "no objection to the shipment of the 260,000 rifles provided some means of payment can be divised [sic]."[89]

Prodded by Bakhmeteff, in late June Vance McCormick asked Wilson to clarify his understanding of Allied and American promises to aid Kolchak. McCormick learned that Wilson approved "of selling to Kolchak's Government, on a credit basis, any available surplus materials which may now be in the hands of the War Department, provided that no formal or diplomatic recognition of the Omsk Government results." Eager to clear the way for such shipments, in July Polk suggested that they would fulfill Wilson's pledge to stand by Russia. "Personally," Polk advised the president, "I feel very strongly that we should translate into action the desire and purpose of the Government to assist Russia which you have so clearly and convincingly formulated from time to time." With Wilson's approval, in the following weeks shipments of weapons, clothing, and food went forward to Siberia and other parts of Russia controlled by anti-Bolshevik forces.[90]

It is difficult to determine with confidence the exact amount of U.S. funds that were disbursed to White armies through the Russian embassy, but the total seems to have been more than $50 million. In June 1919, Polk told a congressional committee that "property of the cost of probably between $25,000,000 and $50,000,000 which has been conserved for the Russian Government" had "been shipped to Russia during recent months."[91] Papers kept by Ughet record these shipments of rifles, machine guns, military boots, and other equipment in great detail. A May 1, 1918, inventory of material that remained in the United States from orders of the Russian Supply Commission found $167,825,425 worth of supplies.

Of this amount, about $77,000,000 worth was shipped to Russia, though a third of it derived from sources other than American credits.[92]

Using the Russian embassy as a channel for aid to anti-Bolshevik movements allowed the Wilson administration to avoid having to request funds from Congress, and it helped to keep this assistance hidden from the press and the American people. Particularly after the Armistice and Republican gains in congressional elections in November 1918, the administration's relations with Congress were strained. In December, after Bakhmeteff and other Russian representatives urged the State Department to provide money or loans to the Kolchak government, Polk "took it up with McCormick and found that there was no way we could make advances without getting into trouble." At the end of the year, when "Ughet spoke of interest coming due on Russian bonds," Polk told him that he "would take it up with [the] Treasury Department," which "hesitated to waive their claim for fear of Congressional investigation."[93]

Anxiety about Congress continued to constrain the administration in 1919. In January, Polk cabled Lansing in Paris, calling his "attention to the political situation" in Washington, where a "critical spirit today is being clearly manifested in regard to Russia." Congressional criticism of the War Trade Board's Russian Bureau as a boondoggle and the maintenance of U.S. troops in Russia raised the danger, Polk wrote, that "Republicans . . . will make attacks on every phase of policy of administration in Russia."[94] In this atmosphere, Polk advised that the administration "give up the possibility of seeking money through appropriation" for patrolling and maintaining the Siberian Railway.[95] In May, members of Wilson's Russian Bureau informed Polk that they "wished to dissolve Russian corporation and turn over money to State Department" because "they were afraid of attack."[96]

In the context of this tension between the executive and legislative branches, as War Trade Board advisor John Foster Dulles noted in a memorandum approved by the president, "it might be exceedingly difficult and embarrassing to secure an appropriation" for operations in Russia. To get around this obstacle, Dulles wrote in April 1919, "the President desires . . . that Russian assets of cash, railway supplies, clothing etcetera, be protected and used for assistance to Russia provided they can be properly applied to some definite constructive plan which does not imply any present recognition of or *obvious* assistance to any Russian Government" (emphasis added). Wilson clearly understood the utility of the Russian embassy in this project: "The President desires," Dulles continued, "Russian diplomatic and consular officials to continue function in this country to the extent that such functioning is materially useful in connection with the liquidation and utilization . . . of Russian assets in the United States."[97]

Although the Russian embassy funneled aid to White forces in Siberia, some prominent anti-Bolshevik Russians in the United States blamed Bakhmeteff for failing to get larger loans, more extensive military assistance, and formal diplomatic recognition for Kolchak's government. One of the harshest detractors, A. A. Bublikov, criticized Bakhmeteff's insistence upon secrecy in the propaganda work of anti-Bolshevik organizations, arguing that in an age that was "democratic par excellence" secretiveness would arouse suspicion among Russians in both America and Russia. Instead, Bublikov held, Bakhmeteff should have followed "the brilliant examples" of Czech and Polish nationalist publicists, and he should have utilized the powerful forces of Russian officers and clergy in America. However, Bakhmeteff and the director of the Russian Information Bureau, A. J. Sack, rejected the course advocated by conservative Russians. Worried that Americans feared the specter of Russian reaction, Bakhmeteff and Sack believed it more useful to combat Bolshevism from a liberal and "Socialist point of view." Being more sensitive than men like Bublikov to Wilson's touchiness and his public relations predicament, Bakhmeteff refrained from applying overt pressure on the administration. The extremely delicate situation in America and the necessity of guarding against accusations of Russian propaganda, Bakhmeteff explained in 1919, forced him to maintain strict secrecy in organizing campaigns to persuade Americans to help free Russia from Bolshevism. Bakhmeteff worried that a high profile campaign would invite a congressional investigation of the financing of the Russian Information Bureau, which was partly funded by the Russian embassy. Thus, the climate of opinion in America constrained Russian as well as American leaders as they sought to support anti-Bolshevik movements.[98]

Soviet Efforts to Expose the Role of the Bakhmeteff Embassy

Despite the confidential nature of the financial relationship between the Russian embassy and the Wilson administration, in 1919 Soviet officials learned much about Bakhmeteff's role in U.S. support for anti-Bolshevik movements. Soon after the Soviet Foreign Commissariat appointed Ludwig Martens as its representative in America, in January 1919, Martens reported that correspondence of the Russian embassy had fallen into his hands. "As you probably already know," Martens announced, "the Bakhmeteff 'embassy' with the permission of the American government" had printed Russian rubles and sent them "to Siberia and probably to European Russia for the financing of counter-revolution." Martens proudly reported that his bureau was "able to expose this activity of Bakhmeteff," in part by distributing a press statement that money "loaned to the Russian Democracy by the American people" was being used "for interventionist propaganda by Bachmeteff" and for weapons contracts. Although the "capitalist press" was "striving not to make of this a scandal," Martens believed that the exposé had produced "a fairly strong impression" on the American public.[99]

Some liberal and socialist publications did criticize the role of the Russian embassy. The liberal weekly the *Nation*, which State Department officials regarded as "a dangerous paper," demanded to know in November 1918 whether the Russian Information Bureau was supported by U.S. credits. In January 1919, the *Nation* urged that "Boris Bakhmetev, the so-called Russian ambassador, be deprived of the diplomatic and financial privileges now accorded him." At the height of the U.S. efforts to support anti-Bolshevik armies, in the summer of 1919, the *New Republic* published charges that the Russian embassy was secretly supported by U.S. funds and that the State Department's refusal to say what Bakhmeteff was doing with that money constituted an un-American "secrecy of diplomacy." Socialist papers such as the New York *Call* went further, repeatedly attacking Bakhmeteff's "counter-revolutionary activities."[100]

However, few mainstream publications joined in publicizing or criticizing Bakhmeteff's use of U.S. funds. In fact, the *Call* and other papers which sympathized with Soviet Russia repeatedly complained that the American press was filled with misinformation emanating from the Russian embassy and the Russian Information Bureau. In the spring of 1919 Martens himself protested that "vilifiers" of Soviet Russia had been aided "with money, political influence, a powerful press, and sympathy of official institutions." Martens's top assistant, Santeri Nuorteva, lamented that whenever the U.S. government seemed ready to reach a "rational settlement" with the Soviet regime it was blocked by "a deluge" of lies by "Russian reactionaries." Hence, Martens seems to have exaggerated his own bureau's success in drawing press and public attention to Bakhmeteff's support of anti-Bolshevik forces.[101]

In April 1919 Martens made his most direct challenge to Bakhmeteff, condemning his use of funds "for purposes openly hostile to the Russian people" and commanding the ambassador to surrender all property and money. On behalf of the Soviet Republic Martens also informed American banks that he claimed all funds deposited in the name of Bakhmeteff and his aides. The State Department quickly countered Martens's gambit by issuing a certificate to Ughet and advising bankers that Martens's claims were "not to be given credence."[102]

While Martens failed to paralyze Ughet's use of American funds, the Soviet bureau gradually developed a fuller understanding of the Russian embassy finances. By April 1919 Martens's staff had seen bills of shipping for munitions sent from America to Siberia and they knew that "the

United States Government is controlling the expenditures of the Bakhmeteff crowd." In January 1920 the bureau explained that "a large part of Russia's debt to the United States," especially "the 187 million dollars which were given by the United States to Mr. Bakhmeteff, have been used by this man for purposes utterly hostile to Russia and in deliberate efforts to besmirch and to overthrow the Soviet Government." Influenced by Martens's reports, Foreign Commissar G. V. Chicherin thought the American people knew, as he did, that Bakhmeteff was "supported and largely financed by the American government." Actually, American citizens knew less about the use of their tax dollars than did Soviet officials, who acquired and carefully read the 1921 Senate Judiciary Committee's Confidential Report on Foreign Loans. The report detailed the Wilson administration's "unbusinesslike" support for White forces through the American Relief Administration and War Department transactions, as well as the Bakhmeteff embassy.[103]

As Lenin himself boasted to a meeting of Soviet officials in February 1920, the Soviet government "by chance came to possess" other evidence on Bakhmeteff's role, including a 1919 telegram in which Bakhmeteff reported State Department assurances that "American policy is one of undeviating support" for the "struggle against the Bolsheviks." Lenin considered these "very interesting documents" useful for unmasking "the allegedly democratic, but in actual fact predatory, powers of the whole world."[104] As a result of such information, Lenin and other Soviet leaders knew that White leaders such as Admiral Kolchak were "receiving the assistance of Britain and America in the form of vast quantities of arms and munitions."[105] However, they were not able during the civil war to utilize such information to disrupt the use of the Russian embassy in Washington as a channel for aid to anti-Bolshevik forces.

In the spring of 1920, after most of the White movements had collapsed, members of Congress began raising questions about the anomalous status of the Russian embassy. Responding to this pressure, Bakhmeteff asked Polk on March 6, 1920, whether he should resign to avoid causing difficulties for the administration. Polk assured the ambassador that the administration "was not embarrassed by his presence" and took steps to help Bakhmeteff evade congressional inquiries. On April 2, troubled by newspaper stories and a lawsuit by Martens, Bakhmeteff asked Polk whether the "Government would be willing to assist to the extent of stating he was Ambassador." Four days later the State Department obliged Bakhmeteff by certifying that he had been recognized continuously since July 1917 while Martens and the Soviet government had never been recognized.[106] Indeed, the Wilson administration never stopped regarding

Bakhmeteff as the ambassador of the Russian people. Only in 1922, after Wilson's second term expired, did a congressional inquiry into the Russian embassy's use of U.S. funds and a new rash of newspaper stories impel Bakhmeteff to resign his post.[107]

In the summer of 1920, two assistant secretaries of the treasury penned a candid review of the Wilson administration's diplomatic and financial relationship with the Russian embassy over the previous two and a half years. "Our understanding of the fiction of the Russian Embassy," they wrote, "was that it represented the 'Russian people' at present submerged under a despotic minority. We had the deepest sympathy, regard for and future faith in this Russian people. . . . On the basis of this feeling we had felt convinced of the wisdom of aiding the continued existence and functioning of the Embassy." After the Kerensky regime was "engulfed in the wave of Bolshevism," the administration had "hoped the Russian people would again find expression" through the movements led by General Denikin, General Iudenich, and Admiral Kolchak. "In the case of Kolchak the U.S. government had approved the Embassy aiding him, hoping that his faction would gather to itself the Russian people."[108]

Thus, the Russian embassy played a crucial dual role in the administration's secret war against Bolshevism. The embassy served a public function as a symbol of "the Real Russia" that the Wilson administration hoped would emerge from the turmoil of civil war.[109] At the same time the embassy served as a secret channel for supplies to anti-Bolshevik forces that the administration could not deliver openly and directly because it feared public opposition and congressional criticism. Bakhmeteff's "tact and discretion," lauded by Lansing, helped Washington to keep faith with "Russia," although the covert support for anti-Bolshevik movements entailed breaking faith with the democratic process in America.

THE BRITISH CONNECTION

AMERICAN COVERT AID TO ANTI-BOLSHEVIKS IN SOUTH RUSSIA, 1917–1918

In the first days of January 1918, Bolshevik newspapers repeatedly charged that American and Allied capitalists were supporting anti-Bolshevik forces in southern Russia with money and supplies. In the most graphic accusation, *Pravda* printed a political cartoon on January 5 that depicted anti-Bolsheviks in Ukraine and along the Don River as monkeys performing for a Kadet Party organ grinder (see page 139). By showing Uncle Sam and Allied imperialists giving the monkeys coins from bulging money bags, the cartoon implied that the United States and the Entente were financing counterrevolutionary forces in south Russia and that White forces were dancing to the tune of foreign supporters.[1]

The Bolshevik suspicion of American and Allied intentions was justified. Three weeks earlier, President Wilson had authorized aid to anti-Bolshevik forces in the Don and Caucasus regions. Since the Wilson administration was unable to give official U.S. funds directly to groups that were neither recognized governments nor belligerents in the war against Germany, it was necessary to find indirect methods of financing. The administration therefore promised British leaders that it would reimburse them for support to the Whites. Over several months, from late 1917 through the spring of 1918, U.S. officials worked with British counterparts in efforts to transmit funds. Although the British and French were only able to deliver a small fraction of the sums they pledged to the anti-Bolshevik officers, the administration appears to have at least partially fulfilled its pledge of reimbursement, and some U.S. representatives became directly involved in transferring money to White forces.[2]

More important than the amount of money transferred is what the attempted financial intervention reveals about the direction, motives, and methods of Wilsonian policy toward Russia in the first months after the Bolshevik Revolution. Some Americans urged Wilson and Lansing not to support the anti-Bolshevik forces because that would mean joining European imperialists in backing reactionary Russian elites against the majority of the war-weary Russian population. The president and secretary of state disregarded such warnings. They were determined to do what they could to support patriotic Russians who would rally around a "strong man," restore order in southern Russia, defend that region against Gemany, and eventually contribute to the reunification of Russia. However, Wilson and his advisors believed they could not openly support anti-Bolshevik forces: to sustain a favorable image of America in Soviet Russia and preserve the American public's faith in the administration's idealistic purposes, the financial support had to be kept secret.

Although American historians have often suggested that the liberal Wilson administration only grudgingly went along with Allied schemes for intervention in Russia, the United States was not dragged by its anti-Bolshevik allies into bankrolling a covert financial intervention in south Russia. American leaders took the initiative in suggesting covert methods to the British and offering to repay them for any aid they gave.[3]

U.S. officials were seeking both to deny resources to Germany and to preserve a non-Bolshevik "nucleus" for the regeneration of Russia. Americans viewed the White forces as both loyal to the Allies and opposed to pacifistic Russian radicalism. Thus, while scholars have often portrayed the effort to support patriotic Russian elements as *either* a strategic move against Germany *or* an effort to extinguish the Soviet regime, it is more accurate to see the Wilson administration's policy as simultaneously anti-German and anti-Bolshevik.[4]

Although the effort failed to sustain powerful military forces in late 1917 and early 1918, it was not a temporary aberration from a Wilsonian "policy of nonintervention."[5] On the contrary, the secret financial initiative was one of the first of the Wilson administration's covert and limited interventions against the Soviet regime.[6]

The Fall of Kerensky and the Rise of Kaledin

In the fall of 1917, as we have seen, American officials became increasingly disturbed by the deteriorating military and political situation in Russia. While maintaining a facade of confidence in the Provisional Government, Wilson and his advisors privately looked for other ways to revive a fighting spirit in Russian armies and buttress non-Bolshevik, pro-Ally parties against the rising tide of radicalism.

Wilson was therefore interested in a November 1 message from British Prime Minister David Lloyd George about protecting Russian soldiers from Bolshevik propaganda by creating separate armies of volunteers "who wish to continue the fight" and by taking "all steps to prevent agitators from getting amongst those soldiers." The British anticipated that the Kerensky government would oppose the plan but thought that Allied and American representatives, together with Russian generals, could still push it through. After reading Lloyd George's cablegram, Wilson asked Secretary of State Lansing, "Has anything further been heard about the independent organization within the army here referred to? It might eventually save the situation, — and Russia."[7] The revolution in Petrograd a few days later made this specific idea obsolete, but in the following weeks Wilson remained sympathetic to plans for salvaging parts of the Russian army and rescuing a democratic Russia from the stormy seas of Bolshevism.

After the Provisional Government was removed from power on November 7, U.S. diplomats in Russia, like officials in Washington, initially pinned their hopes on reports that Kerensky was outside Petrograd rallying troops and would soon regain control of the capital. One of the cars Kerensky and his aides used to leave the city was borrowed from the American embassy after Kerensky said "he desired the car to make a getaway to form [a] junction with the loyal troops sent from the front." However, Kerensky was unable to inspire war-weary soldiers to march against Red Guards south of Petrograd. On November 15, his naval aide came to the U.S. embassy "to say that . . . he was quite defeated; [and] that he had gone to join . . . Cossacks in the South."[8]

When it became clear that Kerensky's frantic efforts had failed, American attention shifted to southern Russia, where Cossacks and patriotic officers were supposedly preparing to attack the Bolsheviks. As early as November 18, the State Department correspondent of the *Washington Post* reported that "officials and entente diplomats believe now that Kerensky's leadership could profitably give way to the leadership of a stronger man." One of the officials who looked for a "strong man" to save Russia, Assistant Secretary of State William Phillips, believed General A. M. Kaledin, leader of the Don Cossacks, was "the man of the hour." "A feeling of misrule is arising among the people," Phillips observed on November 20, "and a military dictatorship is expected soon." Like Phillips, major American newspapers proclaimed Kaledin "Russia's New Man of the Hour" and urged financial support for him. The *Washington Post*, for example, argued that the United States "must stand by Russia" by sending assistance to Kaledin and others who were "trying to restore the nation to sanity and preserve its independence."[9]

Early Proposals for Aid to South Russia

The "booming" of Kaledin in the press was partly based on State Department briefings about dispatches from the American consul in Tbilisi, Felix Willoughby Smith. Born in Russia to American parents in 1872, Smith had joined the consular corps in 1909 and had been stationed at Tbilisi since 1914. On November 9, Smith notified Washington that the Caucasus population and army refused to unite with Bolshevik Russia, but he doubted that they could "hold out much more than five days without financial aid." A week later the consul cabled that, in addition to checking the spread of Bolshevism, "loyal Russians could greatly add to German difficulties" by depriving the Central Powers of Russian food and fuel, and by forming a "nucleus" for a new army. In each message Smith recommended that $10 million be supplied to sustain the patriotic forces of order.[10]

Wilson administration officials in Washington were interested in these reports and began considering ways to implement Smith's recommendations.[11] On November 26, Assistant Secretary of the Treasury Russell Leffingwell informed State Department Counselor Frank Polk that Smith's suggestions were "no doubt worthy of serious and prompt consideration," but he did not discern any recognizable authorities "with whom the Treasury Department could deal in advancing money for the purposes suggested by the Consul." To overcome possible legal or congressional obstacles, Leffingwell advised that "it might be expedient for the Secretary of State to call the attention of the British and French representatives to the suggestions of the Consul with a view to possible action by those Governments along the lines proposed by the Consul."[12]

Interest in the anti-Bolshevik forces in southern Russia was tempered by wariness that assisting such movements could antagonize the regime in Petrograd and contribute to a nationalistic fragmentation of Russia. "Inasmuch as the power of the Bolsheviki seems to be extending," William Phillips worried on November 26, "it strikes me as very dangerous to recognize a portion of Russia antagonistic to the Bolsheviki." On the same day, Phillips helped draft instructions to Smith to "advise how . . . the financial support you propose will not tend to encourage sectionalism or disruption of Russia or civil war. Department cannot encourage tendencies in any of these directions." While former Secretary of State Elihu Root recommended recognizing "the *de facto* government of the Trans-Caucasus" and supporting "anything in Russia which stands by the old Provisional Government," Phillips and others in the department remained "doubtful about doing anything which would tend to break Russia into separate units."[13]

Perhaps anticipating this concern, Smith wired Washington on November 25 that the "local nationalists" who decided to establish a "temporary separate government of Trans-Caucasus" expressed "full loyalty to Russia" and emphasized "that this government was created solely to keep out anarchy until [such] time [as] true representative government of Russia may be established." Noting that the Transcaucasian federation's "power to stop the growth of Maximalists" would "depend upon ability [to] meet obligations," the zealous consul recommended *de facto* recognition and reiterated his appeal for financial aid.[14]

In forwarding this dispatch from Tbilisi to Colonel House in Paris, Lansing mentioned that Smith would "not be given authority to recognize *de facto* government until it is evident that such action will not tend to foster sectionalism or disruption of Russia or civil war." However, the secretary of state thought it was noteworthy that the "government of Trans-Caucasus expressed full loyalty to Russia but definite opposition to Bolshevik government at Petrograd." He also observed that the "British Embassy is recommending to British Government that more financial relief be given." The next day, November 28, Lansing asked for House's advice and a report on the views of his Allied colleagues.[15]

Discussions in London, November 1917

Colonel House had already been conferring with British and French leaders about possible action in southern Russia. Together with his son-in-law, Gordon Auchincloss, House had arrived in England just as reports of the Bolshevik Revolution reached London. On November 8, Auchincloss noted in his diary, there was "very bad news from Russia. Apparently the Kerensky Government has been overthrown and anarchy reigns supreme." Disturbed by the situations in Russia and Italy, Allied officials raised a number of ideas for "resurrecting Russia," which House considered "thoroughly impractical" and "nonsense."[16]

A more feasible-sounding proposal emerged from a meeting on November 20 arranged by Sir William Wiseman, the chief of British intelligence in the United States. Auchincloss stood in for House at this conference with First Lord of the Admiralty Edward Carson, General G. M. W.

Macdonogh, the Director of British Military Intelligence, British secret agent and writer Somerset Maugham, and a Polish Count Horodyski. Horodyski argued that the Allies should "choose one large party in Russia which has power and believes that order should be restored and that the war should be fought to a final victory." He urged the Allies to approach General Kaledin, offer to pay the Cossacks, and encourage them to cooperate with Polish, Romanian, and other forces on the eastern front.

When asked what he thought the U.S. government's attitude would be, Auchincloss first genuflected to Wilsonian principles: "Inasmuch as it was a fixed policy of the United States not to intermeddle with the internal affairs of any friendly country, . . . any proposition looking to the establishment of Kaledin as a Russian Dictator would probably not meet with support." Then, setting his icons of idealism aside, Auchincloss suggested "that the same thing could be accomplished without getting mixed up in the Russian internal and political situation, by ostensibly making the movement in aid of the Government of Romania. Money could be loaned to Romania, and supplies and men could be sent there, and Romania could be used as the rallying ground" for Poles, Cossacks, Armenians, and Georgians. This idea appealed to the British officials present, and Colonel House also endorsed it.[17]

After discussing the Russian situation with Lloyd George and other British leaders on November 21, House noted that there was "a strong element in the Cabinet who wish to recognize Kaledin," but that he "advised against this." The colonel thought the most they could do was "advise Roumania to cooperate with whatever Allied fighting forces were nearest them," and he "strongly urged not mentioning names."[18] Like Auchincloss, House was less concerned with Wilsonian strictures about nonintervention and self-determination than with the opprobrium that might ensue from public knowledge of violation of those tenets. Although little appears to have come from efforts to link Romanian and Don Cossack forces, secretiveness would remain a hallmark of U.S. policy toward south Russia, and House had helped to set in motion a form of covert intervention in Russia.[19]

The War Cabinet was split over policy toward Russia. On one side were Lord Robert Cecil, undersecretary of state for foreign affairs, and other advocates of open assistance to anti-Bolshevik forces who might prevent Russian resources from being used by the Germans. They were opposed by Lloyd George and others who were skeptical about the strength of Kaledin and fearful "that any overt official step taken against the Bolsheviks might only strengthen their determination to make peace, and might be used to inflame anti-Allied feeling in Russia." Divided over whether to work with the Bolsheviks or against them, the British tried to do both.

While avoiding antagonizing the Soviet regime by formally recognizing Kaledin, the British moved to establish secret contact with the Cossack leader.[20]

Secret Discussions in Paris, Early December 1917

At the end of November, House crossed the Channel to participate in a conference with the prime ministers of England, France, and Italy. On December 1, the Allied leaders agreed that a combined French and British mission should be sent to General Kaledin's headquarters with full powers to guarantee Kaledin financial support up to ten million pounds. The secretary of the British War Cabinet understood "that Colonel House intended to take action on the financial side," though this was to be definitely arranged later by Foreign Secretary Arthur Balfour and House.[21]

On December 2, House reported to Lansing that America's allies were inclined "to give encouragement to the trans-Caucasian movement." House considered this "dangerous, because it encourages internal disturbances without our having in mind any definite program or any force to back up a program." However, he also noted that the anti-Bolsheviks might "go to pieces if they are not given money or encouragement." Like Assistant Treasury Secretary Leffingwell a week earlier, House turned to indirect methods of financing the White forces in south Russia. If America could keep its participation secret, House thought, that would minimize the risk involved. Hence, he "declined to commit our government in any way except to say that if England, France and Italy decide after investigation to assist this movement, the United States would advance money for that purpose to these three countries. The United States in making any such advance would not appear in the transaction openly, and if such action on the part of the other powers turned out later on to be a mistake, the United States would occupy a more favorable position, not being committed to the action."[22]

One of the advantages House saw in keeping the American financial role secret was that it would allow the United States to preserve an image in Russia of being less imperialistic than the British and French. Wilson's former campaign consultant was also concerned about American popular sentiment. At the conference in Paris, the colonel stressed that "the forces of public opinion behind the President of the United States attached great importance to the fact that they were making war for idealistic and not for materialistic war aims." Perhaps in part from worry that American liberals would see aid to Cossacks as a violation of Wilson's principles, House told the Allied leaders "that it was very dangerous to have any formal resolution" regarding assistance to anti-Bolshevik leaders and stressed "the danger of having speeches made at the Conference." If speeches were allowed,

House was "sure the Russian question will be ventilated and many indiscreet things said which might make the Conference an instrument for evil rather than good." [23]

Although House downplayed the extent of the commitment he had made, it was a remarkable reflection of the unorthodox nature of American foreign policy that, without consulting the president or secretary of state, an unelected personal representative of Woodrow Wilson had pledged U.S. government funds to support anti-Bolshevik forces of dubious strength and questionable legitimacy. The colonel was not reprimanded for exceeding his authority. Instead, Lansing and Wilson moved to ratify House's action ten days later.

Watchful Waiting in Washington, November 30–December 10, 1917

While Colonel House discussed aiding pro-war and anti-Bolshevik Russian forces with Allied leaders in Paris, Wilson considered the same question with Lansing and other advisors in Washington. When the cabinet took up the Russian situation on November 30, Secretary of the Interior Franklin Lane said that the "Trotsky government might maintain itself and should not be lightly dismissed," but other members of the cabinet "thought it would fail." The president then noted that, in contrast to Trotsky, Cossacks and others in south Russia favored continuing the war, and had asked for help and recognition. Wilson believed it was "too chaotic to act yet," but he was paying sympathetic attention to the efforts of Kaledin and others to organize opposition to the Bolsheviks, whom he found insulting and ridiculously naive at best. [24]

Wilson's early perceptions of the Bolsheviks and anti-Bolshevik forces were influenced by his private advisor on Russian affairs, Charles Crane. In the spring of 1917, Crane had traveled to Russia with the Root Mission and quickly grew disillusioned with the course of the revolution. After his friend Miliukov was forced to resign as foreign minister, Crane became "very much depressed and rather pessimistic." Already in June Crane suggested to Wilson that the United States might have to assume a duty toward backward Russia comparable to the burden it assumed at the turn of the century. "We went into a war to free Cuba and came out of it with a heavy responsibility in the Philippines," Crane reminded Wilson. "The present war is vastly greater and we may come out of it with vastly greater responsibilities for the future of Russia." In subsequent telegrams that reached the White House, Crane suggested that given the "general anarchy," the corrupting influence of German intrigue, and the weak leadership by the "amateurs" of the Kerensky regime, Russia was in dire need of American help. By August Crane concluded that General Kornilov was "the only man who might have saved the regime." When his attempted coup failed, Crane left the country.[25]

On his way to England in September, Crane told a reporter that Russia was "suffering from an overdose of exaggerated modernism in Socialist reform ideas," and suggested that an antidote of sanity might come from southern regions of the country. After Crane arrived back in America on November 30, a reporter took down his remark that "The Lenine-Trotsky and other governments that have sprung up in Petrograd are only 'pantomime governments.'" Wilson conveyed a similarly dismissive attitude toward the Soviet regime three days earlier when he told his cabinet that the "action of Lenin & Trotsky sounded like opera bouffe." In the following weeks, as we shall see, Wilson's thoughts would continue to run parallel to Crane's as he moved to support Cossacks and other forces of order in southern Russia.[26]

Press Secretary Joseph Tumulty probably had the Cossacks in mind when he suggested on November 30 that Wilson might include in an upcoming message to Congress a vow "to aid and stimulate those elements which are in truth seeking democracy" in Russia. "It may be no military advantage immediately to us," Tumulty elaborated, "but we care more for the eventual stability of the Russian republic and the creation of democratic institutions therein than we do for a temporary military advantage." While British and French interest in aiding anti-Bolshevik forces in southern Russia stemmed primarily from a desperate desire to constrain German armies on the eastern front, Tumulty and other Americans were influenced more by a broader vision of a future Russia made safe for democracy and free from German domination. Although Wilson did not openly promise to aid democratic elements in Russia when he addressed Congress on December 4, he did voice the hope that Russians would overcome recent "sad reverses" and resume "the progress of their affairs towards an ordered and stable government of free men."[27]

On the same day that Wilson implicitly expressed sympathy for a restoration of Russian democracy, the U.S. military attaché in Russia, General William V. Judson, warned that "any plan to form fronts with Roumanians, Ukrainians, Kaledines, et cetera, appears most chimerical." It might start an ineffectual civil war that could end in reestablishment of a monarchy, Judson held, but it would be of no conceivable benefit to the Allies. Some Russians, especially of the landed classes, wanted to use Allied aid for "political purposes," but since Russia was "past carrying on war" against Germany, there would be no military gain from such support. Judson had provoked the wrath of Wilson and Lansing by meeting with Trotsky on December 1, and the administration ignored his advice. Instead, Lansing saw Secretary of War Newton Baker "on recalling Judson from Petrograd," and instructed Ambassador Francis that the "President desires

American representatives withhold all direct communication with Bolshevik government." [28]

The administration was more attuned to notes from other American representatives. On December 7, the State Department received a new dispatch from Consul Smith, which argued that unless the United States immediately sent assistance to south Russia, the newly formed states there would "inevitably, for lack [of] currency and in self-defense, shortly submit to Maximalist government." However, if America and her Allies moved quickly to provide funds, they would be "supporting both Russian union and democracy" against the Bolsheviks and Germany. Smith supplemented this appeal with misinformation, stating that election returns throughout Russia indicated a Kadet plurality, and that in Transcaucasia the "entire population" was opposed to the Bolsheviks. Actually, the Kadets received fewer votes than either the Bolsheviks, who won pluralities in Petrograd and Moscow, or the Socialist Revolutionaries (SRs), who triumphed in most rural provinces. In Tbilisi, the Kadets garnered less than 10 percent of the vote, trailing the Mensheviks, Bolsheviks, and SRs. However, Smith's misleading report was the kind of news Washington wanted to hear. [29]

Although Smith's dispatch contained some rays of hope, the secretary of state was still gloomy about the situation in Russia and uncertain about what active steps to take. As he penned a long memorandum on December 7, Lansing *was* sure that the Bolsheviks were a menace, since they sought "to overthrow all existing governments and establish on the ruins a despotism of the proletariat in every country." He had no doubt that the United States should refuse to recognize "these dangerous idealists," and he continued to believe that the government of the "anarchists" in Petrograd "would go to pieces." However, as the Bolsheviks crumbled, Lansing feared that Russia would "break up into separate units" and sink into "a seething cauldron of anarchy and violence." "The only possible remedy," he thought, "would be for a strong, commanding personality to arise who would be able to gather a disciplined military force sufficiently strong to restore order and maintain a government." While Lansing noted sympathetically that Kaledin and General M. V. Alekseev were seeking to organize the Cossacks into an effective army, he worried that many "Cossacks returning from the front are inoculated with Bolshevikism." Hence, although the Cossack leaders and White officers were "the only hope that has appeared," Lansing was against openly supporting them, because their enterprise seemed "too uncertain and the whole situation too chaotic to put faith in any one group or faction." Like Wilson and House a week earlier, Lansing thought it was too early to place money on the Cossacks, though he was leaning toward betting on the Whites in the race for the Russian future. [30]

Ambassador Boris Bakhmeteff encouraged Lansing and other Wilson advisors to make the wager. In a confidential memorandum distributed to Lansing, Creel, and McAdoo by December 7, and to Wilson on December 14, the Russian ambassador passionately urged support for anti-Bolshevik forces in the Caucasus and south Russia. Allaying American concerns about the disintegration of Russia, Bakhmeteff argued that while anti-Bolshevik elements had "seceded for the time being into self-dependent communities," they would contribute eventually to "the reconstruction of Russia." Like Lansing, Bakhmeteff believed "military dictatorship" was necessary to save "the liberties of the people" and reestablish "unity and democratic order in Russia." In an optimistic prediction that seems to have caught Lansing's attention, Bakhmeteff suggested that even the mere promise of supplies such as boots and clothing could be "an effective factor for the re-establishment of order."[31]

Bakhmeteff and his aides were themselves moving to assist non-Bolshevik troops on the southern frontier of Russia. At the request of financial attaché Ughet, in early December the National City Bank transferred half a million dollars from the Russian embassy's American-supported accounts for silver, which would be used to pay Russian soldiers in Persia and the Caucasus. This precipitate action disturbed some Treasury and State Department officials, leading them to urge their superiors to "decide promptly" whether the United States would "give aid to Kaledin and the southern Russians." State Department aide Basil Miles criticized the Russians' use of funds "for purposes which may well be regarded as inimical by the Russian people," and argued that it was "a grave responsibility to direct the City Bank to pay $500,000 for silver to be sent through the British to Kaledin. That involves a question of state."[32]

As the administration neared a decision, left-leaning liberals in Washington opposed support for "a counter-revolution." In a letter to Wilson on December 8, Lincoln Colcord, a correspondent for the *Philadelphia Public Ledger*, charged that the Allies were fostering civil war in Russia, and that in backing Kaledin they were "chasing the illusion of a dictatorial power which can never appear in Russia now." The only alternative Colcord suggested, however, was the faint hope that Lenin and Trotsky might "suffer a change of heart" and "be persuaded to modify their program" of forcing "social revolution upon nations which fundamentally are not prepared for it."[33]

The White House and State Department ignored Colcord's message. They responded more sympathetically to an enthusiastic telegram from Maddin Summers, the hawkish consul general at Moscow. On December 5, Summers received a secret messenger from General Alekseev, and he visited the former commander in chief of the Russian army, General A. A. Brusilov. Based on these contacts, Summers reported that Alekseev and

Kaledin had "formed a well-equipped army of 50,000 cavalry and a trusted infantry force." This was a wild exaggeration: at that time Alekseev commanded only about five hundred officers and Kaledin's Cossacks were of doubtful reliability. Oblivious to the chasm between anti-Bolshevik dreams and realities, Summers conveyed the generals' plans to unite with "Ukrain[ian] troops and loyal elements of the army and people who are flocking to the south," establish a base in Cossack territory, then "send forces to Moscow and St. Petersburg to reestablish order." Summers cited Brusilov's expert opinion that the armies under Alekseev and Kaledin were "more than sufficient to reestablish order and avert further anarchy." Brusilov further told Summers that the British embassy in Petrograd had promised financial support, and he asked "that the United States support them morally and financially" as well.[34]

Lansing and Wilson Decide to Support Kaledin

Summers's telegram reached Washington late in the evening of December 9. Earlier that day, Lansing discussed conditions in Russia with Major Stanley Washburn, who had come to admire many Russian generals while covering the eastern front for the *London Times*.[35] Washburn's comments, Summers's message, and Bakhmeteff's memorandum appear to have resolved Lansing's doubts and galvanized him into action. On December 10, the secretary wrote a five-page brief for Wilson that presented the case for sending assistance to the White forces in southern Russia. It was time to do more than simply watch and wait, Lansing argued, because "the Bolsheviki are determined to prevent Russia from taking further part in the war," and the longer they remained in power the harder it would be "to restore order and military efficiency." With Russia out of the struggle, the war would be prolonged "for two or three years." On the other hand, "with Bolsheviki domination broken the Russian armies might be reorganized and become an important factor in the war by next spring or summer." In this way, "the saving of Russia means the saving to this country of hundreds of thousands of men and billions of dollars."

This military advantage was inextricably connected to the establishment "of a stable Russian Government" through "a military dictatorship," and "the only apparent nucleus for an organized movement sufficiently strong to supplant the Bolsheviki," Lansing noted, were the officers with Kaledin. Troubled by the likelihood "that German intrigues and Bolshevik false representations will speedily impair the morale of Kaledin's followers unless something is done to give them hope," the secretary argued that the United States should promise that "if their movement gains sufficient strength," they would "receive moral and material aid from this Government." Although he was proposing only a conditional pledge of assistance, he thought that "the situation may be saved by a few words of encouragement."

Having reached this conclusion, Lansing turned to the reasons for confidence in the White forces. Citing Major Washburn as his source of information, Lansing reported that the four generals involved—Kaledin, Alekseev, Brusilov, and Kornilov—were either brilliant strategists or popular among the troops, or both. Evoking the American Civil War, when force was necessary to restore the Union, Lansing wrote that Kaledin, in particular, was "a strong character" who "resembles Grant." In addition to these "elements of strength," the secretary believed that the officers would "in all probability obtain the support of the Cadets and of all the bourgoisie [sic] and the land-owning class." Although Lansing knew that Russian soldiers, including Cossacks, had been "infected with Bolshevikism," he evidently still thought that the Russian middle and upper classes would be strong enough to "restore order" and "carry out in good faith Russia's international engagements."[36]

Lansing's position was not an astonishing departure from his previous views. Since the 1890s he had sought to prevent a populist rabble from grabbing power in the United States, and he had longed for a military dictator in Russia since August 1917. More surprising to some was the attitude of the Democratic president.

Wilson was by this point eager to entertain concrete proposals for action. At a cabinet meeting on Tuesday, December 11, Wilson said that he "hate[d] to do nothing about Russia but [was] puzzled how to take hold." Perhaps reluctant to explain his confidential plan in front of other cabinet members who might leak word to the press, Lansing reverted to the position that the situation in Russia was "now too chaotic to make any move." However, that night Lansing returned alone to the White House. There he and Wilson "went over [the] Russian situation particularly [the] strength of [the] Kaledin movement." Practical questions rather than issues of principle appear to have been uppermost in the minds of the former international lawyer and the liberal president.[37]

Wilson evidently liked what he heard about the forces under Kaledin. The next day, Lansing consulted Treasury Secretary McAdoo about "aiding Kaledin" and then sent Wilson a draft telegram to implement the proposal. The president immediately returned it with the succinct comment: "This has my entire approval."[38]

This December 12 cable to Oscar Crosby, the U.S. Treasury representative in London, explained that the movement under Kaledin and Kornilov offered "the greatest hope for the reestablishment of a stable government and the continuance of a military force on the German and Austrian fronts." This movement "should be encouraged," Lansing argued, but aid would have to be given secretly and indirectly: "It would seem unwise for this Government to support openly Kaledine and his party because of the attitude which it seems advisable to take with the Petrograd authorities. . . . Without actually recognizing his group as a *de facto* government, which is at present impossible since it has not taken form, this Government cannot under the law loan money to him to carry forward his movement. The only practicable course seems to be for the British and French Governments to finance the Kaledine enterprise in so far as it is necessary, and for this Government to loan them the money to do so." The secretary of state therefore instructed Crosby to confer with the U.S. ambassador to Britain and Allied authorities, then report whether they were willing to adopt the U.S. proposal "and if so, to what extent financial aid will be required." Lansing closed by reiterating the "importance of avoiding it being known that the United States is considering showing sympathy for the Kaledin movement, much less of providing financial assistance." [39]

The plan for indirect, covert financing of anti-Bolshevik armies in southern Russia was so sensitive that Wilson and Lansing withheld information about it even from their closest aides at the State Department. Wilson had entrusted William Phillips with confidential negotiations with Mexican representatives in 1914, but Phillips was not allowed full information about the proposed assistance to Kaledin. Phillips knew that a message had been sent to Crosby, but, he noted in exasperation, "neither Polk nor I have seen it, although both of us are handling the Russian situation. It is too absurd." [40]

On December 13, Elihu Root called on Lansing to discuss Russian affairs, then stopped to chat with his fellow Republican, Phillips. According to Phillips, Root advised "immediately coming in touch with the forces opposed to the Bolsheviki in Russia, lending them money and giving them comfort, and trying in this way to preserve Southern Russia for the Allies." "It appears," Phillips recorded with dismay, "that the Secretary has adopted these views and that the President has also." [41]

Like Root, Lansing, and Bakhmeteff, Wilson was appalled by the dissolution of order in Russia and looked to the White forces gathering in the south as the main hope for the resurrection of the country. Charles Crane had captured Wilson's imagination with an exaggerated story about how Ambassador Francis faced down a mob in Petrograd by standing at the door of the U.S. embassy with a pistol in his hand and his "colored servant" by his side. On December 14 Wilson repeated the story to his cabinet. At another cabinet meeting four days later Wilson read a telegram from the newly lionized Francis. Navy Secretary Josephus Daniels recorded his impressions of the telegram and Wilson's subsequent commentary: "In Petrograd people broke into winter palace and took all wine & got drunk & went round shooting up the town. . . . Chaos in Russia. . . . Southern Russia the hope. W W wanted to help with money but saw no way with man power unless Roumanian troops could join the Russians who are fighting." [42]

What went through Wilson's mind as he contemplated Russia in chaos? Americans had long drawn parallels between Russia's "dark people" and African Americans, particularly since the nearly simultaneous emancipation of serfs and slaves in 1861 and 1863. In mid-November 1917 Russia's descent into "anarchy" led General Judson to write that the 180 million people in Russia were "mostly ignorant as plantation negroes." Did Wilson silently liken the disorder in Russia to the South during Reconstruction? There is no record of his making such a comparison. However, he certainly thought the situation in Russia called for strong measures to restore order. [43]

Wilson had approved Lansing's proposal for helping Kaledin with money while Colonel House was at sea, en route from France. Upon reaching the United States in mid-December, House evaded journalists' questions about Russia and went quickly to Washington. On December 17, Wilson conferred with both House and Lansing about the Kaledin forces. The next day House communicated Wilson's views to Wiseman in London: "PRESIDENT believes it is essential to give whatever aid is possible to the Polish, Cossacks, and others that are willing to fight Germany, and while he has no power to lend money direct to such un-organised movements he is willing to let France and England have funds to transmit to them if they consider it advisable." [44] Whereas Lansing had originally suggested making U.S. aid to Kaledin conditional upon his movement's gaining "sufficient strength," Wilson and House were now leaving it to the British and French to decide whether funding such forces was "advisable." However, House's message to Wiseman was like Lansing's December 12 cable to Crosby in its recognition that an essential reason for passing the money through America's allies was to get around legislative restrictions on presidential authority.

London and Paris, Late December 1917

In London, Crosby and the U.S. ambassador, Walter Hines Page, were less enthusiastic about the movements in south Russia than Lansing and Wilson were. Following through on the decisions reached in consultation with House at Paris, the British government authorized agents in southern Russia to offer twenty million pounds to two groups. On December 18, Crosby informed Lansing that there were "thus far no results from these authorizations," and the latest news represented the situation as "unpromising." Since the British effort would "accomplish all that can now be considered valuable in this direction," and since the British offers were made independently, Crosby felt that it was "unnecessary for us to offer just now to share liability though British have been given to understand we will consider sharing in any wise effort." Being even more skeptical than Crosby, Page recommended that the United States "decline to risk money in an enterprise so doubtful and about which so little is known either by British Government or ourselves." Page advised waiting until the anti-Bolshevik Russians gave "some hopeful evidence of their strength and spirit."[45]

However, Page also relayed predictions by others that "the Cossacks will win," that the "southern groups are far more important and far stronger than all the rest of Russia," and that the Cossacks were "the coherent organized ultimate masters of Russia." Perhaps in part for that reason, Crosby's suggestion that the United States did not need to advance funds to the British and Page's caution that the White movement in southern Russia was of doubtful strength had little effect on Lansing and Wilson.[46]

Although the American representatives in London urged Washington not to follow through on its pledge to reimburse the Allies, the British and French went ahead on the understanding that they would be repaid. On December 14, the British War Cabinet resolved to provide "any sum of money required for the purpose of maintaining alive in South-East Russia the resistance to the Central Powers." Several days later, after an Interdepartmental Committee reviewed the British financial undertakings in southern Russia, Treasury representative John Maynard Keynes advised Cecil to pin down American support by obtaining "an understanding in writing that the U.S. will share" with the British and French governments "in any expenditure in which we may be involved." Keynes's concern was partly addressed on December 21, when Cecil received a paraphrase of House's message that Wilson was willing to give France and England funds to transmit to Russia.[47]

Despite this assurance of Wilson's support for assistance to Kaledin, some members of the War Cabinet continued to doubt the wisdom of the venture. Trying to convince the fence-sitters, Cecil argued that it was "impossible any longer to go on running two horses; we must decide definitely whether we are to support the Bolsheviks . . . or whether we are to recognise and assist the other *de facto* Governments in Russia." Given British support, he thought, "the forces in Southern Russia had a fair fighting chance of success" against Bolsheviks. However, an unnamed doubter (probably Lloyd George) still pointed to the "danger that by backing a losing horse in Southern Russia, we were destroying any hope of preventing the Germans appearing in Petrograd as the friends and helpers of the all-powerful Bolshevik Government."[48]

Without achieving unanimity, the War Cabinet dispatched Cecil and Lord Alfred Milner to Paris to discuss "the question of providing help for the various Provincial Governments that showed signs of opposing the

Bolsheviki." At the Quai D'Orsay on December 23, Cecil and Milner argued that while it was probably impossible to "induce the Southern Russian Armies to resume the fight" against Germany, supporting those armies might help in "preventing Russian supplies from reaching Germany." The amount of money needed "to pay the Cossacks and Caucasian forces" was not very enormous, though there were great difficulties in exchanging currencies. "If the French could undertake the finance of the Ukraine," Cecil and Milner thought the British "might find the money for the others." They noted pointedly that it was "understood that the United States will assist," and Cecil advised the French that "Mr. Crosby was coming very shortly" to Paris to discuss "the question of financing Southern Russia."[49] The French government had decided on December 20 to provide "a credit of one hundred million francs" to General Alekseev so he could "organise action against Bolsheviks," and the French confirmed that pledge at the conference.[50]

Poole's Intelligence Mission to South Russia, December 1917–January 1918

On December 15, soldiers from Alekseev's small Volunteer Army and Cossacks led by Kaledin captured the city of Rostov from Red forces. Hailing the "victory of Kaledin and loyal troops," Consul General Summers suggested to Washington that the White forces might "liquidate the Bolshevik movement more quickly than expected." To get more direct information about the anti-Bolshevik forces, Summers dispatched Consul DeWitt Poole to southern Russia. Summers informed the State Department that he "was sending Poole unofficially to Rostov ostensibly to investigate commercial situation but in reality to advise the Department of what is occurring," and Washington tacitly approved the mission.[51]

Upon arriving safely in Rostov on December 18, Poole rendezvoused with prominent anti-Bolsheviks who had also come south from Moscow. Although he went "through the motions of pretending to be an American consul," as he disclosed in 1952, his "real function was that of military and political observer" or "an intelligence officer." On December 21, Poole journeyed from Rostov northeast to Novocherkassk, the headquarters of the Don Cossacks. There he met several times with Kaledin, who was deeply troubled by the younger Cossacks who had been "infected with Bolshevism."[52]

The American special consul also conferred with General Alekseev, who was responsible for the finances of the White movement. In telegrams to Moscow and Washington, Poole reported, "From a military point of view, the position of the Don government is lamentably weak."

Alekseev told him that "for the present the Cossacks cannot be counted upon for active military operations," and that the Volunteer Army had practically no infantry or artillery. Nevertheless, Poole recommended financial assistance to these forces. In his view, it was U.S. policy "(1) to hold as many enemy troops as possible upon the Russian fronts, and (2) to assist the Russian people to establish as soon as possible an orderly government representative of their political desires." Since these were the avowed objectives of the White movement, Poole thought it should receive U.S. support. Even with Allied assistance, Poole knew, the White forces would "be quite ineffective against the regular German fighting machine," but he thought they would still have value as "a mobile police force" to restore order in portions of Russia not occupied by German or Soviet troops.[53]

Poole read his reports to Alekseev and showed copies to a French Colonel Hucher and the British General de Candolle. After all approved, Poole sent them to Summers and the State Department. When word came a few days later that the French government was prepared to provide 100 million rubles, Poole joined Hucher in giving Alekseev the good news.[54]

Competing Counsels: Colonel House vs. Robert Lansing and Charles Crane

In the second half of December, according to William Phillips, "the question of the success of the anti-Bolsheviki movement" was "uppermost in everybody's mind" in Washington. Phillips and House were, like Crosby and Page in London, doubtful about the wisdom and effectiveness of aid to Alekseev and Kaledin. "Certainly we must give encouragement to them and do everything we can to preserve what is left of Russia," Phillips granted, but he was bothered that "reports of Kaledin and his army are so conflicting."[55]

House was almost always reluctant to disagree openly with Wilson, but he confided to Phillips that he was "violently opposed" to the "gamble" of aiding Kaledin and had "so advised the President." While the colonel told Phillips "that we must refrain from doing anything which would appear in the future to break Russia," at other times he favored dividing the empire into separate states so that it could never again be a menacing, reactionary force in European politics. House may have worried more about the danger of a powerful Russian military dictator emerging from southern Russia than about the threat of separatism.[56]

At this point House was much more intimate with Wilson than was Lansing.[57] After spending many hours with Wilson on December 17 and 18, House found "the President still antagonistic to Lansing. Lansing constantly does something to irritate him, and generally along the line of taking action without consultation."[58] Yet on the question of supporting anti-Bolshevik forces in south Russia, Lansing had consulted closely with Wilson, and the president more than once approved Lansing's proposal. Despite House's protest, Phillips noted on the day after Christmas, Wilson reaffirmed his approval of the plan. Hence, Phillips wrote, "Our policy in Russia seems at last to be clearly defined. We have secretly telegraphed Crosby to inform the British and French governments that this Government is willing to advance sufficient credit to those governments so that they may send whatever cash may seem necessary to the leaders in southern Russia opposing the Bolshevik regime. It is not considered wise for all the Allied governments to step into the boat at once and the United States is keeping completely in the background so that should the southern Russian developments fail one of the Allies at least would not be in bad."[59]

While overriding House's broader opposition, Wilson and Lansing were acting in accord with the colonel's recommendation that the American hand be hidden in order to limit the possibility for damage to America's idealistic image. As Lansing explained to the British ambassador on December 27, the United States "was the only one of the allies who could hope to exert any influence" in Soviet Russia, and "it would be dangerous and unwise to sacrifice this chance, however slight," by overtly manifesting hostility toward Bolshevism. Hence, the United States planned "to maintain a neutral & expectant attitude" in public while privately working with the British and French along a different line.[60]

This partial acceptance of House's counsel was little consolation to him. Upset that Lansing and others had won out on the issue of aiding anti-Bolshevik forces in south Russia, House confided to his diary on January 2 that he was "in disagreement with the English, French and American governments regarding the policy that should be adopted toward Russia at this time." Although many historians have emphasized House's influence on a supposedly noninterventionist policy toward Soviet Russia, House was reduced to recording for posterity the wisdom of his advice "that literally nothing be done further than that an expression of sympathy be offered for Russia's efforts to weld herself into a virile democracy, and to proffer our financial, industrial and moral support in every possible way."[61]

Unlike House, Wilson and Lansing were not content to do nothing but express sympathy for Russia. Sharing a moral antipathy to Bolshevism and an impatience with disorder in Russia, they were prepared to run risks to support forces of order in southern Russia. Wilson's continuing support for Lansing's position on funding Kaledin was once again reinforced by Charles Crane. On January 3, 1918, Crane gave Tumulty a report by W. C. Huntington, the U.S. commercial attaché in Russia, with a covering note calling it "one of the best comments on present-day Russia I have seen" and suggesting that "perhaps the President would like to read it to the Cabinet." Huntington considered the Bolshevik regime to be "no government at all," expected it to fall, and believed "that soberer forces must follow." Either "a 'strong man' might arise and take charge . . . or the more moderate Socialists . . . might pick up the threads." In late December 1917 and January 1918, Wilson met twice with Crane and continued to retell his anecdotes at cabinet meetings. Crane's contacts with Wilson seem to have bolstered the president's view of the Soviet government as a transitory farce and buttressed his inclination to support the restoration of order in Russia by anti-Bolshevik military forces.[62]

Overcoming Resistance from Subordinates and Obstacles to Funding

After Christmas, the policy of indirectly assisting anti-Bolshevik forces in south Russia continued to encounter practical difficulties and bureaucratic resistance. However, Lansing and Wilson remained convinced that this was the correct course and overrode objections.

On December 27, Crosby reported from Paris on the Allied conference there and criticized the efforts to provide "support of anti-Bolshevik organizations." The British and French leaders, Crosby cabled, fully recognized that the movement in southern Russia against the Petrograd regime was "caused rather by differences in regard to internal Russian questions than because of desire to continue war with Germany." In addition to doubting the utility of the White forces in the struggle against the kaiser, Crosby suspected that the Allies had ulterior, imperialistic motives that had nothing to do with the Great War and that might compromise U.S. interests in southern Russia and the neighboring region. The British and French felt their special interests were so involved that they were reluctant "to use American direction." For these reasons, the assistant secretary of the treasury considered it dangerous to write the Allies a blank check, and he advised that the United States minimize its involvement.[63]

Although Wilson had his own suspicions about Allied policies, he was more concerned with supporting anti-Bolshevik forces in southern Russia than with countering Allied schemes there.[64] Wilson left little evidence of his thoughts about assistance to anti-Bolshevik groups, but his sympathies were reflected indirectly in an exchange with CPI chairman George Creel, one of the most frequent visitors at the White House in late 1917 and early 1918. On December 27, Creel advised Wilson to issue a statement that the United States was ready "to aid in restoration" in Russia "and to build foundations under military strength," but that aid could "only be given in cooperation with a Russian movement that is expressive of the whole people." Creel suggested that a statement along the lines he proposed would strengthen anti-German and anti-Bolshevik forces in southern Russia. Two days later, Wilson thanked Creel for his letter "about the Russian propaganda" and assured him, "You are taking just the right position."[65]

In the first week of 1918, the Wilson administration continued to get encouraging news about the anti-Soviet forces in southern Russia. On New Year's Day, the State Department received a long and important telegram from Consul General Summers which reported that Bolshevik forces had been defeated in the Don region. Based on cables from Consul Poole, Summers informed Washington that with "Milyukov and other popular leaders" present, an anti-Bolshevik Southeastern Federation was "developing strongly." "It has undoubtedly the support of the best element in Russia rapidly concentrating on the south," Summers exclaimed, disregarding the severe tensions in Russia between the "best element" and "popular leaders." The consul general had had ample opportunity in 1917 to observe the intensification of class conflict in Russia. Yet he suggested that the United States could continue its policy of trying to make Russia "safe for democracy" by supporting conservative politicians and reactionary officers in the Don region. "The Russia we welcomed as a democratic nation," Summers argued, "is in the south. The rest is practically at war with us."

To allay Lansing's fear of separatism, Summers reported that the Southeastern Federation "does not seek independence but aims to serve as a nucleus from which Russia may be reconstructed on a federative basis through the action of the Constituent Assembly." While downplaying the regionalism, conservatism, and elitism of the Whites, Summers exaggerated their military significance. Although the soldiers were in pressing need of money and facing a "critical moment," Summers promised that with foreign aid "and continued successes against the Bolshevik element the armies of Kaledin and Alexeev soon will be vastly augmented by large bodies of loyal troops." If given adequate support, Alekseev would "be prepared to undertake an offensive campaign in the spring," and even with less help his troops would be "of the utmost military value" by defending the rich southern region from German depredation. Since the forces in the south could "be expected to act effectively" against both Bolsheviks and Germans, Summers agreed with Poole "that the Government of the United States and the Allies should immediately lend this nucleus all possible moral and material support."[66]

In response to Summers's appeal, Lansing wired only the terse thanks: "Appreciate value of Poole's report and your comment." However, together with similar messages from Consul Smith, the reports from Summers and Poole appear to have sustained Lansing's and Wilson's support for aid to anti-Bolshevik forces in southern Russia.[67]

By January 1, Wilson had seen the memorandum Milner and Cecil had presented at Paris on December 23. The British had proposed a "two-track" policy toward Soviet Russia. On one track, they suggested getting "into relations with the Bolsheviki through unofficial agents" and assuring them "that any idea that we favor a counter revolution is a profound mistake. Such a policy might be attractive to the autocratic governments [of Germany] and Austria but not to the Western democracies or America." Banking on America's idealistic reputation, the British hoped to persuade the Bolsheviks that anti-German, but not anti-Soviet, considerations, made it "necessary to keep in touch . . . with the Ukraine, the Cossacks, Finland, Siberia, the Caucasus, et cetera." Simultaneously, on the other track, the British wanted "to pay the Cossacks and Caucasians and to bribe the Persians," with the understanding "that the United States will assist" in this financing. While dispatching "agents and officers to advise and support the provincial governments and their armies," the War Cabinet somehow hoped "to avoid the imputation as far as we can that we are preparing to make war on the Bolsheviki," and thus preserve the possibility to influence the Soviet regime to resist Germany in northern Russia. After reading the memorandum, Wilson wrote to Lansing: "This seems to me a sensible programme, — except the bribery of Persia, — and I am writing to ask your opinion as to the most feasible and least objectionable way (if there is any) in which we could establish similar unofficial relations with the Bolscheviki [*sic*]." Although the British proposal to "bribe the Persians" violated Wilson's moral sensibility, the plan "to pay the Cossacks and Caucasians" and the duplicitous nature of the two-track policy did not. The president implicitly reaffirmed his approval of reimbursing the Allies for assistance to anti-Bolshevik groups while simultaneously expressing interest in unofficial contacts with the Soviet government.[68]

By this time, the Allies had begun to provide some of the promised funds. On December 31, 1917, the British consul in Tbilisi, Stevens, wired the Foreign Office that one million rubles were being paid to Russian military authorities to support the formation in the Caucasus of a "loyal army . . . and evacuate discontented elements." In addition, Stevens had requested the British Minister at Teheran "to organize purchase of arms etc. up to 3 million roubles" (about 75,000 pounds at a time when one British pound could be expected to buy forty rubles).[69] These sums were merely drops in the buckets of White supply officers, however. Stevens warned that countering the strong Bolshevik influence and establishing White armies would require much greater expenditures by the Allies. Reviewing

Stevens's telegram, George Clerk of the Foreign Office thought the upshot was that the British had to find 150 to 300 million rubles monthly "for 4½ Army Corps which have mostly still to be called into being."[70]

Daunted by the prospect of locating sums of that magnitude in the war-torn and threadbare royal purse, the British sought further assurances from their rich American cousins. On January 2, Cecil prodded Crosby: "It has been intimated to us confidentially that President Wilson is in favour of the provision of Allied support" for the "saner elements" in Russia, and "is willing to let France and England have funds to transmit to them." Noting that the "possibility of indirect assistance from the United States" would "have a very immediate bearing upon the whole question," Cecil asked Crosby to inform him "whether we may in fact count upon such assistance."[71]

It is unclear whether Crosby provided the written guarantee the British wanted. The State Department was certainly aware of Crosby's objections. On January 2, Phillips noted Crosby's criticism of taking sides in a revolution and his prediction "that any support which the Allied governments might extend to the provinces resisting the Bolsheviks will undoubtedly become public." However, that prescient warning did not deter Lansing. Despite the danger, Phillips noted, Lansing was "quite convinced that the course of the Allied governments is the right one."[72]

Lansing's determination to proceed was driven largely by his perception of Bolshevism as an unalterable ideological menace. Analyzing a proclamation by Trotsky, Lansing advised Wilson on January 2 that the Bolshevik call for self-determination throughout the world would result in "international anarchy." The secretary concluded that "Lenine, Trotsky and their colleagues are so bitterly hostile to the present social order in all countries that . . . nothing could be said which would gain their favor or render them amenable to reason."[73]

While Lansing's support for opponents of the Bolsheviks therefore seems unsurprising, Wilson's continuing endorsement of the venture is more intriguing. Lansing's influence has often been minimized by historians who argue that Wilson adopted an accommodating policy toward the Bolsheviks.[74] However, Wilson did not renounce his support for Lansing's proposal of secret aid to Kaledin. Like Milner and Cecil, Wilson seems to have regarded unofficial contacts with the Soviet regime and a vague friendliness toward Russia as a complement, rather than an alternative, to covert aid for anti-Bolsheviks.

On January 3, Wilson received a memorandum from one of the most prominent advocates of a friendly policy toward Soviet Russia, William Boyce Thompson. Recently returned from Russia, where he had led a Red Cross mission and subsidized pro-war propaganda, Thompson argued that the Bolsheviks expressed sentiments that "are common to ninety per cent of the population of Russia, and, in some form, they have come to stay." This perspective led Thompson to criticize the efforts of the Allies "to bring back elements of the old order." Thompson opposed giving "heavy support to the Korniloff and Kaledin movements" because "these movements representing force can never be permanently successful in the Russia of today."[75]

Thompson's views were not warmly received. On January 4, Lansing called Thompson "a crank" and Wilson implied that Thompson's financing of publicity in Russia had been foolish. Lansing and Wilson also dismissed Thompson's criticism of the anti-Bolshevik movements. Navy Secretary Daniels accurately described Wilson administration policy when he observed: "We are with E[ngland] & F[rance] giving all aid possible to those in 'Little Russia,' where there is a fight against Germans & Anarchy. Summers, consul at Moscow, says the only hope is in the men fighting in So. Russia."[76]

Like Daniels, other officials in Washington regarded it as established policy to provide indirect financial support for anti-Bolshevik groups in southern Russia. Around January 8, Basil Miles, chief of the Russian section at the State Department, suggested in a memorandum for Lansing that the United States should "continue its support of elements of law and order in the south," though "on the definite and expressed basis of preserving Russia from Germany and not exploiting Russia to carry on a civil war." Miles thought a neat distinction could be drawn between harmless support for the defense of a non-Bolshevik south Russia and objectionable support for an anti-Bolshevik offensive against Soviet Russia. Since the Americans, the Allies, and the Bolsheviks all knew that the ultimate objective of the White generals was to march on Petrograd, however, it was unlikely that the Bolsheviks could be persuaded that aid to south Russia was strictly anti-German.[77]

By early January, Wilson advisors who had opposed financial aid to the White forces were silent. House and Phillips were confined to venting their frustration in their diaries. Crosby was repeatedly criticized by Treasury Secretary McAdoo and by Wilson for his "inclination to go very much outside his bailiwick"; and on the issue of aiding anti-Bolsheviks in south Russia, Wilson and Lansing compelled Crosby to cooperate.[78] When the French ambassador to Washington "asked about money for Ukraine" on January 11, Polk "told him that his Government could get the information from Crosby." Through January and on into February, Crosby stayed in close touch with British and French efforts to provide assistance in south Russia, and he tried to solve some of the exchange problems. On January 22, for example, Crosby reported that he was still grappling with the difficulties of "efforts to finance southern Russian governments."[79]

In the first weeks of 1918, British officials forged ahead with efforts to support anti-Bolshevik groups in southern Russia. Although the British remonstrated on other occasions when they felt Americans failed to share expenses as pledged, as far as can be ascertained they did not complain that Washington reneged on its promises regarding southern Russia.[80] British representatives seem to have been satisfied with American cooperation in the complicated efforts to fund anti-Bolshevik forces.

On January 4, the Foreign Office thoroughly reviewed British policy toward south Russia. As Sir George Clerk noted, the Treasury had been able to "find means here and there of raising a few hundred thousand roubles," but this was "a mere drop in the ocean" compared to the White generals' request for 500 million rubles. To help the local governments raise money, the British could provide a "formal financial guarantee to a loan," but this would imply diplomatic recognition and therefore risk "a definite rupture with the Government in Petrograd." Clerk did not suggest an answer to this dilemma, but he concluded that "we should be ready to support Kaledine and Alexeieff" with "large sums of money." Clerk's superiors concurred. "We must be prepared in the desperate position in South Russia to take risks," Cecil minuted. He therefore directed British agents to "raise what money they can by any means available and apply it first to help the Armenians and then to Generals Kaledine and Alexeieff."[81]

In the following week, the British consul in Tbilisi received one million rubles from Persia and the British minister at Teheran purchased an additional 2.8 million rubles (at a cost of about fifty thousand pounds) to send to Tbilisi. Despite these successes, continuing exchange problems prompted the British Minister in Romania to suggest that a "strong inter-Allied banking establishment" was needed to support loans and the creation of new currency. He ventured that "an American co-director could be added should America join in expenditure entailed by our action in Southern Russia."[82]

In mid-January, U.S. consul Poole thought the French subsidy of 100 million rubles granted to Alekseev in late December had "disposed of the financial question for the moment," though the French mission actually delivered only 300,000 rubles by that point. After visiting Novocherkassk with Allied officers, Poole reported that the organization of the Volunteer Army was "now proceeding with some vigor," that the "pay of soldiers and officers" had been "substantially increased," and that recruiting centers had been "established at important points in southern and middle Russia." In addition, in a foretaste of his role in covert action later in Moscow, Poole advised that "clandestine preparations" were underway "for counter-B[olshevik] attacks at opportune moments in Moscow and other cities." Yet Poole also warned that, with serious Bolshevik military pressure continuing, there was an "urgent need of cash." Since the disorganization of banking made "realization on French credit difficult," Poole suggested that he could "draw dollar drafts" and "buy considerable amounts of roubles locally."[83]

As far as can be determined, Poole did not receive permission to assist the anti-Bolshevik forces in that way, and the gap between their funds and projected expenses widened. Anticipating a dramatic increase in the size of their forces, the Whites estimated their needs through April at 200 million rubles.[84]

The British and French appear to have provided only a small fraction of that sum in the first half of 1918. On January 22, the British consul in Petrograd reported that methods had been devised to transfer more than eighteen million rubles to south Russia, but such sums arrived only later in the year. In February a French captain arrived with seven million francs, but by then Kaledin's government had fallen.[85]

The Wilson administration had decided to work through London and Paris, rather than Tbilisi. The State Department therefore repeatedly enjoined Consul Smith not to commit the U.S. government, directing him only to "confer closely with British and French representatives" and keep Washington informed. However, sensitive to the urgent needs of the Whites, Smith exceeded his instructions and assured anti-Bolshevik leaders that they would get financial help. In January 1918 Smith belatedly advised his superiors that he had "unofficially" informed his friend, V. A. Kharlamov, a Russian Kadet who headed the Southeastern Federation, that the Allies would "probably soon lend extensive aid" to his government.[86]

Smith's pattern of "exceeding his authority" worried Maddin Summers. The consul general still championed "the movement in the South" as a way of "checkmating Germany" and as "a nucleus . . . to preserve order and save the country." Yet Summers was perturbed that Smith had cracked the shell of secrecy surrounding American policy. Already in late December Trotsky asserted that French and American imperialists had placed a "wager on Kaledin." By early January Soviet leaders had more specific information. On January 10 Summers noted Russian newspaper reports "that the American Consul General and the allied Missions had assured [Kharlamov] . . . that the United States, France, Great Britain and Italy would give moral and material support" to the movement in the southeast.[87]

Like Summers, embassy counselor Butler Wright felt "no little uneasiness" about Smith's "increasing strain of egotism" and his unauthorized promise of aid. Although Wright favored "helping and cheering up the relatively few patriotic Russians," and sympathized with Whites who shot Bolsheviks "without mercy in the attempt to clean the country of this vermin," he believed the United States could not "take sides in what promises to be a fearful civil war." Wright therefore argued that Smith should heed the State Department's November 26 message that it did "not wish to take any action which would tend to foster sectionalism or disruption or civil war."[88]

While Smith's impetuous moves gave these more cautious diplomats heartburn, they did not provoke a direct rebuke from Washington. Smith's insubordination was procedural rather than political. His promise of Allied assistance circumvented the proper channels and compromised the desired secrecy, but it did not contradict U.S. policy.

Willoughby Smith's bossiness and indiscretion vexed British as well as American officials, but they nonetheless worked with him to support anti-Bolshevik forces. On January 24, the Director of British Military Intelligence (DMI) advised the chief military attaché in the Caucasus that Crosby was "pressing for close co-operation" between him and Consul Smith. Since the British hoped for American financial assistance, the DMI directed the attaché to cooperate with Smith. The attaché reported back on January 29 that the well-connected Smith had "agreed to give all possible support and financial advice in which he certainly could help us." Officials in London then gave Crosby a note summarizing the financial situation in the Caucasus and steps they had taken.[89]

In February, the White position on the Don and in the Caucasus turned from precarious to catastrophic. Pro-Bolshevik sentiment was strong among poorer peasants, younger Cossacks who had been radicalized at the front, and workers in industrial towns like Rostov. In addition, many Cossacks regarded bourgeois politicians and reactionary officers from the north as unwelcome intruders in their homeland. Kaledin found his support collapsing, and in despair he shot himself through the heart on February 11. An uprising by workers in Taganrog at the end of January and advances by Red Army units led the White generals to decide to withdraw from the Don. Red forces took over Rostov on February 23 and captured Novocherkassk on the 25th. Generals Kornilov and Alekseev led the badly outnumbered four thousand members of the Volunteer Army south into the Kuban.[90]

These discouraging developments did not halt Anglo-American efforts to bolster anti-Bolshevik forces. At the same time as Washington learned of the setbacks, it finally received confirmation of the transfer of funds to southern Russia. On February 14, Crosby advised Lansing and McAdoo that he had been assured the British government was "doing its best to get money to its representative" in the Caucasus. Crosby detailed several ways the British had authorized and transmitted funds, and he stated that he was "endeavoring to hold [his] action in financial limits." Thus, contrary to studies which concluded that the effort to aid the Whites was aborted in December 1917, it appears that by February Crosby had begun to fulfill the U.S. pledge to reimburse the British. In addition, the U.S. Treasury was the original source of some of the funds the British were transferring. Crosby reported that the British were providing "approximately 38,000 pounds per month" for the "upkeep of forces in Caucasus and Persia," and he indicated that the British were drawing on 3,668,652 ounces of bar silver that the Bakhmeteff embassy had purchased out of U.S. advances and then handed over to British officials in San Francisco.[91]

On February 15, the British consul in Tbilisi asked the Foreign Office to reimburse Willoughby Smith for two million rubles, which Smith advanced to the British from sources in Persia. The U.S. consul regretted that the "development of movement of South Eastern Federation ha[d] been checked by lack of financial support," and he was doing what he could to remedy the problem. Although the sum Smith advanced was small, it is significant that a U.S. representative was actively involved in the financing effort three months after the decision by Wilson, which some historians have dismissed as a momentary flirtation.[92]

The defeat and retreat of anti-Bolshevik troops in south Russia did not cause U.S. and British officials to give up hope that White forces would be able to overthrow the Soviet regime. Maddin Summers thought it was unfortunate that "the only organized and healthy movement in Russia to reestablish order and combat German domination . . . has been disorganized," but believed "those men . . . who have endeavored to save Russia . . . will yet be the ones on whom we must rely to reestablish order and combat Germany."[93]

Charles Crane shared Summers's view. On February 21, Crane drew the attention of President Wilson and Postmaster General Burleson to two reports from Harold Williams in that day's *New York Times*. "While Bolshevism is spreading in the south," Williams wrote, "the reaction against it is growing in the northern centres." Moscow, in particular, had become a safe haven for officers and middle class intellectuals associated with the Provisional Government who were determined to build "a new Russia . . . when the storm is past." With popular discontent growing, Williams thought that "the course of events must necessarily lead to the restoration of a strong Government." Even the Bolsheviks said that "the days of their power are numbered." By commending Williams's "undoubtedly authentic" dispatches Crane evidently sought to counteract disillusionment with Kaledin and bolster the president's faith that orderly self-government eventually would be restored in Russia.[94]

Conclusion

If American and Allied representatives had been able to deliver larger sums to the strapped anti-Bolshevik forces in southern Russia between December 1917 and February 1918, those soldiers would have been better equipped; but more money would not have solved the problem that few men other than former tsarist officers were willing to enlist in the Volunteer Army. In 1919, Britain and the United States did provide more substantial assistance to the much bigger conscripted armies that drove from the south to within three hundred miles of Moscow, yet that campaign faltered, too, in part because urgently needed forces were diverted to suppress uprisings in the rear by peasants and workers. Most of the U.S. aid in 1919 was channeled through the Russian embassy in Washington. Ambassador Bakhmeteff and his agents used U.S. credits to send six shipments of rifles, ammunition, and other materiel, worth more than $16 million, to the anti-Bolshevik forces between May and December 1919.[95]

Since this assistance was provided long after the war against Germany ended in November 1918, it clearly cannot be explained as an effort to constrain the German army. U.S. financial intervention in south Russia did not suddenly become anti-Bolshevik on November 11, 1918.[96] Instead, American efforts to assist White forces in southern Russia were from the beginning both anti-Bolshevik and anti-German in purpose. Over time, anti-Bolshevism increased in importance, while anti-German considerations declined in significance until they became almost irrelevant.

In early 1918, British officials were preoccupied with countering the imminent German military threat, but even then they were able to think about the longer-term problem of the economic and political reconstruction of Russia.[97] Since American diplomats and leaders were more confident than the British that the war would be won on the western front, they were less concerned with resurrecting an eastern front, and more inclined to focus on the Russian future. As Maddin Summers observed in January 1918, the Cossacks and Ukrainians could not be expected "to hold the Central powers in check," but Allied support for those anti-Bolshevik forces could help "check anarchy, help lay foundations for an orderly future and hinder the enslavement of Russia by Germany." Thus, "in making the world safe for democracy," Summers thought, the Allies could "righteously and judiciously also try to make democracy in Russia safe for the world."[98]

Summers did not recognize that "democracy" itself posed severe problems for that crusade, since congressional restrictions on presidential disbursements constrained the Wilson administration's ability to finance anti-Bolshevik movements, while the antiwar, anti-elitist, and nationalist attitudes of peoples on the edges of the former Russian empire made it difficult for White leaders to mobilize popular support. President Wilson and his advisors knew that attempting to support anti-Bolshevik forces in southern Russia through the Allies risked embittering the Bolsheviks, estranging left-leaning Americans, spurring Russian sectionalism, and fostering Allied spheres of influence. However, Wilson and Lansing decided to take the gamble because they believed that it would be possible to keep America's role hidden, that the Soviet regime would soon fall, and that the importance of countering Bolshevism and reorganizing Russian military resistance to Germany outweighed the high chance of failure. Although the wager did not pay off in early 1918, Americans continued to use similar methods as the Russian Civil War spread. After the strongmen in southern Russia proved disappointingly weak, Americans tried to support other strongmen in Siberia. And while it proved impossible to keep all American activity in southern Russia secret from the Bolsheviks, American diplomats and intelligence agents subsequently maintained clandestine contact with and offered encouragement to anti-Bolshevik groups in other parts of Russia.

5

AMERICAN INTELLIGENCE GATHERING, PROPAGANDA, AND COVERT ACTION IN REVOLUTIONARY RUSSIA

When Woodrow Wilson went before Congress in April 1917 to call for a crusade to make the world "safe for democracy," he stressed one of the virtues of democracies like the United States. "Self-governed nations," Wilson proclaimed, "do not fill their neighbor states with spies." Only monarchies and aristocracies, he elaborated, with the "privacy of courts" and the "carefully guarded confidences of a narrow and privileged class," could maintain intelligence organizations to carry out cunning plans of "deception or aggression." Such immoral practices were "happily impossible where public opinion commands and insists upon full information concerning all the nation's affairs."[1]

This notion that the sunlit democracy of the New World was incapable of the shadier practices of the Old World was appealing but inaccurate, as Wilson might have realized had he paused to reflect on his earlier writing about the Mexican-American War or the planters' "revolution" in Hawaii.

From the first days of the United States, presidents authorized covert intervention in foreign lands, and secret agents played vital roles in American territorial expansion. As we have seen, in Wilson's first term, U.S. officials sent spies into neighboring Mexico on a variety of missions, the most sensational being an attempt to assassinate Pancho Villa.[2]

Americans relied more heavily on the methods of secret war as they sought to influence developments in revolutionary Russia. While Wilson suggested that representative institutions blocked statesmen from "the course of intrigue," the fact that the United States was a democracy with an aroused public opinion actually spurred his administration's resort to devious methods. Accountability to Congress for government spending constrained the administration's financing of propaganda, inclining it to utilize private funds. Sensitivity to public attitudes delayed overt intervention, thereby increasing the pressure American representatives in Russia felt to secretly encourage anti-Bolshevik movements and to engage in covert action against German and Soviet forces.

Unaware of these aspects of the secret war against Bolshevism, Americans have often regarded the Wilson era as an age of innocence, untainted by the darker arts of statecraft. Yet experiences with intelligence collection, propaganda, and support for anti-Bolshevik groups during Wilson's presidency had lasting influences on young diplomats and officers who went on to long careers in the State Department and U.S. intelligence organizations.

Although Soviet leaders never learned the full extent of the secret war, they did find out about some of the propaganda efforts, and after capturing the head of one of the U.S. intelligence organizations in Russia they made him a sensational symbol of American hostility to the Bolshevik regime. For decades, Soviet writers treated the American spy Xenophon Kalamatiano as one of the leading villains in a conspiracy by foreign imperialists and domestic counterrevolutionaries to assassinate Bolshevik leaders and overthrow the Soviet government. While those charges were exaggerations and distortions, Americans were indirectly involved in a wider range of conspiracies than the Cheka, the Soviet secret police, ever uncovered or even suspected.[3]

The story of American propaganda, espionage, and covert action in revolutionary Russia thus helps to explain the long rift between American and Russian perceptions of Wilsonian policy. It may also contribute to dispelling illusions about the relationship between democracy and secrecy in American foreign policy.

American Propaganda in Revolutionary Russia

As the United States entered the Great War in the spring of 1917, Wilson's confidential advisor Colonel House talked with the chief British secret service official in America, Sir William Wiseman, about establishing a collaborative relationship between British and American intelligence organizations. In May, House and Wiseman developed plans for a joint venture "to do some effective intelligence work in Russia" and "to start propaganda in Russia to offset German propaganda of like sort." In June, Secretary of State Lansing gave Wilson a copy of the House-Wiseman proposal for "very secretly organized" Anglo-American propaganda campaigns. Lansing noted approvingly that the United States "would not have to appear in the matter at all" and urged that "no stone should be left unturned to counteract the German propaganda in Russia."[4]

Wilson approved the House-Wiseman plan in mid-June. Wiseman then convinced British writer Somerset Maugham to go to Russia as an Anglo-American agent. From Petrograd Maugham passed intelligence through the American diplomatic pouch to Frank Polk, whose position as Counselor of the State Department entailed responsibility for intelligence coordination. Maugham was followed to Russia by several Czech-Americans whom Charles Crane and State Department officials hoped would be able to organize Czechoslovakians in Russia and counteract German influence there. In cooperation with the Czech-Americans, Maugham distributed anti-German and pro-Ally propaganda in Russia and provided financial support to moderate socialists opposed to the Bolsheviks.[5]

Between March and November 1917 American representatives in Russia attempted to launch several other propaganda campaigns to keep Russia in the war and forestall a Bolshevik accession to power.[6] One of those efforts was initiated by an American Red Cross mission, financed by copper magnate William Boyce Thompson, which arrived in Petrograd in early August. The mission had a broad mandate from Washington officials to buttress the Provisional Government against looming chaos and demoralization. Toward that end, Thompson gave $1 million of his own fortune to support the pro-war agitation of a Committee on Civic Education, which included Prime Minister Kerensky's private secretary and the "grandmother of the Russian Revolution," E. K. Breshko-Breshkovskaia. As Raymond Robins, the most dynamic member of the Red Cross mission, later observed, the purpose of Thompson's contribution to the committee was to form "the new culture that would hold the front" and "prevent the bolshevik[s] from ever getting into power in Russia."[7]

Since April 1917, Breshkovskaia had been supporting the publication and distribution of pro-war, pro-Ally newspapers and pamphlets. She received money for that educational work from Arthur Bullard, a left-leaning writer who sailed to Russia in June with the confidential support of the Wilson administration for his publicity work. Thanks to Thompson's generous donation, the Committee on Civic Education was able to conduct a much more extensive campaign in September and October

1917, with leaflets attacking the Bolsheviks, supporting Kerensky, and praising Russia's democratic allies. Thompson and General William Judson, head of the U.S. military mission in Russia in 1917, believed the efforts of the committee and the Red Cross mission delayed the Bolsheviks' "advent to power by a month or more."[8]

American and Russian historians later concluded that Wilson was "highly displeased" by Thompson's disbursements.[9] At the time, however, Wilson and Creel were delighted by Thompson's contributions from his own pocket. On October 12, Creel advised Wilson that he was completing "arrangements for the expenditure of $1,000,000 contributed to Russian publicity by Mr. Thompson." Twelve days later, Wilson signed a letter to Thompson that effusively praised the financier's "helpful interest in Russia's fight for freedom" and lauded the "finely practical" form of his "sympathy." In the same vein, Creel wrote Thompson that "it is a great thing that you are doing, and here in Washington, we have every faith in you."[10]

While Wilson and Creel approved of privately financed propaganda in Russia, they had misgivings about large government-funded ventures. When Thompson urged the administration to appropriate $3 million a month to continue the propaganda campaign, Wilson exploded that he had "gone crazy." Similarly, when the Root Mission had recommended the expenditure of $5 million for propaganda in Russia in August 1917, Wilson deflected the proposal.[11]

What caused Wilson to hesitate? Wilson and his advisors sometimes suggested that moral scruples and political principles inhibited their approach to propaganda in Russia. In May 1917, House and Wiseman pledged that none of the secret missions they proposed "would attempt to interfere in any way with Russian domestic questions." Reviewing the Root Mission's propaganda proposals in August, Creel stiffly opposed "subsidies to any portion of the Russian press." In October, dispatching CPI agent Edgar Sisson to Russia, Wilson instructed him to "guard particularly against any effect of officious intrusion or meddling," and stressed America's "obligation of open dealing."[12]

Yet noninterventionist principles did not keep Wilson and his aides from approving aggressive propaganda campaigns. In October, Creel and Wilson applauded Thompson's subsidies to Breshkovskaia and pro-war Russian newspapers. After the Provisional Government fell, Creel instructed Sisson to "drive ahead full speed regardless [of] expense" along the same line as Thompson's work, by having "Breshkovskaya and others issue statements and translate pamphlets." And as the Bolsheviks came to power, Wilson responded positively to a letter from Root Mission veteran Charles Edward Russell, who argued that it was "perfectly possible" to make the Russian people "have heart in the war" by addressing an American education campaign to "the Russian's passion for democracy." Wilson did not consider this new call for a $5 million propaganda campaign un-justified meddling in Russian affairs. Instead, he deeply appreciated Russell's letter, which ran along the lines of his own thought, and promised to do his best to act along the lines it suggested.[13]

Wilson's resistance earlier in 1917 to expending official U.S. funds on large propaganda campaigns seems to have stemmed less from idealistic principles than from his fear that Congress and the American people would not approve of such activity. In August 1917, Wilson indicated that the U.S. "government should not hand out the money" for propaganda in Russia, "but that the same result should be gained in some round-about way." And in October 1917 Creel asked Thompson to understand that Washington's inability to provide "full support" was not "due to any lack of willingness, but to the iron limitations imposed by our law, and our public opinion."[14]

While such concern about legislative restrictions and American public attitudes inhibited the Wilson administration, it did not prevent Bolsheviks from learning about American support for Breshkovskaia's propaganda campaigns. In December 1917, Breshkovskaia's former secretary published sensational charges that Raymond Robins and other Americans gave her packets of money. Pouncing on the revelations, *Izvestiia* denounced Breshkovskaia for making "humiliating appeals to American imperialists" and being "a paid agent" of "American capitalists." Fearing Bolshevik reprisals, members of the Red Cross mission and the Committee on Civic Education went into hiding.[15]

Many of the American propaganda efforts involved intelligence agents or cooperation with counterintelligence bureaus. In addition to the work of Maugham and Czech-American agent Victor Voska, Raymond Robins "had a secret service organized" to keep him posted on shifting support for the Provisional Government and the Bolsheviks. According to General Judson, the "very efficient secret service organization" formed by Robins was used "to combat the Bolshevicks [sic]." Shortly after reaching Petrograd in November 1917, Sisson reported to Creel that to outward publicity he had added "internal intelligence," and he was "using the only American intelligence service in Russia," men who served him and Robins. Although Sisson did not realize it, American diplomats were at that time working to develop their own "information services" to collect intelligence and maintain clandestine contacts with anti-Bolshevik groups.[16]

Expansion of American Intelligence Collection in Russia, 1917–1918

Soon after the American declaration of war against Germany, the U.S. consul general at Moscow, Maddin Summers, had launched a campaign to hire more consuls, primarily to capitalize on American economic opportunities. In April 1917, Summers stressed to Lansing that Russia was the "greatest of all markets," and that much larger consular staffs were required, "in view of the necessity of gaining a foothold after the war, and of finding a market for our surplus products." Even after the Russian war against Germany faltered, Summers believed Americans could displace the Germans who had previously "held a monopoly of trade." In the fall of 1917, he therefore went ahead with "plans to cover the principal cities in the interior of Russia," in order to be able to assist "American firms wishing to enter these markets." [17]

The effort to augment American consular representation received a further political and military stimulus in November, when the Provisional Government fell and U.S. officials began looking for sources of opposition to the new Soviet regime. As we have seen, American attention focused at first on Cossack and Ukrainian forces in southern Russia. In an important precedent for subsequent intelligence missions by other Americans, Summers dispatched Consul DeWitt Poole ostensibly to investigate the commercial situation, but actually to contact and report on the anti-Bolshevik movement. While Poole went to Rostov in December, Consul Douglas Jenkins was sent to Kiev, where White and Red Guards were battling for control.[18]

A Christmas Eve request from the State Department for more confidential information about political and military conditions in Russia — particularly in regions like the Caucasus that were not under Soviet control — spurred further intelligence collection missions, including a second trip to Rostov by Poole. In February 1918, citing "the distribution of control over Russia among different political factions and the interruption in the ordinary means of communication," the State Department approved Summers's request for more consular officers. In the following weeks he was able to post men throughout Russia and Siberia. Acting along similar lines, Ambassador Francis dispatched a military attaché and a member of the Young Men's Christian Association to north Russia, where they "found anti-bolshevik sentiment strong." The YMCA man predicted that "with Allied encouragement and support," the governments there "would prove a rallying point for the best elements in Russia."[19]

Efforts to Contact, Encourage, and Support Anti-Bolshevik Groups

The purpose of these special assignments was not simply neutral information gathering.[20] By posting consuls throughout Russia, Summers and Francis hoped (1) to learn more about potential sources of opposition to Bolshevism and German influence, (2) to encourage those forces of resistance to act, and (3) to enhance the U.S. position in economic competition with other countries in Russia.

On March 4, Ambassador Francis informed Washington that he had ordered commercial attaché W. Chapin Huntington to Irkutsk to keep him advised concerning the organization of a Siberian republic "on Socialistic lines but independent of Petrograd government." Francis believed that there was "a growing sentiment among the better element of the country against a shameful peace," that "considerable resistance may be expected from the Siberian parties that center in Irkutsk," and that Americans had a duty "to support in every way any party that resents even a passive neutrality" toward Germany. At the same time, Francis remained eager to seize "the tremendous opportunities that may open before us in economic lines." Like Francis, Summers still had "faith in the better class of the people here" and believed that their exasperation with the Bolsheviks and German domination would soon lead them to "drive the enemy from their midst." [21]

Summers and Francis may have thought that by directing their newly deputized consuls to "be discreet" and "avoid creating the impression" of official accreditation, they could preserve a technical neutrality. However, Summers was not a disinterested observer. In confidential instructions to his emissaries, Summers wrote: "We are deeply interested in and vitally affected by the success of the Russian people in their struggle against an autocratic regime which has brought upon them the present unfortunate political state." Summers sympathized with the plight of wealthy Russians, including relatives of his aristocratic Russian wife. "We feel and know that they are still our allies," he explained, "and we know that we can assist them now when they stand in need of friends." [22]

Francis's similar sympathies were evident both in private letters to noble Russian friends, whom he impatiently exhorted to "redeem" Russia from the Bolsheviks and Germans, and in public speeches that promised American assistance to the Russian people if they would repudiate the Treaty of Brest-Litovsk and "organize to resist the encroachments of Germany." On June 6, when Francis was asked about "the remedy for the present deplorable conditions," he pledged that U.S. representatives would "extend aid to the extent of their ability against the common enemy—Germany, whose agents are selfishly attempting to exploit Russia." Francis and other Americans were increasingly convinced in the spring of 1918 that the Bolsheviks were themselves German agents, against whom the "intelligent and property-owning classes" should organize.[23]

While dispatching consuls to establish connections with anti-Bolshevik groups in distant parts of Russia, Summers and Francis themselves communicated with underground organizations in Moscow, Petrograd, and Vologda. Such contacts were requested and approved by the State Department. On March 27, 1918, Francis informed Summers that the department had cabled in his "private cipher" to request information regarding "the whereabouts of Kerensky, Miliukoff, . . . and other conservative leaders." Francis therefore asked the consul general whether he knew "of any organized opposition in Russia to the present bolshevik government." Summers and Poole sent Francis the news they collected about such leaders and groups, and the ambassador relayed the gist of their reports to the State Department. On May 18, for example, Francis cabled Washington, "Poole wires that Kerensky has been in Petrograd now in Moscow incognito of course." [24]

In addition to the investigations by American diplomats, information about anti-Bolshevik forces was gathered by U.S. military officers who reported to Lt. Colonel James A. Ruggles, chief of the American military mission to Russia in 1918. On May 30, for example, Captain E. Francis Riggs sent a report on three "Militant Non-Bolshevick Political Groups": pro-German "Reactionaries"; a "Constitutional-Monarchist Organization" or "'The Pro-Ally Counter-Revolution,'" centered in Moscow; and the "Liberals," "a fusion of parties from Cadets to Social Revolutionists." Skeptical about the military forces of these organizations, Riggs concluded that each of them expected the Bolsheviks "to be overthrown by the unorganized people. They will then step in and supply the organization to restore order after their own manner of thinking." [25]

In early June, Francis requested authorization from Washington to make an announcement about U.S. policy "when Bolshevik Government collapses which may possibly be soon." Believing that the "Russian people require guidance," Francis proposed a statement that would link U.S. diplomatic recognition to free elections, which he thought should be held "by a provisional government composed of unselfish patriotic Russians." President Wilson did not want to "seem to dictate just how the new government should be chosen," but he sympathized with Francis's basic idea. Francis was therefore instructed that "in the event present Soviet government abdicates or is deposed you may announce to the Russian people . . . that this Government will recognize a government of Russia which it has reason to regard as representative of the people of Russia and chosen by their collective action." [26]

Anticipating an anti-Bolshevik revolt, Francis decided to travel from Vologda—where he was keeping a safe distance from the German army and the Bolshevik government—to Petrograd and Moscow. As he advised the State Department, his journey was mainly "for the purpose of ascertaining what organized opposition exists and plans thereof." In Petrograd, the ambassador succeeded in meeting several underground leaders, including industrialists who had formed a clandestine constitutional monarchist group. He also met with a former "Colonel of the General Staff," who told him that "the entire force of the Soviet Government in Russia is less than twenty-five thousand men." Francis advised the State Department, which was then contemplating proposals for military intervention, that that estimate of Soviet weakness was "confirmed from all available sources." Thus, while Americans in Russia knew that anti-Bolshevik forces were small and hesitant, their reports encouraged officials in Washington to believe that limited foreign intervention might be sufficient to secure the removal of the Soviet government.[27]

Although Francis assured Washington that he made no commitment to anti-Bolshevik groups, he and other Americans sought not merely to collect information, but also to encourage and support counterrevolutionaries. In mid-June, Consul Felix Cole informed Francis about the "North-Eastern Sectional Bureau" in Archangel, whose members "hoped to counteract the spread of Bolshevism." On July 10, anticipating Allied intervention in north Russia, Francis reminded Cole of his interest in "anti-Bolshevik organizations" and authorized him to extend "aid to the extent of fifty thousand roubles or even one hundred thousand roubles to aid the Allies in the event you should find worthy objects therefor."[28]

American contact with anti-Bolshevik forces was facilitated by a collaborative relationship between the American and Allied secret services in Russia. French and British agents gave American diplomats reports on secret meetings of anti-Bolshevik groups and U.S. representatives returned such favors. Most of the intelligence gathered by an American "information service," for example, was "made available to the British and French."[29]

Xenophon Kalamatiano and the U.S. "Information Service"

This "information service" had its headquarters in the U.S. consulate general in Moscow, where Xenophon Kalamatiano, an American businessman of Greek-Russian extraction, directed its largest branch. Although Kalamatiano may have begun doing intelligence work for the State Department on an informal basis before 1917, he accepted a more definite assignment from Consul General Summers at about the time the Kerensky regime collapsed.[30] When Summers died suddenly in early May 1918, De-Witt Poole was appointed consul general at Moscow and thus became Kalamatiano's supervisor. In May and June Poole and Francis informed the State Department that they believed the important work of the information service justified continuing "extraordinary expenditures."[31]

The motive for setting up the information service, Poole maintained, was simply an "innocent" desire "to know what was going on." Although their job was simply to gather "the ordinary flow of news," Poole later reminisced, "Bolshevik totalitarian methods of government" made it necessary to organize a network of agents "on the well-known secret service system of cut-outs — that is, only two or three men were to know and have any contact with Kalamatiano. Then each of these men had two or three men in contact with him, and so on down, with the least possible cross-contacting."[32]

The network Kalamatiano organized consisted of about thirty Russian men and women who traveled inside Soviet Russia and reported to him on the conditions they observed. On the basis of these oral and written reports, Kalamatiano typed up "bulletins" that he furnished to the American consulate. "For a period of two or three months," Poole recalled, "excellent reports came in," which he utilized in telegrams to the State Department and Ambassador Francis. Assistant Secretary of State Frank Polk agreed that "this information . . . proved very helpful."[33]

Like Summers, Poole was concerned with laying "the foundation for important subsequent trade between the United States and Russia," and he foresaw economic benefits from the network of consuls and Kalamatiano's information service. On some of their early trips in April and May 1918, Kalamatiano's agents concentrated on conditions of commerce, transportation, and food supply. However, Kalamatiano was unhappy with these reports, and he pushed his agents to get more detailed information about military fronts and the Red Army. Later bulletins focused more on political and military intelligence such as popular moods, numbers of troops, and morale of soldiers. In July Poole reported to Washington that the observers "under the immediate supervision of Mr. X. B. Kalamatiano . . . frequently furnish important military information."[34]

Kalamatiano's organization collected intelligence about the complicated situations on the southern and eastern fronts in the burgeoning civil war. Using these field reports, Kalamatiano and his agents produced several maps for Poole and Francis, one of which marked the military positions of "various forces in Russia as shown by information received at Red Army staff." Red Army intelligence was hardly "the ordinary flow of news." Information from agents who were Red Army officers allowed Poole to send Washington detailed intelligence about the Red Army, including its movements and ammunition shipments.[35]

The U.S. information service also obtained intelligence through the party affiliations of its agents. On June 27, 1918, for example, Kalamatiano relayed to Poole information from an agent apparently linked to the right wing of the Socialist Revolutionary (SR) Party. The agent reported on plans to "turn out the bolshevicks" through an uprising two weeks later, which was "supposed to be in close contact with allies." Thus, U.S. officials seem to have had advance knowledge of the revolt in early July by Boris Savinkov's underground organization, which seized several towns north of Moscow in the vain hope of gaining support from an anticipated Allied military intervention.[36]

Kalamatiano himself directly contacted members of such anti-Bolshevik groups. In mid-May, for example, he met with a "member of a strong organisation working towards the restoration of peace and order," and "urg[ed] the necessity of some action to show the allies that in reality the best forces of the country are against the bolshevicks." Thus, like Francis and Summers, Kalamatiano was not content with purely passive information gathering.[37]

As the civil war escalated in the late spring and summer of 1918, American intelligence operations were increasingly directed against the Soviet regime. After fighting broke out between pro-Ally Czechoslovakian troops and pro-Soviet forces in eastern Russia and Siberia in late May, Poole stressed the utility of the information service in preparing for an expected Allied intervention. "Should we assume a more active policy," he wrote Francis on June 3, "it could be taken over very advantageously by the military." Later in June, Poole directed Consul Jenkins to "work quietly on the political side, developing contact discreetly with the anti-Bolshevik elements; as we may soon have to deal with these in a more definite way." At the same time, he formulated a scheme for sending consular representatives to areas where Allied forces were expected, in order to carry out "a campaign of popular preparations in advance of military movements."[38]

After American troops arrived in north Russia and Siberia in August 1918, U.S. diplomats still emphasized the need "not to interfere in internal Russian affairs." This did not mean that they were neutral in the struggle between Bolshevik and anti-Bolshevik forces, however. In mid-August the first U.S. troops reached Vladivostok on the way to "rescue" Czechoslovakian troops who had helped White forces oust Bolshevik governments between Samara and eastern Siberia. On August 19, Poole stressed to the U.S. vice consul at Samara the "need for care on our part to avoid being drawn into the details of Russian politics." While "letting the Russians select their own government," Poole thought Americans should concern themselves "with military support for the Czechs and the economic rehabilitation of the country." This did not mean an apolitical passivity. "Whenever circumstances force you to reflect a general political preference," Poole instructed the vice consul, "it must naturally be for a sane and progressive liberalism. . . . *Make it clear that the United States stands for true democracy as opposed to absolutism on the one hand and the inverted autocracy of Bolshevism on the other.*" Poole and other Americans may have tried to be neutral in regard to the competition between "sane and progressive" anti-Bolshevik parties, such as the Kadets and the right Socialist Revolutionaries, but they were not neutral in the struggle against Bolshevism.[39]

As American and Allied troops landed at Archangel and Vladivostok, relations between Western diplomats and the Bolshevik government neared a breaking point. While Poole and other officials decided to leave Soviet Russia, arrangements were made for some agents, including Kalamatiano, to stay behind. As Poole later explained, Kalamatiano volunteered to remain in Bolshevik territory because the Soviet government "had become for many purposes and intents an ally of the Imperial Government of Germany," and Kalamatiano planned to furnish information concerning conditions and events in what was effectively "enemy territory."[40]

At the American consulate general in Moscow on August 25, a crucial meeting was held, according to Poole, "to permit the heads of the British, French and American information services, who were to remain in Russia, to see each other and arrange to exchange reports" that could then be sent out of the country.[41] The meeting in Poole's office was attended by Kalamatiano, British agent Sidney Reilly, and three Frenchmen: Consul General Grenard, Colonel de Vertement, and journalist René Marchand.

The day after this coordinating meeting, Poole sent a telegram to Washington that offered a general appraisal of the situation in Russia. "Disaffection from Bolsheviks continues marked," Poole wired. "But opposition to them within the territory they control is taking even less definite form than heretofore because what really anti-Bolshevik elements exist seek to pass behind the Allied lines in north or into Czech country. It is difficult to perceive from what quarter any interior revolt against Bolsheviks may come." Seeing little prospect for overthrowing the Bolshevik government in Moscow, Poole looked to the possibilities for military action from outside the territory controlled by the Soviet government. He assigned priority to efforts to link a variety of anti-Bolshevik forces in southeastern Russia and western Siberia with Allied military expeditions coming from Archangel and Baku. Poole placed special stress on the need to support the Czechs and protect the "much exposed Samara flank."[42]

To gather information about that eastern front, Kalamatiano proposed a special mission to Siberia. Czechoslovakian troops and anti-Bolshevik Russians had been fighting against Red forces along stretches of the Trans-Siberian Railway since May. In August there was an unstable front between Red and White armies along the Volga River and west of the Ural Mountains. Poole and Kalamatiano apparently agreed that on his way to Siberia Kalamatiano would stop in Samara, where the Trans-Siberian Railway crossed the Volga, and where anti-Bolshevik forces were attempting to organize a government. Poole explained the strategic significance of Samara in messages from Moscow on August 26. He urged that the

"Consulate-General be established temporarily at Samara" because it was the "seat of one Siberian Government, a pivotal point economically, and will afford ready access to Moscow when some future friendly Russian Government will permit Consulate General to return there." [43]

Kalamatiano left Moscow on August 30. A week later he reached Samara and began investigating political attitudes and military conditions in the region. While in Samara, Kalamatiano learned that the Cheka had swooped into action in Moscow and Petrograd, and that members of his network had been arrested. He did not yet know of some other complications, though, and he still hoped to be able to report to Poole. Kalamatiano therefore returned to Moscow on September 18. [44]

That morning, Poole finally left the city, eluding the Cheka and barely managing to reach Finland ahead of orders for his arrest. From Helsingfors, Poole cabled the State Department to warn Kalamatiano not to return to Moscow, but his warning was sent too late and failed to reach Kalamatiano. [45]

In separate incidents at the end of August, anti-Bolshevik socialists assassinated the head of the Cheka in Petrograd and shot Lenin in Moscow. As a result, Bolshevik leaders were "much excited and nervous." The Cheka was forced to liquidate plots it had been investigating somewhat earlier than it would have liked. Searching the apartments of Russians who worked for Kalamatiano, Chekists found "masses of material," including reports from field agents of the information service. While Kalamatiano avoided the Cheka units waiting for him at his rooms, he then went to the U.S. consulate and was captured. [46]

During his interrogation and trial, Kalamatiano admitted that he met Allied agents at the consulate on August 25, but he claimed that he "knew nothing as to their business," and said that he "heard nothing of any plots." He further insisted that the purpose of the information service was only to gather commercial data of interest to American firms, though he granted that he had supplied bulletins to Reilly and de Vertement. [47] Kalamatiano's stand was undermined when his interrogators discovered a hiding place inside his cane, from which they took a cipher code, receipts for money, and messages, including instructions to members of his network to encipher reports containing especially important military intelligence. [48]

Soviet officials and writers charged that Kalamatiano and Poole not only organized a clandestine network to gather political and military intelligence for use against the Bolshevik government, but also participated in a plot to use Latvian troops to overthrow the Soviet government, which was masterminded by Reilly and British special envoy R. H. Bruce Lockhart. Since the British and French agents eluded the Cheka or were released in exchange for Bolsheviks held in England, Kalamatiano was left as the main figure in the trial in late November and early December 1918. While Lockhart, Reilly, Grenard, and de Vertement were tried in absentia, Kalamatiano was accused of being aware of their plans and taking a direct part in carrying them out. Later, Feliks Dzerzhinskii, head of the Cheka, asserted that Poole was as deeply involved as the British and French representatives in "not only espionage, but also fighting against Soviet power" through disorganization of the Red Army, destruction of food warehouses, and demolition of bridges. Some Soviet writers went even further, making Kalamatiano out to be "one of the main organizers of the 'consuls' plot,'" and suggesting that the Americans were mixed up in the attempted assassination of Lenin.[49]

At a Senate hearing in 1920, Poole denied that Kalamatiano stayed in Russia "for the purpose of conducting a plot against the Bolshevik Government," and asserted that "everything of that kind was expressly excluded from his activities." Poole also repeatedly and categorically denied that he had any knowledge of or connection to any plot against the Soviet regime. In fact, Poole insisted that at the time he did not even know the names of the British and French agents.[50]

This testimony concealed American contact with Entente agents. On at least one occasion, in July 1918, Reilly carried mail from the U.S. consulates in Petrograd and Moscow to American diplomats in Vologda. When British and French officers and diplomats were arrested in the first week of August, Reilly sent "a warning to the American Consulate," and British secret service money was "safely hidden in the American consulate previous to their arrest." In a confidential message to the secretary of state in 1919, Poole himself admitted that he knew, though "only in a vague way," about the activity of Allied agents, and confessed that he "judged unwisely in permitting Mr. Kalamatiano to come too closely in contact with" the British and French agents.[51]

Poole may or may not have opposed Reilly's plan to use Latvian soldiers to overthrow the Soviet government, but he was not completely ignorant of it. In September 1918, Poole told the British ambassador in Oslo that there was strong suspicion that Reilly had exceeded his instructions and might have been part of a Cheka provocation. The British ambassador wired the Foreign Office that "Reilly advocated encouraging a revolt," but Lockhart, after consulting Poole and the French consul general, "instructed Reilly to limit his efforts to propaganda." Norman Armour, third secretary of the American embassy in Russia, had a different story: "Lockhart had told him he had had opportunity to buy off Lettish troops, [and] that the scheme was known to and approved by the French and American Consuls." On September 9, Poole himself cabled the State Department that there was "some foundation of fact for charges respecting Lettish troops."[52]

Both the Soviet allegations and the American denials centered on the August 25, 1918, meeting at Poole's office in Moscow, attended by Kalamatiano, Reilly, Grenard, de Vertement, and Marchand. The key available pieces of evidence — Reilly's memoir and a letter by Marchand "found" by the Cheka — indicate that the Americans were not present when Reilly discussed his plans with de Vertement and thus tend to exonerate Poole and Kalamatiano from the specific charge of knowingly assisting Reilly's plot to overthrow the Bolsheviks.[53]

However, other evidence suggests that the Soviets had reason to be suspicious and that the Americans were more closely connected to Reilly's organization than they admitted. Two of Kalamatiano's most important agents were Aleksandr V. Friede, a Latvian colonel on the staff of the chief of military communications for the Soviet regime, and his sister, Marie. Colonel Friede testified in November 1918 that when reports from field observers came in, he would work on them, then hand them to his sister, who would deliver them to addresses Reilly had given Kalamatiano. When Marie Friede was arrested, she was carrying a report for Reilly from Kalamatiano's organization. Kalamatiano blamed his own arrest in part on "evident absolute carelessness in connection with Riley's organization" that led the Cheka to the Friedes. While the testimony of other defendants supported Kalamatiano's assertion that the U.S. consulate had no connection to any Allied plots, Friede's did not. As Kalamatiano later recalled, "Friede under cross examination stated that he did know Consul General Poole." Poole apparently jeopardized his insulation from Kalamatiano's operation by meeting directly with the Friedes.[54]

Thus, it seems that Kalamatiano and Poole were neither as innocent as they claimed nor guilty of all the charges Soviet prosecutors and writers leveled against them. Kalamatiano's insistence that he was only gathering economic data is not credible. Although the original organization of his information service was motivated in part by economic interests, after the intensification of civil war in the spring of 1918 the network focused more on gathering military intelligence that could be useful to anti-Bolshevik groups and Allied forces intervening in Russia. On occasion, as when he traveled to Samara and the eastern front in September 1918, Kalamatiano was himself directly involved in gathering political and military intelligence. By supplying this information to Reilly and de Vertement, Kalamatiano became at least an unwitting accomplice in the Allied agents' plans to coordinate anti-Bolshevik risings in Moscow and Petrograd with sabotage and military action elsewhere in Russia. Yet to charge, as some Soviets did, that Kalamatiano knew all about Reilly's plotting, is to go beyond the evidence. To allege that Kalamatiano was the central figure of the conspiracy, as the Soviet prosecutor did at his trial, or to insinuate complicity in the shooting of Lenin, is to strain the evidence even further, especially given Kalamatiano's absence from Moscow between August 30 and September 18.

What Did Washington Know?

Soviet scholars often assumed that the actions of junior American officials were authorized by Washington and represented official U.S. policy.[55] However, the Wilson administration provided its representatives in Russia with only broad guidelines and granted them wide latitude in implementing policy, especially after the Bolshevik Revolution. Lansing requested Francis to gather information about anti-Bolshevik leaders but left it up to the ambassador to decide how to maintain contacts and collect data.[56] Francis, Summers, and Poole were not afraid to accept authority and act on their own responsibility, without waiting for explicit instructions from Washington.[57]

President Wilson was intrigued by aspects of secret service work and spent many hours with his wife coding and decoding confidential dispatches. He was also personally involved in making some decisions about intelligence operations. In August 1917, for example, he decided "to pay out of his own hundred million dollar fund the [State] Department's expenses in connection with intelligence abroad."[58]

However, despite Wilson's tendency to micromanage American foreign policy, he does not seem to have supervised the details of U.S. intelligence activity inside Soviet Russia. In September 1918, Wilson informed Lansing that while he wanted to keep the matter of publicity entirely in his own hands, he "would not think of interfering with the activities of the War Department's intelligence agents."[59]

In early September Francis advised Wilson and Lansing that "the French were prompt to encourage and financially assist every anti-Bolshevik movement," and he recounted some details of French contacts with Savinkov in June, but he did not mention the later collaboration between the U.S. information service and French agents. In mid-October, Wilson appeared to be ignorant of the "Lockhart plot." According to William Wiseman, Wilson agreed with him that "The Bolsheviki . . . were impossible. He had watched with disgust their treatment of Lockhart, who had tried hard to help them."[60]

Wilson, Lansing, and other top State Department officials do not appear to have known the details of Kalamatiano's activities before he was arrested. While Francis, Summers, and Poole did keep Washington generally informed about the costs and activities of the information services in their first months, Poole apparently did not inform either Francis or the State Department about critical developments such as the August 25 meeting at the consulate or Kalamatiano's trip to Samara.[61]

Although top Wilson administration officials had little or no advance knowledge of the most dangerous and controversial activities of the information services, those operations were not wild aberrations from the earlier efforts to gather information about anti-Bolshevik forces that Washington had requested and approved. Even the last unauthorized initiatives of Poole and Kalamatiano are significant as illustrations of how far actual American activity in Russia was from Wilson's pronouncement that "self-governed nations do not fill their neighbor states with spies."

Soviet Views of Kalamatiano

Regardless of how much the Wilson administration knew, the intelligence operations conducted by Kalamatiano and other Americans were bound to affect Soviet perceptions of the United States. Cheka deputy Iakov Peters, who interrogated Kalamatiano, was "very bitter" about Allied support for the Bolsheviks' enemies. Peters told Lockhart in September that "the Americans were the worst compromised" in the consuls' plot, though "for political reasons" the Bolsheviks did not mention Poole or denounce America when they attacked Britain and France for counterrevolutionary conspiracies. As Kalamatiano sensed, there was a struggle between the Cheka "terrorists" and Foreign Commissariat "moderates" over whether he should be executed, permanently imprisoned, or released.[62] After Kalamatiano and Friede were sentenced to death on December 3, 1918, Kalamatiano's lawyer immediately appealed for mitigation of the sentence, arguing that the "Lockhart plot" was not carried out, that Kalamatiano was not connected to it, and that his network gathered commercial rather than military information. Although Friede was executed and Kalamatiano was subjected to mock executions, Soviet leaders decided to use the American as a hostage or in a prisoner exchange. Already in early December Soviet diplomats offered to free Kalamatiano if imprisoned American Socialist Party leader Eugene Debs and a British draft protester were released at the same time.[63]

The Soviet position was formalized in April 1919. After Lenin raised the question of what to do with Kalamatiano, the Bolshevik Central Committee announced, "In view of the possibility of using him as a hostage to exchange in the course of negotiations with the Americans, it has been decided not to shoot him and to hold him in prison." Despite that decision, Soviet officials continued to take different stances. In the summer of 1919 the Cheka categorically declared that it would not free Kalamatiano under any circumstances. Messages from Deputy Foreign Commissar Litvinov staked out a similar position, with shrill assertions that Kalamatiano was a "most dangerous spy" who "can on no account be released," as he was "exceedingly guilty of aiding and abetting Russian reactionaries." In contrast to Litvinov, the Soviet representative in the United States, Ludwig Martens, stressed the allegedly lenient treatment of American prisoners in arguing for improved Soviet-American relations. Along the same line, Foreign Commissar Chicherin assured U.S. leaders that "the Soviet Government will gladly seek a satisfactory resolution of the question." To support his position at home, Chicherin explained to a Chekist in 1921 that Americans were extremely sensitive about the fate of their citizens, and if Kalamatiano was executed "that would extraordinarily strengthen the agitation against Soviet Russia." Since a rapprochement with America had "colossal significance" for Russia, Chicherin continued, "we can not create a pretext for new ferocious agitation against us."[64]

While Soviet leaders sought to extract advantage and avoid damage from the Kalamatiano case, State Department officials who were interested in freeing Kalamatiano were impeded by the Wilson administration's stern nonrecognition policy. Polk, Poole, and others pursued the Soviet offers through a variety of indirect channels, but progress was hindered by the department's fear that direct negotiations would be construed as recognizing the Soviet government. Ultimately, Kalamatiano was traded for food rather than Soviet prisoners. In exchange for famine aid from the American Relief Administration and perhaps in the interest of removing an obstacle to improved relations, the Soviet government released Kalamatiano and several other Americans in August 1921.[65]

U.S. Military Attachés and Sabotage Operations

Kalamatiano's information service was complemented by a separate service based in Petrograd and by parallel operations conducted by U.S. military attachés. Like Kalamatiano, the U.S. officers maintained contact with underground anti-Bolshevik groups and gathered military intelligence. Captain Eugene Prince was especially active in "obtaining information regarding the German and bolshevick battle orders." The military attachés were also interested in keeping food, metals, and other valuable materials in western Russia from falling into the hands of German troops. Particularly in the first months of 1918, Bolshevik officials cooperated with U.S. and Allied efforts to evacuate or purchase such supplies. As the aims of the Bolsheviks and the Western powers diverged later in 1918, however, the U.S. military attachés increasingly relied on propaganda among workers and sabotage to deny resources to both the Germans and the Soviet regime.[66]

"With the approval of the [U.S.] Ambassador," Colonel James A. Ruggles later reported, he cooperated with the French military mission in organizing the destruction of property acquired by the Germans and the provision of support to Czechoslovakian forces fighting the Red Army. To carry out these actions, American and French officers, like Kalamatiano, employed "paid agents, mostly from the Right Wing of the Socialist Revolutionary Party which was bitterly opposed to the Bolshevicks." These agents organized strikes and sabotaged railroads in the German-occupied Ukraine and in eastern European Russia. "When the Bolshevicks started operations against the Czecho-Slovaks and large amounts of artillery and other supplies were being shipped to Kazan and Simbirsk," Ruggles wrote, "numerous explosions on the Moscow-Kazan and Moscow-Simbirsk railroads were effected, causing considerable damage and delay." Agents of the U.S. officers continued this sabotage work for a time after Allied and American representatives left Soviet Russia in July 1918.[67]

U.S. Intelligence Operations in the Petrograd Region, 1918–1919

While Kalamatiano's agents concentrated on the Ukraine and Volga regions, a second special information service, headed by Robert W. Imbrie, vice consul at Petrograd, was established in April 1918 to obtain political and military intelligence in northwestern Russia. Imbrie's organization consisted of about twelve men, most of them former tsarist officers. These agents focused initially on observing German troops in the Baltic region, but to Russians like them and to their American supervisors, the Bolsheviks were as much the enemy as the Germans.[68]

Developments in north Russia between April and August 1918 gradually made the anti-Bolshevik element of Imbrie's information service more explicit. After Allied troops landed on the Murmansk Peninsula in the spring, Imbrie reported, "Agents of proven Anti-Bolshevick belief were despatched there and at frequent intervals brought in information regarding developments on this front." In the summer, when Bolshevik troops opposed an Allied advance from Archangel, other agents reported on the northern front. As a result, Imbrie boasted, "we were in possession of exact information" about the Bolshevik forces, which he transmitted to the U.S. command at Archangel.[69]

Although Imbrie had to leave Petrograd in the summer of 1918, he arranged to continue supervising his information service from Vyborg, Finland. One of Imbrie's leading agents, a former tsarist officer named Rodionoff who had joined the Red Army, regularly came to the Petrograd embassy to draw his salary and to bring military information that the caretakers of the embassy then transmitted to Imbrie.[70]

In 1919, partly because of Imbrie's network, the State Department and Office of Naval Intelligence (ONI) received a regular flow of information about conditions in Petrograd and about the morale and movements of Soviet military and naval forces.[71] Imbrie's dispatches were supplemented by reports from naval attachés whose contacts with anti-Bolshevik Russians allowed them to relay intelligence from inside the Cheka and the Soviet naval counterespionage department.[72]

Much as Kalamatiano's leading agents simultaneously worked for Reilly, at least one of Imbrie's agents—Rodionoff—worked for British agent Paul Dukes. And just as Kalamatiano's link to Reilly led to his arrest, the connection to Dukes led to the liquidation of Imbrie's network.

According to Imbrie's assistant Mrs. Zinaida Mackenzie Kennedy, Dukes organized an anti-Bolshevik conspiracy "on a very large scale" in and around Petrograd in 1919. A British subject born in Russia, Kennedy later informed U.S. officials that the conspiracy involved commanders of the Red Army and the private secretary of Bolshevik leader G. E. Zinoviev. As Mrs. Kennedy explained, the conspirators planned to sabotage Red defenses by blowing up bridges leading to Petrograd, to open the front, and to "let the Whites in without offering them any resistance."[73]

Worried about espionage and subversion in the Petrograd area, Lenin demanded in May 1919 that I. V. Stalin "pay greater attention" and "take extraordinary measures" to expose White plots. Redoubling their efforts, Bolsheviks unearthed one British-financed scheme in June, and in November, a few days after the White army of General Iudenich came close to capturing the city, they uncovered the conspiracy Mrs. Kennedy described. The Cheka arrested many of Dukes's agents and, apparently because Rodionoff accused her of being a spy, Mrs. Kennedy was arrested on November 13. By the end of the month, more Americans were implicated. As Imbrie informed Washington, an agent of his in Cheka headquarters reported the arrest of a Russian officer he had employed in 1918. After obtaining information from the officer through torture, the Bolsheviks "posted for execution" a former American military attaché and Imbrie himself.[74]

As in the case of Kalamatiano, Americans may have had little advance knowledge of the most ambitious plans of British spies and no direct role in their anti-Bolshevik conspiracies, yet the Americans' employees' contacts with British agents led some Soviet officials to suspect a deeper U.S. involvement. Mrs. Kennedy's interrogators wanted to know the names of U.S. agents and the secret plans of the United States. She insisted that she "never took part in any counter-revolutionary movements in Russia," but her protestations of innocence were undermined by written evidence Rodionoff turned over to Soviet authorities.[75] Imbrie distanced himself from anti-Bolshevik plots by telling the State Department that the arrested Russian officer had not been in his employ since 1918. Yet Imbrie's dispatches to the State Department in 1919 demonstrated both his knowledge of and sympathy with underground anti-Bolshevik movements. Thus, Imbrie's work, like Kalamatiano's activity, shows that Soviet charges about American involvement with Russian counterrevolutionaries were not merely propaganda or products of paranoia.

The Influence of Wilson-Era Experiences on America's Cold War Intelligence Establishment

While President Wilson knew little or nothing about American covert activities in Soviet Russia, the broader experience of waging war and countering revolutionary movements in Europe opened Wilson's eyes to the wide use of intelligence services. Campaigning for the League of Nations in September 1919, the president argued that if Americans attempted to stand apart from the League they would have to maintain in peacetime a "militaristic organization of government," including "a system which we have condemned, . . . a spying system." "You cannot watch other nations with your unassisted eyes," Wilson explained. "You have got to watch them by secret agencies planted everywhere." Although Wilson recoiled from this "very ugly picture" of a country that was "not America," he foresaw "with awakened eyes" the national security state of the future.[76]

Although Wilson emerged from his ostensible prewar naiveté,[77] the Wilson era has long been regarded as a time of innocence when the United States did not resort to covert action and was not "experienced in the darker arts of statecraft."[78] In part because of the uncomfortable tension between the Wilsonian ideal of openness and demands for secrecy in foreign affairs, Americans have tended to overlook the history of U.S. intelligence operations before World War II and the Cold War supposedly forced the adoption of un-American practices.[79] Ignorant of the covert actions conducted in Soviet Russia between 1917 and 1920, Americans — including key policymakers — have presumed that the first clandestine operations directed at Russia were defensive responses by the Central Intelligence Agency to the menace of Stalinist subversion.[80] Even specialized scholarly studies have suggested that the foreign intelligence operations conducted by the Wilson administration were part of a World War I aberration with little long-run significance.

In fact, however, the Wilson years were a crucial period in the development of covert action as an instrument of U.S. foreign policy. Many of the men involved in American intelligence operations directed at Bolshevism and Soviet Russia were later prominent figures in U.S. policy toward the Soviet Union and in the establishment of the Central Intelligence Agency. Their experiences during the Russian Revolution and Civil War had lasting influences on their attitudes toward both communism and covert action.[81]

After serving, in effect, as "station chief" in Moscow, DeWitt Poole remained at least periodically in contact with intelligence services. In 1922 he attended a G2 course. During World War II he was director of the Foreign Nationalities Branch of the Office of Strategic Services. In 1947 he warned Americans about the insidious Soviet threat in an article featured in *Life* magazine. From 1949 to 1951 he served as president of the National Committee for a Free Europe, the CIA-funded organization that sponsored Radio Free Europe.[82]

In the last years of the Wilson administration, John Gade watched the international movement of radicals as a naval attaché in Scandinavia and then observed the failure of the anti-Bolshevik Russian Northwestern Army as U.S. commissioner to the Baltic provinces. After the end of the Russian Civil War, the impossibility of further foreign military intervention to overthrow the Soviet government led Gade to argue that "those of us who believe Bolshevism to be a world peril must fight it with other than military means" — especially intelligence work and propaganda. Gade's sense of the importance of intelligence organization and the deficiencies of the American services led him in 1929 to present a detailed proposal for a centralized "National Intelligence Service," which an official CIA history considered a forerunner to William J. Donovan's Office of Strategic Services.[83]

In the summer of 1919, "Wild Bill" Donovan joined a special American mission to investigate conditions in Siberia, where the United States was providing indirect financial and military support to Admiral Kolchak's anti-Bolshevik forces. After observing Bolshevik activity in Siberia, including propaganda and sabotage of railways, Donovan apparently concluded that unconventional measures were needed. "The time for intervention is past," he observed in his diary. "We are a year too late." However, he thought, "We can prevent a shooting war if we take the initiative to win the subversive war."[84]

Back in Washington, Donovan was disappointed by State Department officials' feeling that "they could do nothing further" in Siberia "because they could not be backed by public opinion." Although he thought they should "set out to enlighten public opinion," he recognized that building popular support for military intervention abroad would be difficult. Noting that "many demonstrations" were being made against the embargo on food to Bolshevik Russia, Donovan observed that there was "an unreasonable sympathy for the Bolsheviks, among a great many of the well-to-do pseudo intellectual group."[85]

Like Donovan, John Foster Dulles was aware of public and congressional resistance to Wilson administration policy toward Russia. After being commissioned as a captain and assigned to military intelligence in 1917, Dulles advised the Wilson administration in 1918–19 on economic aspects of U.S. policy toward Russia, including the provision of financial aid to anti-Bolshevik groups and the restriction of trade with Soviet Russia. Dulles's experiences led him to appreciate the importance of intelligence and inclined him toward the use of propaganda and covert action. In a letter to his brother Allen in April 1918, Foster Dulles argued, "One of the secrets of Germany's success is that she uses all possible subsidiary measures to assist the military." He suggested that the United States should also adopt a no-holds-barred war-fighting strategy, employing "blockade, political [warfare], propaganda, etc." Dulles specifically proposed sending "to Russia, Siberia, Persia, Caucasus, etc. small bodies of men which might accomplish something in way of propaganda, making centers of opposition etc." By calling attention to a variety of measures besides conventional military force, Dulles anticipated the strategy of the 1950s more than three decades before he became secretary of state.[86]

In 1956, CIA Director Allen Dulles traveled to Yale University, which was then "contributing able men to American intelligence," to deliver an address on Woodrow Wilson. "My association with Wilson," Dulles remarked, "has had a definite impact upon my own thinking and my approach to . . . international problems." Wilson's use of academic consultants and informal advisors at Paris and his extensive employment of "special envoys and special missions" to Russia, Mexico, and other countries had left a particularly strong impression. "I sometimes wonder why Wilson was not the originator of the plan which led to the creation of the Central Intelligence Agency," Dulles commented. "After all, its task is to do on a worldwide and systematic basis what Wilson was endeavoring to do with special missions as emergencies occurred."[87]

As a diplomat and intelligence gatherer at Vienna and Berne from 1916 to 1918, the young Dulles had witnessed the Wilson administration's use of special agents for investigation, negotiation, and propaganda, and he developed an enthusiasm for "gum shoe work." After the Armistice, Dulles's position as an advisor to Lansing (his uncle) and the other American peace commissioners allowed him to present proposals for intervention in the Baltic region (see chapter 8) and to influence efforts to overthrow a Soviet government in Hungary. In each of these cases, Dulles realized that American principles and public opinion ruled out overt military intervention, thereby requiring him and other advocates of intervention to seek less public, indirect methods. Thus, Dulles's experiences in the Wilson era foreshadowed the interventions and covert actions of the Cold War era, as well as the research and analysis work of the CIA.[88]

Looking back from the Cold War years, Robert Murphy, one of Allen Dulles's colleagues in Switzerland, recalled, "Those Americans were pioneers in their way, experimenting hopefully with primitive forms of intelligence, propaganda, and economic warfare which now are standard features of government."[89] Even Adolf Berle, who denounced America's "undeclared war" against Soviet Russia in 1920, regarded his intelligence work in the Wilson years as a formative experience that gave him special expertise in the later Cold War. When the State Department and CIA geared up for propaganda and covert action in the late 1940s, the involvement of Berle, Allen Dulles, Poole, and many other Wilson administration veterans would make organizations like the National Committee for a Free Europe resemble reunions of the junior advisors from the Paris Peace Conference.[90]

Presidents had used secret agents long before Wilson, but in the Wilson era, when there was much talk about a new, open diplomacy, the United States established much larger intelligence organizations and relied more extensively on covert methods. American intelligence officials sometimes suggested that this turn to secret war was primarily a reaction to or imitation of the "new ideas" of Germans about subversion.[91] However, as we have seen, the Wilson administration's resort to secretive financing of propaganda campaigns and anti-Bolshevik movements was also significantly influenced by congressional restrictions on spending and worries about the attitudes of the American people. U.S. officials relied on secretive methods of intervention not only to respond to their adversaries' activity but also to evade the constraints of American democracy. As the next three chapters will show, concerns about Congress and American public opinion also inhibited more overt forms of intervention, ranging from humanitarian relief missions to military expeditions.

Foreign intervention and the Russian Civil War. Barefoot Russians in Soviet territory, surrounded by anti-Bolshevik Russian and foreign forces, including an American cowboy advancing across Siberia. (Courtesy of the Hoover Institution Archives, Poster Collection)

Military fronts in the Russian Civil War, May 1919. (Adapted from *Soviet Russia*, August 30, 1919)

"Welcome!"
Uncle Sam rushes to
embrace "Russian
Democracy" after
the revolution against
the tsarist autocracy
in March 1917.
(From the *New York
World*, March 24, 1917)

"First Steps in
Self-Government."
Six weeks after the
abdication of Nicholas
II and the formation
of the Provisional
Government,
Americans worried
that Russia was
being led astray
by German-supported
antiwar propaganda
and the turbulent forces
of violence and anarchy.
(From the *New York
World*, April 26, 1917)

"Don't You Know Me, Sister?" Three weeks after the Bolsheviks seized power in Petrograd and called for immediate peace negotiations, Western democracy turns her face away from the Bolsheviks, who are seen as captives of the German kaiser. (From the *New York World*, November 28, 1917)

"The New Autocrat Appears." Although the United States helped the Allies defeat German autocracy, another autocratic menace appeared in the form of Bolshevism, here drawn to resemble L. D. Trotsky, the first Soviet commissar for foreign affairs and later commissar of war. (From the *Los Angeles Daily Times*, December 20, 1918)

"A Nightmare." Before the most severe stages of the Red Scare, a humorous image of an American Bolshevik's dream of the Bolshevization of America. (From the *Los Angeles Daily Times*, February 18, 1919)

"The Bull in the China Shop." During the early weeks of the Paris Peace Conference, Bolshevism seemed the chief threat to American hopes for democracy and stability in the postwar world. (From the *San Francisco Chronicle*, February 22, 1919)

"A Big Job on Hand." Following the establishment of Soviet regimes in Hungary and Bavaria, on a day of pro-Bolshevik marches and street fighting in American cities, Bolshevism seemed to have wrapped its tentacles around all of civilization. (From the *San Francisco Chronicle*, May 1, 1919)

"Kadetskaia Sharmanka" (Kadet Street Organ). Uncle Sam and British and French imperialists toss coins to anti-Bolshevik forces in southern Russia (General Kaledin and the Ukrainian Rada), who perform for the Constitutional Democratic Party organ grinder. (From *Pravda*, January 5, 1918)

Xenophon Kalamatiano, the American businessman and intelligence agent arrested in Moscow in September 1918, convicted of espionage, and sentenced to death in December 1918. (From the Culver Educational Foundation; courtesy of R. B. D. Hartman)

"Bring 'Em Back." Demands for the return of the American Expeditionary Force in Siberia were particularly strong in California, where many families of the soldiers lived. (From the *San Francisco Chronicle*, September 22, 1919)

"At Its Mercy." Relatives of the soldiers from the Great Lakes region who were sent to northern Russia worried that the small American regiment was in grave danger from the increasingly powerful Red Army. Pressure from the relatives and their representatives in Congress precipitated Wilson's decision in February 1919 to withdraw the American Expeditionary Force. (From the *Chicago Tribune*, February 9, 1919)

"Beginning to Ask Questions." Since the Wilson administration did not provide a frank explanation of the American intervention in northern Russia, many of the soldiers did not understand why they were fighting Bolshevik forces there months after the war against Germany ended. (From the *Chicago Tribune*, April 12, 1919)

"Hoover's Idea of Cannon Fodder." In 1919 the Wilson administration relied heavily on Herbert Hoover and the American Relief Administration to use food to stem the spread of Bolshevism. (From the *Los Angeles Daily Times*, January 6, 1919)

"Antanta" (The Entente). Soviet propaganda poster depicting Uncle Sam and British and French capitalists holding the leashes of anti-Bolshevik leaders Denikin, Kolchak, and Iudenich. (Courtesy of the Hoover Institution Archives, Poster Collection)

AMERICAN INTERVENTION IN SIBERIA, 1918–1920

THE SEARCH FOR ANTI-BOLSHEVIK "NUCLEI" AND "STRONG MEN"

On November 10, 1917, three days after the Bolshevik seizure of power in Petrograd and one day after President Wilson discussed the Russian situation with his cabinet, the *New York American* reflected the thinking of some officials in Washington by predicting that "in the event of a civil war in Russia, the rival authority, with the assistance of the allied naval forces, would be expected to obtain control of both Vladivostock [*sic*], the Pacific seaport, and Kola, the Arctic seaport, as bases for operations against the Bolsheviki." In the following weeks, British and French leaders repeatedly proposed sending Japanese and possibly American troops to Vladivostok to prevent Bolsheviks from seizing military supplies there and to create enough of a threat in Siberia to inhibit German transfers of troops from the eastern front to France. While some U.S. officials shared the concerns of the Allies about safeguarding the war materiel and reviving Russian military resistance to Germany, Wilson was reluctant to divert American forces from France to Allied schemes for recreating an eastern front. Wilson did want to help restore a pro-Ally, democratic government in Russia, and assisting the establishment of orderly self-government in Siberia might benefit the Allied cause if Siberians could organize substantial armies. However, the president was constrained in what he could do in Siberia by at least four major problems. First, having proclaimed a commitment to the principles of nonintervention and self-determination, Wilson sought to avoid undermining his moral leadership of American and world opinion by baldly contradicting these tenets. Second, however much Wilson and his advisors disliked the Bolshevik regime, they did not want to push it even closer to Germany by dispatching openly anti-Soviet military expeditions to Russian ports. Third, the president did not want to see tsarism reestablished in Russia, and he worried that his British and French allies might work together with Russian monarchists toward that end. Fourth, Wilson was afraid that Japanese intervention would antagonize non-Bolshevik Russians and jeopardize his efforts to preserve an open door for American commerce in Siberia and Manchuria. Because of these concerns, the president resisted and deferred Allied proposals for sending troops into Siberia for more than six months.

While Wilson hesitated and vacillated about overt military intervention, he showed a consistent interest in indirect methods of assisting Russia. The president first followed the growth of "nuclei" of anti-Bolshevik forces in and around Siberia to see whether any of them were worthy of support. Later, when he sent doughboys to Vladivostok, he tried to restrict their operations to eastern Siberia, where they could protect and quicken the coalescence of White elements without becoming direct combatants. Although conditions in Siberia were extremely complicated and changed rapidly, Wilson insistently tried to distinguish between aiding Russian self-government and fighting Soviet Russia. By emphasizing alleged threats to Czechoslovakian soldiers supposedly stranded in Siberia, Wilson also portrayed the U.S. action as a rescue mission, rather than "intervention." Instead of simply helping the Czech Legion to leave Russia, however, Wilson used them to help White forces organize new governments and armies. Thus, as the president struggled to reconcile conflicting interests and avoid manifold dangers, a persistent anti-Bolshevik impulse underlay the twists and turns of Wilsonian policy. The administration's efforts to conceal this anti-Bolshevik thrust with indirect methods, secrecy, and ambiguous public pronouncements make it appropriate to consider U.S. intervention in Siberia an integral part of America's secret war against Bolshevism, even though the dispatch of troops to Vladivostok was an overt act.[1]

American and Russian Public Opinion and U.S. Resistance to Proposals for Intervention, November 1917–March 1918

When Allied diplomats began raising the idea of sending foreign troops to Vladivostok in late 1917, they found that the threat to military stockpiles and the danger of German domination extending eastward across Russia were overshadowed in the eyes of President Wilson and his top foreign policy advisors by the risk that intervention in Siberia, especially by the Japanese, would antagonize many Russians who bitterly remembered the Russo-Japanese War, hand Germany a propaganda weapon, and alienate important groups of Americans. As British ambassador Sir Cecil Spring Rice discovered in discussions with Lansing in late December 1917, American leaders believed that the United States had "an exceptional position among the Russian masses, and that this capital should be husbanded as much as possible." Spring Rice also deduced that the Wilson administration did "not believe that an expedition to the Far East would be popular in this country, or even pos[s]ible." Meeting with House confirmed that the administration believed "a Japanese expedition to Siberia would arouse hostile sentiment both in Russia and the U.S." This concern about the reaction of Russians and Americans to foreign intervention would be a major constraint on American action in the next half year.[2]

In the aftermath of the Bolshevik Revolution, House and Wilson gave renewed emphasis to the projection of an idealistic image of America's war effort, and they were anxious to avoid taking any public action which might blur that image. At the end of November 1917, in response to Soviet peace proposals and Russian requests for a declaration on Allied war aims, House suggested at an Inter-Allied Conference in Paris that the Allies and the United States proclaim that they were waging war not for purposes of aggression or indemnity, but so "that nations shall have the right to lead their lives in the way that seems to them best." Wilson quickly approved House's resolution. "Our people and Congress will not fight for any selfish aim," Wilson wrote on December 1; "it would be a fatal mistake to cool the ardour of America." Three days later, the president called on Americans to wage war with "greater zeal and enthusiasm" because it was "a war of high principle." Since the principle of self-determination might seem to be contradicted by a foreign military intervention in Russia, American leaders were wary of sanctioning such action.[3]

Wilson and his aides also worried that patriotic Russians would not welcome a Japanese expedition. "Leaving out the ill feeling which it would create in the Bolchiviki Government," House advised the president on February 2, "it would arouse the Slavs throughout Europe because of the race question." While House was particularly sensitive to racial tensions,

Wilson was especially concerned that "middle class and moderate parties in Russia" would be driven to seek protection by Germany in response to a landing of Japanese troops in Siberia.[4]

As this comment suggested, the president and most of his advisors were more interested in the probable responses of "true Russians" than the possible reaction of disloyal subversives like the Bolsheviks. In March, as divided Soviet leaders debated whether they should ratify the Treaty of Brest-Litovsk, Wilson reminded State Department Counselor Frank Polk that he drew a sharp distinction between the Russian people and their Bolshevik rulers. Wilson wanted to "continue to treat the Russians as in all respects our friends and allies against the common enemy" while ignoring the radical regime that pretended to be in power. "There is, in fact, no Russian government to deal with," Wilson declared. Since the United States never recognized "the So-called Soviet government," it did not need to recognize any of the Bolshevik regime's acts.[5]

Japanese Intervention? Yes and No

After the Provisional Government fell in Petrograd, coalitions of Bolsheviks, left Socialist Revolutionaries, and Menshevik-internationalists gradually took over governments in Siberia between November 1917 and February 1918. There were armed struggles for power in Irkutsk and Blagoveshchensk, but in most Siberian cities Bolsheviks and their supporters assumed power peacefully after establishing majorities in urban soviets.[6]

The Wilson administration was disturbed by this extension of Soviet rule and soon considered measures to counter it. On February 19, 1918, the American Minister to China, former University of Wisconsin professor Paul Reinsch, warned that "unless constructive action can be taken Siberia may be controlled by Bolshevik and Germany." Reinsch urged Washington to launch a propaganda campaign to combat Russian misrepresentations of American motives and institutions. Wilson passed Reinsch's telegram on to George Creel, asking him to "consider the feasibility of doing what Reinsch suggests."[7]

When Allied representatives at the Supreme War Council in Paris reiterated their desire for a Japanese intervention in Siberia in mid-February, the United States did not immediately reject the proposition, as it had before. On February 19, the chief U.S. delegate, General Tasker Bliss, drafted Joint Note No. 16, which called for Japanese occupation of the Trans-Siberian Railway between Vladivostok and Harbin. Bliss sympathized with Allied officers who were desperate to take any action that offered the slightest chance of keeping German troops from being transferred out of Russia to the western front. And, as he explained to Washington, the danger of Japanese intervention would be minimized if the expedition halted at Vladivostok or Harbin until the "effect on Russian sentiment both Bolshevik and Anti-Bolshevik is ascertained." [8]

As Bliss informed Chief of Staff Peyton March the next day, he thought the Allied proposal was "fraught with grave possibilities," particularly that once the Japanese were invited into Siberia the United States might have to go to war to make them "get out." Yet Bliss believed that if Allied forces *could* help loyal Russians to organize, intervention would be advisable. Bliss did not think there would be "any great purely military advantage resulting from the occupation of Vladivostok and Harbin," but he favored such a limited intervention if it would promote "a consolidation of sentiment among the Anti-Bolshevists" and if foreign forces could then be withdrawn. [9]

Like Bliss, Lansing believed the desirability of Japanese intervention hinged substantially on whether it would foster the organization of patriotic Russians. He instructed Bliss to "hold off" on presenting the U.S. response to the proposal, in part because he wanted to learn the results of an expected constituent assembly meeting and verify reports that "the sentiment of the people in Siberia is socialistic, but opposed to the Bolsheviki." [10]

By late February the idea of helping pro-Ally Russians to recover power in Siberia was receiving considerable attention in Washington. General William Judson, who had returned from serving as military attaché in Russia, urged sending "at least 50,000" U.S. troops into Siberia "to secure a nucleus from which the well disposed Russians could gather moral support." Although Judson recognized that Bolsheviks were "to many Americans anathema," he hoped to rally "all anti-German Russians," potentially including Bolsheviks, against the Central Powers. Secretary of War Newton Baker took the proposal seriously enough to discuss it with President Wilson. However, as Assistant Secretary of State Breckinridge Long commented, the plan to divert a large force of Americans from France was "impracticable." [11]

With the German army rolling eastward through Russia, and with the Allies pressing for action, Long and other U.S. officials shifted at the end of February toward approving Japanese intervention. Lansing still feared resentment in Siberia and Russia, but he believed that Japan intended to act even without U.S. consent and he thought that securing a pledge of good behavior might restrain her. Wilson shared Lansing's fear of the Siberian reaction and agreed with House on the danger that an Entente-supported Japanese occupation of Siberia would seem the moral equivalent of German occupation of western Russia. However, Wilson did not want to be insensitive to Allied strategic plans. Some members of Wilson's cabinet held that the United States should join in intervention because "if Japan went in she would never come out." Wilson disagreed, arguing that if the United States were to "invade Russia," Germany would "say we are doing exactly what she is doing," and America would lose its "moral position."[12]

Wilson therefore decided (as one cabinet officer recorded) "to keep hands off and let Japan take the blame." On March 1, he handed Lansing a statement explaining that although the United States would not join the Entente in asking the Japanese to intervene, it had "no objection to the request being made" and was confident that Japan had "no purpose but to save Siberia from the invasion of the armies and intrigues of Germany." Wilson's decision appears to have been strongly influenced by a Japanese promise to declare their "disinterestedness," which alleviated some anxiety about Japanese ambitions in the Far East and reduced the amount of ammunition intervention would give to German propagandists.[13]

House had agreed with Wilson on the substance of the March 1 note, but after leaving Washington he changed his mind. On March 2, House saw Ambassador Bakhmeteff, who strongly opposed intervention in Siberia by Japanese troops unless they were accompanied by Allied chaperones.[14] House and Bakhmeteff agreed that it would be "a mistake for the Japanese to go in." On the same day, State Department aide William Christian Bullitt stressed that Wilson could not, like Pontius Pilate, wash his hands of the matter. In a memorandum that House read and sent to Wilson, Bullitt argued that if America stood aside while Japan invaded Siberia, "the President's moral position as leader of the common people of the world will be fatally compromised." Bullitt's idealistic blast revived House's concern that acquiescing in the Japanese expedition would tarnish Wilson's image. On March 3 House therefore cautioned Wilson: "We . . . are likely to lose that fine moral position you have given the Entente cause."[15]

The colonel was concerned about domestic as well as international opinion. He explained to British foreign secretary Balfour on March 4 that approving Japanese intervention would "mean a serious lowering, if not actual loss, of our moral position in the eyes of our own peoples and of the whole world, and a dulling of the high enthusiasm of the American people for a righteous cause. Unless we maintain our moral position we must expect a very formidable anti-war party here, a general weakening of the war effort, and a breaking-up of that practically unanimous support upon which the Administration can now count." At this point Elihu Root, whom House regarded as a bellwether of conservative Republican sentiment, thought Japanese intervention would be a mistake. Hence, House's anxiety about the idealistic Left was not overpowered by pressure from the Right for intervention. The colonel also worried that requesting action by "a yellow race" against "a white one" would result in "American press and public getting out of hand," particularly on the west coast, where anti-Japanese feeling was strong. Analyzing and predicting public opinion was House's specialty, and Wilson still heeded his advice in this area.[16]

Shaken by House's letter and Bullitt's memorandum, Wilson withdrew his tacit approval of the proposed Japanese action. On March 5, he handed Polk a new message to be sent to Tokyo, which stated that even with Japanese pledges of altruism, "the wisdom of intervention seems . . . most questionable" because it would still be fuel for the German propaganda machine.[17]

This reversal did not mean that Wilson and his advisors categorically rejected the idea of a military expedition to help pro-Ally Siberians recover power and organize armed forces. On the contrary, Wilson's note to Tokyo stressed that while he was unable to sanction a Japanese intervention at that time, he realized "the extreme danger of anarchy to which the Siberian provinces are exposed," and he was giving "anxious consideration" to a "possible remedy." Still sympathizing with the original Russian Revolution, "in spite of all the unhappiness and misfortune which has for the time being sprung out of it," Wilson wanted to help Russians return from the Bolshevik deviation to the path of progress.[18]

On March 5, Wilson conferred with Polk about a possible joint Allied intervention involving 14,000 Japanese troops and smaller contingents of American, British, and French soldiers. The exact number of troops was important, Wilson noted, because Russians would "receive the wrong impression unless the virtual equivalence of allies and Japanese were evident from the first." Wilson evidently felt that the Japanese were insisting upon an expedition that was too large and not sufficiently balanced by American and European escorts. Since the Japanese rejected "the very modest programme" the United States proposed, Wilson was "reluctant to act at all."[19]

In this case as at other times, the president's reservations about intervention stemmed less from liberal principles or moral qualms than from pragmatic analysis of the likely consequences of the proposed action and the difficulties of developing a better plan. As Wilson's vacillation and practical consideration of intervention in March showed, he was not absolutely opposed to intervention, but conditionally opposed to excessively direct and offensive forms of interference.[20]

Although Wilson retracted his consent to the specific proposals by the Supreme War Council and the Japanese, he and his advisors continued to look for wiser and more feasible plans. On March 4, Breckinridge Long sent the White House a proposal that grew out of a conversation with a former secretary of the Russian embassy. Long argued that a political base near the Ural Mountains "could be made a nucleus around which would gather . . . individuals and factions which would develop strong antagonism to Germany throughout a large part of Russia." While the main purpose of this scheme was to counter German influence in and economic benefit from Russia, it implicitly envisioned the overthrow of Bolshevism in as much of Russia as possible. The principal defect of Long's plan was that it relied upon Japan "to protect and hold the Trans-Siberia Railroad with a large military force." He sought to offset this by having Ambassador Francis stationed in western Siberia, where he would "become the head of the whole undertaking," in which Japan "would be inextricably identified with the United States." After Wilson finally had an opportunity to read Long's proposal, he wrote on March 14 that it interested him "very much," but because of the "necessary limitations" on U.S. action and the complications involved in cooperation with Japan, it did not seem "practicable."[21]

Although the American concentration on the western front and the dangers of relying on the Japanese made Long's plan unworkable, the president was not unsympathetic to the idea of creating an anti-Bolshevik "nucleus." As William Wiseman reported on March 14, Wilson was "studying feasibility of a joint Japanese American enterprise whereby the United States would collaborate with Russians in reorganization of Russian elements." Wilson did not feel that idealistic and anti-Japanese sentiments would be permanent or immovable obstacles: he assured Wiseman that he was "endeavouring to find a way both to reconcile American people to need for intervention and to allay Russian fears of it."[22]

In mid-March American newspapers were divided about Japanese intervention in Siberia, with papers like the *New York Times* and *San Francisco Chronicle* favoring it and liberal organs like the New York *Evening Post* and the Springfield (Mass.) *Republican* opposed. Over the following months, as Wilson looked for a way to reconcile opponents to the need for action, the press would grow more solidly supportive of intervention.[23]

Like Wilson, Lansing saw several obstacles to intervention in Siberia: the logistical difficulties of extending control to western Siberia, which would be required to obtain any military advantage; the necessity of leaning on the Japanese, who did "not desire to act jointly with the other Governments"; and the danger that "Russian factions now seeking to gain control in Siberia would in all probability harmonize their differences and unite in repelling" the Japanese, who had beaten them in war thirteen years earlier. For these reasons, Lansing noted on March 18, he agreed with Wilson that requesting Japanese intervention would be "unwise and inexpedient," and that the United States had to "await new developments."[24]

As they waited, Wilson and his advisors watched especially for signs that patriotic Russians would welcome a foreign military expedition. On March 19, Lansing sent Wilson a memorandum from Basil Miles, chief of the Russian Division at the State Department, who noted that mass meetings of "socialists and workmen" protesting against Japanese intervention showed that "the Russian peasants and the proletariat have not yet got to the point where they want any uninvited help from the outside." While wealthier Russians, like the laboring classes, opposed intervention by Japan alone, Miles suggested that "the more intelligent classes might favor and be heartened by international intervention in Siberia."[25]

Watching for Nuclei of Anti-Bolshevism

In the late winter and early spring of 1918, several anti-Bolshevik groups had appeared in and around Siberia. In January, liberal and moderate socialist members of a Siberian Regional Duma elected in 1917 gathered in Tomsk. When Bolsheviks suppressed their meeting in early February, these proponents of Siberian autonomy formed an underground Provisional Siberian Government that won the financial support of Siberian cooperatives and began to make plans for a military uprising against the Bolsheviks. Members of this underground cabinet, led by a right Socialist Revolutionary (SR) named Peter Derber, made their way to Harbin and then to Vladivostok, where they contacted Allied representatives, including American consul John K. Caldwell and Admiral Austin M. Knight, commander of the Asiatic Fleet. A more conservative group of anti-Bolsheviks, comprising monarchist officers and diplomats of former Russian governments, clustered in Harbin around the authority of General D. L. Horvath, General Manager of the Chinese Eastern Railway. Grigorii Semenov, a ruthless young Cossack chieftain, headed a third anti-Bolshevik force of Cossacks and Mongols that operated along the Trans-Siberian Railway east of Lake Baikal, near the border with Manchuria.[26]

On March 20, favorably impressed by Derber and his associates, Knight cabled that sentiment throughout Siberia was crystallizing in favor of the "autonomous government," which "would be strongly pro-ally and if established promptly and supported effectively should be able [to] defend [the] whole [of] Siberia against any force that Germany seems likely to send East of Ural Mountains." Wilson's response was coolly neutral: he instructed Navy Secretary Daniels to cable Knight "that Siberians must settle their own government."[27]

However, a month later Wilson showed a warmer interest in learning "*all* that we know about these several *nuclei* of self-governing authority that seem to be springing up in Siberia. It would afford me a great deal of satisfaction," he informed Lansing on April 18, "to get behind the most nearly representative of them if it can indeed draw leadership and control to itself." In the following weeks, "leadership and control," especially of a military force, would prove more important than representativeness in determining which of the Siberian factions warranted attention and support.[28]

In response to Wilson's request, Lansing sent him a memorandum prepared by Basil Miles. Miles reported that the Derber organization, sometimes called the "Tomsk movement," was "weak in leadership" but had "undoubted popular support." The Horvath clique, in contrast, had "no mandate from any body or section of the population within Russia," and was "open to the charge of 'Counter Revolutionary.'" Semenov was "a young Cossack officer who started an independent attempt to produce order by opposing the Bolsheviki." His effort "to put down the Bolsheviki" had "no clear political purpose," but was "supported in funds and munitions by Japanese, British and by Russians who back Horvath." Noting that the Russian ambassador in Washington, Bakhmeteff, regarded "both the Tomsk and Horvath movements as encouraging indications," Miles suggested that "a coalition" of the two rival forces "might offer some promise of gaining popular support."[29]

As Miles's memorandum indicated, the most representative of the three groups was the "Tomsk movement" or Provisional Siberian Government, most of whose members were, like Derber, from the right wing of the Socialist Revolutionary Party. In the November 1917 elections for a national Constituent Assembly, the SRs won between 50 and 60 percent of the vote in eastern Siberia and between 75 and 90 percent in more rural western Siberia. The second most popular party, the Bolsheviks, drew on average about 10 percent of the vote in the various regions of Siberia, while the leading nonsocialist party, the Constitutional Democrats, nowhere polled more than 4 percent of the vote.[30]

Although some Americans in the Far East questioned the legitimacy of the Provisional Siberian Government and misrepresented its members as "extreme socialists," most reports to Washington portrayed them as having considerable popular support. The problem, according to Charles Moser, consul at Harbin, was that there was "no personality among them of sufficient significance as leaders." While they were honest and well-meaning, they seemed "without power and unfitted to cope with situation." More generally, Moser informed Lansing on March 29, democratic schemes for constituent assemblies were for the moment impractical, "as force must restore order in Siberia before stable government can be established."[31]

Searching for a Strong Man

In 1917, as we have seen, many officials in Washington became disillusioned with the weak Kerensky government and began to look for Russian military men who could restore order and assist the reestablishment of stable government. In December 1917 and the first months of 1918, Wilson and Lansing tried to support such anti-Bolshevik officers in south Russia. After their forces proved disappointingly unstable, Americans searching for a Russian "strong man" shifted their attention to Siberia.

While Consul Moser recommended intervention in support of General Horvath as the "only possible solution," Americans showed the greatest enthusiasm for the Cossack leader, Semenov. Wilson's trusted representative in Peking, Paul Reinsch, at times warned Washington that Semenov was a "reactionary military autocrat of the old type," whose troops committed "infringements of personal rights" that "aroused strong opposition among the Russian people." At other moments, however, probably influenced by Semenov's fleeting military victories against Bolshevik forces, Reinsch joined with the majority of American representatives in the Far East in calling for aid to Semenov.[32]

In early February 1918, House and Lansing had learned that the British hoped to supply arms and ammunition to Semenov. Later that month the U.S. military attaché at Peking and the consuls at Peking and Vladivostok urged the administration to give financial assistance to the Cossack forces. Breckinridge Long sympathized with that appeal: in his eyes, "Semenoff's loyal forces" were virtually the only pro-Ally forces of order in Siberia's violent "turmoil." When Semenov briefly advanced into Siberia in early May, American representatives urgently appealed to Washington for aid and intervention in support of Semenov as the best way "to take issue with the Bolshevik movement in Siberia." In their excitement, they overlooked atrocities committed by Cossack forces, claimed Semenov's movement was not monarchical, and even maintained that it had aroused popular enthusiasm.[33]

The closest American observer of Semenov was David Barrows, a professor serving as an intelligence officer in the U.S. Army. Analyzing events in Russia from a U.S. base in Manila, Barrows concluded in December 1917 that "America by her control of supplies could control the forces of Siberia and organize it against the Bolsheviki." He therefore volunteered to inspect anti-Bolshevik forces in Manchuria and Siberia "as a preliminary to military action that our government might take." After reaching northern Manchuria in early April, Barrows later recalled, he "found the most promising anti-Communist force" under Semenov. Some Allied observers regarded Semenov as "brutal." Barrows himself thought Semenov was "tolerably severe," noting that he "executed 7 Bolshevik agitators" on one night. Undeterred, Barrows sent favorable reports to the War Department and to Ambassador Reinsch in Peking. On April 1, for example, Barrows reported that Semenov was "ready to obey any competent Republican anti-Bolshevik Government." Barrows's subsequent reports helped to create the impression that aid to such anti-

Bolshevik forces would cause the fading power of Bolshevism to melt away.[34]

With Semenov reportedly continuing to advance and American observers seeing possibilities for a coalition of anti-Bolshevik forces, Reinsch suggested on May 16 that the time was ripe for American and Allied action that would rehabilitate Siberia as a factor in the war against Germany. Wilson's interest was piqued by the reports of Semenov's success. "Semenov is changing the situation in Siberia very rapidly, apparently," Wilson wrote Lansing on May 20. "Please follow very attentively what Semenov is accomplishing and whether there is any legitimate way in which we can assist."[35]

Lansing immediately responded by sending Wilson a new memorandum from Miles which exclaimed that Semenov's "success has exceeded all expectations," and contrasted him to the earlier disappointing "withering" of Kaledin and Kornilov in south Russia. "Semenoff's policy," Miles reminded the secretary of state and president, "is to keep the Siberian Railway open and overthrow the Bolsheviki." Altogether, Miles concluded, Semenov's 2,500 men seemed "to represent the strongest, most law-abiding, popular and hopeful force active in Siberia against Germany."[36]

After reading this summary, Wilson still felt that "the moment was inopportune" for intervention in Russia, but he noted that the Semenov outfit "was gaining strength and might prove a powerful factor." Wilson did not cite noninterventionist principles as a reason for his hesitation. The potential reconstruction of a non-Bolshevik, anti-German Siberia provided a valid incentive to act. Two pragmatic considerations held Wilson back: insufficient forces to cause Germany to retain troops on her Russian front, and a continuing fear that foreign military operations would be resented by Russians.[37]

By the end of May, the president was prepared to "go as far as intervening against the wishes of the Russian people — knowing that it was eventually for their own good — providing he thought the scheme had any practical chance of success." If America and Britain were able to send a large force into Siberia, Wilson told Wiseman, they might rally the Russian people to defend their country, but substantial Anglo-American forces were not available and relying on the Japanese would unite Russians against foreign intervention. Wilson's aides had not yet been able to develop a workable scheme to get around the logistical and racial obstacles that had blocked intervention since March. At the State Department, Long and Lansing still could "not believe in the practicability of military intervention," since the anti-German and anti-Bolshevik objectives were "too distant" and Japanese intervention "would antagonize the mass of the Russian people."[38]

Using the Czech Legion as an Anti-Bolshevik "Nucleus"

In late May, events in Siberia suddenly made the moment opportune and gave intervention a practical chance of success. Beginning on May 26, fighting broke out along the Trans-Siberian Railway between Bolshevik forces and Czechoslovakian troops on their way from the Ukraine to Vladivostok. These deserters and prisoners of war from the Austro-Hungarian armies had been recruited to fight in Russia on the side of the Allies. In 1917 they were among the most disciplined and effective units remaining in the demoralized armies fighting the Central Powers. After Bolshevik leaders signed the Treaty of Brest-Litovsk, they agreed to allow the Czechs to leave Russia by crossing Siberia. At Vladivostok, the Czechs expected to board ships that would take them to France, where they could resume fighting for the Allies and an independent Czechoslovakia.[39]

Even before wide-scale conflict broke out between the Czech Legion and Bolsheviks, the British, French, and some Americans had begun considering using the Czechs as an anti-Bolshevik nucleus. On May 20, State Department consultant Archibald Cary Coolidge suggested to Lansing that if the United States decided to intervene, "the Czech army now in Siberia might perhaps be taken into our service" as a way to overcome the problem of insufficient American troops and ships. The next day, Basil Miles and Breckinridge Long similarly observed that if the United States decided to support Semenov, the Czech troops "would be most useful" and could be "assisted by American officers."[40]

The Czech legionnaires quickly provided an astonishing display of what relatively small numbers of experienced, disciplined troops could do, given the disorganized state of Russia. By mid-June they gained control of the Trans-Siberian Railway from the Urals to the Pacific, with the exception of a Bolshevik stronghold in Irkutsk and the mountainous region east of Lake Baikal, which held out until late summer. Underground organizations of the Provisional Siberian Government and White officers rose against the Bolsheviks, and, with the crucial assistance of the Czechs, forced them to flee.

Allied and American representatives in Moscow who were in touch with underground anti-Bolshevik organizations may have had advance knowledge of arrangements for cooperation between some Czech officers and the White forces in Siberia. When the fighting erupted, some American representatives in Russia encouraged the Czechs to secure control of Siberia against the Bolsheviks. Although these U.S. officials acted without authorization from Washington, they anticipated rather than contradicted Wilson's will.[41]

The organization of the Czech Legion in Russia had been directed by

Professor Thomas Masaryk, president of the Czecho-Slovak National Council. Masaryk was an old friend of Wilson's staunch supporter Charles Crane. Together with his son Richard, Lansing's personal secretary, Crane urged the administration to consult with Masaryk about action in Russia.

Initially, Masaryk and the administration seemed to be at cross purposes. While the U.S. government had refused to recognize the Soviet regime and was exploring the possibility of supporting anti-Bolshevik forces, Masaryk had advocated *de facto* recognition of the Bolshevik regime and expressed his lack of confidence in their adversaries, including Semenov. In addition, the Czech leader was intent upon transporting his legion to France while U.S. leaders were contemplating using that army to spearhead the reconstruction of Siberia. These different views and aims may help to explain the difficulty the Cranes had in arranging meetings for Masaryk. It was only after the outbreak of fighting between the Czechs and Bolsheviks in Siberia that Lansing and Wilson could find time to see the Czech leader.[42]

When the secretary of state received him on June 3, Masaryk announced that the Czechs did not want to fight against Russians, including Bolsheviks, and he asked for American help in shipping his soldiers to France. Lansing replied that the United States did not have ships available for that purpose. However, the same logistical obstacle to intervention in Siberia could be overcome if the Czechs were "willing to resist Russians who ally themselves with the Germans," since the Czechs were already in Siberia.[43]

Like Lansing, others at the State Department were thinking about utilizing the Czechs in Siberia, not rescuing and evacuating them. On the day of Masaryk's visit, Butler Wright, the former counselor of the American embassy in Petrograd, completed a proposal for intervention in Siberia. Wright's plan centered on having an "Allied Military Police Force of 25,000 men" establish "control of the Trans-Siberian Railroad." He recommended that "the Czecho-Slovak troops now in Siberia and desirous of fighting on the side of the Allies be embraced in this plan."[44]

A week later, Charles Crane recommended that Wilson himself see Masaryk, whom he lionized as "one of the best and wisest of Christians." Crane glowed about Masaryk's "organizing of the Bohemian army in Russia last year — the only organized thing there — and, with anarchy all around him, providing it with food, ammunition and transportation." This letter was well calculated to fire Wilson's imagination and appeal to his sense that a selfless Christian army could help restore order in the midst of a chaotic civil war. On June 11 Wilson promised Crane that he would "try to see Professor Masaryk," adding that he "had been planning to have a joint conference with [Masaryk] and one or two others in order to work out a scheme for the relief of Russia."[45]

Before Wilson met with Masaryk his attention was drawn to ways the Czechs could be utilized for something more than humanitarian relief. In a seminal dispatch, Reinsch advised Washington on June 13 that "it would be a serious mistake to remove the Czecho-Slovak troops from Siberia. With only slight countenance and support they could control all of Siberia against the Germans." In addition to being an effective fighting force, Reinsch suggested, the Czechs were "sympathetic to the Russian population." Wilson was strongly affected by Reinsch's telegram. "There seems to me to emerge from this suggestion the shadow of a plan that might be worked, with Japanese and other assistance," he informed Lansing on June 17. The Slavic kinship between Czechs and Russians alleviated Wilson's fear that Russians would be antagonized by foreign intervention. "These people are the cousins of the Russians," he observed.[46]

The Czech Legion also figured in an elaborate plan for intervention that Wilson received from a friend (possibly Crane) on the same day. This detailed thirteen-page memorandum was prepared by a group of men including Postmaster General Albert Burleson, who was busy fighting sedition in America. The paper suggested that the "Czecho-Slovak army opposing the Bolsheviki" could cooperate with an intervening army of "ten or fifteen thousand American, British, French and Italian troops." Working together with the forces under Semenov and Kolchak, these soldiers could first drive up the Chinese Eastern Railway to its junction with the Trans-Siberian in order to isolate Bolshevik forces in the east. As a second step, the plan envisioned "extending the occupation of the intervening army to Irkoutsk." Thus, "a stable form of government . . . could be established through military intervention, in Asiatic Russia." Although Wilson was somewhat skeptical about how thoroughly informed the authors were about conditions in Siberia, he requested General March's judgment on the military value of the plan on June 19.[47]

He also welcomed Masaryk to the White House that day. According to the Czech leader's notes, the main subject they discussed was "the question of intervention in Russia, whether the Japanese could intervene in Siberia and organize Siberia, and whether our Bohemian troops could be used to that end." Masaryk told Wilson that he did not like the vague plans he had heard for a "small intervention," in which Czech troops would be used as a "'nucleus.'" However, he said that he "would be in favor of renewing the war upon Germany by the whole Japanese army." Alternatively, Masaryk asked the president "to help our men from Russia to be brought to France." Wilson and Masaryk agreed on the danger that the Japanese would seek Russian territory as compensation for their services and both favored a relief mission. Yet they also differed. While Wilson was considering plans for keeping the Czechs in Siberia as part of a limited intervention, Masaryk wanted his men either to be employed in a much larger plan for reconstructing an eastern front, or to be shipped to France.[48]

Despite Masaryk's resistance to the concept of a limited intervention centering around the Czech corps, Wilson's advisors continued to press that idea. Noting that the Czechs were "fighting the Red Guards along the Siberian line with more or less success," Lansing asked Wilson on June 23: "Is it not possible that in this body of capable and loyal troops may be found a neucleus [sic] for military occupation of the Siberian railway?"[49]

Investigating the practicability of this suggestion, on June 25 Lansing asked the U.S. consul at Vladivostok to provide detailed information about the Czech troops there and he invited Masaryk to discuss the "possibility of using Czechs in Siberia." Lansing inquired specifically whether the Czechs would be willing to provide "police" protection for an American economic relief mission to Siberia. Masaryk agreed to this general idea, but he also reiterated that he did not want to fight the Bolsheviks. Instead, he asked Lansing to help "order our relationship to the Bolsheviks peacefully."[50]

While Lansing and others at the State Department were developing definite plans to arm the Czechoslovaks and Russians who might join them, Wilson had not yet adopted that idea. Although Wilson was constantly seeking "a feasible line of action," he had not yet settled on "a practicable method of assisting Russia."[51]

At a hastily convened cabinet meeting on the night of June 25 Wilson seemed to favor a mission to Siberia that would highlight economic assistance and keep any military forces in the background. The plan had been proposed in mid-June by Gordon Auchincloss and it was supported by House. Auchincloss thought military intervention to protect humanitarian work would be much preferable to armed intervention before a relief mission began its work. Like Auchincloss, other administration advisors who favored economic relief regarded it as an "entering wedge" that would open the way for broader action later.[52]

Dispatching a humanitarian mission would also allow the administration to present American action as something other than "intervention." Samuel Harper had campaigned since May against the use of the "ugly" and "malodorous" word "intervention." Ambassador Bakhmeteff advised other anti-Bolshevik Russians to avoid the word "intervention" and speak instead of "active help to Russia," which was more acceptable to American feelings. And on June 26 State Department public relations aide Philip Patchin urged Lansing to change "'intervention' to 'assistance' in dealing with Siberia."[53]

Wilson's first choice to lead a relief mission was John Mott, head of the Young Men's Christian Association, who could symbolize the American spirit of unselfish Christian benevolence. After Mott declined the position on June 27, economic relief plans were put on the back burner. To the dismay of House, Wilson shifted toward seeing military forces as the leading edge of intervention, with an economic commission to follow.[54]

As Wilson contemplated plans for intervention in the last two weeks of June, he received reports that eased his remaining concern about Russian reactions to foreign troops. On June 19, Wilson read a statement by the head of Siberian cooperative societies that Russians were weary of "Bolshevik terror," that there was "a special feeling of friendliness" in Siberia toward America, and that Siberians would welcome Allied intervention if given American assurances about the protection of Siberian interests. Wilson informed Lansing that the statement interested him very much and that the cooperatives might be "of very great service" in what he was "planning to do in Siberia." Five days later, A. I. Konovalov, vice premier in the former Provisional Government, forecast that an Allied commission backed by armed force would serve as a nucleus or rallying point for all constructive elements of Russia. On July 1, Charles Turner Williams, an American Red Cross official who worked in Russia in 1917, predicted to Wilson that "armed intervention in Russia of American, English and French — and some Japanese, if necessary . . . — would result in bringing to the cause of the allies thousands of Russian soldiers, officer[s] and leaders who are only waiting for some such display of force to take sides against the present impossible Bolsheviki." Two days later, Wilson thanked Williams for his letter, which he had "read with interest and profit."[55]

At the end of June, news from Siberia inclined the administration further toward intervention by making it possible to argue that the Czechs were not fighting only or even primarily against Russian Bolsheviks. On June 28, Lansing forwarded to Wilson an exaggerated report from Admiral Knight that in eastern Siberia Czech forces were being "opposed by perhaps 20,000 Austrian [and] German prisoners [of war] armed by Soviet government and commanded by German officers." The Czech representatives who called on Knight were not panic-stricken. They did want to know whether they could expect help from Allied forces and what they should do if they succeeded "in obtaining control of the Siberian Railroad from Vladivostok to the Volga." In passing the dispatch on to Wilson, Lansing highlighted the point that Czech operations were directed "against German and Austrian prisoners of war."[56]

Three months earlier, Lansing had observed that sending "a military expedition against the Germans" would be "manifestly a very different thing from occupying the Siberian Railway in order to control its use by the Russians." In the former case, "Russians could not reasonably complain" of a violation of sovereignty by a force sent to liberate them from German domination. Since March, Wilson had been looking for "a way both to reconcile American people to need for intervention and to allay Russian fears of it." The reports of clashes between Czechs and Central Power POWs offered a way to solve both problems.[57]

Lansing expounded the implications of the new developments in a July 4 memorandum that strongly influenced Wilson's final decision on intervention in Siberia. The Czechs' capture of Vladivostok and their success in western Siberia, Lansing observed, "have materially changed the situation, by introducing a sentimental element into the question of our duty." The image of valiant Czechs fighting against hordes of Huns had captivated the fevered imagination of the American people. This offered the administration a "sentimental" way to present the decision to intervene, toward which it had been moving for other reasons. "Furnishing protection and assistance to the Czecho-Slovaks, who are so loyal to our cause," Lansing argued, "is a very different thing from sending an army into Siberia to restore order and to save the Russians from themselves." It would not be necessary to "consider the attitude of the Bolshevik Siberians," especially since they had made common cause with soldiers of the hated Central Powers.

The plan of action Lansing outlined was not a straightforward mission to rescue and evacuate the Czechs. The fifteen thousand Czechs at Vladivostok were to be armed and supported by Allied troops so that, together with the fifty thousand Czechs west of Irkutsk, they could eliminate the bands of Red Guards and POWs in the Trans-Baikal region and secure control of the entire Trans-Siberian Railroad. Lansing did suggest making a declaration "that as soon as the danger from German and Austrian Aggression is over the military forces will be withdrawn," but he added a crucial qualification: "unless Russia desires further cooperation on their part in resisting the Central Powers and their allies." In other words, if, after the last Siberian Bolshevik forces were crushed, non-Bolshevik Russians requested assistance in combating Soviet forces west of the Urals, the Czech and Allied soldiers might stay in Russia. The conditional nature of this scheme of intervention was also evident in Lansing's recommendation that a commission for social and economic reconstruction "should proceed westward from Vladivostok" behind the Czechs. "The final destination should depend in large measure upon their reception by the Russians and the resistence [sic] made to the military forces."[58]

At a climactic White House meeting on July 6, Wilson approved the central features of Lansing's July 4 proposal. The Czechs at Vladivostok were to be armed and "on sentimental grounds" assisted in "forming a junction with their compatriots in western Siberia." As they cleared the railroad, they were to be backed by seven thousand Americans and seven thousand Japanese, who would "guard the line of communication" but not "advance westward of Irkutsk." The Allied and Czech forces would then "await further developments before taking further steps."[59]

In Russia the next day, however, Czech forces adopted a more aggressively anti-Bolshevik plan. As Czechoslovakian leader Eduard Benes later recalled, the army's executive committee decided on July 7 "to set up an anti-Bolshevik front in the Volga area, to begin an advance against the Soviets and to proceed further into Central Russia," in the hope of eventually "establishing a new Eastern front against the Germans."[60]

In contrast to the Allies, Wilson, Lansing and other Americans thought reestablishing an eastern front was "physically impossible" because of the great distances and limited number of troops.[61] Consequently, they envisioned a more defensive and indirect role for the Czechs, at least initially. After the Legion had cleansed Siberia of Bolshevism and helped loyal Russians to regain their political health, it might be possible to organize Siberian forces to push westward with the Czechs.

Pursuing this line of thinking, Lansing told Japanese ambassador Kikujiro Ishii on July 8 that the United States was gratified by Japanese willingness to furnish arms and ammunition to the Czechs, since "that was the first step in our program." The secretary and the ambassador then considered the possibility that "the Czecho-Slovaks thus aided" could form "a nucleus about which the Russians might rally even to the extent of becoming again a military factor in the war."[62]

By July 8 Wilson was able to tell House that after weeks of "sweating blood over the question what is right and feasible (*possible*) to do in Russia," he finally saw a course of action, "along the double line of economic assistance and aid to the Czecho-Slovaks." Wilson had been prodded to construct a plan of action by persistent pressure from the Allies, whose cooperation he would need in constructing a new world order after the war. More importantly, though, Wilson had won through his torment of doubts to the belief that he was doing what was both right and feasible. Sending large military forces deep into Russian territory without an invitation would have been a blatant violation of liberal principles, but by July Wilson believed that dispatching a smaller and more restrained expedition would be justified because it was what the Russian people desired. The unavailability of sufficient white troops had made such an expedition impractical or unwise in the preceding months, but by July it became feasible because of the presence in Siberia of more than forty thousand Czechoslovakian soldiers. Wilson's long hesitation to intervene had stemmed less from a commitment to the abstract principle of self-determination than from pragmatic consideration of the consequences of various courses of action. As Wilson agonized over "what is right," he was pulled away from strict noninterference by a desire to do what was "possible" to help Russians overcome anarchy, chaos, and radicalism.[63]

Wilson's resolve to come to the aid of Russia received emotional reinforcement from Maria Bochkareva, who had commanded the Women's Battalion of Death in 1917. Her battalion, formed to shame Russian men who declined to fight, had defended the Provisional Government until Bolsheviks seized the Winter Palace and allegedly raped several of the women soldiers. Bochkareva had been in the United States since May 1918 on a British-supported mission to persuade the Wilson administration to send troops to Siberia. When she called at the White House on July 10 she became so worked up about the suffering of the Russian people that she threw herself at Wilson's feet, wrapped her arms around his legs and begged him for military aid to Russia. With tears streaming down his face Wilson assured her of his sympathy.[64]

A week later, in complete seclusion from all advisors, Wilson drafted an *aide-mémoire* on his own typewriter to explain confidentially to the Allies his decisions on the legitimate purposes of the expeditions to Russia. The president doubted that military intervention to deliver an "attack upon Germany from the east" could be "efficacious." He believed that Allied expeditions to Russia should concentrate instead on assisting the economic and political reconstruction of the distressed country and the reconstitution of Russian military forces. Consequently, Wilson sternly declared, military action in Russia was admissible "only to help the Checho-Slovaks [*sic*] consolidate their forces and get into successful cooperation with their Slavic kinsmen and to steady any efforts at self-government or self-defence in which the Russians themselves may be willing to accept assistance." The only other "legitimate object for which American or allied troops" could be employed, he stipulated, was "to guard military stores which may subsequently be needed by Russian forces and to render such aid as may be acceptable to the Russians in the organization of their own self-defence." Wilson carefully left unanswered the questions of *which* Russians were to be assisted and who they were to defend themselves against. However, the Allies and American officials understood that intervention was designed to help Russians liberate themselves from Soviet rule.[65]

This purpose remained central to Wilson administration thinking about Siberia from the Czech-Bolshevik clash in the spring of 1918 through the arrival of American soldiers at Vladivostok in the late summer. As Assistant Secretary of State William Phillips later recalled, "We were led to believe that if the American flag and the Allied flags appeared in Russia, the Russian people would rise against the so-called Bolsheviks and throw them out."[66] Three unofficial advisors played key roles in fostering and sustaining that belief: George Kennan, who was esteemed by Lansing as the greatest American expert on Russia, and Wilson's trusted friends John Mott and Charles Crane.

In late May, just before news of the first Czech-Bolshevik skirmishes reached America, Kennan sent Lansing a letter in which he urged that an

Allied expeditionary force should be sent to eastern Siberia to help Russians "throw off the Bolshevik yoke and to set up an independent, anti-Bolshevik and anti-German government of their own." Kennan predicted that "the people of western Siberia . . . would be so encouraged" that they would take similar action. Like dominoes tumbling toward European Russia, the Siberian revolts "might bring about the overthrow of the Bolsheviki everywhere." Impressed by Kennan's ideas, Lansing gave Wilson the letter, calling it "well worth reading." Ten weeks later Kennan encouraged Lansing to believe that his prophecy was on the verge of fulfillment. On August 9, Kennan hailed the success of the Czechoslovaks, which showed "how weak the Bolsheviki are when opposed by an armed force, and how little popular sympathy and support they have." If the U.S. properly supported "the sane and patriotic Russians," they would "soon put an end to the domination of the Bolsheviki and the Germans." Kennan further predicted "that the arrival of Allied troops — and especially Americans — in eastern Siberia will be welcomed, rather than resented or resisted, by an overwhelming majority of the population, and that with the overthrow of class tyranny in that part of the country, the regeneration of Russia as a true democracy will begin." Heartened by Kennan's assurances, Lansing replied on August 15 that he was glad Kennan approved "of the policy which this Government has adopted," and he hoped that his "prediction as to the friendly welcome of our troops will be realized."[67]

While Kennan stoked Lansing's hopes, Mott and Crane upheld Wilson's faith that an American mission could help Russians to overcome disorder and dissension. Mott, one of the foremost figures in campaigns for the evangelization of the world since the 1890s, felt that despite Russia's bewildering turmoil Americans "must *believe* in Russia" and fulfill their duty to spread the light that "dissipates darkness." After three private meetings with the president in the weeks when he reached his decision to intervene, on July 24 Mott reiterated to Wilson his conviction that "you have been Providentially guided from the beginning in your attitude and policy with reference to Russia and the Russian peoples." The evangelist especially praised Wilson's "sympathy with the aspirations of what have been aptly called 'dark people' groping after larger light and liberty." A week later, Crane also sought to soothe Wilson's "anxiety" about the complicated situation, counseling that in Russia as in Mexico "the political and social cement has run out, . . . and no one is clairvoyant enough to be able to divine how the new cement will be constituted." However, Crane observed, there was "an old tradition that Russia will some day be saved by Siberia," and he predicted to Wilson that "any program you propose will be accepted as the expression of a wisely sympathetic friend." In late August Crane further assured Wilson "that the Russian peasantry are capable of understanding your program, living up to it and even fighting for it."[68]

Leaders of the Czech Legion understood that the regeneration of Russian democracy was part of their mission. In early August, Captain Vladimir Hurban arrived in Washington from Siberia and delivered a detailed report to Masaryk that circulated widely in the administration. Hurban concluded that Russia was "ill" and "exhausted," but the Czech army could "be of great assistance" in the task of "consolidation" and "upbuilding." Masaryk sent Wilson a copy of Hurban's statement and thanked the president for his "decision to help our Czechoslovak Army in Russia." This commitment, Masaryk wrote, guaranteed that "American principles will be realized," since it was "for these principles that our boys are shedding their blood on the endless plains of Russia and Siberia." Wilson "greatly appreciated" this message and was "reassured" that Masaryk approved of what he had done.[69]

The Wilson administration's decision to send U.S. troops to support the Czech forces in Siberia had been influenced by many factors, including insistent Allied pressure for a blow against Germany from Siberia and worries about Japanese territorial aggrandizement. If the United States had not been at war with Germany, Wilson would not have faced the difficult decision. However, when he authorized the U.S. military expedition to Siberia, his primary immediate purpose was not to resurrect an active front against Germany or to rescue the Czechs but to help the Czechs make Siberia safe for Russian democracy.

Public Opinion and the Decision to Intervene

Wilson's decision to sanction a military expedition to Siberia was facilitated by a shift in American opinion, as well as the fortuitous appearance of the Czech Legion. Since March, when the Bolsheviks signed the Brest-Litovsk peace treaty, Germany had transferred more troops from the east and mounted a new offensive that threatened Paris. With the Allies' situation seeming increasingly desperate, Congress and the American people grew more favorable to proposals for expeditions that might, among other things, increase pressure on Germany's eastern front. Leftist publications from the African American socialist Messenger to the Jewish Daily Forward rallied around the Bolshevik government in opposition to foreign intervention, and liberal journals such as the Nation favored sending an economic relief mission but not troops to Russia. However, the majority of American newspapers called for a combined military and humanitarian expedition by the United States (and Japan, if necessary) to rescue Russia from Bolshevik and German domination.[70]

Already at the end of May, Breckinridge Long noted that "pleas for intervention in Siberia" were coming from all sides. Urging Wilson to take "decisive action in Russia," former Treasury Department official Samuel Bertron argued in June that "the demand for it is of the same character and is as wide-spread as it was for war in April, 1917." A State Department survey at the beginning of July concluded that American newspapers were "unanimous in urging some kind of action at once," and that "the great majority . . . are frankly in favor of Allied armed intervention." In the face of this tidal wave of interventionist sentiment, William Bullitt doubted that the president would "be able to hold to his vision of what is right."[71]

Mounting criticism of Wilson's procrastination caused his advisors to worry about political repercussions. In early June former president William Howard Taft and other prominent Republicans, such as Senator Miles Poindexter, published articles in major newspapers demanding immediate military intervention in Russia. On June 13, one day after seeing the chairman of the Democratic Party about the "Russian situation and politics," Lansing advised Wilson that "the very active propaganda now being carried on in the press," combined with impatience in Congress and Allied expectations, made it necessary to announce steps "to stand by Russia and to assist the Russian people." Lansing's assistant Gordon Auchincloss worried about a "Republican drive for Russian intervention as a campaign issue" and feared that "the Russian situation may yet prove very embarrassing" to Wilson unless he were to take some action, such as sending a relief mission to Siberia.[72]

Although editorials favoring armed intervention in the *New York Times* and other papers heightened the sense of urgency in the administration, they did not dictate a change of policy. In fact, the press campaign for intervention may have provoked increased resistance from the stubborn president. As French ambassador Jusserand observed in July, Wilson believed that articles "appearing in the American press in favor of intervention in Siberia with imposing force" had been "inspired by London," and he "spoke with a marked bitterness caused by the efforts to make him go where he did not want to go."[73] Political pressure did not suddenly convert Wilson from a steadfast commitment to nonintervention to a reluctant acquiescence in intervention. Instead, he waited until he had a feasible plan for providing assistance to Russia that could be presented as something other than "intervention."

When the decision to send military expeditions to Siberia and north Russia was finally made public in early August, most Americans accepted it, with many editors prophesying that "awakening" Russians would rally around the expeditions. While the *Nation* repeatedly complained that the "mystery and evasion" surrounding Wilson's decision contradicted his declarations against secret diplomacy, his secretiveness and vagueness made it difficult to criticize his course of action. Wilson's explanation that

U.S. forces would give friendly assistance to the Russian people and rescue stranded Czechoslovaks, along with press censorship and prosecution of government critics, helped to restrict protests to a small minority of radicals.[74]

Standing by the American Plan

After consenting to Allied expeditions to Siberia in support of the Czechs, Wilson stubbornly clung to his conception of a limited, indirect intervention in the face of pressure to enlarge the number of Allied troops and commit them to more aggressively anti-Bolshevik operations. Two days after Wilson circulated his *aide-mémoire*, the British ambassador advised London that Wilson feared "once American troops are in Russia action may be taken by French or British which would in his view be interference with Russian domestic affairs — or that otherwise he may be drawn into a much more extensive operation than he intends." Wilson's apprehension was warranted. Less than a month later, even before most of the American and Allied troops arrived at Vladivostok, the British were already urging an increase in the number of Japanese troops, citing the allegedly "critical position" of the Czechs. Indignant, Wilson insisted that "it should . . . be left to a later time and other circumstances, not yet developed, to consider radical alterations of the whole scale and character of action in Siberia." Despite his anger, Wilson did not rule out sending more soldiers later if they were less urgently needed in France, if the first wave of Allied troops were welcomed as liberators by Siberians, and if the consolidation of power by pro-Ally Russians made it feasible to expand the scope of military operations.[75]

Some of Wilson's appointees at the State Department, who were more openly anti-Bolshevik than the president, favored dispatching additional doughboys sooner rather than later. On August 17, Lansing directed Breckinridge Long to draft a memorandum on the necessity for "enlargement" of "military activity in Siberia." Noting that the Czechs were facing stiff resistance from about 25,000 Bolsheviks and POWs along the railroad east of Lake Baikal, and that the Japanese were planning "to send a larger military force," Long drily observed, "The situation in Siberia is developing in a direction which differs somewhat from the policy outlined by the President." Instead of resisting the flow of events, Long recommended that the United States adapt to it by approving "an increased military expedition" and allowing American forces "to engage in military activities" further from their base at Vladivostok than had been envisioned originally.[76]

To avoid provoking the president, Lansing revised Long's draft to advise only that "the situation is getting beyond our control and that unless we revise or modify our policy to meet these new conditions we will be placed in a very embarrassing situation, especially so if any disaster should occur to the Czechs in the west." Wilson was frustrated by the divergence from his intentions. In exasperation he cried that "the other governments are going much further than we and much faster, — are, indeed acting upon a plan which is altogether foreign from ours and inconsistent with it." If Long underplayed the divergence between American and Allied policy, Wilson, in his frustration, exaggerated it.[77]

On August 22, Lansing passed along to Wilson a French proposal for an "inter-Allied civilian board" in Russia, which would "decide the political disputes, give the economic, financial, and technical directions, [and] define the relations between the Allied Governments and the local authorities." Lansing said he felt this proposal was "unwise" and would "impress our action in Siberia with the character of intervention rather than relief of the Czechs." Wilson adamantly agreed with Lansing's suggestion that the United States should decline to participate in the proposed Allied High Commission. He asked the secretary to "make it plain to the French ambassador that we do not think cooperation in *political* action necessary or desirable in *eastern* Siberia because we contemplate no political action of any kind *there*, but only the action of friends who stand at hand and wait to see how they can help."[78]

As in his Mexican policy earlier, Wilson persuaded himself that limited military intervention by altruistic Americans in support of a people's efforts to liberate itself from despotic or alien rule was not, in fact, "intervention." Although Lansing was less prone to such self-deception, he worried that British and French involvement in Siberia would create a bad "impression . . . because of the secret support and encouragement" the Allies had "given to factions in various parts of Russia." According to William Phillips, Lansing told Ambassador Jusserand "that the French were not invited because they were identified with factions within Russia, especially the Seminoff revolutionary [*sic!*] forces." Phillips and Lansing knew that the United States had also favored "secret support and encouragement" to anti-Bolshevik factions, particularly in south Russia, but they believed they had kept such sympathies at least partially hidden and preserved a more idealistic image that could be "expedient" in minimizing Russian resistance to foreign intervention. In contrast, Lansing told the British ambassador, Lord Reading, "In Russia the British were regarded as imperialistic and unsympathetic to the revolution." Hence, Lansing feared that the participation of the British and French in Siberia would "give the enterprise the character of interference with the domestic affairs of Russia and create the impression that the underlying purpose is to set up a new pro-Ally Government in Siberia, if not in Russia."[79]

Lansing's aides at the State Department were less concerned than Wilson was to constrain the activity of America's Allies. Breckinridge Long's attention was drawn more to the way the British and Japanese could serve as whipping boys who would incur the odium for some of the work to be done in Siberia. Phillips believed that Wilson had promised in the *aide-mémoire* "that the Allied governments were free to take their own course," and he worked to hold the president to this presumed pledge not to limit the expeditions by the Allied governments. In the same vein, Polk advised the Allies "that they had an entirely free hand in Siberia and that nothing in our action must be taken to indicate that we had any objection to their coming in." [80]

Hemmed in by his own State Department and badgered by the Allies, Wilson increasingly felt trapped. William Wiseman thought there was a danger that Wilson was "beginning to feel that the Allies are trying to rush, even trick, him into a policy which he has refused to accept" by changing the expedition "into a full-fledged military intervention with the object of reconstituting the Eastern Front." Wilson's suspicions were well founded: this was, in fact, precisely what the Allies were doing. Wiseman had "always thought that time and circumstances would modify the President's original policy regarding Russia," but he was concerned that the Allies were pushing too hard too soon. [81]

Although Wilson sensed that the Allies were trying to manipulate him and that the Japanese were wriggling out of the straitjacket he made for them, he did not halt the shipment of troops and supplies to Siberia. In August, Lansing and Polk repeatedly reminded the president of the need to send the Czechoslovakian soldiers "clothing to survive a Siberian winter," and in September Wilson approved funds for provisions to the Czechs. Lansing also gave Wilson George Kennan's recommendations about how to equip American forces for "the rigorous winter which our men will have to endure in eastern Asia." Clearly, the State Department did not expect to "rescue" the Czechs in the near future. [82]

Mission Accomplished, the Czechs Winter in Siberia

By early September, Japanese troops backed by American detachments had chased Red forces out of the region around Vladivostok, and the Czechs had crushed the remaining Bolshevik and POW resistance near Lake Baikal. The Allies and Czechs controlled the railroad from the Pacific to the Volga, and the surrounding territory was at least nominally under the administration of non-Bolshevik Russians. [83]

In June Wilson had asked Masaryk whether Czech troops could be used to "organize Siberia." In mid-July he had expressed the hope that they would "consolidate their forces and get into successful cooperation with their Slavic kinsmen." Later in July he did not object when word came that the Allies planned to send "Czech-Slovaks from neighborhood of Vladivostok to western Siberia."[84] By the end of August the Czechs had achieved all of those objectives.

Masaryk therefore took up with the administration the question of the further deployment of the Czech Legion. On August 28 he suggested to the State Department that instead of abandoning the front west of the Urals, the Czechoslovak army, reinforced by the Allies, should hold the line between the Volga River and Lake Baikal.[85]

Breckinridge Long and Lansing addressed the issues raised by Masaryk on September 5, discussing "whether it is now advisable to change [U.S. policy] & allow Czechs to move westward & with Russians to fight west of Urals." For them, this was a practical question: they decided to seek more "information as to present conditions morale, etc." In contrast, Wilson vehemently opposed having the Czechs push further west of the Ural Mountains. The president was enraged by a report that British General F. C. Poole, commander of the Allied forces in north Russia, had asked the Czechs to capture Perm and Viatka "in order to effect a junction with the Allies at Vologda," and that the Czechs were "meeting unexpected and strong resistance" as they tried to carry out the plan. Furious, Wilson denounced "the utter disregard of General Poole and of all the Allied governments . . . of the policy to which we expressly confined ourselves in our statement about our action in Siberia." Wilson informed Lansing that it was "out of the question to send reenforcements [sic] from eastern Siberia . . . to Perm; and we have expressly notified those in charge of those forces [at Vladivostok] that the Czecho-Slovaks must (so far as our aid was to be used) to [sic] be brought out eastward, not got out westward."[86]

Although Wilson's aide-mémoire had mentioned "safeguarding the rear of the Czecho-Slovaks operating from Vladivostok," rather than evacuating them from that port, he no doubt sincerely believed that he was being consistent with his previous injunctions. Wilson did not stipulate in September that the Czechs had to be brought out immediately, nor did he take any steps to provide ships to evacuate them from Vladivostok. The Czechoslovakian troops might still be useful in protecting and steadying efforts at self-government in Siberia. However, Wilson was incensed by the British use of the Czechs in a blatant campaign to overthrow the Bolshevik regime and reconstitute an eastern front against the Central Powers. This was in his view an outrageous violation of the conditions set forth in the aide-mémoire.

Gordon Auchincloss suggested that the way to deal with this problem was not to withdraw but to provide more active support to the Czechs. In a letter Lansing gave Wilson on September 9, Auchincloss warned the president that "reactionary influences in Russia and elsewhere are at work to shake off your leadership," and that retreating would allow imperialists "to make use of Russia rather than to serve her." While Auchincloss expressed concern about the Allies, he was heartened by the "extraordinarily favorable military situation" in Siberia, where "Bolsheviki opposition [had] broken down" and there was "close cooperation between Czech [troops] and the Central Siberian Army." This showed that "our confidence in the Czech forces has been justified." Since "a Russian military force of equal strength has joined them," and since the Czechs had been embraced by the civilian population of Siberia, Auchincloss concluded "that the Russians are entirely satisfied to cooperate with the Czechs in Russia and that assistance to the Czechs amounts to assistance to the Russians." Instead of recommending withdrawal of the Czechs, Auchincloss and Lansing therefore stressed the need to "get them military supplies" and to provide for the "relief of the civilian population in Siberia."[87]

A week later Wilson authorized $1.5 million for supplies to the Czechs and addressed the issue of what to do with them now that they had fulfilled their initial function. Like Auchincloss, Wilson was pleased that "the railroad is open and under control of our friends from Vladivostok all the way to Samara." Although Wilson did not candidly acknowledge the nature of the enemy, he was satisfied that "the hostile forces which were said to be in the intervening regions are dispersed or cowed and under control." Yet Wilson still sensed "that some influence is at work to pull absolutely away from the plan which we proposed and to which the other governments assented, and proceed to do what we have said we would not do, namely form a new Eastern front." With this suspicion in mind, the president informed Lansing on September 17 that while it might "be necessary to leave some portion of the Czecho-Slovak troops in Western Siberia," by the time winter closed the country Americans "should insist that the Czecho-Slovaks be brought out eastward to Vladivostok and conveyed to the Western front in Europe, if necessary, according to the original agreement made with them." The tide had turned in favor of the Allies in France, but Wilson and his top military advisors were still adamantly against diverting energy and resources from winning the war on the western front. The president also remained opposed to having Czech and American soldiers fight on the frontlines in a direct assault on the Soviet government. Keeping even part of the Czechoslovakian troops in Siberia offered the Japanese an excuse to stay, and Wilson was anxious about what Japan was "now proposing to do with the large army she has sent to Siberia." For these reasons, he was inclined to withdraw the Czechs, though he was not ready to insist on that.[88]

This inclination sharpened the next day, when Wilson read reports that the military position of the Czechs west of the Urals was far more precarious than their position in Siberia. Galvanized by news of the "defeat of the Czecho-Slovaks by the Bolsheviks" at Kazan, Wilson directed Lansing to inform the Allies that "we shall insist, so far as our cooperation is concerned, that if the Czecho-Slovak troops cannot maintain themselves in Western Siberia, they withdraw to Eastern Siberia and there await the determination of the best military disposition of their forces." [89]

This letter marked the first time Wilson recognized in writing that the Czechs were fighting Bolsheviks, rather than some vague, nameless enemy. His antipathy toward the Soviet government became more open in the following days. On September 20 he revised and approved a declaration by Lansing of America's "abhorrence" of the Red Terror. That message expressed support for anti-Bolshevik movements, saying that it was "the earnest desire of the people of the United States to befriend the Russian people and lend them all possible assistance in their struggle to reconstruct their nation upon principles of democracy and self-government." Wilson also authorized the publication of the Sisson Documents, which claimed to show that the Bolsheviks were paid German agents. British officials and some State Department advisors believed the papers were forgeries, but Wilson satisfied himself that they were genuine. On September 24 Wilson admitted to House that "their publication meant a virtual declaration of war upon the Bolsheviki Government." [90]

A war of words was one thing, but a shooting war was another. Wilson still could not countenance participating in an overt military crusade against Soviet Russia. Consequently, he favored removing the Czechs from Siberia, unless they could be used safely for constructive purposes there.

While Wilson believed his position was consistent with the July *aide-mémoire*, State Department officials thought otherwise. William Phillips considered the president's insistence that the Czechs come eastward a breach of his pledge not to criticize "any independent action" of the Allies. With Lansing's concurrence, Phillips reminded Wilson of that promise. He suggested that the United States should make it clear "that we will not send forces into the interior to support the Czecho-Slovaks and that in our opinion they should proceed to a zone of safety," but not insist on their withdrawal. Wilson quickly admitted that this was "quite right" and agreed merely "to urge the advisability" of the Czechs retiring eastward.[91]

Masaryk professed to be in entire agreement with Wilson "that the restoration of an Eastern Front was absolutely out of the question," and that the Czechs west of the Urals should "retire through Siberia as soon as that could be done with safety." However, at the same time he signed an agreement with French General Charles Maurice Janin that pulled in the opposite direction. This document raised the specter of a Red massacre of Allied forces in north Russia and Western citizens in Moscow and stipulated that the Czech "army should not retire over the Ural [Mountains] before the Allied troops and citizens are saved." Despite recent victories by the Bolsheviks, Masaryk entertained the idea of a junction between the Czech Legion and the north Russian expedition. Even if it were necessary to retreat over the Ural Mountains, the Czech leader was leaning away from evacuation to France. "If we can hold Siberia," Masaryk wrote, "that should have the political effect of placing the whole of Siberia under one government and enabling the Russians there to organize an army." On September 23, Masaryk perplexed Lansing by requesting reinforcement of the Czechs so that "the part of Russia leading up to Archangelsk can be held, and Siberia saved from the Germans," while denying that this plan "in any way impl[ied] the restoration of the Russian front."[92]

As Lansing was pondering Masaryk's latest proposal, an important cable arrived from Roland Morris, Wilson's ambassador to Japan, who had been sent to survey the situation in Siberia. Morris reported that the Czech forces on the Volga front were "seriously menaced," and that General William S. Graves, the commander of the American Expeditionary Force (AEF), consequently felt he should move to Omsk and form a base there for the winter in order to support the Czechs to the west. Morris strongly supported Graves's proposal. He believed that "such movement would be entirely consistent with the policy" announced by Wilson, since it would be "the only practicable way . . . to render assistance to the Czech forces . . . and to open up the field for social and economic action." Morris warned that if the United States did not support the Czechs along the Volga, that region would "revert to a condition of anarchy" and Allied generals would be free to proceed "with impracticable plans to create by force a new Russian Army and a new Eastern front."[93]

Lansing was particularly struck by the danger that if the Czechs withdrew east of the Urals, Russians in the Volga region would "be at the mercy of the Red Guards." On September 24 he wrote Wilson that "we must assume that the Czecho-Slovak force west of the Urals will remain there and do the best that they can to protect the friendly Russian communities from Bolshevik excesses."[94]

With winter about to descend on Siberia, it was no longer possible to put off a decision about the deployment of Czech and American forces. House, who "disagree[d] almost entirely with the manner in which the President ha[d] handled the Russian situation," visited the White House at an opportune moment to counter the recommendations of Lansing, Morris, and Masaryk. On September 24, House and Wilson pored over a map, trying to figure out the best disposition for the Czech army.[95]

Two days later, after conferring with General March and Lansing, Wilson communicated his judgment. Splitting the difference between proposals for withdrawal and forward deployment, the president authorized General Graves "to establish his headquarters at some such place as Harbin [about five hundred kilometers northwest of Vladivostok] where he can be in touch with an open port during the winter," yet simultaneously "safeguard the railways and keep the eastward routes open for the Czechs."

Wilson disapproved the suggestion that Graves move to "Omsk or any other point in the far interior, because, strongly as our sympathies constrain us to make every possible sacrifice to keep the country on the Volga front out of the hands of the merciless Red Guards," that was impossible. The Czechs, Wilson advised, "should retire to the eastern side of the Urals," where they could be secure and block German access to Siberian supplies. Noting that the people of north Russia had failed to rally around the Allied nucleus there, Wilson declared that the United States could not "cooperate in an effort to establish lines of operation and defence through from Siberia to Archangel."[96]

Wilson had spoken. In vain, Masaryk protested that Wilson's decision represented a reversal of the administration's press release of August 3, which had accepted the westward move of Czechoslovak troops.[97] Although Wilson had authorized aid to the Czechs and assistance to Russian "efforts at self-government or self-defence," he was disappointed by the initial Russian responses to foreign military expeditions and was unwilling to run the risks required to support Czech and anti-Bolshevik Russian forces west of the Urals. Like other presidents later in the century, Wilson agreed to wager on a limited intervention but refused to throw in more chips when the stakes were raised.

In the following months, Wilson became increasingly preoccupied with a peace settlement to end the Great War. Other U.S. officials in Siberia and Washington would watch closely as Russians in Siberia attempted to strengthen their governments and armies in the continuing civil war. Although the Wilson administration repeatedly admonished its representatives in Russia not to take sides in the struggle between conservative and moderate socialist anti-Bolshevik groups, U.S. officials would show preferences between those elements in Siberia.[98]

Limited Support for Socialistic Democracy in Siberia

As Czechoslovak and White forces defeated the Bolsheviks in the summer of 1918, nineteen local governments appeared between the Volga and Vladivostok, most of them dominated by Socialist Revolutionaries. The leading contender for rule of the whole region was the relatively conservative Provisional Siberian Government (PSG), which established its headquarters at Omsk and governed western and central Siberia starting in July. Through protracted negotiations, the various governments were gradually unified by September, with SRs retaining a leading role, though the balance of power shifted toward Kadets and monarchists at Omsk. In late September, the PSG was succeeded by a five-member Directorate (including two SRs) that aspired to be an all-Russian government.

One might have expected the Wilson administration to be deeply pleased by these developments. In April 1918 Wilson had expressed a desire to support the most nearly representative authority in Siberia, and in May he had told the French ambassador in Washington that his goal was "the formation in Siberia of the kind of government which our agents could help to stand on its own feet."[99]

However, the overturning of Soviet power in Siberia left the Wilson administration facing the major dilemmas of a limited intervention in support of Russian democracy during a civil war. Given the popular inclinations toward regional autonomy and socialism, would representative governments in Siberia be compatible with the American goal of a reunited Russia that would fulfill its financial obligations and offer stable conditions for capitalist development? Could a democratic Siberian government, unlike the Provisional Government of 1917, raise strong armies and fight effectively? Where was the line between legitimate assistance to Russian self-government, on the one hand, and illegitimate interference in Russian affairs or outright intervention in the civil war?

Numerous reports to Washington indicated that the PSG was the most representative governmental organization in Siberia. On June 28, for example, Lansing brought to Wilson's attention information from Admiral Knight that the Bolsheviks had been replaced by a new government which was "wholly Russian but anti-Bolshevik," made up largely of delegates elected to a constitutional convention, and "supported by a large majority of people including entire peasant population."[100] Most cables from Siberia also indicated that the SR-dominated government had a fairly good claim to authority. From the first days of the PSG, non-Bolshevik civilian and military leaders informed American representatives that the Constituent Assembly elections of November 1917 were the foundation of political legitimacy in Siberia, and that the convening of the assembly was the primary goal of the new Siberian government.[101]

Americans familiar with Russia repeatedly advised Wilson of the popularity of the moderate socialists and the need to intervene on their side rather than in support of Russian reactionaries. On June 24, for example, Wilson received a memorandum from William T. Ellis, a journalist who had been in Russia in 1917. Ellis stressed that peasants and workers were "obsessed by the spirit of the revolution," and that American intervention would have to be sympathetic to the aspirations of this "ninety per cent of the people of Russia." If foreign powers allied themselves with the "thoroughly discredited Cadet party, or with the representatives of business and autocracy," Ellis warned, "they would at once alienate the bulk of the Russian population." Even the more conservative George Kennan advised that "a sympathetic comprehension . . . of Socialistic ideals" would be essential "in dealing with a population in which there is a very considerable admixture of Social Revolutionists."[102]

Sensitive to "the danger of the Vladivostok movement being tied up with the reactionary party in Russia," Frank Polk told British representatives in July that the administration wanted to avoid giving the impression "that we were lining up with the reactionaries," such as the Horvath group at Harbin. Wilson, similarly, was suspicious of monarchists and did not want to see "a return to the old regime in Russia."[103]

Despite these concerns, the advice about the SRs, and the favorable information about the Siberian governments, the United States did not give them significant assistance and rejected all pleas for recognition or even informal statements of support. Although the administration authorized Ambassador Bakhmeteff in July and September to use his American-supplied fund to send weapons and money to Siberia, it said that it could not itself send supplies to the Omsk regime, because "there was no government in Russia which we could recognize." President Wilson set up an informal committee to aid the Czech troops in Siberia, but not the Omsk government or its army. Not until October 28 did the administration allow rifles to be turned over to the Siberian army, though many more rifles were authorized earlier for the Czechs.[104]

If the United States was thus somewhat stingy with supplies to the Omsk government, it was still more reluctant to offer verbal support. In August, the State Department declined to acknowledge the PSG's telegrams requesting recognition and aid. Wilson's reluctance to interfere with Russian selection of an anti-Bolshevik government helps to explain his hands-off approach while there were many contending organizations in the summer of 1918. But even after the unification of the Siberian governments, the State Department continued to insist that its representatives follow the declared policy of "strict impartiality." In practice absolute nonintervention was an impossibility: even sincere efforts to be neutral had political repercussions. The cold receptions Americans gave SR leaders were interpreted as signs of disapproval and attributed to the failure of the SR governments. On October 11, Bakhmeteff told Polk that the U.S. position "was misunderstood in Siberia, as they thought that we were too neutral." In response to this prodding, the State Department declared on October 17 that it was watching "with interest and hope for the future the various efforts which are being made to restore law and order under a stable government." However, the United States was not at that time "prepared to recognize any new government in Russia," and on November 5 Lansing stiffly refused to accept a French invitation to join in a statement promising "moral support" and "material assistance" to the Omsk government.[105]

The administration understandably hesitated to extend formal diplomatic recognition until a new government for *all* of Russia had been established. Thus, Polk told Bakhmeteff on November 9 that the United States could not "recognize the Omsk Government, as that was purely in Siberia." Similarly, Wilson doubted the feasibility of "recognizing and receiving delegates from the Omsk government" because of the "at least temporary disintegration of Russia" into separate parts. However, opposition to the dismemberment of Russia was not the only reason for Washington's diffidence toward the "All-Russian Directorate" at Omsk, which was dedicated to the reunification of Russia under one central government.[106]

The Wilson administration's slowness to support the moderate socialists stemmed also from perceptions that they wasted energy in long-winded factional strife and lacked a single powerful leader. However, the SRs' weakness was as much a product as a cause of American and Allied coolness toward them. The refusal to recognize the Siberian government and Allied representatives' scheming with reactionary officers seriously undermined the position of the democratic socialists. Despite professions of neutrality, some American diplomats were neutral in neither thought nor deed. In early September, for example, American consul general Ernest Harris joined his Allied counterparts in urging the removal of General A. N. Grishin-Almazov, who had organized the Siberian army along democratic lines, after he complained of minimal Allied assistance and suggested that the Allies needed Russia more than Russia needed the Allies.[107]

The cool response to the SRs by some American officials may have stemmed in part from disappointment in the military forces they gathered and an unduly pessimistic view of their chances of success against the Red Army. Consul General Harris sometimes reported from the former Bolshevik stronghold of Irkutsk that the people showed no enthusiasm "for recruiting or for continuation [of] war." In mid-September, after Bolshevik forces defeated Czech troops at Kazan, Wilson and Lansing complained about the failure of "large forces of Russians" to gather in either north Russia or Siberia.[108]

Yet most of the information from U.S. representatives in Siberia indicated an "extraordinarily favorable military situation." On September 9, Lansing had sent Wilson encouraging reports that a large number of Russians were mobilizing. Similarly, in late October, Charles Crane wrote to his son at the State Department that the "Omsk Government ha[d] organized an excellent army of about one hundred and fifty thousand young soldiers and it could be easily doubled or trebled if equipment were forthcoming."[109]

Wilson took a relatively patient approach toward the forming of Siberian armies: he wanted to give the Russians time to regroup before pressing them into offensive military action. Lansing and his aides had been more sharply disappointed by the failure of the Kerensky regime to revitalize the Russian army after the fall of the tsar, and this led them to expect other moderate socialists to fail to raise an effective anti-Bolshevik army. One State Department advisor, Jerome Landfield, who was linked by marriage and friendships to the Russian nobility, confessed in October 1918 that he was "not very enthusiastic over any of the attempted civil governments thus far formed," because he thought the Russian people were still "suffering from the effects of their socialistic debauch" and he doubted that "any popular government . . . can possibly re-establish real order and discipline or cooperate in the formation of an effective army."[110]

Such prejudices were more important than the few negative reports about the Siberian army. The attitudes of U.S. diplomats and State Department officials toward Siberian forces in the summer and fall of 1918 were shaped primarily by three factors: (1) discomfort with the SRs' economic policies; (2) distaste for their socialist ideology; and (3) preference for leadership by a military man who would move more decisively to "restore order."

American consular officials and businessmen in Russia were deeply disturbed by the way the revolutions of 1917 contributed to the disorganization of the economy. During the war, American exports to Russia had increased dramatically, from only $31 million in 1914 to over $500 million worth of American products in 1917. Many American businessmen began to see great opportunities in Russia for buying raw materials, running factories using cheap Russian labor, and exporting American manufactured goods. Siberia, in particular, seemed "our new land for development," as Interior Secretary Franklin Lane put it. However, the revolutions aggravated industrial disruption, brought precipitous declines in productivity, and dimmed American enthusiasm. Before Ernest Harris was appointed consul general at Irkutsk in May 1918 he had worked for the National City Bank, and in touring Russia he "saw on every hand the evidence of factory stagnation due primarily to the enjoyment of new-found liberty, which was based upon the idea that it was practically no longer necessary to work." In 1918 Harris, like other consular officials, worried that the "Social Revolutionary element" would "foment strife and impede the progress of the country along the lines of sound and rational democracy."[111]

Americans were also troubled by the possibility that the SRs would follow economic policies similar to the Bolsheviks' nationalization of foreign companies and repudiation of the foreign debt. Harris was personally affected when the Soviet government took over banks in Petrograd and Moscow in 1917. In 1918 he sought assurances from Siberian leaders that their conception of "order" did not include nationalizing "private banks and other industries." While the PSG repudiated the sweeping Bolshevik program of nationalization, the moderate socialists did envision a more limited program, including a government bank and nationalization of the mines and ore in Siberia.[112]

Although Wilson and Lansing did not express specific concern about Siberian economic policies, their broader attitudes were based on information from American diplomats in Russia. Harris was, as Lansing wired on October 23, "the Government's highest responsible authority at present available in Siberia for reliable information to guide its decisions and conclusions." Dispatches from Harris and other American representatives led Lansing to conclude, in a November 5, 1918, letter to Wilson, that in Siberia "a considerable industrial and social uneasiness persists, fraught with danger for the future." [113]

On one important economic issue Wilson and Lansing definitely shared Harris's concern. American bankers had loaned $233 million to the tsar during the war, and the U.S. government advanced nearly $200 million in loans and credits to the Provisional Government in 1917. Within a few days of the Bolshevik repudiation of the foreign debt in January 1918, Treasury Secretary McAdoo suggested to Lansing and Wilson that "we should make it a condition of recognition of any Government in Russia that its obligations to the United States should be respected." One of the reasons Harris recommended against recognition of the Omsk government was that, in its program, "nothing was said about Russia's foreign debt and how same was to be paid." In formulas similar to earlier messages to Mexican leaders, Lansing repeatedly declared in October and November 1918 that the United States desired to see in Russia "a government which is able to protect individual rights and to perform its international obligations," and Wilson approved of such statements. [114]

In addition to such economic considerations, broader ideological differences figured in the disdain for the moderate socialists expressed by American representatives in Siberia. Although the right SRs guaranteed "personal liberty and private ownership rights," being "socialistic" only in favoring land reform, support for cooperatives, and government control of some major industries, they were nonetheless branded as "extreme socialists." In fact, American diplomats repeatedly portrayed them as being almost indistinguishable from Bolsheviks. On September 24, for example, Lansing forwarded to Wilson a dispatch from Harris which shrilly maintained that the program of the SRs was "so radically socialistic" that it was "practically the Bolshevik plan." [115]

The skepticism and scorn that Lansing, Harris, and other U.S. diplomats felt about Siberian governments in 1918 were fed by their disillusionment with the Provisional Government of 1917. If the Russian people were left entirely to themselves, Harris argued in July 1918, they would "not be able to rise above the governmental status which obtained during the Kerensky fiasco." Much like Lansing, Harris decided that Russia's generals were the only men who "really had the power to save Russia" from the despotism of the "scum of humanity." He therefore favored "a military dictatorship" which would allow leaders of the Kadet Party and officers like Admiral Kolchak "to inaugurate a safe and conservative republic."[116]

The search for such a strongman continued in the fall of 1918. On September 23, Harris lamented that "no strong men have come forward in any of the governments as yet." On November 6 he wrote Lansing that he preferred military to civilian leaders, "for it is only through the police work of a well-disciplined army that law and order ever will be restored in Siberia and Russia."[117]

Backing Kolchak's March on Moscow

Near midnight on November 17, 1918, Cossack officers arrested leading SRs in Omsk, including two members of the Directorate. Early the next day, while British soldiers deployed to prevent Czech forces from rescuing the SRs, the council of ministers in Omsk decided to replace the Directorate with a dictatorship. The ministers selected as dictator Admiral A. V. Kolchak, who had favorably impressed American officials while on a naval mission to the United States in the fall of 1917. Soon after Kolchak took power, American consuls reported that the situation in Siberia was improving, that order was finally being restored. Consul General Harris informed Washington that, in contrast to the SRs, Kolchak promised to fulfill all financial obligations previously incurred by non-Bolshevik governments, including the repayment of foreign loans with interest. By early December Harris encouraged Washington to support and perhaps eventually recognize Kolchak.[118]

While Harris and other conservative Americans believed the anti-Bolshevik cause was strengthened by the Omsk putsch, it aggravated the declining morale of the Czechs (who sympathized with the democratic socialists) and it led many SRs to side with the Bolsheviks as a lesser evil than reaction. This disaffection was noted by Carl Ackerman, an American journalist on a semi-official mission in Siberia. In early January 1919, Ackerman advised the State Department that "the reason the intellectuals and liberals of Russia are turned against us is because we did not show an interest in the government which they tried to form." Since the overthrow of the Directorate, military morale and popular support had deteriorated: "Neither the Czech soldiers . . . nor the Russian people . . . sympathize with the Kolchak Government," Ackerman reported. General Graves had a similar impression: he informed Washington that "the consensus of opinion is that if it were not for Allied troops [Kolchak] would be quickly overthrown."[119]

State Department officials disregarded such warnings. On January 8, 1919, Lansing approved of the idea of a declaration that the United States and the Allies desired to assist the Kolchak government through "economic and financial aid and the furnishing of military supplies," although he had rejected a similar statement when SRs were in the Omsk government only two months earlier. Later in 1919, the United States did provide such assistance to Kolchak, by "lending good offices to the Russian Embassy in shipping Russian rifles and boots" to the Kolchak armies, and by facilitating the purchase of railroad cars and locomotives with American credits. This support was much more generous than that given to the armies and regimes led by moderate socialists in Siberia.[120]

In late 1918 and early 1919, several of Wilson's advisors urged him to send more American troops to Siberia and deploy them further inside the country. U.S. soldiers were subsequently assigned to guard the Trans-Siberian Railroad as far west as Lake Baikal, but Washington did not expand the size of the American Expeditionary Force. Sending more troops would have given the Japanese an excuse to increase their forces, and Congress and the American people increasingly questioned the purpose of the AEF after the Armistice in Europe. Wilson was also influenced by reports that foreign intervention was causing Russians to rally around the Soviet government. In this context, an ambivalent Wilson considered withdrawing American troops and leaving Russia "to settle her own affairs." The Allied interventions, he told the Supreme War Council on February 14, 1919, "were not assisting any promising effort to establish order throughout Russia." [121]

In late March and April, however, reports reaching Paris indicated that Kolchak was "winning" against the Bolsheviks in the East. By early May, Kolchak's armies advanced to within fifty miles of the Volga and many expected them to take Moscow in the near future. Most major American newspapers were pleased by the success of anti-Bolshevik forces, and apart from the socialist New York *Call* few papers actively opposed recognition of Kolchak. With this "new situation," some U.S. officials, particularly Acting Secretary of State Frank Polk, pushed for more active cooperation by U.S. forces with Kolchak's armies and advocated recognition of the admiral's government.[122]

General Graves's strict construction of Wilson's *aide-mémoire* as requiring him to remain aloof from conflicts between Russian factions had led reactionary supporters of Kolchak to claim that Americans sympathized with the Bolsheviks. In March, Polk criticized Graves's conservative interpretation of his instructions, suggested that the situation was "somewhat beyond" the general, and recommended that Graves be directed to use the influence he had from the presence of American forces "to insist upon a policy of moderation," as opposed to the extremes of Bolshevism and "counter revolution." After Lansing echoed Polk's suggestions, Wilson authorized the proposed directions to Graves, provided that Secretary of War

Baker approved them. However, Baker and Chief of Staff March were determined to support Graves and resist efforts to expand the activities of the Siberian expedition. Baker warned in early April that the proposed instructions would require "a very large force" and "increase the frequency" of conflicts with "elements of the native population." Lansing and Wilson then agreed with Baker that American and Japanese forces should be restricted to the vicinity of the railway and used "to suppress local violence by conflicting Russian forces" only when clashes with Cossacks or Red partisans affected railway operations.[123]

Amid continuing reports that the limited U.S. intervention was "a source of weakness to Kolchak," Baker advised Wilson in May that "either General Graves should be directed to cooperate with the Kolchalk [*sic*] government or he ought to be withdrawn." On May 9, immediately after receiving Baker's message, Wilson told the British and French prime ministers, "We must either act with Kolchak or withdraw." If the United States sent more troops, Wilson noted, "Japan will do the same." Since he also did "not have confidence in Admiral Kolchak," Wilson was inclined to "withdraw from Russia." As John Foster Dulles commented, Wilson unfortunately had "the idea that Kolchak is a dictator." Dulles and other U.S. advisors who did not "really care a damn about the Democratic conditions" wished Lloyd George would tell Wilson "the Admiral is the White Hope of Russia." Lloyd George did so, stressing optimistic reports about Kolchak's military advances. "If Admiral Kolchak can join us, it is the end of Bolshevism," he exclaimed. "If Kolchak is on the point of succeeding, now is the time to impose our conditions and to negotiate with him." Bowing to the greater experience of the British "in far-flung expeditions," Wilson postponed his decision on Siberia.[124]

In the following weeks, Kerensky and other Russian socialist critics of Kolchak compared him to brutal Mexican leaders Wilson had refused to recognize, argued that the admiral was dominated by monarchist officers, and predicted that aid to such reactionary forces could not lead to the regeneration of a democratic Russia. However, the democratic socialists and likeminded American liberals failed to block the movement toward greater support of the Omsk regime. Wilson had been disenchanted by Kerensky's ineptitude in 1917 and he felt nagging doubts that "backward" Russia, with her darkly "ignorant" peasants, could be made fit for democracy without forceful leadership. Hoping that Kolchak would prove strong enough to control his reactionary advisors, Wilson joined the Allies in soliciting from Kolchak promises to hold free elections as soon as he reached Moscow, respect "civil and religious liberty," and accept the independence of Finland and Poland. (As junior advisor A. A. Berle confided, the United States could not recognize Kolchak "unless we could justify to our own public opinion the liberal character of his government.") On May 23,

1919, Wilson also sought confirmation of "the alleged declaration by Admiral Koltchak, recognizing Russia's debt as an obligation." After all these assurances arrived in June, Wilson and the Allied leaders publicly promised Kolchak assistance "with munitions, supplies and food." Wilson said this pledge did not amount to *de facto* recognition, but he did consider it a promise of continued "countenance and support."[125]

This support was given. On June 24, Wilson ordered that whatever remained from $5 million originally allotted for civilian relief in north Russia should be distributed in Siberia. Also in June, $5 million worth of credit was extended to Russian cooperatives for the purchase of War Department surplus material such as clothing and shoes.[126] Most importantly, the financial arrangement between the Wilson administration and Ambassador Bakhmeteff allowed the Russian embassy to send the Kolchak regime millions of dollars worth of rifles, machine guns, ammunition, and other supplies that had been purchased with credits extended to the Provisional Government in 1917.

The Wilson administration's ability to provide more direct military aid and more extensive economic assistance was limited by legal restrictions and resistance in Congress. In May 1919, discussing with Allied leaders the question of sending military supplies to Siberia, Wilson claimed: "It is not I who needs to be persuaded, but the Congress of the United States, which until now has shown itself hostile to the idea of any intervention in Russia." Wilson suggested that the attitude in Congress would change if Kolchak replied satisfactorily to the Allies' questions, but many congressmen remained critical of intervention in Siberia after Kolchak provided the desired assurances. In Paris in late June, when Wilson reviewed plans to "continue to send supplies and munitions to the anti-Bolshevist forces," he agreed with one advisor about "the importance of telling the Congress the whole story and said he would appeal for funds upon his return." A major congressional appropriation would permit not only more arms shipments to Kolchak but also "a great constructive program," centering on the Trans-Siberian Railway, which would prevent Japan from "monopolizing Siberia." However, the climate of hostility and suspicion on Capitol Hill discouraged Wilson from making that appeal. On June 27, the Senate adopted a resolution requesting the president to state the reasons for keeping U.S. soldiers in Siberia. A month later the administration responded that U.S. troops were needed to protect the Trans-Siberian Railway from partisan bands and keep that "artery of trade" open so economic assistance could be provided. Not satisfied by that response, congressmen introduced further resolutions in August and grilled State Department officials in committee hearings.[127]

If Wilson and his advisors had called for more aggressive military intervention against Soviet Russia or had campaigned openly for more generous funding of anti-Bolshevik movements they probably could have mobilized significant support. Henry Cabot Lodge, chairman of the Senate Foreign Relations Committee, and other influential senators believed that if the United States was going to intervene in Russia it should have intervened with sufficient forces to be effective. Many newspaper editors agreed. In July, for example, the New York *Tribune* asked, "if Lenine is our enemy why not do something really worth while to end his career of terrorism and savagery?" Even the anti-interventionist *New Republic* conceded, "It might be possible to respect a policy which declared the Soviet government an enemy of the human race and made war against it." Since the administration failed to provide a candid and satisfying explanation of why U.S. troops were in Siberia, however, opponents of intervention such as Raymond Robins had opportunities to win over anti-Bolshevik audiences, and by the fall most American newspapers favored bringing the boys home.[128]

As Wilson toured the country in September, denouncing Bolshevism and urging support for a League of Nations, Senate critics who followed him made U.S. intervention in Siberia an emotional core of their rebuttals of the president. In Des Moines, for example, a crowd of eight thousand people "jumped to their feet and gave way to a ringing demonstration" when Republican senator Hiram Johnson of California declared that Bolshevism was bred, not by opponents of the League, but by the men in power who violated the Constitution, with undeclared wars. "Bolshevism," Johnson shouted, "is born in the bosoms of the women whose sons were drafted for a war with Germany and are sent across the waters to be shot down in Siberia." While other members of Congress made similar speeches and pro-Soviet radicals organized meetings to protest against U.S. intervention in Russia, dock workers in Seattle refused to load rifles the War Department and Russian embassy were shipping to Siberia.[129]

Given that congressional and public opposition to intervention, the Wilson administration decided to postpone a request for substantial military and economic assistance to the Kolchak government that might cost votes for the League. While the aid program was delayed, Kolchak's position worsened.

Soon after Wilson decided to "bet on" the Omsk government, as he put it at a press conference in June, Kolchak's armies were "chased eastward" across Siberia. Although Kolchak's military situation deteriorated further in the late summer of 1919, State Department and consular officials pressed even harder for aid and formal recognition to bolster the collapsing White government. Despite reports that the Omsk regime lacked popular support, Breckinridge Long felt that "the waning power of Kolchak" had to be restored, since "it is a question of Kolchak or Bolshevism."[130]

In September Bakhmeteff informed the State Department that Kolchak's aides were complaining that delays of recognition and supplies were causing substantial harm to the prestige of the Omsk government and fostering rising anti-American sentiment among White officers. In response to such complaints, Long assured Bakhmeteff that the United States had dispatched "a message of encouragement from the President which was to be orally communicated to Kolchak." Later that month, just before Wilson collapsed on a speaking tour, he approved the sale "upon a credit basis" of clothing and other equipment for Kolchak's armies, which were said to be "driving the Bolsheviki back toward the Urals." After General Graves held up a shipment of rifles to Kolchak's forces because of conflicts between American units and marauding Cossacks, Secretary of War Baker encouraged Graves to release the rifles, observing: "President feels that his agreement to support Kolchak . . . ought to be carried out if possible." A week later, Frank Polk told a former Russian embassy aide that he thought U.S. recognition of Kolchak would still be considered and that "if it had not been for the President's illness recognition would have been granted."[131]

After Wilson suffered a stroke on October 2, State Department advisors struggled to overcome governmental paralysis and do whatever possible to keep Kolchak's anti-Bolshevik forces alive. As Lansing observed on October 9, experts on Russia both inside and outside the department were making "a determined effort . . . to have this Government recognize Kolchak as the head of a *de facto* government." Ambassador Bakhmeteff, who lobbied for recognition and expanded aid in almost daily meetings with State Department officials, tried to persuade Lansing that there was no wide public protest against the presence of American troops in Siberia. However, Lansing responded that the opposition was more widely spread than Bakhmeteff thought and he suggested that the ambassador talk with senators and congressmen. Lansing's realism and training as an international lawyer also figured in his cautious position. Although he considered it "a decision which may mean the salvation of Russia," he ruled against recognition for the moment because he did "not think that the Bolsheviks have been decisively beaten or that the Kolchak Government has as yet shown sufficient evidence of permanency or stability."[132]

This was an understatement. Kolchak's government abandoned Omsk to the Red Army in the second week of November, and the White retreat quickly became a chaotic flight. In early 1920, Czechoslovakian troops handed Kolchak over to socialists in Irkutsk in order to secure their long-delayed departure from Siberia. The admiral was subsequently interrogated by a Bolshevik-dominated Military-Revolutionary Committee and then executed on February 6.

There were many reasons for the defeat of Kolchak's armies and the demise of his government. While many of his soldiers at the front were barefoot and inadequately fed, corrupt members of his bloated staff diverted desperately needed Allied and American supplies for their own profit, and wealthy Russians who congregated in Omsk carried on as if under the old regime, "still drinking and dancing and eating and motoring and whoring," as one appalled American recorded. Atrocities committed by White forces and Cossack raiders in the rear turned whole villages into partisan bands. Believing that questions of political reforms had to be postponed until after a military victory over Bolshevism, Kolchak ignored the social and economic dimensions of the struggle. Many peasants were reluctant to fight at all, and fears that the reactionaries who surrounded Kolchak wanted to restore the old order spurred desertions from his armies. After White officers reintroduced traditional military discipline and put epaulets back on their shoulders, many peasant recruits concluded that Kolchak "wants Russia to have a Tsar again," and at the first opportunity returned to their villages to protect their land. As Lansing recognized in October 1919, Kolchak did not "have the confidence or support of the Siberian people. They appear to fear if he succeeds that the old regime will be reestablished." [133]

Wilson and Polk had understood that foreign intervention on the side of the conservative Russian elite would alienate the bulk of the population. But disillusionment with the Kerensky regime and discomfort with the Siberian SRs led the Wilson administration to be lukewarm toward the more popular political leaders in Siberia between June and November 1918, and more sympathetic to Kolchak's military dictatorship.

When Consul General Harris had argued that the programs of "radical" SRs and Bolsheviks both seemed "incomparably worse than what the blackest forces of reaction might inaugurate," he was preaching to the converted: if forced to choose, Lansing preferred the orderly and elitist German form of autocracy to the Bolshevik "despotism of ignorance," which was "productive of disorder and anarchy." [134] Many of Wilson's friends and advisors agreed with Lansing. Cyrus McCormick, for example, advised Wilson that "the Czar's regime was bad but it was better than the present condition of unendurable tyranny, disorder and general murder." In contrast, Wilson believed, at least until early 1919, that a "restoration of the old order" would be "even more disastrous" than the Bolshevik regime. However, as Wilson tried to steer between reaction and radicalism, with many of his crew on the starboard side, his ship of state listed heavily to the right. In the late spring and summer of 1919, despite fears that Kolchak would establish a reactionary government in Moscow, Wilson authorized increased support for Kolchak's armies and publicly proclaimed that the Bolsheviks were crueler than the tsar. While Wilson had been more reluctant than his State Department advisors to back the White forces, he ultimately shared the view that Bolshevism was a greater menace than the risk of a reversion to tsarism.[135]

Hostility toward Bolshevism led Lansing and his aides to strive to the end to breathe life back into anti-Bolshevik campaigns. On November 30, Lansing conceded that "the Kolchak Government is practically done," and that American troops would have to be withdrawn. However, looking for a surrogate anti-Red force, he decided "we ought not to raise any objection to Japan sending a sufficient force to check the Bolshevik advance[,] for the spread of Bolshevism in the Far East would be a dreadful menace to civilization." Breckinridge Long urged the evacuation of U.S. soldiers, but through the end of 1919 he was opposed by the chiefs of the Russian and Far Eastern Divisions. After Long finally got Wilson to authorize withdrawal on December 27, 1919, he encountered bitter resentment from his colleagues.[136]

George Kennan was also upset by the Wilson administration's failure to support the White cause in Siberia more aggressively. In January 1920 Kennan expostulated with Lansing that in 1918 he had "contemplated an active force, that would help the loyal Russians to overthrow the Bolsheviki and the Germans, not a passive force that would sit with folded hands in barracks for a year and a half." In response, Lansing asked Kennan to understand that "it was not lack of sympathy which prevented the employment of a large active force in Siberia but conditions which simply rendered such a course out of the question." The secretary explained that the public, Congress, and military leaders were opposed to sending troops to Siberia or declaring war on Russia. Hence, Lansing concluded, "We were bound hand and foot by the circumstances."[137]

Like Kennan and Lansing, Wilson had wanted to help pro-Ally Russians overturn Bolshevik rule in Siberia as a first step toward the restoration of orderly self-government throughout Russia, but he had not been free to render unlimited assistance. In the first half of 1918, Wilson and his advisors had hesitated to intervene in Siberia because of their reluctance to divert troops from winning the war in France, the concern that military intervention would chill idealistic enthusiasm for the war against Germany, the worry that Japanese forces would provoke a "yellow peril" reaction from patriotic Russians, and the fear that Japan would carve out a sphere of influence in eastern Siberia. Neither those dangers nor liberal principles led Wilson to be categorically opposed to intervention. From March through May 1918 he had looked for ways to intervene that Americans and Russians would accept, showing particular interest in the Cossack forces of Semenov, but he had not found a practicable course of action. In June Wilson and his advisors thought that the Czechoslovakian legion in Siberia offered a solution, since supporting the Czechs and their Russian kinsmen could be presented as something other than "intervention," and since utilizing the Czechs to organize Siberia obviated the need to rely on large Japanese forces. While the Czechs and anti-Bolshevik Russians succeeded in deposing Bolsheviks throughout Siberia, the Wilson administration failed to consolidate that achievement by providing speedy and substantial assistance to Siberian governments in the summer and fall of 1918. U.S. support for moderate socialist and liberal efforts to stabilize a non-Bolshevik Siberia was limited by scruples about interfering in non-Bolshevik Russian affairs, concerns about socialist and separatist tendencies in Siberian governments, and inclinations to favor a military strongman over more popular but less vigorous civilians. After Admiral Kolchak became the Supreme Ruler at Omsk, American officials worked more energetically to help the White cause, but they found that the Kolchak regime lacked popular support in Siberia. They also ran into strong resistance from Congress and the American people, in part because they failed to provide candid explanations of U.S. objectives. Thus, at each stage, the Wilson administration found itself constrained by conditions in Russia and America. While many of Wilson's advisors would have liked to do much more to aid the anti-Bolshevik cause, a limited, indirect intervention was the best they could do. The small U.S. expedition and the many shipments of supplies to anti-Bolshevik forces were enough to provoke dissent at home and resentment in Soviet Russia, but not sufficient to secure the goal of a reunited democratic Russia.

7

FIGHTING, BUT NOT A WAR

AMERICAN INTERVENTION IN NORTH RUSSIA, 1918–1919

We are not at war with Russia. — Woodrow Wilson, February 1919

The real truth was, we were waging war against Bolshevism. Everybody knew that. Yet no Allied government ever stated that that was its policy in intervening. — Captain Hugh S. Martin, August 1919

On August 2, 1918, anti-Bolshevik forces overthrew the local Soviet government at Archangel (Arkhangel'sk) while, by prearrangement, Allied warships sailed into the port from the White Sea. Fifty sailors from the *USS Olympia* arrived by August 4, and twenty-five of them joined British troops in chasing retreating Bolsheviks down the railroad line toward Vologda. At the beginning of September, forty-five hundred doughboys from the 339th Infantry Regiment, nicknamed "Detroit's Own," reached north Russia. Two of these three battalions from the Great

Lakes region were sent south from Archangel to fight on the front lines against the Red Army, nearly two hundred miles inside Russia.

American members of the Allied expedition suffered over five hundred casualties before they were withdrawn from north Russia in June 1919.[1] In the "Battle of Armistice Day," between November 11 and 14, 1918, six hundred Americans, Canadians, and Scots stationed in trenches and blockhouses at Tulgas were attacked by about twenty-five hundred Bolshevik troops. "We licked the Bolo good and hard," Sergeant Silver Parrish recorded, "But lost 7 killed & 14 wounded. . . . The Bolo lost about 475 men."[2] Near Shenkursk in late January 1919, one platoon of forty-three Americans incurred thirty-two casualties. "It's a real war now," Sergeant John Crissman commented in his diary.[3]

President Woodrow Wilson did not share that view. Although he was responsible for sending U.S. troops to Archangel, he declined to consider that an act of war. Leaving the Paris peace discussions in February 1919, Wilson urged Colonel Edward House to insist in meetings with Allied representatives that "we are not at war with Russia and will in no circumstances that we can now foresee take part in military operations there against the Russians."[4] Wilson's statement was not a result of sheer ignorance. The White House and State Department had been informed about the deployment of U.S. troops, and the battles were reported in American newspapers. Although Wilson knew that American units were in conflict with Soviet forces, he was stubbornly determined to differentiate between limited, defensive operations near the ports and aggressive military campaigns into the heart of Russia.[5]

For six months after the Bolsheviks came to power in Petrograd, Wilson had resisted Allied pressure to dispatch American forces to north Russia. The president and his military advisors were firmly convinced that the war against Germany was going to be won on the western front, and they believed that Russian war-weariness made it impractical to try to re-create an eastern front. Wilson and his aides saw somewhat more value in proposals for American soldiers to guard military supplies at Russia's northern ports and prevent Germany from turning Murmansk and Archangel into submarine bases.[6] The president's resistance to intervention was also eroded by repeated appeals from his desperate allies.[7] However, the Allied intervention in north Russia was not merely a sideshow of the Great War, and Wilson's May 1918 authorization of an American military expedition was not simply a reluctant departure from nonintervention wrung out of him by Allied arm-twisting.[8]

Understanding of the U.S. expedition to Archangel has been obscured by the postulation of a false dichotomy between Wilson's principle of self-determination and his attitudes toward intervention. Wilson did think that a massive invasion would violate the ideal of self-government, and in the spring of 1918 he worried that even a smaller intervention would seem to contradict his liberal ideals. However, devotion to noninterventionist principles influenced Wilson less than practical analysis of ways to help Russia in her time of trouble. Unlike the proposals for expeditions to Siberia, the question of intervention in north Russia was not complicated by the danger that Japanese participation would provoke a "yellow peril" backlash. Wilson still feared that military intervention might unite Russian factions in a nationalistic reaction against the Allies, yet by the summer of 1918 he was persuaded that many Russians would welcome American assistance in restoring order and reorganizing their armed forces. Thus, he came to believe that a limited, indirect intervention to help the Russian people overcome domination by Bolsheviks and Germans would not contradict, but rather facilitate self-determination.[9]

When Wilson agreed to send American soldiers to Archangel, then, he sought not only to conciliate his Allies, but also to help the Russian people liberate their country from an allegedly alien and tyrannical regime. Wilson and his advisors did not authorize intervention under the illusion that it had been invited by Bolshevik leaders and would be welcomed by the Soviet government.[10] Wilson did want to avoid making the anti-Bolshevik thrust of the military expedition obvious and explicit, but it was implicit from the beginning.[11]

After an anti-Bolshevik government assumed power in Archangel in August, Wilson opposed British interference in politics there. However, he believed that support for the northern government against the Soviet regime did not constitute illegitimate intervention in Russia's internal affairs. When few Russians volunteered for military service at Archangel, Wilson was disappointed, and when foreign intervention seemed to be helping the Bolsheviks strengthen their control of central Russia, he tried to hold American forces back from any further drives into the Russian interior. Thus, Wilson tried to limit the scope of Allied intervention, particularly after it appeared to backfire, but he was neither unsympathetic to British hopes for an anti-Bolshevik national revival nor unaware of British plans to link the north Russian and Siberian theaters.[12] The Archangel expedition was not simply a result of cunning Allied leaders manipulating innocent and ignorant Americans into a misadventure. Wilson and his advisors wittingly acquiesced in the Arctic intervention in part because they hoped to encourage the resurrection of responsible republicanism and accelerate the demise of Bolshevik despotism. In this light, American intervention in north Russia can be seen as a part of the broader U.S. policy toward the Russian Civil War rather than a peculiar aberration from Wilsonian principles.

Early Proposals for Intervention, November 1917–March 1918

Even before the Kerensky government fell, British and American officials began recommending foreign intervention in Russia to help restore political stability and rebuild military forces. On the first day of November 1917, a British high commissioner suggested to President Wilson that he might consider sending U.S. troops to Russia. On November 6, after reporting that Bolsheviks were preparing a demonstration in Petrograd, Ambassador Francis inquired what Washington officials would think of "sending two or more army divisions via Vladivostok or Sweden" to Russia's aid if he could get the Russian government to consent or make such a request. Francis thought that the "moral effect of American troops on Russian front" would be beneficial, "as millions of sensible Russians only need encouragement to organize."[13]

Francis's cable did not trigger any immediate action by Washington, but it contained two ideas that would be central to American thinking about intervention in Russia over the following months. First, Wilson and many of his key advisors would develop increasing faith in the notion that sending American soldiers to Russia could inspire "sensible Russians" to expunge defeatist radicalism, retake control of their destinies from German agents, and revive their country's fighting spirit. Implicit in this notion was the illusory assumption that in Russia, as in America, there was a large body of sober citizens that could be mobilized through patriotic appeals to squelch an ignoble, disloyal minority. A second, related expectation was that the presumed democratic majority could in some way signal its consent to foreign intervention in its behalf.

Until March 1918, when the Soviet regime under duress accepted harsh German peace terms, proposals for expeditions to Russia focused mainly on possible action through Siberia. After Bolshevik leaders signed the Treaty of Brest-Litovsk and Germany launched a new offensive in the west, Allied leaders gave more attention to the idea of intervention in north Russia. On March 18, Foreign Secretary Balfour suggested to Wilson that "since Russia cannot help herself she must be helped by her friends," and that such help could be supplied through Russia's northern ports, as well as Siberia.[14]

The Wilson administration did want to help Russia to help herself. Despite the Bolshevik seizure of power, Secretary of State Lansing commented on January 6, Americans remained confident that "the spirit of democracy continues to dominate the Russian people." They still had faith that the "democratic impulse" would lead Russia to "a stable government and to the protection of individual rights and an orderly national life." The United States therefore desired to render assistance, "provided its aid is acceptable to the Russian people," Lansing added four days later.

In a similar spirit, Wilson announced in his Fourteen Points speech his desire "to assist the people of Russia to attain their utmost hope of liberty and ordered peace." [15]

However, as Wilson told his press secretary in February, the United States could not "interfere with the form of government in any other government. That would be in violent contradiction of the principles we have always held, earnestly as we should wish to lend every moral influence to the support of democratic institutions in Russia." In early 1918, administration officials felt themselves limited to hoping for "a change for the better to be brought about without foreign intervention." [16]

If Russians themselves initiated a change of government, though, the United States could come to their assistance. This was the implicit thrust of a new appeal Wilson made to the Russian people over the heads of Soviet leaders on March 11. Although the United States was unhappily not yet in a position to render direct and effective aid, Wilson assured "the people of Russia" that his government would "avail itself of every opportunity that may offer to secure for Russia once more complete sovereignty and independence in her own affairs." [17]

The Congress of Soviets sarcastically responded in kind, expressing "to all peoples perishing and suffering from the horrors of imperialistic war its warm sympathy and firm belief that the happy time is not far distant when the laboring masses of all countries will throw off the yoke of capitalism and will establish a socialistic state of society." Wilson's statement evoked more enthusiastic responses from Russians outside Soviet territory. Patriotic Russian societies in Paris appreciated the message. The Provisional Government's ambassador to France approved of it. And a Russian count told the U.S. ambassador in Paris that "the President's words would have a lasting effect in their encouragement to the more thoughtful Russian people which class still was in large majority." [18]

While many influential non-Bolshevik Russians remained anxious about Japanese intervention in Siberia, they favored American intervention to help the Russian people free themselves from Soviet rule. In early March, for example, the State Department received a letter from Leo Pasvolsky, editor of *Russkoye Slovo*, who argued that because of the Bolshevik usurpation of power and German intervention in Russian internal affairs, the Constituent Assembly could not meet without Western aid and protection. If the United States helped Russians to convene the assembly, however, Pasvolsky predicted that it "would become a political center around which all the constructive elements in the country would flock." [19]

Although Ambassador Bakhmeteff opposed solitary Japanese intervention in Siberia for the sake of Allied strategic interests, he told State Department officials that he approved of intervention in Russia if U.S. troops participated and the operations pursued not "a military end but a political one." In a March 5 statement that foreshadowed Wilson's explanation of his decision to intervene in July 1918, Bakhmeteff excluded "every thought of creating a military front against Germany" and urged that intervention should assist "national elements of Russia in their endeavor of consolidation and organization." Military forces should be followed by economic assistance, Bakhmeteff suggested, and to reduce Russian fears of foreign intervention, "the action should be preceded by a joint declaration of the Allies" expressing their friendly purpose.[20]

The suggestions from Bakhmeteff and Pasvolsky harmonized with the Wilson administration's desire to assist Russia, but Wilson had yet to see a practical way to render that service. In July, Wilson's *aide-mémoire* would parallel each of Bakhmeteff's recommendations, but in March the Allied proposals for intervention involved undesirable reliance on Japanese forces, and Wilson was not yet convinced that Russians would embrace Allied military expeditions.

Intervention by Invitation?

In the first months of 1918, Allied officials sought to persuade their American counterparts that the Russian people — at least "all the orderly elements" — would welcome foreign aid against "anarchy" and German oppression. Perhaps in part because they had been surprised by the extent of nationalist resistance to American intervention in Mexico between 1914 and 1916, U.S. leaders required more definite assurances that Russians desired America's help. As Wiseman noted on March 15, the president wanted to see "a sympathetic reply from some body of opinion in Russia." With Lansing and House taking similar positions, the British ambassador, Lord Reading, reported that the Americans were making Russian assent to intervention an indispensable feature of American policy.[21]

Although the British special representative in Moscow, R. H. Bruce Lockhart, had been reporting that Trotsky opposed Japanese intervention in Siberia, in March it suddenly appeared that Trotsky took a different view of Allied intervention in north Russia. In late February and early March, while the German army was advancing through European Russia, Finnish White Guards allied with Germany seemed to menace the railway line between Petrograd and Murmansk. Given this threat, the local Murmansk Soviet asked the central Soviet government whether it should accept assistance from Allied warships and missions. Believing that both Petrograd and Murmansk were in danger, Trotsky wired the Murmansk Soviet: "You must accept any and all assistance from the Allied missions and use every means to obstruct the advance of the plunderers."[22]

Washington learned of this development when Lt. Hugh Martin, an assistant U.S. military attaché, cabled that several hundred British marines had landed at Murmansk, and that he had seen "a telegram from Trotsky approving of concerted action." After attending meetings between Murmansk Soviet leaders and Allied officers, Martin reported that Allied forces planned "to cooperate with red army in defense of Murmansk" and that "American aid would be most welcome."[23]

Wilson and his advisors did not jump to accept the reported invitation from Trotsky. On April 2, Basil Miles noted that over two weeks earlier the British, who had landed troops in the north "with the full consent and approval of Trotsky," had requested an American warship at Murmansk. Wilson warily agreed to have a warship sent to Murmansk, if one was available nearby. While he desired to seem cooperative to his allies, he did not want to sacrifice resources needed for the war against Germany, and he feared being drawn into a morass.[24]

Although the Soviet government had bowed in March to German demands for huge cessions of land and resources, in the spring the German army remained the nearest and greatest threat to Bolshevik hopes to hang on to power while waiting for revolution to spread to Germany and beyond. Hence, Lenin as well as Trotsky considered Allied aid desirable in case of a new German attack and even the mere prospect of Allied intervention seemed useful as a counterweight to German pressure. Throughout April the Wilson administration received conflicting information about the Soviet attitude toward Allied intervention. On April 2 came word that Trotsky and the new commissar for foreign affairs, Chicherin, had said that since Russia was involved in a life and death struggle with Germany she would welcome help from the Allies, as long as they promised not to support anti-Bolshevik groups and sent troops to escort Japanese forces in Siberia. Wilson found nothing "at all persuasive" in this and other papers he returned to Lansing on April 4. Soon thereafter, Trotsky reportedly gave orders "to resist the invasion" of Japanese and British soldiers at Vladivostok. Lord Reading, who relied on Wiseman's more intimate contacts with House and Wilson, thought this news would "serve to harden" American opposition to Japanese intervention unless there was a "request from Russian Government for this assistance."[25]

The views of the Soviet government actually carried more weight with House than with Wilson. House concurred with British officials that the possibility "to get Trotzky [sic] and his associates to agree" to Allied intervention altered the situation. Changing American domestic conditions influenced House's shift. His earlier concern that military intervention in Russia would divide Americans, reduce support for Wilson, and lessen enthusiasm for the war had diminished. He was becoming increasingly confident in the unity of Americans, "even the socialists and pacifists," behind Wilson's crusade against German militarism. On April 24, therefore,

House advised Wilson: "Balfour has sent an entirely new proposal regarding Russia—one that I think you will approve."[26]

The pragmatic House underestimated Wilson's aversion to shaking hands with men like Trotsky. Although Wilson agreed on April 25 to reconsider the problem of intervention in Russia "viewed by the new light upon it," he was anxious to avoid being led "into a trap by Trotzsky." Even if Trotsky honestly favored Allied intervention, Wilson thought Trotsky's power was ebbing and doubted whether he was fully authorized to speak for the Soviet government. An even more important source of Wilson's anxiety about cooperating with the Bolsheviks was his expectation that CPI agent Edgar Sisson would soon arrive from Russia with documents which would prove that Trotsky and Lenin were paid agents of Germany.[27]

Whatever interest Wilson and his advisors may have had in a Soviet invitation was quickly submerged by a new wave of reports that the slippery Trotsky was "losing his influence." As British and German leaders grew more and more impatient with Soviet maneuvers it became increasingly difficult for Bolsheviks to balance the "imperialists" against each other. By May 1, Wiseman confessed that he doubted the feasibility of "an invitation from Trotsky," since Germans would in response "probably turn his government out of Moscow and Petrograd." A few days later the Bolshevik leadership decided to tilt toward resisting the Allies and yielding to German ultimata.[28]

As the prospects for intervention by invitation from Trotsky dimmed, Lansing and Wilson saw more friction and hostility than possibilities for cooperation with the Soviet regime. In early May Lansing thought the Bolshevik government was seeking the withdrawal of British troops from Murmansk, and he complained that the Bolsheviks would not permit Washington to send cipher messages to its representatives in Russia. In general, Reading commented, "The view here is that the Bolshevik Govt. wishes to pick a quarrel with the U.S.G.," and recent developments had not encouraged "the President to believe in Trotzsky's good intentions towards Allies." Even without the latest irritations, Reading sadly informed London, Wilson still would have declined the British proposals for intervention at Archangel and Vladivostok because "the moment was not opportune" and he was not convinced "that a sufficient military advantage would be gained."[29]

With Reading's persistent lobbying beginning to annoy Wilson, French ambassador Jusserand tried a new approach. At the White House on May 8, Jusserand explained that the French wanted to abandon the idea of an appeal for intervention from the Bolsheviks. Focusing on anti-Bolshevik rather than Bolshevik opinion, Jusserand asserted that "the most influential Russians, originally hostile" to foreign intervention, "now recommend it." Hence, there was hope that an inter-Allied expedition would be well received by Russians and "it would be easy to advance far into the interior."[30]

Ambassador Francis seconded that assessment. The general dissatisfaction with Bolshevik rule he observed on a trip to Moscow encouraged him to believe that the "majority of Russian people would welcome Allied intervention." There was still a possibility that the Soviet regime would "request Allied assistance," but Francis urged that "Allied intervention should not be delayed," regardless of the Soviet attitude.[31]

Just at this moment, with attention turning toward the reception by non-Bolshevik Russians and away from the reaction of the Soviet regime, Wilson's suspicions about the Bolsheviks were reinforced by the arrival of long-awaited evidence that they were German agents. CPI Director George Creel apprised Wilson on May 9 that Sisson had returned from Russia with original documents from Bolshevik headquarters in Petrograd that were "absolutely conclusive, and contribute the most amazing record of double-dealing and corruption." That night Sisson's report was placed in Wilson's hands.[32]

Although the Wilson administration waited until September 1918 to publish the Sisson Documents, the information from Creel and Sisson, combined with reports that anti-Bolshevik Russians desired Allied intervention, appears to have made the president more receptive to proposals for military expeditions to north Russia. After meeting with Wilson on May 10, Lansing was able to give Reading some good news the following morning. Since intervention in northern Russia did not involve the "racial difficulty" in Siberia, there was more reason to hope that people in north Russia would welcome Allied forces. Intervention in the north would also receive more favorable consideration, Lansing said, because Americans "could understand the military advantage" of action closer to Europe. The secretary was more dubious about getting an invitation from the Bolsheviks. To clear up this question, Reading requested an expression of Wilson's views on whether such an invitation "was not advisable."[33]

To the frustration of the frantic Allies, Wilson showed no eagerness to take up this issue. Before the president offered any response, Lansing told Reading that he "could see no objection to securing a request from Trotsky that we should intervene via Murmansk," where there was no strong anti-Bolshevik force available as an alternative. However, he advised Wilson that he was "not sure that this is expedient in view of the uncertainty of Trotsky's power." Lansing more firmly opposed acting upon a request from Trotsky for intervention in Siberia, because that "would array us against [Cossack leader] Semenoff and the elements antagonistic to the Soviets."[34]

The widening civil war in Russia made it increasingly difficult to envision intervening in a neutral way and posed more sharply than before the question of which Russians the United States wanted to support. Lockhart advised the Allies to work with the Bolsheviks. Although Lenin's one ambition was to protect "the system of Soviet organization," which he thought would "be adopted in the future by the whole of Europe," this revolutionary was a ruthless *realpolitiker* who acknowledged that Russian and Allied interests were similar as long as they were faced by the German danger. Hence, Lockhart suggested, if the Allies assured Lenin they would not try to overthrow the Soviet government, there was a good chance that Lenin would cooperate against the Germans.[35]

Lockhart's recommendation clashed with the preponderant sentiment among U.S. officials in Russia and Washington. Whether Lenin and Trotsky were dupes of the kaiser or not, they were not going to cling to power much longer, according to dispatches that reached Wilson and Lansing on May 21. Military attaché Ruggles advised that although it was still "very desirable" to gain Bolshevik consent to Allied intervention, that was "not now considered of vital importance due to increasing opposition of workmen[,] peasants." Ambassador Francis agreed that "opposition to Bolshevik domination [was] increasing" and cited a French officer's view that "Bolshevism is dead." In the same week Postmaster Burleson asked Tumulty to show Wilson a *Baltimore Sun* editorial which argued that "the Bolsheviki cannot hold on and we cannot help them to hold on." What Russia needed, the *Sun* argued, was "a rallying point and true democratic leaders" who would give "a hearty welcome" to foreign intervention.[36]

Although British representatives continued to suggest that the Bolsheviks would wink at Allied intervention in north Russia, Lansing advised Wilson that those messages did not "present facts or arguments sufficient to warrant a change in our present policy." While some ambiguity remained about the Bolshevik attitude toward foreign intervention, Wilson expressed his deep distrust of the Bolsheviks quite unambiguously in an interview with the British ambassador on May 22. Wilson thought Trotsky might be amenable at one moment to Allied intervention, Reading informed the Foreign Office, "but President regards him as absolutely untrustworthy. . . . The President's expression was that the only certainty in dealing with such a man was that he would deceive you." While Wilson was not interested in an invitation from the despicable Trotsky, he was by then prepared to approve a limited intervention in northern Russia. Like Lansing, Wilson distinguished "between intervention in Siberia and intervention to protect Murmansk and Archangel."[37]

On May 26, General Tasker Bliss informed Washington that his colleagues on the Supreme War Council (SWC) were probably going to approve an occupation of the ports of Murmansk and Archangel by the British navy and four to six British, French, and possibly American battalions. Bliss planned to vote in favor of the proposal, "unless instructed to the contrary," because he believed there was a "pressing danger to these ports." He also believed that military intervention in Russia would not encounter the resistance it would have met a few months earlier, since "all opposition parties are unanimous in demanding foreign action against Germany." While patriotic Russians would cheer Allied forces, Bliss thought the Bolsheviks would probably acquiesce rather than fight.[38]

Within two days Wilson approved the idea of military action in north Russia to protect military stockpiles, divert German forces, and encourage pro-Ally Russians to organize. On May 28, Secretary of War Baker and Chief of Staff March relayed Wilson's reply to Bliss: the president was "heartily in sympathy with any practical military effort which can be made at and from Murmansk or Archangel." Responding to Bliss's concern about an Allied desire to reimpose "the old regime" in Russia, Wilson stipulated that Allied expeditions should be predicated "upon the sure sympathy of the Russian people and should not have as their ultimate object any restoration of the ancient regime or any other interference with the political liberty of the Russian people."[39]

It is improbable that Wilson had the Bolsheviks in mind when he expressed concern about the sympathy of the Russian people. At the moment Wilson authorized intervention in north Russia, the administration received new accusations of a German-Bolshevik conspiracy. On May 27, the State Department learned that Ambassador Francis saw daily "evidences that [the] Soviet government submits to German demands without protest," and was "almost convinced that Lenin and possibly Trotsky are pliable tools if not responsive German agents." The next day Lansing handed Wilson a letter from Russian expert George Kennan, who argued vehemently against recognizing, aiding, or cooperating with the Bolsheviks, "even if they make a show of fighting the Germans." There was "no good reason for believing in the sincerity of the Bolsheviki when they assume an anti-German attitude," Kennan wrote. The Bolsheviks had "been playing into the hands of the Germans ever since they acquired power," and "they number[ed] in their ranks hundreds of pro-Germans and German agents."[40]

Beyond the issue of German-Bolshevik ties, Kennan made the case for intervention on behalf of Russian democracy. The Bolsheviks' authority, he argued, was "not recognized by anything like a majority of the Russian people; they obtained what power they have by criminal violence, and they are retaining it by a system of terrorism which prevents the majority of the nation from giving expression to its will." Hence, the United States "should not hesitate to take sides against the Bolsheviki." Allied intervention in Russia would not be "a case of taking the side of one 'faction' against another faction, it is a case of taking the side of a majority of the Russian people against a minority of criminal usurpers."[41]

The advice from Kennan and Francis, combined with Wilson's suspicion of Bolshevik duplicity, makes it very unlikely that when Wilson agreed to send American soldiers to north Russia he was significantly influenced by a belief that Trotsky had invited such action.[42] Reports from Russia may have led Wilson to believe that the Bolsheviks were too weak to resist Allied intervention, but he was not seeking to cooperate with them. The president did not need an invitation from the Soviet regime to reconcile intervention in Russia with his commitment to the principle of self-determination because he believed that the Bolsheviks had stolen power from the rightful democratic government and did not truly represent the Russian people. Regardless of whether they were being paid by Germany, Lenin and Trotsky were not patriotic Russians but treacherous ideologues whose only allegiance was to an international revolution.[43]

The view of the Bolsheviks as German agents became increasingly popular as the administration resolved its doubt about intervention in north Russia and Siberia. Edgar Sisson illustrated the appeal of the conspiracy theory to policymakers facing a complicated situation. "The moment we base an analysis upon the fact that the present leaders of the Russian Bolsheviki government were installed by Germany for German use against the nations at war with Germany," Sisson observed at the end of May, "every previous confusion falls into its orderly place. We know what we face, and thereby it is easier to decide what to do." Instead of "courting the present Bolsheviki leaders," Sisson urged the rescue of "the Russian people from their present control." The United States should call "upon Russians themselves to rise and stand with us against their German masters and against such Bolsheviki leaders as are servants of those German masters."[44]

Like Sisson and Kennan, Butler Wright, the former counselor of the embassy in Petrograd, refuted the notion that it was dangerous to intervene "without the invitation — or at least the tacit acquiescence — of the present 'Bolshevik' *de facto* authorities." Wright had departed from Russia via Siberia in March 1918, and by June he was working at the State Department. As the highest-ranking American diplomat to return from Russia, Wright had considerable influence on State Department Russian policy in the late spring and early summer of 1918. In a June 3 memorandum, Wright argued that it was increasingly evident that the Soviet authorities "are not representative of the will of the people; and, whether or not they are directly in the pay of Germany, they are solely Maximalist Internationalists, without the slightest conception of *patriotism*." Consequently, it mattered little "whether their invitation or acquiescence is obtained." Instead, the Allies should look to the "better elements" of the population, who were "seeking for a nucleus about which to rally and ultimately create a government worthy of recognition."[45]

Instead of distinguishing whether the Bolsheviks were German agents or international revolutionaries, Wright, like Sisson and others in Washington, treated both points as counts in an indictment of Bolshevik illegitimacy. As Wright confidentially and colorfully explained, "the German odor" was part of the "almost wholly *circumstantial* evidence" that guided State Department policy. The "stench" of German intrigue, the sense that the Bolsheviks were "losing ground and growing 'panicky,'" and the belief that Russia was "becoming nauseated after its debauch" together led Wright to conclude "that any one who can give them Bromo Seltzer will be welcome." Idealistic Americans were best fitted to give that aid, Wright believed, since "we have a better brand of Bromo Seltzer than any one else."[46]

Although Wilson did not comment in early June on the Bolsheviks' relations with Germany, two decisions he made on June 10 showed that he did not think the Soviet regime worthy of recognition and that he hoped other elements might create a new government. The Soviet government had announced that it was nominating a representative to serve in Washington and promote "intimate friendship between our peoples." Ambassador Francis advised Washington to ignore this communication, and Wilson concurred. In addition, Wilson authorized Francis to announce, upon the abdication or removal of the Soviet government, that the United States would "recognize a government" which seemed "representative of the people of Russia."[47]

As Wilson and his advisors looked beyond the Bolsheviks for signs of a resurgence of Russia's democratic spirit, representatives of the former Provisional Government, Russians in exile, and Allied leaders encouraged the administration to believe that a U.S. expedition would help to mobilize anti-Bolshevik forces. On June 10, Ambassador Bakhmeteff gave Lansing a resolution by the Kadet Party that called for intervention against the Bolsheviks and on the side of Russian democracy. Ten days later, Wilson received a petition signed by former officials of the Provisional Government, leaders of cooperatives, writers, and others. They argued that since Bolshevik tyranny prevented people in Soviet Russia from expressing their opinion, it was the duty of Russians who were abroad to request foreign intervention. If the Allies sent troops, they would "constitute a sound nucleus around which those Russians may gather who desire as far as they are able to help the Allies."[48]

On July 3, Lord Reading passed on to Wilson a Supreme War Council resolution, drafted by British leaders, which argued "that the best Liberal and Democratic elements in Russia are beginning to lift their heads and to get into touch with one another," partly because of "disgust with autocratic methods of the Bolshevists," and partly because of "growing fear of German domination." Although Wilson could not be that candid or explicit, he espoused similar hopes the next day. In a Fourth of July address, Wilson lamented that "the people of Russia" were "for the moment unorganized and helpless," but implicitly expressed the wish that Russians would follow the liberating example of the American Revolution and achieve independence from their temporary overlords.[49]

By the beginning of July tensions in northern Russia had reached a breaking point. Local Russian leaders in Murmansk who embraced one hundred American sailors and accepted larger British contingents were denounced as outlaws by Lenin and Chicherin. The State Department received clear evidence that additional Allied forces would not be welcomed by the Bolshevik regime in Moscow or its representatives in north Russia. On June 24 came word that the top Soviet commissar in Archangel had announced "that the arrival of a foreign warship, especially with an armed crew, . . . will be regarded as commencement of military operations which may lead to serious consequences." In forwarding this news, Consul Felix Cole mentioned that he had advised the British to withdraw "until entry can be made with a sufficient strength to guarantee quick certain occupation." On the same day, the State Department learned that Foreign Commissar Chicherin had requested Allied vessels to leave the northern ports. Lansing directed Francis to make no reply and take no action regarding Chicherin's request.[50]

Chicherin feared that an unopposed Allied invasion of north Russia would provoke a German-Finnish counterattack on Russian territory. He also knew that German leaders required proof of Soviet resistance to the Allies before Germany would be responsive to Soviet needs for grain from Ukraine and security against Germany's Finnish and Cossack allies. On June 24 Chicherin urged War Commissar Trotsky to shift troops from the western front against Germany to the northern front against an impending English attack. On July 12 Chicherin protested to Consul General Poole against American representatives' signature of a treaty with the "mutinous" Murmansk Soviet for the purpose of organizing "an armed incursion of foreign forces into Russian territory." At the end of July Chicherin warned Poole that any foreign ship attempting to dock at White Sea ports "will be fired upon." Poole acknowledged Chicherin's notes and relayed them to his superiors.[51]

If the Wilson administration's approval of the Allied expedition to Archangel had hinged on a belief that the Bolshevik government had invited it, the information it received in June and July should have dispelled any illusions and caused the administration to reconsider. Instead of being surprised by the idea of Bolshevik resistance, Washington decided to ignore it, and preparations for intervention went forward. On August 2 the

State Department learned from Francis that the Allied flotilla then sailing into Archangel would "be resisted if Bolsheviks [are] still in control." Francis urged expediting the dispatch of U.S. troops who would arrive a month later.[52]

As Wilson's decision to intervene in north Russia was carried out in the summer of 1918, he repeatedly expressed his lack of interest in cooperative relations with the Bolsheviks. "I don't think you need fear any consequences of our dealings with the Bolsheviki," he assured one senator on July 24, "because we do not intend to deal with them." Two weeks later, Wilson reiterated his view that "the Russian people . . . have no government." And on August 14, he explained that "after the revolution [of March 1917], the Government of the United States recognized the revolutionary government and received its Ambassador [Boris Bakhmeteff] here," but the United States had "recognized no subsequent government in Russia" and did not accept the government of Lenin and Trotsky.[53] Thus as the American expeditionary force moved toward Archangel, Wilson did not believe U.S. troops would aid the Bolsheviks. Instead, he hoped American soldiers could assist the reemergence of representative and patriotic Russians who had been submerged since the Bolsheviks seized power.

Limited Intervention to Restore Democracy

In April 1914, convinced that the Mexican dictator Huerta had been propped up by foreign interests and was on his last legs, Wilson authorized a limited military intervention at Veracruz to help the people of Mexico reestablish an authentic government. In the summer of 1918, convinced that the expiring Bolsheviks had betrayed Russian interests and obstructed Russian self-government, Wilson approved a limited Allied intervention to restore rather than contradict the process of self-determination. If American and Allied troops could secure base areas around the northern ports where anti-Bolsheviks could congregate, he believed, they would be helping and liberating the Russian people instead of interfering in their internal political affairs.

Wilson articulated this conception of intervention on July 16 when he drafted a confidential statement to the Allies of the limits and purposes of American action in north Russia and Siberia. While Wilson opposed Allied hopes for an aggressive "military intervention" to re-create an eastern front against Germany because that would "be merely a method of making use of Russia, not a method of serving her," he approved the creation of a security zone where Russian democracy could be regenerated. "The only legitimate object for which American or Allied troops can be employed," Wilson declared, "is to guard military stores which may subsequently be needed by Russian forces and to render such aid as may be acceptable to the Russians in the organization of their own self-defence." By making "it safe for Russian forces to come together in organized bodies in the north," Wilson hoped to test the capacity of the Russians for self-government and the formation of military forces. If they established order and showed good morale, they might merit further support. But Wilson warned that the United States "can go no further than these modest and experimental plans." He specifically excluded the possibility of using large numbers of American soldiers to push through Soviet territory and attack the Germans on the eastern front. To allay possible Russian concerns, Wilson called on his Allies to join him in abjuring "any interference of any kind with the political sovereignty of Russia" and promising that they had "the single object" of helping "the Russian people in their endeavour to regain control of their own affairs."[54]

Wilson's pronouncement thus echoed his expressions of a desire "to assist the people of Russia to attain their utmost hope of liberty and ordered peace" in his Fourteen Points speech and his March 11 message to the people of Russia. As in those previous statements, on July 16 Wilson looked beyond the Bolshevik regime to the Russian people. He did not say that the Soviet government had invited foreign intervention. Instead, he declared that intervention was "in the interest of what the Russian people themselves desire."[55]

Since the Russian ambassador in Washington, Boris Bakhmeteff, had urged that the United States intervene to render a political service rather than to pursue the selfish military interests of the Allies, he sympathized with the gist of Wilson's statement, which was released to the press on August 3. As Bakhmeteff later reminisced, he "was very much opposed" to the idea of forcing the Russian people back into the war against Germany, but he favored "intervention of a different kind." Seeing signs of "spontaneous outbursts of anti-Bolshevik revolt," Bakhmeteff advised that if American troops were sent to establish "a political beachhead," then "there would be a ground where the nationalist elements in Russia could . . . organize, where they could form an army, and where they could fight Bolshevism if it were necessary." Bakhmeteff recommended "this mild form of intervention" in conversations with Wilson's advisors early in the summer of 1918. Although Bakhmeteff thought Wilson's *aide-mémoire* was "a rather vague statement," he was pleased that it expressed a desire "to give an opportunity for national consolidation" and "to help the Russian people."[56]

Of course, Wilson did not send American troops to Archangel solely or simply to restore democracy. He also saw some value in guarding the military supplies that the Allies had sent while Russia was still in the war. However, the administration knew that the Soviet government had removed most of the materiel by June 1918, and Wilson did not feel that preservation of the stockpiles was crucial to the defeat of Germany.[57] Wilson noted in his *aide-mémoire* that the supplies might "subsequently be needed by Russian forces," but he refrained from spelling out that they might be needed against Bolsheviks as well as Germans.

The U.S. agreement to an Allied expedition was also influenced by pressure from the British and French, who were frantically seeking ways to keep German forces in the east and who insinuated that Wilson's resistance to military intervention was giving comfort to the enemy.[58] However, Wilson did not accept the Allies' arguments about the possibility of offensive operations from northern Russia in the near future. As Wilson told Reading in March, he believed that "the decision must be on [the] western front," and he reiterated that view to Jusserand in June. On June 24, Chief of Staff March advised Wilson that the Allied plan for intervention in north Russia presented somewhat greater "possibilities from the military standpoint" than the impractical plan for Siberia. But March stressed that "all responsible military opinion believes that the War will be won or lost on the western front, . . . that any substantial diversion of troops from that one object is a serious military mistake," and that none of the Allies would "ever be able to reconstitute Russia into a military machine."[59] When March and Secretary of War Baker conferred with Wilson "about the Murmansk expedition" in July they could not "see the military value of the proposal," so they assumed "that other considerations moved in favor of it." Impressed by his military advisors' counsel, Wilson emphasized in his *aide-mémoire* that intervention in Russia "would be of no advantage whatever in the prosecution of our main design, to win the war against Germany."[60]

Lacking faith in the military utility of the expedition to north Russia, Wilson consented to it largely for political reasons: to appease the Allies and to assist Russian democrats. Viewing Russia as a captive nation, Wilson decided to gamble that foreign troops, especially Americans, would be welcomed as liberators by the Russian people.

On July 19, the State Department received a prescient warning that the odds were against this wager from the consul at Archangel, one of the few U.S. representatives who understood Russian and knew the local conditions. "Intervention can not reckon on active support from Russians," Felix Cole predicted. "All the fight is out of Russia," he explained. "The only men who will fight are a few Red Guards and Red Army men, and their best stomach for fighting is against the *bourgeois* in their own land. Some Russian officers and *bourgeois* volunteers would undoubtedly rally to an Allied anti-Soviet movement but more for their pocketbooks than for Russia or for hate of Germany."[61]

Cole's warning did not cause U.S. officials to change their minds about intervention at Archangel. On July 22, Wilson's final approval of the dispatch of three battalions of American infantry to north Russia was telegraphed to Paris.[62]

Anglo-American Cooperation and Conflict

Long before Wilson and his aides sent U.S. troops to Archangel, they knew that British leaders planned not only to defend that port, but also to drive southeast to link up with Czechoslovakian and anti-Bolshevik Siberian forces. While Wilson tried at times to limit the geographical scope of Allied military action, he also condoned some penetration south from Archangel. The president worried that the British might push too far, too fast, without sufficient participation from Russian forces. But he decided to take that chance, hoping that large numbers of Russians would rally around Allied forces and then gradually liberate territory from Bolshevik and German domination. Hence, while British and American objectives contrasted, they were not as different as black and white.[63]

British and American leaders began to give frequent attention to proposals for action in northern Russia in April 1918. Foreign Secretary Balfour suggested to Lansing in mid-April that while the presence of Allied forces at Russian ports would be of some use in preventing German seizure of military stockpiles there, to keep Germany from transferring divisions to France, the Western powers would also need to create "some definite and important pro-Ally force in Russia." This might be feasible, Balfour ventured, because "a large proportion of the Russian people . . . regard intervention by the Allies as their only hope of rescue from domination by Germany on the one side and from anarchy on the other." Balfour was uncertain then and later about how intervention would affect relations with the Soviet government, but he was clear that securing the northern ports should be only the initial objective, with the creation of a Russian army and the stirring of "a national revival" as ultimate goals.[64]

Balfour's ideas were not utterly repugnant to Wilson. Like Balfour's proposals, Wilson's assent to military action in north Russia in late May was predicated upon evoking an enthusiastic response from Russians. Wilson did not strictly limit his authorization to guard duty "at" the ports. Instead, he explicitly sanctioned military efforts "*from* Murmansk or Archangel," provided that "the Russian people" showed "sympathy" for such campaigns.[65]

Balfour pounced on the news that Wilson was more favorable to intervention in north Russia than in Siberia. In a message the president received on May 31, Balfour argued that it was vital "to retain Murmansk, if we desire to retain any possibility at all of entering Russia," though he also suggested that at least the initial military operations would "only be of ir-regular character." The idea of "entering Russia" did not deter Wilson from reiterating on June 1 that the United States "was entirely willing to send troops to Murmansk."[66]

Two days later, the Supreme War Council (SWC) approved Joint Note 31, which stated that Allied intervention in north Russia was justified, not only by an imminent German threat, but also because "the majority of the Russian parties" had requested Allied occupation of the ports. The Allied representatives did not limit the proposed military action to "the land de-fence of the maritime bases." Instead they specified that Allied forces would also defend "important points on the railway lines leading to those ports," and they argued that occupation of Murmansk and Archangel was "an indispensable corollary of Allied intervention in Siberia." Intervention in the north was necessary, the Joint Note stated quite plainly, to "protect the flanks of the Allied Armies which may eventually operate in Siberia and facilitate and expedite liaison with them." The SWC clearly antici-pated a campaign from Murmansk and Archangel "to penetrate into the heart of Russia in order to watch its political evolution, to keep in touch with the various nationalities and to combat German influence."[67]

This note was signed by the American military representative, General Tasker Bliss, an astute and highly respected officer.[68] It is not plausible that Bliss failed to understand the note and had no idea that it envisioned operations into the interior of Russia.[69] Instead, as Bliss informed Baker and March in July, he felt the Joint Note was in line with the instruction he received that Wilson was "heartily in sympathy with any practical mili-tary effort which can be made at and from Murmansk or Archangel," as long as the "sympathy of the Russian people" was assured.[70]

Before a copy of the Joint Note reached the War Department, the Brit-ish secretary of state for war, Lord Alfred Milner, dispatched a request for larger U.S. forces. Milner gathered that Wilson was favorable to keeping the northern ports under Allied control in order to preserve the "only means of access to European Russia." In the near term, Milner reported, General F. C. Poole expected to "at least make sure of the ports themselves and of the railway lines connecting them at any rate for some distance." Given friendly relations with natives dependent on the Allies for food, there was reason to hope that with the active assistance of local Russians, the "small Allied force may in time become [the] nucleus of [a] larger one."[71]

These features of Milner's message were not a sharp departure from the earlier exchanges between Balfour, Reading, and Wilson. Secretary of War Baker did not raise his eyebrows at Milner's expectation of controlling the region surrounding the ports or his hope to expand the size of the force, though he and March were disturbed by Milner's request to divert more U.S. forces from France to north Russia and place them under British command.[72]

As Wilson pressed for confirmation that the French supreme commander, Marshal Ferdinand Foch, approved the diversion of American troops to Russia, the U.S. military representative in Paris called attention to a crucial point of divergence between Allied and American plans. Bliss clearly understood that the Allies had in mind a "double purpose" of preventing the Germans from using the northern ports as submarine bases and retaining the only open routes for access to central Russia. An "advance from these ports to districts of any allied political importance would be wholly impracticable," Bliss informed March on June 23, unless it was "supported in major part by Russian element." Echoing Wilson's earlier thought that any military effort should proceed only with the support of the Russian people, Bliss recommended that "until definite assurance is had that such assistance will be obtained the allied forces maintained at those ports should be sufficient only for defense" or for destruction of the military stores and port facilities.[73]

On June 27, Ambassador Jusserand produced a telegram from Foch approving the dispatch of American soldiers to Russia because it would not cause an "appreciable diminution of the number of troops to be sent to France." Given this clarification, Wilson promised to give the problem his full attention.[74]

While the president deliberated, on July 2 the British presented to the SWC a resolution carefully crafted to win Wilson's final consent. "Practically all elements of the Russian population," it argued, "except the dwindling minority of Bolshevists, now recognize that intervention of some kind is necessary and inevitable." If the Allies didn't go in, the Germans would. Unless the Allies provided Russian "Liberal and Democratic elements" with military support "and a base upon which to rally, the Reactionary forces, backed by German bayonets, will inevitably crush the movement for national freedom and regeneration." The British paper cleverly played on Wilson's political sympathies, allaying his concern that intervention might restore the tsarist regime by casting monarchists along with Bolsheviks as pro-German. Appealing to Wilson's oft-expressed desire to help the Russian people, the resolution argued that in order to "bring effective assistance to Liberal Russia," the Allies had to "occupy Murmansk and Archangel in order to retain the bridge heads into Russia from the north from which forces can eventually advance rapidly to the centre of Russia." Fostering and assisting "the national movement in Russia" in this way would help "to reform an Eastern front or at least to sustain a vigorous spirit of independence in the occupied territories behind the German line." Thus, the SWC resolution (which the French and Italian representatives approved) made it clear that the purpose of Allied intervention would be both anti-Bolshevik and anti-German.[75]

Reading gave Wilson the complete text of the SWC paper on July 3. Although the resolution mentioned a rapid advance "to the centre of Russia," linked action in north Russia to action in Siberia, and betrayed British hopes for future "additions of Allied forces," it did not spark any outbursts from Wilson.[76]

On July 6, Wilson learned from Bliss that Sir Eric Geddes, First Lord of the Admiralty, had reported to the SWC that the British commander at Murmansk, General Poole, wanted — besides the three thousand troops he already had — "six *additional* battalions" in order to be able "to take possession of Archangel" as soon as the ice cleared. "With this force as a nucleus," Poole believed that he could "rally one hundred *thousand* Russian troops between Archangel and Vologda inclusive." British military planners plainly envisioned the possibility that the Allied expedition might "proceed inland with considerable American forces." Although Bliss may have indicated some personal reservations with the italics, he recommended American concurrence.[77]

Wilson discussed this latest proposal with the British ambassador on July 8. When Reading remarked that "Murmansk was quite a small matter," Wilson replied that "it was small at present but in view of Sir Eric Geddes's memorandum it was a very risky proceeding and . . . although it might be advisable to take the risk we must be prepared to support the troops there and no one could say what this might mean both in men and supplies." The president was clearly aware of, and anxious about, the open-endedness of the British proposal. But he was willing to take a chance in the hope that enough Russians would rally to the Allied banners to make the venture a success.[78]

Wilson was very busy in the spring and summer of 1918. He had to decide many other questions besides intervention in Russia and, as he told House, his "over-burdened mind" mind was "becoming 'leaky.'"[79] Wilson may have had difficulty remembering the details of proposals for action in north Russia. However, he would have to have been a very careless reader to have missed the repeated mention of military action inside Russia, not just at the ports themselves.

While Wilson may have forgotten later about aspects of the proposals, at the time he responded to specific language they contained. On July 2, Balfour argued that "an adequate military force must be employed," then repeated that it was "imperative that force shall be adequate in number and in character." Two weeks later, Wilson replied in his *aide-mémoire* that the United States was "not in a position . . . to take part in organized intervention in adequate force from either Vladivostock or Murmansk and Archangel." Wilson's rejection of providing forces large enough to re-create an eastern front showed that he had read the Allied proposals.[80]

Wilson and his aides recognized the tension between their cautious and patient approach to intervention and the bolder, more ambitious visions of the British. Wilson gambled that he could control his allies and limit the expeditionary forces to indirect, supporting roles while waiting for anti-Bolshevik and anti-German Russian forces to coagulate around the Allied "nucleus." British leaders had less respect for Russian sovereignty and less faith in the Russian people. However, they at least partly shared Wilson's notion of rallying nationalist Russian forces, and by stressing that these elements would be liberal and democratic, the British thought they could get the president's consent. Members of the War Cabinet were also willing to give rhetorical assurances that they would not countenance interfering with Russian self-government or fostering political reaction. Once the American forces were in far-off north Russia, they thought, it would be possible to deploy them in a more direct and aggressive campaign than Wilson had sanctioned. Although the British hoped to bend Wilson to their purposes, they found that he was not pliable. When Reading pressed the cabinet's case for increasing the size of the expeditions, Wilson agreed that the authorized forces "were insufficient to cope with the Russian situation viewed as a military problem but repeated his opinion that it was not possible to send an adequate force there." The president clung to his view of intervention as being not a way of restoring an eastern front against Germany, but a means of "coming to the assistance of Russia."[81] While American and British conceptions of intervention thus differed dramatically, they had a common initial objective of securing the northern ports and promoting the organization of anti-Bolshevik Russians.[82]

"The Murmansk and Archangel plan," as General Bliss observed on July 12, was "a *compromise*" between the American idea of a limited expedition and British plans for more aggressive intervention. Bliss thought that realization of the maximum British objectives would be delayed because "a force large enough to move South" could not be sent in from the outside, "but would have to be raised in the country from friendly Russians." He therefore agreed with his Allied colleagues "upon a small force . . . sufficient to hold the Northern ports during the coming winter," when Russian units would be organized. Bliss believed this program was consistent with the instructions he had received at the end of May, because he assumed "that no military movement from these places to the South can be made if Russians are not sympathetic." Later, harsh words would be fired from Washington to London because Americans believed British commanders did not make sufficient efforts to secure the sympathy of the local population before thrusting southward from Archangel.[83]

On August 18, Bliss wired to Washington a copy of the instructions the War Office issued to the British commander of Allied forces in north Russia. General Poole was informed that his "main object" was "to cooperate in restoring Russia with the object of resisting German influence and penetration, and enabling the Russians again to take the field side by side with their Allies." Specifically, he should try to organize an "armed force to resist the Germans" and support "any administration which may be disposed to be friendly to the Allies." Since it would not be possible to send more troops before winter, full achievement of the Allied objectives depended upon rallying "Russians in sufficient numbers." Poole was not directed to confine his operations to the vicinity of the ports. Instead, he was instructed that his "immediate aim should be to establish communications with the Czechs, and assisted by them probably secure control of the . . . river and railroad lines of communications between Archangel and Viatka." If it was not possible to break through "Bolshevist" forces to link up with the Czechs, Poole was to concentrate on organizing Russian units to help in "the immediate defense of Archangel during the ensuing winter months."[84]

Bliss did not accompany these instructions with any indignant commentary, and he later noted that the directives were "quite in accord with the original intention" of the SWC. The British plans also do not appear to have set off any alarm bells in Washington. They were not totally irreconcilable with a press release the administration issued on August 3 which stated that American troops could be used in operations "*from* Murmansk and Archangel" to aid "Russians in the organization of their own defence."[85]

Wilson may not have seen the War Office instructions to General Poole. He had read earlier plans, including the SWC resolution of July 2, which clearly envisioned an effort to link the north Russian and Siberian theaters. However, in September the president exploded in anger when he learned that Poole had asked Czech troops to advance from near the Ural Mountains to meet Allied forces driving south from Archangel, and that the Czechs were meeting "unexpected and strong resistance." Allied officers who thought they could not rely on mobilizing Russians to augment their forces were already citing the Czechs' heavy losses in calls for reinforcements. "This illustrates in the most striking way," Wilson fumed to Lansing on September 5, "the utter disregard of General Poole and of all the Allied governments . . . of the policy to which we expressly confined ourselves." The Allied campaign had disregarded Wilson's emphasis upon securing the cooperation of the Russian people, had led the Czech Legion into major battles, and had given the Allies leverage to demand more U.S.

troops. In his outrage and alarm at significant direct fighting between foreign forces and Russians, Wilson seemed to forget what he knew earlier about the risks involved in the action to which he consented.[86]

In north Russia, Ambassador David Francis was responsible for implementing U.S. policy. When Francis arrived at Archangel from Vologda in late July, a British officer told him that plans had been made "for a counter revolution" and that it might embarrass both the leaders of the coup and foreign diplomats if they were in Archangel at that time. The ambassador took the hint and left for Murmansk. He returned in August, after anti-Bolshevik forces deposed the local Soviet government and Allied troops occupied Archangel.[87]

Francis detested Bolsheviks. "[I]f these damned bolsheviks are permitted to remain in control of the country," he seethed on August 4, "it will not only be lost to its devoted people but bolshevik rule will undermine all governments and be a menace to society itself." Helping the Russian people to overthrow the Bolsheviks was not, in his view, illegitimate meddling in Russian politics, because he was impartial toward the various anti-Bolshevik factions. "The Russian people are divided between a Monarchy and a Socialistic Republic," he wrote at the end of July, "and I am not interfering in the slightest degree in any way."[88]

Since communication with Washington had been difficult and infrequent, Francis informed Lansing, he had acted according to his best judgment while adhering to "the general line of our policy." Although Francis found the administration's August 3 press release "mystifying on first reading," he pledged "to follow policy outlined when American troops arrive." Privately, Francis struck a wilier pose, confiding to assistant military attaché Hugh Martin that he planned to put his "own construction" on the press release: he intended to permit General Poole to send American troops out to all points where munitions were stored and to aid the Czechoslovaks.[89]

Francis was not as bold and devious as he liked to make out. He used some discretion in interpreting the loose guidelines from Washington, but he was careful to cover himself. In a letter to Lansing on August 27, Francis openly stated his intention to encourage American troops to proceed to Vologda and perhaps even to Petrograd and Moscow, in order to recover war supplies that the Soviet government treacherously transferred from Archangel. "Furthermore," Francis announced, "I shall encourage American troops to obey the commands of General Poole in his effort to effect a junction with the Czecho-Slovaks and to relieve them from the menace which surrounds them; that menace is nominally Bolshevik but is virtually inspired and directed by Germany." This announcement of a potentially very sweeping and aggressive deployment of U.S. forces did not reach

Washington until October 15. In speedier telegrams, Francis revealed less of his ambitious anti-Bolshevik dreams, but he did make it clear that the American units were not simply sitting in Archangel.[90]

On September 2, the State Department received word from Francis that General Poole had used his small initial force to dispatch "expeditions 100 miles south on Vologda Railroad and 200 miles up Dvina River toward Kotlas," but was "awaiting reenforcements before attempting further advance." Among the forces rushed south were twenty-five American sailors, at least one of whom had been wounded. This news did not provoke a protest from Washington.[91]

Anticipating the arrival of three American infantry battalions, Francis wired on September 3: "I do not know what instructions these troops have, but if General Poole asks my approval I shall not object to his sending them to the interior in accordance with objects set forth in the Department's declaration of August 3rd." This telegram reached the State Department on September 6 and arrived at the White House three days later. Although Wilson had denounced Poole's aggressive use of the Czechs on September 5, neither Wilson nor Lansing expressed any perturbation at Francis's indication that U.S. soldiers would be sent south from the White Sea.[92]

Wilson and Lansing *were* disturbed by other information in the cable from Francis, however. The new government at Archangel, headed by an old populist, N. V. Chaikovskii, was utterly dependent on foreign support. It would not have come to power "if Allied forces had not landed," Francis reported; "neither would it survive if Allied troops [were] taken away." Chaikovskii and other moderate socialist leaders of the Supreme Administration of the Northern Region complained profusely to Francis that their power was being undermined by Russian military officers and Allied officials. They were particularly upset by the appointment of a French officer as military governor of Archangel and his order that the militia "arrest anyone accused by a citizen of Bolshevik propaganda." Francis was unsympathetic. He told Chaikovskii "that there was nothing objectionable" in the order; "in fact such is law in America." Yet the ambassador also felt that the Allies were being unnecessarily abrasive. The British disposition to treat the Chaikovskii government contemptuously might invite comparisons to German conduct in Ukraine. In addition to wanting to preserve a moral distinction between the Allied intervention and the German depredation, Francis felt that he had to back Chaikovskii and his naive, impractical colleagues in order to preserve popular support for the Allies in the north. The overthrow of the Chaikovskii regime "would prolong civil dissension, strengthen Soviet Government and Bolsheviks generally, and would injure Allied cause." Since the north Russian government was mobilizing an army to fight Germany, it "should be protected and encouraged." If Russians in the north believed that the Allies came as "conquerors," they would "recklessly resist" rather than join the Allies.[93]

Francis's fear of a coup was warranted. Shortly after midnight on September 5–6, with the complicity of Allied commanders, Russian officers seized the socialistic leaders and sent them to an island on the White Sea. Francis acted quickly to reverse the coup, successfully demanding the return of Chaikovskii and the other ministers. However, he could not undo the damage to the socialists' prestige and to popular confidence in Allied intentions.[94]

On September 9, Lansing called in the chargé of the British embassy, Colville Barclay, to warn that General Poole's attitude was causing the United States considerable concern. Lansing specifically cited the report that "Poole had appointed a French Colonel as Military Governor of Archangel and that the latter had issued an order prescribing the arrest of anyone guilty of Bolshevist propaganda." Although the Wilson administration was then arresting and prosecuting domestic "Bolsheviks," it could not sanction such action being directed by foreigners in Russia. That would cross the line between assistance to Russian self-government and domineering intervention. Lansing explained that U.S. policy "had been consistently to allow Russians to work out their own salvation," and that Washington opposed interference with the local Russian government. Lansing was speaking for Wilson, who "took a serious view" of the matter. In fact, Wilson was so disturbed that he threatened to secede from the expedition. "Unless there was a change in the high handed attitude adopted by General Poole," Barclay reported, the United States "would seriously have to consider the withdrawal of the U.S. contingent from General Poole's command."[95]

What aroused Wilson and Lansing most was the warning from Francis that the Allies' imperialistic arrogance would strengthen the Soviet government and Bolsheviks generally. To avoid such a backlash, Lansing elaborated on September 12, Americans had hoped intervention in north Russia would be "for the purpose of aiding and not of coercing the inhabitants." Hence, they were appalled by Poole's indifference "to the rights and feelings of the Russian communities with which he comes in contact."[96]

These concerns resembled Wilson's stipulation in late May that intervention in north Russia should proceed "upon the sure sympathy of the Russian people." This was consistently the primary condition for American participation. If the British heeded that stipulation, the administration was willing to let American troops be used some distance inside Russia.

On September 11, Lansing and Wilson learned from Francis that after the three American battalions debarked on September 4, they were divided, with one battalion sent down the railroad toward Vologda, one ordered up the Dvina River toward Kotlas, and one assigned to guard duty in Archangel. Neither Wilson nor Lansing protested against the dispatch of American forces into the interior. Conveying the telegram from Francis to Wilson, Lansing commended "the tact and judgment with which Mr. Francis has conducted himself in very trying circumstances." [97]

Particularly trying was the political insensitivity of the British commander. Francis had reiterated his fear that General Poole's "military and colonizing instincts together with his contempt for sovereign government and his general mistrust of Russians will handicap American policy in Russia." Lansing's response to this danger was to suggest to Wilson that the commander of the American forces, Colonel George Stewart, be ordered to consult closely with Francis. Stewart had in fact already called on Francis, although that did not dispel his uncertainty. After he finally received a copy of the August 3 press release on October 5, Stewart underlined the sentence that U.S. troops could be used to render aid to Russians' organization of their self-defense, but neither he nor the navy's top representative received clarification of how supporting Russian self-government should affect relations with the Bolsheviks. Ultimate responsibility for the lack of clear guidance belonged not to Francis or the military staffs in Washington, but to the commander in chief who composed the vague *aide-mémoire*. [98]

While Wilson and Lansing did not object to the forward deployment of American forces in north Russia, Americans did resist pressure in September for additional troops. Bliss opposed a request for five thousand more soldiers because he believed the British were trying to manipulate the United States and their proposal departed from the plan previously approved by the SWC. In mid-September, when the French asked the United States to send five additional battalions to Murmansk, Secretary of War Baker joined Bliss in urging Wilson to refuse that request. [99]

Before ruling on this question, Wilson read two important letters from Bliss. In the first, written on August 22, Bliss, like Wilson, drew a sharp distinction between a friendly expedition to help the Russian people and a direct war against Soviet Russia. Bliss recollected that General Poole had declared "that if he moved south with a small force, . . . he would rally to him en route to Vologda at least 100,000 friendly Russians." If the Russians proved friendly and rallied to Poole, Bliss thought that would be well and good. However, if Russians proved hostile, Poole would, "by continuing his advance, put himself in an attitude of war with Russia." On September 7 Bliss sharpened the contrasts, heightened the sense of danger, and brought the situation up to date. Bliss recalled that if Poole "got the assistance of a sufficient force of friendly Russian volunteers, and also of the Czechs," he was authorized to try to get possession of the railway and river lines to the southeast. If the Russians did not volunteer in sufficient numbers and he could not get in touch with the Czechs, however, "he was then to confine himself to the defense of Archangel during the winter." Since the latter situation had arisen, Bliss told the American representative on Foch's staff that "Poole was engaging in a campaign which we had never contemplated nor recommended and that it was up to him to obey his instructions and confine himself to the defense of the Arctic ports."[100]

Like Wilson, Bliss discerned clear moral imperatives in ambiguous situations. Bliss expected the British commander to be as attentive as he and Wilson were to the difference between rallying Russian forces for a drive down the railroad and river, on the one hand, and an unsupported campaign into the interior by Allied troops, on the other. This distinction was vital because of the potential impact on the Russian people and world opinion.

As Bliss chewed over the situation in north Russia, Major Francis Riggs arrived in Paris with a message from Ambassador Francis urging the sending of reinforcements. Riggs thought that additional forces would allow General Poole to "force himself" from Archangel to more populous regions where he could secure volunteers, get into contact with the Czechs, and as a result "practically conquer Western Russia and re-establish a front against the Germans." If the Allies did not send sufficient forces to reestablish the eastern front, Riggs warned, the Germans would "get a great many recruits out of Russia," in part because of a Russian reaction against the limited intervention. Indignant, Bliss commented: "If we had stayed at Murmansk and Archangel, as I supposed we were to do, we would not have given German propaganda the opportunity of saying that the Allies were engaged in an invasion of Russia with a view to ulterior objects repugnant to the Russian people."

Bliss acutely perceived the central practical and moral dilemmas of American intervention in north Russia. If the United States was to intervene "for the purpose of getting at Germany we must go with a force sufficient for that purpose," he wrote, but that was not feasible because the United States did not have enough shipping to transport and maintain an adequate force. Effective action was also fettered by American moral idealism: "an invasion of Russian [sic] was repugnant to the intentions of the United States." (Bliss did not add that a limited intervention to help anti-Bolshevik Russians organize self-government and self-defense might have the same counterproductive effects as an intervention to restore an eastern front undertaken with insufficient forces.)[101] Wilson shared the suspicions and anxieties vented by Bliss. After carefully reading the general's letter, Wilson informed March "that the judgments expressed are my own also."[102]

Galvanized by the communications from Bliss and Francis, Wilson moved to rein in American operations in north Russia. When he authorized U.S. participation, Wilson had been uncertain about the response of the Russian people, and he conceived of the initial phase of intervention as an "experimental" probe.[103] By the middle of September, the experiment had yielded some firm conclusions.

"What has happened at Kazan in the defeat of the Czecho-Slovaks by the Bolsheviks," Wilson wrote Lansing on September 18, "taken in connection with the latest advices from Archangel, makes the situation in Northern Russia and Siberia quite clear." Wilson was familiar with the British hopes for the Arctic expedition, and he concluded that they were not being realized. General Poole predicted, Wilson recalled, "that large forces of Russians would gather and that the only function of the Allied forces would be to hold Murmansk and Archangel in their rear and see that they were accessible for the shipment of supplies. Not only has this not happened, but . . . they are finding it difficult to make the local authorities function in any independent way, and . . . the situation is not at all what it was anticipated that it would develop into." Wilson had been willing to send American troops to help secure base areas where anti-Bolsheviks could gather and be equipped from military stockpiles. If the Russians had greeted the Allied forces with patriotic enthusiasm and had recovered their military vigor, he might have been willing to continue taking chances. However, since the Russian response was disappointing and the Allies were interfering in internal (non-Bolshevik) Russian politics, Wilson decided to reduce the risks he was running. The United States would not throw any more soldiers into the venture, he informed Lansing. In addition, Wilson wanted the Allies to abandon the more ambitious goals of the Supreme War Council plan and retreat to the minimum objectives that had been specified at Paris and underscored in his *aide-mémoire*. Hence, he asked Lansing to inform the Allies that the United States would not be a party to impractical and unwise attempts to form an eastern front, and that "the most we are ready to do is to assist to hold Archangel or Murmansk, as the exigencies of the winter dictate, until the spring."[104]

After meeting with Lansing and General March on September 25, Wilson announced his decisions about how American forces should be deployed during the approaching winter. The most important factor in Wilson's judgment was his perception that non-Bolshevik Russians had not moved with great energy to organize governments and armies. Since it was plain that "no gathering of any effective force by the Russian[s] is to be hoped for," Wilson decreed, "we shall insist with the other governments, so far as our co-operation is concerned, that all military effort in that part of Russia be given up except the guarding of the ports themselves and as much of the country round about them as may develop threatening conditions." Although Wilson clearly proscribed further use of U.S. soldiers to form a junction with the Czechs, he left some ambiguity about how far inside Russia Americans could be deployed to prevent "threatening conditions" from developing.[105]

Wilson took pains to make it clear that he was not rebuking Ambassador Francis. He asked Lansing to "commend the course [Francis] has taken — a thoroughly American course which I have entirely admired — and impress upon him the fact that we are following, not the course of our choice, but the course of stern necessity." Wilson may have been thinking primarily of Francis's efforts to contain and undo Allied interference in Russian internal affairs. It is also conceivable that, with an eye to domestic political repercussions, Wilson wanted to avoid criticizing the former Missouri governor. Yet Wilson does not seem to have felt any urge to upbraid Francis. It seems very unlikely that the hot-tempered Wilson violently objected to Francis's authorization of the use of American forces in the interior but then completely stifled all expression of his irritation, even in confidential correspondence.[106]

A week later, Wilson did inform Lansing that he had "very serious doubts" about an American-financed legion of Russian troops that Francis wanted to organize. Francis believed that the involvement of American officers in training a Russian battalion would "convince Russians that an army is not inimical to liberty as our government has been model since the revolution [of March 1917] for all democratic Russians except Bolsheviks." Wilson did not disagree with this notion. His objections to the "American Slavic Legion" were practical and pecuniary rather than principled. The president was reluctant to part with the $1.3 million Francis requested. He voiced no moral opposition to financing anti-Bolshevik forces, but thought that sum would "go a very little way," and since the United States could not "supply any more money for such purposes," the Legion would be difficult to sustain. "We cannot maintain an army, our own or another, in Northern Russia, much as we would wish to do so," Wilson concluded, "and while I would wish Francis to know how much we admire the spirit and success with which he has guided matters at Archangel, I think we ought to apprise him very definitely of the limiting facts."[107]

The British and French were not happy with the way Wilson constrained the deployment of American forces in Russia. If the Bolsheviks massacred their opponents, the French ambassador cried to Lansing, the "blood will be on your head, not on ours [!]." Jusserand wrung out of the defensive Lansing an assurance that Wilson would not "take umbrage" if the Allies seized upon a possible "Russian awakening." On October 2, Jusserand extracted a similar concession from Wilson that the United States would not look unfavorably upon Allied efforts to relieve "the danger to the Czechs" and avoid giving "encouragement to the Bolsheviks." The ambassador was unduly optimistic, however, when he declared, "The door remains open to us." For Wilson also expressed to Jusserand his abiding anxiety that the Allies were "entering on a very risky business," and would ask for aid that he would "in conscience not know how to give," though it would "be ghastly . . . to refuse."[108]

While Wilson was drawing back from the riskier aspects of intervention in Russia, he remained willing to cooperate with the Allies in safer, more defensive operations. Even at the height of his anger with British political interference at Archangel, Wilson threatened only to remove American units from British control; he never threatened and does not appear to have contemplated seriously a complete withdrawal of U.S. forces from Russia before ice sealed the port of Archangel for the winter.

By September 1918, increasing confidence in victory over the kaiser offered Wilson an opportunity to argue more convincingly than before that military action in Russia was not necessary to win the Great War. At the end of August, Wilson and his advisors had learned that General John Pershing, commander of American forces in France, believed "the defeat of Germany" was "certain." If Wilson had consented to intervention in Russia only to placate the desperate British and French, he now had a chance to declare that since the German pressure on the Allies had been relieved he was going to bring American boys home from Russia. Since the port of Archangel would not freeze until November, there was still time to order the withdrawal of the U.S. battalions. However, even the specter of Americans being trapped in north Russia and captured by the Bolsheviks did not prod Wilson into ordering their evacuation.[109]

Wilson decided to leave American forces in their snow trenches not only because he needed to show the Allies a cooperative spirit, but also because his goal of helping to restore orderly democracy in Russia harmonized with the minimum objectives of the Allies. On October 3, the president received a Supreme War Council statement of Allied military plans for the fall of 1918 and 1919. This strategic study, signed by General Bliss, declared that the Allied objectives in northern Russia and eastern Siberia were to prevent the Central Powers from exploiting Russian resources; to assist the Czechs; to rebuild an eastern front if circumstances permitted; and, more immediately, "to collect round nuclei of Allied forces all anti-German elements of resistance; to train these elements; to organize them, and so to make them into a force fit to fight against Germany." By this point, Wilson was more concerned with designing terms for German surrender than with organizing armies to defeat the kaiser's minions, but the idea of rallying non-Bolshevik Russian forces around an Allied nucleus was consistent with his *aide-mémoire*. Wilson was also probably relieved that the SWC agreed with him that the extent of military action from Archangel should be restricted, at least for the near future. Passing the SWC paper on to Wilson, General March noted with delight that the Allied military representatives concurred with "the military policy of the United States, with reference to practically every theatre of war." With the British and French seeming to come around to his conception of a limited intervention, Wilson decided to leave the question of Russia to the Paris Peace Conference.[110]

At the scene of intervention, there was still some danger that military operations would exceed the limits Wilson sought to impose. In Archangel, Ambassador Francis confided to General Poole on October 2 that he would "take a very liberal view" of his instructions that U.S. troops were to be used only to defend the country surrounding the port. And Poole still hoped to reach Vologda in order to open up a line to Viatka. But in London the War Office agreed with Wilson and his military advisors that the improved situation on the western front made it unnecessary to press action in Russia. Dispatching General Edmund Ironside to replace Poole, Sir Henry Wilson instructed him, "Your business in North Russia is to hold the fort until the local Russians can take the field."[111]

By restricting the use of American troops in north Russia to the defense of a vaguely defined security zone where Russians could organize, the Wilson administration sought to avoid blatant belligerency toward Soviet Russia. Wilson and his advisors knew that Americans were fighting Bolsheviks but they did not want to admit that fact in public. Francis touched this problem in late August when he wrote Lansing: "The intervention we are now making in Russia is the only intervention we could make without declaring war against Russia, and we cannot do that and be consistent with the position we have maintained — that we consider the Russian people to be our Allies still."[112] A month later, after "Detroit's Own" had been sent into action, Francis inquired as to "whether a state of war exists between the United States and Bolshevik government." In response, the secretary of state declared, "The Government of the United States has never recognized the Bolshevik authorities and does not consider that its efforts to safeguard supplies at Archangel or to help the Czechs in Siberia have created a state of war with the Bolsheviki." While Lansing personally would have preferred a more forthright policy, Wilson insisted upon ignoring the Bolsheviks, even when they were shooting at and being shot by Americans. He stubbornly resisted facing the fact that his objective of making Russia safe for democracy necessarily involved hostilities with the Soviet regime.[113]

British and French officials who were not wedded to the Wilsonian ideal of self-determination failed to appreciate the importance Americans attached to limiting the scope of intervention. Exasperated by Allied pressure to expand the size and sphere of military operations in Russia, General Bliss complained in October: "It seems difficult to make some people here understand that the United States is actuated by any *principle* or that it has any conscientious policy. I think that the reason is that some of them do not believe there is any connection between 'policy' and their conscience."[114]

Like Bliss, Wilson could not divorce moral scruples from military and diplomatic action, and he was loath to acknowledge any contradiction between his principles and his policies. This was one of the primary reasons why, as the British observed in 1919, "The United States Government made a distinction between fighting Russia and being at war with Russia." Wilson insisted upon this fastidious distinction through the end of American military involvement in north Russia. At Paris on June 17, 1919, Wilson asked his fellow heads of state: "Are we at war with Bolshevik Russia?" When Lloyd George pointed out that "British troops are in Archangel," Wilson insisted that "the operations in which Allied troops participated in Russia don't constitute a state of war in the legal sense of the word. There has been no declaration of war."[115]

Immediate Impact of Intervention at Archangel

The Wilson administration restricted the scope of American action in northern Russia not only in obeisance to legal niceties and liberal principles but also because Wilson and his advisors feared that more direct intervention would provoke a nationalistic reaction which might strengthen the positions of the Bolsheviks and Germans. Ironically, however, fear of a massive invasion still pushed Soviet leaders to request secret military assistance from Germany in August, while the limitations on the size and range of the expedition contributed to the other result Washington sought to avoid: the small, ineffective intervention helped the Bolsheviks to consolidate their power.

In the summer of 1918, many Bolshevik leaders despaired of hanging onto power much longer. British special consul Lockhart reported in June, based on conversations with two high Soviet officials, that the Bolsheviks understood that their reign was coming to an end, and that they had decided to go down without compromising themselves by inviting either German or Allied intervention. Similarly, U.S. consul general DeWitt Poole advised Washington: "The Bolsheviks are apparently making preparations for a last stand." At the beginning of August, Captain William B. Webster of the American Red Cross observed that "the feeling in Petrograd is that this Government will not last long, being squeezed to death between British and German pinchers [*sic*]." Webster, whose relief work involved frequent contacts with Soviet officials, reported rumors "that even the Red Guard is ready to turn towards the Allies' side," and that "a ship is standing in harbour with steam up ready to convey the Soviet leaders into a place of safety."[116]

With the Bolsheviks floundering in stormy seas, the Allies tossed them a lifebuoy. The small expeditionary force that sailed into Archangel at the beginning of August was not strong enough to overthrow the Soviet regime by itself, but it gave the Bolsheviks an opportunity to portray their domestic political opponents as collaborators with imperialist invaders. A Bolshevik newspaper in Petrograd, for example, declared on August 8 that anti-Soviet forces, from monarchists to socialists, were "summoning foreign conquerors to help, to restore the bourgeois power," promising concessions in return. Although the paper portrayed the situation as dangerous, it also showed a degree of cockiness, announcing that "the French and the British are unable to send over here any great forces; they are relying on help from our home enemies."[117]

In Moscow, the news that the Allies had landed at Archangel provoked excited reactions. "For several days the city was a prey to rumour," Lockhart remembered. "The Allies had landed in strong force. Some stories put the figure at 100,000. . . . Even the Bolsheviks lost their heads and, in despair, began to pack their archives." Deputy Foreign Commissar Karakhan, whom Lockhart encountered, "spoke of the Bolsheviks as lost," though they would go underground rather than surrender. By August 10, however, the Bolsheviks realized how small the Allied expedition was. That afternoon a relieved, smiling Karakhan assured Lockhart, "The situation is not serious. The Allies have landed only a few hundred men." On August 14 the front page of *Pravda* featured a banner headline proclaiming that the "Archangel invaders" had been smashed in a battle on the river front and that such military successes were bringing smiles to the faces of Red troops. In Lockhart's view, the "direct effect" of landing without sufficient force to reach the capital "was to provide the Bolsheviks with a cheap victory, to give them a new confidence, and to galvanise them into a strong and ruthless organism." At the same time, the weak intervention diminished Allied "prestige among every class of the Russian population."[118]

American diplomats and military officers agreed with Lockhart that the small expedition was counterproductive. In late August, Consul General Poole cabled Washington that the "indecisive tone" of the administration's press statement, which the Bolshevik press published, and the "leisurely nature of advance from the north tend to bolster Bolsheviks up." Since the expedition was "forced by lack of men to stop and await the mobilization and training of Russian troops," assistant military attaché Hugh Martin recalled, "we gave the Bolsheviks time in which to bring up heavy reinforcements and strengthen their positions to such an extent that we were never able to continue their [*sic*] advance." In addition, "the weakness of our intervention gave to the Bolsheviks one of their most powerful weapons of propaganda."[119]

Some Americans had predicted that an anti-Soviet military intervention would backfire. In June 1918, after returning from Russia, journalist William T. Ellis advised Navy Secretary Daniels and President Wilson that "the master word of the bolsheviks is 'counter revolution.' Whenever they can persuade the people that the revolution is menaced, and that there is a danger of a return to anything like the old order, then they may be sure of the support of the masses." Allied military intervention, Ellis warned, "would give the bolsheviks the best excuses for reasserting their leadership."[120]

Wilson tried to ensure that Allied intervention would be in sympathy with the Russian people and not for restoring the old order, but by September 1918 there was reason to believe that Ellis's prophecy was being fulfilled. On September 22, Albert Rhys Williams, a Congregationalist minister who enlisted in the Bolshevik cause in Petrograd in 1917, gave Colonel House a memorandum which argued that Allied intervention in Russia had caused the Bolsheviks to "become bitterly hostile and sullen. Revolutionary fanaticism has been driven deeper into their spirits and the class antagonism . . . is stronger than before." This led Williams to conclude that either a massive direct invasion or complete nonintervention would be wiser than limited intervention.[121]

Although Major Allen Wardwell of the American Red Cross in Moscow did not share Williams's sympathy for the Bolsheviks, he agreed that either using sufficient force to destroy the Soviet government or staying out of the civil war entirely would have been better than "trying to straddle" the question of intervention. Wardwell found the Wilson administration's August 1918 press release "hardly frank": "they say they are not in favor of intervention, but are coming in solely to protect military supplies + Czechs. Of course this is utter rot." The humane thing to do, he thought, was to go to war with the Bolsheviks and restore order in Russia. "If we are fighting these people," he wrote, "lets [*sic*] say so and get it over for the sake of the great mass of the population who really don't care so much about political parties, but would like to eat and live free from extraordinary disturbances!"[122]

In the immediate aftermath of the Allied landing at Archangel, Soviet leaders considered themselves in a state of war with the "Anglo-French imperialists," but, perhaps in part because only a handful of U.S. sailors had gone ashore, they maintained a different view of the United States. "The Bolshevik leaders here," Webster wrote from Petrograd on August 6, "are especially anxious at this time to cultivate our friendship as they seem to feel, rightly or wrongly, that America will possibly be the only country in which they can seek a place of safety in case they are forced to leave this country, if overpowered by the White Guard." In Moscow, Wardwell noted on August 27 that while the Soviet government had "arrested the English and French residents," Americans "so far have not been touched." Lockhart, who spent much of September in the custody of the Cheka, enviously observed that "the Bolsheviks showed no animosity against the Americans. Their name was always excluded from the official protests against the alleged atrocities by the French and British troops in North Russia." The British agent saw this as a clever and sophisticated tactic. "The Bolsheviks," he recalled, "knew that President Wilson, who was a historian and who therefore remembered Napoleon, was very lukewarm in his attitude toward the Russian policy of the Allies. They were determined to do nothing to prejudice that attitude." [123]

Although Soviet leaders had long been skeptical or cynical about Wilson's idealistic rhetoric, they had sought to differentiate Americans from European imperialists in public statements and official diplomatic contacts. Foreign Commissar Chicherin had taken pains in the spring and summer of 1918 to stress his respect for representatives of the "land of puritan revolutionary pioneers" and emphasize Soviet hopes for friendly cooperation with the United States. After Chicherin learned that Wilson had agreed in principle to intervention, he focused on reported disagreements among the Western allies about the form and scale of the expeditions and worked to preserve cordial relations with American diplomats. Immediately after the Allied landing at Archangel in early August, Chicherin politely asked Consul General Poole, "seeing that you have declared that your people does not wish to overthrow the Soviets," to explain "what Britain really wants from us." While Chicherin maintained a conciliatory attitude toward America until September, Lenin launched scathing attacks on Wilson's hypocrisy. In his August 20, 1918, "Letter to American Workers," Lenin attacked Wilson as "the head of the American multi-millionaires and servant of the capitalist sharks" who had "given their approval — whether direct or indirect, open or hypocritically concealed" to intervention. In October, after larger U.S. forces reached Archangel and Vladivostok, Lenin prompted Chicherin to send a sarcastic note to Wilson. "The Russian people," Chicherin charged, had not received the "assistance to the independent expression of their will" that Wilson had promised them. Instead, they had "met with a revival of the Russian counter-revolution which had already become a corpse." However, Soviet leaders were not entirely displeased, for this "opened the eyes of the workmen and peasants of Russia as to the aims of the Russian counter-revolution and of its foreign assistants," and as a result, they were fighting "splendidly against your invasion and the advance of your allies." More temperately, Chicherin's deputy Litvinov asserted in December 1918 that Soviet leaders "at first respected [Wilson's] impartiality and believed in his desire to help Russia. . . . But the intervention at Archangel had placed American motives in a bad light and suggested that the president's belief in the right of a people to regulate its own political affairs was not sincere."[124]

While Wilson's secretiveness and vagueness about his objectives and his restriction of the number of American troops did not keep the Archangel expedition from antagonizing the Bolsheviks, the atmosphere of secrecy and the small size of the expedition did undermine the mobilization of anti-Bolshevik forces. Problems arose even before the American regiment reached northern Russia. In June former Prime Minister Kerensky had left Russia via Murmansk on a mission for the Party of Socialist Revolutionaries and other democratic anti-Bolshevik groups to secure formal commitments that an Allied intervention would respect Russian sovereignty and territorial integrity. Kerensky expected a friendly reception from American representatives, who he thought shared Russian ideals more than European leaders did. However, upon reaching Paris in July Kerensky learned that Lansing did not want him to come to the United States, and he was unable to meet with the American ambassador to France. Lower-ranking Americans also treated Kerensky coolly, suspecting that he was "taking drugs," talking "rubbish," and might be part of "some sort of game put up by Trotsky." This treatment did not inspire confidence in Kerensky and his Russian associates. On July 30, 1918 — two weeks after Wilson privately drafted his *aide-mémoire*, but several days before the administration released an abbreviated version to the press — V. A. Maklakov, the Russian ambassador in Paris, warned Ambassador Bakhmeteff that the secrecy surrounding the Allied decision to intervene was raising doubts and suspicions among anti-Bolshevik groups both inside Soviet Russia and abroad. Having discussed the issue with Kerensky, who was in touch with a "democratic bloc" in Moscow, Maklakov wired that "intervention, performed clandestinely, creates strong arguments against it and has hurt the feelings of many of those who were its ardent partisans." The democratic coalition in Moscow urged that "an open declaration to Russia" be issued without further delay to assuage fears about foreign territorial aggrandizement and political interference, and to enlist the cooperation of the Russian people.[125]

Although no such declaration was promulgated before the tiny Allied expedition reached Archangel on August 2, residents of the port initially greeted the foreign forces "with joyous enthusiasm," according to assistant military attaché Martin. However, as soon as the Russians "began to realize the weakness of our force," Martin recalled, "there was a perceptible decrease in their enthusiasm." Archibald C. Coolidge, a special representative of the State Department in north Russia, agreed that the Allies were at first "welcomed as liberators" by at least the wealthier classes, but the fervor soon died, since the number of foreign troops was very small, their southward advance quickly halted, and food relief was "slow in coming." Consul Felix Cole similarly observed that the Allies were welcomed by "the peasantry, and the city 'intelligents' and *bourgeois*," but "the working class was patently absent," and the rest of the populace soon sank back into apathy.[126]

On September 20, 1918, Wilson received a caution from a Red Cross worker in north Russia that "unless the Allies [*sic*] program of intervention is made strong enough not to appear ridiculous, it is fore-doomed to failure." Jesse Halsey recognized that "intervention is not the word to use," and he noted approvingly that "the troops have paid attention to the feelings of the people." However, friendly relief work was not sufficient. Substantial foreign forces were needed, in part because of the disheartening fact that "the moderately well to do classes hold aloof from everything that is going on in Russia except what is immediately before them."[127]

Wilson thought enough of Halsey's statement to take a copy of it with him to Paris. He was undoubtedly more sympathetic to the ideas of avoiding the word "intervention" and attending to Russian feelings than to the recommendation of stronger foreign military forces. Only a few days before receiving Halsey's memorandum, Wilson had ruled out sending reinforcements to north Russia. In late September and again in October Chaikovskii appealed for more American troops to enable him "to form a serious Russian army" and to strengthen the faltering "struggle against Bolshevism."[128] However, discouraged by the reported apathy of anti-Bolsheviks and later troubled by the rise of nationalist support for the Bolsheviks, Wilson refused to expand the size or scope of American intervention.

American Public Opinion, Congress, and Intervention in North Russia

Anxiety about opposition from the American people and Congress also figured in Wilson's rejection of proposals to wage war against Bolshevism more aggressively. In the summer and fall of 1918 government censorship and patriotic inhibitions checked criticism of intervention in Russia. However, even then there was significant popular agitation against the two Russian expeditions. In September 1918, "reading American papers on Allied intervention in Russia," Ambassador Francis observed that "sentiment [was] divided." After the Armistice of November 11, the domestic division widened. Many soldiers who had expected to fight Germans in France but found themselves fighting "Bolos" in north Russia did not understand why they remained in the frozen north after Germany had been defeated. By the end of the year, as Secretary of War Baker informed Wilson, "wild stories" were circulating that U.S. troops were "exposed to conflict with Russian forces which outnumber them 'fifteen to one.'" Parents of the soldiers from Michigan, Wisconsin, and Illinois pressed their congressional representatives to bring their sons home or at least secure an explanation of the expedition. On December 12, 1918, Republican senator Hiram Johnson of California introduced a resolution to require the secretary of state to explain why American soldiers were fighting in north Russia even though the State Department press release in August 1918 had disavowed armed intervention in Russia and Congress had not declared war. Although the resolution was bottled up in the Foreign Relations Committee for the next two months, Johnson's sarcastic speech mocking Wilson's "wonderful" but "disingenuous" words launched a major challenge to the administration's policy toward Russia.[129]

Knowledge of the opposition at home did not prevent Ambassador Francis from insistently urging a larger military intervention. Although Francis had to leave Archangel in late October for urgent medical treatment in England, after his surgery the elderly Ambassador wanted to go back to Petrograd along with 50,000 American soldiers and comparable Allied forces "to restore order in the interest of humanity and consequently to suppress bolshevism." This mission was necessary, Francis argued, because the Bolsheviks "were endeavoring to promote a world wide social revolution, and . . . if it succeeded in Russia, it would be a menace . . . to every European country and would not spare even our own."[130]

Like Francis, Wilson was disturbed by "the susceptibility of the people of Europe to the poison of Bolshevism," and in December a note from Wilson encouraged Francis to believe that they were thinking along the same lines. However, Wilson was actually leaning away from further intervention, though he put off withdrawal of the Archangel expedition for the next three months. When Francis finally received the favor of a meeting with the president in February 1919, Wilson told him "that sending American soldiers to Russia after the armistice had been signed would be very unpopular in America." Francis' plan to enlist volunteers in a great crusade was much too public a course for Wilson, who doubted that there would be sufficient "public sentiment to support" military action against Bolshevism. The Ambassador was directed to keep quiet about Russia.[131]

Assistant Secretary of State Breckinridge Long sympathized with Francis about the need for active intervention in Russia. At the end of 1918, the aristocratic Missouri lawyer concluded that "looking, not at Russia but at Bolshevism, . . . the peacefully inclined and orderly establishments for government everywhere have a right—perhaps a duty—to unite and intervene to establish order in Russia." However, Long realized that the administration had a major public relations problem. Long had "felt for some time that our policy in Russia and Siberia was not understood, and that the misinterpretations placed upon it, especially our 'making war against the Bolshevics' were making trouble for us at home." After conferring with his State Department colleagues, Long drafted a statement for the press. Instead of stressing America's anti-Bolshevik duty he placed "emphasis on the protection of military stores, bringing of help to the Czecho-Slovaks in Siberia—etc." Even so, Long was unable to win Wilson's approval to release the statement.[132]

Although Long expressed frustration about not being able to wage a more "aggressive battle" to forestall attacks on the administration, he was himself reluctant to be fully candid with the American people. While he agreed with Francis about the menace of Bolshevism, particularly "its internationalism and its consequent denial of patriotism, family ties, blood relatives and traditions," he was ambivalent about making a public declaration of ideological antipathy. After having dinner with his fellow Missourian, "Governor" Francis, Long commented in his diary, "I think he can do a good deal to bring a popular understanding of Bolshevism, but I fear he will paint too bleak a picture, which *may* react."[133]

Since Long, Wilson, and others held back from organizing an anti-Bolshevik crusade and refrained from elucidating their private thinking, the administration's difficulties with Congress and public opinion persisted. Anticipating a new surge of pressure from Congress in February, Frank Polk groaned that Senator Johnson was "going to make it very disagreeable for the Administration" by demanding that the Archangel expedition be withdrawn. Although Polk tried to coach Democratic senators on how to respond, he complained that Johnson had "considerable support" and was attracting "considerable public attention by showing our men are being killed and no policy has been announced." Colonel House was even more sensitive to "the demands of the public in the United States and England" for the return of the expeditions, which William Bullitt cited in calling for withdrawal. In late January, House advised Wilson to consider Bullitt's arguments that U.S. soldiers should be brought home from north Russia, since few Russians had "rallied around this force," and it was serving "merely to create cynicism in regard to all our proposals and to stimulate recruiting for the Red Army." Two weeks later, Secretary of War Baker advised Wilson that "public opinion" in America was "very insistent upon the return of our troops." On the same day Bullitt presented his case again, pointing to the "Johnson resolution for withdrawal" that was before the Senate and the fact that the "American press is becoming increasingly bitter over the situation of our men at Archangel."[134]

The bitterness of the press was fostered by the administration's secretiveness. On January 25, 1919, the liberal editors of the *Dial* demanded: "How much longer will the American public endure our shameful intervention in Russia? . . . [I]f our Government does not see fit to put a stop to this anti-American adventure, the American people will put a stop to it themselves." The more conservative *Chicago Tribune* also criticized the administration's policy. On February 5, 1919, the *Tribune* observed that "The opinion has been pretty general here in America that the full truth about operations in Russia is either being withheld or distorted." Reflecting common sentiment in the region from which the men of the north Russian expedition came, the *Tribune* lamented that "our men are dying for a cause, the purpose of which they are no more certain than we in America. America has not declared war on Russia, but Americans are killing Russians or are being killed by them."

The Wilson administration's failure to explain the objectives of the Archangel expedition sowed similar confusion and opposition in the Senate. On February 13, when Senator Johnson once again took the floor, he read exposés published by the *Chicago Tribune* in order to stir smoldering resentment of Wilsonian secrecy and reignite debate on the withdrawal of American soldiers from Russia. Frazier Hunt, a correspondent who left Archangel to escape censorship of his dispatches, reported that Americans in north Russia were "absolutely ignorant" of any reason for being there. "From the start the expedition lacked the thrill of the drive that a great, honest stated purpose would have given," Hunt argued. He alleged that the only statements the Wilson administration had made "were false in fact and were given to lull not only the Russian people into a false security but to lull the American people as well." Countering Johnson's reading of Hunt's charges, defenders of the administration maintained that the United States had intervened "by invitation of loyal Russians," and that American troops were needed to protect those Russian allies from the savage Bolsheviks. However, the administration's point man, Democrat Gilbert Hitchcock of Nebraska, betrayed deep perplexity when he claimed American forces were cooperating with "the Russian Soviets," and even staunch proponents of intervention like Republican Porter McCumber of North Dakota agreed with Johnson that "the Government should say why we are there." Playing on the indignant feelings of many senators that Wilson had usurped Congress's power to declare war, Johnson warned that allowing the president to wage undeclared war would establish a dangerous precedent. On February 14, advocates of withdrawal very nearly won: Vice

President Thomas Marshall had to break a tie vote in order to table Johnson's resolution.[135]

At Paris, Colonel House cited such congressional resistance and public distrust in America when he opposed a proposal by Winston Churchill to enlarge and intensify the military campaigns against Bolshevism. In a forceful speech on February 17, the colonel argued that the tie vote in the Senate, combined with the general anti-interventionist sentiment in America, made it impossible for American representatives to agree to the proposal made by Churchill. As House informed Wilson, he further "pointed out that under existing legislation the United States could not employ any of her resources against Russia for we are not at war with Russia."[136]

Since the armistice with Germany, Wilson and his State Department advisors had ignored and resisted War Department moves to withdraw American forces from north Russia. The president had also declined to make public any statement explaining U.S. policy toward the Bolsheviks and Russia. Now, prodded by the uproar at home, Wilson had to face the failure of the limited intervention at Archangel. Few Russians had rallied around the American flag. The morale of the American soldiers in north Russia was very low. Although some British and French leaders wanted to wage war more vigorously, they could not enlist enough volunteers among their countrymen to strangle Bolshevism. Even if he and his Allies could have raised sufficient forces for an outright war on Bolshevism, Wilson's scruples and American public opinion blocked that course. The inadequate forces already sent to north Russia seemed to be strengthening the Bolshevik regime. Unable and unwilling to eradicate Bolshevism with blatant military force, Wilson decided in favor of the "earliest practicable withdrawal" of the American expedition.[137]

As American troops departed from Archangel in June 1919, Wilson set his policy in historical perspective. Reminding anti-Bolshevik aides Vance McCormick and Herbert Hoover that "Europe had made a great mistake when they attempted to interfere in the French Revolution," Wilson drew the lesson that "the Russian people must solve their own problems without outside interference." Wilson also could have cited Edmund Burke's opposition to British intervention in revolutionary America. In 1893 Professor Wilson had recapitulated Burke's argument that "the use of force alone is but *temporary*. It may subdue for a moment; but it does not remove the necessity of subduing again: and a nation is not governed which is perpetually to be conquered." In addition, if force failed, "no further hope of reconciliation" would be left. Such wisdom may have contributed to Wilson's aversion to a massive military invasion, but it did not keep him from succumbing to the temptations of limited intervention. On the same afternoon that Wilson edified McCormick and Hoover about noninterference in revolutions, he discussed his agreement with the Allies to "continue to send supplies and munitions to the anti-Bolshevist forces," particularly in Siberia.[138]

After the American North Russian Expeditionary Force finally returned to the United States, Wilson relied on other methods to help anti-Bolshevik forces in the Russian Civil War. American troops remained in Siberia, in part to secure Admiral Kolchak's supply line; the Russian embassy in Washington continued to ship supplies to White armies; and American humanitarian organizations provided aid to soldiers in anti-Bolshevik forces. Thus, while the American-Soviet fighting in north Russia stopped, America's secret war against Bolshevism continued.

FOOD AS A WEAPON AGAINST BOLSHEVISM

AMERICAN "HUMANITARIAN" INTERVENTION IN THE BALTIC REGION, 1919

In the summer of 1919, as the Russian Civil War entered its climactic phase, the *USS Democracy* and six other American ships steamed into the Gulf of Finland with about 18,000 tons of flour, 1,500 tons of bacon, and thousands of tons of other foodstuffs. On July 16, Herbert Hoover, head of the American Relief Administration (ARA), agreed to deliver these supplies "to the representatives of the Provisional Government of Russia" in Baltic ports such as Vyborg, Reval (Tallinn), Riga, and Libau (Liepaja), in exchange for promissory notes. According to the formal document Hoover signed with Lt. General E. Hermonius, the agreement was "made solely for humanitarian purposes," and the food was to be distributed "in accord with the dictates of humanity." [1]

This was a curious document. The original Provisional Government had been overthrown in November 1917. The Baltic ports were in July 1919 under the jurisdiction, not of any Russian regime, but of Finnish, Estonian, and Latvian nationalist governments who were anxious about harboring anti-Bolshevik movements dedicated to restoring Russia's imperial greatness. No Russian provisional government could hope to pay for the U.S. aid unless the Soviet regime was overthrown and a new government was installed in Russia. The ARA supplies were not delivered to Russian civilian relief officials but to officers of the anti-Bolshevik Russian North-western Army, who deeply appreciated the U.S. aid. Thanking Hoover, one White general observed that "the North-Western Russian Army, which is fighting against the Bolshevism in the direction of Petrograd for the restoration of lawful order of things in Russia, is now existing practically upon American flour and bacon."[2]

The ARA shipment of food to the Northwestern Army was one of the principal ways Americans sought to affect the course of the civil war in the turbulent Baltic region. With the American people averse to direct U.S. military intervention and with Congress increasingly critical of Wilson administration expenditures of public funds, U.S. leaders had to utilize a variety of other measures to influence developments along the Baltic Sea. In addition to delivering provisions to anti-Bolshevik Russian forces, U.S. officials withheld such supplies from Bolshevik-controlled territories, participated in an undeclared blockade of Soviet Russia, approved the use of German troops to contain and roll back Bolshevism, authorized the sale of weapons to Baltic nationalist governments, and attempted to transfer war materiel from American or German stocks to Russian units.

These tactics were often morally controversial and they led American officials to the margins of legality and honesty. Hoover loathed the "plague" of Bolshevism and sincerely believed that "no greater relief of human misery could be undertaken than the occupation of Petrograd" and the suppression of the Soviet regime. However, like other policymakers he felt compelled to bow to the moral sensibility of the American people by portraying relief projects for Russia as purely altruistic, apolitical programs to alleviate civilian suffering.[3] With this tension between public pronouncements and actual policies, and with the reliance on evasive, indirect methods, the "humanitarian" intervention in the Baltic region fit into the broader pattern of America's secret war against Bolshevism.

Origins of the Civil War in the Baltic States

As the First World War ground to a close in the fall of 1918, the former Russian provinces along the Baltic Sea were plunged in turmoil. Torn by internal conflicts between radical socialist and more conservative nationalist forces, Estonia, Latvia, and Lithuania were also affected by the receding tide of German influence and the rising tide of Soviet influence.

In Estonia, the Bolshevik party had had significant support in 1917 among landless peasants, workers in Tallinn, and Russian soldiers and sailors. During the November 1917 elections to the Russian Constituent Assembly, the Bolsheviks drew a 40 percent plurality of the vote in Estonia. After two months of Soviet rule, however, the Bolsheviks' internationalist orientation and dictatorial policies had antagonized many Estonians. When nationalist parties showed increased popularity in January 1918 elections to the Estonian parliament, the Bolsheviks suspended the balloting. A month later, as German troops advanced through Estonia, Bolshevik leaders fled and nationalists seized the opportunity to declare Estonia's independence in the few hours before German soldiers marched into Tallinn. After German leaders signed the Armistice of November 11, 1918, a Center-Left government established at Tallinn won wide approval with its combination of nationalism and a land reform program providing for the division of estates of German-speaking barons. In late November and December 1918, the Red Seventh Army advanced from Soviet Russia, established the Estonian Workers' Commune at Narva, and threatened Tallinn. However, with crucial assistance from the British navy, Finland, and the anti-Bolshevik Russian Northern Corps, the Estonian nationalists rallied sufficient forces to hold a front running between Narva and Pskov.[4]

In Latvia, the most industrialized Baltic province, Bolsheviks demonstrated broad popular support, particularly from the relatively large class of urban workers, land-hungry peasants, and soldiers hardened by front-line fighting. In the November 1917 elections, Bolsheviks won 72 percent of the votes in Latvia, and they ruled the unoccupied northeastern section until the German offensive of late February 1918. Throughout 1918 the Soviet regime relied on disciplined divisions of Latvian riflemen to retain power in Petrograd and Moscow. In January 1919, many of these units were used to form an army of Soviet Latvia that spearheaded the establishment of a Latvian Socialist Soviet Republic in Riga. Until the Germans returned in May 1919, Bolsheviks could glory in the way Red Latvia "transformed the Baltic Sea into the Sea of Social Revolution," while Latvian nationalists had to issue their rival claims to power from the southwestern port of Libau.[5]

The German occupation of Lithuania since 1915 prevented much revolutionary agitation in that region, which was in any case predominantly agricultural and offered Bolsheviks few opportunities to appeal to urban workers. After the German collapse in the fall of 1918, Lithuanian Bolsheviks formed a Soviet Socialist Republic at Vilnius which received some backing from Red Army units that arrived in the city by January 1919. However, the Lithuanian Bolsheviks had less popular support and controlled less territory than their Latvian counterparts. Their short-lived regime was challenged by Lithuanian nationalists who benefited from German protection, and it was ultimately deposed by Polish forces in April 1919.[6]

Early American Responses to the Threat of Bolshevism in the Baltic

Even before the Armistice, dispatches reaching Washington from the Baltic region forecast "an outbreak of Bolshevism" when the German army of occupation withdrew. In early December, according to naval intelligence, the Bolsheviks were "gaining ground daily" along the Baltic. By the middle of January, peace commission advisors informed President Wilson in Paris that "the Bolshevists . . . have swept the Baltic provinces." In these months, Baltic nationalist groups issued numerous appeals to the Allies and the United States for assistance against the Soviet governments at Narva, Riga, and Vilnius, and for protection from the danger of further Red Army offensives.[7]

Some American diplomats desperately wanted to send U.S. forces to the Baltic region. When Allen Dulles arrived in Paris at the end of 1918 to serve as an advisor to his uncle, Secretary of State Lansing, he "was rather stirred up about the situation in Lithuania and Poland . . . and submitted a number of memoranda advocating intervention to prevent the union of the Russian and German Bolsheviki." Dulles argued that "immediate military assistance" was vital if the Allies wanted "to utilize the still-existent anti-Bolsheviki forces of Lithuania." All the Poles and Lithuanians needed, according to Dulles, was "a small army as a nucleus for their own forces."[8]

However, to most American officials, military intervention in the Baltic region by the United States was almost unthinkable. Direct military action would be costly and it would risk American casualties. If undertaken in conjunction with allies, it would bring political entanglements and conflicts comparable to those experienced in north Russia and Siberia. If designed to support anti-Bolshevik armies led by former tsarist officers it would risk contributing to the restoration of the Russian monarchy.[9]

Even if Wilson administration officials had wanted to run those risks, that course was virtually impossible. American soldiers were eager to return from Europe to the United States, not to embark on new crusades. As Allen Dulles regretfully recognized, "There is a strong reaction against intervention by American troops and I very much doubt whether anything of this nature can be undertaken on our part. The cry is now to get the troops home." Difficult questions were being raised in Congress and in the press about the continued presence of "Sammies" in Russia. Using military force directly against the Soviet regime would alienate potential political support for the Wilson administration among liberals and socialists in Europe as well as the United States. Commenting on this climate, State Department Counselor Frank Polk advised Lansing and Wilson in January 1919, "It is obvious that great difficulty would be encountered at home by any of the Allied Governments sending troops to Russia." Along the same line, the president stressed to Clemenceau and Lloyd George in April that "United States public opinion would not tolerate sending any more troops" to Russia.[10]

The rising antipathy to Bolshevism in the United States in the year of the Red Scare did not lead to greater public support for military intervention, as it was counterbalanced by a rise in isolationist sentiment. "Our people are not prepared for us to undertake the military policing of Europe while it boils out its social wrongs," Hoover wrote to Wilson in April. "I have no doubt that if we could undertake to police the world . . . that we would be making a great contribution to civilization, but I am certain that the American people are not prepared for any such a measure." In this context, Wilson administration officials looked for other weapons to contain or extinguish the fires of Bolshevism.[11]

Wilson's liberal advisors devoted special attention to promoting the use of food supplies as an alternative to military intervention. State Department aide William C. Bullitt advised Lansing and Wilson in November 1918 that "famine and economic disorganization" were "the parents of Bolshevism in Russia . . . [and] in Western Europe, and that the roots of Bolshevism can be cut only by food and restoration of economic life, and not by arms." The strongest supporter of Bullitt's position among Wilson's top counselors was Colonel House. Although House privately believed that "military intervention . . . could be successfully accomplished" with "a mercenary army of very small proportions," in meetings with Allied statesmen he argued that "military intervention was impossible" and favored food as "the remedy" for Bolshevism.[12]

More conservative figures hoped to see economic aid used as a complement to military intervention. William Chapin Huntington, former commercial attaché in Russia, warned that "economic, without military, assistance is useless in a country so torn with strife and so completely anarchical as Russia." In a similar vein, Cyrus H. McCormick Jr., head of the International Harvester company, advised Wilson that "food can best be supplied and economic help rendered by an increase in the number of Allied soldiers placed . . . to do police duty." McCormick recommended that the United States should at the same time channel aid through "a National Patriotic Russian Army under the command of any one of several capable, efficient, loyal Generals." In February 1919, Ambassador Francis tried to persuade Wilson to approve a plan for Allied missions to return to Petrograd, "accompanied by 100,000 Allied troops and abundant food." Vance McCormick, head of the War Trade Board, also suggested "sending food to Petrograd with sufficient troops to protect distribution."[13]

Ultimately, neither the proponents of economic aid to cure Bolshevism nor the advocates of combined military and economic intervention to eradicate the Soviet regime were able to implement their desired policies. Lansing, who saw the obstacles to direct armed intervention more clearly than other conservatives, identified an intermediate option and antici- pated the future course of U.S. policy when he wrote on October 28, 1918: "Food will defeat the Bolshevik movement, food with arms and ammu- nition. Somehow we must supply them." In a letter to Wilson on Novem- ber 26, Lansing borrowed Bullitt's idea about the need to "cut to the root of the sore and relieve the misery and exhaustion which form such a fertile soil for its rapid growth." But Lansing added a harshly anti-Bolshevik twist, stressing that "we must set our faces sternly against anarchy and the class tyranny and terror of Bolshevism," and give "economic assistance" only to "elements desiring to maintain democratic principles." Whereas Bullitt and House sought to rule out the use of force, Lansing observed that what the United States resisted was "a purely military intervention." In 1919, the United States neither dispatched food to Moscow to moderate the Soviet regime nor sent soldiers to combat the Red Army directly, but it provided both food and weapons to check Bolshevism along the Baltic.[14]

While Wilson's advisors disagreed about proposals for conciliating or fighting Bolshevik leaders, a consensus developed behind the idea of using food "to prevent bolshevikism & anarchy," first in central Europe, and then in the Baltic region. Herbert Hoover, a wealthy engineer who had directed a Siberian mining venture before the revolutions of 1917 and headed the commission for relief in Belgium during the war, became the leading exponent of using food to stabilize political conditions in Europe. Following the defeat of Germany, Hoover increasingly focused on the urgent problems of combating the seductive "fallacy" of Socialism and returning political and economic leadership from misguided radicals to practical liberals. In the first week of 1919, Hoover stressed that "strong liberal relief is today the only hope of stemming the tide of Bolshevism, without the expenditure of lives and vast sums on military action." Hoover specifically cited the desperate food scarcity in the Baltic states and the need in Finland for "help to prevent a renewed rise of Bolchevism" after the White victory in the civil war there. Augmenting the consensus, Republican peace commissioner Henry White informed the chairman of the Senate Foreign Relations Committee and other Re- publican politicians that since military occupation was impractical, the "only effective barrier now apparently possible against [Bolshevism] is food relief."[15]

In the wake of the victory over Germany, Wilson's mind was "not clear as to what is the immediate proper course in Russia." At the end of 1918 Wilson and British Prime Minister David Lloyd George were uncertain "how far the so-called invasion of Esthonia or Poland was a direct invasion by Bolshevik forces, from outside, or an internal Bolshevik rising in those countries." However, the president did favor the "restoration of orderly governments in the Baltic States." And by the beginning of 1919, with foreign military intervention reportedly causing Russians to rally around the Soviet regime, he was convinced that Bolshevism "cannot be stopped by force but it can be stopped by food."[16]

Financial and Legal Constraints on American Relief Work

American policymakers did not have unlimited funds at their disposal to beat back Bolshevism. After the Armistice, it became increasingly difficult for the administration to seek appropriations from the House and Senate. The congressional well was drained by the "isolationist" retrenchment following the wartime crusade and poisoned by rising bitterness between the executive and legislative branches. Wilson's relations with Congress, strained by his unsuccessful appeal for Democratic majorities in the November 1918 elections and aggravated by his failure to make prominent Republicans peace commissioners, grew even more tense in the course of 1919. The president's personal diplomacy at Paris and his evasiveness about American policy toward Russia were perceived by many in Congress as arrogant infringements of their constitutional prerogatives. By the middle of June, Lansing, troubled by the president's "liability to exceed his authority," commented that the "temper of Congress is such that he might be impeached."[17]

Even at the beginning of 1919, Wilson and his aides had trouble persuading Congress to provide funds to prevent destitute regions in Europe from succumbing to Bolshevism. In January, when the administration was fending off pressure for the withdrawal of U.S. troops from Russia, the president asked Congress for an immediate appropriation of $100 million to provide food and other urgent supplies "to such populations in Europe, outside of Germany, as may be determined upon by me from time to time as necessary." Presenting this request, Wilson sought to appeal "to the great sense of charity and good will of the American people toward the suffering, and to place this act upon a primarily humanitarian basis."[18]

Sensing that his colleagues would balk at the amount and the wide discretion demanded by the president, Swagar Sherley, chairman of the House Appropriations Committee, advised that "it would be difficult to get this money without facts" about how the relief would be administered, what contributions the Allies would make, and what provisions for repayment would be made. In an initial vote, the committee was evenly divided, and there was reported to be considerable opposition to the appropriation in the House and Senate.[19]

Joining the battle to pry open the public purse, the president's men stressed the great danger to western civilization from the East. "The peril to Western Europe if Bolshevism prevails in Central Europe is very real," the peace commissioners wired from Paris on January 3. The Red menace could "only be met by . . . relieving the food and economic situation" and "reestablishing sane governments capable of resisting the advance of Bolshevism from Russia." [20] Shifting from the president's stress on charity, the commissioners emphasized that relief funds would serve U.S. interests by making it easier to dispose of surplus wheat and pork. They also thought it would be "well to impress upon Congress . . . that entirely aside from a humanitarian standpoint it is necessary to feed even Germany in order to prevent starvation and anarchy and the necessity of an extended military occupation." [21]

Wilson and his advisors did not suggest that building bulwarks against Bolshevism would involve provisioning armies to fight Red troops. On the contrary, their lobbying messages indicated that distributing food to starving civilians would avoid the need for military operations and preserve distance between the United States and violent conflicts in central and eastern Europe. [22]

Supporters of the relief appropriation in Congress echoed and supplemented the administration's arguments. Some urged that the U.S. government, "the richest in all the world," could surely afford "a paltry $100,000,000" to fulfill its Christian, humanitarian duty. Others asserted that there was "no better business proposition" because the generous gesture would build goodwill abroad and open doors to American trade. Partisan Democrats stressed that the nation was still technically at war, that the president was commander in chief, and that nothing should be done to embarrass him at the momentous meetings in Paris. Most insistent, though, was the argument that food shipments would "stem the wave of bolshevism" by giving "an element of permanency to the new governments of the liberated peoples," thus avoiding the need to have "our boys . . . fight another war." Again and again, proponents of the food bill stressed that it would stabilize and pacify Europe, thereby helping "to get our soldiers home as speedily as possible." [23]

Despite these arguments, the appropriation was attacked in debates that stretched into late January. Especially on the Republican sides of the Capitol chambers, resentment of the president's "autocratic" or "imperial" power spurred resistance to allowing Wilson or Hoover to be responsible for disbursing the funds. [24] Many doubted that bread could stop the spread of Bolshevism, and there was heated opposition to "buying Bolshevists into good behavior." "I am opposed to feeding anything but hot lead to murderous Bolshevists," roared Arizona Democrat Henry F. Ashurst on January 20. However, even such fire-breathing anti-Bolsheviks as Illinois Republican Lawrence Sherman, who thundered that "the way to deal with those of the Trotzky variety in this country was with military force," did not advocate military intervention in Russia, preferring to "let them work it out." Democrat Thomas Hardwick of Georgia expressed the prevailing sentiment when he stated that U.S. soldiers "ought not to be employed in policing Europe." Hence, while Democrat William King of Utah favored "feeding peoples and equipping those who are fighting Bolshevism," most of his colleagues were wary of anything that might lead to new entanglements in faraway places. In one of the few references to the Baltic states in the protracted speechmaking, Hiram Johnson voiced his suspicion that "to-day we are building Esthonia and Ukrainia and Lavonia and Lithuania and creating a new Poland and Finland, . . . the props of all of which we are told are to be in the future American bayonets." [25]

In spite of this resistance, Congress passed the relief appropriation by the end of January, and in February Wilson established the American Relief Administration, with Hoover as director, to distribute the food. However, the trouble involved in procuring the $100 million stood as a warning that it would be very difficult to approach Congress for further funds in the future. In addition, the presentation of the relief effort as a humanitarian alternative to military involvements and the fears of congressmen that it would lead to such embroilments created potential difficulties concerning how the money would be used. [26]

Constrained by limited resources and seeing urgent needs for action to counter the spread of Bolshevism in eastern Europe, Wilson's advisors considered ways to escape the straitjacket of congressional restrictions. On February 6, 1919, for example, Hoover advised Wilson that unfortunately there were "no American funds under the law" available for feeding Russian POWs in Germany. Since "taking care of these prisoners" would "prevent them from going back to Russia . . . and joining in the Bolshevik army," and would therefore serve "a military purpose," Hoover suggested that it was "the proper duty of the American army to furnish supplies" for the POWs. Although Wilson did not think that use of army provisions would be justified, Hoover persisted in pressing the idea. [27]

In the following months, Wilson's aides continued to explore the limits of the laws, searching for loopholes and clever ways to procure funds for anti-Bolshevik causes. At a meeting of the American peace commissioners on February 20, Lansing observed that approving the Estonian, Latvian, and Lithuanian nationalist governments' requests for credits and supplies "was at present impossible, as no legislative action permitting this had ever been passed." However, a week later, when Hoover reviewed with the commissioners the "complicated" and "very difficult" problem of shipments to the Baltic provinces, Lansing had a brainstorm. He suggested that Hoover consult his nephew John Foster Dulles, "who had large experience in similar cases on the War Trade Board," which oversaw shipments of supplies to anti-Bolshevik forces in Siberia. On March 20, the commissioners agreed that "it would be advisable to feed and give prompt economic assistance to Finland, Estonia, Poland, Czecho-Slovakia and the liberated sections of Latvia and Lithuania," though they were uncertain "whether satisfactory financial arrangements could be made to pay for this food," since Congress would not convene for some time.[28]

The problem of constricted means grew even more acute. The American delegates to the peace conference recognized that extensive "military assistance to the Anti-Bolshevik forces in Russia" and an "economic offensive . . . against Bolshevik Russia" would "require ratification" — certainly by the president and "probably by Congress." Yet, as the Treasury Department advised Wilson in May, "public sentiment" in America was "in no mood to tolerate the assumption by government of further financial burdens in aid of Europe."[29]

Even the existing funds were due to be cut off. As Hoover explained to Wilson in June, the ARA's congressional appropriation would expire by the first of July. To deal with this looming deadline, Wilson approved the transfer of one million dollars from other funds in order to cover the expenses of relief work after June 30, 1919. Hoover specified that the Baltic region would be one of the principal areas for this continued work.[30]

When the heads of delegations in Paris discussed how "to pay Russian and Lettish troops" in Latvia on July 8, Lansing regretted that the United States had no funds for that purpose. "American laws were very stringent on the subject of spending money," Lansing explained. "Until July 1st, while the president was in Paris, there had been funds which he could spend at his discretion," but after Wilson's departure "there were no funds available."[31]

Since Wilson and his advisors were reluctant to stir up controversy by seeking large new appropriations from Congress, they tried creative methods of financing shipments, explored ways to transfer materials from existing stockpiles, and encouraged action by forces that would not have to be paid from U.S. funds. Legal and financial constraints thus significantly shaped the forms of American intervention in the Baltic states.

Political Conditions for "Humanitarian" Aid

In his Fourteen Points speech, President Wilson pledged an attitude of "unselfish sympathy" toward Russia and promised to provide her with "assistance . . . of every kind that she may need and may herself desire." In 1919 Wilson sometimes similarly suggested that he had no animus against the Soviet government and wanted above all to provide economic assistance to the Russian people in a spirit of Christian charity. After a luncheon with British publisher Lord Northcliffe in March 1919, for example, Wilson informed Lady Northcliffe that the cure for Bolshevism was not force but the redressing of grievances. He urged her to "remember the Bible supplication: 'Give us this day our daily bread.'"[32]

However, a Christian spirit of evenhanded succor to the evil and the good did not prevail among top American relief officials, let alone among diplomats and military officers. In a book written during the summer of 1919, Henry P. Davison, chairman of the War Council of the American Red Cross (ARC), remembered that in 1917 "the Red Cross went 'to war' . . . to hold the Russians to the cause of right" and save them from "chaos." Davison's belief that freebooting "revolutionists" were not "the real Russia" allowed him to view ARC support for Allied and American troops who were fighting Red forces as a moral duty rather than political intervention. Davison did not envision cooperating with the Soviet regime in relief efforts; instead he wanted to know "what could be done in Russia without working with the Bolsheviks."[33]

Although ARC officials in the Baltic region stressed that their "mission was of a strictly humanitarian nature," it was only when "large areas of Finland and the three Baltic states . . . had been liberated from the Bolsheviks" that the Red Cross considered "sending a commission to undertake relief work in those countries." As Loy Henderson recalled, the Red Cross "had been militarized in the war," and its activities were closely coordinated with U.S. diplomacy and military strategy. The repatriation of Russian prisoners of war, for example, was delayed in order to avoid adding men to the ranks of Bolshevik armies, and American officials emphasized "weeding out future Bolshevist propagandists" from POWs to be repatriated to the Baltic region. Red Cross officials were careful to ascertain that supplies they distributed to civilians in the Baltic would not "be handed over to the Russian Bolsheviks," but they felt no compunction about turning over to the Russian Northwestern Army thousands of suits of underwear and pairs of socks.[34]

ARC activity in the Baltic states, as in in north Russia, south Russia, and Siberia, was guided more by enthusiasm for anti-Bolshevik campaigns than by impartial humanitarianism. In June 1919 one Red Cross captain reported glowingly on the struggle of "the little army of Lithuania . . . to free the country from Bolshevism" and noted that "Mr. Hoover's men . . . are following every Military advance here as quickly as the Railroad bridges can be repaired." In November, Lt. Colonel Edward Ryan, ARC commissioner for western Russia and the Baltic states, received a medal from General N. N. Iudenich in recognition of Red Cross medical supplies and other support to the Russian Northwestern Army. Ryan thanked Iudenich for the honor, expressed sympathy for his cause, and hoped to be able to do more for his army in the future.[35]

Although American relief efforts were strongly influenced by anti-Bolshevik sentiment, Hoover and other U.S. officials maintained that U.S.

plans "should have no political objective or other aim than the maintenance of life and order." Hoover, Wilson, and other American leaders believed that, in contrast to the greedy designs of Old World representatives, enlightened Americans sought no special privileges and did not intervene in the contests between orderly political forces within foreign countries. In their eyes, Bolshevism was beyond the pale of legitimate political activity, and using food shipments to preserve "order" against such radicalism did not constitute selfish intervention. In this sense, acting "to prevent revolution" or thwart Bolshevism was considered "humanitarian."[36]

In his typically blunt manner, Robert Lansing summarized the political conditions for relief work in a proposed statement he submitted to Wilson on November 21, 1918. "In all parts of Russia where the people desire to safeguard the principles of democratic freedom won by their Revolution," Lansing wrote, "the United States purposes [sic]to assist by all the means in its power." However, the United States could not "take part in measures which would tend to prolong" Bolshevik control of Russian territory. It could not render assistance to that part of Russia "until the authorities at Moscow and Petrograd definitely abandon government by mass terror and murder and at the same time obligate themselves . . . to restore order and the due process of law and set up a government based on the freely expressed will of the whole people." Wilson deferred issuing such a statement because he did not want to preempt discussions with Allied leaders and because of his general aversion to public clarifications of his ambiguous policy toward Russia. Nonetheless, Lansing's paper was a candid exposition of attitudes shared by almost all U.S. diplomats. At Paris in February 1919, Lansing approved a "statement of the principles constituting the policy of the United States," prepared by junior aide Christian Herter (who forty years later succeeded John Foster Dulles as secretary of state), which included the announcement that "the Associated Governments have firmly resolved to do all in their power to protect the newly constituted and friendly states bordering on Russia from the aggression of invading armies recruited from within Russia and to send to these states all assistance possible including food and other supplies." While Wilson vacillated and hedged, most officials responsible for carrying out American policy hewed to a more consistent line of treating Bolsheviks as dangerous untouchables.[37]

The Hoover-Nansen Proposal

For a brief period in March and April 1919, American officials in Paris did consider proposals for extending relief to territory controlled by the Soviet government. During the first three months of the year, foreign military intervention in Russia seemed to have blown upon the fires of Bolshevism, causing them to burn hotter and throw off dangerous sparks. In late March and early April, the flames appeared to leap into central Europe with the establishment of Soviet republics in Hungary and Bavaria. Alarmed U.S. and Allied representatives discussed the possibility of wider applications of American flour to smother the blazes.

Formal statements prepared by Hoover and others stressed "humanitarian" motives for offering to send food to Bolshevik Russia. An April 9 letter from the Big Four to Norwegian explorer Fridtjof Nansen, who was acting as an intermediary, emphasized that the delivery of food to Russia was offered "without thought of political, military, or financial advantage," and did not have "any other aim than the 'humanitarian purpose of saving life.'"[38]

However, political considerations were uppermost in the minds of the men who struggled to shape the proposals. House and Bullitt saw the offer of relief and an armistice to the Bolsheviks as a way to check "the advance of Bolshevism westward" and begin developing a *modus vivendi* with the Soviet government.[39] Most American officials, though, were more interested in the possibilities for weakening and undermining the Bolshevik regime, and they opposed any language or form of communicating the proposals that might appear to condone, recognize, or strengthen it.

Hoover conceived of tightly conditioned food distribution in Soviet Russia as a way to quarantine and eliminate the Bolshevik contagion. On March 28, Hoover recommended to Wilson that relief to Russia be predicated upon "assurances that the Bolsheviki will cease all militant action across certain defined boundaries and cease their subsidizing of disturbances abroad." Containment of the plague was essential, Hoover explained in a press release in late April: "The newly born democracies of Siberia, Kuban, Finland, Esthonia, Lettlandt, Livonia, . . . and other nationalities which surround Bolshevik Russia must have a breathing spell to build up some stability." While Soviet Russia's neighbors gained strength, relief workers could irradiate the breeding ground of the disease. In this way, Hoover believed, "Bolshevism will die out much more quickly."[40]

Some historians have suggested that Wilson was inclined to conciliate the Bolsheviks and that this put him at odds with Hoover, who tried to "sabotage" the relief plan.[41] However, the divergence between the two men should not be exaggerated. While Wilson vacillated between the positions of Bullitt and Hoover, on balance Wilson was closer to Hoover.

To avoid "giving Lenin the power that would be conferred upon him by distribution of hundreds of thousands of tons of wheat," as Lloyd George put it, the Council of Four stipulated on April 9 that the "distribution should be solely under the control of the people of Russia themselves." Local communities and a neutral commission, not Moscow, would be in charge. As Wilson said, distribution "by a neutral organization" was "an essential condition." This provision of foreign food, Hoover anticipated, would counterbalance the Bolsheviks' use of food rations to lure army recruits, reward supporters, and starve class enemies.[42]

The final text of the Big Four offer was an ambiguous compromise. A draft by House aides Gordon Auchincloss and David Hunter Miller required the Red Army to cease fighting without comparably restraining White forces. Bullitt protested that the one-sided Auchincloss-Miller armistice proposal was "absolutely unfair" and tried to require an evenhanded "cessation of all hostilities within the territory of the former Russian Empire." However, at the insistence of the French, who were supporting anti-Bolshevik armies on the southern and western frontiers of Russia, the wording was changed to "within definitive lines in the territory of Russia." Although the letter also specified "a complete suspension of the transfer of troops and military material of all sorts to and within Russian territory," it was still possible to interpret the proposal as requiring a Bolshevik cease-fire but not an end to foreign intervention or a halt by White armies.[43]

In May, Soviet leaders rejected the proposal. Lenin and Chicherin particularly objected to what they regarded as a unilateral armistice, designed to prevent Red Army "successes." They were willing "to discuss cessation of hostilities" only as part of a comprehensive discussion of their relations to their adversaries, "that is in the first place to the Associated Governments." Wilson commented to Clemenceau and Lloyd George that Soviet leaders "were perfectly correct in claiming that the Allies were supporting Koltchak and Denikin, and not putting pressure on them to stop fighting," but he was not prepared to push very hard for a more evenhanded policy.[44]

Before the Soviet rejection was received, the Hoover-Nansen Plan had already met fierce resistance from anti-Bolshevik Russian leaders in Paris, French politicians and newspapers, and conservative Britons. When the signatures of the four heads of state were finally secured in late April, the French and British refused to send the telegram to Moscow, and it had to be dispatched from Berlin. By then the Allies and most Americans had lost interest in the relief proposal. House had tried to use Allied leaders' fear of Bolshevism to build support for a settlement with Soviet Russia, but that fear faded with news that Admiral Kolchak's armies were advancing from Siberia. In early May Vance McCormick suggested to Nansen that in view of the apparent success of Kolchak, he might withdraw the relief offer.[45]

Economic and Military Aid to Anti-Bolshevik Nationalists in the Baltic Region

The wrangling in Paris over the terms of possible relief to Soviet Russia did not entail a suspension of aid to various anti-Bolshevik forces. While leaders in Paris debated, American officials in France and in the field worked to deliver food only to areas liberated from Bolshevik control.

In March 1919, the American Commission to Negotiate Peace dispatched a Mission to the Baltic Provinces, led by Lt. Colonel Warwick Greene. After reaching Libau, in the southwest portion of Latvia not controlled by Red forces, Greene wired an urgent request for food and relief officials. This was "very important," Greene advised the peace commissioners in April, "as sections freed from Bolshevists must be provided with adequate food ration. Otherwise we are nourishing bolshevism behind fighting front." The U.S. commissioners sympathized with Greene's recommendations. They informed him in late May that Hoover had been directed to continue providing food "to all nonbolshevist areas in the Baltic region without respect to political control."[46]

In May 1919, anti-Bolshevik Russian and Estonian troops pushed from Estonia into Soviet territory and seemed for a time to be rolling toward Petrograd. The advance raised an urgent question about how the people of Petrograd would be fed once they were liberated. In response, Hoover announced at the end of the month that his instructions were "to feed all people where sufficiently orderly government is established and maintained." "We shall not be far behind the mine sweepers that the British Navy are sending into the Gulf of Finland to clear the channel," he promised, "if Petrograd is captured by the Russian Army now operating against the Bolsheviks southwest of the city."[47]

In the view of many U.S. representatives, food shipments were not an inherent human right but a reward for preserving "orderly" politics and waging war against Bolshevism. Thus John Gade, the U.S. naval attaché assigned to the Baltic mission, argued in May 1919 that Estonia was "unquestionably worthy of assistance in various forms," since it had "fought its own hard fight against Bolshevism with courage and persistency." However, disturbed by "steadily increasing radical tendencies" in Estonian politics, Gade urged that if Estonian leaders carried out "communistic promises" of land reform or concluded peace with the Soviet regime, U.S. aid should be halted. Hoover was of like mind: if the Estonians would not give reasonable support to anti-Bolshevik Russian forces, he cabled, "we will lose our interest very promptly in Esthonians."[48]

In the Baltic region, as in other parts of the former Russian empire, Americans faced the problem that popular self-government might lead to something uncomfortably akin to Bolshevism. In November 1918, Lansing suggested to Wilson that "in distinguishing between representatives of order and any others, we do not at all oppose socialistic movements or governments as such but only where they are definitely undemocratic and unrepresentative of the majority will." In practice, however, the popularity of socialist programs was one of the things that alarmed U.S. officials and led them to intervene in local politics. Thus, Warwick Greene recognized in April 1919 that the provisional government of Latvia, based in Libau, had "no mandate from the people of Latvia" and "would be overthrown immediately if there were popular election." When the provisional government was deposed by conservative Balts, Greene urged Allied insistence upon the reinstatement of the centrist regime because it was the best available bulwark against Bolshevism. After the regime was reestablished, Greene explained to one of its leaders that while "America does not wish to interfere or intervene in the internal politics of Latvia, . . . American sympathies are with the people of Latvia in their efforts toward self-determination and in their struggle against the destructive force of Bolshevism." Promoting "a political and social truce . . . to enable a vigorous prosecution of the war against Bolshevism" did not, in Greene's mind, constitute intervention.[49]

American assistance to anti-Soviet forces along the Baltic was not limited to such political support and "humanitarian" supplies of food, clothing, and medicine. As anti-Bolshevik armies advanced toward Petrograd between May and October 1919, the United States also provided them with weapons and approved naval support in the rear of their operations. Thus, after liberals' hopes to extend economic relief to Soviet Russia had been dashed, American policy increasingly resembled the combined military and economic intervention that had been advocated by conservative advisors in late 1918 and early 1919.

On May 7, 1919, an officer fresh from the Baltic states roused Vance McCormick and Herbert Hoover by reporting that Estonian and other forces were making a "great fight against Bolshevists," but if Americans failed to "send assistance immediately they will fall into the hands of the Bolshevists." McCormick immediately planned to see President Wilson about the matter. On the same day, Hoover sent a memorandum to the Big Four about the situation at Riga, where the Latvian "Bolshevik Government," in part because it was "unable to provide foodstuffs," had been compelled to withdraw its troops. With that army still lurking in the vicinity, and with "anarchy" in the city, Hoover suggested that an Allied "naval escort" and "military protection" were required to safeguard delivery of food to the newly liberated capital.[50]

Seeking an immediate response, Hoover urged Wilson on May 9 "to take some more definite action with regard to . . . the three Baltic States." Ignoring the 1917 election results and the fact that the Latvian Soviet had ruled most of Latvia for several months, Hoover flatly asserted that "the population in none of these states is Bolshevik." "In many places," he continued, "they are putting up a good fight to try and establish their independence of the Moscow tyranny." To assist this fight, the ARA director recommended that the United States and the Allies send naval forces to "protect the relief of all the [Baltic] coastal towns" and "furnish military supplies to the established governments so as to enable them to maintain order in the interior and to defend their borders."[51]

Occupied with other matters, Wilson initially had Hoover's proposal referred to the Council of Ten, which set up a committee to study the issue. On May 13, that committee, including Hoover, determined that "as the despatch of Allied troops to the Baltic Provinces was out of the question, the only alternative was the organization of such native forces and volunteers from outside as might be obtainable." The committee further decided, according to Hoover, that the equipment and training of these forces "for defense against the Bolsheviks and for the retirement of the Germans from their territories" should be assisted by a credit of ten million pounds and supervised by an Allied military mission under British command.[52]

After further prodding from Hoover, Wilson finally read his May 9 letter "with deep interest and concern" and presented it to the Council of Four. Following a suggestion from Lloyd George, Wilson directed Hoover to confer with British Admiral George Hope about the feasibility of his program. Moving rapidly, Hoover saw the admiral and "urged that naval destroyers be sent at once." By the end of May, Hoover had accomplished his main objectives: an Allied military mission was dispatched to the Baltic states, followed by British and American destroyers.[53]

To support anti-Bolshevik forces in the Baltic region, the United States also authorized sales of weapons to the armies that were pushing Red units back to the north and east. On May 23, the Council of Foreign Ministers approved a recommendation presented by Hoover that arms and munitions, as well as food and clothing, should be provided to the Baltic states. Wilson and the Allied prime ministers affirmed that decision on May 24, after they received a military briefing that "the Esthonians had made a considerable advance, and, if aided by a rising in Petrograd, might even hope to capture that city." The American mission in Paris further approved of the sale of rifles by U.S. companies "to Finland and that portion of Esthonia and Latvia which is non-Bolshevik."[54]

The Council of Four returned to the question of providing military aid to the Baltic states on June 13. When Wilson asked, "Is there reason to send munitions to the local forces?" Lloyd George reminded him, "We have done it already." Wilson quickly concurred: "We must continue." He formally agreed with Lloyd George and Clemenceau "that the local national forces in the Baltic Provinces should be supported with equipment, arms, ammunition, clothing, and supplies generally."[55]

Thus, on two occasions Wilson personally approved of military aid to anti-Bolshevik forces, some of which he knew were seeking to capture the old Russian capital. Although Wilson sometimes expressed frustration at the difficulty of forming a policy toward the kaleidoscopic Russian situation, his decisions in the late spring of 1919 were consistent with the prevailing direction that had been set in December 1917 when he first approved of financial assistance to anti-Bolshevik forces in southern Russia.

A Moral Blockade against Bolshevik Russia

The flip side of a policy of shipping food and weapons to anti-Bolshevik forces was an effort to keep supplies from reaching people and armies in Bolshevik-ruled territories. In 1918, the U.S. War Trade Board, Federal Reserve Board, and Shipping Board had imposed strict controls on the licensing, financing, and shipping of goods to Russia, which allowed them to block almost all exports to Soviet Russia while permitting trade with White regions. After the Armistice, U.S. officials reaffirmed most of those controls. While preserving U.S. freedom of action, they pressed for closer coordination with the Allied Blockade Committee, which decided to do everything possible to discourage and obstruct commerce with Bolshevik Russia. In 1919, the Wilson administration maintained its effective ban on trade with Soviet Russia, although legal complications prevented it from joining a formal Allied blockade.[56]

Discussions of blockade issues by Allied and American officials often centered on the Baltic Sea. Since anti-Bolshevik military operations in north Russia, Siberia, and south Russia effectively precluded supplies from reaching the Bolsheviks from those areas, the Baltic ports were the only possible breaches in the wall. Despite the Royal Navy's domination of the Baltic, British leaders worried that some neutral ships might slip through at the very moment when the starving city of Petrograd appeared ready to succumb. Ensuring that no supplies reached Red territory seemed a necessary complement to the military operations by the small White forces under General Iudenich.

Free trade had long been a cardinal American principle. Wilson had made it the second of his Fourteen Points, calling for "absolute freedom of navigation upon the seas, . . . alike in peace and in war."[57] This position created a potential for some friction with the world's greatest sea power. Although British and American officials shared a desire to hasten the demise of the Bolshevik regime, tension over freedom of the seas hindered cooperation in economic warfare against Soviet Russia.

In early 1919, Wilson and some of his liberal aides seemed inclined to remove restrictions on trade with Russia. After returning from Moscow in March, Bullitt argued that lifting the blockade against Soviet Russia and delivering supplies regularly to the Russian people would give the Western nations a powerful hold over Russians by making them fear that the delivery of supplies might be stopped. About the same time, Wilson told his fellow heads of state in Paris, "The only way to kill Bolshevism is to establish the frontiers and to open all the doors to commerce."[58]

Wilson's statement was not followed by action to open commerce with Soviet Russia. In March his top aides *were* working to lift the Allied blockade in the Baltic, but *only* to allow goods to go to non-Bolshevik areas. On March 15, Vance McCormick and other U.S. representatives on the Blockade Committee "tried to free Poland, Esthonia, Lettland and Lithuania from further blockade restrictions" in order "to discourage Bolshevism" along the Baltic. For two weeks British delegates resisted this move, prompting Americans to suspect that their cousins were seeking "some trade advantage." However, on March 28 U.S. officials managed to push through a relaxation of the blockade for Estonia and Poland, contingent upon guarantees that no commodities would be "exported to Germany and Bolshevik Russia." Three weeks later, U.S. and Allied delegates "authorised the relaxation of the blockade in the case of Latvia," with the stipulation that "food should not be landed unless reasonable security existed that it would reach the people and not the Bolshevists."[59]

Lansing and McCormick were not knowingly violating Wilson's instructions or sabotaging his policy. Their actions were broadly consistent with Wilson's reliance on economic sanctions as a method of combating Bolshevism and enforcing the will of the great powers.

In December 1918 Wilson had announced that if any country refused to listen to a prospective league of nations, the offender "should be boycotted absolutely by the other powers. . . . Their frontiers would be hermetically sealed." Elaborating, Wilson said that "the alternative to war" was "the boycott," which could be used against "a state that had been guilty of wrong-doing. Under this plan no nation would be permitted to be an outlaw, free to work out its evil designs against a neighbor or the world."[60]

Although Wilson's anger at Bolshevik wrongdoing ebbed in early 1919, by the late spring he was firmly convinced that Soviet Russia was a dangerous outlaw, and he explicitly approved commercial punishment of Bolshevik wickedness. When the Council of Four discussed the lifting of restrictions on trade with Germany on May 9, Wilson agreed with the prime ministers "that the removal of the Blockade would not apply to Bolshevist Russia."[61]

The continued use of this stick against the Bolsheviks was made difficult by the fact that the United States had never declared war against Soviet Russia and by the conclusion of peace with Germany. As the members of the Supreme Economic Council (SEC) observed on June 7, "restrictions upon commercial intercourse with Bolshevist Russia" had been maintained "by legislation under the War Powers Laws of the various Governments." This legislation would lapse "with the termination of the state of war," and the SEC "felt that there would be great difficulty in securing from the respective legislative bodies the special legislation necessary to enable the restrictions to be continued in force solely against Bolshevist Russia." When the Council of Four considered the SEC note on June 17, Wilson pointed out that "a legal blockade could not be established after peace had been made." While Lloyd George regarded the "hostilities" in north Russia as being virtually a war, Wilson insisted that "this did not constitute a legal state of war, since there had been no formal declaration of war. Consequently, there was no legal basis for a blockade." [62]

Although the president was emphatic about these points of international law, he was not averse to finding other ways to achieve the same end. Hence, he agreed with the other members of the Council of Four to end the blockade formally and technically but leave the public impression that it was still in place. While "measures are not still to be taken to prevent commodities from reaching Bolshevik Russia or Hungary," the Big Four resolved, "there should be an abstention from any positive measures or public announcements indicating a resumption of such trade." In addition, at Wilson's suggestion, the heads of state agreed that the SEC "should be asked . . . whether . . . means could be found for preventing war material from being carried by sea from Germany to Bolshevik Russia." [63]

At a press conference ten days later, on June 27, Wilson indicated that he had no objections to trade with the Bolsheviks. "There really is no blockade against Russia," Wilson declared. "Theoretically, Russia is free to trade now." In practice there was "nobody to trade with," and "the uncertainty of credit" posed a "real difficulty." But Wilson said he would "raise the war-time prohibition" if he could and wished Congress would do so. Perhaps influenced by the presence among the correspondents of several Soviet sympathizers, including Herbert Bayard Swope and Lincoln Steffens, Wilson stressed that he had taken "particular pains not to interfere with revolutions," and that "it's absolutely none of my business what kind of government another country has." [64]

As was often the case, Wilson's remarks contrasted sharply with the actions of his administration. Only one day before his press conference, a presidential proclamation had revoked all executive orders and proclamations dealing with currency exports and financial transactions, *except in regard to Bolshevik Russia.* On July 14, the War Trade Board sternly announced that the removal of the blockade of Germany two days earlier did not modify restrictions against trade with "that portion of Russia under the control of the Bolshevik authorities." [65]

Although the United States was thus obstructing commerce with Soviet Russia, Wilson irritated Allied leaders by continuing to oppose a formal blockade. When the Allies made a new request in late July for American cooperation in prohibiting neutral ships from sailing to Baltic ports without the permission of the Allied navies, Wilson and Lansing clarified that domestic political considerations as well as constitutional constraints hindered the United States.[66] Conveying Wilson's answer to the Allies, Lansing cabled that while the president fully understood "the reasons for employing war measures to prevent the importation of munitions and food supplies into the portion of Russia now in the hands of the Bolsheviks, he labors under the difficulty of being without constitutional right to prosecute an act of war such as a blockade affecting neutrals unless there has been a declaration of war by the Congress of the United States against the nation blockaded." If Wilson agreed to the Allied proposal, Lansing explained confidentially to the American mission in Paris, it "would arouse serious criticism by Congress" of the president for exceeding his constitutional powers and interfering in the domestic affairs of Russia. "With the present partisan feeling in Congress," Lansing continued, "while the ratification of the Treaty of Peace is undecided, any action which would bring a new controversy or a new excuse for criticism would be manifestly unwise." These legal and political constraints did not prevent Wilson from indicating another method of keeping supplies from reaching the Bolsheviks. Although Wilson could not participate in a formal prohibition of trade, he could endorse a voluntary, moral embargo. He therefore suggested a joint note to neutral governments that would set forth "the menace to such countries and to the world of any increase of the Bolshevik power," and that would request the neutrals "to take immediate steps to prevent trade and commerce with Bolshevik Russia." Lansing added that Washington "could deny clearance to all American vessels for the Baltic ports . . . as well as passports to persons seeking to visit those regions." If other governments took the same action it "would accomplish the same purpose as a hostile blockade." A week later the heads of delegations in Paris accepted Wilson's proposal for "measures which should be equivalent to a Blockade of Russian Baltic ports."[67]

The Wilson administration's inability to join in a formal blockade did not signify a departure from its "policy of non-intercourse with the Bolshevik territory." In August, John Foster Dulles met with Polk about "steps to prevent commercial intercourse with bolshevist Russia," and then attended other conferences to implement the policy. At the end of September, Polk and other heads of delegations in Paris followed Wilson's suggestion and approved a note to neutral governments asking them to cooperate in preventing commerce with Bolshevik Russia because of the "grave danger" posed by the "avowed hostility of the Bolsheviki toward all governments." During Iudenich's fall campaign to seize Petrograd, the State Department continued to refuse export licenses and clearance papers for shipments to Soviet Russia.[68]

At one point during the Paris Peace Conference, Wilson told his fellow heads of state, "If it were up to me alone, I would have lifted the blockade a long time ago." However, when Wilson was freed from the constraints of coalition diplomacy he maintained what amounted to a blockade of Soviet Russia. After White armies failed to overthrow the Bolsheviks, the Wilson administration continued to apply the Trading with the Enemy Act to prohibit "the shipment of coin, bullion, and currency to that part of Russia under the control of the so-called Bolshevik Government." Although the Allies lifted their blockade, Wilson remained stubbornly opposed to trade with Soviet Russia. As Secretary of the Navy Daniels noted after a cabinet meeting in May 1920, Wilson "did not believe we should open trade relations with Russia, for it would soon involve recognition of Soviet government." [69]

Wilson might have done more "to kill Bolshevism," as he put it in March 1919, by opening "all the doors to commerce." In June he opposed reimposition of the blockade against Germany because that would "only produce Bolshevism." Yet that insight did not lead him to remove the barriers to trade with Soviet Russia that gave Soviet leaders an excuse for economic hardships.[70]

Unleashing the Finns?

With little money and no U.S. troops available to influence events in the Baltic region, some American officials were interested in using foreign forces to combat Bolshevism. Two of the possible proxies were the Finnish army and German soldiers.

In 1918, with the assistance of German troops, former Russian general Karl Gustav von Mannerheim led White forces to victory in the Finnish civil war. In February 1919, Mannerheim offered Allied and American leaders a proposition. His troops could "easily take Petrograd unassisted," he suggested, "if the Allies were prepared to support him and to provision the city." Elaborating this proposal, Mannerheim told a U.S. naval attaché that his army was "capable of defeating the Bolsheviki in northern Russia," and he was "willing to commence hostilities immediately if encouraged . . . by the Allies and assured that the United States would hasten sending food supplies to Finland." A few weeks later the White Finns added a condition, stating that "Finland would expect the Murman Peninsula as a reward for taking Petrograd."[71]

Robert Imbrie, Vice Consul at Vyborg, was enthusiastic about the possibility of launching an anti-Bolshevik campaign from Finland. In addition to the White Finns, he informed the State Department, Russian anti-Bolsheviks in Finland had "perfected a military organization numbering, they state, 10,000 men." Their objective was "the capture of Petrograd and afterward Moscow and the overthrow of the Bolsheviks." All these Russians needed was "sufficient food to supply Petrograd and Moscow once they are taken"; in return they would "be guided by the wishes" of the United States and would give Washington "the preferential interest . . . both politically and economically."[72]

While Imbrie readily accepted the exaggerated claims of anti-Bolshevik Russians, other U.S. officials were more cautious. The U.S. consul at Helsinki even condemned the idea of encouraging operations from Finland as "the height of folly." More temperately, Frank Polk informed Imbrie that the State Department did not have "adequate information regarding Russian Whites." While Washington was "not in a position to offer any support or assistance," it wanted to be kept advised of developments.[73]

Herbert Hoover was more eager to assist the White Finns. In addition to respecting the Finns' honesty and work ethic, Hoover was impressed by their "sturdy fight to get on a basis of liberal democracy," as he described it to Wilson in April. To support the White Finns, Hoover arranged for food shipments on credit, delivered with American naval protection. He also persuaded Wilson to grant diplomatic recognition to help the White government consolidate its position and enable Finns to use bank deposits in New York to pay for food.[74]

In the spring, General N. N. Iudenich took over efforts to organize Russian anti-Bolshevik forces on Finnish soil. His negotiations with Mannerheim for Finnish support were difficult and protracted, particularly because conservative Russian patriots like Iudenich were reluctant to recognize Finnish independence. Finally, a Iudenich-Mannerheim agreement on June 19 seemed to open the way for a joint attack on Petrograd.[75]

In anticipation of the occupation of Petrograd, ARA officials in Finland and Estonia signed agreements with Iudenich and other Russian leaders in late June for the delivery of food to "such regions as were cleared of the Bolsheviks." As an ARA man informed Hoover, the operation then awaited word of the Allies' attitude. From Vyborg, Imbrie renewed his appeal for U.S. sanction of Finnish action. "If our Government desires the fall of Petrograd and the overthrow of the Bolsheviks," Imbrie cabled on July 2, "such intimation should be conveyed to the Finns together with an approval for their advance." On July 7, Lansing and the other heads of delegations in Paris decided to inform Mannerheim that, while they did not want to put "any pressure on the Finnish Government," they "would have no objection" to his commencing operations against Petrograd.[76]

By the time this message was sent, however, the window of opportunity for seizing Petrograd was closing. Admiral Kolchak rejected the Iudenich-Mannerheim agreement, saying that only the Russian Constituent Assembly, which would meet after removal of the Bolshevik regime in Moscow, could recognize Finnish independence. Later in July, Mannerheim lost the Finnish presidency in elections that showed the strength of center-left parties who were opposed to intervention in the Russian Civil War.[77]

When Iudenich's efforts to capture Petrograd faltered in the fall, British, French, and some American representatives pressed the Finns to support the Russian campaign. However, perhaps because of the riskiness of the venture, the possibility of Soviet retaliation against Finland, and awareness of turmoil in Finnish domestic politics, Lansing insisted that "the attitude of the United States in this matter is entirely noncommittal."[78]

Using and Being Used by the Germans

In January 1918, Wilson declared that his peace program would require "the evacuation of all Russian territory." At that time, the Soviet regime appeared to Wilson to be a transitory farce, and the German occupation of Russian territory threatened a long-term domination of Russian markets and resources. Ten months later, with Germany suing for peace amid revolutionary turmoil, Lenin was still in power and Bolshevism seemed to Wilson and other Americans to be a poisonous menace. Allied and American representatives, including Colonel House, feared that evacuation of German troops from the western provinces of the former Russian empire would allow Bolshevism to slither across those lands. To guard against this danger, the Armistice signed on November 11 provided that German soldiers would continue to occupy Russian territory until they were directed to withdraw by the Allies.[79]

Some Russians immediately protested. In a memorandum that Wilson read in mid-November, the Interparty League for the Restoration of Free Russia, a union of non-Bolshevik and non-monarchist Russians in the United States, demanded that "the Clause of the Armistice according to which the German armies should remain temporarily on Russian soil, as the guardians of order in Russia, should be declared as void and annulled." However, when Wilson and Allied leaders prepared the peace treaty in the spring of 1919, they decided to allow German forces to remain for a while longer. Article 433 stipulated that to guarantee the abrogation of the Brest-Litovsk Treaty and "to ensure the restoration of peace and good government in the Baltic Provinces and Lithuania," all German troops in those territories should return to Germany "as soon as the Allied and Associated powers thought the moment suitable."[80]

The diplomatic representatives of Baltic nationalist governments were divided over the maintenance of German soldiers in their countries, with the stronger Estonian groups often demanding withdrawal while the weaker regimes in Latvia and Lithuania tended to favor retaining German units to defend against a Bolshevik advance. Ideally, Baltic nationalists would have liked Allied troops to replace the Germans, but if that was not possible they were alarmed by the idea of a precipitate German withdrawal. In the last days of 1918, Latvian nationalist leader Karlis Ulmanis even signed an agreement with German representatives that promised Latvian citizenship to *Freikorps* volunteers who would fight against Red forces in Latvia.[81]

Wilson and his advisors were ambivalent about leaving German forces in the Baltic states. In addition to worrying that the troops would assist the extension of German economic domination of the region, U.S. officials were troubled by the way German soldiers protected the privileges of Baltic barons and participated in intrigues against local governments, thereby complicating the task of buttressing nationalist dikes against the Red flood tides. Despite these concerns, the greater fear of Bolshevism and the perceived weakness of Baltic nationalist movements led Americans to support the retention of German units in Latvia and Lithuania.

Once the defeat of Germany seemed assured in the fall of 1918, most U.S. leaders concluded that Bolshevism was a more dangerous threat than Prussianism. In October 1918, disturbed by public and congressional demands for excessively tough or vindictive treatment of Germany, Wilson asked, "Had you rather have the Kaiser or the Bolsheviks"? Shortly before the German surrender, Lansing observed that "Bolshevism" was a bigger menace than "Absolutism" and concluded that "a Bolshevik Germany" would be "worse, far worse, than a Prussianized Germany."[82]

Much as he had qualms about aggressive foreign military intervention in north Russia and Siberia, Wilson had scruples against using German troops offensively. On March 29, 1919, Wilson rejected a German offer that if the Allies provided locomotives they would "drive the Bolsheviks out of Riga," arguing "that we would become allies of the Germans against our former allies, who have not attacked us."[83] However, Wilson's principled statement did not prevent American policy from taking the form of a de facto alliance with German forces against Soviet Russia. By sanctioning the defensive use of German troops, Wilson, House, and Lansing permitted them to remain in positions where they could subsequently engage in offensive actions.

German troops were employed most actively in Latvia. In March 1919, with a Soviet regime in power in Riga and most of northern Latvia, U.S. officials contemplated inserting and supporting German forces on the southwest coast. In April, the head of the U.S. Baltic mission recommended that German forces in southern Latvia be allowed "to supply themselves by sea . . . to maintain their forces now operating against Bolshevists." The Council of Four subsequently decided to allow provisions to reach the Germans, though it refused to permit reinforcements.[84]

The risks of playing with fire were soon brought home to American officials when German forces assisted aristocratic Balts in deposing the Latvian provisional government at Libau on April 16. Faced with this complication, Lansing and the Allied foreign ministers discussed whether to stop sending supplies for military operations to the Germans, noting that in that event "they cannot hold back the Bolshevists." Despite the German political intrigue, the Council of Foreign Ministers agreed "to continue to allow coal from Germany to go through, provided it was only used for supplying the front now set up against the Bolshevists." In Latvia, "food distribution was temporarily held up" as a sign of displeasure with the Germans, who then allowed the restoration of the Latvian provisional government. The German-supported coup led some U.S. advisors to urge immediate evacuation of the German troops. However, American representatives in the field stressed that this was not feasible, since the "immediate departure of German forces [would] deliver [the] country to bolshevism unless replaced by other forces."[85]

American officials hoped that eventually the German forces could be replaced by a Latvian army, but in the meantime they were prepared to make further use of the Germans. Less than two weeks after the coup at Libau, U.S. military advisors suggested that Germans, together with Balts, Letts, and Russians, "could advance and take Riga, especially with naval assistance." In a reversal of the usual ratio of moral sensitivity, American officials' qualms about enlisting German assistance were faint and fleeting in comparison to the queasiness experienced by some of their Allied counterparts. At a meeting of the Council of Foreign Ministers on May 9, Hoover urged joint action to secure Riga and prevent "the Bolsheviks" from returning. "[A] humanitarian policy," Hoover argued, "would allow the Germans to do the work on land in co-operation with the British Navy acting at sea." French Foreign Minister Pichon objected that accepting German cooperation would be "very bad from a moral point of view." Foreign Secretary Balfour thought "it was rather a strong order to expect the British and German forces to co-operate." However, Lansing threw heavy punches in support of Hoover's proposal, hitting the British for being reluctant "to co-operate with the Germans purely for fear of giving the latter some economic advantages," and charging that they "would be wholly responsible for the deaths that would occur" if Hoover's plan were rejected. In stark contrast to Wilson's remarks of March 29, Lansing argued that "paradoxical as it might seem, the Allied and Associated Governments were, by the Armistice, Allies of Germany in the Baltic provinces." Rebutting Balfour's statement that "the Germans had been behaving disgracefully in the Baltic provinces," Lansing blandly maintained that "there existed no danger of German misbehaviour."[86]

While waiting for warships to be sent to Riga, Hoover impatiently encouraged additional action to terminate the "anarchy of wholesale massacre and murder" there. According to Hoover, around May 20 he sent a telegram to German General Rüdiger von der Goltz, "asking him to occupy Riga," and then dispatched food shipments to follow the Germans into the city. Wilson does not appear to have condemned either the German occupation of Riga or Hoover's encouragement of it.[87] On May 23, after learning that the Germans had occupied Riga, the Council of Foreign Ministers implicitly affirmed that action. With Hoover and Lansing speaking for the United States, the foreign ministers agreed that "the Germans shall be required to withdraw from Lettland and Lithuania as soon as it is possible to replace them there by organised local forces, but they should remain where they are till further orders."[88]

On June 13, spurred by reports that German units were causing new complications by moving northward into Estonia, the Council of Four decided that the Germans should be ordered to evacuate southern Latvia at once, and to complete the evacuation of former Russian territory "with the least possible delay." To meet "the danger of Bolshevism breaking through to the Baltic and Scandinavia," U.S. and Allied officers proposed expanded support for Baltic nationalist forces to cover the German withdrawal. Wilson agreed with Lloyd George and Clemenceau that this support should be provided. When this assistance was slow to materialize, however, American officers warned that abrupt withdrawal of the German troops would endanger "the internal security" of the Baltic regions, invite "a fresh Bolshevist aggression from Russia," and then allow Bolshevism to "threaten Western Europe."[89]

In the summer and fall of 1919 officials in Paris became more resolute in demanding German withdrawal, but German commanders evaded the orders. Instead of returning to Germany, many *Freikorps* soldiers joined a "West Russian Army" nominally led by Russian Colonel P. M. Bermondt-Avalov, though organized by German officers. Frank Polk indirectly assisted those enlistments by resisting a demand "for the evacuation . . . of individual Germans, who, after being demobilized, had joined Russian units." Other U.S. officials considered aiding the forces under Bermondt-Avalov through the transfer of arms and ammunition Germany had captured in Russia during the war.[90]

While British officers such as General Sir Hubert Gough believed the German menace "was far more serious than the danger of Bolshevism" in the Baltic region, U.S. officials often took the opposite position. Allen Dulles reflected the priorities of many Americans, including Lansing, when he suggested in October 1919 that the problem of "establishing an orderly government in Russia" had to be resolved before Americans could work on "establishing a barrier against German penetration." Dulles therefore argued that the United States should "support all anti-Bolshevist elements — Baltic provinces, Kolchak, Denikin, Yudenitch, — until Bolshevism is out of the way, and then endeavor to support the orderly element or elements in Russia which are most likely to successfully combat German penetration." Although Wilson showed more reluctance to utilize German forces, Lansing, Hoover, and other officials who were formulating U.S. policy eagerly employed troops of the old enemy, Germany, against the new and greater enemy of Bolshevism.[91]

American Policy toward Baltic Nationalism: Self-Determination vs. Anti-Bolshevism

One reason for the Red victory in the Russian Civil War was the Soviet readiness to play the nationalities card. Lenin and other Bolsheviks were willing to relinquish claims to rule non-Russian groups along their borders, at least in the short-run, if that would hasten world revolution or promote the survival of the regime in Moscow. Appearing to champion self-determination helped the Soviet regime to divide its enemies by playing on tensions between ethnic nationalists and Russian imperialists.[92]

Some U.S. officials argued that America should have trumped Lenin's ace by actively supporting the aspirations of the various nationalities for independence and diplomatic recognition. "The only way to get the Lithuanians, Letts, and Esthonians to fight against Bolshevism," Allen Dulles argued, "is to encourage their nationalistic feelings." Other junior advisors who believed the Bolsheviks "were there to stay" wanted to combine protection of "the Baltic barrier," negotiation with the Bolsheviks, and abandonment of White leaders such as Kolchak. Those advisors had an ally in Colonel House, who feared that a reunited Russia under "a great military figure" would be "a menace to the world" and therefore preferred "to see this great Empire fall into several states."[93]

However, President Wilson sympathized more with the squarely legalistic views of his secretary of state on the nationalities problem. Wilson and Lansing were willing to give aid and encouragement to anti-Bolshevik nationalists in the Baltic states, but, confident that the Soviet regime could not survive, and committed to the resurrection of Russia as a large economic and political unit, they were unwilling to extend diplomatic recognition to separatist movements.

Attempting to reconcile national self-determination with the White cause of restoring a great Russia, Lansing and like-minded U.S. officials promoted the idea of national autonomy within a Russian federation. In contrast to House, they were reluctant to abandon the idea of liberating the Russian people from Bolshevism and did not want to settle for the containment of Soviet Russia inside a ring of smaller independent states. "Convinced that Bolshevik domination cannot continue," and worried that "if Russia was broken up into small independent states, they would become a prey to German intrigue and economic penetration," Lansing thought Americans should "look ahead to the time when the Russian people will be free . . . and able to rebuild under enlightened rulers."[94]

Wilson agreed with Lansing that the United States should help Russia to emerge from her civil war with her union restored (apart from the separate nations of Poland and Finland, which had demonstrated their capacities for self-government). As a result, House found in 1918 that he was "not in agreement with the President as to leaving Russia intact." While the colonel wanted "to see Siberia a separate republic, and European Russia divided into three parts," Wilson hoped to restore the territorial integrity and political independence of a Russia that would be open to American trade and investment from the Pacific to the Baltic, not carved into exclusive enclaves.[95]

The sixth of Wilson's Fourteen Points promised "Russia . . . an unhampered and unembarrassed opportunity for the independent determination of her own political development." By the end of the Great War, however, "Russia" was no longer a singular entity. In October 1918, therefore, Walter Lippmann and Frank Cobb attempted to apply Wilson's vague pledge to the Baltic states and other areas of the former Russian empire. They recommended granting recognition and providing assistance to the "provisional governments" on the Russian periphery. Wilson had a major reservation about the Lippmann-Cobb analysis, as he cabled House: "Admission of inchoate nationalities to peace-conference most undesirable." To Wilson, the peoples on the borderlands of Russia were not fully formed nations. They were not worthy of diplomatic recognition or capable of standing alone.[96]

As he prepared to leave for Paris in November, Wilson doubted whether it was feasible, given the "at least temporary disintegration of Russia into at least five parts, . . . to have Russia represented at the peace table." Lansing seized the moment to press for devotion to Russian territorial integrity. He suggested that the United States should "urge that Russian questions be considered as parts of a whole and not as separate problems resulting from what may prove, for the most part, temporary disintegration."[97]

Aboard the ship to France, surrounded by idealistic young advisors, Wilson waffled. According to his physician, Wilson said his policy toward Russia had to be altered. Since Russia had "broken up into several different states," it would "be necessary to follow the principle of self-determination in ascertaining under what sovereignty these various states desire to come."[98]

At Paris, many of the American experts on Russian questions advocated recognition of the Baltic states. In late April, for example, Harvard historians Samuel Eliot Morison and Robert H. Lord argued that the United

States and its allies should no longer delay collective recognition of the nationalist governments of Latvia, Lithuania, and Estonia, which urgently needed moral support to help them defend themselves against Bolshevism.[99] A month later, in a memorandum Lansing shared with Wilson, Morison presciently warned that providing the Estonian government with food and arms to ward off Bolshevism, but leaving the nature of Estonian-Russian relations to be settled when a non-Bolshevik central Russian government was established, would probably backfire by leading the Estonians to negotiate with the Soviet government for a peace treaty that would recognize Estonian sovereignty. Morison therefore believed the United States and its allies should either (1) require prospective rulers of Russia to guarantee Estonian autonomy within a future Russian federation, or (2) recognize Estonian independence, with Russian rights such as access to the Baltic to be guaranteed in a Russian-Estonian treaty.

To Lansing, a stickler on questions of recognition and legitimacy, neither of the alternatives proposed by Morison was feasible or compatible with the recognition of Admiral Kolchak's government that was then under discussion at Paris. While the secretary thought something "might be tried" in the way of mediating between Estonia and Russia, he favored continuing "the present policy" of deferring "the final regulation of the status of Esthonia until after the restoration of a stable government in Russia." As Morison observed, his initiatives were blocked "because everyone hoped to wake up some day and learn Russia had gone 'democratic' again, when she would reproach us for helping to dismember her." Frustrated by the U.S. adoption of a Russian policy that seemed both impractical and unjust, Morison resigned from his position as an advisor to the peace commission on June 15.[100]

In the interest of maintaining the "anti-Bolshevist front" along the Baltic, General Tasker Bliss did seek assurances from Russian leaders that they would respect the "autonomy of Esthonia, Latvia and Lithuania." In response, Ambassador Bakhmeteff called attention to Admiral Kolchak's statement "assuring . . . the autonomy of the various nationalities," which would mean "Provincial Self-Government." However, Bakhmeteff stressed the Russians' understanding that "the United States authorities consider these [Baltic] Provinces as a part of Russia, it being contrary to the intentions of the United States to encourage by any action the dismemberment of Russia."[101]

This was, in fact, U.S. policy. According to Lansing, Wilson said in June that "while he desires the maximum of autonomy and self-government for the Baltic Provinces he does not understand that . . . any commitment has been made as to their independence but that on the contrary the sovereignty of Russia remains unimpaired." Especially after his return from Paris to Washington, Wilson left policy toward the Baltic region largely in the hands of Lansing and other State Department advisors. In meetings of the U.S. peace commissioners on June 30 and July 2, Lansing firmly declared that the United States "was not in favor of independence" for the small states bordering on Russia, "but that it was in favor a single Russia, in which the various portions should have a certain degree of autonomy."[102]

This attitude, shared by many U.S. representatives in the Baltic states, was influenced by economic considerations, a predisposition to favor Russians over other ethnic groups, and a desire to eradicate, not merely confine, Bolshevism. For economic and strategic reasons, Americans argued, Russia had to have access to Baltic ports, through which her commerce could pass out to the Atlantic and across to America. The Baltic peoples, U.S. officials further maintained, were too inexperienced in self-government and too inclined to Bolshevism to be allowed to rule themselves. "Unlike the Finns," Hoover recalled in his memoirs, the people of the "Back Blocs" had "had no experience in self-government." In part because of this inexperience, it was held, self-determination would lead to Bolshevik or at least Bolshevistic governments. "The red tide could not be held by any bulwarks which any of these native races could maintain," reported Lt. Robert Hale. "Esthonia and Latvia were themselves permeated with the Bolshevistic poison and were far too weak within to have any strength without."[103]

These political fears and economic calculations contributed to the U.S. decision to side with Russian advocates of "Russia, One and Indivisible," when they came into conflict with Baltic nationalists. In August 1919, British generals who sought to secure Estonian cooperation with the Northwestern Army's impending offensive against Petrograd bullied General Iudenich into a "preliminary declaration" recognizing the independence of Estonia. Bakhmeteff quickly disavowed this reported agreement, informing the State Department that Iudenich had no authority to take that step. Estonians, not satisfied by the preliminary recognition granted under duress, sought de jure recognition from the Allies at Paris. When the Allies resisted, the Estonians accepted an offer from the Soviet government to begin peace discussions. In response, Bakhmeteff emphasized to the State Department "the extreme seriousness of the situation created in the rear of general Yudenich's army" by the Estonian move. He urged the United States to "cease all material and moral support" of the Estonian government if it made peace with Soviet authorities.[104]

As the Northwestern Army advanced toward Petrograd in September and October, Bakhmeteff met frequently with State Department officials who sympathized with his position and agreed with his advice. In mid-October Lansing noted that he was "disposed to share the Ambassador's views" that the Baltic states "cannot be made an effective barrier against

German penetration into Russia; the effective barrier is Russia itself and the wisest policy would, therefore, be to protect the integrity of Russia [by] supporting the Russians rather than the separatist movements." On October 23, at the climax of the Iudenich campaign, the State Department endorsed Bakhmeteff's suggestion of an ultimatum to the Baltic governments. It urged the British government, which "had been foremost in supporting the Baltic separatist movements," to threaten to terminate such support in order "to influence their course of action with respect to the Bolsheviki."[105]

American Aid to Iudenich's March on Petrograd, Summer–Fall 1919

In the second half of 1919, U.S. military and diplomatic representatives shifted their attention from supporting nationalist groups in the Baltic states to backing the drive by the Russian Northwestern Army to capture Petrograd. Whereas American officials had spoken in the spring about the defensive objective of protecting local nationalist forces, in the summer many called for a more offensive policy.

In June, Lt. Colonel Greene returned from the Baltic states to Paris in order to argue that the United States and the Allies should switch from what he regarded as "an inactive policy" to "an active and aggressive campaign for the defeat of Bolshevism and the reconstruction of Russia." On July 5, an agitated Greene warned the American commissioners that "the summer is slipping by and with it the chance for finally clearing the Baltic Provinces of Bolshevism, capturing Petrograd and organizing an aggressive movement against Bolshevism." To seize the opportunity, Greene recommended that "vigorous steps be taken immediately" to provide "credits, supplies and munitions" to anti-Bolshevik Russian forces.[106]

General Bliss was preeminently responsible for answering such appeals in Paris, and on July 1 he was charged with the oversight of all Russian matters dealt with by the American peace commission. While Greene and other U.S. officers were animated by the desire to drive the Red Army deep into Soviet territory, Bliss was primarily concerned with holding the line against Bolshevism. This attitude led some to believe that Bliss favored a policy of nonintervention and neutrality toward the warring Russian factions. Yet Bliss sympathized with proposals to provide military aid to White forces.[107]

Writing to Ambassador Bakhmeteff on Independence Day, Bliss observed that the approaching withdrawal of German forces and the critical situation in the Baltic region called "for a firm military and political policy in order to maintain this anti-Bolshevist front and not to jeopardize the gains that have already been made from the Bolshevists." Stabilizing this front, Bliss continued, required "the immediate support and strengthening of the Russian Volunteer anti-Bolshevist forces." Searching for a practical way to do this, Bliss asked Bakhmeteff for information about "the measures the representatives of Admiral Kolchak at Paris would propose in order to finance, organize, and support the anti-Bolshevist forces in the Baltic Provinces and Lithuania."[108]

Bakhmeteff replied on July 8, after consulting with other anti-Bolshevik Russians in Paris, including Sergei Sazonov, a former tsarist foreign minister who was serving as minister of foreign affairs for Kolchak's government. Agreeing with Bliss on the need "to support and develop anti-bolshevist action" along the Baltic front, Bakhmeteff wrote that "the most important operation at the present moment consists in the capture of Petrograd." To accomplish this objective, the Kolchak regime was "prepared to assume liabilities towards the U.S. Government resulting from delivery of munitions, materials and food to the anti-bolchevist [sic] forces."[109]

As the American peace commissioners considered this proposition and the appeals by Lt. Colonel Greene, they probed the possibilities for transferring arms from U.S. stockpiles in France to the armies under Iudenich. This method, they realized, involved walking a thin legal line. On July 15, they decided that they could not "properly advise the Liquidation Commission," which had authority over the stockpiles, on the disposal of U.S. property in France, which was "prescribed in a law of Congress." While the peace commissioners were not willing to stick their necks out, they hoped the Liquidation Commission would decide the "sales" were legal and "be glad to make them."[110]

The Wilson administration could not simply give the weapons to the anti-Bolshevik forces. As Lansing noted on July 25, since the "Secretary of War cannot, by law, dispose of surplus munitions, except by sale," it was necessary to coordinate aid to Iudenich with the Kolchak regime, which had assumed responsibility for Russian debts to the United States.[111]

Although Bliss did what he could to support the Russians' negotiations with the U.S. Liquidation Commission, the Commission hesitated since it did not know whether Washington would favor selling supplies for the Russian army in the Baltic region.[112] Across the Atlantic, Bakhmeteff took up the case. Spurred by intimations that British support for Iudenich was going to be curtailed, Bakhmeteff pressed U.S. officials to counterbalance the prospective reductions with American arms. On August 4, emphasizing that the "capture of Petrograd and successful development of anti-Bolshevik action around the Baltic" was of "paramount importance for the whole cause of the liberation and pacification of Russia," Bakhmeteff urged Lansing to nudge the chairman of the Liquidation Commission to release the weapons to "representatives of Admiral Kolchak on relatively liberal conditions." Perhaps in part because of the Wilson administration's troubled relations with Congress, Lansing was not willing to take this potentially controversial step. Lansing conferred with Secretary of War Baker, an opponent of military intervention in Russia, and they decided not to approve Bakhmeteff's request.[113]

Despite that decision, the idea of transferring materials from France was not yet dead. Only three days later, the State Department, prodded again by Bakhmeteff, asked Polk to confer with Bliss and the Liquidation Commission "with a view to supplying the forces acting under General Yudenitch with military equipment from American supplies in France." After investigating, Bliss informed Washington that the Liquidation Commission furnished fifty-five three-ton trucks for the Northwestern Army, but that no further supplies would be forthcoming because the surplus stores had been turned over to the French. According to Bliss, the trucks were to be used for "distributing food to civilian population in rear of Yudenitch army." However, the trucks had been ordered by the army, and once they arrived the army used them for military purposes. In October 1919, as the Northwestern Army drove toward Petrograd, Iudenitch declined to yield the trucks for the transportation of food, saying they were absolutely essential to the success of his army.[114]

In addition to seeking materiel from U.S. sources in France, Russian representatives approached U.S. officials about having Germany turn over to Iudenich military supplies that it had captured from Russian armies during the Great War. After looking into the matter, Bliss reported that until the peace treaty with Germany came into force, "legally no war material in the possession of Germany can be demanded," and that only non-German arms, "little of which probably will be serviceable, can be given to Russia." Despite that pessimistic analysis, Russian diplomats continued to pursue the matter and sympathetic U.S. officials tried to help them. Weeks of inquiries by U.S. diplomats culminated on October 11, when Polk and the other heads of delegations decided that "the Interallied Commissions of Control . . . should direct, if they found it possible, that Russian arms, munitions, and war material retained by Germany should be delivered to the Russian Armies recognized by the Allied and Associated Governments."[115]

A simpler method for providing supplies to the Northwestern Army was to ship them on credit. On July 16, Hoover and the head of the Russian Central Supply Commission in Paris, General Hermonius, agreed that the "Provisional Government of Russia" would issue special treasury notes for supplies from the United States. A month later, Bliss informed Washington that the ARA "has furnished 22,200 tons [of] food to the civilian population in the rear of army of General Yudenich and has taken in exchange securities furnished by the Kolchak Government."[116]

Hoover's office claimed that the food was always "sent with [the] specific understanding that it was for the civilian population." In his memoirs, Hoover asserted that he "did not particularly like the looks of the [Iudenich] expedition," and insisted that the ARA "would feed only civilians and that the British would have to get food for the White Russian troops." Hoover left the impression that the White soldiers received almost no food directly from the ARA, except when they "plundered some of our storehouses in their retreat."[117]

Actually, much of the ARA food was delivered directly to the Northwestern Army with the enthusiastic cooperation of Hoover's representatives. On June 11, ARA officers agreed to furnish the entire ration for the Russian corps because "it looked as if this was a 'military adventure' offering genuine 'assurance of definitely re-establishing order and freeing the territory . . . from Bolshevist control.'" Pleased that ARA "supplies reached [the] Northern Army," Hoover wired his men: "Glad our food is winning in the cause of law and order." Thanking Hoover for this assistance, General A. P. Rodzianko observed in July that "a regular food supply of the starving population and the Army is at least as important as rifles and ammunition in our fight for the liberation of our great country from the red terror." In Washington, Ambassador Bakhmeteff expressed gratitude to Lansing that "the distribution of victuals . . . under the control of General Youdenitch . . . has greatly contributed to the success of the national forces and has led to a decomposition of the Bolshevik lines."[118]

By August 10, all of the supplies the ARA had prepared for the Baltic states had been distributed. Since the chief of the Baltic mission of the ARA "was convinced that Petrograd could not possibly be relieved until late in the fall," he closed down the operation. However, American assistance to the Northwestern Army continued, largely because Wilson administration officials strongly sympathized with the army's anti-Bolshevik cause. On August 18, U.S. representatives suggested to Sazonov that they might be able to provide the Northwestern Army with surplus U.S. Army uniforms. Later in August, Bakhmeteff presented Iudenich's request "that priority in delivering the flour should be given to his troops" rather than Estonian civilians. In response, Lansing asked Hoover to inform him "what arrangements, if any, can be made to supply General Youdenich whose movement is regarded as of great importance."[119]

Hoover's answer contradicted his assertions that the ARA fed only civilians. On August 30, Hoover wired Washington that a steamship was arriving at Tallinn "for General Yudenitch's adjutant with 5,000 tons flour." In addition, Hoover noted, "General Yudenitch has some 10,000 tons of flour and beans stored at Viborg and Narva which will supply bread to his present army and civil population for next two or three months." Thanks to the ARA, then, the Northwestern Army did not face an immediate food crisis. However, since Hoover recognized that Iudenich would "soon be out of bacon," and the ARA had "no more money or supplies," he urged a special effort. Believing that "Yudenitch could at an early date take Petrograd," Hoover argued "that it is wholly illogical to support Kolchak and not to support Yudenitch with arms and supplies."[120]

Although there had been sharp disagreements over Russian policy in the spring, by the fall of 1919 top American officials were united behind the policy of providing as much support to anti-Bolshevik armies as limited resources and domestic political conditions permitted. As Assistant Secretary of State Breckinridge Long told Bakhmeteff on September 4, "We wanted to help Deniken [sic] and Yudinich [sic] and any other movements on the soil of the old Russian Empire which might be strongly against Bolshevism."[121]

The consensus on this policy included the president. Although Wilson was preoccupied with the struggle for ratification of the Versailles treaty, many of his speeches on his Western tour included denunciations of Bolshevism and expressions of his desire to help the Russian people. "There is not a day goes by," Wilson mourned in Minnesota on September 9, "that my heart is not heavy to think of our fellow beings in that great, pitiful Kingdom of Russia, without form, without order, without government." To help the Northwestern Army restore order, the president authorized the Shipping Board to charter to Ambassador Bakhmeteff 45,000 tons of shipping for transporting arms and equipment from British and French ports to General Iudenich's forces.[122]

On September 28, Iudenich launched a final offensive to seize Petrograd. Although the Northwestern Army consisted of barely fifteen thousand men, for three weeks it rolled rapidly toward the old capital. By October 21, Iudenich's vying commanders had raced to within rifle range of the suburbs, and their troops could see the golden dome of St. Isaac's cathedral in the center of the city.[123]

As Iudenich's forces advanced, Wilson's diplomatic advisors agonized over the persistent problem of limited resources to support anti-Bolshevik ventures. In Paris on September 26, Sazonov saw Polk to ask that at least thirty thousand additional tons of foodstuffs be held ready in anticipation "of the fall of Petrograd." Otherwise, "all military operations might be stopped by the lack of food supplies for the famine-stricken population of Petrograd." Polk forwarded the request to Washington, though he was a bit skeptical about the chances of taking Petrograd and he "pointed out that there would be serious difficulties in connection with our Government financing the plan." Responding to Polk on October 2, Acting Secretary Phillips elaborated on the administration's constraints. "We have no funds with which to finance any further food supplies," Phillips confirmed, "and although we anticipate requesting the President to present a general plan to Congress we cannot predict its attitude."[124]

A month later, State Department officials were still considering seeking a congressional authorization to loan Russia $100 million. However, with Wilson bedridden following a stroke, and with many congressmen uncooperative, no action could be taken to make further funds available for the White movements. Hence, when Polk received two anti-Bolshevik leaders on October 22 he had to tell them "that all appropriations made by Congress for relief are exhausted and that under existing laws no credits" could be extended. On the same day, after Lt. Col. Greene urged sending "an army, or at least a general staff, to the Baltic States," Polk noted in exasperation: "He cannot get it through his head that Congress is not ready to spend any money whatever for these purposes."[125]

Despite these difficulties, in mid-October, when premature reports reached Washington "that the White Forces have occupied Petrograd," U.S. officials became extremely excited. Believing the "release of Petrograd from Bolshevists control imminent," some of them hurriedly prepared to send to the city food stocks left in Finland and Estonia.[126]

In addition, State Department aides collaborated with the Russian ambassador to find a way to authorize new credits without a congressional appropriation. With Wilson still incapacitated, the cabinet met in his absence on October 21 and discussed an emergency application by Bakhmeteff to purchase on credit twenty-nine thousand tons of flour from the U.S. Grain Corporation. The cabinet members agreed "that everything possible should be done to effect this transaction." The next day DeWitt Poole drafted a letter for the president that approved the Russian embassy's application for "relief of the civilian population of Petrograd and such adjoining regions as may be freed from Bolshevik control." Reflecting the Red Scare climate, the letter expounded that "economic relief of this character is the most effective means of limiting the spread of Bolshevism and of protecting, thereby, the Government of the United States from the dangers of subversive propaganda."[127]

Wilson had been near death only a few days before, but he was apparently strong enough to sign the letter. By November 1 definite arrangements had been made with the U.S. Grain Corporation to provide flour for the Petrograd area "in the event of its liberation." The State Department also approved plans to move to Petrograd foodstuffs that it and the ARA had delivered earlier to Vyborg and Tallinn. However, this plan, too, was conditioned upon the fall of Petrograd. When Red forces commanded by Trotsky drove the Northwestern Army back from the outskirts of the city at the end of October, then chased them all the way into Estonian territory in November, American officials' hopes were dashed and their more ambitious plans were suspended.[128]

Despite the withering of such hopes in the winter of 1919–20, Americans in the Baltic states provided support for the remnants of the Northwestern Army and continued to see the political value of food shipments. At the end of November, John Gade, head of the American Mission to the Baltic Provinces, urged the State Department to assure Iudenich's forces of a reliable food supply so that the Russians would be able to fend off disarmament by the Estonians and "continue the struggle" against the Soviet government.[129]

In Washington, too, political considerations continued to guide the distribution of American humanitarian aid. On December 13, Lansing heard the Finnish minister describe the "desperate state of Esthonia," but "told him we could not give aid, and that I opposed cutting up Russia." Two days later, Lansing informed Gade that the thirty thousand tons of flour and other foodstuffs "forwarded during Yudenich's drive against Petrograd" could "only be disposed of by Russians under our control and with our consent." Lansing directed that food "stores should continue to be used" for "assisting Yudenich."[130]

In addition to providing the Northwestern Army with food, medicine, and clothing, U.S. officers intervened with Estonian officials regarding passports and transportation for Iudenich's men. Iudenich and his aides valued the American supplies and support. In November, Iudenich decorated Gade with the order of St. Stanislaus as a sign of the "deep appreciation of the sincere interest of our Great Ally, the United States shown through your goodselves towards the Russian North-West Army in its fight against the enemies of humanity—the Bolsheviks." Gade and other U.S. representatives were equally effusive about their devotion to the Northwestern Army, which they worked "eagerly and constantly" to help. Thus, while Iudenich's campaign failed, it was not because of lack of sympathy from American officials.[131]

The Failure of the Northwestern Army

The Russian Northwestern Army's inability to capture Petrograd stemmed from many shortcomings. The squat, rotund, and aging Iudenich was unable to provide vigorous military leadership or even control his bloated corps of quarreling officers. Like many former tsarist generals, he lacked diplomatic tact and political finesse. His monarchist views did not help to win the support of Allied leaders or the confidence of peoples on the western fringes of the former Russian empire. The fifteen thousand men in the Northwestern Army were vastly outnumbered by the more than fifty thousand Red troops hurriedly drawn from other fronts once Iudenich threatened Petrograd. Racing to be first to enter the former capital, one of Iudenich's generals failed to carry out orders to cut the railway line to

Moscow, thereby allowing Red reinforcements to arrive. A supporting naval campaign by British and Estonian forces failed to seize the fortress of Krasnaia Gorka after some Royal Navy ships were diverted to counter a threat to Riga from Bermondt-Avalov's renegade Russian and German units.[132]

Beyond these military fiascoes there was a failure to win popular support. Some Northwestern Army commanders launched pogroms and white terrors in the areas they occupied. Iudenich was unwilling to endorse land reform or democracy—his slogan was "Against the Bolsheviks, without Politics." Together, the brutality and rigidity of the Whites made them unable to enlist the enthusiasm of peasants, workers, and intellectuals. As Gade reported in December 1919, the people of the Baltic states and liberated regions of Russia did not receive "firm guarantees as to the future, . . . and as a consequence the advancing armies have had discontented conditions in their rear, when all their attention and strength should have been devoted to the enemy in front. The spectre of despotism haunts the liberated peasants and many of the soldiers actually fighting in the White armies."[133]

The Failure of American "Humanitarian" Intervention in the Baltic States

American leaders had been unable to dispatch U.S. military forces to the Baltic states, had postponed an appeal for funds that Congress seemed unlikely to grant, and had been prohibited by law from giving weapons to foreign armies. Unable to intervene directly and openly, American officials attempted to support anti-Bolshevik forces in the Baltic region through a variety of limited and indirect methods, ranging from "humanitarian" aid to the use of German soldiers as proxies. Many of these half-measures backfired. Condoning the continued German occupation of Baltic lands and resisting the evacuation of German volunteers contributed indirectly to the disruption of Iudenich's fall campaign by German-Russian marauders' attack on Riga. Giving preferential support to former tsarist officers and sympathizing with their desire to restore a greater Russia antagonized Baltic nationalist governments whose backing was essential to capture Petrograd.

In addition, as Commander Gade observed near the end of 1919, "Allied intervention and the blockade have been important weapons in the hands of the Soviet leaders, . . . for purposes of propaganda. The result has been that a patriotic wave has swept through Soviet Russia, resulting in the present strong Soviet Army." Bolshevik leaders' appeal to "National ideals," as well as workers' fears of the reactionary nature of the Whites, helped to explain why "the Petrograd population supported the Soviet

Government wholeheartedly when Judenitsch advanced." Instead of spurring the starving people of Petrograd to revolt against Bolshevik rule, the blockade provided an excuse for the hardships of life in Soviet Russia and thus helped "to keep alive Bolshevism." If the blockade were "abandoned and supplies permitted to enter," Gade concluded, "the people would soon find out that the rottenness of the whole structure was at fault and that they had been listening to false prophets." [134]

The ideological antipathy to Bolshevism and the desire to help patriotic Russians replace the Soviet government that inspired John Gade and other U.S. representatives were not the only influences on American policy toward the Baltic region in 1919. U.S. officials were also troubled by German hegemonic aspirations, concerned about possible British commercial domination, opposed to splitting Russia into weak, insolvent fragments, and worried about the monarchistic inclinations of Russian military commanders. To American representatives in the Baltic states, it sometimes seemed that policymakers in Paris and Washington were distracted by such concerns from the main objective of stemming the Red tide.

However, the drive to contain and if possible roll back Bolshevism was throughout 1919 the predominant element in U.S. policy, the principal goal, to which other concerns were repeatedly subordinated. Thus, despite their distrust of the recently defeated German army, Americans endorsed continued German military occupation of Lithuania and Latvia when it seemed necessary to keep those lands out of the hands of Bolsheviks. Although Americans worried about British economic exclusiveness and imperial bossiness, they cooperated with British officials and ceded to them the senior positions on Allied commissions sent to the Baltic. Even those Americans who were most resistant to recognizing the independence of the Baltic states were willing to discuss arrangements for substantial autonomy within a loose Russian federation in order to keep Estonian, Latvian, and Lithuanian nationalists in the anti-Bolshevik camp. Yet, despite professions of support for self-determination, most U.S. officials sympathized more with patriotic Russians' plans to overthrow the Soviet regime and restore Russia as a great power than with the aspirations of Baltic nationalists. And even liberal U.S. policymakers who dreaded a restoration of tsarism were prepared to overlook the political leanings of former tsarist officers as they arranged for aid to the Russian Northwestern Army.

Wilson was more reluctant than his vehemently anti-Bolshevik advisors to approve some steps, such as the offensive employment of German troops. Unable to manage all aspects of U.S. foreign relations, Wilson was compelled to delegate substantial authority on policy toward the Baltic region to Hoover, Lansing, and other aides, and their initiatives accounted for some of the most aggressive moves, such as the U.S. support for the occupation of Riga. However, the anti-Bolshevik thrust of American policy was not merely a product of the devolution of decision making from Wilson to adamantly anti-Bolshevik subordinates. The president personally approved of aid to the Russian Northwestern Army, authorized arms shipments to other anti-Bolshevik forces in the Baltic region, and endorsed a moral embargo on trade with Soviet Russia. Wilson concurred with Hoover's policy of using food as a weapon against Bolshevism, which was implemented in central as well as eastern Europe.[135] Like almost all U.S. officials, Wilson agreed with Hoover that shipments of food and other supplies should be wrapped in political conditions and used to support the forces of order against the forces of anarchy, chaos, and radicalism. Thus, the "humanitarian" intervention in the Baltic region cannot be satisfactorily explained as a result of sabotage by reactionary underlings or an aberration from Wilsonian policy; it must be understood as a part of America's broader struggle against Bolshevism.

THE STRUGGLE AGAINST INTERVENTION

SOVIET POLICY TOWARD AMERICA, 1917–1920

Through all of our foreign policy of the last year runs the red thread of striving for a rapprochement with America. . . . We have not missed a chance to note our special desire to establish contact with America. — Maxim Litvinov, May 1919

Bolshevism is a mistake and it must be resisted as all mistakes must be resisted. If left alone it will destroy itself. It cannot survive because it is wrong. — Woodrow Wilson, September 1920

Foreign intervention in the Russian Civil War confirmed and aggravated longstanding Bolshevik expectations that capitalist powers would attempt to crush the world's first socialist state, and American participation in the Allied military expeditions provoked Bolshevik officials in some critical moments to class the United States with other "imperialist" foes.[1] Yet Lenin and other Soviet leaders did not regard America as just another capitalist country. Nor did they dismiss the United States as an unimportant nation.[2] From 1917 to 1920 the leaders of Soviet Russia repeatedly differentiated America from the Entente powers and offered preferential treatment to American businessmen and statesmen. Soviet officials viewed such special attention to America as the most promising way to break through the economic blockade, political isolation, and military encirclement of Soviet Russia. Bolshevik approaches to Americans were not merely cynical ploys; while Lenin and other key figures believed the revolution in Russia would not be secure until it ignited revolution around the world, including the United States, they simultaneously hoped for substantial economic relations with capitalist America.

Some Soviet appeals encouraged Wilson and his more liberal advisors to consider negotiations with the Bolshevik regime, and Soviet offers to buy American products attracted the attention of many businessmen. However, Soviet representatives simultaneously made extraordinary efforts to support pro-Bolshevik propaganda among workers and socialists in the United States, which angered American leaders and reinforced their opposition to diplomatic and economic relations with Soviet Russia. While Soviet officials sincerely sought to separate the struggle against intervention from the promotion of revolution, that distinction was as implausible to U.S. leaders as the American differentiation between supporting Russian self-government and intervening in Russian internal affairs was to Bolshevik leaders. While Soviet historians often contrasted the peace-loving policy of Soviet Russia to the interventionist policy of the Wilson administration, before 1920 many Soviet leaders were not much more reconciled to peaceful coexistence with capitalism than most American leaders were resigned to living with a Bolshevik Russia.[3] Examining the assumptions, tactics, and results of Soviet policy toward America highlights the way that U.S.-Soviet relations from early on took the form of "war in peace," a political and ideological struggle short of open war.

Lenin, the dominant figure in the development of Soviet foreign policy strategies from March 1918 through the end of the Wilson administration, was guided by several major assumptions about the United States, which most other Soviet leaders shared.[4] The United States was the most advanced of the capitalist countries, Lenin believed. That made the United States the most desirable source of modern technology and assistance to Soviet economic development. But it also meant that capitalism dominated America "more than anywhere else." The concentration of production and accumulation of capital had given industrial monopolies and a couple of banks enormous power and funds for "bribery" of government officials. By robbing the Philippines and attempting to rob Mexico,

American capitalists had shown themselves to be "no better" than European monarchs. Hence, American multimillionaires could be expected to be as reactionary and hostile to a socialist state as other imperialists.[5]

However, Soviet leaders could utilize three factors to deflect or mitigate American hostility. First, American capitalists would be driven by the imperatives of their extraordinarily productive system to export their products, invest their surplus capital, and exploit Russia's vast resources. Hence, they would seize economic opportunities in Soviet Russia and even pressure the U.S. government to establish diplomatic relations with the Bolshevik government. Second, the economic development of America and Japan had created severe conflicts of interest that made war between them inevitable and allowed astute communists "to play one side off against the other." Such inter-imperialist contradictions would make it difficult for the imperialist powers to unite in a military crusade against Soviet Russia. Third, since America was a democracy, "the freest" of the capitalist countries, Bolsheviks could exploit the contradictions between capitalism and democracy by rousing popular opposition to intervention in Russia. Although Lenin became more cynical and sarcastic about American democracy after the United States entered the Great War and especially after Wilson sent military expeditions to Russia, he and other Soviet leaders still believed that they had special opportunities to appeal to citizens of the "great democratic social republic."[6]

Influenced by these ideas about the American economy and polity, Soviet leaders pursued a multifaceted strategy toward the United States that involved highlighting tensions between the United States and Japan, dramatizing lenient treatment of American prisoners, dangling deals in front of American businessmen, offering to repay Russian debts, appealing to the liberal principles of U.S. leaders, and encouraging American sympathizers to protest against intervention in Russia and press for diplomatic relations between the two countries. Some of these approaches seemed at times to be effective. In the end, however, Soviet officials had to reckon with their inability to break down the Wilson administration's barriers to diplomatic and economic relations.

Soon after the Bolsheviks took power in Petrograd, L. D. Trotsky, the commissar for foreign affairs, articulated some of the central tenets about America that would influence Soviet policies over the next three years. Although Trotsky had been in New York for only the first three months of 1917, he confidently explained that "finance imperialists" dictated U.S. foreign policy, including American intervention in the Great War. "The sober calculations of the American Stock Exchange" would not necessarily lead to intervention against Soviet Russia. America could tolerate the existence of the Soviet government, since it would be satisfied by the exhaustion of its warring European rivals and "interested in investing its capital in Russia." Thus, while Trotsky did not "believe in the platonic sympathy for the Russian people" expressed by Americans, he expected that their own interests, particularly their competition with German and British capitalists, would lead them to seek "friendly relations" with Soviet Russia. Rivalry with Japan for the markets and resources of the Far East would also lead the United States to oppose Japanese intervention in Siberia, Trotsky believed. Hence, when Japan threatened to land troops at Vladivostok in January 1918, Trotsky suggested alerting the American embassy to the way such action would damage American as well as Russian interests.[7]

In the spring of 1918, following the Soviet signing of the harsh Brest-Litovsk peace treaty, Trotsky's responsibilities shifted from revolutionary diplomacy to the creation of the Red Army. G. V. Chicherin, an eccentric, aristocratic figure who had worked in the tsarist foreign office before joining the revolutionary movement, became the new foreign commissar. With the cosmopolitan and pragmatic Chicherin carrying out Lenin's directives, Soviet foreign policy shifted toward increased reliance on traditional diplomacy to ensure the survival of the Soviet state.

Soviet policy toward the United States continued to be influenced by assumptions about American economic drives. In March and April 1918 Soviet officials had intensive discussions with Americans in Moscow, particularly Raymond Robins, about bases for trade with the United States. By May 1918 Soviet foreign trade advisors prepared a plan that Lenin hoped would lead to the development of Soviet-American economic relations and simultaneously pit the interests of American capitalists against Japanese and German encroachment on Russian territory. Robins carried the plan to the United States and lobbied vigorously on its behalf. However, as we have seen, Wilson and Lansing did not believe in the legitimacy or permanence of the Soviet regime, and they did not respond to the invitation to take the place of "exhausted" Germany as Russia's leading trade partner.[8]

Some liberals and many socialists in America had been calling for diplomatic and economic relations with Soviet Russia since soon after the Bolshevik Revolution. In their efforts to stand by Soviet Russia, American radicals, including many Russian and Jewish immigrants, formed societies to promote cooperation, gathered supplies to send to Russia, and passed resolutions of solidarity. As pressure for U.S. intervention in Russia mounted in 1918, friends of Bolshevik Russia stepped up their activity, organizing numerous meetings to protest against intervention. Santeri Nuorteva, a Finnish revolutionary who established the Finnish Information Bureau in New York in March 1918, was particularly active in distributing propaganda in favor of the Red governments of Russia and Finland. Although the Soviet government did not give Nuorteva funds or instructions at that stage, it sought to encourage such activity by sending couriers to the United States with appeals to the American people. By August 1918, Chicherin believed that "a strong anti-interventionist movement" was developing, particularly in western states, where rivalry with Japan was sharpest. However, pro-Soviet activists such as John Reed who protested against intervention in Russia were harassed and arrested in the summer of 1918, and the Wilson administration censorship of leftist publications was so severe that the People's Council of America, one of the principal pro-Bolshevik pacifist organizations, was forced to shut down temporarily in the fall.[9]

In pursuit of the strategy of distinguishing the United States from other capitalist countries, Lenin and especially Chicherin often did not mention America in indictments of "Entente conspiracies" or "Anglo-French imperialism." As late as September 2, 1918 — shortly before the main body of U.S. troops reached Archangel — Chicherin explained that while the Soviet government was taking measures against "Anglo-French" intrigue and intervention, "our attitude is entirely different towards American citizens." Although America "was compelled by its Allies to agree to participate in intervention," Chicherin continued, "its decision is not regarded by us as irrevocable."[10]

Beyond the hard-headed calculation that the United States was the weakest link in the tightening chain of capitalist encirclement, some Bolsheviks felt until the fall of 1918 that American liberals were idealistic and progressive enough to justify hopes for cooperation. Mikhail Borodin, a veteran of the 1905 revolution whose Bolshevism softened during his years of exile in Chicago, remembered that he was not the only one who was "infatuated" by the notion that "among American liberals there were honest people" with whom one could work constructively. Bolshevik leader Nikolai Bukharin "was right," Borodin recalled, "when he said there was something patriarchal in our relations to Wilson." After leaving the United States in July 1918, Borodin journeyed to Moscow and created a short-lived Russian-American friendship society. Then, carrying Lenin's "Letter to American Workers," Borodin started to return to America. In that period when ideological lines had not yet hardened into rigid fronts, Borodin hoped to cooperate on a propaganda campaign with Americans, including CPI chairman George Creel, at the same time as he sought to deliver Lenin's propaganda message. Waiting in Norway for some word from Washington that never came, Borodin grew frustrated by the way the U.S. government seemed to be building walls between Americans and Russians. He was also outraged by Americans' merciless criticism of Russia, including their publication of documents alleging a German-Bolshevik conspiracy. By October 1918, as he informed Lev Karakhan of the Foreign Commissariat, he had "lost all illusions about the possibility of legal work through Creel and others." Saying that the best of the Americans had turned out to be "cowards and phrase-mongers," Borodin declared that he was "finished" with Wilson. (In the following year Borodin became a key figure in Soviet efforts to stimulate and support communist movements in the Americas.)[11]

As hopes for cooperation faded and after efforts to deter American participation in Allied military intervention in Russia failed, Soviet leaders relied more heavily on revolutionary appeals to workers. Although Lenin recognized in August 1918 that dramatic assistance from "American revolutionary workers" would "probably not come soon," he still urged them "to play an exceptionally important role as uncompromising enemies of American imperialism." Chicherin ordinarily emphasized the impossibility of exporting revolution and the necessity of separating official diplomacy from nongovernmental agitation. Yet if the United States refused to negotiate, Chicherin threatened Wilson in October 1918, Soviet Russia would summon workers of all countries to a final fight.[12]

In a phase of extreme vexation and anger, Soviet leaders lashed out at the United States as well as the Allies. In October 1918, after the arrival of U.S. military expeditions at Vladivostok and Archangel, the arrest of American intelligence agents in Moscow, and the publication of the Sisson Documents, Soviet officials lumped the "Anglo-French, American, and Japanese imperialist robbers" together and argued that "the chains which the Anglo-American and Japanese-American robbers bring to the people are no better than the Austro-German chains." Later in October Chicherin bitterly attacked the contradiction between American support for "the Russian counter-revolution" and Wilson's Fourteen Points promise to assist independent Russian self-government. He also sarcastically inquired what economic or territorial concessions Wilson and his allies demanded in exchange for peace with Soviet Russia, and implied that America was just as greedy as the British and French. In November and December 1918 Lenin continued that sarcastic line, mocking the "'humane'" and "'philanthropic'" policies of the "Tiger Wilsons and Co.," scorning the "illusion" of democracy in Britain, France, and America, and attacking the compound of "Anglo-American imperialism."[13]

As the Great War ended, Lenin was acutely aware that the Soviet state had been able to survive for a year because of "the split of international imperialism" into two camps that were so enmeshed in their "mortal combat" that neither side could muster large forces against Soviet Russia. The Allied victory raised the danger that "Anglo-American troops" would now be free to throttle "the world revolution."[14]

Although Lenin argued that British and American hostility was aroused by the growth of Bolshevism into "a world force," that did not cool his passion to infect workers in the West with "the germ of Bolshevism." The collapse of the Central Powers at the end of the war refired his hopes for "world Bolshevism." "When the German revolution came," he declared in December 1918, "everyone realised that revolution was sweeping the whole world, that Britain, France and America were also going the same way — along our path!" In those months Lenin showed little hope for an accommodation with the United States, which the war had degraded "to the level of semi-militarist, despotic Germany," and which was led by a president who (Lenin asserted) had proclaimed, "'Our enemy is now world Bolshevism.'" Instead, Lenin hoped to restrain U.S. intervention by exposing it to the American people, particularly to American workers, about whom he had little information. Lenin viewed that struggle against intervention as a complement rather than an alternative to revolutionary agitation: the main international challenges facing Soviet Russia, he announced on November 8, were "broadening the revolution in other countries" while "warding off imperialism."[15]

In the fall of 1918 Lenin and other Bolsheviks formed a Russian Communist Party Bureau to support and coordinate the work of foreign revolutionaries. Three months later, in January 1919, Soviet leaders issued an appeal for the formation of a Communist International to conduct similar tasks more aggressively. While encouraging and subsidizing proletarian seizures of power, the Comintern was also intended "to safeguard the socialist revolution" from "the alliance of capitalist States" that were organizing to strangle the revolution.[16]

In this stage of sharp conflict and ominous foreboding, Lenin argued that American democratic institutions did not mean much when pacifists were "shot in the streets." However, Lenin still believed that the United States was "the world's most democratic republic," and that perspective suggested that a peace offensive directed at America would offer the best prospect for disrupting a united anti-Bolshevik crusade by the Western powers. Although the Armistice and the German revolution seemed to narrow the future to either world revolution or the strangulation of Bolshevism, before the end of the year Soviet diplomats renewed their special efforts to appeal to America.[17]

Isolated by an Allied blockade that contributed to severe food shortages and encircled by anti-Bolshevik armies (including the White forces who captured the strategic northern city of Perm in December 1918), Bolshevik leaders believed that Soviet Russia desperately needed to escape the "iron ring" surrounding her. Since Russia did not have the strength to break the ring by itself, foreign policy advisors argued in a report on January 1, 1919, the country needed help from the outside. That aid would not come from England, France, Germany, Japan, or the neutral countries, which were in the hands of the Entente. Only the United States might help the Soviet regime, since America needed to market its products, invest its capital profitably, weaken the influence of England in Europe, and prepare for the "inevitable" war with Japan. Soviet officials expected the United States to face a severe postwar economic crisis, and they hoped Americans would recognize that friendship with Russia would open "colossal possibilities" for trade and investment in big projects like railroad construction. Anticipating that America would clash with England over many issues, especially freedom of the seas, at the impending peace conference, the Soviet advisors naively imagined that America might call Soviet Russia to its side. Their calculation of America's interests led them to hope that America might eliminate the blockade of Soviet Russia and cut off aid to anti-Bolshevik forces. Such "support" from the United States was absolutely necessary, Soviet officials concluded: "the fate of Soviet Russia" hung on establishing relations with the United States. Soviet leaders would pursue such a breakthrough in two principal ways: through direct appeals to American officials and through agitation by Soviet representatives in the United States.[18]

In November and early December 1918, American officials, like their Allied counterparts, had ignored repeated appeals for negotiations from Chicherin. On Christmas Eve, however, Chicherin's deputy, Maxim Litvinov, sent a conciliatory letter to President Wilson that won a positive response. Like earlier Soviet messages, Litvinov's letter played on American economic interests, mentioning Soviet Russia's readiness to "go to any length of concessions" and to seek foreign advice on "how to exploit her natural riches." Undoubtedly more attractive to Wilson was Litvinov's respectful tone. Instead of denouncing Wilsonian hypocrisy, as Chicherin had in October, Litvinov went out of his way to "express confidence in the good will of the American Government," pledged to refrain from revolutionary agitation in Western countries after a peace agreement, and sought to explain the aspiration of the Russian people for "economic liberty without which political liberty is of no avail to them." Litvinov appealed to Wilson's desire to hear both sides in the Russian Civil War and played on his fear that a White victory would mean a "restoration of Monarchy."[19]

More than any other Soviet peace proposal, Litvinov's courteous note and his subsequent discussions with U.S. representative William Buckler encouraged Wilson to consider peace discussions with the Bolsheviks and other Russian groups as an alternative to military intervention, which then seemed ineffective and even counterproductive. At a meeting of the Council of Ten in Paris on January 21, 1919, Wilson argued that "by opposing Bolshevism with arms they were in reality serving the cause of Bolshevism"; the foreign armies allowed Soviet leaders to claim that the Allies wanted to destroy Russia, enslave the Russian people, and restore the monarchy. In 1914, after American intervention at Veracruz provoked a nationalistic reaction among Mexicans, Wilson had blocked more aggressive military operations and accepted an offer of mediation by Argentine, Brazilian, and Chilean diplomats as an alternative way to secure the elimination of General Huerta. In 1919, similarly, Wilson suggested that withdrawing the armies and opening talks with all Russian groups might be the best way to "bring about a marked reaction against Bolshevism." The next day Allied leaders approved a proclamation drafted by Wilson that invited "every organised group" of Russians to a conference at the island of Prinkipo in the Sea of Marmora.[20]

While the Soviet government accepted the invitation, anti-Bolshevik Russians, encouraged by French leaders, rejected negotiations with Bolsheviks. Wilson did not push very hard against such resistance. As junior advisor Samuel Eliot Morison later commented, the president got "cold feet." Wilson first hesitated to send an official invitation to Moscow since that "would be tantamount to a recognition of the Bolshevik Government." What he was seeking, he explained, "was not a rapprochement with the Bolsheviks." Wilson was then disturbed that the invitation "attracted the factions least desirable, to the exclusion of those which might restore order." In addition, he was angered by the Bolsheviks' "insulting" message of acceptance, which offered to buy off the grasping Western imperialists with debt settlements and territorial cessions.[21]

Soviet peace proposals often included such offers to pay at least some of Russia's foreign debts, which contrasted with Lenin's vows to Soviet audiences not to "pay for the old rulers." The Soviet government's repudiation of responsibility for foreign loans in 1918 undermined the credibility of its new position under the duress of foreign intervention. Some liberal American representatives took the offers seriously, but most U.S. officials greeted them with skepticism or contempt.[22]

While doubts about the sincerity of the Soviet pledges limited the middle ground between Soviet and American leaders, the discussions of peace contributed to Lenin's perception in January that imperialist attacks were "slacking off." The sense that the Allies' were wavering on intervention in Russia, combined with the worsening situation on the eastern front against Kolchak's forces, spurred new initiatives by Soviet diplomats.[23]

Although Soviet Russia was almost completely cut off from the West in 1919, Soviet antennae were tuned to notes of discord within as well as between imperialist powers. Thus, in January 1919 Chicherin pounced on the news that many members of Congress felt "that American troops should be withdrawn from Russia as soon as possible." Seizing the opportunity, Chicherin, in a January 12 appeal to the State Department, expressed the "hope that the peaceloving views of the . . . senators will be shared by the American Government" and lead to the "opening [of] peace negotiations."[24]

A few days later Soviet foreign policy advisors moved beyond such individual salvos by outlining a broad campaign to prod the Wilson administration to recognize the Soviet government and renounce moral and material support for the enemies of Soviet Russia. The outline started from the view that American society as a whole was sincerely well disposed toward Soviet Russia. With remarkable optimism, the Soviet officials held that the U.S. government was inclined to recognize the Soviet regime, though it had not been able to depart from the views of its allies, particularly the French, during the war. The top priority task in America, then, was to mobilize sufficient public pressure so that the Wilson administration would grant diplomatic recognition. The most effective way to do this was to establish contacts with business circles in New York and Chicago, who would "compel their government" to cooperate in the creation of political conditions conducive to their financial and economic operations. At the same time, the Soviet advisors recommended, the widest possible propaganda campaign should be unleashed, and one point it should stress was the way Russia's former allies were supporting anti-Bolshevik forces, "the enemies of the Russian people." Turning from this optimistic plan to the worst-case scenario of active military intervention by the United States and its allies, the Soviet officials anticipated organizing street demonstrations in America. They considered it especially important to organize the defense of Soviet Russia in conjunction with members of Congress who were known to be sympathetic.[25]

As the authors of the memorandum recognized, their plans would have to be elaborated by people "on the spot." The campaign against intervention and for diplomatic and economic relations with America would be spearheaded by Ludwig Martens, whom the Foreign Commissariat designated in January 1919 as its representative in the United States. Martens was a veteran Russian revolutionary who had worked in America as an engineer since 1916. His key aide was Santeri Nuorteva, who headed the diplomatic department of Martens's Soviet Russian Information Bureau in New York.

During the Red Scare, American officials accused Martens of inciting strikes and distributing propaganda to overthrow the U.S. government.[26] Soviet leaders denied such charges, and later Soviet scholars portrayed Martens's mission as a straightforward effort to apply Lenin's principles of peaceful coexistence, which they backdated.[27] Neither of those views accurately described the main thrust of Martens's work.

The Foreign Commissariat was closer to the truth when it informed Martens for the record that he was its representative "for the defense of the interests of the Soviet Republic and above all for the struggle against intervention and for commercial goals." The "struggle against intervention" involved propaganda, but it was geared to the defense of Soviet Russia and the improvement of American-Soviet relations more than the instigation of revolution. The Foreign Commissariat did not hide its enthusiasm about how "the American workers' movement has moved far ahead," and it expressed the "hope that in the nearest future in America will be created a united Communist Party." However, it instructed Martens that his mission concerned "purely governmental questions or commercial tasks, and not communist ones." Martens's activity generally harmonized with those instructions. His abstention from conflicts among leftists in America created friction with radical Russian immigrants who believed the Soviet bureau should be dedicated to advancing the revolutionary socialist movement. In response, Chicherin rebuked leaders of the Russian Federation for their "extremely damaging" criticism of Martens's nonrevolutionary work and heatedly informed them that Martens was a representative of the Foreign Commissariat, not of the Communist Party or of the Communist International.[28]

As early as January 1919, Red-hunters asserted that thanks to tsarist jewels smuggled to America by Bolshevik couriers, Martens and his associates had vast sums to spend on revolutionary propaganda, and some historians have accepted such assertions.[29] Bolshevik couriers were in fact bringing diamonds as well as currency to America, and the jewels and money were intended to support communist movements as well as the Soviet bureau. However, at least in 1919 these transfers yielded only small sums and Martens and his aides repeatedly complained of a desperate shortage of funds. While officials in Moscow tried to arrange for $6,000 to be sent from Norway to the New York bureau each month, Litvinov also noted the Soviet government's extreme difficulty in acquiring foreign currency and suggested that Martens might make do with a reduced staff.[30]

Despite the limits of its funds, by late January 1919 Martens's bureau was already very actively engaged in agitation against American intervention in Russia. One of the bureau's methods was to distribute pro-Bolshevik information through socialist publications. Although Martens expressed disappointment with socialist periodicals' limited use of material the bureau sent them, he "took other measures" so that radical publications "would receive wide distribution." Martens specifically mentioned *Class Struggle*, the left-wing socialist paper, and the *Liberator*, a monthly journal edited by Crystal and Max Eastman, which regularly denounced intervention in Russia and criticized Wilsonian policies.[31]

To counteract "the campaign of misrepresentation carried on against Soviet Russia by reactionary elements" such as Ambassador Bakhmeteff's associates, the Soviet bureau also distributed its own publications. In March 1919 Nuorteva began issuing a regular bulletin of news and commentary, and in June Martens's staff started publishing the weekly *Soviet Russia*. Maintaining a calm, reasonable tone, the paper refuted accusations about Bolshevik policies such as the alleged nationalization of women, argued that the Soviet government had popular support and would defeat the Whites, and publicized opportunities for trade with Soviet Russia.[32]

A third line of action by the Soviet bureau involved encouraging socialist organizations and arousing American workers. While the Socialist Party's effort against intervention was weak, Martens reported, the campaign among immigrant workers "was carried on with great enthusiasm." "Even in the conservative unions of the AFL," Martens glowed, "if our men managed to penetrate, the mood became anti-intervention." In addition to such direct action, Martens's bureau distributed Soviet leaders' appeals to workers not to trust their rulers and to exert pressure to halt attacks against revolutionary Russia.[33]

Such efforts to mobilize American workers seemed to many Bolsheviks to be succeeding in 1919, as a wave of strikes rose month by month. At the First Congress of the Communist International in March, Boris Reinstein, representing the American Socialist Labor Party, declared that "the Russian revolution has exerted an enormous influence upon the proletarian masses in America." Although Reinstein had been away from the United States for almost two years, he asserted that the awakening proletariat had "had a very significant impact upon the American government," causing Wilson in the preceding months to adopt "a different posture" toward the Soviet government. Perhaps influenced by news of the general strike called by the Seattle Central Labor Council in February, Lenin exulted that even in America "Soviet-type councils" were "being set up everywhere" and would sooner or later "take power into their own hands." Such signs of the "growth of the revolutionary movement" throughout the world gave him confidence in the confrontation with capitalist powers that were outwardly stronger than Soviet Russia, but were weakened and constrained by their internal divisions.[34]

In this period of opportunity and danger, when the creation of a Soviet government in Hungary kindled Bolshevik hopes that communism would soon "triumph all over the world," while Kolchak's advance from Siberia heightened the threat from White armies and their foreign supporters, Lenin conceived of peace proposals less in terms of establishing a basis for peaceful coexistence with the West than in terms of a new Brest-Litovsk agreement to buy time for the spread of Bolshevism. It was "inconceivable for the Soviet Republic to exist alongside of the imperialist states for any length of time," Lenin declared on March 18. "One or the other must triumph in the end."[35]

Although Lenin counted the United States among the imperialist states, he also differentiated it from the others. A few days earlier in March, State Department aide William Bullitt had arrived in Russia. While Secretary of State Lansing and President Wilson viewed Bullitt's trip as only an information-gathering mission, Bullitt and Colonel House hoped it would lead to a peace settlement with Russia. After many discussions with Litvinov and Chicherin, on March 14 Bullitt met with Lenin and received Soviet terms for an armistice on all fronts — which would have limited Bolshevik rule to central European Russia. In exchange for the withdrawal of foreign troops from Russian territory, the cessation of foreign military assistance to anti-Bolshevik groups, and the lifting of the blockade, Soviet leaders pledged not to overthrow the anti-Bolshevik governments around them and to repay Russia's foreign debts. When Bullitt returned to Paris on March 25, House supported the tentative agreement, but Wilson declined to meet with Bullitt and refused to release his report, which seemed "dangerous" at a time when many Americans vehemently opposed dealing with the Bolsheviks. By April 3, junior advisors in Paris learned, Wilson decided he would "not negotiate with Bolshevists" — a decision Bullitt blamed on Wilson's "Whig" or "Gladstonian" view of Bolshevism as a disease. Despite the disappointing outcome of the Bullitt mission, Lenin discerned that Wilson was more amenable to negotiations than the French and that the friction between Wilson and Clemenceau had helped to brake foreign intervention in Russia. Thus, although Soviet Russia was "fighting Wilson" and the United States was aiding the Bolsheviks' enemies, it continued to seem important to make special appeals to Americans.[36]

While Soviet leaders sent messages from Moscow to American leaders, the Soviet bureau in New York sought formal relations with the Wilson administration and established contacts with American businessmen. When Martens presented his credentials to the State Department in March 1919 he stressed in an accompanying message that the Soviet government was "prepared at once to buy from the United States vast amounts of finished products" and "to go to any length of concessions as far as the real interests of other countries are concerned." The Wilson administration did not respond directly to Martens. Instead it informed businessmen that it had not recognized Martens, warned that export licenses would not be granted for shipments to Soviet Russia, and cautioned against deals with Bolsheviks that future Russian governments would not respect.[37]

Despite those countermeasures, Martens was very enthusiastic about the prospects for his mission in April. He reported to Moscow that almost the whole "bourgeois press" had greeted his appointment as a very important step and that his office was besieged by representatives of numerous firms and banks, who were thirsting for the opening of relations with Soviet Russia. The crisis of overproduction, the partial closing of European markets, and the fear that England would capture the Russian market were all creating very favorable ground for his work. This labor was definitely geared toward a political objective. "I am doing everything possible here," Martens wrote, "in order to bring the necessary pressure to bear on Washington through industrial and banking circles."[38]

Litvinov and other Soviet leaders "were extremely pleased" by Martens's letter. In late May, Litvinov, then head of the department for America at the Commissariat for Foreign Affairs, encouraged Martens to continue his work and confirmed the Soviet government's readiness "to give all economic concessions to Americans in preference to other foreigners."

Litvinov recognized that this strategy had not yet paid off. Despite the conciliatory approaches and offers of special concessions to Americans, he wrote, America had unfortunately "identified itself with the rabid policy of Clemenceau and practically participated in all the military and diplomatic attacks," as well as the economic blockade, against Soviet Russia. Soviet officials had discussed peace terms with Buckler and Bullitt, agreed to participate in the proposed Prinkipo conference, and even consented to the Hoover-Nansen food relief plan under certain conditions, but all these proposals, Litvinov suspected, had the goal of lulling public opinion in the West and masking preparations for further intervention. Although Soviet leaders received clandestine reports on U.S. policymaking from Americans in Paris, they were uncertain about the depth of American antipathy and they had not firmly established how actively America was participating in the various forms of foreign intervention.[39]

In that climate of uncertainty, Soviet leaders and representatives were prey to wild rumors and fears. On June 1, when Trotsky heard a report that "the League of Nations has 'flooded' Siberia with Entente troops, American ones among them," he considered it "essential to verify this announcement immediately by organising a reconnaissance in depth into Siberia." In July, a member of Martens's diplomatic department reported on confidential information "that an attempt will be made by concerted sea and air forces to destroy the crops of Soviet Russia and Soviet Hungary." According to the far-fetched report, American navy yards were working day and night on special submarines that would be used in the attack.[40]

Although Soviet officials thus sometimes worried that the United States was preparing much more aggressive action in Russia, they tended to see "an attitude of reluctance" to intervene among Americans, and that encouraged them to pursue the policy of differentiating America from its imperialist allies. Overlooking the Soviet lumping of the United States with other capitalist powers in the fall of 1918, Litvinov informed Martens in May 1919 that Soviet foreign policy in the past year had been striving consistently for a rapprochement with America. "Even during the past year of intervention," Litvinov explained, "our relations to American official and unofficial representatives have been distinguished from relations to the representatives of other allies. We have not missed a chance to note our special desire to establish contact with America."[41]

Soon after Litvinov sent his upbeat dispatch, Martens's optimism began to fade. In June, agents of a New York legislative committee that was investigating seditious activity raided his headquarters and confiscated many papers. Although the Lusk Committee returned some of his commercial department's correspondence with American firms by July, Martens sent a gloomy report to Moscow. Struggling against the Lusk Committee in the courts was draining and the capitalist press was using Lusk Committee material to conduct a "dirty campaign" against his bureau. The general vilification of Soviet Russia had assumed "unbelievable dimensions," and liberal circles were reduced to despondent whimpering. No significant radical movement was visible among workers. Samuel Gompers's "reactionary band" had dominated an American Federation of Labor convention that passed only a very weak resolution for the withdrawal of U.S. troops from Russia while rejecting demands for a lifting of the blockade. In sum, the outlook seemed bleak.[42]

While Martens grew disheartened about the prospects for Soviet-American relations, he continued to carry out the Soviet policy. Although communications from Moscow had been sporadic and delayed, he reported to Chicherin in August 1919 that he understood very well "the tactic which you have maintained all along in relation to the United States — that in the final analysis the United States remained the one capitalist country" with which it was possible to hope to establish relations. "Unfortunately," Martens wrote, "those hopes had not yet been justified," and he doubted that they would be fulfilled in the near future. Although he expected Wilson's "ambiguous game" of unofficial war to continue, Martens promised to follow Litvinov's instructions about offering special concessions and debt repayment arrangements.[43]

Lenin was more optimistic. As the Red Army defeated Admiral Kolchak's forces in the late summer and fall of 1919, Lenin discussed his hopes for economic relations, "*especially* with America," not merely as a ploy to gain a breathing space, but as an opening to a relatively long period of co-existence during which socialist Russia would offer concessions to capitalists and receive technical help from more advanced countries. Lenin's rising confidence about this prospect stemmed not only from the Red military victories but also from his perception that "American opponents of the war against Russia" were "not only workers, but mainly bourgeois."[44]

In spite of the intensifying Red Scare, with its police raids and demands for the expulsion of the Martens bureau, in the fall of 1919 Soviet representatives in America regained hopes for a breakthrough. After their founding conventions in September 1919, the Communist Party and

Communist Labor Party launched propaganda campaigns against the blockade of Soviet Russia. Dockworkers in Seattle and Baltimore refused to load shipments of weapons to White forces. Citing a resolution of the United Mine Workers and a campaign by women suffragists against the blockade, Nuorteva asserted that public opinion was developing in favor of intercourse with Soviet Russia. Nuorteva further believed that American firms, with whom Martens claimed to have signed deals worth $20 million, were exerting great pressure for the opening of trade relations. Red Army victories and the opening of peace negotiations between Soviet Russia and the Baltic states had caused "ruling spheres" to become "depressed," Martens reported to Moscow; "they feel that intervention has broken down. And 'society' is notably inclined to leave Russia in peace."[45]

Although the American government ignored a proposal for peace negotiations that Lenin drafted in December 1919, in early 1920 officials at the Foreign Commissariat still found it "difficult to suppose that a full isolation from America can continue for long" and hoped that "in the near future" Martens's energetic work would reap success. Chicherin suggested to Washington in February that the Red Army's defeat of Kolchak's forces in Siberia, combined with the growth of popular movements against foreign intervention, highlighted the alternative of relations between the United States and Soviet Russia, which would allow Americans to play a gigantic role in the reconstruction of Russian economic life. The Wilson administration did not reply to Chicherin's renewed request for peace negotiations.[46]

While American officials spurned such appeals, Soviet leaders continued to dangle special deals in front of Americans through the last months of the Wilson administration. In the most infamous case, Soviet leaders offered Los Angeles engineer Washington Vanderlip a concession to develop the resources of Kamchatka. As Lenin assured Bolshevik activists troubled by the idea of inviting in foreign exploiters, concessions were "a new form of warfare" for a period when the duel between communism and capitalism was shifting from the military front to the economic sphere. The Soviet government signed a tentative agreement with Vanderlip, Lenin explained, because it hoped it would (1) lead Republican presidential candidate Warren Harding to recognize the Soviet government after he was elected, (2) spur conflict between America and Japan, and (3) attract American investment essential to Soviet economic development. Wilson's State Department responded to the new gambit by once again warning American businessmen and investors against hazarding deals with the unrecognized Bolshevik regime that might be repudiated by future Russian governments.[47]

By the summer of 1920, Martens had become embittered by such resistance. In a draft of a letter to new secretary of state Bainbridge Colby,

Martens complained that despite the friendliness of the American people and the interest of American businessmen in trade, all of his efforts to establish commercial relations had been frustrated by the U.S. government, with its policy of prohibiting trade.[48]

Since the spring of 1919 State Department advisors, accurately appraising the political purpose of the Soviet trade mission, had urged Wilson to deport Martens and publicly explain the U.S. government's unwillingness to sanction commercial intercourse with Bolsheviks. In that way, Washington could simultaneously safeguard control of internal American affairs and help the Russian people to regain control of their affairs. Although Wilson considered Martens "pestiferous," he thought it "wise to go carefully" with the deportation case and sought assurances that the evidence was "abundant" and "complete." In December 1920, Wilson finally approved the expulsion.[49]

Facing imminent deportation proceedings against Martens, Chicherin finally concluded that "for the time being Russia will have to get along without that cooperation with American industries which we expected." As a parting shot, Chicherin directed Martens to cancel all orders with U.S. firms before leaving the country. That punitive action, Chicherin explained, would apply pressure on the wide bourgeois circles that hoped for trade relations with Soviet Russia and that were bound to prove stronger than the petty bourgeois and farming circles who had elected Wilson. Thus, while Soviet leaders were interested in economic relations with the most advanced capitalist country, they placed a higher priority on achieving a political and diplomatic breakthrough, and they still believed that economic interests would ultimately determine American foreign policy. The petty bourgeois, Chicherin predicted, would be unable to resist "the iron course of history."[50]

Although the Soviet strategy toward the United States did not lead the Wilson administration to abandon its hostility to Bolshevism, establish diplomatic relations with the Soviet government, or allow economic relations to flourish, Soviet leaders claimed success in the struggle against intervention. Reflecting on the Red victories in December 1919, Lenin argued that the "miracle" that Soviet power "held out for two years in a backward, ruined and war-weary country," in the face of German and Allied hostility, stemmed from the "international solidarity of the working people," who refused to fight in Russia and demonstrated against intervention at home. Soviet historians similarly maintained that the protests of American workers, together with the Soviet proposals for peace and economic cooperation, significantly influenced the Wilson administration's withdrawal of U.S. troops from Russia.[51]

Some American officials certainly were disturbed by the "Hands Off Russia" campaign waged by American unions and radical socialists.[52] However, the agitation by militant workers and communist parties (which had fewer than 100,000 members at their peak in the fall of 1919) had less influence on Wilson administration decisions than the broader anti-interventionist and isolationist sentiment among Americans. Although the administration arrested and even deported many immigrant "Bolsheviks," it was not willing to make a public case for intervention against Bolshevism in Russia. It therefore failed to build support for its policy. Instead, it provoked rising suspicion in Congress and among the American people that it was pursuing a secretive and un-American course. As journalist William Hard observed, "the overwhelming mass" of Americans were "instinctively absolutely anti-Bolshevik," but "interventionist anti-Bolshevism" had to be inculcated because "Americanism" was instinctively against aggressive military intervention in distant Russia.[53] While Wilson authorized the publication of the Sisson Documents, that was not sufficient to persuade most Americans that they had a mission or duty in Russia. The Wilson administration consequently had to rely on secretive and indirect methods of supporting anti-Bolshevik forces.

Lenin often derided "bourgeois democracy" as "merely freedom for the capitalists," yet he recognized the importance of the fact that none of the Western governments dared to say to their parliaments "that they were declaring war on Russia," and he noted the American charges that Wilson had "violated the Constitution" by "waging war on Russia without declaring war." Although Lenin usually emphasized working-class opposition to war against Bolshevik Russia, he knew that radical weeklies with their small circulation were faint voices in comparison to the mass-circulation daily newspapers, and in some speeches he acknowledged that more significant resistance to the blockade and intervention had come from the "bourgeois intelligentsia" and "the middle sections of the population." In December 1919, after Soviet Russia parried the most dangerous thrusts of the foreign-supported White armies, Lenin even counted the Bolsheviks' ability "to win over, within the Entente countries, the petty bourgeoisie and educated townsfolk" as the "greatest of our victories."[54]

While the war-weariness of people in the West was more important than positive Bolshevik victories in the struggle for hearts and minds, Lenin had been right to anticipate that the tension "between imperialism and the republic" could check the organization of anti-Soviet crusades and help to protect the first socialist state. In the ominous days at the end of the First World War, Lenin feared that "Anglo-American imperialism" had "perfectly mastered the art of using the form of the democratic republic."[55] However, the tension between democracy and foreign intervention remained, as American public opinion constrained the Wilson administration's provision of support to anti-Bolshevik forces in 1919, the decisive year of the Russian Civil War.

While the United States was the most hesitant participant in military intervention in Russia, it was also the capitalist power that proved most stubbornly resistant to the temptations of Soviet sirens. Soviet leaders had difficulty understanding why their policy toward the United States did not produce the diplomatic breakthrough and economic benefits they hoped for. To Lenin it was obvious that America needed Russian raw materials, that Russia needed American manufactured goods, and that America's economic and strategic conflicts with England and Japan gave it an interest in relations with Soviet Russia, which was reemerging as a great power. He therefore found incomprehensible the Wilsonian policy of a "pious refusal" to deal with Soviet Russia, by which America gained nothing. Since they had simplistically pictured Wall Street interests dominating American foreign policy, Soviet leaders were baffled by the Wilson administration's resistance to economic pressures and inducements. To Chicherin America's policy was "a puzzle, its relations with Russia a paradox." He sometimes blamed "alien influences" — tsarist diplomats and "bourgeois Russian emigrants in the United States" — for distributing false information that obscured the Wilson administration's perception of America's "real interests." On other occasions Chicherin classed Wilson as the representative of a petty bourgeois utopian element deluded by a fantastic ideology. In general, Soviet officials maintained that Wilsonian policy was "senseless" and unreasonable.[56]

Ignoring the possible effect on American leaders of Soviet encouragement of proletarian revolution, Lenin, Chicherin, and other Soviet officials asserted that there were no obstacles to peaceful and cooperative relations on the Soviet side. Rejecting the "utterly ridiculous" charge that the Soviet regime was endeavoring to overthrow the U.S. government by force, Chicherin dismissed American hostility "as a psychological curiosity seemingly inspired by a panicky animal fear which we refuse to regard seriously." By 1923 Chicherin thought "the main and perhaps insuperable obstacle to agreement between America and Russia" was Soviet revolutionary propaganda, but such thinking did not guide Soviet activity while Wilson was president.[57]

Soviet leaders' stress on the economic drives behind American foreign policy did not prepare them to comprehend Woodrow Wilson, who sought to rise above narrow interests in his "unselfish" quest to steady "the whole process of history."[58] In February 1919, recalling the Bolsheviks' insulting insinuation that Western statesmen were driven by financial concerns and territorial greed, Wilson supposed that since the

Bolsheviks "know they have no high motives, they do not believe that any-body else has."[59]

Wilson's smoldering anger at Bolshevik aspersions and his sense that Bolshevism posed a fundamental threat to international stability con-tributed to his increasingly rigid opposition to relations with the Soviet regime. After British and American troops left Russia, the British govern-ment entered negotiations with Soviet representatives for a trade agree-ment, but instead of following suit the Wilson administration expressed its disapproval. With Wilson's consent, in August 1920 Secretary of State Colby issued "the Colby Note," an open letter to the Italian ambassador in Washington, which anathematized the Soviet regime as the negation of American political principles and moral values. Written largely by the anti-Bolshevik socialist John Spargo, the note formalized and publicized the Wilsonian excommunication of Bolshevik heretics in part to make it difficult for a future Republican president to undo Wilsonian policy and admit Soviet Russia to the Western congregation.[60]

Even after the release of the Colby Note, Wilson himself remained re-luctant to speak candidly in public about his attitudes toward Bolshevism. When newspaperman William Hawkins sought Wilson's "opinion regard-ing Bolshevism" in September 1920, the president stipulated that the con-versation must be "confidential." "I do not fear Bolshevism," Wilson then confided, "but it must be resisted. Bolshevism is a mistake and it must be resisted as all mistakes must be resisted. If left alone it will destroy itself. It cannot survive because it is wrong."[61]

By the fall of 1920, when the Red Army drove the last significant White forces from the Crimea, Wilsonian resistance to Bolshevism was narrowed to relying primarily upon the maintenance of the nonrecog-nition policy and an undeclared embargo on trade. The Wilson admin-istration's limited and secretive efforts to support anti-Bolshevik groups did not lead to the removal of the Soviet regime, the restoration of democracy, or even the containment of Bolshevism in the heartland of European Russia. Since many of those efforts did not remain secret from Bolshevik leaders, they gave Soviet representatives opportunities to de-nounce Wilsonian violations of pledges about open diplomacy and self-determination and to present themselves as more faithful practitioners of such principles. While Martens and Nuorteva carefully refrained from direct revolutionary agitation, their one-sided statements ignored the way secret Soviet emissaries smuggled funds into the United States and the way Bolshevik leaders urged American radicals to develop a revolu-tionary movement. Soviet agents were even less effective in stimulating revolution in the United States than American representatives were in supporting Russian counterrevolutionaries, but both sides engaged in clandestine subversion.[62]

Lenin and Wilson sought to move the world along opposite tracks — the road to world Bolshevism and the road away from revolution. Given the intensity of their political and ideological conflict, there was little chance that the two governments could resolve their differences and set off together on an alternative path. At the same time, Soviet Russia was unable to do much to promote revolution in America and the United States was unwilling to launch massive military campaigns to overthrow the Bolshevik regime. Yet each government, underestimating the longevity of its rival, lacked the foresight to refrain from the limited and secretive actions that exacerbated their inevitable suspicion and antagonism.

CONCLUSION

"I do not know that I rightly understand Bolshevikism," Secretary of War Newton Baker confessed to Woodrow Wilson in November 1918. "So much of it as I do understand I don't like, but I have a feeling that if the Russians do like it, they are entitled to have it and that it does not lie with us to say that only ten percent of the Russian people are Bolsheviks and that therefore we will assist the other ninety percent in resisting it." Wilson sometimes expressed a similar feeling "that Russia should be left to settle her own affairs in her own way," at least "so long as she does not become a menace to others." In his most passionate assertion of the right of self-determination, Wilson declared to members of the Democratic National Committee in February 1919 "that any people is entitled to any kind of government it damn pleases, and that it is none of our business to suggest or to influence the kind that it is going to have." While that might leave "a very riotous form of government" in power, Wilson argued that the principle of nonintervention should be respected, "even with regard to Russia."[1]

Wilson's vehement statement seemed to align him with liberal advisors such as Colonel House, who suggested that the United States should refrain from military intervention in Russia, establish de facto relations with the Bolsheviks, cease supporting anti-Bolshevik armies if the Soviet government promised not to overthrow its neighbors, and offer economic assistance to alleviate distress throughout Russia. That position had many virtues. It would have been clear and understandable to Americans, even those who passionately disagreed. It recognized that Russia was too vast to be pacified by foreign armies and it acknowledged the difficulty of enforcing the principle of self-determination in a country torn by civil war. Finally, it offered opportunities for the early stabilization of conditions in eastern Europe and the gradual moderation of Soviet policies.

Yet Wilson did not follow that advice. At the peak of the wartime pressure for military expeditions to Russia, in June 1918, even Newton Baker believed his preferred course of letting the Russians "settle their own affairs" was "impossible."[2] Many international pressures made it extremely hard to abstain from intervention. Americans saw urgent needs for action to counter German propaganda in Russia, block German exploitation of Russian resources, foil German domination of Russian markets, appease British and French desperation for a revived eastern front, prevent Japanese closure of the "open door" in Siberia, and preserve Russian territorial integrity. Such concerns about the demands and ambitions of allies and enemies did not simply compel Wilson to violate his principles and inter-vene against his better judgment. Wilson was also impelled to intervene by his faith in a democratic Russia, his "infinite longing to be of some ser-vice" to the Russian people, his confidence that deluded Soviet leaders could not last, his revulsion at the "poison" of Bolshevism, and his convic-tion that the Bolshevik regime was a violent perversion, rather than a gen-uine expression, of Russian self-determination.[3]

Soon after the revolution against tsarism in March 1917, influenced by Charles Crane and other informal advisors, Wilson decided that Russia had been silently prepared for a miraculous transformation from decadent autocracy to militant democracy. Hence, at the start of his crusade to make the world "safe for democracy" in April 1917, Wilson expressed the con-viction that Russians were "democratic at heart." After Bolsheviks pushed Russia's shaky liberal government from power in November 1917, Wilson's friends, State Department officials, and Russian representatives repeatedly suggested to him that real, loyal Russians only needed slight assistance and encouragement to regain control of their destinies from treacherous usurpers. Although early efforts to support anti-Bolshevik forces in south-ern Russia failed, in the summer of 1918, Wilson agreed to dispatch small American military expeditions to north Russia and Siberia in part because he still hoped such modest U.S. aid would inspire Russians who admired America to overcome war-weariness, expunge fevered radicalism, and re-store democracy to their country. A year later, despite his disillusionment with democratic socialists who faltered in 1917 and notwithstanding his belief that order had to be restored by a strong military leader before "backward" Russia would be ready for responsible self-government, Wil-son still maintained that "the Russian people" were "in their local life a very democratic people." At Paris in 1919, Wilson did not know where Azerbaijan was, but he determined immediately that a delegation of gentlemen from Azerbaijan spoke "the same language" he did "in respect of ideas" and "conceptions of liberty." Like other delegations "from all over the world," the Azerbaijanis, Wilson concluded, sought "the guid-ance and the help and the advice of America." Wilson never developed a clear conception of how America could help peoples of the former Russian empire transcend bitter class and national antagonisms, but through the end of the Russian Civil War he embraced a vague faith that by providing food, clothing, and weapons to anti-Bolshevik groups the United States could contribute to the reestablishment of orderly self-government.[4]

In addition to being animated by dreams of Russian democracy, Wil-son could not stomach the "intolerable tyranny" of Bolshevism and could not sit still while the Russian conflagration threatened to spread across the globe. Insulted by Soviet propaganda, fearful that the Russian revolution-ary example would lead the world down the wrong path, and increasingly convinced that the "mistake" of Bolshevism had to be resisted, Wilson rejected proposals for diplomatic relations and political settlements with the Soviet government. Even in his speech to the Democratic National Committee Wilson decried the "ugly poisonous thing called Bolshevism," recognized the impossibility of establishing peace "if we left half of Europe and half of Asia at war," and expressed his wish to help the Russians, rather than "leave the country in a state of chaos." [5]

Some American leaders who shared Wilson's moral and ideological antipathy toward Bolshevism favored open and direct action against the Soviet regime. Secretary of State Robert Lansing proposed a blunt public refusal to recognize the Soviet government. Ambassador David Francis, other U.S. diplomats, and conservative politicians, like many British and French officials, called for large, aggressive military campaigns to reorganize Russian resistance to Germany and eradicate the menace of Bolshevism. However, Wilson could not approve of full-scale military intervention in Russia. That would risk pushing the Bolsheviks into the arms of the Germans and provoking a nationalistic backlash in which Russians would rally around the Soviet regime. Even more importantly, a direct invasion would contradict Wilson's declared commitment to the principle of self-determination, alienate his supporters on the Left, and jeopardize his moral leadership of world opinion. As Wilson's ambassador to Denmark observed, a blatant campaign to "put down Lenin's Government . . . by sheer force" would have been "very difficult to recommend to liberals in our country and elsewhere." [6] For similar reasons, Wilson was reluctant to publicly condemn the Bolsheviks and he could not openly provide military and financial assistance to anti-Bolshevik forces.

Torn between conflicting impulses, prodded by competing counsels, and buffeted by rapidly changing situations, Wilson did not hold consistently to a clear and firm strategy. He was at times uncertain about the specific path to take, but also deliberately vague about the direction in which he was moving. A series of ambiguous pronouncements—his Fourteen Points speech, his March 1918 message to the Russian people, his *aide-mémoire* of July 1918, and his invitation of Russian leaders to a conference at Prinkipo—created considerable confusion about his intentions. Wilsonian policy was also shrouded by a misty combination of self-deception and expedient fictions: that Ambassador Bakhmeteff represented the unbroken spirit of the Russian people; that the United States, unlike the Old World powers, did not stoop to espionage and subversion; that Bolsheviks were German agents; that American forces went to Siberia to rescue Czechoslovakian legionnaires from German prisoners of war; that American soldiers in north Russia were not involved in warfare against the Red Army; and that American aid to the Baltic region was distributed for purely philanthropic purposes. However, underneath all the fog and vacillation, Wilson's decisions showed a recurring pattern, as he repeatedly approved efforts to support anti-Bolshevik movements, escalating from financial assistance to small military expeditions but halting short of outright war. Instead of either accepting the Bolshevik regime or declaring war against it, Wilson and other Americans tried to influence the kind of government Russians had through propaganda campaigns, moral encouragement of patriotic Russians, financial support for anti-Bolshevik groups, limited military expeditions to Russian ports, weapons shipments to White armies, and "humanitarian" assistance to forces fighting against the Red Army.

Those secretive efforts were not strange aberrations in Wilsonian foreign policy. From the first year of his presidency Wilson had been confronted by new constraints on statecraft that shaped his approach to intervention. In an age when modern methods of communication were weaving the world into a single tight web, educated publics were increasingly attentive to international affairs, and Americans were deeply divided about how to respond to dramatic foreign revolutions, Wilson and his closest aides felt they had to move carefully to avoid offending important constituencies and exacerbating domestic divisions. While the Progressive Era has long been regarded as a period of idealistic publicity—the time when "the attack on secrecy reached its peak"—it was precisely then that American statesmen resorted more extensively to the instruments of secret war.[7] First in Mexico from 1913 to 1917 and then in Russia from 1917 to 1920, American officials experimented with and came to rely heavily upon indirect and covert forms of intervention. Those methods were often unsuccessful or counterproductive. Nevertheless, young Americans who participated in the Wilson administration's operations employed similar techniques during the later Cold War confrontation with international communism. Thus, among the most significant legacies of the Wilson years were the formative experiences that inclined men such as Allen and John Foster Dulles to rely on propaganda and covert action when they led the Central Intelligence Agency and State Department in the 1950s.

With his profound understanding of American institutions and values and his magnificent gift for resonant rhetoric, Wilson was in some respects superbly equipped to face the challenges of foreign policy leadership in an era of heightened public involvement. Yet despite his extraordinary persuasive abilities, Wilson showed an aversion to laying the case for intervention before the American people that would be characteristic of subsequent, less talented presidents. While Wilson often stressed his desire to make public opinion the arbiter of international relations, he repeatedly refused to inform Americans fully and candidly about his policy toward revolutionary Russia. If Wilson had addressed Congress and the American people honestly and directly, he might have mobilized support for a course of strict nonintervention or a policy of more aggressive and effective intervention. Instead, Wilson and his advisors evaded public and congressional scrutiny of relations with Russia, thereby fostering suspicion about their objectives and severely constraining financing for their initiatives.

Wilson's unwillingness to be frank with Congress and the American people also undermined support for his highest priority, the League of Nations. As Wilson traveled across the United States in September 1919 urging U.S. entry into the League, he was trailed by Senate critics who roused emotions about the continuing U.S. military intervention in Siberia. In Chicago, for example, Senator Hiram Johnson argued that at the very moment Wilson claimed the League would prevent future wars, "American youths . . . were being slain . . . in Siberia, in a war not declared by the American people or the American Congress, but directed in secrecy at Paris by what now constitutes the league of nations." Johnson, Idaho senator William Borah, Wisconsin senator Robert LaFollette, and other progressives distrusted Wilson's "secret" and "concealed" policy toward Russia. They saw the U.S. military expeditions to north Russia and Siberia as ominous signs that membership in a League would mean American involvement in further interventions around the world to support the status quo and thwart revolutionary change. While Wilson did not lose the treaty fight simply because of the opposition of the "peace progressives," his secretive efforts to make Russia safe for democracy significantly eroded support for the League in American democratic institutions.[8]

Wilson's reliance on constricted and clandestine means to pursue an avowedly impartial policy increased the likelihood of failure abroad as well as disillusionment at home. While nothing Americans could have done would have resolved the tensions between conservative officers and socialist civilians that fractured anti-Bolshevik movements, the official neutrality and tacit partiality alienated both groups. The limited, indirect, and covert interventions in the Russian Civil War were far from sufficient to support the confident organization of anti-Bolshevik forces. American efforts thus failed to fulfill Wilson's wish "to assist the people of Russia to attain their utmost hope of liberty and ordered peace."[9] The secret war against Bolshevism did not hasten the collapse of communism. On balance, it did more to help the Bolsheviks survive and consolidate their control over Soviet Russia, since the many forms of foreign intervention helped the Bolsheviks to justify ruthless class terror and to portray their Russian adversaries as tools of rapacious imperialists.

If the Allies and the United States had been able to send larger military forces to Russia, particularly before the expansion of the Red Army in late 1918, they might have succeeded in overthrowing the Soviet regime. However, in 1918 American leaders were very reluctant to divert major forces from the war against Germany. Even then massive foreign intervention probably would have triggered widespread Bolshevik guerrilla warfare that would have required maintaining a large army of occupation for many years.[10] Since Wilson was unwilling to face those risks and costs, he would have been wiser to keep faith with his promise to Russia of "an unhampered and unembarrassed opportunity for the independent determination of her own political development," and to allow economic connections to draw Russia back "into the society of nations."[11] Few arguments can be made for the half-way measures of the Wilson administration. While the limited and covert interventions failed to overturn the Bolshevik regime, they exacerbated the fears of hostile encirclement and foreign subversion that buttressed the Soviet government for seven decades.[12]

In the wake of the Cold War and the collapse of the Soviet system Woodrow Wilson continues to be a central figure — perhaps *the* central figure — in American thinking about international relations. For many, Wilson represents an inspiring liberal internationalism committed to the principles of self-determination and nonintervention. Others invoke Wilson as an exemplar of humanitarian intervention around the world or as a paragon of the carefully defined and restricted use of force.[13] However, the history of America's secret war against Bolshevism shows that Wilsonian policy toward Russia cannot stand as a model of either principled, steadfast nonintervention or adept, tightly controlled limited intervention. Wilson and his advisors neither abstained from intervention in the Russian Civil War nor solved the complicated problems of how a democracy can intervene to promote self-government in foreign countries. Instead, they repeatedly and painfully straddled the horns of those dilemmas, succumbing to the illusions that they could support anti-Bolshevik movements but keep that secret from idealistic Americans; that they could provide friendly assistance to forces of order without becoming entangled in civil war; that they could intervene without interfering. Thus, at the beginning of the Soviet-American conflict, amid popular demands for a new, open diplomacy, the Wilson administration epitomized a limited, secretive, and ineffective style of intervention, one that unsuccessfully sought to evade the constraints of democracy at home as it pursued American interests and promoted American values abroad. Wilson and his aides did not find satisfactory solutions to the problems of intervention in the global "whispering gallery." It remains for Americans living in the information age to learn from the experiences of the Wilson era and come to treat with greater candor the dilemmas of intervention and democracy.

NOTES

ABBREVIATIONS USED IN NOTES

ARA   American Relief Administration
ARC   American Red Cross
AVPRF Archive of the Foreign Policy of the Russian Federation
CAB   War Cabinet Papers, Public Record Office, London
CPI   Committee on Public Information Records, RG 63, National Archives, Washington, D.C.
DVP   Ministry of Foreign Affairs of the USSR, *Dokumenty vneshnei politiki SSSR,* Moscow, 1959– .
FRUS   U.S. Department of State, *Papers Relating to the Foreign Relations of the United States, Russia, 1918–1919,* 4 volumes, Washington, D.C., 1931–1947
GARF   State Archive of the Russian Federation
HIA   Hoover Institution Archives, Stanford University, Stanford, California
LC   Library of Congress, Washington, D.C.
MID   Military Intelligence Division
NA   National Archives, Washington, D.C.
ONI   Office of Naval Intelligence
PPC   *Papers Relating to the Foreign Relations of the United States: The Paris Peace Conference, 1919,* 13 volumes, Washington, D.C., 1942–1947
PPWW Ray Stannard Baker and William E. Dodd, eds., *The Public Papers of Woodrow Wilson: War and Peace,* 2 volumes, New York, 1927
PWW   Arthur S. Link, et al., eds., *The Papers of Woodrow Wilson,* 69 volumes, Princeton, 1966–1993
RG   Record Group
SD   State Department
SHSW State Historical Society of Wisconsin
WC   War Cabinet
WWLL Ray Stannard Baker, *Woodrow Wilson, Life and Letters,* 8 vols., Garden City, N.Y., 1927–1939

INTRODUCTION

1. Address of Sept. 6, 1919, PPWW, 2:15.

2. Address of Dec. 4, 1917, PPWW, 1:133–39.

3. "Let There Be Light," in Link, *Wilson: The New Freedom,* 76–77; Address of May 27, 1916, PWW 37:113–16; Address of Jan. 8, 1918, PPWW 1:159. For accounts of Wilson's devotion to a new, open diplomacy, see esp. Knock, *To End All Wars*; Mayer, *Wilson vs. Lenin,* 8, 34–35, 56, 331, 357–58 (but note also 392).

4. Notes on "Philosophy of Politics," quoted in Bragdon, *Wilson,* 263; "The True American Spirit," ca. Oct. 27, 1892, PWW 8:39; House Diary, Feb. 14, 1913, PWW 27:112–13.

5. Draft memoir on Wilson, Cary T. Grayson Papers; Sir William Wiseman to Arthur Cecil Murray, July 4, 1918, PWW 48:523–25; House Diary, Sept. 12 and Dec. 18, 1917, House Papers; Lansing, "Effect of Secret Diplomacy on the Public Mind," April 4, 1919, Lansing Papers, LC.

6. See House Diary, July 4, Aug. 7, and Aug. 15, Sept. 3, 1917; Wilson remarks to Wiseman in Oct. 1918, PWW 51:351; Israel, *Nevada's Key Pittman*, 36; and William Wiseman to Lord Robert Cecil, July 18, 1918, PWW 49:11–13. For contrary views of the Wilsonian policymaking process, see Link, *Wilson: Revolution, War, and Peace*, 17; and McFadden, *Alternative Paths*, 9.

7. William Phillips Journal, Dec. 31, 1917. For similar complaints, see Gordon Auchincloss Diary, June 18, 1918; Samuel Eliot Morison Diary, June 6, 1919.

8. *Nation*, July 27, 1918; Ray Stannard Baker Diary, April 12 and 25, 1919 (omitted from PWW 58:142–3).

9. For different views, see Link, *Woodrow Wilson*, 95–96; Unterberger, *Intervention Against Communism*, 22; Calhoun, *Power and Principle*, 2.

10. Nicolai, *German Secret Service*, 10, 266–69; Katz, *Secret War in Mexico*, x.

11. See, for example, Link, *Woodrow Wilson*; Knock, *To End All Wars*, 313; Pipes, *Russia Under the Bolshevik Regime*, 64.

12. See esp. Williams, "American Intervention in Russia."

13. House Diary, April 26, 1917, May 30, 1917, Sept. 27, 1918.

14. "Proekt doklada ob otnosheniiakh s Soedinennymi Shtatami," n.d. (late 1920), f. 129, op. 4, d. 6, ll. 18–19, AVPRF.

15. Draft of letter from Martens to Secretary of State Colby, June 19, 1920, f. 507, op. 56, d. 5, ll. 3–9, AVPRF.

16. Khrushchev, *Khrushchev in America*, 111–12; *Los Angeles Times* and *New York Times*, Sept. 20, 1959.

17. *New York Times*, May 29, 1972; "Vystuplenie R. Niksona po Tsentral'nomu televideniiu," *Pravda*, May 29, 1972.

18. *New York Times*, Jan. 26, 1984.

19. David K. Shipler, "The View from America," *New York Times Magazine*, Nov. 10, 1985, 48.

20. See, for example, Kennan, *Russia and the West*, v–vi; Kennan, "Soviet Historiography"; Kennan, "American Troops in Russia: The True Record," 42; Sivachev and Yakovlev, *Russia and the United States*, 44; Gvishiani, *Sovetskaia Rossiia i SShA*, 3–14; Kunina, "V Kollokvium istorikov SSSR i SShA," 213; and Unterberger, *Intervention Against Communism*.

21. Soviet scholars and "revisionist" historians discussed some of the secretive forms of intervention in articles and chapters of books on broader topics. See esp. the works by Ganelin, W. A. Williams, Maddox, Levin, and Gardner cited in the bibliography.

22. See, for example, Phillips Journal, Dec. 12, 1917; Wilson remarks on May 20, 1919, in Link, *Deliberations of the Council of Four*, 2:123; and Fowler, *British-American Relations 1917–1918*, 165, 197.

23. Woodrow Wilson Foundation Broadcast, Jan. 1, 1949, Box 221, Allen Dulles Papers. On the Dulles-Jackson-Correa report, see Jeffreys-Jones, *CIA and American Democracy*, 57; Ranelagh, *Agency*, 164–67; and Darling, *Central Intelligence Agency*, esp. 307.

CHAPTER ONE

1. Address of Jan. 8, 1915, PWW 32:38–9. For similar statements see PWW 35:314; and Baker, *WWLL*, 6:74.

2. My views have been strongly influenced by Gardner, *Safe for Democracy*. For contrasting interpretations, see Unterberger, "Wilson and the Bolsheviks"; Link, *Woodrow Wilson*, 9–10, 95–97; Graber, *Crisis Diplomacy*, esp. 151–53; Knight, *U.S.-Mexican Re-*

lations, 106–16; Calhoun, *Power and Principle,* 191; and Calhoun, *Uses of Force,* 6, 77–79, 129.

3. Wilson, *Division and Reunion,* 147–54; Wilson, *History of the American People,* 4:122, 118; Baker, *WWLL,* 6:74. See also PWW 48:257.

4. Wilson, *History of the American People,* 5:240–44; "Mr. Cleveland's Cabinet," ca. March 17, 1893, PWW 8:164.

5. Memorandum for an interview, ca. Dec. 18, 1895, PWW 9:365; Wilson, *History of the American People,* 5:244–48; Baker, *WWLL,* 2:24, 285.

6. Wilson, *History of the American People,* 5:270–75; "The Statesmanship of Letters," Nov. 5, 1903, PWW 15:41.

7. "Our New Foreign Policy," May 15, 1902, Box 79, Lansing Papers, LC.

8. Wilson, *History of the American People,* 5:255; "Democracy and Efficiency" [ca. Oct. 1, 1900], PWW 12:18; Speech on Feb. 3, 1906, PWW 16:297–98; *History of the American People,* 5: 296. For further discussion, see Diamond, *Economic Thought of Wilson,* and Williams, "Frontier Thesis and American Foreign Policy."

9. Newspaper report of Wilson's speech on Dec. 1, 1903, PWW 15:58–59. See also PWW 15:142–43.

10. See "Democracy and Efficiency," ca. Oct. 1, 1900, PWW 12:19; address of May 3, 1902, PWW 13:362; Beale, *Theodore Roosevelt,* 455.

11. Wilson to Mary Allen Hulbert Peck, Feb. 28, 1912, PWW 24:218; House, *Philip Dru,* 280–85; House Diary, Jan. 18, 1913, PWW 27:64.

12. Diary of Josephus Daniels, March 11, 1913, PWW 27:169–70; Statement on Relations with Latin America, March 12, 1913, PWW 27:172; Tumulty, *Wilson as I Know Him,* 144–45.

13. Samuel G. Blythe, "Mexico: The Record of a Conversation With President Wilson," April 27, 1914, PWW 29:521, 524. See also Page to Wilson, Nov. 2, 1913, PWW 28:484–85; Wilson to Page, Dec. 6, 1913, PWW 29:19–20.

14. "The Ideals of America," Dec. 26, 1901, PWW 12:222–23; Wilson address of Dec. 12, 1900, PWW 12:44; Edward G. Lowry, "What the President is Trying to Do for Mexico," Jan. 1, 1914, PWW 29:97; Meyer, *Huerta,* 121; Franklin Lane to Wilson, March 13, 1916, PWW 36:301; Smith, *United States and Revolutionary Nationalism,* 90–91; Blythe, "Mexico," April 27, 1914, PWW 29:522.

15. Statement for the press, March 25, 1916, PWW 36:364–66. See also Oct. 27, 1913, speech at Mobile, PWW 28:450–51; Spring Rice to Grey, Feb. 7, 1914, PWW 29:230; Wilson to Lansing, Aug. 31, 1915, PWW 34:382–83.

16. Press conference, July 21, 1913, PWW 28:57; Diamond, *Economic Thought of Wilson;* Levin, *Wilson and World Politics,* 13–22; Sklar, *United States as a Developing Country,* 102–42; Smith, *United States and Revolutionary Nationalism,* 34–35.

17. Delbert James Haff to Wilson, May 12, 1913, PWW 27:419–25; Wilson's "Draft of Instructions to Henry Lane Wilson," May 15, 1913, PWW 27:435; John Bassett Moore to Wilson, May 15, 1913, PWW 27:437–40; Link, *Wilson: The New Freedom,* 351–53.

18. House Diary, May 2, 1913, PWW 27:383; Instructions to John Lind, Aug. 4, 1913, PWW 28:110.

19. House Diary, Oct. 14, 1913; Address in Mobile, Alabama, Oct. 27, 1913, PWW 28:448–52; Gardner, *Safe for Democracy,* 54–55; Link, *Wilson: The New Freedom,* 366–73.

20. House Diary, Oct. 30, 1913, PWW 28:478; Draft of a war address to Congress, PWW 28:479–81; Link, *Wilson: The New Freedom,* 375–80; Augustus Bacon to Wilson, Nov. 4, 1913, PWW 28:488.

21. House Diary, Oct. 27, 1913; Wilson to Mary Allen Hulbert, Feb. 1, 1914, PWW 29:211; Haley, *Revolution and Intervention,* 190, 219–20; Knight, *U.S.-Mexican Relations,*

105; Smith, *United States and Revolutionary Nationalism*, 64–66 and 84; Tate, "Pershing's Punitive Expedition," 62; Link, *Wilson and the Progressive Era*, 247, 237, 241; and Harbaugh, "Wilson, Roosevelt, and Interventionism," esp. 231–59.

22. Bryan to Walter Hines Page, Nov. 19, 1913, PWW 28:566.

23. Bryan to Special Commissioners (drafted by Wilson), June 3, 1914, PWW 30:137–39; Wilson to Walter Hines Page, Jan. 29, 1914, PWW 29:196–97. See also PWW 29:206–7.

24. Phillips, *Ventures in Diplomacy*, 60–62; Phillips to Wilson, Jan. 28, 1914, PWW 29:187–89; House Diary, Jan. 21, 1914, PWW 29:160; Cabrera to Phillips, Jan. 28, 1914, PWW 29:193–95; Wilson remarks at press conference, Feb. 26, 1914, PWW 29:296.

25. See, for example, Bryan to American Consulate in Monterey, Mexico, July 20, 1914, PWW 30:290, and Bryan to Carothers and Silliman, July 23, 1914, PWW 30:297–98.

26. Grieb, *United States and Huerta*, 118; Hill, *Emissaries to a Revolution*, 347, 363, 332–33, 367; Tate, "Pershing's Punitive Expedition," 66.

27. Hale to Wilson, Dec. 31, 1913, PWW 29:90–91; Hale to Wilson, Jan. 13, 1914, PWW 29:130; Wilson to Hale, Jan. 15, 1914, PWW 29:133–34; Lazaro de la Garza to Felix A. Sommerfeld, June 27, 1914, PWW 30:220–21; Wilson to Bryan, with enclosure, Aug. 5, 1914, PWW 30:346–47; Grieb, *United States and Huerta*, 61; Meyer, *Huerta*, 125. For a contrary view, see Knight, *Mexican Revolution*, 2:31.

28. Wilson's Jan. 31, 1914 announcement, PWW 29:207.

29. House Diary, Jan. 16, 1914, PWW 29:135; Wilson to Page, Jan. 29, 1914, PWW 29:196–97. See also Bryan to Lind, Jan. 18, 1914, PWW 29:137–38.

30. Spring Rice to Sir William Tyrell, March 9, 1914, PWW 29:324–25.

31. Spring Rice to Grey, Feb. 7, 1914, PWW 29:228–31; Draft of an address to Congress, ca. Oct. 31, 1913, PWW 28:479; Wilson to Page, June 4, 1914, PWW 30:143; Lansing to Wilson, Aug. 10, 1915, quoted in Haley, *Revolution and Intervention*, 173–74; House Diary, Aug. 30, 1914, PWW 30:463; House Diary, Sept. 23, 1915, *Intimate Papers of Colonel House*, 1:224.

32. Spring Rice to Sir Edward Grey, Feb. 7, 1914, PWW 29:229.

33. Edwin Ludlow to House, April 29, 1913, paraphrased in PWW 27:405; Luis Cabrera to William Phillips, Jan. 30, 1914, PWW 29:205–6; William Kent to Wilson, April 24, 1914, PWW 29:499–500; Bryan to William Wesley Canada, April 21, 1914, PWW 29:477; Wilson "Remarks to Mexican Editors," June 7, 1918, PWW 48:255, 257; Quirk, *Affair of Honor*, 70; Address to Congress, April 20, 1914, PWW 29:471–74.

34. Quirk, *Affair of Honor*, 68, 114; Link, *Wilson: The New Freedom*, 400–405; Knight, *U.S.-Mexican Relations*, 105; Garrison to Wilson and Wilson to Garrison, both Aug. 8, 1914, PWW 30:360–62.

35. Hart, *Revolutionary Mexico*, 283–312; Draft of Lansing to Arredondo, June 20, 1916, enclosed in Wilson to Lansing, June 18, 1916, PWW 37:256. See also Hill, *Emissaries to a Revolution*, 363.

36. House Diary, March 30, 1916, PWW 36:381; Statement to the press, March 25, 1916, PWW 36:365.

37. Wilson to House, June 22, 1916, PWW 37:281; Haley, *Revolution and Intervention*, 225; Calhoun, *Uses of Force*, 40–43; House Diary, Oct. 30, 1913, PWW 28:476–78; press conference, Feb. 26, 1914, PWW 29:291–92; Aide-mémoire of July 17, 1918, *FRUS, 1918, Russia*, 2:287–90; Samuel G. Blythe record of April 27, 1914, interview, PWW 29:516; Wilson to Secretary of War Garrison, Aug. 8, 1914, PWW 30:362; and Hill, *Emissaries to a Revolution*, 334, 359.

38. For efforts to define "intervention," see Schraeder, *Intervention in the 1980s*, 2; and Hoffman, "The Problem of Intervention," in Bull, *Intervention in World Politics*, 7–28.

39. Lind to Bryan, Jan. 7, 1914, and "Notes from conversation with Lind," ca. Jan. 8, 1914, PWW 29:110; Lind to Wilson, Jan. 10, 1914, PWW 29:118–27.

40. Department Intelligence Officer to Major R. H. Van Deman, Sept. 14, 1916, M.I.D. file 9700-22, RG 165, NA. For a broader discussion, see Katz, *Secret War in Mexico*, esp. 433–41.

41. Harris and Sadler, "Termination with Extreme Prejudice: The United States Versus Pancho Villa," in *Border and the Revolution*, 8–16; R. H. Van Deman to Leland Harrison, Sept. 25, 1916, M.I.D. file 9700-23, RG 165, NA; Adjutant general to Scott, April 23, 1916, quoted in Hall and Coerver, *Revolution on the Border*, 67.

42. Essay on Caribbean policy and remarks on U.S. foreign policy, July 1917, Box 8, Lansing Papers, Princeton.

43. Cf. Knock, *To End All Wars*, 27; Cooper, *Warrior and the Priest*, 268; Clements, "Wilson's Mexican Policy, 1913–15"; Unterberger, "Wilson and the Russian Revolution," in Link, *Wilson and a Revolutionary World*, 49–50.

44. Mobile Address, Oct. 27, 1913, PWW 28:448–49; Draft of an Address to Congress, ca. Oct. 31, 1913, PWW 28:479; Remarks to Mexican Editors, June 7, 1918, PWW 48:257. On American enthusiasm about trade and investment in Russia, see Washburn, *Victory in Defeat*, 156, 171; and Tuve, "Changing Directions in Russian-American Economic Relations, 1912–1917."

45. Wilson to Lansing, May 27, 1919, and Lansing to Wilson, May 28, 1919, Lansing Papers, LC, vol. 43.

46. Wilson remarks on June 6, 1919, PWW 60:215; Address to Congress, April 2, 1917, PPWW 1:13; Address of Sept. 10, 1919, PPWW 2:101. For the views of Wilson's Cabinet members and informants, see Smith, *United States and Revolutionary Nationalism*, 138; Root to Secretary of State, June 17, 1917, *FRUS, 1918, Russia*, 1:122; Joshua Butler Wright Diary, July 2 and Dec. 4, 1917; W. T. Ellis to Josephus Daniels, June 21, 1918, in Daniels to Wilson, June 24, 1918, PWW 48:410–13.

47. Knock, *To End All Wars*, 29–30; Foner, *Bolshevik Revolution*, 50, 133.

CHAPTER TWO

1. Fourteen Points speech, Jan. 8, 1918, PPWW 1:155–59; Herbert Bayard Swope in the *New York World*, Jan. 11, 1918, quoted in Lasch, *American Liberals*, 79–81; Hankey's Notes of a Meeting of the Council of Ten, Jan. 22, 1919, PWW 54:204–5.

2. Address to Congress, April 2, 1917, PPWW 1:12; address at Des Moines, Sept. 6, 1919, PPWW 2:15. See also PPWW 2:6, 10, 70, 84–85, 100–101, 107–8, 143, 193.

3. "Bolshevism and Russia," Box 18, Ray Stannard Baker Papers, Princeton.

4. For an example of the former view, see Williams, "American Intervention in Russia," 32; for different statements of the latter interpretation, see Link, *Wilson: Revolution, War, and Peace*, 95–96; PWW 54:vii–viii; Unterberger, "Wilson and the Bolsheviks," 71–73; Knock, *To End All Wars*, 145, 156.

5. See esp. Mulder, *Wilson*.

6. Diary entry, July 16, 1877, PWW 1:279; essay on Bismarck, PWW 1:307–8.

7. "The Road Away from Revolution," *Atlantic Monthly*, Aug. 1923, PPWW, 2:536–39.

8. Confidential Journal, Dec. 28, 1889, PWW 6:462–63. My views have been influenced by Mulder, *Wilson*, 170, 259, 263, 265. See also Bragdon, *Wilson*, 195–97.

9. Ross, "Socialism and American Liberalism"; Crunden, *Ministers of Reform*, 12–13, 70–71; "Socialism and Democracy," ca. Aug. 22, 1887, PWW 5:561.

10. Marginal notes on Richard T. Ely's *The Labor Movement in America* and "Socialism

and Democracy," ca. Aug. 22, 1887, both in PWW 5:559–62; Wilson, *The State*, 658–59. See also Bragdon, *Wilson*, 183–84.

11. "Nature of Democracy in the United States," May 17, 1889, PWW 6:228.

12. Elson, *Guardians of Tradition*, 139–40, 290; Hunt, *Ideology*, 96–97; Williams, *America Confronts*, 44, 64, 7, 17, 32; Curtis, "American Opinion"; Thompson and Hart, *Uncertain Crusade*. For a different view, see Davis, *Revolutions*.

13. "Self-Government in France," Sept. 1879, PWW 1:516–17, 536–38.

14. Good, "America and the Russian Revolutionary Movement"; "Mr. Gladstone, A Character Sketch," April 1880, PWW 1:633–34.

15. Memoranda for "The Philosophy of Politics," ca. Jan. 26, 1895, PWW 9:129; Lecture on Democracy, Dec. 5, 1891, PWW 7:366; lecture notes from late 1893, PWW 8:409; "Princeton in the Nation's Service," Oct. 21, 1896, PWW 10:30.

16. Notes for "Philosophy of Politics," n.d., quoted in Bragdon, *Wilson*, 261; "University Training and Citizenship," ca. June 20, 1894, PWW 8:594; "Edmund Burke: The Man and His Times," ca. Aug. 1893, PWW 8:337–38.

17. "The Banker and the Nation," Sept. 30, 1908, quoted in Bragdon, *Wilson*, 349–50; News report of an address at Oberlin College, March 22, 1906, PWW 16:341; Address to the National Democratic Club, April 16, 1906, PWW 16:365.

18. Wilson, *New Freedom*, 24–40.

19. "Edmund Burke," Aug. 1893, PWW 8:337–38; "A Calendar of Great Americans," ca. Sept. 1893, PWW 8:373; Address in Trenton, N.J., Oct. 9, 1911, PWW 23:435.

20. Samuel G. Blythe, "Mexico: The Record of a Conversation with President Wilson," April 27, 1914, PWW 29:520. See also Spring Rice to Grey, Feb. 7, 1914, PWW 29:229 and Wilson to Walter Hines Page, June 4, 1914, PWW 30:143; Wilson statement to Frank Worthington, Dec. 28, 1918, in Bell to Winslow, Dec. 31, 1918, PWW 53:574–75.

21. Hartig, "Robert Lansing," 10, 15, 16, 51, 52; Grose, *Gentleman Spy*, 36.

22. Hartig, "Robert Lansing," 22; "Clubs of the French Revolution," first prepared in Nov. 1891, rewritten in Jan. 1922, Box 79, Lansing Papers, LC.

23. Lansing notes on *Commonwealth and Empire* (1902), by Goldwin Smith; "Trusts and Socialism," May 7, 1902; "The Party of Obstruction," May 9, 1902; "Democracy and Republicanism in America," May 24, 1902; "Trusts," May 4, 1902, Lansing Papers, LC; Hartig, "Robert Lansing," 39–45.

24. "Trusts," May 4, 1902; "Trust Remedies," May 5, 1902, Lansing Papers, LC.

25. House, *Philip Dru: Administrator*, 1, 8, 11–12, 44–45; Seymour, *Intimate Papers of Colonel House*, 1:152–58; House Diary, Jan. 17 and 22, 1913; Neu, "Wilson and Colonel House," 251; House Diary, May 24, 1917.

26. House, *Philip Dru*, 276; House Diary, March 17 and April 19, 1917.

27. Osborn, *Wilson*, 19, 24, 27, 97; Bragdon, *Wilson*, 79; Wilson, *History of the American People*, 5:60; Mulder, *Wilson*, 69, 73, 175; Link, *Wilson and the Progressive Era*, 66; Link, *Wilson: The New Freedom*, 243–54; Diary of Josephus Daniels, Oct. 15, 1918, PWW 51:344–45. See also PWW 15:58–59, and Bragdon, *Wilson*, 231.

28. "Nature of Democracy in the United States," May 17, 1889, PWW 6:234; "Princeton in the Nation's Service," Oct. 21, 1896; PWW 10:24; *A History of the American People*, 5:212; Bragdon, *Wilson*, 260, 348.

29. Higham, *Strangers in the Land*, 190, 192–93, 243, 199–200; Gwynn, *Letters and Friendships of Sir Cecil Spring Rice*, 422–23; Sarasohn, *Party of Reform*, 208–12.

30. Dinnerstein, Nichols, and Reimers, *Natives and Strangers*, 136; Higham, *Strangers in the Land*, 160–61, 277–81.

31. May, *Great Expectations*; May, *End of American Innocence*, vii, 393; Kennedy, *Over Here*, esp. 229; Lears, *No Place of Grace*, esp. xvi and 25; Crunden, *Ministers of Reform*, ix.

32. "Clubs of the French Revolution," 41–42; "National Menaces," June 16, 1903, Box

79, Lansing Papers, LC.

33. "The Positive in Religion," *North Carolina Presbyterian*, Oct. 25, 1876, quoted in DeYoung, "Religious Speaking," 113. See also "Work-Day Religion," Aug. 11, 1876, PWW 1:175–77; and "Princeton in the Nation's Service," Oct. 21, 1896, PWW 10:20.

34. Newman, "Hegelian Roots," 191–202; Link, "Wilson: Presbyterian in Government," in Hunt, *Calvinism and the Political Order*, 157–74; Link, *Higher Realism*; Mulder, "'Gospel Of Order,'" 223–47; "Calendar of Great Americans," ca. Sept. 1893, PWW 8:372; Speech to the New England Society, Dec. 22, 1900, PWW 12:53–54.

35. "Calendar of Great Americans," ca. Sept. 1893, PWW 8:372; Thompson, *Presidents I've Known*, 292; Draft memoir on Wilson, chapter 16, Cary T. Grayson Papers; Randolph Bourne, "Puritan's Will to Power" (April 1917), in Resek, *War and the Intellectuals*, 156–61; Hart, "Connoisseur of 'Rabble-Rousing,'" 197–202.

36. House Diary, Feb. 24, 1918; Diary of Raymond Fosdick, Dec. 11, 1918, PWW 53:366.

37. Tumulty to Wilson, May 21, 1917, PWW 42:360–61; "This Is a People's War," June 14, 1917, PPWW 1:60–67; Grubbs, *Struggle for Labor Loyalty*, 25, 92; William Lamar to Albert Burleson, enclosed in Burleson to Wilson, Aug. 8, 1917, PWW 43:394.

38. Gompers to Tumulty, Nov. 9, 1917, PWW 44:556; Address of Nov. 12, 1917, PWW 45:11–17.

39. Spring Rice to Balfour, Nov. 30, 1917, Gwynn, *Letters and Friendships of Sir Cecil Spring Rice*, 2:415–16.

40. State of the Union Message, Dec. 4, 1917, PWW 45:194–202; Lansing to Edward N. Smith, Dec. 20 and 27, 1917, Vol. 33, Lansing Papers, LC; Statement by Robert Lansing, Dec. 4, 1917, PWW 45:205–7.

41. Cronon, *Cabinet Diaries of Josephus Daniels*, 253–54; PWW 45:341–42.

42. Memorandum by Steffens, ca. Dec. 28, 1917, PWW 45:381–84.

43. Spring Rice to Balfour, Jan. 4, 1918, *Letters and Friendships of Sir Cecil Spring Rice*, 422–23. See also PWW 45:458.

44. Gompers to Wilson, Feb. 9, 1918, enclosing "Chief Danger of Revolutions and Revolutionary Movements in Eastern Europe: Revolutions in Western Europe," PWW 46:310–13; Wilson to Lansing, Feb. 13, 1918, PWW 46:334; Lansing to Wilson, Feb. 15, 1918, PWW 46:349–50.

45. House Diary, Feb. 24 and Jan. 9, 1918; Wiseman to Reading, Feb. 12, 1918, PWW 46:333–34.

46. Breckinridge Long Diary, Feb. 23, 1918.

47. Cronon, *Cabinet Diaries of Josephus Daniels*, 285.

48. Unaddressed letter by Edgar Sisson, May 31, 1918, Vol. 21, Albert S. Burleson Papers.

49. Jusserand to Pichon, Sept. 12, 1918, PWW 49:538–39; Salvatore, *Euguene V. Debs*, 290–96; Polenberg, *Fighting Faiths*, 43–55; Wiseman notes of an interview with the president, Wednesday, Oct. 16, 1918, PWW 51:347. See also Grant Squires to Wilson, Nov. 9, 1918, and Wilson to Squires, Nov. 12 1918, PWW 53:20–21, 55.

50. Wilson statement to Frank Worthington, Dec. 28, 1918, in Bell to Winslow, Dec. 31, 1918, PWW 53:574–75.

51. Notes of a meeting of the Council of Ten, Jan. 16, 1919, PWW 54:102.

52. Diary of Dr. Grayson, March 10, 1919, PWW 55:471.

53. Remarks to Democratic National Committee, Feb. 28, 1919, PWW 55:314; "Bolshevism and Russia," Box 18, Ray Stannard Baker Papers, Princeton. See also Ray Stannard Baker Diary, Jan. 8, 1918, LC; Samuel Eliot Morison Diary, April 9, 1919.

54. Cyrus McCormick was so impressed by Col. Ruggles's Aug. 9, 1919, letter that he sent copies to Basil Miles, Samuel Harper, Samuel Bertron, and other influential figures. Box 115, McCormick Papers, SHSW.

55. Root address in "Russia: The International Problem," pamphlet issued by the American-

Russian Chamber of Commerce, 1919; Francis, *Russia From the American Embassy*, 334–35, 349.

56. Lansing to Wilson, Aug. 7, 1919, enclosing Poole's "Memorandum Concerning the Purposes of the Bolsheviki Especially with Respect to a World Revolution," PWW 62:203–5; Wilson to Lansing, Aug. 21, 1919, returning a separate memorandum from Poole, PWW 62:441–48.

57. Wilson to Lansing, Aug. 14, 1919, PWW 62:281; Wilson speeches of Sept. 1919 in PWW 63 and PPWW 2.

58. Address of Sept. 9, 1919, PPWW 2:85; "Nature of Democracy in the United States," May 17, 1889, PWW 6:230, 233; Address of Sept. 11, 1919, PPWW 2:108; "Self-Government in France," Sept. 1879, PWW 1:523; Address of Sept. 6, 1919, PPWW 2:6.

59. "Memorandum on the Russian Situation and the Root Mission," Aug. 9, 1917, and "Memorandum on the Russian Situation," Dec. 7, 1917, Lansing Papers, LC; see also William Phillips Journal, Dec. 21, 28, and 31, 1917.

60. Addresses of Sept. 6, 9, 12, and 25, 1919, PPWW 2:15, 143, 78, 83, 400; "Immigration," undated, but probably early 1920s, Box 13, Lansing Papers, Princeton; Coben, "Study in Nativism"; Bennett, *Party of Fear*.

61. Higham, *Strangers in the Land*, 280; Singerman, "American Career of the *Protocols*," 48–78; Long Diary, Nov. 2, 1919; Memoranda in M.I.D. files 10110-920/128, 245-3, 245-1, and 245-9, RG 165, NA; Crane to Winslow, March 11, 1919; Crane to Charles Parmelee, Dec. 5, 1918; Crane memorandum of Feb. 12, 1919, Richard T. Crane Papers; Spring Rice to Foreign Office, Dec. 17, 1917, PWW 45:316; "The Spread of Bolshevism in the United States," July 26, 1919, Lansing Papers, Princeton.

62. John A. Gade, "Inside Red Russia," 234; unsigned memorandum of May 15, 1919 from Herbert Hoover Archives, Box 19, ARA Papers, HIA.

63. Healy, "Tsarist Anti-Semitism"; Higham, *Strangers in the Land*, 285; Wilson to Clarence Darrow, Aug. 9, 1917, PWW 43:400. See also Wilson to Lansing, Aug. 24, 1917, PWW 44:38–39; and Grubbs, *Struggle for Labor Loyalty*, 71.

64. Lane and Wall, *Letters of Franklin K. Lane*, 297–98. House seems to have been more skeptical of such conspiracy theories. See House Diary, Dec. 31, 1918.

65. Higham, *Strangers in the Land*, 278–79; "Tendency Toward Communistic Ideas," Sept. 1, 1919, Lansing Papers, Princeton; Harper, *Russia I Believe In*, 129; McFadden, *Alternative Paths*, 313.

66. Hartig, "Robert Lansing," 135–36; Baker to Wilson, July 1, 1918, PWW 48:475–76; "Confidential Summary Report of the Progress of Radicalism in the United States and Abroad," Jan. 17, 1920, Vol. 51, Lansing Papers, LC; Murray, *Red Scare*, 178–80; Grayson Diary, March 10, 1919, PWW 55:471.

67. Carrie Chapman Catt to Wilson, May 4, 1917, PWW 42:215; Wilson to Jessie Woodrow Wilson Sayre, June 22, 1917 and editorial note, PWW 42:560–61; Dudley Malone to Wilson, Sept. 7, 1917, PWW 44:167; Edith Bolling Wilson, *My Memoir*, 138.

68. Ernest Poole to George Creel, Feb. 15, 1918, CPI 1-A1, NA; Russell Campbell, "Nihilists and Bolsheviks," 28; Ross, "Struggles for the Silent Screen," 349; Allen Dulles to Mother, June 4, 1918, Box 5, and Ellis Dresel to Joseph Grew, Jan. 10, 1919, Box 7, Allen Dulles Papers; Lasch, *American Liberals*, 121–22; Francis to Lansing, Aug. 2, 1918, *FRUS, 1918, Russia*, 2:505–6; "Francis Confirms All the Horrors of Bolshevism," *New York Times*, March 9, 1919; "Decree of the Free Association of Samara on the Question of the Ownership of Women," May 11, 1918, Francis Papers; *Congressional Record*, 65th Congress, Third Session, Vol. 57: 1969–72, 4885–87; *Soviet Russia*, Aug. 2 and Sept. 6, 1919.

69. Smith, *Seeds of Secularization*; Sermons of April 27 and Dec. 6, 1919, Walter Hays Papers, Palo Alto, Calif.; Marsden, *Fundamentalism and American Culture*, 153–64, 208–9.

70. See, for example, Randolph Bourne, "Puritan's Will to Power" in Resek, *War and the Intellectuals*, 156–61.

71. "Memorandum on the Russian Situation," Dec. 7, 1917; "Memorandum on Absolutism and Bolshevism," Oct. 26, 1918, Lansing Papers, LC. See also the April 1919 entry in "Scraps," Box 8, Lansing Papers, Princeton.

72. Letters of Aug. 7 and 22, 1919, Vol. 45, Lansing Papers, LC.

73. Diary entry for Sunday, Dec. 30, 1917, Carton 3, David Prescott Barrows Papers, Bancroft Library, University of California at Berkeley. On Barrows's "Puritan" upbringing, see "Memoirs of David Prescott Barrows, 1873–1954," Bancroft Library.

74. Barrows diary, Feb. 3, 1918; "Are Berkeley Socialists Bolshevists?" July 31, 1919, pamphlet, Bancroft Library.

75. Declaration Against Recognition of the Russian Soviets, New York City, March 29, 1920, Vol. 52, Lansing Papers, LC. Declaration signers included Lyman Abbott, Charles W. Eliot, and John Hays Hammond.

76. Lansing to Kennan, May 28, 1918, Vol. 35, Lansing Papers, LC; Travis, *George Kennan and the American-Russian Relationship, 1865–1924*, 4–5; Kennan to Joseph M. Price, Aug. 5, 1918, enclosed in Kennan to Lansing, Aug. 6, 1918, Vol. 37, Lansing Papers, LC; Kennan to Lansing, May 26, 1918, Box 4, Lansing Papers, Princeton.

77. "The Reminiscences of DeWitt Clinton Poole," Oral History Transcript, 1952, Columbia University, 10, 92, 127; Poole to Chicherin, Sept. 4, 1918, AVPRF, f. 129, op. 2, p. 1, d. 3, l. 76.

78. "Russian Bolshevism," ca. March 1919, Vol. 54, Carton 3, Barrows Papers; Barrows to W. T. Hornaday, Sept. 17, 1919, Box 3, Barrows Papers.

79. Diary of Ray Stannard Baker, April 11, 1919, PWW 57:240–41; Wilson addresses of Sept. 6 and Sept. 15, 1919, PPWW 2:13, 200; Sklar, "Wilson and the Political Economy," 18; Address of Sept. 6, 1919, PPWW 2:15.

80. Cf. Kennan, *Russia and the West*, 181.

81. Hard, *Raymond Robins' Own Story*, 4; Robins addresses, March 20, 1919, p. 80, and March 22, 1919, p. 95, Box 43, Robins Papers, SHSW; David Parry, *The Scarlet Empire* (1906), discussed in Conn, *Divided Mind*, 83–89.

CHAPTER THREE

1. Address of May 18, 1918, PWW 48:53–54.

2. Reading to Balfour, May 23, 1918, PWW 48:133–34; Lasch, *American Liberals*, 102–3; C. H. McCormick Jr. to House, June 10, 1918, and to Wilson, Sept. 13, 1918, Box 116, McCormick Papers, SHSW.

3. Wilson Remarks to Mexican Editors, PWW 48:257. See also PWW 54:103n.

4. In *The Decision to Intervene*, 322–23, Kennan recognized the importance of the Russian embassy, but like other historians he did not describe its part in American policy. Important exceptions to the general neglect of Bakhmeteff's role are Maddox, "Wilson, the Russian Embassy and Siberian Intervention"; Maddox, *Unknown War with Russia*; Killen, "Search for a Democratic Russia"; and Killen, *Russian Bureau*. For a denial that "a supposed deal between the State Department and the Russian Embassy" was ever concluded, see Walsh, "Secretary of State Lansing."

5. See esp. Hasegawa, *February Revolution*.

6. Diary of Joshua Butler Wright, Feb. 26, 1917; Francis to Secretary of State, Feb. 25, 1917, *FRUS, 1918, Russia*, 1:1; Francis, *Russia from the American Embassy*, 65. For a more thorough discussion of the attitudes of American diplomats in Russia, see Foglesong, "Missouri Democrat in Revolutionary Russia."

7. Francis to Secretary of State, March 14, 1917, *FRUS, 1918, Russia*, 1:1–2; Francis, *Russia from the American Embassy*, 66–68; Wright Diary, March 13 and 18, 1917.

8. Francis to Secretary of State, March 18, 1917, *FRUS, 1918, Russia*, 1:5–6; Lansing to Wilson, March 19, 1917, PWW 41:425–27; House to Wilson, March 17, 1917, PWW 41:422–23.

9. William Phillips Journal, March 15, 1917; Harper to Richard Crane, March 15, 1917, and Milton Bronner, "Crane and Harper Tell Why New Russia Will Succeed," Box 3, Folder 12, Harper Papers; Harper remarks in Moline, Illinois, May 14, 1917, Box 4, Folder 5, Harper Papers.

10. Charles R. Crane to Wilson, May 18, 1914, PWW 30:46; McCormick to Harper, March 22, 1917, Box 3, Folder 12, Harper Papers; William Phillips Journal, March 16, 1917. On Crane's enthusiasm, see also Levy and Urofsky, *Letters of Louis D. Brandeis*, 4:276–77.

11. Lansing Memorandum of Cabinet Meeting, March 20, 1917, PWW 41:436–44; Lansing to Francis, March 20, 1917, *FRUS, 1918, Russia*, 1:12; Francis, *Russia from the American Embassy*, 93; Cronon, *Cabinet Diaries of Josephus Daniels, 1913–1921*, 119, 121.

12. *New York World* editorials, March 4, 17, 18, and 25, 1917; Link, "That Cobb Interview."

13. Lansing Memorandum of Cabinet Meeting, March 20, 1917, PWW 41:436–44. See also Lansing to Wilson, March 19, 1917, PWW 41:425–27 and Gardner, *Safe for Democracy*, vii.

14. Address of April 2, 1917, PPWW 1:11–13.

15. See, for example, *New York World*, March 17 and 18, 1917.

16. Richard Crane to Samuel Harper, April 19, 1917, Harper Papers; Memorandum by John Howard Whitehouse, April 14, 1917, PWW 42:67; *FRUS, 1918, Russia*, 3:1–10.

17. Bakhmeteff, "Reminiscences," 279, 327; Caffery to Secretary of State, June 15, 1917, *FRUS, 1918, Russia*, 1:157. According to B. I. Nikolaevskii, Bakhmeteff was a Menshevik in the first years of the century and left the party after 1907. "Vo Vtoroi Gosudarstvennoi Dume," Box 10, item 75, p. 7, Nikolaevskii Collection, HIA. I am indebted to Ziva Galili for this reference.

18. Francis to Secretary of State, April 28, 1917, *FRUS, 1918, Russia*, 1:153–54; Charles R. Crane, "Chicago Leader Tells the Story of a New Nation," *Chicago Herald*, May 22, 1917, Harper Papers. See also Joshua Butler Wright Diary, May 13, 1917.

19. Wilson to Breckinridge Long, May 7, 1917, Long Papers; *War Memoirs of Robert Lansing*, 332.

20. Long Diary, June 18, 1917; Phillips Journal, June 21, 1917.

21. *New York Times*, July 1, 7, and Sept. 4, 1917.

22. *New York Times*, July 1 and Sept. 5, 1917; *Boston Globe*, Aug. 22, 1917. Regarding American notions of the *mir*, see Lasch, *American Liberals*, 3n; 135.

23. SD file 701.6111/174, NA; PWW 43:100–101.

24. *FRUS, 1918, Russia*, 3:11; Francis to Secretary of State, July 18, 1917, *FRUS, 1918, Russia*, 1:160–61. See also Kennan, *Russia Leaves the War*, 25; Heenan, *Russian Democracy's Fatal Blunder*, 52, 56.

25. Winship to Secretary of State, May 8, 1917, *FRUS, 1918, Russia*, 1:50; Browder and Kerensky, *Russian Provisional Government*, 2:1120–34; Bakhmeteff, "Reminiscences," 309. On the relationship between the war and the demise of the Provisional Government, see Wade, *Russian Search for Peace*, and Heenan, *Russian Democracy's Fatal Blunder*.

26. Ganelin, *Rossiia i SShA 1914–1917*, 266–76; *FRUS, 1918, Russia*, 3:14–18.

27. Seymour, *Intimate Papers of Colonel House*, 3:25.

28. Bakhmeteff, "Reminiscences," 327, 306.

29. House Diary, July 22 and Aug. 19, 1917; Seymour, *Intimate Papers of Colonel House*, 3:25, 156–58; House to Wilson, July 23, 1917, PWW 43:248–49.

30. House Diary, Aug. 19, 1917.

31. Lansing Desk Diary, April 11, 1917; Kennan to Lansing, May 23 and June 3, 1917; Lansing "Memorandum on the Russian Situation and the Root Mission," Aug. 9, 1917, Lansing Papers, Princeton.

32. House to Wilson, July 23, 1917, PWW 43:248–49; FRUS, 1918, Russia, 3:22; Ganelin, Rossiia i SShA, 344.

33. Lansing to Bakhmeteff, Aug. 15, 1917, PWW 43:475–76; Wilson to the President of the National Council Assembly at Moscow, Aug. 24, 1917, PWW 44:38; William Phillips Journal, Aug. 24, 1917.

34. Foglesong, "Missouri Democrat in Revolutionary Russia," 36–37; Breckinridge Long to Francis, Sept. 14, 1917, Francis Papers; Lansing Desk Diary, Box 3, Lansing Papers, Princeton. See also Bakhmeteff, "Reminiscences," 278, 276–77, 283.

35. Bakhmeteff summary of conversation with Lansing, Sept. 21, 1917, Box 3, Lansing Papers, Princeton; Memorandum of Aug. 9, 1917, Lansing Papers, Princeton. See also Lansing to Wilson, Oct. 3, 1917, PWW 44:297–98.

36. FRUS, 1918, Russia, 3:23–27; Table prepared in the Treasury Department, Dec. 25, 1917, Russell Leffingwell letterbooks.

37. Polk Diary, Nov. 2, 1917. See also Phillips Journal, Nov. 5, 1917.

38. Washington Post, Nov. 9, 1917.

39. Phillips Journal, Nov. 8–16, 1917; Lansing Desk Diary, Nov. 11, 1917. See also Washington Post, Nov. 9, 1917.

40. Creel to C. E. Russell, Nov. 9, 1917, CPI 1-A1, Box 21, RG 63, NA; Cronon, Cabinet Diaries of Josephus Daniels, 234; Washington Post, Nov. 9, 1917; New York American, Nov. 10, 1917; New York World, Nov. 10, 1917; Washington Post, Nov. 11, 1917.

41. Wilson to Charles E. Russell, Nov. 10, 1917, PWW 44:558; Bakhmeteff, "Reminiscences," 344–45.

42. Washington Post, Nov. 10, 1917; New York Times, Nov. 10 and 11, 1917; New York American, Nov. 10 and 11, 1917; Phillips Journal, Nov. 9, 1917.

43. Bakhmeteff, "Reminiscences," 344.

44. Washington Post, Nov. 11, 1917; Phillips, Ventures in Diplomacy, 88; New York Times, Nov. 11, 1917. See also Polk Diary, Nov. 16, 1917.

45. Address of Nov. 12, 1917, PWW 45:14; Washington Post, Nov. 13, 1917.

46. Bakhmeteff, "Reminiscences," 345–46.

47. Ibid., 347–48.

48. Wilson to Frank Clark, Nov. 13, 1917, PWW 45:39.

49. Bakhmeteff, "Reminiscences," 349. Wilson's Appointment Books record a meeting with Creel at 3:00 p.m. on Wednesday, Nov. 21, 1917. Wilson Papers, LC, Series I, Reel 3.

50. SD file 701.6111/199, NA; Long Diary, Nov. 23; Phillips Journal, Nov. 23; Lansing Desk Diary, Nov. 23 and 24, 1917; Bakhmeteff, "Reminiscences," 349, 350, 351.

51. Lansing Desk Diary, Nov. 24, 1917; "Bakhmeteff Stays; Disowns Bolsheviki—Russian Envoy's Stand Tacitly Approved by Lansing," New York Times, Nov. 25, 1917.

52. Polk Diary, Nov. 14, 1917; Polk testimony before House of Representatives Committee on Expenditures in the State Department, June 27, 1919, Box 33, Folder 695, Polk Papers; Telegram to House, written for Lansing by Polk, SD file 861.51/242a; House response, FRUS, 1918, Russia, 3:28; Francis to Secretary of State, Nov. 24, 1917, and attached memorandum from Basil Miles on "Financial Aid to Russia," file 861.51/245, NA.

53. SD file 861.51/250; also in RG 39, box 182, folder 41, NA.

54. John C. Gardiner (vice president, National City Bank) to Leffingwell, Nov. 23, 1917, RG 39, Box 186, Folder 84, NA. See also Lansing Desk Diary, Nov. 26, 1917.

55. Bakhmeteff, "Reminiscences," 350; Bakhmeteff to Lansing, Nov. 24, 1917, file 701.6111/199, NA; New York Times, Nov. 25, 1917. Bakhmeteff's letter circulated widely in

the administration: it bears the stamps of an assistant secretary, the Division of Near Eastern Affairs, the Bureau of Foreign Agents and Reports, and the War Trade Board.

56. Bakhmeteff, "Reminiscences," 351 and 397; Lansing Desk Diary, Nov. 23, 1917; Polk Diary, Jan. 5, 1918.

57. Bakhmeteff, "Reminiscences," 351–52; Polk Diary, Nov. 26, 1917. On Ughet's activity see also Records of the Russian Supply Committee and its Successor Offices in the United States, 1914–22, RG 261, NA.

58. Treasury Department files, RG 39, Box 182, Folder 41, NA; SD file 861.51/253, NA; Leffingwell to National City Bank, Nov. 25, 1917, Leffingwell Papers; Polk testimony before House Committee on Expenditures in the State Department, June 27, 1919, Box 33, Polk Papers. See also Ughet to Eliot Wadsworth of the Treasury Department, May 26, 1922, Bakhmeteff Papers, Box 44.

59. See Polk testimony, June 27, 1919, Box 33, Polk Papers, 10–11; Leffingwell to Polk, Dec. 4 [?], 1917, Leffingwell Papers.

60. Trotsky speech of Nov. 8/21, 1917, in Wade, *Documents of Soviet History*, 1:46; Cronon, *Cabinet Diaries of Josephus Daniels*, 243, 244. See also Phillips Journal, Nov. 27 and Dec. 2, 1917.

61. Heaton, *Cobb*, v, xvi.

62. Tumulty to Wilson, Nov. 30, 1917, PWW 45:165; Address of Dec. 4, 1917, PWW 45:199.

63. Statement by Lansing, Dec. 4, 1917, PWW 45:205–7; Phillips Journal, Dec. 3, 1917; Lansing, *War Memoirs*, 340–45.

64. Bakhmeteff Memorandum, enclosed in Basil Miles to Elihu Root, Dec. 8, 1917, Root Papers, Box 136.

65. Ibid. Miles believed the memorandum had been brought to the attention of Lansing, McAdoo, and Creel. See also Bertron to Lansing, Dec. 7, 1917, Box 3, Lansing Papers.

66. Bertron to Wilson, Dec. 12, 1917; Wilson to Tumulty, ca. Dec. 13, 1917, PWW 45:282–83

67. Kennan, *Decision to Intervene*, 327. For a suggestion about the legacy of the embassy memorandum, see Killen, *Russian Bureau*, 18.

68. See McAdoo to Newton Baker, Dec. 17, 1917, Polk Papers, Box 33; McAdoo to Lansing, Leffingwell letterbooks; Report on Activities of the Russian Supply Committee, RG 261, Box L 37, NA, chapter VII, pp. 7–8; and Polk Diary, Dec. 17, 1917.

69. Treasury Department files, Box 186, Folder 91; Box 182, Folder 41, RG 39; SD file 861.51/260, NA; Bakhmeteff to Maklakov, Dec. 15/28, 1917, Box 9, Russia Posol'stvo (U.S.) Papers, HIA.

70. Bakhmeteff to House, Nov. 30, 1917, Seymour, *Intimate Papers of Colonel House*, 3:330–31; House Diary, Dec. 22 and 31, 1917, and Jan. 9, 1918; Creel to Wilson, Dec. 27, 1917, Creel Papers, Vol. 1.

71. Address of Jan. 8, 1918, PWW 45:535–37; Gwynn, *Letters and Friendships of Sir Cecil Spring Rice*, 422–25; Bakhmeteff to Maklakov, Dec. 15/28, 1917, Box 9, Russia Posol'stvo (U.S.) Papers, HIA; Bakhmeteff, "Reminiscences," 361; Bakhmeteff to House, Dec. 19, 1917, and Jan. 4, 1918, House Papers, Box 10, Folders 280 and 281.

72. Wilson to Lansing, Jan. 1, 1918, PWW 45:417. For further discussion of this phase, see Kennan, *Russia Leaves the War*, 385–94.

73. Phillips Journal, Jan. 4, 1918; Polk Diary, Jan. 14, 1918; Lansing Desk Diary, Jan. 15, 1918.

74. Wiseman to Reading, Feb. 12, 1918, relaying a message from House, and Wilson to Lansing, Feb. 13, 1918, PWW 46:333–34.

75. Marginal notes by Lansing on Phillips to Lansing, Feb. 19, 1918, *FRUS, 1918, Russia,*

1:383; Long Diary, Feb. 23, 1918. Lansing's Desk Diary and Wilson's Appointment Book record a meeting between them on Feb. 22.

76. PPWW 1:191; Polk Diary, March 11, 1918; House Diary, March 11, 1918.

77. Wilson to Phillips, May 8, 1918, Series 4, Case 64, Reel 194, Wilson Papers.

78. *New York Times*, June 12, 1918; Lomonosov press statement, June 10, 1918; Bakhmeteff to Lansing, June 12 and 20, 1918; Lansing to Bakhmeteff, June 13 and 26, 1918; Lansing certificate, June 21, 1918; Lomonosov to Lansing, June 24, 1918, Box 37, Folder 3, Russia Posol'stvo (U.S.) Papers, HIA. According to a Soviet scholar, Wilson differed from the State Department, writing on June 26 that it would be a mistake to interfere in the Bakhmeteff-Lomonosov dispute. See Gvishiani, *Sovetskaia Rossiia i SShA*, 150.

79. "An Appeal to President Wilson from the Russian Citizens Living in the United States," July 4, 1918, Posol'stvo (U.S.) Papers, HIA; Address of July 4, 1918, PPWW 1:232–33; Bakhmeteff, "Reminiscences," 364; Bakhmeteff to Maklakov, July 5 and 8, 1918, Box 9, Posol'stvo (U.S.) Papers, HIA; *Aide-mémoire* of July 17, 1918, FRUS, *1918, Russia*, 2:287–90; Gvishiani, *Sovetskaia Rossiia*, 151. Maklakov credited Bakhmeteff with having eased the path to intervention. See Maklakov cables to Bakhmeteff, esp. June 20, 1918, Box 9, Posol'stvo (U.S.) Papers, HIA.

80. Wilson to Lansing, Aug. 22, 1918, PWW 49:312; Polk Diary, Nov. 14, 1918; Lansing to Wilson, Nov. 9, 1918, PWW 53:6; and "Memorandum on the Russian Situation" by Commercial Attaché W. C. Huntington, in W. C. Redfield to Wilson, Nov. 22, 1918, PWW 53:179.

81. Lansing to Masaryk, Oct. 25, 1918, Richard T. Crane Papers, Box 2, Folder 14. For further discussion, see chapter 8.

82. Lansing, *War Memoirs*, 278; Polk Diary, Aug. 23, 1919, recording remarks to S. D. Sazonov.

83. Message of April 3, 1918, in SD file 861.00/1373, NA. For further examples, see Polk to the American embassy in Tokyo, March 13, 1919, file 861.00/1335c, NA, and Phillips Journal, Aug. 13, 1918.

84. Polk Diary, Dec. 2, 1918; Senate Judiciary Committee, *Foreign Loans and Authority for Making Same*, 91.

85. A. A. Berle to Dad and to Mother, May 25, 1919, Box 2, Berle Papers; Diary of Vance McCormick, Feb. 24, Jan. 15, Feb. 28, March 11, April 26, May 29, June 5, June 14, and June 21, 1919, HIA.

86. Polk Diary, Oct. 26, 1918.

87. Albert Rathbone to Basil Miles, April 24, 1919; unsigned letter to Rathbone, April 25, 1919, and Miles to Polk, April 25, 1919, in American Embassy-Russia, Miscellaneous Correspondence, Box 2, RG 84, NA; *New York Times*, June 18, 1919. See also Polk testimony to House Committee on Expenditures in the State Department, June 27, 1919, Box 33, Polk Papers.

88. Phillips to American mission Paris, March 22, 1919, and American mission to Miles, Phillips, March 26, 1919, SD files 861.24/128b and 861.24/129, NA; Crossed-out handwritten note, dated April 18, 1919, on American mission Paris to Miles, Phillips, March 26, 1919, file 861.24/129; Caldwell to Secretary of State, April 5, 1919; American mission Paris to Washington, April 12, 1919; Polk to Ughet, April 15, 1919, SD files 861.24/134, 861.24/136, and 861.24/136.

89. Ughet to Polk, April 10, 1919; Polk to American mission Paris, April 19, 1919, SD file 861.24/138; Polk to American mission Paris, May 26, 1919; American mission to Washington, June 3, 1919; American mission Paris to Washington, June 28, 1919, SD files 861.24/138, 861.24/149, 861.24/153.

90. Vance McCormick Diary, June 21 and 23, 1919, HIA; Polk to Wilson, July 12, 1919, SD file 861.24/155, NA.

91. Polk testimony to House Committee on Expenditures in the State Department, June 27, 1919, Box 33, Polk Papers, p. 11.

92. Ughet to Wadsworth, June 3, 1922, Bakhmeteff Papers, Box 44; Anonymous, "*Aide-mémoire*," March 1, 1920, Box 182, Long Papers. Copies of contracts and tables of purchases and shipments are contained in the Bakhmeteff Papers, in the papers of the Russian embassy, HIA, and in the Records of the Russian Supply Committee, Box K9, RG 261, NA. See also SD file 753.0000/2-350, NA; *Congressional Record*, Vol. 60, No. 73, Feb. 26, 1921.

93. Polk Diary, Nov. 20, Dec. 2, 4, 19, and 28, 1918.

94. See, for example, remarks of Senator Kenyon, Jan. 18, 1919, *Congressional Record*, 65th Congress, 3rd session, Vol. 57:1659.

95. At a protest on June 20, 1919, Max Eastman cited Polk's confidential Jan. 24, 1919, telegram to Lansing as evidence that Wilson was waging "a private war" against Lenin and Trotsky. *New York Times*, June 21, 1919.

96. Polk Diary, May 28, 1919.

97. Dispatch from the American mission in Paris to Washington, April 16, 1919, Box 6, Folder 16, Vance McCormick Papers, Yale University. On Dulles's draft, the words "exceedingly" and "embarrassing" were crossed out. A paraphrase of this telegram, with the word "obvious" underlined, is in Folder 83, Box 186, RG 39, NA.

98. Bublikov to S. S. Novoselov, Aug. 1918, Box 19, Folder 7; Bublikov to Bakhmeteff, Sept. 19, 1919, Box 18, Folder 11; Bakhmeteff to Maklakov, July 5, 1918, Box 9; Sack to Oustrialov, Oct. 12, 1919, Box 26, Folder 5; Bakhmeteff to Sazonov, Oct. 9, 1919, and press statement, Nov. 26, 1919, Box 18, Posol'stvo (U.S.) Papers, HIA; record of Dec. 25, 1919, meeting between Bakhmeteff and Senator Joseph Frelinghuysen, Box 36, Bakhmeteff Papers; and accounting records, Box 9, Posol'stvo (U.S.) Papers, HIA.

99. Martens to "Dear Comrades," Jan. 29, 191[9], f. 04, op. 3, d. 122, ll.1–4, AVPRF; "Who Spends the Russian People's Money and How?," n.d., Folder 18, Russian Soviet Bureau Seized Files.

100. Note by A. Adee, attached to Lansing to Villard, Oct. 8, 1918, SD 861.00/3940c, NA; *Nation*, Nov. 16, 1918, and Jan. 4, 1919; *New Republic*, Aug. 13, 1919; Foner, *Bolshevik Revolution*, 154, 102.

101. Foner, *Bolshevik Revolution*, 40, 104, 151; Martens address of May 22, 1919, Folder 22, and Nuorteva to Wright, June 2, 1919, Folder 9, Russian Soviet Bureau Seized Files.

102. Martens to Bakhmeteff, April 10, 1919, Martens to Bankers Trust Company, n.d., Polk to Coudert Brothers, April 19, 1919, Ughet to Bakhmeteff, April 26, 1919, Box 10, Posol'stvo (U.S.) Papers, HIA; Polk to Lansing, April 15 and Lansing to Polk, April 17, 1919, *FRUS, 1919, Russia*, 142–43.

103. Nuorteva [?] to Hillquit, April 20, 1919, Russian Soviet Bureau Seized Files; Secretary of Russian Soviet Government Bureau to Mr. John Milholland, Jan. 15, 1920, f. 507, op. 56, d. 14, l. 21, AVPRF; Chicherin to Martens, Dec. 17, 1920, f. 129, op. 4, d. 6, AVPRF; Copy of *Confidential Report on Foreign Loans*, with marks in margins, f. 04, op. 3, d. 128, AVPRF. The Soviet government also acquired the multivolume reports of the Agent of the Ministry of Finance attached to the Russian embassy in Washington and Bakhmeteff's correspondence with the Ministries of Foreign Affairs of the Archangel and Omsk governments. See f. 5863/5881, op. 1, dd. 1–7; f. 200, op. 1, dd. 29, 131–33; and f. 200, op. 1, dd. 134–36, 251, 330, GARF.

104. Report to All-Russia Central Executive Committee, Feb. 2, 1920, in Lenin, *Collected Works*, 437–42.

105. Report of April 3, 1919, in Lenin, *Collected Works*, 30:320–22.

106. Polk Diary, March 6; March 11; April 2, 1920; Bainbridge Colby certificate of April 6, 1920, Box 96, Folder 10, Posol'stvo (U.S.) Papers, HIA.

107. *New York Times*, April 16, April 30, May 5–9, June 5 and June 20, 1922, and *Congressional Record*, May 8, 1922, 7080-81.

108. Memorandum of a conference with Ughet by Nicholas Kelley and Van Merk-Smith, Aug. 6, 1920, RG 39, Box 186, Folder 80, NA.

109. See William Hard, "Anti-Bolsheviks: Mr. Bakhmetev," *New Republic*, Aug. 13, 1919.

CHAPTER FOUR

1. Summers to Francis, Jan. 14, 1918, *FRUS, 1918, Russia*, 1:340.

2. Robert Warth similarly deduced that U.S. "aid was forthcoming," though he did not examine the question in depth. See *The Allies and the Russian Revolution*, 193, 186. Several subsequent scholars concluded that no U.S. aid was actually sent. See Kennan, *Russia Leaves the War*, 178–81; Trask, *United States in the Supreme War Council*, 101–2; Fowler, *British-American Relations*, 118; and Gaddis, *Russia*, 67–68.

3. For a different view see Warth, *Allies and the Russian Revolution*, 185–88.

4. American historians often emphasized anti-German motives. See, for example, Kennan, "Soviet Historiography," 306. For works that stress anti-Bolshevik motives, see Gakaev and Kirienko, "Razzhiganie Antantoi," 66–81; Gambashidze, *Iz istorii politiki SShA v otnoshenii Gruzii 1917–1920*; Williams, "American Intervention in Russia, 1917–1920," 40–43.

5. Link et al., "Introduction," PWW 45:vii.

6. For similar views, see Williams, *American-Russian Relations*, 117–27; Levin, *Wilson and World Politics*, 67; Maddox, *Unknown War with Russia*, 35–37; and Gardner, *Safe for Democracy*, 152–58.

7. Wilson to Lansing, around Nov. 3, 1917, PWW 44:496–97.

8. Telegram from Francis received Nov. 10, 1917, PWW 44:532; William Phillips Journal, Nov. 9–16, 1917; Diary of Joshua Butler Wright, Nov. 7, 1917; Kerensky, *Russia and History's Turning Point*, 437–48; Buchanan, *My Mission to Russia and Other Diplomatic Memories*, 2:212–13; Kennan, *Russia Leaves the War*, 71–73; Wright Diary, Nov. 15, 1917.

9. Albert W. Fox, "Francis Heard From . . . Strong Man Wanted to Upset Plans [of Bolsheviks]," *Washington Post*, Nov. 18, 1917; Phillips Journal, Nov. 20, 1917; *New York American* and *New York Times*, Nov. 21, 1917; *Washington Post*, Nov. 29, 1917; Strakhovsky, *American Opinion*, 40–41.

10. *Register of the Department of State*, 131; Consul at Tbilisi to Secretary of State, Nov. 9 and 18, 1917, *FRUS, 1918, Russia*, Vol. 2:580–81.

11. For contrary views that Smith had little or no influence on U.S. policy, see Kennan, "Soviet Historiography," 305–6; Kazemzadeh, *Struggle for Transcaucasia, 1917–1921*, 79–80, 53, 97.

12. Leffingwell to Polk, Nov. 26, 1917, SD file 861.00/1344, NA.

13. Phillips Journal, Nov. 26, 1917; Lansing to Smith (written by Miles and Phillips), Nov. 26, 1917, SD file 861.51/244, NA; *FRUS, 1918, Russia*, 2:582; Phillips Journal, Nov. 28, 1917.

14. *FRUS, 1918, Russia*, 2:582–83.

15. Lansing to House, Nov. 27 and 28, 1917, *FRUS, 1918, Russia*, 2:582–83.

16. Gordon Auchincloss Diary, Nov. 8. 1917; House Diary, Nov. 8–13, 1917. On the impracticality of British proposals, see Woodward, *Trial by Friendship*, 140.

17. Auchincloss Diary, Nov. 20, 1917. See also Kettle, *Allies and the Russian Collapse*, 118.

18. House Diary, Nov. 20 and 21, 1917.

19. See Foglesong, "America's Secret War Against Bolshevism" (dissertation), 197n.

According to the American Minister to Romania, the Wilson administration authorized $50 million to pay 200,000 Russian soldiers to join an American-led army, with which "Ukrainia might have been saved from Bolshevism, and the Bolshevik government itself might have been overthrown," but the approval arrived "too late for any action." Vopicka, *Secrets of the Balkans*, 142–43, 158n.

20. WC 286, Nov. 29, 1917, CAB 23/4; WC 280, Nov. 22, 1917, CAB 23/4; Lloyd George, *War Memoirs*, 2:1540; House Diary, Nov. 21, 1917; Ullman, *Intervention and the War*, 43; WC 281, Nov. 23, CAB 23/4; Tyrkova-Williams, *Cheerful Giver*, 199–200.

21. Notes of a Conversation at Paris, Dec. 1, 1917, p. 4, CAB 28/3; WC 289, Dec. 3, 1917, CAB 23/4; Ullman, *Intervention and the War*, 45–46; Note on Progress of Paris Conference, Dec. 3, 1917, p. 2, CAB 28/3:19.

22. House to Lansing, Dec. 2, 1917, Box 8, Folder 270, Polk Papers.

23. Notes of Conversations at Paris, Dec. 1 and 3, 1917, CAB 28/3; House Diary, Nov. 27, 1917.

24. Cronon, *Cabinet Diaries of Josephus Daniels*, 244.

25. Frederic M. Corse to Samuel Harper, May 30, June 12, 1917, Box 4, Folder 8, Harper Papers; Charles Crane to Wilson, June 21, 1917, PWW 43:13; Richard Crane to Tumulty, July 11, 1917, enclosing a copy of Crane's telegram of July 6, PWW 43:149–50; Telegram of July 21, 1917, PWW 43:298–99; Memoirs of Charles R. Crane, 201–2, Crane Papers.

26. *New York Times*, Sept. 26 and 27, 1917; *Washington Post*, Dec. 1, 1917; Cronon, *Cabinet Diaries of Josephus Daniels*, Nov. 27, 1917, 243.

27. PWW 45:165, 196, 199.

28. Judson's Dec. 4, 1917, cable to the War Department, cited in PWW 45:219; Lansing Desk Diary, Dec. 6, 1917, LC; Lansing to Francis, Dec. 6, 1917, *FRUS, 1918, Russia*, 1:289.

29. Smith to Washington, Dec. 4, 1917, *FRUS, 1918, Russia*, 2:584–85; Radkey, *Election*; Rosenberg, *Liberals in the Russian Revolution*, 274–76; Suny, "Social Democrats in Power," 333; Suny, *Transcaucasia*, esp. 239–58.

30. "Memorandum on the Russian Situation," Dec. 7, 1917, Lansing Papers, LC. Emphasis added.

31. Bakhmeteff Memorandum in Miles to Root, Dec. 8, 1917, Box 136, Root Papers, and with Tumulty to Wilson, Dec. 14, 1917, PWW 45:288–95.

32. Pidhainy, "Silver and Billions," 15–16; Miles memorandum, Dec. 11, 1917, and Leffingwell to McAdoo, Dec. 10, 1917, in Senate Judiciary Committee, *Foreign Loans and Authority for Making Same*, 99–100.

33. Colcord to Wilson, Dec. 8, 1917, PWW 45:250–53.

34. Summers to Secretary of State, Dec. 6, 1917, received Dec. 9, 7:55 p.m., *FRUS, 1918, Russia*, 2:587; Ganelin, *Sovetsko-Amerikanskie Otnosheniia*, 72.

35. Lansing Desk Diary, Dec. 9, 1917; Washburn, *Victory in Defeat*, 172–73, 179, 154.

36. Lansing to Wilson (enclosing Summers's telegram of Dec. 6), Dec. 10, 1917, Lansing Papers, Princeton; SD file 861.00/807a, NA.

37. Cronon, *Cabinet Diaries of Josephus Daniels*, 249; Lansing Desk Diary, Dec. 11, 1917.

38. Lansing Desk Diary, Dec. 12, 1917; Wilson to Lansing, Dec. 12, 1917, PWW 45:274–75.

39. Lansing to American embassy, London, Dec. 12, 1917, in PWW 45:274–75.

40. Phillips Journal, Dec. 13, 1917.

41. Lansing Desk Diary, Dec. 13, 1917; Phillips Journal, Dec. 13, 1917.

42. Cronon, *Cabinet Diaries of Josephus Daniels*, 250, 252; Foglesong, "Missouri Democrat," 22, 39.

43. Rand, "America Views Russian Serf Emancipation"; Poole, *Dark People*; Judson to War College, Nov. 14, 1917, File 2070-6, RG 165, NA.

44. *New York Times*, Dec. 16, 1917; House Diary, Dec. 17, 1917; House to Wiseman,

18.12.17, Box 123, Folder 4326, House Papers; Lansing Desk Diary, Dec. 17, 1917.

45. Crosby and Page to Lansing, Dec. 18, 1917, *FRUS, 1918, Russia,* 2:591–92.

46. Page to Lansing, Dec. 21, 1917, *FRUS, 1918, Russia,* 2:595–96.

47. Dec. 20, 1917, record of Dec. 19 conference, F.O. 371/3283:7–8; Letter to Mr. Oliphant of the Foreign Office, communicating Keynes's views to Cecil, F.O. 371/3283:6–7; "ED" to Lord R. Cecil, 21.12.17, F.O. 371/3283:8.

48. WC 304, Dec. 21, 1917, CAB 23/4.

49. Notes of conference of Dec. 23, 1917, CAB 28/3:55. Page forwarded a copy of this memorandum to Lansing on Dec. 29. SD file 861.00/3478, NA. On Milner's views, see Golin, *Proconsul in Politics,* 556–57.

50. Lord Bertie to London, Jan. 3, 1918, F.O. 371/3283:36–37. See also Torrey, *General Henri Berthelot,* xxix; 136.

51. Kenez, *Civil War in South Russia,* 65; Lincoln, *Red Victory,* 79–80; Summers to Lansing, Dec. 15 and 18, 1917, *FRUS, 1918, Russia,* 2:590, 593; Poole, "Reminiscences," 138–40; Lansing to Francis, Dec. 24, 1917, *FRUS, 1918, Russia,* I:324.

52. Poole, "Reminiscences," 141, 86, 167, 170; Poole report of Jan. 26, 1918, *FRUS, 1918, Russia,* 2:609.

53. Poole, "Reminiscences," 143–48. On Jan. 18, Summers sent Poole's telegrams to Lansing with the recommendation that they "should be read *in extenso.*" *FRUS, 1918, Russia,* I:349.

54. Kennan, *Russia Leaves the War,* 181.

55. Phillips to Harper, Dec. 18, 1917, Box 4, Folder 15, Harper Papers.

56. Phillips Journal, Dec. 24 and 26, 1917; House Diary, April 28, 1917; Sept. 19, 1918; Oct. 28, 1918.

57. See Wilson to House, Dec. 16, 1917, PWW 45:313.

58. House Diary, Dec. 18, 1917.

59. Phillips Journal, Dec. 26, 1917. See also Phillips, *Ventures in Diplomacy,* 88–89, and Phillips, "Reminiscences," 76.

60. Spring Rice to Foreign Office, Dec. 27, 1917, PWW 45:369.

61. House Diary, Jan. 2, 1918.

62. Huntington report of Nov. 21–26, 1917, in C. Crane to Tumulty, Jan. 3, 1918, Wilson Papers, Reel 194; entries for Dec. 21, 1917, and Jan. 4, 1918, in Cronon, *Cabinet Diaries of Josephus Daniels,* 250, 254, 262. Crane met with Wilson on Dec. 26, 1917 and Jan. 2, 1918. *New York Times,* Dec. 27, 1917; Wilson appointment books, Wilson Papers.

63. Crosby to Lansing and McAdoo, Dec. 27, 1917, *FR, 1918, Russia,* 2:597–600.

64. Although Christine White stresses Anglo-American friction and economic motives for intervention, she acknowledges that the Wilson administration did little to support American interests in south Russia. See White, *British and American Commercial Relations,* esp. 63–64, 74.

65. Creel to Wilson, Dec. 27, 1917, and Wilson to Creel, Dec. 29, 1917, in Vol. 1, Creel Papers. On the frequency of Creel's visits to the White House, see Wilson's Appointment Books, Wilson Papers.

66. Summers to Lansing, Dec. 29, 1917, *FRUS, 1918, Russia,* 2:601–3.

67. Lansing to Summers, Jan. 8, 1918; Smith to Lansing, Jan. 8, 1918, *FRUS, 1918, Russia,* 2:605–6.

68. Wilson to Lansing, Jan. 1, 1918, PWW 45:417–19.

69. In the first quarter of 1918, one pound sterling was worth about 45 rubles. Arnold, *Banks, Credit, and Money,* 85.

70. Stevens to London, Dec. 31, 1917, and G.R.C[lerk] minute of 1-1-18, F.O. 371/3283. See also Barclay to London, Dec. 31, 1917, F.O. 371/3283:38–39.

71. Cecil to Crosby, Jan. 2, 1918, F.O. 371/3283:11–12.

72. Phillips Journal, Jan. 2, 1918.

73. Lansing to Wilson, Jan. 2, 1918, PWW 45:427–30; Trotsky proclamation, "To Peoples and Governments of Allied Countries," PWW 45:411–14.

74. Unterberger, "Wilson and the Bolsheviks"; Walsh, "Secretary of State Robert Lansing," iii, 28, 215, 249–50; Knock, *To End All Wars*, 313n.

75. "Memorandum of the Present Situation in Russia," Jan. 3, 1918, PWW 45:442–47.

76. Cronon, *Cabinet Diaries of Josephus Daniels*, Jan. 4, 1918, 262.

77. Miles, "Memorandum for the Secretary of State," c. Jan. 8, 1918, PWW 45:543–45.

78. McAdoo for Crosby, Jan. 2, 1918, Oscar Crosby Papers, LC; Wilson to McAdoo, Jan. 9, 1918, PWW 45:546. See also PWW 46:358–59.

79. Polk Diary, Jan. 11, 1918; SD file 861.00/987, NA.

80. See, for example, Wiseman to House, April 24, 1919, Box 123, Folder 4331, House Papers.

81. F.O. 371/3283:100–111.

82. Stevens to London, Jan. 10, 1918; Marling to London, Jan. 12, 1918; Barclay to London, Jan. 11, 1918, F.O. 371/3283: 196–97, 190, 212.

83. Poole to State Department, Jan. 14, 1918, enclosed in Francis to Lansing, Feb. 6, 1918 (received May 2 [!], 1918), *FRUS, 1918, Russia*, 2:613; Jan. 18, 1918, telegram in Poole, "Reminiscences," 149; Account Book of the Volunteer Army, HIA; Keep, *Debate on Soviet Power*, 379.

84. Poole to Francis, Jan. 26, 1918, *FRUS, 1918, Russia*, 2:613.

85. Lindley to London, Jan. 22, 1918, F.O. 371/3283:305; Crosby for Lansing and Secretary of Treasury, Feb. 6, 1918, Box 187, Folder 110, RG 39, NA; Keep, *Debate on Soviet Power*, 379; "Account Book of the Volunteer Army," HIA. By June 1918, the Allies had handed over 10 million rubles. "Doklad o Poezdke v Moskvu," Alekseev Papers, HIA.

86. Lansing to Smith, Dec. 15 and 28, 1917, *FRUS, 1918, Russia*, 2:590, 600–601; Lansing Desk Diary, Dec. 28, 1917, LC; Smith to Kharlamov, Dec. 5/18, 1917, in Smith to Secretary of State, Jan. 9, 1918 (received March 18, 1918), *FRUS, 1918, Russia*, 2:606–7. On Kharlamov, see Suny, *Baku Commune 1917–1918*, 74n.

87. Summers to Wright, Jan. 10, 1918, Reel 10, in Kesaris, *Confidential U.S. Diplomatic Post Records, Part 1, Russia, 1914–1918*; Trotsky remarks of Dec. 14 (27), 1917, in Keep, *Debate on Soviet Power*, 216.

88. Wright to Summers, Jan. 16, 1918, in Kesaris, *Confidential U.S. Diplomatic Post Records*, Reel 10, 173–77; Wright Diary, Jan. 1; Feb. 19; Jan. 23, 1918; Wright to Smith, Jan. 18, 1918, in Kesaris, *Confidential U.S. Diplomatic Post Records*, Reel 10, 180–82.

89. DMI to CMA, 24/1/1918; CMA to DMI, Jan. 29, 1918, F.O. 371/3283:374–75.

90. See Kenez, *Civil War in South Russia*; Mawdsley, *Russian Civil War*; Lincoln, *Red Victory*.

91. Crosby for Lansing and McAdoo, in Page to Lansing, Feb. 14, 1918, SD 861.00/1101, NA; *FRUS, 1918, Russia*, 2:619–20. For more detailed discussion, see Pidhainy et al., "Silver and Billions"; Hodge, "American Diplomacy."

92. Stevens to London, Feb. 15, 1918, F.O. 371/3283:466; Smith to Washington, Feb. 12, 1918, paraphrased in Lord Reading to Foreign Office, Feb. 21, 1918, F.O. 371/3283:507–8. A crucial part of Smith's dispatch was omitted in *FRUS, 1918, Russia*, 2:618–19.

93. Summers to Secretary of State, Feb. 22, 1918, *FRUS, 1918, Russia*, 1:385–86.

94. Crane to Tumulty, Feb. 21, 1918, PWW 46:411.

95. Brinkley, *Volunteer Army and Allied Intervention in South Russia 1917–1921*, 373–74.

96. Cf. Ulam, *Expansion and Coexistence*, 84.

97. See, for example, WC 304, Dec. 21, 1917, CAB 23/4:273.

98. Summers to Francis, Jan. 14, 1918, enclosed in Summers to Secretary of State, Jan. 18 (received March 2), *FRUS, 1918, Russia*, 1:339.

CHAPTER FIVE

1. Address of April 2, 1917, PPWW, Vol. 1:12.

2. Knott, "Lifting the Veil"; Ameringer, *U.S. Foreign Intelligence*; O'Toole, *Honorable Treachery*. For the U.S. involvement in Mexico, see chapter 1.

3. The most thorough Soviet accounts of the Kalamatiano case are Kravchenko, *Pod imenem Shmidkena*, 162–91; Rudnev and Tsybov, *Sledovatel' Verkhovnogo Tribunala*, 102–37; Golinkov, *Krushenie antisovetskogo podpol'ia v SSSR*, 2:146–56 and 243–47; and Shteinberg, *Ekab Peters*, 66–107. For a detailed analysis, see Foglesong, "Xenophon Kalamatiano."

4. House to Polk, March 11 and April 23, 1917, Box 8, Polk Papers; House Diary, May 15–19, May 30, 1917; "Russia," memorandum by Wiseman, May 15, 1917, Box 182, House Papers; Lansing to Wilson, June 8, 1917, PWW 42:463.

5. House Diary, June 15–16, 1917; Auchincloss to Francis, Aug. 4, 1917, Box 33, Folder 672, Polk Papers; "Intelligence and Propaganda Work in Russia July to Dec. 1917," Jan. 19, 1918, Box 10, Folder 261, William Wiseman Papers; Jeffreys-Jones, "W. Somerset Maugham"; Calder, *W. Somerset Maugham*; Voska and Irwin, *Spy and Counterspy*, 212–40.

6. For a detailed analysis, see Foglesong, "German 'Intrigue,' U.S. Intelligence, and American Propaganda in Revolutionary Russia."

7. Edward N. Hurley to Hermann Hagedorn, May 3, 1932, Box 18, Hagedorn Papers; Hagedorn, *Magnate*, 183–84; Newton Baker to Wilson, Aug. 13, 1917, PWW 43:455; Bullard to Creel, Dec. 7/20, 1917, CPI 1-A1, NA; Salzman, *Reform and Revolution*, 175–76; "Russia," address by Robins to City Club of Chicago, March 20, 1919, Box 43, Robins Papers, SHSW.

8. Bullard, "German Gold in Russia," March 1918 memorandum, Bullard Papers; Mal'kov, "Bol'sheviki i 'Germanskoe Zoloto,'" 42–52; Creel to Wilson, May 10, 1917, PWW 42:267; Wilson to Creel, May 14, 1917, PWW 42:290–91; Wilson to Lansing, May 14, 1917, PWW 42:289; Lansing to Wilson, May 23, 1917, PWW 42:377–78; Lansing to Wilson, June 14, 1917, PWW 42:507–9; Polk to Francis, June 19, 1917, Francis Papers; Thompson, "Memorandum of the Present Situation in Russia," Jan. 3, 1918, PWW 45:447; Judson to Burleson, April 10, 1919, Vol. 23, Burleson Papers; Judson, June 18, 1919, report to the Secretary of War, MID file 2070-12, NA.

9. Kennan, *Russia Leaves the War*, 54, 59; Ganelin, *Rossiia i SShA 1914–1917*, 386–87.

10. Creel to Wilson, Oct. 12, 1917, PWW 44:367; Wilson to Thompson, Oct. 24, 1917, PWW 44:435; Creel to Thompson, Oct. 24, 1917, CPI 1-A1, Box 23, NA. See also Sisson, *One Hundred Red Days*, 33.

11. Creel to Wilson, Oct. 22, 1917, PWW 44:434; Hagedorn, *Magnate*, 219; Root to Lansing, June 17, 1917, FRUS, 1918, Russia, 1:120–22.

12. "Russia," memorandum by Wiseman, May 15, 1917, House Papers, Box 182; Creel to Wilson, Aug. 20, 1917, PWW 43:529; Wilson to Sisson, Oct. 24, 1917, PWW 44:435–36.

13. Creel to Sisson, Dec. 3, 1917, PWW 45:194; Charles Edward Russell to Wilson, Nov. 7, 1917; Wilson to Russell, Nov. 10, 1917; and Wilson to Creel, Nov. 10, 1917, PWW 44:557–58.

14. William Phillips Journal, Aug. 30, 1917; Creel to Thompson, Oct. 24, 1917, CPI 1-A1, Box 23, NA. On House's view that propaganda "could not be carried on directly by the American government," see Hagedorn, *Magnate*, 218.

15. Sisson, *One Hundred Red Days*, 44–48; Judson to Secretary of War, June 18, 1919, p. 3, MID file 2070-12, RG 165, NA. See also Hagedorn, *Magnate*, 240.

16. "Russia," Address by Raymond Robins, March 20, 1919, p. 32, Robins Papers, SHSW; Salzman, *Reform and Revolution*, 410, note 16, 196; Judson report to Secretary of War, June 18, 1919, p. 3, MID file 2070-12, NA; Fike, "Influence of the Creel Committee," 95.

17. Summers to Lansing, April 25, Oct. 15, and Nov. 7, 1917, files 125.6314, 125.6314/182, and 125.0061/48, NA.

18. Summers to Secretary of State, Dec. 15, 1917, *FRUS, 1918, Russia*, 2:590; Poole, "Reminiscences," 139–40, 170.

19. Lansing to Francis, Dec. 24, 1917, *FRUS, 1918, Russia*, 1:324; Lansing to Wilson, Feb. 9, 1918, PWW 46:301; Francis to Secretary of State, March 4, 1918; Jesse Halsey to Francis, March 15, 1918; Box 32, Francis Papers.

20. For a different view, see Langbart, "'Spare No Expense.'"

21. Francis to Huntington, March 3, 1918, and Summers to Francis, March 20, 1918, Francis Papers.

22. Summers to Francis, March 27 and April 10, 1918, Francis Papers. Regarding Summers's in-laws, see Foglesong, "Missouri Democrat," 32–33.

23. Francis to Countess Lillian Nostitz of Petrograd, April 16, 1918; Francis to Mr. Edward A. Weyde in Moscow, May 3, 1918; addresses by Francis in Vologda, May 29 and July 4, 1918; remarks by Francis in Petrograd, June 6, 1918, Francis to Baroness Ixkull of Petrograd, May 25, 1918, Francis Papers.

24. Francis to Summers, March 27, 1918, Box 32, Francis Papers; Poole to Francis, June 15, 1918 and Poole to State Department, July 12 and 17, 1918, in Kesaris, *Confidential U.S. Diplomatic Post Records*, Reel 9, 354–64; Francis to Secretary of State, May 18, 1918, Francis Papers.

25. Captain E. F. Riggs, "Notes on Militant Non-Bolshevick Political Groups," May 30, 1918, Riggs Papers.

26. Francis to Washington, June 3, 1918, enclosed in Polk to Wilson, June 6, 1918; Wilson to Polk, June 10, 1918, PWW 48:276–78.

27. Earl M. Johnston to Sarah, June 1, 1918, Johnston Papers; Francis to his son Perry, June 4, 1918, Francis Papers; Francis to Lansing, June [2], 1918 (received June 14), *FRUS, 1918, Russia*, 1:549–50; Francis to Poole, June 10, 1918, Francis Papers; Francis to Secretary of State, June 9 and 11, 1918 (received June 24 and June 15), *FRUS, 1918, Russia*, 1:558, 560–61.

28. Cole to Francis, June 14 and June 19, 1918, in Kesaris, *Confidential U.S. Diplomatic Post Records*, Reel 10, 962–73; Francis to Cole, July 10, 1918, Francis Papers.

29. Francis appointment book, April 26–May 9, 1918, and Dumas to Poole, May 27, 1918, Francis Papers; Kesaris, *Confidential U.S. Diplomatic Post Records*, Reel 10, 954–56; René Marchand testimony in Moscow in 1922, f. 1005, op. 1a, d. 362, GARF; Poole to Francis, June 3, 1918.

30. Kalamatiano to Secretary of State, Nov. 20, 1921, file 125.6313, NA.

31. Poole, "Reminiscences," 209; Kalamatiano to Secretary of State, Sept. 14, 1921, file 123K121/1; Poole to Secretary of State, May 13, 1918, file 125.6313/207, NA; Francis to Poole, June 15, 1918, Francis Papers.

32. Poole to Secretary of State, Oct. 5, 1918, file 811.20261/2, NA; Poole, "Reminiscences," 209–10; Poole testimony, in U.S. Senate, *Russian Propaganda*, 360–61, 362, 376.

33. Kalamatiano, "Report on so-called 'Lockhart Trial' in Moscow, Dec. 1918," given to the Commissioner of the United States at Riga, Aug. 22, 1921, NA; Poole, "Reminiscences," 210; Polk to American mission, Paris, June 7, 1919, Confidential File 811.20261/48, NA.

34. Poole to Secretary of State, Aug. 26, 1918 and Feb. 5, 1919, files 125.6313/235 and 125.6315/56, NA; Kesaris, *Confidential U.S. Diplomatic Post Records*, Reel 9, esp. 679, 656, 857; Poole to Secretary of State, July 26, 1918, file 861.00/2633, NA.

35. Poole to Francis, June 21, 1918, Francis Papers; Kesaris, *Confidential U.S. Diplomatic Post Records*, Reel 9, 582–95, 619, 648, 683, 709, 852; Shteinberg, *Ekab Peters*, 80; Rudnev, *Sledovatel' Verkhovnogo Tribunala*, 121, 127.

36. Kesaris, *Confidential U.S. Diplomatic Post Records*, Reel 9, 620, 582–95, 450–54; Lincoln, *Red Victory*, 141–46; Spence, *Boris Savinkov*, 207–12.

37. Kesaris, *Confidential U.S. Diplomatic Post Records*, Reel 9, 688, 477–88.

38. Poole to Francis, June 3, 13, and 16, 1918, Francis Papers, Box 33.

39. Langbart, "'Spare No Expense,'" 326–27; Poole to Williams, Aug. 19, 1918 (emphasis added), forwarded to Secretary of State, Sept. 21, 1918, file 861.00/3014, NA.

40. Poole to Secretary of State, Feb. 8, 1919, file 811.20261/33, NA.

41. Ibid.

42. Poole to Secretary of State, Aug. 26, 1918 (received Sept. 16), *FRUS, 1918, Russia*, 1:580–81.

43. Poole, "Reminiscences," 210; Poole message of Aug. 26, 1918, forwarded to Washington, Sept. 7, 1918, file 125.6313/235, NA; Poole to Washington, Aug. 26, 1918, enclosed in Findlay to British Foreign Office, Sept. 19, 1918, F.O. 371, Vol. 3336, 487–88.

44. Kalamatiano report to Poole, Oct. 26, 1918, enclosed in Poole to Secretary of State, Feb. 8, 1919, file 811.20261/33, NA; statement of Mrs. Kalamatiano, Jan. 26, 1921, file 361.11/3660, NA; and Kalamatiano statement in Riga, Aug. 22, 1921.

45. Poole, "Reminiscences," 210–11.

46. Allen Wardwell Diary, Aug. 31, 1918; Peters, "Vospominaniia," 93–123; Kalamatiano statement in Riga, Aug. 22, 1921.

47. Golinkov, *Krushenie antisovetskogo podpol'ia v SSSR*, 154; *Izvestiia*, Dec. 1, 1918; Kalamatiano statement at Riga, Aug. 22, 1921.

48. Peters, "Vospominaniia," 117; Kravchenko, *Pod imenem Shmidkena*, 171; Rudnev and Tsybov, *Sledovatel' Verkhovnogo Tribunala*, 117–18; Golinkov, *Krushenie antisovetskogo podpol'ia v SSSR*, 154–55; *Izvestiia*, Nov. 26, 1918; Poole, "Reminiscences," 211.

49. Kravchenko, "Pervyie shagi VChK," 97; Golinkov, *Krushenie antisovetskogo podpol'ia v SSSR*, 244–46; *Izvestiia*, Nov. 26–Dec. 5, 1918; Khatskevich, *Soldat velikikh boev*, 255–56; Seleznev, *Krakh zagovora*, 56–57; Ostriakov, *Voennye Chekisty*, 31.

50. U.S. Senate, *Russian Propaganda*, hearing of March 3, 1920, 350–77.

51. Norman Armour to Robert Imbrie, July 20, 1918, Box 4, RG 84, NA; Hill report of Nov. 26, 1918, F.O. 371, Vol. 3350:31; Poole to Secretary of State, Feb. 8, 1919, file 811.20261/33, NA.

52. Kettle, *Sidney Reilly*, 46; Lockhart, *British Agent*, 320; Armour's comments reported by the British Minister to Stockholm, Sept. 7, 1918, F.O. 371, Vol. 3336; Poole to Washington, Sept. 9, 1918, *FRUS, 1918, Russia*, 1:668.

53. Reilly, *Adventures*; Marchand, *Allied Agents in Soviet Russia*; Foglesong, "Xenophon Kalamatiano," 172–73.

54. *Izvestiia*, Nov. 29, 1918; Kalamatiano report to Poole, Oct. 26, 1918; Golinkov, *Krushenie antisovetskogo podpol'ia v SSSR*, 152; Hill report of Nov. 26, 1918, F.O. 371, Vol. 3350:39; Kalamatiano statement at Riga, Aug. 22, 1921.

55. See Kennan, "Soviet Historiography and America's Role in the Intervention"; Kunina, "V kollokvium istorikov SSSR i SShA," 213; Fursenko, "Podgotovka amerikanskoi interventsii," 55, 57.

56. Lansing to Francis, March 25, 1918, Francis Papers.

57. Francis to Poole, June 28, 1918, Francis Papers; Poole, "Reminiscences," 171.

58. Baker, *WWLL*, 5:307, 316–17, 6:52–53, 144–45; William Phillips Journal, Aug. 14 and Dec. 20, 1917. See also House Diary, June 15, 1917.

59. Wilson to Lansing, Sept. 5, 1918, PWW 49:447.

60. Francis to Washington, Sept. 3, 1918, enclosed in Lansing to Wilson, Sept. 9, 1918, PWW 49:491; Wiseman notes of an interview with Wilson, Oct. 16, 1918, PWW 51:351.

61. Phillips Journal, July 30, 1918; Earl Johnston letter of Sept. 5, 1918, Johnston Papers; *FRUS, 1918, Russia*, 2:367–70; Poole to Washington, Oct. 5, 1918, file 811.20261/2, NA;

Polk messages of Jan. 28 and June 7, 1919, see *FRUS, 1919, Russia*, 168, and Confidential File 811.20261/48, NA.

62. Allen Wardwell Diary, Sept. 4, 8, and 21; Young, *Diaries of Sir Robert Bruce Lockhart*, 1:44–45, Lockhart, *Memoirs of a British Agent*, 338–40; Kalamatiano report to Poole, Oct. 26, 1918.

63. "Proshenie" to Presidium VTsIK, Dec. 1918, f. 1235, op. 93, d. 207, ll. 167–9, GARF; *Izvestiia*, Dec. 7, 1918; Christensen to Norwegian Department of Foreign Affairs, June 4, 1920, file 811.20261/176, NA; *FRUS, 1919, Russia*, 168.

64. Khatskevich, *Soldat velikikh boev*, 255; *FRUS, 1919, Russia*, 186–87; *FRUS, 1920*, 3:670–75, 679–80; Members of the Collegium of the NKID to Sletov, Aug. 6, 1919, f. 4, op. 3, d. 123, AVPRF; Martens to Wadsworth in *Soviet Russia*, Nov. 15, 1919; Chicherin to Davydov of V.Ch. K., Feb. 22, 1921, f. 04, op. 3, d. 122, l. 33, AVPRF.

65. *New York Times*, July 28 and 31; Aug. 1, 9, and 11, 1921.

66. Captain E. Prince to Director of Military Intelligence (DMI), Sept. 3, 1919, M.I.D. file 2560-8, RG 165, NA; Earl Packer oral history, Foreign Affairs Oral History Program, Lauinger Library, Georgetown University.

67. Ruggles reports to DMI, Dec. 6, 1919, and Jan. 18, 1920, MID file 2560-17; also on microfilm reel M924, roll 2, NA.

68. Imbrie, "Memorandum Regarding the 'Information Service' Established in Petrograd," Dec. 3, 1918, 811.20261/8, NA; Imbrie reports in Francis Papers, in Kesaris, *Confidential U.S. Diplomatic Post Records*, Reel 9, 492–96, and in the Correspondence of the Consular Officer Assigned to Petrograd, April-Aug. 1918, Box 4, RG 84, NA.

69. Imbrie memorandum of Dec. 3, 1918. The U.S. embassy in Vologda told Imbrie on June 27, 1918, that his reports were "proving of great value." Box 4, RG 84, NA.

70. Imbrie to Francis, May 20, 1918, Box 4, RG 84, NA; Kennedy, "Memorandum on British Counter-Revolutionary Activities in Russia, about 1919," Feb. 25, 1921, enclosed in John W. Davis to Secretary of State, March 1, 1921, file series 361, NA; also in M.I.D. file 9771-245, RG 165, NA.

71. See, for example, Imbrie report, March 17, 1919, Box 552, C-10-h, RG 38, NA, and April 20, 1919, Reg. #12439, WA-6, RG 45, NA.

72. See esp. dispatch from Stockholm, Jan. 12, 1919, Box 552, C-10-h, RG 38; and John Gade's May 1919 report on efforts to disarm garrisons at Petrograd and Kronstadt in anticipation of the occupation of Petrograd, M.I.D. file 10058-316/39–40, NA.

73. Kennedy, "Memorandum on British Counter-Revolutionary Activities in Russia, about 1919." See also Joseph Shaplen's account of an interview with Dukes, "Playing Hide and Seek with the Bolshevik Secret Police," *New York Tribune*, March 20, 1921; and Dukes, *Red Dusk and the Morrow*, viii–x.

74. Lenin, *Collected Works*, 29:402–3; Stalin, *Works*, 4:272–78; Kennedy memorandum of Feb. 25, 1921, and separate thirty-five-page report, file 361.1123, NA; Imbrie to Secretary of State, Nov. 29, 1919, 361.1123 K58, NA; Registers of Communications Received from Military Attachés and Other Intelligence Officers, M1271, NA.

75. Kennedy memorandum and report, file 361.1123, NA.

76. Speech at St. Louis, Sept. 5, 1919, PPWW 1:634–45.

77. Ibid. Wilson declared that he "did not know" until America entered the war "that Germany was not the only country that maintained a secret service."

78. Brown, *Last Hero*, xi; xvii.

79. See Sayle, "Historical Underpinnings," 1.

80. See, for example, Kennan, "Morality and American Foreign Policy," 214; Kennan, *Memoirs*, 48; and Knott, "Lifting the Veil," 10, citing the Iran-Contra Committee report of 1987.

81. Robert F. Kelley, who served as a military attaché on the edges of Russia from 1919 to

1921, went on to head the Russian Division of the State Department, where he instilled anti-communism in the first generation of Soviet experts. M.I.D. file 2693, NA; Propas, "Creating a Hard Line Toward Russia," 209–26.

82. M.I.D. file 2277-22-9 39, Aug. 31, 1922, NA; biographical entry on Poole in guide to collections of SHSW; O'Toole, *Encyclopedia of American Intelligence*, 375–76; Smith, *Shadow Warriors*, 212–13, 412; Poole, "Balance of Power," *Life*, Sept. 22, 1947.

83. John A. Gade, "Russia from Its Baltic Window," 56; Troy, *Donovan and the CIA*, 2–5.

84. July 16, 1919, entry and undated fragment in "Siberian Trip" notebook and "The Omsk Journey," William J. Donovan Papers, USAMHI, Box 95B.

85. Donovan to Roland Morris, Nov. 16, 1919, Box 2, Morris Papers.

86. John Foster Dulles record card, M.I.D. Name Index, M1194, NA; 1919 diary, Box 278, John Foster Dulles Papers; J. F. Dulles to Allen Dulles, April 4, 1918, Box 5, Allen Dulles Papers.

87. "Woodrow Wilson: Prophecy and Perspective for the Present," Nov. 27, 1956, Box 226, Allen Dulles Papers.

88. Ibid.

89. On Dulles's recognition that "there is not the flicker of a hope of having American troops sent into Hungary" and his advocacy of other measures against Hungarian Bolshevism, see Dulles to Hugh Wilson, April 4, 1919, Box 8, memoranda of March 24 and April 1, 1919, Box 6, Allen Dulles Papers; Lansing to Wilson with enclosure, March 24, 1919, PWW 56:238–41.

90. A. A. Berle, "Our Undeclared War," *New Republic*, June 16, 1920; Schwarz, *Liberal*, 23–32, 169, 306. In addition to Berle, Poole, Donovan, and the Dulles brothers, Cold Warriors whose careers extended back to the Wilson administration included Norman Armour, Christian Herter, and William C. Bullitt.

91. "History and Development of Bolshevism," Nov. 28, 1918, M.I.D. file 10058-285, RG 165, NA.

CHAPTER SIX

1. For different interpretations, see esp. Unterberger, *United States*, 263, and Kennan, *Decision to Intervene*.

2. Breckinridge Long Diary, Jan.-Feb. 1918; PWW 46:213–15, 219–20, 236; Spring Rice to Foreign Office, Dec. 22 and 27, 1917, PWW 45:347, 370.

3. House to Wilson, Nov. 30, 1917, *Intimate Papers of Colonel House*, 3:281–82; House Diary, Nov. 30 and Dec. 1, 1917; Wilson to House, Dec. 1, 1917, PWW 45:176; Message on the State of the Union, Dec. 4, 1917, PWW 45:201–2.

4. House to Wilson, Feb. 2, 1918, PWW 46:214–15; Lord Reading to Foreign Office, Feb. 15, 1918, PWW 46:353–55. Wilson's aides shared this fear. See PWW 46:35, 219–20, 339–41.

5. Wilson to Polk, March 10, 1918, Lansing Papers, Princeton.

6. Snow, "Russian Revolution in Transbaikalia"; Snow, *Bolsheviks in Siberia*; White, *Siberian Intervention*. For opposite interpretations that stress the violence and unpopularity of the Bolsheviks, see Morley, "Russian Revolution," and Dotsenko, *Struggle for a Democracy*.

7. Wilson to Creel, Feb. 21, 1918, PWW 46:407.

8. Bliss to Washington, Feb. 19, 1918, PWW 46:391–92.

9. Bliss to March, Feb. 20, 1918, Box 33, Folder 674, Polk Papers.

10. Lansing to American embassy, Paris, Feb. 20, 1918, Bliss Papers. For a different view

of Washington's response to Bliss, see Trask, *United States in the Supreme War Council*, 106.

11. Judson Memorandum, Feb. 26, 1918, enclosed in Crowell to Wilson, March 5, 1918, PWW 46:532–37; Breckinridge Long Diary, March 1, 1918.

12. Long Diary, Feb. 25 and 26, 1918; Lansing to Wilson, Feb. 27, 1918, PWW 46:474–75; House Diary, Feb. 25, 1918; Cronon, *Cabinet Diaries of Josephus Daniels*, 285.

13. Lane and Wall, *Letters of Franklin K. Lane*, 266–67; Breckinridge Long Diary, March 2, 1918; Wilson note of March 1, PWW 46:498–99.

14. Lansing Desk Diary, Dec. 21, 1917; Breckinridge Long Diary, Feb. 25, 1918; Polk Diary, March 1, 1918, Bakhmeteff to Ambassador in Tokyo, March 2, 1918, Box 17, Russia Posol'stvo (U.S.) Papers, HIA; House Diary, March 2–3, 1918.

15. House Diary, March 2 and 3, 1918; Bullitt memorandum in Polk Papers, Box 33, Folder 675; and House Papers, Box 182, Folder 132; House to Wilson, March 3, 1918, PWW 46:518. At House's request, Auchincloss sent Wilson a copy of the Bullitt memo. Auchincloss Diary, March 3, 1918; PWW 46:510n.

16. Wiseman to Balfour, March 4, 1918, enclosing House to Balfour, PWW 46:530–31; Seymour, *Intimate Papers of Colonel House*, 1:29. See also Wiseman, "Notes for a Cable from the Ambassador to the Foreign Office," March 9, 1918, PWW 46:590–91.

17. Wilson note, sent as Polk to Morris, March 5, 1918, PWW 46:545; House Diary, March 4–5, 1918; Auchincloss Diary, March 3 and 5; Polk Diary, March 4–5.

18. Wilson note, sent as Polk to Morris, March 5, 1918, PWW 46:545.

19. Wilson memorandum, March 5, 1918, PWW 46:544.

20. For a different view, see Unterberger, *United States*, 220.

21. Long memorandum of March 2, 1918, conversation with John Sookine [Sukin], PWW 46:513–15; Long to Wilson, March 4; Wilson to Long, March 14, 1918, Long Papers, Box 186.

22. Wiseman to Sir Eric Drummond, March 14, 1918, PWW 47:35–36.

23. Strakhovsky, *American Opinion*, 57–58.

24. "Memorandum on the Proposed Japanese Military Expedition Into Siberia," March 18, 1918, Lansing Papers, LC.

25. Basil Miles, "Effect of Japanese Intervention on Public Opinion in Russia," March 18, 1918, in Lansing to Wilson, March 19, 1918, PWW 47:67–69.

26. Snow, *Bolsheviks in Siberia*, 226–27; Dotsenko, *Struggle for a Democracy*, 20–21; Kennan, *Decision to Intervene*, 58–65; Lincoln, *Red Victory*, 96–97, 255.

27. PWW 47:92–93; Cronon, *Cabinet Diaries of Josephus Daniels*, 292.

28. *FRUS: The Lansing Papers*, 2:360; PWW 47:357.

29. Lansing to Wilson, April 22, 1918, PWW 47:397–99.

30. Radkey, *Election*, 16, 77.

31. *FRUS, 1918, Russia*, 2:117–18, 120, 93.

32. Ibid., 2:93, 54, 141, 147–48, 158–61.

33. Balfour to Wiseman for House, Feb. 2, 1918, PWW 46:220–21; Lansing Diary, Feb. 8, 1918; *FRUS, 1918, Russia*, 2:47–48; Long Diary, March 12, 1918; Morris to Lansing, May 16, 1918, and other messages in *FRUS, 1918, Russia*, 2:150–63. For the view that "the United States was absolutely opposed to the support of Semenov," see Unterberger, *United States*, 82.

34. Diary entry for Dec. 30, 1917, David Prescott Barrows Papers, Carton 3, v. 52a, p. 66; "Memoirs of David Prescott Barrows, 1873–1954," 142; Diary entries for April 17–21, 1918, Barrows Papers, Carton 3, v. 53; Barrows's reports in files 2275-D-2 and 2070-555, Military Intelligence Division, RG 165, NA. See also Barrows to Reinsch, May 18, 1918, Paul Reinsch Papers, Box 5.

35. PWW 48:72–73. Although the situation in Siberia was complicated, Lansing under-

stood that the groups the United States was watching were "Anti-Soviet." See Lansing to Wilson, May 10 and May 16, PWW 47:591–92; PWW 48:37–38.

36. Lansing to Wilson, May 21, 1918, enclosing memo by Miles, PWW 48:104–5.

37. British ambassador's summary of Wilson's remarks of May 22, 1918, PWW 48:133–34.

38. Wiseman report of May 29, 1918, interview with Wilson, PWW 48:203–4; Breckinridge Long Diary, May 31, 1918.

39. See Kennan, *Decision to Intervene*, chapter 12; Unterberger, *United States*; Fic, *Bolsheviks and the Czechoslovak Legion.*

40. Coolidge, "Report on American Relations with Russia Since the Triumph of the Bolsheviki," May 20, 1918, Lansing Papers, Princeton, Box 4; Miles memorandum, May 21, 1918, PWW 48:106; Unterberger, *United States*, 131.

41. Aug. 16, 1919, report of Consul Alfred R. Thomson in Box 2, Harris Papers; Unterberger, *United States*, 201; Klimenko, *Bor'ba s kontrrevoliutsei v Moskve*; Poole to Vice Consul at Samara, June 18, 1918, Harris Papers, HIA.

42. Richard Crane to Wilson, May 7, 1918, enclosing Masaryk to Charles Crane, April 10, 1918, PWW 47:548–51; Masaryk, *Making of a State*, 192–94.

43. Lansing Desk Diary, June 3, 1918; Czech sources cited in Kalvoda, "Masaryk in America in 1918," 89; "Memorandum on Intervention in Russia," June 12, 1918, Lansing Papers, LC.

44. Wright memorandum for Division of Near Eastern Affairs, June 3, 1918, Albert S. Burleson Papers, Vol. 21.

45. Crane to Wilson, June 9, 1918, Charles R. Crane Papers, Box 1; PWW 48:283.

46. *FRUS, 1918, Russia*, 2:206–7; PWW 48:335.

47. "Memorandum," June 17, 1918, Burleson Papers, Vol. 21; Wilson to Baker, June 19, 1918, PWW 48:357.

48. Copy of Masaryk's notes, typewritten in English, Box 2, Richard Crane Papers; English translation of Masaryk's handwritten Czech notes, Kovtun, *Masaryk and America*, 57. See also George Tom Molesworth Bridges to Lord Reading, June 18, 1918, PWW 48:352–54; and Masaryk, *Making of a State*, 183–84. For a different view of the Wilson-Masaryk meeting, see Unterberger, *United States*, 222.

49. PWW 48:398.

50. *FRUS, 1918, Russia*, 2:224; Lansing Diary, June 25, 1918; quotations from Masaryk's Czech notes in Kalvoda, "Masaryk in America in 1918," 90n., 95; Unterberger, *United States*, 228.

51. Reading to Balfour, June 27, 1918, PWW 48:453–54; Wilson to S. R. Bertron, June 25, 1918, PWW 48:422; Wilson to C. E. Russell, July 3, 1918, PWW 48:492. Cf. Wilson to Lincoln Colcord, July 9, 1918, PWW 48:568.

52. *New York Times*, June 27, 1918, PWW 48:432–34; Auchincloss Diary, June 13, 1918; Alexander Legge to Samuel Harper, July 6; Harper to Mott, July 13, Aug. 12 and 17, 1918, Box 5, Harper Papers.

53. Harper to Richard Crane, May 21, 1918, Richard Crane Papers; Harper to New York Times, June 23, 1918, Harper Papers; Bakhmeteff to Maklakov, July 1, 1918, Russia Posol'stvo (U.S.) Papers, HIA; Lansing Diary, June 26, 1918.

54. Mott to Wilson, June 27, 1918, Box 100, Mott Papers; Wilson to Reading, July 3, 1918, PWW 48:511–13; William Phillips Journal, July 8, 1918; July 16 *aide-mémoire*, PWW 48:626–27; House Diary, Aug. 17, 1918, PWW 49:281.

55. PWW 48:358–60, 408, 479, 493.

56. Lansing to Wilson, June 28, 1918, PWW 48:458–60.

57. "Memorandum on German Domination in Siberia and the Possible Means of Over-

coming It," March 22, 1918, and addendum of April 6, 1918, Lansing Papers, LC; Wiseman to Sir Eric Drummond, March 14, 1918, PWW 47:35.

58. "Memorandum on the Siberian Situation," July 4, 1918, Box 2, Lansing Papers, Princeton. Wilson may have received recommendations similar to Lansing's points about German POWs when he met John Mott on July 5. Samuel Harper had advised Mott that a mission to Siberia "would have to be protected, not necessarily against Bolsheviki, in any case one would not have to say this, but against hooligans and Germans." Harper to Mott, July 2, 1918, Box 5, Harper Papers.

59. "Memorandum of a Conference at the White House in Reference to the Siberian Situation," July 6, 1918, Box 2, Lansing Papers, Princeton.

60. Benes, *My War Memoirs*, 359, 370.

61. Lansing memorandum of July 6, 1918, Lansing Papers, Princeton.

62. PWW 48:559–60.

63. Wilson to House, July 8, 1918, PWW 48:549–50.

64. Abraham, *Alexander Kerensky*, 203, 321; Reading to London, May 29, May 31, and June 20, 1918, F.O. 371/3332: 446–57; Baker, *WWLL*, 8:271–72; William Phillips Journal, July 11, 1918. See also Wilson to Bochkareva, July 1, 1918, PWW 48:475.

65. Draft of an *aide-mémoire*, July 16, 1918, PWW 48:626. Wilson's generals and aides recognized that the passage about steadying Russian efforts at self-government was the crucial section. See Graves to Harris, Oct. 25, 1918, PWW 51:448; Polk to Lansing, Jan. 6, 1919, PWW 53:633.

66. Phillips, "Reminiscences," 76.

67. Kennan to Lansing, May 26, 1918, Box 4, Lansing Papers, Princeton; Lansing to Kennan, May 28, 1918, Vol. 35, Lansing Papers, LC; Lansing to Wilson, May 28, 1918, Lansing Papers, Princeton; Kennan to Lansing, Aug. 9, and Lansing to Kennan, Aug. 15, Vol. 38, Lansing Papers, LC.

68. Mott, "A View of the Situation in Russia," Jan. 4, 1918, in *Missionary Review of the World*, 174–79, Mott Papers; Mott to Harper, July 17, 1918, Box 5, Harper Papers; Mott to Wilson, July 24, 1918, PWW 49:79; Crane to Wilson, Aug. 1 and 29, 1918, Box 1, Crane Papers.

69. Report of Capt. V. S. Hurban, Aug. 6, 1918, Box 9, Bakhmeteff Papers; Masaryk to Wilson, Aug. 5 and 6, and Wilson to Masaryk, Aug. 7, 1918, PWW 49:194, 203; Kovtun, *Masaryk and America*, 58–59.

70. Foner, *Bolshevik Revolution*, 22, 94–101; *Current Opinion*, April 1918; *Daily Palo Alto Times*, June 29, 1918; *Chicago Tribune*, July 6, 1918, reprinting "Words Will Not Rescue Russia" editorial from *Boston Transcript*; *Nation*, July 6, 1918; Strakhovsky, *American Opinion*, 62–63, 69.

71. Long Diary, May 31, 1918; Bertron to Wilson, June 24, 1918, PWW 48:414–15; State Department Periodical Report, July 5, 1918, 861.00/1161, NA; Bullitt to House, June 24, 1918, Box 21, Folder 679, House Papers.

72. Strakhovsky, *American Opinion*, 63–64; Lansing to Wilson, June 13, 1918, PWW 48:305; Lansing Desk Diary, June 11 and 12, 1918; Auchincloss Diary, June 29, 1918.

73. Jusserand to Paris, July 24, 1918, PWW 49:93. See also House Diary, June 22, 1918.

74. Press release of Aug. 3, PWW 49:170–72; *Nation*, July 27, Aug. 3, 10, and 24, 1918; Polenberg, *Fighting Faiths*; Roberts, "American Opinion Regarding Allied Intervention in Siberia"; Strakhovsky, *American Opinion*, 75–76.

75. Reading to Balfour, July 19, 1918, in PWW 49:36; Wilson to Lansing, Aug. 14, 1918, PWW 49:248–49; Phillips Journal, Aug. 12 and 14, 1918.

76. Long Diary, Aug. 17, 1918 and Memorandum for the Secretary, Aug. 17, 1918, Long Papers.

77. Lansing to Wilson, Aug. 18, 1918, and Wilson to Lansing, Aug. 23, 1918, PWW 49:282–83, 332.

78. Lansing to Wilson, Aug. 22, 1918, and Wilson to Lansing, Aug. 23, 1918, PWW 49:323, 332. See also Wilson to Lansing, Sept. 2, 1918, Long Papers.

79. Phillips Journal, July 9, 1918; Lansing to Polk, Aug. 3, 1918, Vol. 37, Lansing Papers, LC. See also Lansing Desk Diary, July 9, 1918.

80. Long Diary, Feb. 26, April 13, and Dec. 20, 1918; Phillips Diary, July 20, Aug. 14, Aug. 5, Sept. 20, 1918; Polk Diary, Aug. 8, 1918.

81. Wiseman to Reading, Aug. 23, 1918, PWW 49:345; remarks of Foreign Secretary Balfour, Aug. 12, 1918, Imperial War Cabinet 29B, "Secret" minutes, CAB 23/44.

82. Polk to Wilson, Aug. 3; Lansing to Wilson, Aug. 18, 22, and 29, 1918; PWW 49:176–77, 282–84, 320, 383.

83. See White, *Siberian Intervention*, and Mawdsley, *Russian Civil War*, esp. 100.

84. Reinsch to Secretary of State, July 24, 1918, and Wilson to "Mr. Counselor," July 26, 1918, Breckinridge Long Papers. Wilson did express irritation at Japanese unilateralism.

85. "The Situation in Russia and the Military Help of the Allies and the United States," Box 2, Folder 26, Richard Crane Papers; State Department copy, file 763.72/1172 1/2, NA. Wilson returned Masaryk's memorandum to Lansing on Oct. 7, 1918. PWW 51:97n.

86. Long Diary, Sept. 5, 1918; Wilson to Lansing, Sept. 5, 1918, PWW 49:448.

87. Lansing to Wilson, with enclosures, Sept. 9, 1918, PWW 49:491–94; Auchincloss Diary, Sept. 9, 1918.

88. Wilson to Lansing, Sept. 17, 1918, PWW 51:25–26.

89. Wilson to Lansing, Sept. 18, 1918, PWW 51:50–51.

90. Wilson to Lansing, Sept. 20, 1918, PWW 51:78; House Diary, Sept. 24, 1918.

91. Phillips Journal and Lansing Diary, Sept. 20, 1918; Lansing to Wilson, Sept. 21, 1918, and Wilson to Lansing, Sept. 23, 1918, PWW 51:87, 91.

92. Lansing to Wilson, Sept. 21, 1918, PWW 51:86–87; "Agreement with General Janin on the Situation in Siberia," Sept. 21, 1918, Box 2, Folder 14, Richard Crane Papers; copy to Wilson, PWW 51:95–96; Masaryk to Lansing, Sept. 23, 1918, PWW 51:96–97.

93. Morris to Washington, Sept. 23, 1918, PWW 51:98–101.

94. Lansing to Wilson, Sept. 24, 1918, PWW 51:97–98.

95. House Diary, Sept. 24, 1918.

96. Lansing Diary, Sept. 25; Auchincloss Diary, Sept. 26; Wilson to Lansing, Sept. 26, 1918, PWW 51:121–22.

97. Masaryk, "Some Notes on the Memorandum of Sept. 27, 1918," Box 10, Wiseman Papers; copies to Lansing and Bakhmeteff, File 861.00/2900 1/2, NA; Box 9, Bakhmeteff Papers.

98. For different views see Levin, *Wilson and World Politics*, 110; Unterberger, *United States*, 325.

99. PWW 48:202, 276–77.

100. PWW 48:458–60. For similar reports, see *FRUS, 1918, Russia*, 2:342–43, 380; for two challenges to the government's representativeness, see 375, 405.

101. Caldwell to Washington, July 15, 1918, *FRUS, 1918, Russia*, 2:282; reports in Box 2, Harris Papers.

102. Ellis to Daniels, enlcosed in Daniels to Wilson, June 24, 1918, PWW 48:411; Lansing to Wilson, Aug. 22, 1918, enclosing Kennan to Lansing, Aug. 18, 1918, PWW 49:320–21.

103. Polk Diary, July 12 and 17, 1918; Wilson to William Fellowes Morgan, July 1, 1918, PWW 48:472.

104. *FRUS, 1918, Russia*, 2:384, 385; Gvishiani, *Sovetskaia Rossiia i SShA*, 151–52; Mad-

dox, *Unknown War with Russia*, 82–83.

105. *FRUS, 1918, Russia*, 2:335, 362, 382–83; PWW 49:332; Paraphrase of cable received by Russian embassy from Vladivostok, Sept. 27, 1918, Box 9, Russia Posol'stvo (U.S.) Papers, HIA; Lansing Diary, Oct. 3, 1918; Polk Diary, Oct. 11, 1918; Lansing to Bakhmeteff, Oct. 17, 1918, *FRUS, 1918, Russia*, 2:413; Lansing to Jusserand, Nov. 5, 1918, *FRUS, 1918, Russia*, 425.

106. Polk Diary, Nov. 9, 1918; Wilson to Lansing, Nov. 20, 1918, PWW 53:136. On the prevalence of national and international over regional concerns among Siberian SRs, see Pereira, "Regional Consciousness."

107. Maddox, *Unknown War with Russia*, 66; Pereira, "'Democratic Counterrevolution,'" esp. 80–81; *FRUS, 1918, Russia*, 2:309–14, 386–87, 392, 404, 414–15, 420–21, 397–98; Bullard to House, Dec. 7, 1918, Box 21, Folder 672, House Papers; Dotsenko, *Struggle for a Democracy*, 41; L. Gray to Minister of Foreign Affairs, Omsk, Sept. 12, 1918 and Note from foreign consuls to Minister of Foreign Affairs, Sept. 2, 1918, both in f. 200, op. 1, d. 127, GARF.

108. PWW 51:101, 95–98; PWW 49:152.

109. PWW 49:479, 491–94; *FRUS, 1918, Russia*, 2:380; Charles Crane to Richard Crane, Oct. 22, 1918, Box 1, Charles Crane Papers. See also Paraphrase of Cable received by the Russian embassy from Vladivostok, Sept. 27, 1918, Box 9, Russia Posol'stvo (U.S.) Papers, HIA; Varneck and Fisher, *Testimony of Kolchak*, 147.

110. House Diary, Oct. 28, 1918; Landfield to Samuel Harper, Oct. 4, 1918, Harper Papers; "Operation Kaleidoscope: A Melange of Personal Impressions," Jerome Barker Landfield Papers.

111. Libbey, "American-Russian Chamber of Commerce," 236; Lane comment at Cabinet meeting, March 1, 1918, PWW 46:515; "Economy — Effects of Revolution," Box 2, Harris Papers; "The Allies in Siberia," Box 5, Harris Papers; Harris to Secretary of State, July 29, 1918, *FRUS, 1918, Russia*, 2:312–13.

112. Record of June 4, 1918, interview at Nizhneudinsk, Box 2, Harris Papers; Dotsenko, *Struggle for a Democracy*, 21.

113. *FRUS, 1918, Russia*, 2:417; PWW 51:598.

114. Gaddis, *Russia*, 52; Schuman, *American Policy*, 298; PWW 46:65; Harris to Secretary of State, Nov. 1, 1918, *FRUS, 1918, Russia*, 2:421; *FRUS, 1918, Russia*, 2:413, 425; PWW 51:481–82.

115. *FRUS, 1918, Russia*, 2:293, 335–36, 385–86, 407–8, 273, 430; J. Paul Jameson, Sept. 14, 1918 report, Box 1, Harris Papers; PWW 51:102; *FRUS, 1918, Russia*, 2:387.

116. Harris to Washington, July 29, 1918, *FRUS, 1918, Russia*, 2:312–13; "The Allies in Siberia," 1921 report to State Department, Box 5, Harris Papers. See also Consul at Chita to Secretary of State, Sept. 14, 1918, Box 1, Harris Papers; and *FRUS, 1918, Russia*, 2:375.

117. *FRUS, 1918, Russia*, 2:387, 427.

118. Lincoln, *Red Victory*, 242–44; Mawdsley, *Russian Civil War*, 108–11; Weeks and Baylen, "Admiral Kolchak's Mission"; *FRUS, 1918, Russia*, 2:446–47, 455–56, 458–60.

119. Ackerman report in Polk to Lansing, Jan. 6, 1919, PWW 53:628, 630; Graves to Adjutant General of the Army, Dec. 29, 1918, in Newton Baker to Wilson, March 3, 1919, PWW 55:399.

120. *FRUS, 1919, Russia*, 323, 331, 336.

121. See Lansing Diary, Nov. 6, 1918; Polk Diary, Nov. 19, 1918; Cyrus McCormick to Wilson, Nov. 29, 1918, Box 53, Mott Papers; PWW 53:254–57; PWW 54:91–95, 102–3, 173; PWW 53:575; PWW 55:181.

122. PWW 57:575; Polk Diary, April 8 and May 24, 1919; Strakhovsky, *American Opinion*, 99.

123. Polk to Lansing, March 13, 1919, enclosing Graves telegraph of March 5, PWW

55:493–95; Homer Slaughter, "The American Expeditionary Force in Siberia as a Part of Allied Intervention in 1918," lecture at the Army War College, 1934, Box 6, Leroy W. Yarborough Papers, USAMHI, esp. p. 26; Lansing to Wilson, March 21, 1919, PWW 56:152–53; Wilson to Lansing, March 28, 1919, PWW 56:371; Baker to Wilson, April 4, 1919, PWW 56:576–77; Peyton C. March, "Reminiscences," lecture at Army War College, April 6, 1934, USAMHI, 10, 15; Lansing to Wilson, April 7, 1919; Wilson to Lansing, April 8, 1919; Lansing to Washington, April 11, 1919, enclosed in Lansing to Wilson, April 12, 1919, PWW 57:94–95, 134, 313–15.

124. Baker to Wilson, May 7, 1919, enclosing May 4 message from Graves, PWW 58:569–71; Notes of a Meeting of the Council of Four, May 9, 1919, PWW 58:571–78; Samuel Eliot Morison Diary, May 10, 1919.

125. Morison Diary, May 14, 1919; Kerensky and others to Wilson, May 14, 1919, PWW 59:150–56; Morison to Wilson, June 10, 1919, Box 1, A. A. Berle Papers; Wilson comments on June 6, 1919, PWW 60:215; Wilson to Tumulty, May 16, 1919, PWW 59:189; Dispatch to Admiral Kolchak, May 26, 1919, PWW 59:543–46; Berle to Mother, May 25, 1919, Box 2, Berle Papers; FRUS, 1919, Russia, 356; PWW 59:436–37, 545; Polk Diary, June 4, 1919; Cronon, Cabinet Diaries of Josephus Daniels, 500; FRUS, 1919, Russia, 368, 361.

126. FRUS, 1919, Russia, 383–84, 387.

127. Notes of a Meeting of the Council of Four, May 24, 1919, PWW 59:463n.; Wilson to President of Senate, July 22, 1919, PWW 61:579–82; "President's Response to Senate Resolution as to the Reasons for Retaining American Troops in Siberia," July 25, 1919, Box 187, Long Papers; H. Res. 258, Aug. 22, 1919; Memorandum of Statements to the Committee on Foreign Affairs of the House of Representatives by Breckinridge Long, Aug. 29 and 31, 1919, Long Papers; Vance McCormick Diary, June 23, 1919, HIA; Congressional Record, 58:1473, 1864, 3140, 4324, 4815. For detailed discussion of the unfulfilled plans for economic aid to Siberia, see Killen, Russian Bureau, and Bacino, "Reconstructing Russia."

128. Congressional Record, 57:3262, 3342, 58:4900; New York Tribune editorial, quoted in Sack to Omsk, July 28, 1919, Box 26, Russia Posol'stvo (U.S.) Papers, HIA; New Republic, July 16, 1919, p. 343; Robins to Gumberg, April 11 and May 14, 1919, Gumberg Papers; Strakhovsky, American Opinion, 105–6.

129. San Francisco Chronicle, Sept. 16, 1919; Senator William Borah speech, Sept. 5, 1919, Congressional Record, 58:4896–4902. Breckinridge Long Diary, Sept. 20, 1919; Foner, Bolshevik Revolution, 204–5.

130. Notes of a press conference, June 27, 1919, PWW 61:244; FRUS, 1919, Russia, 408–10, 434–36, 445–46; Lansing Diary, Aug. 16 and 25; Oct. 20 and 27, 1919; Long Diary, Aug. 1, 1919.

131. Paraphrase of Sookine to Bakhmeteff, Sept. 1, 1919, Bakhmeteff to Phillips, Sept. 18, 1919; Sazonov to Bakhmeteff, Sept. 6, 24, and 27 1919, and paraphrases, Box 18, Russia Posol'stvo (U.S.) Papers, HIA; Memorandum of Conversation with the Russian Ambassador, Sept. 4, 1919, Box 182, Long Papers; Phillips to Wilson, Sept. 19, 1919, SD 861.24/181B, NA; Phillips to Crowell, Sept. 24, 1919, SD 861.24/184B; Miles and Phillips to Wilson, Sept. 24, 1919, American embassy—Russia papers, RG 84, NA; Baker to Graves, Sept. 26, 1919, Baker Papers; Polk Diary, Oct. 1, 1919.

132. "The Suggested Recognition of the Kolchak Government," Oct. 9, 1919, Box 2, Vol. 2, Lansing Papers, Princeton; Record of Bakhmeteff meeting with Lansing, Oct. 9, 1919, Box 36, Bakhmeteff Papers.

133. F. C. MacDonald (secretary to Ambassador Morris), "The Omsk Journey," Box 95B, Donovan Papers, USAMHI; Pereira, "White Power"; Dotsenko, Struggle for a Democracy, 101; Varneck and Fisher, Testimony of Kolchak, 142, 272–77; "The Suggested Recognition of the Kolchak Government," Oct. 9, 1919, Lansing Papers, Princeton. See also "Siberian Trip," Box 95B, W. J. Donovan Papers; Long Diary, July 30 and Aug. 23, 1919.

134. Harris to Secretary of State, Dec. 10, 1918, *FRUS, 1918, Russia*, 2:459–60; *FRUS, Lansing Papers*, 2:352–53. See also Lansing to Root, Oct. 28, 1918 and Lansing to Charles Hotchkiss, Nov. 13, 1918, Volumes 39 and 40, Lansing Papers, LC.

135. Wilson remarks to Council of Ten, Jan. 16, 1919, PWW 54:102; Cyrus McCormick to Wilson, Nov. 29, 1918, copy enclosed in McCormick to Mott, Dec. 6, 1918, Box 53, Folder 983, Mott Papers; Wilson, expression of "misgivings lest Admiral Koltchak might be under reactionary influences," May 24, 1919, PWW 59:461; Wilson speeches of Sept. 1919, PWW 63:70, 145, 152.

136. "Advisability of Withdrawing Our Troops From Siberia," Nov. 30, 1919, Lansing Papers, Princeton; Breckinridge Long Diary, Dec. 22 and 27, 1919.

137. Kennan to Lansing, Jan. 24, 1920, and Lansing to Kennan, Feb. 2, 1920, George Kennan Papers.

CHAPTER SEVEN

1. "Casualties — 339th Infantry," George Evans Stewart Papers; Dupuy, *Perish by the Sword*, 191; Cudahy, *Archangel*, 211; Moore, Mead, and Jahns, *History of the American Expedition*, 296.

2. Sgt. Silver Parrish, "The Shanghied Expedition," Bentley Historical Library. On the soldiers' experiences, see esp. Gordon, *Quartered in Hell*; Halliday, *Ignorant Armies*; Doolen, *Michigan's Polar Bears*; and Goldhurst, *Midnight War*.

3. Diary of John S. Crissman, Jan. 22 1919, quoted in Rhodes, "Anglo-American Intervention," 382.

4. Wilson to House, c. Feb. 23, 1919, PWW 55:229–30.

5. For different views see Link, *Woodrow Wilson*, 97; Unterberger, "Wilson and the Bolsheviks," 86.

6. See Kennan, *Decision to Intervene*, esp. 271–76; and Strakhovsky, *Intervention at Archangel*.

7. Trani, "Wilson and the Decision to Intervene"; Silverlight, *Victor's Dilemma*; Kennan, *Russia and the West*.

8. For different views, see Long, "American Intervention in Russia," 49, 66; Link, *Woodrow Wilson*, 18–19; Unterberger, "Wilson and the Bolsheviks," 71.

9. For a similar view, see Levin, *Wilson and World Politics*, 96, 198. For other treatments of the Archangel expedition as at least partly motivated by anti-Bolshevism, see Williams, *Russian-American Relations*; Williams, "American Intervention in Russia"; and Gardner, *Safe for Democracy*.

10. Cf. Link et al., PWW 48:vii; Unterberger, "Wilson and the Bolsheviks," 76–82; Kennan, *Decision to Intervene*, 267, 270.

11. For different views, see Long, "American Intervention in Russia," 67; Rhodes, *Anglo-American Winter War*, 127; Long, "Civil War," 178, 444; Trani, "Wilson and the Decision to Intervene," 443–44; Kennan, *Russia and the West*, 105; and Kennan, *Decision to Intervene*, 14.

12. Cf. Kennan, *Russia and the West*, 73; Kennan, *Decision to Intervene*, 268–71, 276, 418.

13. House to Wilson, July 23, 1917, PWW 43:248–49; Reading to Lloyd George and Others, Nov. 2, 1917, PWW 44:494–95; Francis to Secretary of State, Nov. 6, 1917, *FRUS, 1918, Russia*, 1:220–21.

14. Message for the President from Balfour, March 18, 1918, PWW 47:61–63.

15. "Memorandum on Non-recognition of a Russian Government," Jan. 6, 1918; "Statement," Jan. 10, 1918, Box 4, Lansing Papers, Princeton; Address of Jan. 8, 1918, PWW 45:536.

16. Wilson to Tumulty, c. Feb. 23, 1918, PWW 46:422; Memorandum of Feb. 8, 1918, drafted by Breckinridge Long, E. T. Williams, and Basil Miles, enclosed in Lansing to Wilson, Feb. 9, 1918, PWW 46:301–4.

17. Message to Congress of Soviets, March 11, 1918, PWW 46:598.

18. Summers to Lansing, March 15, 1918, SD file 861.00/1309, NA; *FRUS, 1918, Russia,* 1:399–400; PWW 47:79–80; Ambassador Sharp to Secretary of State, March 21, 1918, SD file 861.00/1343, NA. On the approval of Ambassador Maklakov, see file 861.00/1302.

19. Leo Pasvolsky to Senator Robert Owen, March 4, 1918, SD file 861.00/1275, NA.

20. Polk Diary, March 1, 1918; Paraphrase of Bakhmeteff to Maklakov, March 5, 1918, SD file 861.00/1334, NA.

21. Sharp to Lansing, Feb. 19, 1918, PWW 46:388–89; Wiseman to Drummond, March 14, 1918, PWW 47:35–36; "Memorandum on German Domination in Siberia and the Possible Means of Overcoming It," March 22, 1918, Lansing Papers, LC; Reading to Drummond, March 27, 1918, PWW 47:170–71.

22. Message from Frazier for the President, March 19, 1918, PWW 47:59–61; Trotsky message of March 1/14, in Kennan, *Decision to Intervene,* 46.

23. Francis to Secretary of State, March 11, 1918, *FRUS, 1918, Russia,* 2:470; Summary of message from Martin by Col. Ruggles, March 12, 1918, enclosed in Lansing to Wilson, March 25, 1918, PWW 47:140–41.

24. Miles Memorandum, April 2, 1918, Box 33, Folder 677, Polk Papers; Polk to Lansing, April 2, 1918, PWW 47:226–27; Balfour to Reading, March 12, *FRUS, 1918, Russia,* 2:470–71; Wilson to Lansing, April 4, 1918, Box 33, Folder 677, Polk Papers; PWW 47:246; Daniels to Wilson, April 5, 1918, PWW 47:263; Wilson to Daniels, April 8, 1918, PWW 47:290.

25. Debo, *Revolution and Survival,* 252–58; Goldin, *Interventsiia,* 22–32; Wilson to Lansing, April 4, 1918, PWW 47:241; Reading to Balfour, April 7, 1918, PWW 47:281.

26. House Diary, April 24, 1918; see also Balfour to Reading, April 23, 1918, PWW 47:412; House to Wiseman, April 25, 1918, PWW 47:436; and Fowler, *British-American Relations, 1917–1918,* 176; House to Wiseman, May 12, 1918, Box 123, Folder 4328, House Papers; House to Wilson, April 24, 1918, PWW 47:417.

27. Reading to Balfour, April 25, 1918, PWW 47:440–41.

28. Wiseman to House, April 27, 1918, Box 123, Folder 4328, House Papers; Wiseman to House, May 1, 1918, Box 123, House Papers, enclosed in House to Wilson, May 3, 1918, PWW 47:503–5; Reading to Balfour, May 2, 1918, PWW 47:496; Debo, *Revolution and Survival,* 258–62; Goldin, *Interventsiia,* 33.

29. Reading to Balfour, May 6, 1918, PWW 47:544.

30. Jusserand to French Foreign Ministry, n.d., PWW 47:585–86; Wilson Appointment Books, Wilson Papers.

31. Francis to Secretary of State, May 8, 1918 (received May 9, 8:19 p.m.), *FRUS, 1918, Russia,* 2:473.

32. Creel to Wilson, May 9, 1918, George Creel Papers; Sisson, *One Hundred Red Days,* 430.

33. Wilson Appointment Books; Lansing Diary, May 10, 1918; Lansing to Wilson, May 11, 1918, PWW 47:605.

34. Lansing to Wilson, May 16, 1918, PWW 48:37–38.

35. Paraphrases of telegrams from Lockhart, in Lansing to Wilson, May 16, 1918, PWW 48:39–41.

36. Lansing to Wilson, May 21, 1918, enclosing Ruggles to Milstaff, May 11, 1918, PWW 48:96; Telegram from Francis, May 11, 1918, enclosed in Miles to Lansing, May 21, 1918, PWW 48:112–14; *Baltimore Sun,* May 21, 1918, Wilson Papers, Series 4, Case 64, Reel 194.

37. Lansing to Wilson, May 21, 1918, enclosing Balfour to Reading, May 15, and para-

phrase of Lockhart to London, May 15, 1918, PWW 48:99–104; Reading to Balfour, May 23, 1918, PWW 48:133–34. A week later Wilson reiterated that "an oral or secret arrangement with Trotsky would be no good since he would repudiate it." Wiseman to Drummond, May 30, 1918, PWW 48:203–4.

38. Bliss to Secretary of War, May 26, 1918, enclosed in Newton Diehl Baker to Wilson, c. May 28, 1918, PWW 48:179–81.

39. "Memorandum for the Adjutant General" by Chief of Staff Peyton March, May 28, 1918, enclosed in Baker to Wilson, c. May 28, 1918, PWW 48:178–82.

40. Francis to Secretary of State, May 23, 1918, *FRUS, 1918, Russia,* 1:538; Kennan to Lansing, May 26, 1918, Box 4, Lansing Papers, Princeton.

41. Kennan to Lansing, May 26, 1918; Lansing to Wilson, May 28, 1918, Box 4, Lansing Papers, Princeton (also PWW 48:183–87); Lansing to Kennan, May 28, 1918, Vol. 35, Lansing Papers, LC.

42. For opposite views, see Link et al., PWW 48:vii; Kennan, *Russia and the West,* 70; Unterberger, "Wilson and the Bolsheviks," 78.

43. For a different view of the Wilson administration's reconciliation of self-determination and intervention, see Lasch, "American Intervention in Siberia," 220–21, 217, 205n.

44. Unaddressed letter by Sisson, May 31, 1918, Vol. 21, Burleson Papers.

45. Harper to Charles Crane, July 17, 1918; Harper to John R. Mott, July 2, 1918, Box 5, Folder 11, Harper Papers; Memorandum of June 3, 1918, Vol. 21, Burleson Papers.

46. Wright to Samuel Harper, June 20, 1918, Harper Papers.

47. Polk to Wilson, June 8, 1918, enclosing Francis to Lansing, June 5, 1918, PWW 48:264–65; Wilson to Polk, June 10, 1918, PWW 48:276; Lansing to Francis, June 12, 1918, and Wilson to Polk, June 10, 1918, PWW 48:276–77.

48. Lansing forwarded the Kadet resolution to Tumulty for Wilson on June 19, 1918, PWW 48:364–65; Ariadna Tyrkova et al. to the President of the United States, enclosed in Charles Edward Russell to Wilson, June 20, 1918, Wilson Papers, Reel 195.

49. Reading to Wilson, July 3, 1918, PWW 48:493–501; "The Four-Point Speech," July 4, 1918, PPWW 1:231–35.

50. Goldin, *Interventsiia,* 40–46; Lockhart dispatch of June 18, enclosed in Balfour to Reading, June 20 1918, PWW 48:379–81; Cole to Secretary of State, June 21, 1918, *FRUS, 1918, Russia,* 2:486–87; Chicherin to Poole, June 14, 1918, f. 129, op. 2, d. 2., l. 13, AVPRF; Francis to Secretary of State, June 16, 1918 (received June 24), and Secretary of State to Francis, July 6, 1918, *FRUS, 1918, Russia,* 2:486, 495.

51. Chicherin to Trotsky, June 24, 1918, f. 5, op. 1, d. 2070, l. 1, Russian Center for the Preservation and Study of Documents of Contemporary History; Freund, *Unholy Alliance,* 19–20; Chicherin to Poole, July 12 and 30, 1918, f. 129, op. 2, p. 1, d. 2, l. 27 and l. 34, AVPRF; Poole to Chicherin, July 13 and 31, 1918, f. 129, op.2, p. 1, d. 3, l. 52 and l. 66, AVPRF.

52. Francis to Secretary of State, Aug. 1, 1918 (rec'd Aug. 2), *FRUS, 1918, Russia,* 2:505.

53. Wilson to James Hamilton Lewis, July 24, 1918, PWW 49:74; Jusserand to French Foreign Ministry, Aug. 7, 1918, PWW 49:211; Wilson to Russell Benjamin Harrison, Aug. 14, 1918, PWW 49:247.

54. Draft of an *aide-mémoire,* July 16, 1918, PWW 48:624–27.

55. Fourteen Points speech, Jan. 8, 1918, and Message to the People of Russia through the Soviet Congress, March 11, 1918, PPWW 1:158, 191; draft of an *aide-mémoire,* July 16, 1918, PWW 48:626.

56. Bakhmeteff, "Reminiscences," 368–70.

57. See Francis to Secretary of State, March 31, 1918, Box 33, Folder 677, Polk Papers; Francis to Secretary of State, April 24, 1918, *FRUS, 1918, Russia,* 2:472; Arthur Bullard to House, June 1918, Box 21, Folder 672, House Papers; Auchincloss Diary, July 16, 1918;

and Kennan, *Decision to Intervene*, 249, 248.

58. Balfour to Reading, May 28, 1918, enclosed in Lansing to Wilson, May 31, 1918, PWW 48:206–8.

59. Reading to Balfour, March 19, 1918, PWW 47:82; Jusserand to Pichon, received June 6, 1918, PWW 48:252–55; March Memorandum of June 24, 1918, enclosed in Newton Baker to Wilson, June 24, 1918, PWW 48:418–21. See also March, *Nation at War*, especially 113, 133–39, 152–53.

60. Baker to Bliss, July 9, 1918, PWW 48:577; Draft of an *aide-mémoire*, July 16, 1918, PWW 48:625. See also Baker foreword to Graves, *America's Siberian Adventure*, ix.

61. Cole to Francis, June 1, 1918, *FRUS, 1918, Russia*, 2:477–84. On Cole, see Rhodes, "A Prophet in the Russian Wilderness."

62. March to Bliss, July 22, 1918, PWW 49:57.

63. For the contrary view, see Kennan, *Russia and the West*, 73; Kennan, *Decision to Intervene*, 271, 418.

64. Balfour to Reading, April 15, 1918, handed to Lansing on April 19, PWW 47:355–57; Balfour to Reading, April 18, 1918, PWW 47:366–69.

65. March to Bliss, May 28, 1918, PWW 48:182 (emphasis added). Since March and Baker were both more reluctant to intervene than Wilson was, it is unlikely that they were responsible for adding the expansive word "from."

66. Balfour to Reading, May 28, 1918, enclosed in Lansing to Wilson, May 31, 1918, PWW 48:206–8; Memorandum by Lansing on June 3, 1918, about a conference with Wilson on June 1, PWW 48:236; Lansing Desk Diary, June 3, 1918.

67. Joint Note No. 31, June 3, 1918, printed in PWW 48:287–88.

68. See Wilson to Baker, June 19, 1918, quoted in Kennan, *Decision to Intervene*, 367n.; March to Wilson, Sept. 12, 1918, PWW 49:529–30; Palmer, *Bliss, Peacemaker*, 158–59.

69. For the opposite view, see Kennan, *Decision to Intervene*, 366–67.

70. March to Bliss, May 28, 1918, PWW 48:182; Bliss to Baker and March, July 12, 1918, PWW 48:599–602.

71. Balfour to Reading, June 11, 1918, PWW 48:285–86. On June 13, Lansing saw Reading "on memo in re troops needed at Murmansk." Lansing Diary.

72. Baker to Bliss, June 15, 1918, PWW 48:330–31; March, *Nation at War*, 133–35.

73. Bliss to March, June 23, 1918, PWW 48:401–3.

74. Telegram from Foch, June 27, 1918, and Jusserand to Pichon, c. June 27, 1918, PWW 48:445–47.

75. Balfour to Reading, July 2, 1918, enclosed in Reading to Wilson, July 3, 1918, PWW 48:493–501, quoted at 497–98; also in *FRUS, 1918, Russia*, 2:241–46.

76. Reading to Wilson, July 3, 1918, PWW 48:493.

77. Bliss message of July 5, enclosed in Baker to Wilson, July 6, 1918, PWW 48:536–38.

78. Reading to Balfour, July 8, 1918, PWW 48:565–66. See also Reading to Balfour, July 19 and 21, 1918, PWW 49:36, 52.

79. House Diary, Aug. 19, 1918.

80. Balfour to Reading, July 2, 1918, enclosed in Reading to Wilson, July 3, 1918, PWW 48:493–501; Draft of an *aide-mémoire*, July 16, 1918, PWW 48:624–27. Polk noted that Wilson's statement was "in reply to questions of the Supreme War Council as to our going into Russia." Polk Diary, July 16, 1918.

81. Lloyd George to Reading, July 18, 1918, PWW 49:9–11; Balfour to Reading, July 22, 1918, PWW 49:57–60; "Secret" record of Imperial War Cabinet 29B, Aug. 12, 1918, CAB 23/44; Reading to Balfour, July 23, 1918, PWW 49:67–68.

82. For different views see Fowler, *British-American Relations*, 164–65; Trask, *United States in the Supreme War Council*, 127.

83. Bliss to Secretary of War and Chief of Staff, July 12, 1918, PWW 48:599–602.

84. Bliss to Secretary of War and Chief of Staff, Aug. 18, 1918, PWW 49:285–86.

85. Bliss to March, Sept. 3, 1918, enclosed in March to Wilson, Sept. 12, 1918, PWW 49:529–31; "Statement to the press *in re* American-Japanese action in Siberia," c. Aug. 3, 1918, PWW 49:170–72 (emphasis added).

86. Wilson to Lansing, Sept. 5, 1918, enclosing Harris to Washington, Aug. 30, 1918, PWW 49:448.

87. Francis to Secretary of State, July 27, 1918 (received Sept. 19), SD file 124.61/47, NA.

88. Francis to McCully, Aug. 4, 1918, Francis Papers; *Russia from the American Embassy*, 266.

89. Francis to Secretary of State, July 27, 1918, SD file 124.61/47, NA; Francis to Secretary of State, Aug. 23, 1918, *FRUS, 1918, Russia*, 2:513–14; Francis to Hugh Martin, Aug. 23, 1918, Francis Papers. While the August 3 press release sanctioned action "from Murmansk and Archangel," an earlier message from Polk stated that the United States would "not take part in any expedition into Russia from" Murmansk. Polk to Cole, July 30, 1918, *FRUS, 1918, Russia*, 2:504.

90. Francis to Secretary of State, Aug. 27, 1918 (received Oct. 15), *FRUS, 1918, Russia*, 2:515–16.

91. Francis to Secretary of State, Aug. 23, 1918 (received Sept. 2), *FRUS, 1918, Russia*, 2:513–14.

92. Francis to Secretary of State, Sept. 3, 1918 (received Sept. 6), *FRUS, 1918, Russia*, 2:517–19; Lansing to Wilson, Sept. 9, 1918, PWW 49:491–97.

93. Francis to Secretary of State, Sept. 3, 1918, *FRUS, 1918, Russia*, 2:518; see also 516–17.

94. Francis to Secretary of State, Sept. 6, 1918, *FRUS, 1918, Russia*, 2:521–22; Kotsonis, "Arkhangel'sk, 1918," 539.

95. Barclay to Foreign Office, Sept. 9, 1918, PWW 49:508.

96. Lansing to American embassy, London, Sept. 12, 1918, PWW 49:516–17.

97. Francis to Washington, Sept. 10, 1918, enclosed in Lansing to Wilson, Sept. 11, 1918, PWW 49:517–19.

98. Ibid.; Telegram to Francis, Aug. 17, 1918, received by Col. Stewart, Oct. 5, 1918, Stewart Papers; Weeks, *American Naval Diplomat*, 140–42.

99. Bliss to March, Sept. 3, 1918, enclosed in March to Wilson, Sept. 12, 1918, PWW 49:529–32; Message from Baker enclosed in Lansing to Wilson, Sept. 16, 1918, PWW 51:17.

100. Bliss to Baker, Aug. 22, 1918, enclosed in Crowell to Wilson, Sept. 17, 1918, PWW 51:33–38; Bliss to March, Sept. 7, 1918, PWW 51:52–55.

101. Bliss to March, Sept. 7, 1918, PWW 51:52–55.

102. Wilson to March, Sept. 18, 1918, PWW 51:51.

103. Wilson draft of an *aide-mémoire*, July 16, 1918, PWW 48:626.

104. Wilson to Lansing, Sept. 18, 1918, PWW 51:50–51.

105. Wilson Appointment Books; Lansing Diary, Sept. 25, 1918; Auchincloss Diary, Sept. 26, 1918; Wilson to Lansing, Sept. 26, 1918, Box 33, Folder 687, Polk Papers; also PWW 51:121–22.

106. Wilson to Lansing, Sept. 26, 1918. Lansing fulfilled Wilson's request with gushing enthusiasm. *FRUS, 1918, Russia*, 2:546.

107. Francis to Secretary of State, Sept. 29, 1918, *FRUS, 1918, Russia*, 2:549–50; Wilson to Lansing, Oct. 2, 1918, PWW 51:178.

108. Jusserand to Paris, Sept. 28, 1918, PWW 51:152–53; Jusserand to Pichon, Oct. 3, 1918, PWW 51:209–10.

109. Bliss to Secretary of State and Col. House, Aug. 30, 1918, enclosed in Lansing to Wilson, Aug. 31, 1918, PWW 49:403–4; Bliss to March, Sept. 7, 1918, returned by Wilson

to March, Sept. 18, 1918, PWW 51:51-55.

110. March to Wilson, Oct. 3, 1918, enclosing Joint Note No. 37, Sept. 10, 1918, PWW 51:195-203; Wiseman notes of an interview with Wilson, Oct. 16, 1918, PWW 51:347-52.

111. Poole to War Office, Oct. 2, 1918; quoted in Rhodes, "Anglo-American Intervention," 376-77.

112. Francis to Secretary of State, Aug. 27, 1918 (received Oct. 15), Francis Papers. This portion of Francis's letter was not printed in FRUS, 1918, Russia, 2:515-16.

113. Francis to Secretary of State, Sept. 23, 1918, and Lansing to Francis, Sept. 27, 1918, FRUS, 1918, Russia, 2:543-44, 548; Wilson to Polk, March 10, 1918, Lansing Papers, Princeton.

114. Bliss to Baker, Oct. 9, 1918, enclosed in Baker to Wilson, Oct. 24, 1918, PWW 51:425-28.

115. Williams, American-Russian Relations, 171; Link, Deliberations of the Council of Four, 2:484.

116. June 12, 1918, message from Lockhart, relayed in Balfour to Reading, June 1918, Box 10, Folder 263, Wiseman Papers; Poole to Secretary of State, June 22, 1918, FRUS, 1918, Russia, 1:565-66; Webster to Wardwell, Aug. 12, 1918, Box 2, Wardwell Papers.

117. Translation of New Petrograd Gazette, Aug. 8, 1918, Box 2, Wardwell Papers. On August 4, Pravda similarly proclaimed that the Allies and tsarist officers at Murmansk sought to restore the Russian monarchy.

118. Young, Diaries of Sir Robert Bruce Lockhart, 1:39; Lockhart, Memoirs of a British Agent, 308-11; Pravda, Aug. 14, 1918.

119. Poole to Secretary of State, Aug. 26, 1918, FRUS, 1918, Russia, 1:580-81; Captain H. S. Martin, "Memorandum for Colonel Ruggles," Archangel, Aug. 20, 1919, Box 33, Folder 696, Polk Papers. For similar conclusions that weak intervention strengthened Bolshevism, see Lt. H. J. Costello, "Menace to World, Our Men in Russia See in Bolshevism: Regret Their Failure to Deal It Death Blow," Red Cross World, July 31, 1919, Box 2, Wardwell Papers; Ambassadorial Diary of John W. Davis, 58.

120. William Thomas Ellis to Josephus Daniels, June 21, 1918, enclosed in Daniels to Wilson, June 24, 1918, PWW 48:410-13.

121. Albert Rhys Williams, "Memorandum for Colonel House," Sept. 22, 1918, Wilson Papers, Reel 100.

122. Diary entry for Aug. 27, 1918, Box 3, Wardwell Papers.

123. Cole reports of July 22 and Sept. 10, 1918, FRUS, 1918, Russia, 2:500-502, 527-30; Webster to Wardwell, Aug. 6, 1918, Box 2, Wardwell Papers; Wardwell Diary, Aug. 27, 1918, Box 3, Wardwell Papers; Lockhart, Memoirs of a British Agent, 313, 339.

124. Lenin, Selected Works, 452-63; Chicherin to Francis, May 6, May 26, July 4, 1918; Chicherin to Poole, July 4, Aug. 5, 1918, f. 129, op. 2, p. 1, d. 2, ll. 8, 10, 22, 23, 37-50, AVPRF; Chicherin conversation with Karakhan by direct wire, c. July 1918, f. 159, op. 1, d. 43, ll. 9-10, RTsKhIDNI; Chicherin to Wilson, Nov. 2, 1918, PWW 51:555-61; Buckler Notes of Conversations with Litvinov in Jan. 1919, Vol. 41, Lansing Papers, LC.

125. Abraham, Kerensky, 337-41; Kerensky, Russia and History's Turning Point, 497-99; FRUS, 1918, Russia, 1:567-68, 578-79; Hugh Gibson Diary, July 6-19, 1918, HIA; Maklakov to Bakhmeteff, July 30, 1918, Box 9, Posol'stvo (U.S.) Papers, HIA. Like Lansing and other State Department officials, Wilson was averse to having former Provisional Government leaders visit the United States. See Wilson to Lansing, Aug. 3 and 22, 1918, PWW 49:175, 312; Polk Diary, Aug. 6 and Nov. 14, 1918.

126. Lockhart, Memoirs of a British Agent, 311; Captain H. S. Martin, "Memorandum for Colonel Ruggles," Archangel, Aug. 20, 1919, Box 33, Folder 696, Polk Papers; A. C. Coolidge, "The Archangel coup d'etat," c. mid-Sept. 1918, Breckinridge Long Papers; Cole

to Secretary of State, Sept. 10, 1918, *FRUS, 1918, Russia,* 1:527–30. For further analysis, see Long, "Civil War"; Kotsonis, "Arkhangel'sk, 1918"; Weeks, *American Naval Diplomat,* 142, 151.

127. Undated "Statement of Mr. Jesse Halsey," enclosed in Senator John Sharp Williams to Wilson, Sept. 20, 1918, Wilson Papers, Reel 100. According to a handwritten note on these documents, Halsey's statement was "originally among papers brought back by WW from Paris."

128. Chaikovskii to Wilson, Sept. 29, 1918, and Chaikovskii to Bakhmeteff, Oct. 22, 1918, Box 18, Russia Posol'stvo (U.S.) Papers, HIA.

129. Francis to Washington, Sept. 3, 1918, enclosed in Lansing to Wilson, Sept. 9, 1918, PWW 49:496; Bliss to Baker, Aug. 22, 1918, enclosed in Crowell to Wilson, Sept. 17, 1918, PWW 51:36; Baker to Wilson, Jan. 1, 1919, PWW 53:580–84; Rhodes, "The Anglo-American Intervention at Archangel," 384–85; letters to Johnson, Carton 12, Johnson Papers; *Congressional Record,* Vol. 57:342–46.

130. Francis to Lansing, Jan. 1 and 11, 1919, Vols. 40 and 41, Lansing Papers, LC.

131. Bullitt notes of Wilson's remarks on Dec. 9, 1918, Box 21, Folder 681, House Papers; Francis, *Russia From the American Embassy,* 306, 310; Notes of Meetings of Council of Four, March 27, 1919, PWW 56:328–29; Polk to Francis, April 21, 1919, Box 41, Francis Papers. Like Wilson, Bliss viewed American public opinion as a major constraint on action against Bolshevism. See Bliss Diary, Jan. 22, 1919, and Bliss Memorandum to House, Feb. 17, 1919, in Palmer, *Bliss, Peacemaker,* 369.

132. Breckinridge Long Diary, Jan. 21, 1919; Dec. 31, 1918.

133. Long Diary, Jan. 29, Feb. 12, 25, and 28, 1919.

134. Polk to Auchincloss, Feb. 4, 1919, Series I, Box 1, Polk Papers; Polk Diary, Jan. 4 and Feb. 12, 1919; Polk to Lansing, Feb. 4, 1919, PWW 54:487; Bullitt Memorandum on "Withdrawal of American Troops from Archangel," Jan. 30, 1919, Box 21, Folder 682, House Papers; House to Wilson, n.d., PWW 54:348–49; Bullitt to House, Feb. 11, 1919, Box 21, Folder 682, House Papers; Baker to Wilson, Feb. 11, 1919, PWW 55:81.

135. *Congressional Record,* Vol. 57:3258–65; 3334–42.

136. Auchincloss Diary, Feb. 18, 1919, and Feb. 19, including text of House to Wilson, Feb. 18, 1919.

137. *FRUS, 1918, Russia,* 2:574; Lasch, *American Liberals,* 171; Lansing to Wilson, Nov. 21, 1918, PWW 53:151–52; Polk to Lansing, Jan. 6, 1919, PWW 53:627–32; Lansing to Wilson, Jan. 9, 1919, PWW 53:706; Wilson comments at a Council of Ten Meeting, Jan. 16, 1919, PWW 54:103; Wilson to the American Commissioners, Feb. 19, 1919, PWW 55:208.

138. Vance C. McCormick Diary, June 23, 1919, HIA; "Edmund Burke: The Man and His Times," c. Aug. 1893, PWW 8:336.

CHAPTER EIGHT

1. Special Agreement between the ARA and the Provisional Government of Russia, July 16, 1919, Box 18, Folder 119, N. N. Iudenich Collection, HIA; also in *FRUS, 1919, Russia,* 693–96.

2. Anonymous, undated note regarding the Hoover-Hermonius agreement, Box 18, Iudenich Collection; Major-General Rodzianko to Hoover, in C. Krusenstiern to E. H. Foreman, ARA, Reval, July 26, 1919, Box 13, Iudenich Collection.

3. Hoover statement sent to Secretary of State by Polk, Aug. 30, 1919, *FRUS, Russia, 1919,* 707. See also Patenaude, "Hoover's Brush with Bolshevism," 3–4.

4. Page, *Formation of the Baltic States,* 69–82; Arens, "Revolutionary Developments," 242–75; Mawdsley, *Russian Civil War,* 116; Lincoln, *Red Victory,* 287.

5. Page, *Formation of the Baltic States*, 62–67; Ezergailis, *Latvian Impact on the Bolshevik Revolution*; Mawdsley, *Russian Civil War*, 117; *Izvestiia*, Dec. 25, 1918, quoted in Page, *Formation of the Baltic States*, 135.

6. Mawdsley, *Russian Civil War*, 118; Page, *Formation of the Baltic States*, 130–34. For a Soviet interpretation, see Zhugzhda, "Imperialisticheskaia."

7. William C. Bullitt, "The Bolshevist Movement in Europe," Nov. 2, 1918, PWW 51:563; Naval Attaché Stockholm to ONI, Dec. 4, 1918, RG 45, WA-6 Russia, Box 706, Folder 4, NA; R. H. Lord, "The Present Situation of the Bolshevists in Russia," in S. E. Mezes to Wilson, Jan. 16, 1919, PWW 54:91–96; Chargé in Denmark to Secretary of State, Jan. 24, 1919, *FRUS, 1919, Russia*, 667.

8. Dulles to Christian A. Herter, Jan. 6, 1919, Box 7, Allen W. Dulles Papers; Dulles, "Lithuania and Poland—The Last Barrier Between Germany and the Bolsheviki," Dec. 30, 1918, *FRUS, 1919: The Paris Peace Conference* [PPC] Vol. 2:481–83; Lansing Desk Diary, Dec. 30, 1918, LC. Gordon Auchincloss and Sir William Wiseman drafted another plan for "sending forces" to the Baltic states. Auchincloss Diary, Feb. 16, 1919.

9. Hoover listed these reasons for his opposition to an "invasion of Russia" in *Memoirs: Years of Adventure*, 412.

10. Dulles to Herter, Jan. 6, 1919, Allen Dulles Papers; Bullitt to Lansing, Nov. 8, 1918, "The Bolshevist Movement in Western Europe," PWW 53:6–9; G. S. Macfarland to Wilson, Nov. 25, 1918, PWW 53:199; Polk to Lansing, Jan. 11, 1919, enclosed in Lansing to Wilson, Jan. 15, 1919, PWW 54:83; Notes of a Meeting of the Council of Four, April 30, 1919, PWW 58:266.

11. Hoover to Wilson, April 11, 1919, PWW 57:271–74, quoted at 273.

12. Bullitt to Lansing, Nov. 8, 1918, "The Bolshevist Movement in Western Europe," enclosed in Lansing to Wilson, Nov. 9, 1918, PWW 53:6–9; House Diary, Jan. 8, 1919; PWW 53:694.

13. W. C. Huntington, "Memorandum on the Russian Situation," in W. C. Redfield to Wilson, Nov. 22, 1918, PWW 53:169–80, quoted at 173 and 178; Cyrus H. McCormick Jr. to Wilson, Nov. 29, 1918, enclosed in N. D. Baker to Wilson, Nov. 30, 1918, PWW 53:254–57; Francis to Lansing, House, Bliss, and White, Feb. 23, 1919, PWW 54:234–35; Vance McCormick Diary, Jan. 30 and March 4, 1919, HIA.

14. "Memorandum on Post-Bellum Conditions and Bolshevism," Oct. 28, 1918, Lansing Papers, LC; Lansing to Wilson, Nov. 26, 1918, PPC, 1:270–71.

15. Cronon, *Cabinet Diaries of Josephus Daniels*, 348; Hoover speech, Sept. 16, 1919, American Institute of Mining and Metallurgical Engineers *Monthly Bulletin*, no. 154, Oct. 1919, 6–7; Hoover to Wilson, Dec. 20, 1918, PWW 53:453–54; Hoover cables of Jan. 5 and Jan. 6, 1919, PWW 53:648–50; White to Lodge, Jan. 8, 1919, PPC 2:711–12.

16. Wilson to Grenville Macfarland, Nov. 27, 1918, PWW 53:221; Draft Minutes of a Meeting at 10 Downing Street, Dec. 30, 1918, PWW 53:561; Davis and Fleming, *Ambassadorial Diary*, 5; PWW 54:103, 183; Wilson to Tumulty, Jan. 10, 1919, PWW 53:709. See also PWW 55:161; PWW 56:127.

17. Lansing Desk Diary, June 16, 1919.

18. Message for the Secretary of the Treasury from the President, Jan. 1, 1919, PPC, 2:692–93.

19. Telegrams from Polk to Commission to Negotiate Peace, reporting advice of Representative Swagar Sherley, Jan. 4 and 6, 1919; PPC, 2:698, 707.

20. Commission to Negotiate Peace to Acting Secretary of State, Jan. 3, 1919, PPC, 2:698. On the bipartisan dimension of the Red peril appeal, see Commissioner White to Senator Lodge, Jan. 8, 1919, PPC 2:711–12.

21. Commission to Negotiate Peace to Acting Secretary of State, Jan. 6, 1919, PPC,

2:705–7. For a study that emphasizes desires to dispose of the farm surplus, see Best, "Food Relief as Price Support."

22. See, for example, Lansing to Polk, Jan. 20, 1919, PPC 2:723; Wilson to Tumulty, Jan. 10, 1919, PWW 53:709; Lansing to Polk for Sherley, Jan. 9, 1919, PPC, 2:716–17.

23. *Congressional Record*, Jan. 13–28, 1919, 65th Cong., 3rd sess., Vol. 57, Pt. 2:1339–40, 1363, 1362, 1656, 1360, and 1808.

24. *Congressional Record*, Vol. 57, esp. 1361, 1965, 1340–41, 1359–60, 1341–43, 1659–60, 1794.

25. *Congressional Record*, Vol. 57:1857, 1750, 1969, 1968, 1793, 1798.

26. On Jan. 13, H.R. 13708 received 242 yeas, with 73 nays and 114 not voting. In the Senate on Jan. 24, the vote was: 53 yeas, 18 nays, and 25 not voting. *Congressional Record*, Vol. 57:1373, 1995–96. Two years later, some members of Congress denounced the use of funds to support Polish troops against the Red Army. See *Congressional Record*, Jan. 4, 1921, p. 922.

27. Hoover to Wilson, Feb. 6, 1919, PWW 54:515; Wilson to Hoover, Feb. 7, 1919, and Hoover to Secretary of War Newton Baker, Feb. 28, 1919, in O'Brien, *Two Peacemakers in Paris*, 63–64.

28. Minutes of the Daily Meetings of the Commissioners Plenipotentiary [hereafter Minutes of Commissioners], Feb. 20, Feb. 26, and March 20, 1919, Box 265, Tasker Bliss Papers.

29. "Note from American Delegates on Propositions in British Memorandum on Allied Economic Policy in Russia," Supreme Economic Council, June 10, 1919, ARA Papers, Russian Operations, Box 19, Folder 6, HIA; Norman Davis to Wilson, May 9, 1919, enclosing Leffingwell to Davis, May 7, 1919, PWW 58:595.

30. Hoover to Wilson, June 21 and 22, 1919, *Two Peacemakers in Paris*, 186–89.

31. Notes of a Meeting of the Heads of Delegations, July 8, 1919, PPC, 7:48–49.

32. Fourteen Points speech, Jan. 8, 1918, PWW 45:537; Grayson Diary, March 29, 1919, PWW 56:407.

33. Davison, *American Red Cross*, 265–78; editorial in *The World's Work* 40, no. 3 (July 1920); Wardwell Diary, Nov. 12, 1918.

34. Baer, *A Question of Trust*, 53, 38, 12, 17–18, 24; Representatives of Lithuanian Estate to ARC Captain C. S. Paine, 26.4.1919; Memorandum from Lt. Col. E. W. Ryan to Captain A. E. Franklin, ARC, Reval, May 25, 1919, both in file 949.4, Box 874, American National Red Cross Papers, RG 200, NA; Ryan to John Gade, Dec. 18, 1919, File 814.2, Vol. 6, American Mission, Riga, RG 84, NA; Minutes of Commissioners, April 12, 1919, Box 265, Bliss Papers. The Soviet government protested the Allied and American encouragement of POWs to join White forces. DVP, 2:37–38, 296–97.

35. Fike, "The Influence of the Creel Committee and the American Red Cross on Russian-American Relations, 1917–1919," 107–8; Dulles, *American Red Cross*, 211; Telegram from Captain Russell, June 22, 1919, June 24, file 949.08, Box 874, RG 200, NA; Lt. Col. Edward W. Ryan to Iudenich, Nov. 19, 1919, Box 6, Iudenich Papers, HIA. For lists of materials the Northwestern Army received from the ARC, see Box 8, Folder 6, Iudenich Collection.

36. Memorandum by Messrs. Hoover, Davis, and Cotton, "Analysis and Comparison of the Plans of President Wilson and the Plans of the Allied Representatives," [c. Dec. 13, 1918] PPC, 2:659; Hoover to Acting Food Administrator Rickard, Jan. 4 and 5, 1919, PPC 2:703–5; Col. O. N. Solbert to Bliss, April 28, 1919, PPC, 12:152; Hoover remarks to Council of Foreign Ministers, May 9, 1919, PPC, 4:689; Hoover to Groome, May 20, 1919, *Documents of the American Relief Administration European Operations* [*Documents of ARA*], 16:354.

37. "Proposed Statement Regarding Russian Situation," enclosed with Lansing to Wil-

son, Nov. 21, 1918, PWW 53:151–53; Polk to Lansing, Jan. 6; Lansing to Wilson, Jan. 9; Wilson to Lansing, Jan. 10, 1919, PWW 53:627, 706, 709; Gordon Auchincloss Diary, Feb. 17, 1919.

38. April 9, 1919, letter to Nansen, in Nansen to Lenin, April 17, 1919, PWW 57:438–39; House Diary, April 19, 1919; Hoover to House, April 19, 1919, enclosing statement dated April 18, PWW 57:503–8; Wilson to Hoover, April 23, 1919, PWW 58:41–42; *Two Peacemakers in Paris*, 125–32. For a detailed discussion, see Thompson, *Russia, Bolshevism, and the Versailles Peace*, 251–54.

39. House Diary, April 5, 1919.

40. Hoover to Wilson, March 28, 1919, PWW 56:375–78; Hoover statement of April 21, 1919, PWW 58:42; "Hoover Press Statement," April 19, 1919, Box 19, Folder 6, ARA Papers, Russian Operations, HIA.

41. Schulte Nordholt, *Wilson*, 308–9; Link, PWW 57:505n.; viii.

42. Mantoux's Notes of a Meeting of the Council of Four, April 9, 1919, PWW 57:165; April 9 letter to Nansen in Hoover, *Memoirs*, 416; "Hoover Press Statement," April 19, 1919, ARA Papers, HIA. For the contrary view that the plan was to send food "to Russia through the Bolshevik government," see PWW 57:viii; 505n.

43. Thompson, *Russia*, 252–55; Bullitt draft of a letter to Nansen, April 7, 1919, PWW 57:93–94; letter to Nansen, April 9, 1919, Hoover, *Memoirs*, 416; Vance McCormick Diary, April 21, 1919, HIA.

44. Chicherin to Nansen, relayed by Nansen to Hoover, May 14, 1919, PPC, 5:743–47; Notes of a Meeting of the Council of Four, May 20, 1919, PWW 59:301.

45. Lansing Desk Diary, April 19, 1919 (noting Bakhmeteff's opposition to a "bargain as to cessation of hostilities"); Gilbert Close, Memorandum for the President, c. April 17, 1919, PWW 57:440; Thompson, *Russia*, 260; House Diary, March 25, 1919; Rickard to American mission, Paris, April 30, 1919, Box 19, Folder 6, ARA Russian Operations, HIA; Vance McCormick Diary, April 24 and May 7, 1919, HIA.

46. Message from Greene, April 12, PPC, 12:139–41; American mission to Greene, May 26, 1919, PPC, 12:197–98; Hoover to Heath, May 26, 1919, Box 326, Herbert Hoover Papers, HIA; PPC, 4:756.

47. Col. C. Krusenstein [*sic*] to ARA, Reval, May 19, 1919, *Documents of ARA*, 15:189–91; Hoover announcement, May 1919, Box 19, Folder 6, ARA Russian Operations, ARA Papers, HIA.

48. Report by John Gade, endorsed by Warwick Greene and sent to Paris on May 3, 1919, PPC, 12:154–72, quoted at 155–56; Greene to Grew, July 9, 1919, PPC, 12:213–15; Hoover for Groome, July 7, 1919, *Documents of ARA*, 17:172; Phillips to Commission to Negotiate Peace, Sept. 20, 1919, *FRUS, Russia, 1919*, 712; Minutes of Commissioners, Sept. 26, 1919, Box 265, Bliss Papers.

49. Lansing to Wilson, Nov. 26, 1918, PPC, 1:270–71; Greene to Commission to Negotiate Peace, April 13 and 22, 1919; Greene to Mr. Andreas Needra, May 1, 1919, PPC, 12:139–41, 144–47, 182–83.

50. Vance McCormick Diary, May 7, 1919, HIA; Memorandum of May 7, 1919, Hoover, *Memoirs*, 373.

51. Hoover to Wilson, May 9, 1919, in *Two Peacemakers*, 149–51.

52. Hoover, *Ordeal*, 129.

53. Wilson to Hoover, May 21, 1919, PWW 59:347; Hankey's Notes of a Meeting of the Council of Four, May 20, 1919, PWW 59:303–4; PPC, 5:737; Hoover, *Ordeal*, 130; PPC, 12:197.

54. Crowell to Secretary of State, April 30, 1919, *FRUS, 1919, Russia*, 675; Polk to American mission, Paris, May 13, 1919, file 861.24/139, NA; Notes of a Meeting of Foreign Ministers, May 23, 1919, PPC, 4:752–63; Hankey's Notes of a Meeting of the Council of Four,

May 24, 1919, PWW 59:465–67; American mission Paris to Polk, May 24, 1919, SD file 861.24/148, NA; PPC, 11:182; *FRUS, 1919, Russia*, 678.

55. Mantoux's Notes of a Meeting of the Council of Four, June 13, 1919, PWW 60:500; Hankey's Notes, June 13, 1919, PWW 60:498.

56. Leffingwell to Secretary of State, June 21, 1918, Folder 98: Trade with Russia Prohibited, Box 186, RG 39, NA; Gaworek, "Allied Economic Warfare Against Soviet Russia," 200–206; Gaworek, "From Blockade to Trade."

57. PWW 45:536.

58. Memorandum by Bullitt, c. March 28, 1919, PWW 56:387–91; Notes of a Meeting of the Council of Four, March 27, 1919, PWW 56:328.

59. Vance McCormick Diary, March 15, 19, and 28, 1919, HIA; Lansing Desk Diary, March 28, 1919; Notes of a Meeting of the Council of Foreign Ministers, March 28, 1919, PPC, 4:522–35; April 19, 1919, PPC, IV, 585–93. On Feb. 16, 1919, Gordon Auchincloss and Sir William Wiseman envisioned "Drawing an economic cordon around Russia." Auchincloss Diary.

60. Wilson remarks quoted in Diary of William Bullitt, Dec. 9 [10], 1918, PWW 53:350–51; Isaiah Bowman, "Memorandum on Remarks by the President to Members of the Inquiry on December 10, 1918," PWW 53:354–55.

61. Hankey's Notes of a Meeting of the Council of Four, May 9, 1919, 10:30 a.m., PWW 58:563–54; PPC, 5:521–22.

62. Note from SEC for Council of Heads of States, in Vance McCormick to Wilson, June 7, 1919, PWW 60:281–82; Notes of a Meeting of the Council of Four, June 17, 1919, PWW 60:624–26.

63. Notes of a Meeting of the Council of Four, June 17, 1919, PWW 60:624–26; see also 639.

64. Notes of a Press Conference by W. E. Weyl, June 27, 1919, PWW 61:240–45.

65. Carter Glass to Wilson, Aug. 25, 1919, PWW 62:498–99; War Trade Board Resolution 802, July 14, 1919, PWW 62:424.

66. White to Wilson, July 27, 1919, PWW 62:14–16.

67. Lansing to Wilson, with instruction to the American Commission, Aug. 1, 1919, PWW 62:108–10; Notes of a Meeting of the Heads of Delegations, Aug. 8, 1919, PPC, 7:634–35.

68. Lansing to Wilson, Aug. 1, 1919, PWW 62:108–10; Diary entries for Aug. 18, 19, and 23, 1919, Box 278, John Foster Dulles Papers; Dulles to Polk, Aug. 18, 1919, Box 33, Polk Papers; Polk to Lansing, Oct. 1, 1919, *FRUS, 1919, Russia*, 159–60; Phillips to Polk, Sept. 9, 1919; Phillips to Senator Wadsworth, Nov. 1, 1919, *FRUS, 1919, Russia*, 157, 161; Phillips to Senator Lenroot, Sept. 13, 1919, *FRUS, 1919, Russia*, 158.

69. Notes of a Meeting of the Council of Four, June 17, 1919, PWW 60:621; Lansing to British Chargé Lindsay, Jan. 10, 1920, *FRUS, 1919, Russia*, 163; Cronon, *Cabinet Diaries of Josephus Daniels*, 526. In June 1920 Wilson decided that formal restrictions on trade with Russia should be lifted, though businessmen should be warned not to expect any government aid. Norman Davis to Bainbridge Colby, June 25, 1920, Davis Papers. On State Department hindrance of trade with Soviet Russia after July 1920, see J. Hoff Wilson, *Ideology and Economics*, 35–36.

70. Wilson remarks of March 27, 1919, PWW 56:328–29; Wilson comments on June 13, 1919, PWW 60:499.

71. Minutes of a Meeting of the Council of Ten, Feb. 15, 1919, PPC, 4:10–11; Chargé in Denmark to Acting Secretary of State, Feb. 20, 1919; Acting Secretary of State to Ambassador in France, March 18, 1919, *FRUS, 1919, Russia*, 669, 674.

72. Imbrie to Acting Secretary of State, March 2, 1919, *FRUS, 1919, Russia*, 670.

73. Consul at Helsingfors to Acting Secretary of State, March 6, 1919; Polk to Imbrie,

March 8, 1919, *FRUS, 1919, Russia,* 671, 673. See also PPC, 4:664.

74. Hoover to Wilson, April 26, 1919, *Two Peacemakers,* 142–43; Hoover, *Memoirs,* 363–67; Hoover, *Ordeal,* 124–27; Link, *Deliberations of the Council of Four,* 1:399; Samuel Eliot Morison Diary, Feb. 28, 1919 and Morsion to Thornwell Haynes, May 15, 1919, Morison Papers. See also PWW 58:177, 319, 404; and PPC, 4:664.

75. Smith, *Finland,* 134–52. On Iudenich's background, see Drujina, "History of the North-West Army," 29–37.

76. Hoover to American Consul Helsingfors, July 2, 1919, Box 326, Hoover Papers, HIA; Telegram to Hoover from Heath, sent as Haynes to American mission, Paris, June 21, 1919, Box 326, Hoover Papers, HIA; Imbrie to Acting Secretary of State, July 2, 1919, *FRUS, 1919, Russia,* 683; Notes of a Meeting of Heads of Delegations, PPC, 7:38–39; see also Peace Commission to Acting Secretary of State, July 16, 1919, *FRUS, 1919, Russia,* 691. On British and American reluctance to push the Finns into a risky operation, see Morison Diary, May 30, June 3, and July 17, 1919.

77. Smith, *Finland,* 154–58; *FRUS, 1919, Russia,* 707; Virmavirta, "Karl Gustav Emil' Mannergeim," 64.

78. Gade to Polk, Oct. 23, 1919, File 124.6, and Gade to Norman Hapgood, American Minister to Denmark, Nov. 1, 1919, File 800, Vol. 6, American Mission, Riga, Gade, RG 84, NA; Haynes to Lansing, Nov. 3, 1919; Lansing to the Chargé in Sweden, Nov. 5, 1919, *FRUS, 1919, Russia,* 735–37.

79. Fourteen Points speech, PWW 45:537; Lippmann-Cobb Memorandum, enclosed in House to Wilson, Oct. 29, 1918, PWW 51:498–99; Unfug, "German Policy," 86–119.

80. *New York Herald,* Sept. 6, 1918; Wilson to Lansing, Nov. 20, 1918, PPC, 1:268–70; Article 433, PPC, 13:726 and PPC, 12:225. Wilson discussed drafts of the article with Clemenceau and Lloyd George on May 3, 1919. See PWW 58:390–403. Before the Armistice, anti-Bolshevik Russians had called for the evacuation of German troops. See *FRUS, 1918, Supplement 1,* 1:356, 435–38.

81. PPC, 2:467–68, 480–81, 485; *FRUS, 1918, Russia,* 2:838–55; Waite, *Vanguard of Nazism,* 100–104.

82. Cronon, *Cabinet Diaries of Josephus Daniels,* Oct. 21, 1918, pp. 342–43; "Memorandum on Absolutism and Bolshevism," Oct. 26, 1918, Lansing Papers, LC.

83. Notes of a Meeting of the Council of Four, March 29, 1919, PWW 56:413.

84. Minutes of the Commissioners, March 3, 1919, Box 265, Bliss Papers; PPC, 11:89–90; Greene to Paris, April 11, 1919, PPC, 12:138–39; Remarks of Balfour, April 16, 1919, PWW 57:392.

85. Greene message of April 20, 1919, PPC, 12:141–44; Waite, *Vanguard of Nazism,* 111–15; Vance McCormick Diary, April 19, 1919, HIA; Notes of a Meeting of Foreign Ministers, April 19, 1919, PPC, 4:593; Col. O. N. Solbert to Bliss, April 28, 1919, PPC, 12:150–53; Hoover, *Ordeal,* 131; Hoover, *Memoirs,* 372–73; R. H. Lord and S. E. Morison memorandum for the Commissioners Plenipotentiary, April 23, 1919, PPC, 12:147–50; April 20, 1919 message from Greene, PPC, 12:144–47.

86. Col. O. N. Solbert to General Bliss, April 28, 1919, PPC, 12:150–53; Notes of a Meeting of Foreign Ministers, May 9, 1919, PPC, 4:690–91.

87. Hoover, *Memoirs,* 374–76; Hoover, *Ordeal,* 131, 132; Warwick Greene report, June 3, 1919, *FRUS, 1919, Russia,* 679–80. Whatever messages Hoover may have sent had little influence on von der Goltz, who had long been determined to recapture Riga. See von der Goltz, *Meine Sendung,* 191–97; Waite, *Vanguard of Nazism,* 114–18; Williams, "Die Politick der Alliierten," esp. 158; Hiden, *Baltic States.*

88. Notes of a Meeting of Foreign Ministers, May 23, 1919, PPC, 4:748–62.

89. Notes of a Meeting of the Council of Four, June 13, 1919, PWW 60:498–500; Recommendation by Commission on Baltic Affairs, June 7, 1919, PWW 61:161–63; Greene to

Grew, June 28, 1919, *FRUS, 1919, Russia,* 682–83. See also Dawley to Grew, June 22, 1919, PPC, 12:202–6; Morison Diary, June 16, 1919.

90. Wilson discussion with Lloyd George, June 12, 1919, PWW 60:475; PPC, 7:41, 48, 405, 428, 557–58; PPC, 8:204, 793–94; PPC, 13:743; Notes of a Meeting of the Heads of Delegations, Sept. 18, 1919, PPC, 8:257; Memorandum to J. C. Grew by R. Tyler, Oct. 2, 1919, File 820, RG 84, NA. Waite, *Vanguard of Nazism,* 122–30; Page, *Formation of the Baltic States,* 160–65; Sullivan, "1919 German Campaign," 33–40. John Gade hoped "rebellious Russians under Bermont may be induced to . . . join Yudenitch's forces." Gade to Polk, Oct. 23, 1919, File 824.6, Vol. 6, American Mission, Riga, RG 84, NA.

91. Notes of a Meeting of the Heads of Delegations, Sept. 18, 1919, PPC, 8:254–58; A. W. Dulles Memorandum for Mr. Dresel, Oct. 22, 1919, Box 6, Allen Dulles Papers.

92. On the manipulative Soviet nationality policy in relation to the Baltic region, see Degras, *Soviet Documents,* 1:157–58, 171–75; Debo, *Survival and Consolidation,* 97–102.

93. Memorandum for Mr. Dresel, Oct. 22, 1919, Box 6, Allen Dulles Papers; Samuel Eliot Morison Diary, Feb. 12 note and Feb. 19, 1919, entry; House Diary, Oct. 28, 1918. For further discussion, see Fike, "United States and Russian Territorial Problems"; Killen, "Self-Determination vs. Territorial Integrity," 78.

94. Lansing to Samuel Eliot Morison, May 31, 1921, Morison Papers.

95. House Diary, Sept. 19, 1918.

96. Fourteen Points speech, Jan. 8, 1918, PWW 45:537; Lippmann-Cobb Memorandum, enclosed in House to Wilson, Oct. 29, 1918; Wilson to House, Oct. 30, 1918, PWW 51:498–99, 511.

97. Wilson to Lansing, Nov. 20, 1918; Lansing to Wilson, Nov. 26, 1918, PPC, Vol. 1:268–71. See also *FRUS, 1918, Russia,* 2:852, 856.

98. Diary of Dr. Grayson, Dec. 8, 1918, PWW 53:338.

99. Lord and Morison to the Commissioners Plenipotentiary, April 23, 1919, PPC, 12:147–50.

100. Lansing to Wilson, May 27, 1919, and summary of Morison to Lansing, May 26, 1919, PWW 59:547–49; PPC, 4:667; Morison Diary, March 13, 1919, note; Morison to Grew, June 15, 1919, PPC, 11:591. See also Morison Diary, June 12–16 and "Memoranda-1919."

101. Bliss to Bakhmeteff, July 4, 1919; Bakhmeteff to Bliss, July 8, 1919, *FRUS, 1919, Russia,* 683–87; Kolchak to Clemenceau, June 4, 1919, PWW 60:141–44.

102. Secretary of State to Commission to Negotiate Peace, Oct. 15, 1919, *FRUS, 1919, Russia,* 723–24; Minutes of the Commissioners, June 30 and July 2, 1919, Box 265, Bliss Papers; PPC, Vol. 11:261–64.

103. Lt. Robert Hale, "Report of the Mission to Finland, Esthonia, Latvia, and Lithuania on the Situation in the Baltic Provinces," Paris, July 23, 1919, Document No. 105, *Senate Documents,* Vol. 15, 66th Cong., 1st sess., 6, 8; Hoover, *Ordeal,* 130, 127. See also A. A. Berle Jr., "American Economic Intervention in Russia," Dec. 10, 1918, PPC, Vol. 2:471; PPC, 1:65; Gelfand, *Inquiry,* 211.

104. Ullman, *Britain and the Russian Civil War,* 269; Russian Embassy to Department of State, Aug. 29, 1919, *FRUS, 1919, Russia,* 705–6; Russian Embassy to Department of State, Sept. 18, 1919, *FRUS, 1919, Russia,* 710–11.

105. Records of Bakhmeteff meetings with Miles, Phillips, and Long, Sept.-Oct. 1919, Box 36, Bakhmeteff Papers; Secretary of State to Commission to Negotiate Peace, Oct. 15, 1919, *FRUS, 1919, Russia,* 723–24; Phillips to Davis, Oct. 23, 1919, *FRUS, 1919, Russia,* 727–28.

106. Greene to Grew, June 30 and July 5, 1919, PPC 12:207–12, 213–15. For a similar recommendation, see Dawley to Commission to Negotiate Peace, July 19, 1919, PPC, 12:217–22.

107. Minutes of the Commissioners, July 1, 1919, Box 265, Bliss Papers; Grew Diary, Oct. 8, 1919.

108. Bliss to Bakhmeteff, July 4, 1919, Box 1, Bakhmeteff Papers.

109. Bakhmeteff to Bliss, July 8, 1919, Bakhmeteff Papers; *FRUS, 1919, Russia,* 684–87.

110. Minutes of the Commissioners, July 11 and 15, 1919, Bliss Papers.

111. Lansing to Imbrie, July 25, 1919, *FRUS, 1919, Russia,* 692–93.

112. Bliss Diary, July 23 and 29, 1919.

113. Bakhmeteff to Lansing, Aug. 4, 1919, Box 5, Bakhmeteff Papers; *FRUS, 1919, Russia,* 696–98; Lansing Desk Diary, Aug. 4, 1919. On the tense relations with Congress, see PWW 61:353, 579–82; Breckinridge Long Diary, Aug. 29 and 30, 1919.

114. Ellis Loring Dresel to Frederic Dolbeare, Aug. 14, 1919, Dresel Papers; Minutes of Commissioners, Aug. 11, 1919, Box 265, Bliss Papers; also in Box 326, Hoover Papers, HIA; PPC, 11:375–76; Minutes of the Commissioners, Aug. 12, 1919, Box 265, Bliss Papers; Telegram prepared by Bliss, sent as Polk to Secretary of State, Aug. 12, 1919, *FRUS, 1919, Russia,* 700–701; Memorandum from Lt. Col. Dawley to Chief of the Diplomatic Section, Russian North-Western Army, July 28, 1919, Box 13, Iudenich Collection; Telegram from Reval to American mission, Paris, Oct. 20, 1919, Box 18, Folder 119, Iudenich Collection, HIA.

115. Baron Schilling to Polk, Aug. 20, Polk to Bliss, Aug. 26, Memorandum for Polk, Aug. 28, and Polk to Schilling, Aug. 29, 1919, Box 33, Folder 699, and Box 2, Folder 58, Polk Papers; Grew Diary, Oct. 2, 1919; Grew, *Turbulent Era,* 397–400; Polk Diary, Oct. 8, 1919; Notes of a Meeting of Heads of Delegations, Oct. 11, 1919, PPC, 8:580–81; Bliss to Polk, Oct. 12, 1919, Box 2, Folder 59, Polk Papers.

116. Special Agreement between ARA and Provisional Government of Russia, July 16, 1919, Box 18, Iudenich Collection; *FRUS, 1919, Russia,* 693–96; Commission to Negotiate Peace to Secretary of State, Aug. 12, 1919, *FRUS, 1919, Russia,* 700.

117. *FRUS, 1919, Russia,* 700; see also Hoover to Secretary of State, received Aug. 7, 1919; Imbrie to Secretary of State, Aug. 13, 1919, *FRUS, 1919, Russia,* 698–99, 701; Hoover, *Memoirs,* 418–19.

118. Anonymous memorandum, c. July 1919, Box 18, Folder 119, Iudenich Collection; Aug. 6, 1919, letter by Major General Krusenstiern, Box 13, Iudenich Collection; Van Arsdale Turner, "Feeding the Russian Northwestern Army," *Documents of ARA,* 15:181–88; Sazonov to Iudenich, June 27, 1919, quoted in Drujina, "The History of the North-West Army of General Yudenich," 130; Hoover for Groome for Powers, July 7, 1919, *Documents of ARA,* 17:172; Major-General Rodzianko to Hoover, in C. Krusenstiern to E. Howell Foreman of the ARA, Reval, July 26, 1919, Box 13, Iudenich Collection, HIA; Bakhmeteff to Lansing, Aug. 4, 1919, *FRUS, 1919, Russia,* 696–98.

119. "Report of the operations of the Baltic Mission," May 15 to Aug. 1, 1919, by John C. Groome, Box 19, ARA Papers, European Operations, HIA; Sazonov to Iudenich, Aug. 18, 1919, Iudenich Collection, cited in Drujina, "The History of the North-West Army of General Yudenich," 130; Lansing to Hoover, Aug. 25, 1919, *FRUS, 1919, Russia,* 705.

120. Hoover to Lansing, Aug. 30, 1919, *FRUS, 1919, Russia,* 707.

121. Breckinridge Long Diary, Sept. 4, 1919.

122. Wilson address, Sept. 9, 1919, PWW 63:134; Lansing to Bakhmeteff, Sept. 4, 1919, enclosing Lansing to Shipping Board, Box 22, Russia Posol'stvo (U.S.) Papers, HIA; Phillips to Commission to Negotiate Peace, Sept. 9, 1919, *FRUS, 1919, Russia,* 709.

123. Mawdsley, *Russian Civil War,* 199; Lincoln, *Red Victory,* 295–97.

124. Polk Diary, Sept. 26, 1919; Polk to Secretary of State, Sept. 29, 1919; Phillips to Polk, Oct. 2, 1919, *FRUS, 1919, Russia,* 714, 721.

125. Lansing Desk Diary, Nov. 3, 1919; Commission to Negotiate Peace to Acting Secretary of State, Oct. 23, 1919, *FRUS, 1919, Russia,* 729–31; Polk Diary, Oct. 22, 1919.

126. Imbrie to Secretary of State, Oct. 18, 1919; Commission to Negotiate Peace to Acting Secretary of State, Oct. 23, 1919, *FRUS, 1919, Russia,* 725, 729–31.

127. Lansing, "Memorandum to Be Read to the President," Oct. 22, 1919, PWW 63:588–89; letter from Wilson to Barnes, President of the Grain Corporation, Oct. 22, 1919, PWW 63:589–90; Lansing Desk Diary, Oct. 21 and 22, 1919.

128. PWW 63:590n. (cf. *FRUS, 1919, Russia,* 733); Phillips to Senator Wadsworth, Nov. 1, 1919, *FRUS, 1919, Russia,* 161–62; Commission to Negotiate Peace to Acting Secretary of State, Oct. 23, 1919; Phillips to Commission, Oct. 25, 1919, *FRUS, 1919, Russia,* 729–31, 733.

129. Gade to Polk, Oct. 23, 1919, File 124.6; Col. T. W. Hollyday to Gade, Dec. 15, 1919, File 127, File 800; Gade to Secretary of State, Nov. 27, 1919, File 820, Vol. 6, American Mission, Riga, RG 84. See also Nov. 24 entry in the diary of Gade's secretary, Maj. Edward Peck Curtis.

130. Lansing Desk Diary, Dec. 13, 1919; Lansing to Gade, Dec. 15, 1919, *FRUS, 1919, Russia,* 748–49.

131. Gade to Col. Krusenstiern, Jan. 4, 1920; Iudenich to Gade, Nov. 26, 1919, Box 8, Folder 8; Gade to Col. Krusenstiern, Dec. 2, 1919, Box 8, Folder 48. There are lists of materials received in these papers.

132. Gade to Secretary of State, Nov. 15, 1919, File 800, Volume 6, American Mission, Riga, RG 84, NA; Lincoln, *Red Victory,* 285–98; Mawdsley, *Russian Civil War,* 197–201; Drujina, "History of the North-West Army," esp. 37, 39, 87, 140–43; Gade, "Russia from Its Baltic Window," 56.

133. Mawdsley, *Russian Civil War,* 197; Gade to Secretary of State, Dec. 18, 1919, File 800, Volume 6, American Mission, Riga, RG 84. See also Edward Peck Curtis Diary, Dec. 3, 1919; Drujina, "History of the North-West Army," 130.

134. Gade to Secretary of State, Dec. 18, 1919, RG 84, NA. See also Gade, "Inside Red Russia," 237.

135. See Mayer, *Politics and Diplomacy of Peacemaking;* Rothbard, "Hoover's 1919 Food Diplomacy in Retrospect," in Gelfand, *Herbert Hoover;* Hopkins, "Politics of Food"; Smallwood, "Banquo's Ghost," 289–307; and Chavez, "Hoover and Food Relief."

CHAPTER NINE

1. Nation, *Black Earth, Red Star,* 2, 6, 10; Carr, *Bolshevik Revolution,* 17–18; Cohen, *Bukharin and the Bolshevik Revolution,* 66.

2. For a different view, see Kennan, *Russia Leaves the War,* 31; Kennan, *Decision to Intervene,* 222–23, 133.

3. See, for example, Gvishiani, "Martens Mission"; Gvishiani, *Sovetskaia Rossiia,* esp. 4, 243, 314; Reikhberg and Shapik, "L. K. Martens," 98, 100.

4. On the relationship between Lenin and Chicherin, see Uldricks, *Diplomacy and Ideology,* 27–31; O'Connor, *Diplomacy and Revolution,* 49–50; Debo, *Revolution and Survival.*

5. Lenin, "The Results and Significance of the U.S. Presidential Elections," Nov. 9, 1912, *Collected Works,* 18:402–4; Lenin, remarks to correspondent of *The World,* Feb. 21, 1920, DVP, 2:380; Gromyko and Ponomarev, *Soviet Foreign Policy,* Vol. 1:79–80; Lenin, "A Caricature of Marxism," 1916, and "'Disgrace' as the Capitalists and the Proletarians Understand It," April 23 (May 6), 1917, *Collected Works,* 23:46–47, 24:221.

6. Lenin, report on foreign policy, May 14, 1918, and speech of Dec. 6, 1920, *Collected Works,* 27:367–68, 31:442–43; Meijer, *Trotsky Papers,* 1:623; Lenin, "The Successes of the American Workers," Sept. 1912, and "The Results and Significance of the U.S. Presidential Elections," Nov. 1912, *Collected Works,* 18:335–36, 402–4; Lenin, "A Caricature of Marx-

ism and Imperialist Economism," 1916, *Collected Works*, 23:44–46; Lenin, speech of Nov. 8, 1918, "The Valuable Admissions of Pitirim Sorokin," Nov. 20, 1918, and speech of Dec. 9, 1918, *Collected Works*, 28:151–64, 185–94, 334.

7. Trotsky report to the Central Executive Committee, Nov. 8 (21), 1917, and speech of Nov. 30, 1917, Degras, *Soviet Documents on Foreign Policy*, 1:4–8, 13; Trotsky to Chicherin, Jan. 31, 1918, Meijer, *Trotsky Papers*, 1:17–19.

8. Plan by the Commission on Foreign Trade of the Supreme Economic Council, May 12, 1918, DVP, 1:286–94. For different views of the plan, see McFadden, *Alternative Paths*, esp. 118–22; Kennan, *Decision to Intervene*, 221–25.

9. Foner, *Bolshevik Revolution*, 28–39, 56; Kostiainen, "Santeri Nuorteva and the Origins of Soviet-American Relations," 3, 6; Chicherin to Trotsky, Aug. 19, 1918, "secret," f. 5, op. 1, d. 2070, l. 3, Russian Center for the Preservation and Study of Documents of Contemporary History; Rosenstone, *Romantic Revolutionary*, esp. 325–30; Grubbs, *Struggle for Labor Loyalty*, 127–28.

10. Lenin, speech of July 29, 1918, *Collected Works*, 28:17–33; Degras, *Soviet Documents on Foreign Policy*, 1:103–4.

11. Jacobs, *Borodin*; Borodin to L. M. Karakhan, Sept. [Oct.] 2, 1918, f. 04, op. 3, d. 136, ll. 1–3, AVPRF.

12. Debo, *Revolution and Survival*, esp. 89, 297; Carr, *Bolshevik Revolution*, Vol. 3, esp. 88, 109; Lenin, "Letter to American Workers," Aug. 1918, *Selected Works*, 462; Chicherin report of Sept. 2, 1918, and circular note of Sept. 10, 1920, Degras, *Soviet Documents on Foreign Policy*, 1:101, 210; Chicherin to Wilson, Oct. 24, 1918, PWW 51:560–61.

13. "Resolution of the All-Russian Central Executive Committee on the International Situation," Oct. 3, 1918, Degras, *Soviet Documents on Foreign Policy*, 1:111–12; Chicherin to Wilson, Oct. 24, 1918, f. 129, op. 2, g. 1, AVPRF; PWW 51:555–61; Lenin, speeches of Nov. 6, Nov. 27, and Dec. 9, 1918, and "The Valuable Admissions of Pitirim Sorokin," Nov. 20, 1918, *Collected Works*, 28:149, 209, 234, 185–94.

14. Lenin, *Collected Works*, 28:102, 118–19, 132, 146, 159. See also Fischer, *Russia's Road*, 32.

15. Lenin, report of Nov. 27, 1918, speeches of Nov. 8 and Dec. 9, 1918, "The Valuable Admissions of Pitirim Sorokin," Nov. 20, 1918, speech of Dec. 14, 1918, *Collected Works*, 28:216, 161, 337, 188, 331, 156, 218, 152, 162, 354–62, 151.

16. Volkogonov, *Lenin*, 391–92; Degras, *Soviet Documents on Foreign Policy*, 136–37.

17. Lenin, speech of Dec. 14, 1918, *Collected Works*, 28:360.

18. "K Voprosu o Nashikh Snosheniiakh s Soedinennymi Shtatami Ameriki," Jan. 1, 1919, f. 130 (Sovnarkom), op. 3, d. 177, ll. 147–48, GARF. On the Soviet loss of Perm on Dec. 24, 1918, see Lincoln, *Red Victory*, 249–50.

19. Lansing to Wilson, Nov. 21, 1918, PWW 53:151–52; Chicherin note of Dec. 2, 1918, DVP, 1:593–95; Debo, *Survival and Consolidation*, 22–26; McFadden, *Alternative Paths*, 175–80; Litvinov to Wilson, Dec. 24, 1918, PWW 53:492–94.

20. Notes of meetings of Council of Ten, Jan. 21 and 22, 1919, PWW 54:183, 204–5.

21. Samuel Eliot Morison Diary, note to entry for March 5, 1919 (see also entries for Feb. 12 and 20, 1919); Hankey's Notes of a Meeting of the Council of Ten, Feb. 1, 1919, PWW 54:415; News Report of a Press Conference, Feb. 14, 1919, PWW 55:161; Wilson remarks to Democratic Committee, Feb. 28, 1919, PWW 55:319; Chicherin reply to the Prinkipo proposal, Feb. 4, 1919, in Degras, *Soviet Documents on Foreign Policy*, 1:137–39. For a different view, see McFadden, *Alternative Paths*, 201.

22. Lenin, speech of Dec. 14, 1918, *Collected Works*, 28:356; Bullitt to Lansing and House, March 10, 1919, f. 04, op. 3, d. 121, ll. 11–12, AVPRF; Bullitt to Wilson, Lansing, and House, March 16, 1919, PWW 55:540–45; Phillips, *Between the Revolution and the West*, 35; Lenin, answers to an American journalist's questions, July 20, 1919, *Collected Works*, 29:517; William Phillips's acid comments to Lansing, March 25, 1919,

PWW 56:548–50.

23. Lenin, speech of Jan. 17, 1919, and "Letter to Workers of Europe and America," Jan. 21, 1919, *Collected Works*, Vol. 28:397, 435.

24. Chicherin to Secretary of State, Jan. 12, 1919, f. 129, op. 3, p. 2, d. 1, ll. 4–5, AVPRF; DVP, 2:24–26.

25. "K Voprosu o Programme Deiatel'nosti Sovetskavo Pravitel'stva Soedinennikh Shtatov," Jan. 15, 1919, f. 130, op. 3, d. 177, ll. 151–52, GARF.

26. Attorney General Palmer charge at a cabinet meeting, April 14, 1920, PWW 65:186–87; *FRUS, 1919, Russia*, 147; White, "'Riches Have Wings,'" 129–30. Strakhovsky, *American Opinion About Russia*, 88, concurred with the indictment.

27. Nuorteva statements of May 3 and June 16, 1919, Russian Soviet Bureau Seized Files, Folder 22; Gvishiani, "The Martens Mission," 62; Reikhberg and Shapik, "L. K. Martens."

28. Chicherin to Martens, Dec. 17, 1920, f. 129, op. 4, d. 6; Statement by the People's Commissary for Foreign Affairs, Jan. 15, 1920, f. 04, op. 3, d. 123, l. 175; Draft of Chicherin to Central Executive Committee of Russian Federation, Aug. 28, 1919, f. 04, op. 3, d. 123, l. 70, AVPRF. See also Martens to Senator Wadsworth, Nov. 5, 1919, *Soviet Russia*, Nov. 15, 1919, p. 14; N.K.I.D. to Martens, Jan. 16, 1920, f. 04, op. 3, d. 123, l. 74, AVPRF.

29. "Bolshevist Fund Here: Federal Officials Report Lenine Sent $500,000 for Propaganda," *New York Times*, Jan. 7, 1919; New York State, *Revolutionary Radicalism*, 1:646; Murray, *Red Scare*, 47–48; Kostiainen, "Santeri Nuorteva and the Origins of Soviet-American Relations," 5, 9–10. See also McFadden, *Alternative Paths*, 276–77, 406 n.66.

30. Dubrovsky to Moscow, deciphered Sept. 25, 1919; Martens to Reinstein for Chicherin, March 11, 1919; Martens to Chicherin, April 5, 1919, Martens to Chicherin, July 2, 1919, f. 04, op. 3, d. 122, ll. 34, 36–37, 74–75, 80, AVPRF; Martens to Chicherin, July 24, 1919, Nuorteva to Martens, July 2, 1919, f. 04, op. 3, d. 123, ll. 17 and 39–41; Roy, "Michel Borodine en Amerique (1919)," 112; Jacobs, *Borodin*, 65, 72; Draper, *Roots of American Communism*, 236–41; Litvinov to Martens, May 27, 1919, f. 04, op. 3, d. 122, l. 68, AVPRF. (This section of the letter was not printed in DVP, 2:176–77.) Martens told the Lusk Committee that he received $50,000 from Soviet Russia between March and July 1919. New York State, *Revolutionary Radicalism*, 1:655. Lenin later acknowledged that Martens desperately needed the $7,000 provided by a sympathetic American manufacturer. Lenin to Emerson Jennings, April 5, 1921, *Leninskii Sbornik*, 39:281.

31. Martens to "Dear Comrades," Jan. 28, 191[9], f. 04, op. 3, d. 122, ll. 1–4, AVPRF; Cook, *Crystal Eastman*, 294–302.

32. Nuorteva announcement, March 1919, Box 1, Folder 16, Russian Soviet Bureau Seized Files.

33. Folders 21 (Socialists) and 23 (Sympathizers), Russian Soviet Bureau Seized Files; Martens to "Dear Comrades," Jan. 28, 191[9], f. 04, op. 3, d. 122, ll. 1–4, AVPRF; "Soviet Russia Appeals to Workingmen in Allied Countries [reproduction of Chicherin proclamation of April 22, 1919]," Russian Soviet Bureau Seized Files, Folder 18.

34. Riddell, *Founding the Communist International*, 79; Draper, *Roots of American Communism*, 148–53; Lenin, *Collected Works*, 29:20, 145, 258, 284. For more on Soviet leaders and revolution in America, see Lazitch and Drachkovitch, *Lenin and the Comintern*, 47, 143, 153, 379. As late as October 1920 Lenin believed American workers and farmers were moving toward Communism. Interview with S. Kh. Agurskii, *Leninskii Sbornik*, 39:248.

35. Lenin, *Collected Works*, 29:197, 146–53.

36. Ray Stannard Baker Diary, March 29, 1919, PWW 56:425; Wilson to Tumulty, July 17, 1919, PWW 61:509; Priezd Bullitta v RSFSR, f. 04, op. 3, d. 121, AVPRF; Bullitt and Freud, *Thomas Woodrow Wilson*, 253, 271–72; Tumulty to Wilson, April 2, 1919, PWW 56:551; Samuel Eliot Morison Diary, April 3 and 9, 1919; Debo, *Survival and Consolidation*, 44–50; McFadden, *Alternative Paths*, 218–43; Lenin, *Collected Works*,

29:195, 244, 258, 306, 284.

37. Martens message in Phillips to Lansing, March 25, 1919, PWW 56:548–50; American-Russian Chamber of Commerce *Service Bulletin*, May 14, 1919, f. 507, op. 5, g. 17, ll. 1–4, AVPRF; *FRUS, 1919, Russia*, 133–44; War Trade Board to Ughet, May 1, 1919, with "stock letter" to businessmen ("not for publication"), Box 96, Folder 10, Russia Posol'stvo (U.S.) Papers, HIA.

38. Martens to Moscow, April 5, 1919, f. 04, op. 3, d. 122, ll. 36–37, AVPRF.

39. Litvinov to Martens, May 27, 1919, f. 04, op. 3, d. 122, ll. 68–70, AVPRF. On Stalin's similar suspicion, see "Imperialism's Reserves," March 16, 1919, *J. V. Stalin: Works*, Vol. 4:254–57. On the clandestine reports from Paris, see unsigned letter of April 30, 1919, apparently by Lincoln Steffens, sent by courier, f. 04, op. 3, d. 121, ll. 28–29, AVPRF; message from Bullitt in Shklovsky to Chicherin, April 17, 1919, f. 04, op. 3, d. 127, l. 30.

40. Trotsky to Skliansky, June 1, 1919, *Trotsky Papers*, 1:507; Report to Martens by the Diplomatic Department, July 7, 1919, f. 04, op. 3, d. 123, ll. 7 and 48, AVPRF.

41. Nuorteva report to Martens, Aug. 7, 1919, f. 04, op. 3, d. 123, ll. 45–47, AVPRF; Litvinov to Martens, May 27, 1919, f. 04, op. 3, d. 122, ll. 68–70, AVPRF; DVP, 2:176–77.

42. Martens to Chicherin, July 2, 1919, f. 04, op. 3, d. 122, ll. 74–75, AVPRF. On the AFL see Grubbs, *Struggle for Labor Loyalty*, 134–35; Foner, *Bolshevik Revolution*, 36–37.

43. Martens to "Dear Comrades," Aug. 7, 1919, f. 04, op. 3, d. 123, l. 63, AVPRF; DVP, 2:234–35.

44. Lenin, *Collected Works*, 30:50, 30, 39.

45. Nuorteva report to Martens, Nov. 20, 1919; Martens to Chicherin, Nov. 20, 1919, f. 04, op. 3, d. 123, ll. 73 and 71–72, AVPRF; White, *British and American Commercial Relations*, 138.

46. Lenin, draft resolution on foreign policy, Dec. 2, 1919, Lenin, *Collected Works*, 30:191–92, 549n.; NKID to Martens, n.d. (c. Jan. 1920), f. 04, op. 3, d. 123, l. 74; Note of Feb. 24, 1920, DVP, 2:387–88.

47. Parry, "Washington B. Vanderlip, the 'Khan of Kamchatka'"; Records of Soviet agreement with Vanderlip in Nov. 1920, f. 129, op. 4, d. 12; f. 0129, op. 3, d. 10, p. 102; and f. 04, op. 3, d. 125, AVPRF; Lenin, speech of Dec. 6, 1920, *Collected Works*, 31:438–59.

48. Draft of Martens letter to Bainbridge Colby, June 19, 1920, f. 507, op. 56, d. 5, ll. 3–9, AVPRF.

49. Polk to Lansing, June 5, 1919, *FRUS, 1919, Russia*, 144–45; Wilson to Lansing, June 12, 1919; Lansing to Wilson, June 14, 1919; Wilson to Lansing, June 17, 1919, PWW 60:484, 566–67, 641; Diary of Josephus Daniels, Dec. 14, 1920, PWW 66:504.

50. Chicherin to Martens, Dec. 17, 1920, f. 129, op. 4, d. 6, ll. 4–5, AVPRF; Undated report to the Collegium of the Narkomindel, f. 04, op. 3, d. 122, ll. 6–8, AVPRF; Chicherin to Martens, Dec. 17, 1920, Chicherin speech at the Eighth Congress of Soviets, 1920, *Stat'i i rechi po voprosam mezhdunarodnoi politiki*, 177. Despite Chicherin's instruction, Martens's departure did not halt the development of American-Soviet commerce. See White, *British and American Commerical Relations*, 139.

51. Lenin, speech of Dec. 5, 1919, *Collected Works*, 30:207–19; Krasnov, *Klassovaia Bor'ba v SShA*, 199, 241–42; Gvishiani, *Sovetskaia Rossiia i SShA*, 314. See also Foner, *Bolshevik Revolution*, 41; Zolotukhin and Malkov, "Oktiabrskaia revoliutsiia," 156, 159.

52. See, for example, Richard Crane to Walter Rogers, Feb. 12, 1919, Box 2, Folder 26, Crane Papers.

53. "Pitiless Publicity About Russia," *New Republic*, July 9, 1919, 299–300; Hard, "Anti-Bolsheviks: Mr. Bakhmetev," *New Republic*, Aug. 13, 1919; Hard to Gumberg, 6.24.1919, Box 1, Gumberg Papers.

54. Lenin, speech of Dec. 5, 1919, report of Dec. 2, 1919, report of Feb. 2, 1920, and speech of March 1, 1920, *Collected Works*, 30:207–19, 173, 316, 390–91. For further discus-

sion, see Thompson, "Lenin's Analysis of Intervention."

55. Lenin, "A Caricature of Marxism and Imperialist Economism," 1916, and "The Valuable Admissions of Pitirim Sorokin," Nov. 20, 1918, *Collected Works*, 23:47, 28:190.

56. Lenin, interview with Louise Bryant, Oct. 13, 1920, *Leninskii Sbornik*, 37:254–55; Lomonosov, expression of inability to understand self-denying U.S. policy, May 22, 1919, Russian Soviet Bureau Seized Files, Folder 12; Chicherin speech at the Eighth Congress of Soviets, 1920, *Stat'i i rechi po voprosam mezhdunarodnoi politiki*, 176; Chicherin, report to the Central Executive Committee, Jan. 27, 1922, in Degras, *Soviet Documents on Foreign Policy*, 1:291–92; Draft of a report on relations with the United States, n.d. (c. Dec. 1920), f. 129, op. 4, d. 6, ll. 18–19; March 21, 1921 telegram from the All-Russian Central Executive Committee to President Harding, f. 04, op. 3, d. 126, l. 6, AVPRF.

57. Lenin, reply to a correspondent's questions, Feb. 18, 1920, *Collected Works*, 30:366; Martens speech, May 22, 1919, Russian Soviet Bureau Seized Files, Folder 22; Chicherin to Martens, Dec. 17, 1920, f. 129, op. 4, d. 6, AVPRF; Chicherin report of talk with Norman Hapgood, May 8, 1923, f. 04, d. 150, ll. 6–7, AVPRF. See also Belevich and Sokolov, "Foreign Affairs Commissar Georgy Chicherin," 92, 94.

58. Remarks to Democratic National Committee, Feb. 28, 1919, PWW 55:320, 314.

59. Diary of Raymond Fosdick, Dec. 11, 1918, PWW 53:366.

60. John Spargo to Bainbridge Colby, July 31, 1920; Colby to Wilson, Aug. 9, 1920, with Wilson approval of the "excellent" note, Box 3, Colby Papers; Radosh, "John Spargo," 559–60; Debo, *Survival and Consolidation*, 263.

61. William H. Hawkins, "Confidential Report" of interview with Woodrow Wilson, Sept. 27, 1920, Bainbridge Colby Papers.

62. Statement of May 8, 1919, Address by Martens, May 22, 1919, Nuorteva speech of May 3, 1919, Russian Soviet Bureau Seized Files, Folders 9 and 22; ECCI to IWW, Jan. 1920, Degras, *Communist International*, Vol. 1:71–72.

CONCLUSION

1. Newton Baker to Wilson, Nov. 27, 1918, PWW 53:228; Report of Wilson remarks on Dec. 28, 1918, PWW 53:575; Remarks to Democratic National Committee, Feb. 28, 1919, PWW 55:319.

2. Baker to Wilson, June 19, 1918, Reel 195, Wilson Papers.

3. Address of Sept. 11, 1919, PPWW 2:107.

4. Address of April 2, 1917, PPWW 1:12; Address of Sept. 11, 1919, PPWW 2:107; Addresses of Sept. 10 and 18, 1919, PPWW 2:94–95, 259–60.

5. Remarks to Democratic Committee, Feb. 28, 1919, PWW 55:314–19.

6. Hapgood to Wilson, May 26, 1919, PWW 59:518.

7. Rourke, *Secrecy and Publicity*, 24.

8. *San Francisco Chronicle*, Sept. 11, 1919; Lower, "Hiram Johnson"; Lower, *Bloc of One*; Thelen, *Robert M. LaFollette*, 148–52; Johnson, *Peace Progressives*.

9. Fourteen Points speech, Jan. 8, 1918, PPWW, 1:158.

10. For Lenin's comments on these points, see *Collected Works*, 30:209; Lenin, "Letter to the Workers of Europe and America," Jan. 21, 1919, *Collected Works*, 28:435.

11. Fourteen Points speech, Jan. 8, 1918, PPWW, 1:159.

12. For different perspectives on the legacy of intervention and civil war, see Thompson, "Allied and American Intervention"; Fitzpatrick, "Civil War"; and Lel'chuk and Pivovar, "Mentalitet Sovetskogo."

13. Knock, *To End All Wars*, 276; Smith, *America's Mission*; Walter Isaacson, "Sometimes, Right Makes Might," *Time*, Dec. 21, 1992; Calhoun, *Uses of Force*.

BIBLIOGRAPHY

PRIMARY SOURCES

Manuscript Collections

Ann Arbor, Michigan
Bentley Historical Library, University of Michigan
    Robert Granville Letters
    Silver Parrish Diary

Berkeley, California
Bancroft Library, University of California
    David Prescott Barrows Papers
    Hiram Johnson Papers
    Jerome B. Landfield Papers
    Edward T. Williams Papers

Cambridge, Massachusetts
Baker Library, Harvard University
    Thomas William Lamont Papers
Houghton Library, Harvard University
    Ellis Loring Dresel Papers
    Joseph Clark Grew Papers
    David F. Houston Papers
    Walter Hines Page Papers
    William Phillips Papers
    John Reed Papers
    Oswald Garrison Villard Papers
Pusey Library, Harvard University
    Samuel Eliot Morison Papers

Carlisle, Pennsylvania
U.S. Army Military History Institute
    William J. Donovan Papers
    Peyton C. March Reminiscences
    Leroy W. Yarborough Papers

Chicago, Illinois
Joseph Regenstein Library, University of Chicago
    Samuel N. Harper Papers

Hyde Park, New York
Franklin D. Roosevelt Library
    Adolf A. Berle Papers
    Franklin D. Roosevelt Papers

Madison, Wisconsin
State Historical Society of Wisconsin
  Alexander Gumberg Papers
  Cyrus H. McCormick Jr. Papers
  DeWitt Clinton Poole Papers
  Paul S. Reinsch Papers
  Raymond Robins Papers

New Haven, Connecticut
Divinity School Library, Yale University
  John R. Mott Papers
Sterling Library, Yale University
  Gordon Auchincloss Papers
  Edward M. House Papers
  Vance C. McCormick Papers
  Frank Polk Papers
  William Wiseman Papers

New York, New York
Bakhmeteff Archive, Columbia University
  Boris A. Bakhmeteff Papers
  Charles R. Crane Papers
  E. Francis Riggs Papers
  Allen Wardwell Papers
New York Public Library
  George Kennan Papers

Palo Alto, California
Hays Family Collection
  Walter G. Hays Sermons, 1899–1920

Princeton, New Jersey
Mudd Library, Princeton University
  Norman Armour Papers
  Ray Stannard Baker Papers
  Arthur Bullard Papers
  Allen W. Dulles Papers
  John Foster Dulles Papers
  Cary T. Grayson Papers
  Robert Lansing Papers
  John Van Antwerp MacMurray Papers
  Joshua Butler Wright Diaries

Rochester, New York
University of Rochester Library
  Edward Peck Curtis Diary

St. Louis, Missouri
Missouri Historical Society
  David R. Francis Papers
  Earl M. Johnston Papers

San Mateo, California
San Mateo County Historical Association Museum
   William S. Strobridge Collection
   Iler Watson Collection

Stanford, California
Hoover Institution Archives
   Mikhail V. Alekseev Papers
   American Relief Administration Papers
   William S. Barrett Papers
   Louis Edgar Browne Papers
   John K. Caldwell Papers
   George H. Emerson Papers
   Edith M. Faulstich Collection
   Hugh S. Gibson Papers
   William S. Graves Papers
   Ernest L. Harris Papers
   Herbert Hoover Papers
   Nikolai Nikolaevich Iudenich Collection
   Joseph B. Longuevan Papers
   Louis Loucheur Papers
   Vance C. McCormick Diary
   Sergei P. Melgunov Papers
   Russian Provisional Government Embassies: Posol'stvo (U.S.) Papers

Washington, D.C.
Lauinger Library, Georgetown University
   Richard T. Crane Papers
Library of Congress
   Carl William Ackerman Papers
   Newton Diehl Baker Papers
   Ray Stannard Baker Papers
   Tasker H. Bliss Papers
   William E. Borah Papers
   Albert Sidney Burleson Papers
   Bainbridge Colby Papers
   George Creel Papers
   Oscar Crosby Papers
   Josephus Daniels Papers
   Norman H. Davis Papers
   Hermann Hagedorn Papers
   George Kennan Papers
   Robert Lansing Papers
   Russell C. Leffingwell Papers
   Breckinridge Long Papers
   William G. McAdoo Papers
   Roland S. Morris Papers
   Elihu Root Papers
   Joseph P. Tumulty Papers
   Woodrow Wilson Papers

West Point, New York
United States Military Academy Library
  Frederick Carroll Papers
  George Evans Stewart Papers

Government Records

Great Britain
Public Record Office (microfilm)
  Cabinet Office. Eastern and Middle East Committees, 1918. CAB 27.
  Cabinet Office. International Conferences, 1918. CAB 29.
  Cabinet Office. Memoranda, 1917–1918. CAB 24.
  Cabinet Office. Minutes, 1917–1918. CAB 23.
  Cabinet Office. Miscellaneous records. CAB 1/25; 1/27; 1/28.
  Foreign Office. Confidential Print: Russia and the Soviet Union. F.O. 418.
  Foreign Office. Correspondence, Political: Russia. 1918. F.O. 371.
  Foreign Office. Embassy and consular archives. United States of America
    correspondence. 1916–1918. F.O. 115.
  War Cabinet. Allied War Conferences, 1917–1918. CAB 28.

New York, New York
New York State Archives
  Records of the Joint Legislative Committee to Investigate Seditious Activities (Lusk
    Committee).
  Russian Soviet Bureau Seized Files, 1918–1919.

Russia
Archive of the Foreign Policy of the Russian Federation (AVPRF), Moscow
  Fond 4/04. Secretariat of the People's Commissar for Foreign Affairs G. V. Chicherin.
  Fond 129. Referentura for the United States of America.
  Fond 507. L. C. A. K. Martens in the United States of America.
State Archive of the Russian Federation (GARF), Moscow
  Fond 130. Soviet of People's Commissars.
  Fond 200. Ministry of Foreign Affairs, Omsk.
  Fond 1005. Supreme Court of the RSFSR.
  Fond 1235. VTsIK.
Russian Center for the Preservation and Study of Documents of Contemporary History
  (RTsKhIDNI)
  Fond 5. Secretariat of V. I. Lenin.
  Fond 76. Dzerzhinskii, F. E.
  Fond 159. Chicherin, G. V.

United States
National Archives
  RG 39: Records of the Treasury Department. Country File: Russia.
  RG 45: Naval Records Collection of the Office of Naval Records and Library, Subject
    Files, 1911–1927, WA-6 Russia.
  RG 59: General Records of the Department of State.
  RG 63: Records of the Committee on Public Information.
  RG 84: American Embassy, Consulates, and Missions to Russia.

RG 120: Records of the American Expeditionary Forces (World War I), 1917–23
(Historical Files of the American Expeditionary Forces, North Russia, 1918–1919.
M924).
RG 165: Records of the War Department General and Special Staffs.
Military Intelligence Division records.
RG 200: American National Red Cross Papers.
RG 395: Records of U.S. Army Overseas Operations and Commands, 1898–1942
(Historical Files of the American Expeditionary Forces in Siberia, 1918–1920. M917).
Records of the Department of State Relating to the Internal Affairs of Russia and the
Soviet Union, 1910–1929 (M316).
Records of the Department of State Relating to Political Relations Between the United
States and the Soviet Union, 1910–1929 (M333).

Published Documents

Bane, Suda L., ed. *Documents of the American Relief Administration European Operations,*
vols. 15–17. Stanford, Calif., 1952.
Belov, G. A., et al., eds. *Iz istorii Vserossiiskoi Chrezvychainoi komissii 1917–1921gg —
sbornik dokumentov.* Moscow, 1958.
Browder, Robert Paul, and Alexander F. Kerensky. *The Russian Provisional Government.*
3 vols. Stanford, Calif. 1961.
Challener, Richard D., ed. *United States Military Intelligence.* New York, 1979.
Chicherin, G. V. *Stat'i i rechi po voprosam mezhdunarodnoi politiki.* Moscow, 1961.
Degras, Jane, ed. *The Communist International 1919–1943: Documents.* Vol. 1, *1919–1922.*
London, 1956, 1971.
———. *Soviet Documents on Foreign Policy.* Vol. 1, *1917–1924.* London, 1951.
Institut Marksizma-Leninizma pri TsK KPSS. *Leninskii Sbornik.* 40 vols. Moscow,
1924–85.
Keep, J. L. H., ed. *The Debate on Soviet Power: Minutes of the All-Russian Central
Executive Committee of Soviets.* Oxford, 1979.
Kesaris, Paul, ed. *Confidential U.S. Diplomatic Post Records. Part 1. Russia, 1914–1918.*
Frederick, Md., 1982.
Link, Arthur S., ed. *The Deliberations of the Council of Four (March 24–June 28, 1919).
Notes of the Official Interpreter Paul Mantoux.* 2 vols. Princeton, 1992.
Ministerstvo Inostrannykh Del SSSR. *Dokumenty Vneshnei Politiki SSSR.* Moscow, 1959.
New York State Senate Joint Legislative Committee Investigating Seditious Activities.
Revolutionary Radicalism. 4 vols. Albany, 1920.
Riddell, John, ed. *Founding the Communist International: Proceedings and Documents of
the First Congress, March 1919.* New York, 1987.
U.S. Congress. *Congressional Record.* Washington, D.C., 1917–20.
U.S. Department of State. *Papers Relating to the Foreign Relations of the United States.
1918, Russia.* 3 vols. Washington, D.C., 1931–32.
1918, Supplement I. Vol. 1. Washington, D.C., 1933.
1919, Russia. Washington, D.C., 1937.
Paris Peace Conference. 13 vols. Washington, D.C., 1942–47.
———. *Register of the Department of State.* Washington, D.C., 1918–32.
U.S. Senate Committee on Foreign Relations. *Russian Propaganda.* 66th Cong., 2nd sess.,
1920.
U.S. Senate Committee on the Judiciary. *Bolshevik Propaganda.* 65th Cong., 3rd sess.,
1919.

————. *Confidential Report on Foreign Loans.* 67th Cong., 1st sess., 1921.

————. *Foreign Loans and Authority for Making Same.* 67th Cong., 1st sess., 1921.

U.S. Senate Documents. Document No. 105: Lt. Robert Hale, "Report of the Mission to Finland, Esthonia, Latvia, and Lithuania on the Situation in the Baltic Provinces," Paris, July 23, 1919. Vol. 15. 66th Cong., 1st sess., 1919.

Wade, Rex A., ed. *Documents of Soviet History.* Vol. 1, *The Triumph of Bolshevism, 1917–1919.* Gulf Breeze, Fla., 1991.

Letters, Diaries, Memoirs, and Contemporary Writings

Albertson, Ralph. *Fighting Without a War: An Account of Military Intervention in North Russia.* New York, 1920.

Baer, George W., ed. *A Question of Trust. The Origins of U.S.–Soviet Diplomatic Relations: The Memoirs of Loy W. Henderson.* Stanford, Calif., 1986.

Baker, Ray Stannard, and William E. Dodd, eds. *The Public Papers of Woodrow Wilson: War and Peace.* 2 vols. New York, 1927.

Bakhmeteff, Boris A. "The Reminiscences of Boris A. Bakhmeteff." Oral History Research Office, Columbia University, 1950.

Benes, Eduard. *My War Memoirs.* London, 1928.

Berle, Beatrice Bishop, and Travis Beal Jacobs, eds. *Navigating the Rapids, 1918–1971: From the Papers of Adolf A. Berle.* New York, 1973.

Buchanan, George. *My Mission to Russia and Other Diplomatic Memories.* Boston, 1923.

Bullard, Arthur. *The Russian Pendulum: Autocracy–Democracy–Bolshevism.* New York, 1919.

Bullitt, William C. *The Bullitt Mission to Russia.* New York, 1919.

Chicherin, Georgii. *Two Years of Foreign Policy.* New York, 1920.

Colby, Bainbridge. *The Close of Woodrow Wilson's Administration and the Final Years.* New York, 1930.

Cook, B. W., ed. *Crystal Eastman on Women and Revolution.* New York, 1978.

Creel, George. *How We Advertised America.* New York, 1920.

————. *Rebel at Large.* New York, 1947.

Cronon, E. David. *Cabinet Diaries of Josephus Daniels.* Lincoln, Neb., 1963.

Crosby, Oscar T. *International War: Its Causes and Its Cure.* London, 1919.

Cudahy, John. *Archangel: The American War with Russia.* Chicago, 1924.

Daniels, Josephus. *The Wilson Era.* 2 vols. Chapel Hill, N.C., 1944–46.

Davis, Julia, and D. A. Fleming, *The Ambassadorial Diary of John W. Davis: The Court of St. James's 1918–1921.* Morgantown, W.V., 1993.

Davison, Henry P. *The American Red Cross in the Great War.* New York, 1920.

Dotsenko, Paul. *The Struggle for a Democracy in Siberia, 1917–1920.* Stanford, Calif., 1983.

Dukes, Paul. *Red Dusk and the Morrow: Adventures and Investigations in Red Russia.* New York, 1922.

Foner, Philip S., ed. *The Bolshevik Revolution: Its Impact on American Radicals, Liberals and Labor.* New York, 1967.

Francis, David R. *Russia from the American Embassy.* New York, 1921.

Gade, John A. *All My Born Days: Experiences of a Naval Intelligence Officer in Europe.* New York, 1942.

————. "Inside Red Russia." *The World's Work* 40 (July 1920): 233–37.

————. "Russia from Its Baltic Window." *North American Review* 213 (January 1921): 52–64.

von der Goltz, Rüdiger. *Meine Sendung in Finnland und im Baltikum.* Leipzig, 1920.

Gordon, Dennis, ed. *Quartered in Hell: The Story of the American North Russian Expeditionary Force, 1918–1919*. Missoula, Mont., 1982.

Graves, William S. *America's Siberian Adventure, 1918–1920*. New York, 1931.

Grew, Joseph C. *Turbulent Era: A Diplomatic Record of Forty Years*. Boston, 1952.

Gwynn, Stephen L., ed. *The Letters and Friendships of Sir Cecil Spring Rice*. London, 1929.

Hard, William. *Raymond Robins' Own Story*. New York, 1920.

Harper, Paul V., ed. *The Russia I Believe In: The Memoirs of Samuel N. Harper, 1902–1941*. Chicago, 1945.

Hill, George A. *Go Spy the Land*. London, 1932.

Hoover, Herbert. *The Memoirs of Herbert Hoover*. New York, 1951.

———. *The Ordeal of Woodrow Wilson*. New York, 1958.

House, Edward M. *Philip Dru: Administrator*. 1912. Reprint, New York, 1920.

Ironside, Lord Edmund. *Archangel, 1918–1919*. London, 1953.

Kerensky, Alexander F. *Russia and History's Turning Point*. New York, 1965.

Khrushchev, Nikita. *Khrushchev in America*. New York, 1960.

Lamont, Thomas. *Across World Frontiers*. New York, 1951.

Lane, Anne Wintermute, and Louise Herrick Wall, eds. *The Letters of Franklin K. Lane: Personal and Political*. New York, 1922.

Lansing, Robert. *The Peace Negotiations: A Personal Narrative*. Boston, 1921.

———. *War Memoirs of Robert Lansing*. Indianapolis, 1935.

Latsis, M. Y. *Dva goda bor'bii na vnutrennom fronte*. Moscow, 1920.

Lenin, V. I. *Collected Works*. New York, 1927–45.

———. *Lenin on the United States*. New York, 1970.

———. *Selected Works*. 1968. Reprint, Moscow, 1975.

Link, Arthur S., ed. *The Deliberations of the Council of Four*. Princeton, 1992.

Link, Arthur S., et al., eds. *The Papers of Woodrow Wilson*. 69 vols. Princeton, 1966–93.

Lloyd George, David. *War Memoirs of David Lloyd George*. London, 1936.

Lockhart, Robert Bruce. *Memoirs of a British Agent*. London, 1932.

Mal'kov, P. D. *Zapiski komendanta Kremlia*. Moscow, 1987.

March, Peyton C. *The Nation at War*. New York, 1932.

Marchand, René. *Allied Agents in Soviet Russia*. London, 1918.

Masaryk, Thomas G. *The Making of a State: Memories and Observations*. New York, 1927.

Maynard, C. *The Murmansk Venture*. London, 1928.

Meijer, Jan, ed. *The Trotsky Papers, 1917–1922*. The Hague, 1961.

Miller, David Hunter. *My Diary at the Conference at Paris*. 21 vols. Washington, D.C., 1928.

Moore, Joel R., Harry Mead, and Lewis Jahns. *The History of the American Expedition Fighting the Bolsheviki*. Detroit, 1920.

Murphy, Robert. *Diplomat Among Warriors*. New York, 1964.

Nicolai, W. *The German Secret Service*. London, 1924.

Noulens, Joseph. *Mon ambassade en russie sovietique, 1917–1919*. 2 vols. Paris, 1933.

O'Brien, Francis William, ed. *Two Peacemakers in Paris: The Hoover-Wilson Post-Armistice Letters 1918–1920*. College Station, Tex., 1978.

Pershing, John J. *My Experiences in the World War*. 2 vols. New York, 1931.

Peters, Iakov. "Vospominaniia o rabote v VChK v pervyi god revoliutsii." *Proletarskaia revoliutsiia* no. 10 (October 1924): 5–32. Reprint, *Byloe* 2 (1933): 93–123.

Phillips, William. "The Reminiscences of William Phillips." Oral History Research Office, Columbia University, 1972.

———. *Ventures in Diplomacy*. Boston, 1952.

Poole, DeWitt C. "The Reminiscences of DeWitt C. Poole." Oral History Research Office, Columbia University, 1952.

Poole, Ernest. *The Dark People: Russia's Crisis.* New York, 1918.

Reilly, Sidney. *The Adventures of Sidney Reilly.* London, 1931.

Reinsch, Paul S. *An American Diplomat in China.* New York, 1922.

Resek, Carl, ed. *War and the Intellectuals: Essays by Randolph S. Bourne 1915–1919.* New York, 1964.

Roy, M. N. "Michel Borodine en Amerique (1919)." In *Contributions a L'Histoire du Comintern,* published under the direction of Jacques Freymond. Geneva, 1965.

Sadoul, Jacques. *Notes sur la revolution bolchevique.* Paris, 1926.

Savinkov, Boris. *Borba s bolshevikami.* Warsaw, 1920.

Seymour, Charles, ed. *The Intimate Papers of Colonel House.* 3 vols. Boston, 1928.

Sisson, Edgar. *One Hundred Red Days.* New Haven, Conn., 1931.

Stalin, J. V. *Works.* Vol. 4. Moscow, 1953.

Steffens, Lincoln. *The Autobiography of Lincoln Steffens.* 2 vols. 1931. Reprint, New York, 1958.

Thompson, Charles Willis. *Presidents I've Known and Two Near Presidents.* Indianapolis, 1929.

Tumulty, Joseph P. *Woodrow Wilson as I Know Him.* New York, 1921.

Tyrkova-Williams, Ariadna. *Cheerful Giver: The Life of Harold Williams.* London, 1935.

Varneck, Elena, and H. H. Fisher, eds. *The Testimony of Kolchak and Other Siberian Materials.* Stanford, Calif., 1935.

Vopicka, Charles J. *Secrets of the Balkans: Seven Years of a Diplomatist's Life in the Storm Centre of Europe.* Chicago, 1921.

Voska, Emanuel Victor, and Will Irwin. *Spy and Counterspy.* New York, 1940.

Ward, John. *With the "Die-Hards" in Siberia.* New York, 1920.

Washburn, Stanley. *Victory in Defeat: The Agony of Warsaw and the Russian Retreat.* New York, 1916.

White, D. F. *Survival: Through War and Revolution in Russia.* Philadelphia, 1939.

Wilson, Edith Bolling. *My Memoir.* Indianapolis, 1938.

Wilson, Woodrow. *Division and Reunion 1829–1889.* 1893. Reprint, New York, 1907.

———. *A History of the American People.* New York, 1901.

———. *The New Freedom.* 1913. Reprint, Englewood Cliffs, N.J., 1961.

———. *The State.* Boston, 1889.

Young, Kenneth. *The Diaries of Sir Robert Bruce Lockhart, 1915–1918.* London, 1973.

Newspapers and Magazines

Chicago Tribune, 1918–19

Daily Palo Alto Times, 1917–18

Izvestiia, 1918

Los Angeles Times, 1918–19

Nation, 1918–19

New Republic, 1919–20

New York American, 1917

New York Times, 1917–21

New York World, 1905, 1917–18

Pravda, 1918

Sacramento Bee, 1917–19

San Francisco Bulletin, 1905

San Francisco Call, 1918–19

San Francisco Chronicle, 1918–19

Soviet Russia, 1919–20
Struggling Russia, 1919–20
Washington Post, 1917

SECONDARY SOURCES

Abraham, Richard. *Alexander Kerensky: The First Love of the Revolution.* New York, 1987.

Abrams, Richard. "United States Intervention Abroad: The First Quarter Century." *American Historical Review* (1974): 72–102.

Aleksentsev, A. I. "F. E. Dzerzhinskii vo Glave Voisk VChK (1918–1919gg.)." *Istoriia SSSR* no. 6 (1988).

Allison, William. "Into the Cauldron: David R. Francis, Felix Cole, and American Intervention in North Russia, 1918–1919." *Gateway Heritage* 14, no. 3 (Winter 1993–94), 16–31.

Ambrosius, Lloyd E. "The Orthodoxy of Revisionism: Woodrow Wilson and the New Left." *Diplomatic History* 1, no. 3 (Summer 1977): 199–214.

———. *Wilsonian Statecraft: Theory and Practice of Liberal Internationalism During World War I.* Wilmington, Del., 1991.

———. *Woodrow Wilson and the American Diplomatic Tradition: The Treaty Fight in Perspective.* Cambridge, 1987.

———. "Woodrow Wilson's Health and the Treaty Fight, 1919–1920." *International History Review* 9, no. 1 (February 1987): 73–84.

Ameringer, Charles D. *U.S. Foreign Intelligence: The Secret Side of American History.* Lexington, Mass., 1990.

Andrew, Christopher. *Her Majesty's Secret Service: The Making of the British Intelligence Community.* New York, 1986.

Arens, Olavi. "Revolutionary Developments in Estonia in 1917–1918 and Their Ideological and Political Background." Ph.D. dissertation, Columbia University, 1976.

Arnold, Arthur Z. *Banks, Credit, and Money in Soviet Russia.* New York, 1937.

Bacino, Leo J. "Reconstructing Russia: The Political Economy of American Assistance to Revolutionary Russia, 1917–1922." Ph.D. dissertation, Northern Illinois University, 1993.

Baker, Ray Stannard. *Woodrow Wilson: Life and Letters.* 8 vols. New York, 1927–39.

Barnet, Richard J. *Intervention and Revolution: The United States in the Third World.* New York, 1968.

Beale, H. K. *Theodore Roosevelt and the Rise of America to World Power.* Baltimore, 1956.

Belevich, Yelena, and Vladimir Sokolov. "Foreign Affairs Commissar Georgy Chicherin." *International Affairs*, no. 3 (1991): 90–99.

Beliavskaia, I. A. "Kollokvium istorikov SSSR i SSha." *Voprosy Istorii* (February 1985): 157–62.

Bell, Sidney. *Righteous Conquest: Woodrow Wilson and the Evolution of the New Diplomacy.* New York, 1972.

Bennett, David H. *The Party of Fear: From Nativist Movements to the New Right in American History.* New York, 1990.

Berk, Stephen Michael. "The Coup D'Etat of Admiral Kolchak: The Counterrevolution in Siberia and East Russia, 1917–1918." Ph.D. dissertation, Columbia University, 1971.

Best, Gary Dean. "Food Relief as Price Support: Hoover and American Pork, January–March 1919." *Agricultural History* 45, no. 2 (April 1971): 79–84.

———. *The Politics of American Individualism: Herbert Hoover in Transition, 1918–1921.* Westport, Conn., 1975.

Biskupski, M. B. "Re-Creating Central Europe: The United States 'Inquiry' into the Future of Poland in 1918." *International History Review* 12, no. 2 (May 1990): 249–79.

Bradley, John. *Allied Intervention in Russia.* New York, 1968.

Bragdon, Henry Wilkinson. *Woodrow Wilson: The Academic Years.* Cambridge, Mass., 1967.

Brands, Henry William Jr. "Unpremeditated Lansing: His 'Scraps.'" *Diplomatic History* 9, no. 1 (Winter 1985): 25–33.

Brinkley, George. *The Volunteer Army and Allied Intervention in South Russia, 1917–1921.* Notre Dame, Ind., 1966.

Browder, Robert P. *The Origins of Soviet-American Diplomacy.* Princeton, 1953.

Brown, Anthony Cave. *The Last Hero: Wild Bill Donovan.* New York, 1982.

Bull, Hedley, ed. *Intervention in World Politics.* Oxford, 1984.

Bullitt, William C., and Sigmund Freud. *Thomas Woodrow Wilson: A Psychological Study.* Boston, 1967.

Burnham, John C. "The Progressive Era Revolution in American Attitudes Toward Sex." *Journal of American History* 59 (March 1973): 885–908.

Calder, Bruce J. *The Impact of Intervention: The Dominican Republic During the U.S. Occupation of 1916–1924.* Austin, Tex., 1984.

Calder, Robert L. *W. Somerset Maugham and the Quest for Freedom.* London, 1972.

Calhoun, Frederick. *Power and Principle: Armed Intervention in Wilsonian Diplomacy.* Kent, Ohio, 1986.

———. *Uses of Force and Wilsonian Foreign Policy.* Kent, Ohio, 1993.

Campbell, Russell. "Nihilists and Bolsheviks: Revolutionary Russia in American Silent Film." *The Silent Picture,* no. 19 (1974).

Capelotti, P. J. *Our Man in the Crimea: Commander Hugo Koehler and the Russian Civil War.* Columbia, S.C., 1991.

Carley, Michael J. "The Origins of French Intervention in the Russian Civil War, January–May 1918: A Reappraisal." *Journal of Modern History* 48 (September 1976): 413–39.

———. *Revolution and Intervention: The French Intervention and the Russian Civil War, 1917–1919.* Montreal, 1983.

Carr, E. H. *The Bolshevik Revolution.* 3 vols. New York, 1951–53.

Chamberlin, W. H. *The Russian Revolution, 1917–1921.* 2 vols. London, 1935.

Chavez, Leo Eugene. "Herbert Hoover and Food Relief: An Application of American Ideology." Ph.D. dissertation, University of Michigan, 1976.

Cherry, George L. "American Metropolitan Press Reaction to the Paris Commune of 1871." *Mid-America* 32, no. 1 (January 1950): 3–12.

Clements, Kendrick A. *The Presidency of Woodrow Wilson.* Lawrence, Kans., 1992.

———. *Woodrow Wilson: World Statesman.* Boston, 1987.

———. "Woodrow Wilson's Mexican Policy, 1913–1915." *Diplomatic History* 4, no. 2 (Spring 1980): 113–36.

Coben, Stanley. "A Study in Nativism: The American Red Scare of 1919–20." *Political Science Quarterly* 79, no. 1 (March 1964).

Cockfield, Jamie H., ed. *Dollars and Diplomacy: Ambassador David Rowland Francis and the Fall of Tsarism, 1916–1917.* Durham, N.C., 1981.

Cohen, Stephen F. *Bukharin and the Bolshevik Revolution.* New York, 1974.

Cohen, Warren. "America and the May Fourth Movement: The Response to Chinese Nationalism, 1917–1921." *Pacific Historical Review* 35, no. 1 (February 1966): 83–100.

Conn, Peter. *The Divided Mind: Ideology and Imagination in America, 1898–1917.* Cambridge, Mass., 1983.

Cooper, John Milton. *The Warrior and the Priest: Woodrow Wilson and Theodore Roosevelt.* Cambridge, Mass., 1983.

Cooper, John Milton, and Charles E. Neu, ed., *The Wilson Era: Essays in Honor of Arthur S. Link.* Arlington Heights, Ill., 1991.

Corson, William R., and Robert T. Crowley. *The New KGB: Engine of Soviet Power.* New York, 1985.

Crunden, Robert M. *Ministers of Reform: The Progressives' Achievement in American Civilization, 1889–1920.* New York, 1982.

Curtis, Eugene N. "American Opinion of the French Nineteenth-Century Revolutions." *American Historical Review* 29, no. 2 (January 1924): 249–70.

Darling, Arthur B. *The Central Intelligence Agency,* University Park, Penn., 1990.

Davis, David Brion. "American Equality and Foreign Revolutions." *Journal of American History* 76, no. 3 (December 1989): 729–52.

———, ed. *The Fear of Conspiracy: Images of Un-American Subversion from the Revolution to the Present.* Ithaca, N.Y., 1971.

———. *Revolutions: Reflections on American Equality and Foreign Liberations.* Cambridge, Mass., 1990.

Davis, Donald E., and Eugene P. Trani. "An American in Russia: Russell M. Story and the Bolshevik Revolution, 1917–1919." *The Historian* 36, no. 4 (August 1974): 704–21.

———. "The American YMCA and the Russian Revolution." *Slavic Review* 33, no. 3 (September 1974): 469–91.

Debo, Richard K. "Lockhart Plot or Dzerzhinsky Plot?" *Journal of Modern History* 43, no. 3 (September 1971): 413–39.

———. *Revolution and Survival: The Foreign Policy of Soviet Russia, 1917–1918.* Toronto, 1979.

———. *Survival and Consolidation: The Foreign Policy of Soviet Russia, 1918–1921.* Montreal, 1992.

Deutscher, Isaac. *The Prophet Armed. Trotsky: 1879–1921.* New York, 1954.

DeYoung, Harry Rine. "A Study of the Religious Speaking of Woodrow Wilson." Ph.D. dissertation, Wayne State University, 1965.

Diamond, William. *The Economic Thought of Woodrow Wilson.* Baltimore, 1943.

Dinerstein, Herbert S. *Intervention Against Communism.* Baltimore, 1967.

Doolen, Richard M. *Michigan's Polar Bears.* Ann Arbor, 1965.

Draper, Theodore. *The Roots of American Communism.* New York, 1957.

Drokov, S. V. "Aleksandr Vasil'evich Kolchak." *Voprosy Istorii* (January 1991): 50–67.

Drujina, Gleb. "The History of the North-West Army of General Yudenich." Ph.D. dissertation, Stanford University, 1950.

Dugdale, Blanche E.C. *Arthur James Balfour.* New York, 1936.

Dulles, Foster Rhea. *The American Red Cross: A History.* New York, 1950.

Dupuy, R. Ernest. *Perish by the Sword: The Czechoslovakian Anabasis and Our Supporting Campaigns in North Russia and Siberia, 1918–1920.* Harrisburg, Penn., 1939.

Dziak, John J. *Chekisty: A History of the KGB.* Lexington, Mass., 1988.

Elson, Ruth Miller. *Guardians of Tradition: American Schoolbooks of the Nineteenth Century.* Lincoln, Neb., 1964.

Erickson, John. "The Origins of the Red Army." In *Revolutionary Russia,* edited by Richard Pipes. Cambridge, Mass., 1968.

———. "Some Military and Political Aspects of the 'Militia Army' Controversy, 1919–1920." In *Essays in Honour of E. H. Carr,* edited by C. Abramsky. London, 1974.

———. *The Soviet High Command: A Military-Political History.* London, 1962.

Etheredge, Lloyd S. *Can Governments Learn? American Foreign Policy and Central*

American Revolutions. New York, 1985.

Ezergailis, Andrew. *The Latvian Impact on the Bolshevik Revolution.* Boulder, Colo., 1983.

Farnsworth, Beatrice. *William C. Bullitt and the Soviet Union.* Bloomington, Ind., 1967.

Feldman, Egal. "Prostitution, the Alien Woman and the Progressive Imagination." *American Quarterly* 19, no. 2, pt. 1 (Summer 1967).

Fic, Victor M. *Bolsheviks and the Czechoslovak Legion: Origin of Their Armed Conflict.* New Dehli, 1978.

Fike, Claude E. "The Influence of the Creel Committee and the American Red Cross on Russian-American Relations, 1917–1919." *Journal of Modern History* 31, no. 2 (June 1959): 93–109.

―――. "The United States and Russian Territorial Problems, 1917–1920." *The Historian* 24, no. 3 (May 1962): 331–46.

Filene, Peter. *Americans and the Soviet Experiment, 1917–1933.* Cambridge, Mass., 1967.

Fischer, Louis. *Russia's Road from Peace to War: Soviet Foreign Relations, 1917–1941.* New York, 1969.

―――. *The Soviets in World Affairs: A History of the Relations Between the Soviet Union and the Rest of the World, 1917–1929.* 2 vols. Princeton, 1951.

Fishbein, Leslie. *Rebels in Bohemia: The Radicals of The Masses, 1911–1917.* Chapel Hill, N.C., 1982.

Fitzpatrick, Sheila. "The Civil War as a Formative Experience." In *Bolshevik Culture: Experiment and Order in the Russian Revolution,* edited by Abbot Gleason, Peter Kenez, and Richard Stites. Bloomington, Ind., 1985.

Fleming, Peter. *The Fate of Admiral Kolchak.* London, 1963.

Floto, Inga. *Colonel House in Paris.* Princeton, 1980.

Foglesong, David S. "America's Secret War Against Bolshevism: United States Intervention in the Russian Civil War, 1917–1920." Ph.D. dissertation, University of California, Berkeley, 1991.

―――. "German 'Intrigue,' U.S. Intelligence, and American Propaganda in Revolutionary Russia." Paper presented at the American Association for the Advancement of Slavic Studies Convention, Honolulu, November 21, 1993.

―――. "A Missouri Democrat in Revolutionary Russia: Ambassador David R. Francis and the American Confrontation with Russian Radicalism, 1917." *Gateway Heritage* 12, no. 3 (Winter 1992): 22–43.

―――. "Xenophon Kalamatiano: An American Spy in Revolutionary Russia?" *Intelligence and National Security* 6, no. 1 (January 1991): 154–95.

Footman, David. *Civil War in Russia.* London, 1961.

―――. *Siberian Partisans in the Civil War.* Oxford, 1954.

Fowler, Wilton B. *British-American Relations, 1917–1918: The Role of Sir William Wiseman.* Princeton, 1969.

Freund, Gerald. *Unholy Alliance: Russian-German Relations from the Treaty of Brest-Litovsk to the Treaty of Berlin.* New York, 1957.

Fry, Michael G. "Britain, the Allies and the Problem of Russia 1918–1919." *Canadian Journal of History* 2, no. 2 (September 1967): 62–84.

Fursenko, A. A. "Podgotovka amerikanskoi interventsii v Sovetskuiu Rossiiu." *Voprosy Istorii* (June 1986): 53–61.

Gaddis, John Lewis. *Russia, the Soviet Union, and the United States: An Interpretive History.* New York, 1978.

Gakaev, Zh.Zh., and Yu.K. Kirienko. "Razzhiganie Antantoi grazhdanskoi voini na Donu i Severnom Kavkaze." In *Imperialisticheskaia interventsiia na Donu i Severnom Kavkaze,* edited by I. I. Mints. Moscow, 1988.

Galili, Ziva. *The Menshevik Leaders in the Russian Revolution.* Princeton, 1989.

Gambashidze, Givi. *Iz istorii politiki SShA v otnoshenii Gruzii 1917–1920.* Tbilisi, 1960.

Ganelin, R. Sh. *Rossiia i SShA 1914–1917.* Leningrad, 1969.

———. *Sovetsko-amerikanskie otnosheniia v kontse 1917–nachale 1918g.* Leningrad, 1975.

Gardner, Lloyd C. *Safe for Democracy: The Anglo-American Response to Revolution, 1913–1923.* New York, 1984.

———. *Wilson and Revolutions, 1913–1921.* Washington, D.C., 1976.

———. "Woodrow Wilson and the Mexican Revolution." In *Woodrow Wilson and a Revolutionary World, 1913–1921,* edited by Arthur S. Link. Chapel Hill, N.C., 1982.

Gaworek, Norbert Horst. "Allied Economic Warfare Against Soviet Russia From November 1917 to March 1921." Ph.D. dissertation, University of Wisconsin, 1970.

———. "From Blockade to Trade: Allied Economic Warfare Against Soviet Russia, June 1919 to January 1920." *Jahrbücher für Geschichte Osteuropas* 23, H. 1 (1975): 39–69.

Gelfand, Lawrence E., ed. *Herbert Hoover: The Great War and Its Aftermath.* Iowa City, 1974.

———. *The Inquiry: American Preparations for Peace, 1917–1919.* New Haven, Conn., 1963.

George, Alexander L., and Juliette L. George. *Woodrow Wilson and Colonel House: A Personality Study.* New York, 1956.

———. "*Woodrow Wilson and Colonel House:* A Reply to Weinstein, Anderson, and Link." *Political Science Quarterly* 96, no. 4 (Winter 1981–82): 641–65.

George, Brian T. "The State Department and Sun Yat-sen: American Policy and the Revolutionary Disintegration of China, 1920–1924." *Pacific Historical Review* (1977).

Gilderhus, Mark T. *Diplomacy and Revolution: U.S.-Mexican Relations Under Wilson and Carranza.* Tucson, Ariz., 1977.

———. *Pan American Visions: Woodrow Wilson in the Western Hemisphere, 1913–1921.* Tucson, Ariz., 1986.

Gleason, Abbott, Peter Kenez, and Richard Stites, eds. *Bolshevik Culture: Experiment and Order in the Russian Revolution.* Bloomington, Ind., 1985.

Goldhurst, Richard. *The Midnight War: The American Intervention in Russia, 1918–1919.* New York, 1978.

Goldin, V. I. *Interventsiia i anti-bol'shevistskoe dvizhenie na Russkom Severe, 1918–1920.* Moscow, 1993.

Golin, A. M. *Proconsul in Politics: A Study of Lord Milner in Opposition and in Power.* New York, 1964.

Golinkov, David L. *Krushenie antisovetskogo podpol'ia v SSSR.* 2 vols. Moscow, 1980.

Good, Jane. "America and the Russian Revolutionary Movement, 1888–1905." *Russian Review* 41, no. 3 (July 1982): 273–87.

Graber, D. A. *Crisis Diplomacy: A History of U.S. Intervention Policies and Practices.* Washington, D.C., 1959.

Green, David. *Shaping Political Consciousness: The Language of Politics in America from McKinley to Reagan.* Ithaca, N.Y., 1987.

Grieb, Kenneth J. *The United States and Huerta.* Lincoln, Neb., 1969.

Gromyko, A. A., and B. N. Ponomarev, eds. *Soviet Foreign Policy 1917–1980.* 2 vols. Moscow, 1981.

Grose, Peter. *Gentleman Spy: The Life of Allen Dulles.* New York, 1994.

Grubbs, Frank L. *The Struggle for Labor Loyalty: Gompers, the A.F. of L., and the Pacifists, 1917–1920.* Durham, N.C., 1968.

Guhin, Michael A. *John Foster Dulles: A Statesman and His Times.* New York, 1972.

Gvishiani, L. A. "The Martens Mission." *International Affairs* (October 1964): 62–65, 98.

————. *Sovetskaia Rossiia i SShA 1917–1920.* Moscow, 1970.

Haefner, Lutz. "The Assassination of Count Mirbach and the 'July Uprising' of the Left Socialist Revolutionaries in Moscow, 1918." *Russian Review* 50, no. 3 (July 1991): 324–44.

Hagedorn, Hermann. *The Magnate: William Boyce Thompson and His Time, 1869–1930.* New York, 1935.

Haley, P. Edward. *Revolution and Intervention: The Diplomacy of Taft and Wilson with Mexico, 1910–1917.* New York, 1970.

Hall, Linda B., and Don M. Coerver. *Revolution on the Border: The United States and Mexico, 1910–1920.* Albuquerque, N.M., 1988.

Halliday, E. M. *The Ignorant Armies.* New York, 1958.

Harbaugh, William Henry. "Wilson, Roosevelt, and Interventionism, 1914–1917: A Study of Domestic Influences on the Formulation of American Foreign Policy." Ph.D. dissertation, Northwestern University, 1954.

Harris, Charles H. III, and Louis R. Sadler. *The Border and the Revolution.* Las Cruces, N.M., 1988.

Hart, D. G. "A Connoisseur of 'Rabble-Rousing,' 'Human Folly,' and 'Theological Pathology': H. L. Mencken on American Presbyterians." *American Presbyterians* 66, no. 3 (Fall 1988): 195–204.

Hart, John Mason. *Revolutionary Mexico: The Coming and Process of the Mexican Revolution.* Berkeley, 1987.

Hartig, Thomas H. "Robert Lansing: An Interpretive Biography." Ph.D. dissertation, Ohio State University, 1974.

Hasegawa, Tsuyoshi. *The February Revolution: Petrograd, 1917.* Seattle, 1981.

Healy, Ann. "Tsarist Anti-Semitism and Russian-American Relations." *Slavic Review* 42, no. 3 (Fall 1983): 408–25.

Healy, David. *Gunboat Diplomacy in the Wilson Era: The U.S. Navy in Haiti, 1915–1916.* Madison, Wisc., 1976.

Heckscher, August. *Woodrow Wilson: A Biography.* New York, 1991.

Heenan, Louise Erwin. *Russian Democracy's Fatal Blunder: The Summer Offensive of 1917.* New York, 1987.

Hiden, John W. *The Baltic States and Weimar Ostpolitik.* Cambridge, 1987.

————. "From War to Peace: Britain, Germany and the Baltic States 1918–1921." *Journal of Baltic Studies* 19, no. 4 (Winter 1988): 371–82.

Higham, John. *Strangers in the Land: Patterns of American Nativism 1860–1925.* 1963. Reprint, New York, 1975.

Hilderbrand, Robert C. *Power and the People: Executive Management of Public Opinion in Foreign Affairs, 1897–1921.* Chapel Hill, N.C., 1981.

Hill, Larry D. *Emissaries to a Revolution.* Baton Rouge, La., 1973.

Hodge, Larry G. "American Diplomacy Towards Transcaucasia During the Russian Revolution, March 1917–March 1918." *New Review: A Journal of East European History* 15, no. 1–2 (1975): 20–38.

Hofstadter, Richard. *The Age of Reform.* New York, 1955.

————. *The American Political Tradition and the Men Who Made It.* 1948. Reprint, New York, 1973.

————. *The Paranoid Style in American Politics.* New York, 1965.

Hogenhuis-Seliverstoff, Anne. *Les Relations Franco-Soviétiques 1917–1924.* Paris, 1981.

Hopkins, C. Howard. *John R. Mott, 1865–1955: A Biography.* Grand Rapids, Mich., 1980.

Hopkins, George W. "The Politics of Food: United States and Soviet Hungary, March–August 1919." *Mid-America* 55, no. 4 (October 1973): 245–79.

Hunt, Michael H. *Ideology and U.S. Foreign Policy.* New Haven, Conn., 1987.

Ioffe, G. Z. *Kolchakovskaia avantiura i ee krakh.* Moscow, 1983.

Isaacson, Walter. "Sometimes, Right Makes Might." *Time,* December 21, 1992.

Israel, Fred. *Nevada's Key Pittman.* Lincoln, Neb., 1963.

Jacobs, Dan N. *Borodin: Stalin's Man in China.* Cambridge, Mass., 1981.

Jeffreys-Jones, Rhodri. *American Espionage: From Secret Service to CIA.* New York, 1977.

———. *The CIA and American Democracy.* New Haven, Conn., 1989.

———. "W. Somerset Maugham, Anglo-American Agent in Revolutionary Russia." *American Quarterly* 28, no. 1 (Spring 1976).

Johnson, Robert David. *The Peace Progressives and American Foreign Relations.* Cambridge, Mass., 1995.

Kalvoda, Josef. "Masaryk in America." *Jahrbücher für Geschichte Osteuropas* 27 (1979): 85–99.

Katz, Friedrich. *The Secret War in Mexico: Europe, the U.S., and the Mexican Revolution.* New York, 1981.

Kazemzadeh, Firuz. *The Struggle for Transcaucasia, 1917–1921.* Westport, Conn., 1951.

Keep, John. "1917: The Tyranny of Paris over Petrograd." *Soviet Studies* 20, no. 1 (July 1968).

Kenez, Peter. *The Birth of the Propaganda State: Soviet Methods of Mass Mobilization, 1917–1929.* New York, 1985.

———. *Civil War in South Russia, 1918.* Berkeley, 1971.

———. "The Ideology of the White Movement." *Soviet Studies* 32, no. 1 (January 1980): 58–83.

Kennan, George F. "American Troops in Russia: The True Record." *Atlantic Monthly* 203 (1959): 36–42.

———. *Memoirs 1925–1950.* Boston, 1967.

———. "Morality and American Foreign Policy." *Foreign Affairs* (Winter 1985–86): 205–18.

———. *Russia and the West Under Lenin and Stalin.* Boston, 1961.

———. *Soviet-American Relations, 1917–1920.* 2 vols. Vol. 1, *Russia Leaves the War.* Princeton, 1956. Vol 2., *The Decision to Intervene.* Princeton, 1958.

———. "Soviet Historiography and America's Role in the Intervention." *American Historical Review* 65, no. 2 (January 1960): 302–22.

Kennedy, David. *Over Here: The First World War and American Society.* New York, 1980.

Kettle, Michael. *Russia and the Allies 1917–1920.* 3 vols. Vol. 1, *The Allies and the Russian Collapse, March 1917–March 1918.* London, 1981. Vol. 2, *The Road to Intervention, March–November 1918.* London, 1988. Vol. 3, *Churchill and the Archangel Fiasco, November 1918–July 1919.* London, 1992.

———. *Sidney Reilly.* New York, 1983.

Khatskevich, A.F. *Soldat velikikh boev: Zhizn' i deiatelnost' F.E. Dzerzhinskogo.* Minsk, 1987.

Khromov, S. S., ed. *Grazhdanskaia voina i voennaia interventsiia v SSSR.* Moscow, 1983.

Killen, Linda. *The Russian Bureau: A Case Study in Wilsonian Diplomacy.* Lexington, Ky., 1983.

———. "The Search for a Democratic Russia: Bakhmetev and the United States." *Diplomatic History* 2, no. 3 (Summer 1978): 237–56.

———. "The Search for a Democratic Russia: The Wilson Administration's Russian Policy, 1917–1921." Ph.D. dissertation, University of North Carolina, Chapel Hill, 1975.

———. "Self-Determination vs. Territorial Integrity: Conflict within the American

Delegation at Paris over Wilsonian Policy Toward the Russian Borderlands."
Nationalities Papers 10, no. 1 (Spring 1982): 65–78.

Klimenko, V. A. *Bor'ba s kontrrevoliutsei v Moskve, 1917–1920.* Moscow, 1978.

Knight, Alan. *The Mexican Revolution.* Vol. 2. Cambridge, 1986.

———. *U.S.-Mexican Relations, 1910–1940: An Interpretation.* San Diego, 1987.

Knock, Thomas J. *To End All Wars: Woodrow Wilson and the Quest for a New World Order.* New York, 1992.

Knott, Stephen F. "Lifting the Veil: The Roots of American Covert Activity." Ph.D. dissertation, Boston College, 1991.

Koenker, Diane P., William G. Rosenberg, and Ronald Grigor Suny, eds. *Party, State, and Society in the Russian Civil War.* Bloomington, Ind., 1989.

Kolonitskii, Boris I. "Antibourgeois Propaganda and Anti-'Burzhui' Consciousness in 1917." *Russian Review* 53, no. 2 (April 1994): 183–96.

Koltz, Arno W. F. "British Economic Interests in Siberia During the Russian Civil War, 1917–1920." *Journal of Modern History* 48 (September 1976): 483–91.

Kostiainen, Auvo. "Santeri Nuorteva and the Origins of Soviet-American Relations." *American Studies in Scandinavia* 15 (1983): 1–14.

Kotsonis, Yanni. "Arkhangel'sk, 1918: Regionalism and Populism in the Russian Civil War." *Russian Review* 51, no. 4. (October 1992).

Kovtun, George J. *Masaryk and America: Testimony of a Relationship.* Washington, D.C., 1988.

Krasnov, I. M. *Klassovaia Bor'ba v SShA i dvizhenie protiv antisovetskoi interventsii (1919–1920gg.).* Moscow, 1961.

Kravchenko, Vladimir F. "Pervie shagi VChK (Novoe o zagovore Lokkarta)." *Sovetskoe gosudarstvo i pravo* (March 1967): 97–102.

———. *Pod imenem Shmidkena.* Moscow, 1970.

Krenn, Michael L. *U.S. Policy Toward Economic Nationalism in Latin America, 1917–1929.* Wilmington, Del., 1990.

Kunina, A. E. "V Kollokvium istorikov SSSR i SShA." *Novaia i noveishaia istoriia* no. 1 (1985): 212–16.

Kuz'min, G. V. *Razgrom interventov i belogvardeitsev v 1917–1922gg.* Moscow, 1977.

Langbart, David A. " 'Spare No Expense': The Department of State and the Search for Information about Bolshevik Russia, November 1917–September 1918." *Intelligence and National Security* 4, no. 2 (April 1989): 316–34.

Lasch, Christopher. "American Intervention in Siberia: A Reinterpretation." *Political Science Quarterly* 77, no. 2 (June 1962).

———. *The American Liberals and the Russian Revolution.* New York, 1962.

———. *The New Radicalism in America 1889–1963.* New York, 1965.

Lazitch, Branko, and Milorad Drachkovitch. *Lenin and the Comintern.* Vol. 1. Stanford, Calif., 1972.

Lears, T. J. Jackson. *No Place of Grace: Antimodernism and the Transformation of American Culture 1880–1920.* New York, 1981.

Leggett, George. *The Cheka: Lenin's Political Police.* Oxford, 1981.

———. "Lenin's Reported Destruction of the Cheka Archive." *Survey* 24, no. 2 (Spring 1979): 193–99.

Lel'chuk, V. S., and E. I. Pivovar. "Mentalitet Sovetskogo obshchestva i 'kholodnaia voina.'" *Otechestennaia istoriia* 6 (1993).

Levin, N. Gordon. *Woodrow Wilson and World Politics: America's Response to War and Revolution.* New York, 1968.

Libbey, James K. *Alexander Gumberg and Soviet-American Relations, 1917–1933.* Lexington, Ky., 1977.

————. "The American-Russian Chamber of Commerce." *Diplomatic History* 9, no. 3 (Summer 1985).

Lincoln, W. Bruce. *Red Victory*. New York, 1989.

Link, Arthur S. *The Higher Realism of Woodrow Wilson and Other Essays*. Nashville, 1971.

————. "That Cobb Interview." *Journal of American History* 72 (June 1985): 7–17.

————. *Wilson: The New Freedom*. Princeton, 1956.

————. *Woodrow Wilson and the Progressive Era*. New York, 1954.

————. "Woodrow Wilson: Presbyterian in Government." In *Calvinism and the Political Order*, edited by George L. Hunt. Philadelphia, 1965.

————. *Woodrow Wilson: Revolution, War, and Peace*. Arlington Heights, Ill., 1979.

Listikov, S. V., and I. A. Kurtov. "Kollokvium istorikov SSSR i SShA." *Amerikanskii ezhegodnik* (1985): 246–255.

Little, Richard. *Intervention: External Involvement in Civil Wars*. London, 1975.

Lockhart, Robin B. *Reilly: Ace of Spies*. New York, 1967.

Long, John W. "American Intervention in Russia: The North Russian Expedition, 1918–19." *Diplomatic History* 6, no. 1 (Winter 1982): 45–67.

————. "Civil War and Intervention in North Russia, 1918–1920." Ph.D. dissertation, Columbia University, 1972.

Lower, Richard C. *A Bloc of One: The Political Career of Hiram W. Johnson*. Stanford, Calif., 1993.

————. "Hiram Johnson and the Progressive Denouement, 1910–1920." Ph.D. dissertation, University of California, Berkeley, 1969.

————. "Hiram Johnson: The Making of an Irreconcilable." *Pacific Historical Review* 41 (1972): 505–26.

Luckett, Richard. *The White Generals*. Edinburgh, 1971.

Lyandres, Semion. "The 1918 Attempt on the Life of Lenin: A New Look at the Evidence." *Slavic Review* 48, no. 3 (Fall 1989): 432–48.

McFadden, David W. *Alternative Paths: Soviets and Americans, 1917–1920*. New York, 1993.

————. "Hiram Johnson, Raymond Robins, and the Struggle for an Alternative American Policy Toward Soviet Russia, 1918." *Peace and Change* 18, no. 1 (January 1993): 50–77.

Mackay, Ruddock. *Balfour: Intellectual Statesman*. New York, 1985.

MacLaren, Roy. *Canadians in Russia, 1918–1919*. Toronto, 1976.

Maddox, Robert J. *The Unknown War with Russia*. San Rafael, Calif., 1977.

————. *William E. Borah and American Foreign Policy*. Baton Rouge, La., 1969.

————. "Woodrow Wilson, the Russian Embassy and Siberian Intervention." *Pacific Historical Review* 36 (November 1967): 435–48.

Mal'kov, Viktor L. "Bol'sheviki i 'Germanskoe Zoloto'. Nakhodki v Arkhivakh SShA." *Novaia i noveishaia istoriia* (September-October 1993): 42–52.

————, ed. *Pervaia Mirovaia Voina*. Moscow, 1994.

Marsden, George M. *Fundamentalism and American Culture: The Shaping of Twentieth Century Evangelicalism: 1870–1925*. New York, 1980.

Mawdsley, Evan. *The Russian Civil War*. Boston, 1987.

May, Elaine Tyler. *Great Expectations: Marriage and Divorce in Post-Victorian America*. Chicago, 1980.

May, Henry. *The End of American Innocence*. New York, 1959.

Mayer, Arno J. *The Politics and Diplomacy of Peacemaking: Containment and Counterrevolution at Versailles, 1918–1919*. New York, 1967.

————. *Wilson vs. Lenin: Political Origins of the New Diplomacy, 1917–1918*. Cleveland, 1964.

Meyer, Michael C. *Huerta: A Political Portrait.* Lincoln, Neb., 1972.

Miller, Robert M. *American Protestantism and Social Issues, 1919–1939.* Chapel Hill, N.C., 1958.

Minaev, Vladislav N. *Kovarnye metody inostrannykh razvedok.* Moscow, 1940.

———. *Tainoe stanovitsia iavnym.* Moscow, 1960.

Mints, I. I. *God 1918.* Moscow, 1982.

Morley, James. *The Japanese Thrust into Siberia, 1918.* New York, 1954.

———. "The Russian Revolution in the Amur Basin." *American Slavic and East European Review* 16 (December 1957): 450–72.

Mosley, Leonard. *Dulles: A Biography of Eleanor, Allen, and John Foster Dulles and Their Family Network.* New York, 1978.

Mulder, John M. "'A Gospel of Order': Woodrow Wilson's Religion and Politics." In *The Wilson Era: Essays in Honor of Arthur S. Link,* edited by John Milton Cooper and Charles E. Neu. Arlington Heights, Ill., 1991.

———. *Woodrow Wilson: The Years of Preparation.* Princeton, 1978.

Murray, Robert K. *Red Scare.* Minneapolis, 1955.

Nation, R. Craig. *Black Earth, Red Star: A History of Soviet Security Policy, 1917–1991.* Ithaca, N.Y., 1992.

Neu, Charles E. "In Search of Colonel Edward M. House: The Texas Years, 1858–1912." *Southwestern Historical Quarterly* 93 (July 1989): 25–44.

Newman, Simon P. "The Hegelian Roots of Woodrow Wilson's Progressivism." *Journal of Presbyterian History* 64, no. 3 (Fall 1986): 191–201.

Nezhinskii, L. N. "Vneshnaiia Politika Sovetskogo Gosudarstva v 1917–1921 godax: Kurs na 'Mirovuiu Revoliutsiiu' ili na Mirnoe Sosushchestvovanie?" *Istoriia SSSR* no. 6 (1991): 3–26.

Nordholt, Jan Willem Schulte. *Woodrow Wilson: A Life for World Peace.* Berkeley, 1991.

Norton, Henry. *The Far Eastern Republic of Siberia.* London, 1923.

O'Connor, Timothy. *Diplomacy and Revolution: G. V. Chicherin and Soviet Foreign Affairs, 1918–1930.* Ames, Ia., 1988.

O'Neill, Thomas J. "Business, Investment and Revolution in Russia." Ph.D. dissertation, McGill University, 1987.

Osborn, George C. *Woodrow Wilson: The Early Years.* Baton Rouge, La., 1968.

Osgood, Robert E. *Ideals and Self-Interest in America's Foreign Relations.* Chicago, 1964.

Ostriakov, S. Z. *Voennye Chekisty.* Moscow, 1979.

O'Toole, G. J. A. *The Encyclopedia of American Intelligence and Espionage.* New York, 1988.

———. *Honorable Treachery: A History of U.S. Intelligence, Espionage, and Covert Action from the American Revolution to the CIA.* New York, 1991.

Page, Stanley W. *The Formation of the Baltic States: A Study of the Effects of Great Power Politics Upon the Emergence of Lithuania, Latvia, and Estonia.* New York, 1970.

Parrini, Carl P. *Heir to Empire: United States Economic Diplomacy, 1916–1923.* Pittsburgh, 1969.

Parry, Albert. "Washington B. Vanderlip, the 'Khan of Kamchatka.'" *Pacific Historical Review* 17, no. 3 (August 1948): 311–30.

Patenaude, Bertrand M. "Herbert Hoover's Brush with Bolshevism." Kennan Institute Occasional Paper no. 248. June 1992.

Pereira, Norman G. O. "The 'Democratic Counterrevolution' of 1918 in Siberia." *Nationalities Papers* 16, no. 1 (Spring 1988): 71–94.

———. "Regional Consciousness in Siberia Before and After October 1917." *Canadian Slavonic Papers* 30, no. 1 (March 1988): 112–33.

———. "White Power During the Civil War in Siberia (1918–1920): Dilemmas of Kolchak's War Anti-Communism." *Canadian Slavonic Papers* 29, no. 1 (March 1987).

Perez, Louis A. Jr. *Intervention, Revolution, and Politics in Cuba, 1913–1921*. Pittsburgh, 1978.

Phillips, Hugh D. *Between the Revolution and the West: A Political Biography of Maxim M. Litvinov*. Boulder, Colo., 1992.

Pidhainy, Oleh S., Loventrice A. Scales, and Alexander S. Pidhainy. "Silver and Billions: American Finances and the Bolshevik Revolution." *New Review: A Journal of East European History* 14 (1974): 1–47.

Pipes, Richard. *Russia Under the Bolshevik Regime*. New York, 1993.

———. *The Russian Revolution*. New York, 1990.

———. *Struve: Liberal on the Right, 1905–1944*. Cambridge, Mass., 1980.

Polenberg, Richard. *Fighting Faiths: The Abrams Case, the Supreme Court, and Free Speech*. New York, 1987.

Propas, Frederic L. "Creating a Hard Line toward Russia: The Training of State Department Soviet Experts, 1927–1937," *Diplomatic History* 8 (1984): 209–26.

Pruessen, Ronald W. *John Foster Dulles: The Road to Power*. New York, 1982.

Quirk, Robert. *An Affair of Honor: Woodrow Wilson and Vera Cruz, 1914*. New York, 1962.

Raat, W. Dirk. "U.S. Intelligence Operations and Covert Action in Mexico, 1900–47." *Journal of Contemporary History* 22, no. 4 (October 1987): 615–37.

Radkey, Oliver H. *The Agrarian Foes of Bolshevism: Promise and Default of the Russian Socialist Revolutionaries, February to October 1917*. New York, 1958.

———. *The Election to the Russian Constituent Assembly of 1917*. Cambridge, Mass., 1950.

———. *The Sickle Under the Hammer: The Russian Socialist Revolutionaries in the Early Months of Soviet Rule*. New York, 1963.

Radosh, Ronald. "John Spargo and Wilson's Russian Policy, 1920." *Journal of American History* 52 (December 1965): 548–65.

Raeff, Marc. "An American View of the Decembrist Revolt." *Journal of Modern History* 25, no. 3 (September 1953): 286–93.

Rand, Larry. "America Views Russian Serf Emancipation 1861." *Mid-America* 50, no. 1 (January 1968): 42–51.

Ranelagh, John. *The Agency*. New York, 1987.

Rauch, Georg von. *The Baltic States: The Years of Independence. Estonia, Latvia, Lithuania 1917–1940*. Berkeley, 1974.

Reikhberg, G. E., and B. S. Shapik. "L. K. Martens." *Voprosy istorii KPSS* 1 (1965): 97–101.

———. "Amerikanskie senatori sudiat sovetskogo predstavitelia." *Istoriia SSSR* 7, no. 2 (1963): 81–89.

Rhodes, Benjamin D. "The Anglo-American Intervention at Archangel, 1918–1919: The Role of the 339th Infantry." *The International History Review* 8, no. 3 (August 1986): 367–88.

———. *The Anglo-American Winter War with Russia*. New York, 1988.

———. "A Prophet in the Russian Wilderness: The Mission of Consul Felix Cole at Archangel, 1917–1919." *Review of Politics* 46, no. 4 (1984): 388–409.

Richard, Carl J. "'The Shadow of a Plan': The Rationale Behind Wilson's 1918 Siberian Intervention." *Historian* 49, no. 1 (November 1986): 64–84.

Roberts, Beth Alene. "A Study of American Opinion Regarding Allied Intervention in Siberia." M.A. thesis, University of Hawaii, 1938.

Rogin, Michael Paul. "Max Weber and Woodrow Wilson: The Iron Cage in Germany and America." *Polity* 3, no. 4 (Summer 1971): 557–75.

Rosenberg, William G. *Liberals in the Russian Revolution: The Constitutional Democratic Party, 1917–1921*. Princeton, 1975.

Rosenstone, Robert. *Romantic Revolutionary: A Biography of John Reed*. New York, 1975.

Ross, Dorothy. "Socialism and American Liberalism: Academic Social Thought in the 1880s." *Perspectives in American History* 11 (1977–78).

Ross, Steven J. "Struggles for the Silent Screen: Workers, Radicals, and the Political Uses of Silent Film." *American Historical Review* 96, no. 2 (April 1991).

Rourke, F. E. *Secrecy and Publicity: Dilemmas of Democracy.* Baltimore, 1961.

Rudnev, Daniil M., and Sergei I. Tsybov. *Sledovatel' Verkhovnogo Tribunala.* Tallin, 1971.

Salvatore, Nick. *Eugene V. Debs: Citizen and Socialist.* Chicago, 1982.

Salzman, Neil V. *Reform and Revolution: The Life and Times of Raymond Robins.* Kent, Ohio, 1991.

Sarasohn, David. *The Party of Reform: Democrats in the Progressive Era.* Jackson, Miss., 1989.

Sayle, Edward F. "The Historical Underpinnnings of the U.S. Intelligence Community." *International Journal of Intelligence and Counterintelligence* 1, no. 1 (Spring 1986): 1–27.

Schraeder, Peter J., ed. *Intervention in the 1980s: U.S. Foreign Policy in the Third World.* Boulder, Colo., 1989.

Schuman, Frederick L. *American Policy Toward Russia Since 1917.* New York, 1928.

Schwarz, Jordan A. *Liberal: Adolf A. Berle and the Vision of an American Era.* New York, 1987.

Seleznev, G. K. *Krakh zagovora.* Moscow, 1963.

Senn, Alfred Erich. *The Emergence of Modern Lithuania.* New York, 1959.

Service, Robert. *The Bolshevik Party in Revolution: A Study in Organisational Change, 1917–1923.* London, 1979.

Shaffer, Robert. "Jews, Reds, and Violets: Anti-Semitism and Anti-Radicalism at New York University, 1916–1929." *Journal of Ethnic Studies* 15, no. 2 (Summer 1987): 47–83.

Shishkin, V. I. *Iz Istorii interventsii i grazhdanskoi voiny v Sibiri i na Dal'nem Vostoke 1917–1922gg.* Novosibirsk, 1985.

Shteinberg, Valentin A. *Ekab Peters.* Moscow, 1989.

Siegel, Katherine A. S. "Loans and Legitimacy: Soviet-American Trade and Diplomacy, 1919–1929." Ph.D. dissertation, University of California, Santa Barbara, 1991.

———. "Technology and Trade: Russia's Pursuit of American Investment, 1917–1929." *Diplomatic History* 17, no. 3 (Summer 1993): 375–98.

Silverlight, John. *The Victors' Dilemma: Allied Intervention in the Russian Civil War.* New York, 1972.

Singerman, Robert. "The American Career of the *Protocols of the Elders of Zion.*" *American Jewish History* 81, no. 1 (September 1981): 48–78.

Sivachev, N. V., and N. N. Yakovlev. *Russia and the United States: U.S.-Soviet Relations from the Soviet Point of View.* Chicago, 1979.

Sklar, Martin J. *The United States as a Developing Country.* Cambridge, 1992.

———. "Woodrow Wilson and the Political Economy of Modern United States Liberalism." *Studies on the Left* 1, no. 3 (1960): 17–47.

Smallwood, James. "Banquo's Ghost at the Paris Peace Conference: The United States and the Hungarian Question." *East European Quarterly* 12, no. 3 (1978): 289–307.

Smith, B. F. *The Shadow Warriors.* New York, 1983.

Smith, C. Jay Jr. *Finland and the Russian Revolution, 1917–1922.* Athens, Ga., 1958.

Smith, Gary Scott. *The Seeds of Secularization: Calvinism, Culture, and Pluralism in America, 1870–1915.* Grand Rapids, Mich., 1985.

Smith, Robert F. *The United States and Revolutionary Nationalism in Mexico, 1916–1932.* New York, 1972.

Smith, Tony. *America's Mission: The United States and the Worldwide Struggle for Democracy in the Twentieth Century.* Princeton, 1994.

Snow, Russell E. *The Bolsheviks in Siberia, 1917–1918.* Cranbury, N.J., 1977.

————. "The Russian Revolution in Transbaikalia, 1917–1918." *Soviet Studies* 23 (October 1971): 201–15.

Spence, Richard B. *Boris Savinkov: Renegade on the Left.* New York, 1991.

Startt, James D. "The Uneasy Partnership: Wilson and the Press at Paris." *Mid-America* 52, no. 1 (January 1970): 55–69.

Stewart, George. *The White Armies of Russia: A Chronicle of Counter-Revolution and Allied Intervention.* New York, 1933.

Strakhovsky, Leonid. *American Opinion About Russia, 1917–1920.* Toronto, 1961.

————. *Intervention at Archangel.* Princeton, 1944.

————. *The Origins of American Intervention in North Russia, 1918.* Princeton, 1937.

Stults, Taylor. "George Kennan: Russian Specialist of the 1890s." *Russian Review* 29, no. 3 (July 1970): 275–85.

Sullivan, Charles L. "The 1919 German Campaign in the Baltic: The Final Phase." In *The Baltic States in Peace and War, 1917–1945,* edited by V. Stanley Vardys and Romuald J. Misiunas. University Park, Penn., 1978.

————. "The German Role in the Baltic Campaign Spring 1919." *Baltic Review* 36 (October 1969): 40–62.

Suny, Ronald Grigor. *The Baku Commune 1917–1918.* Princeton, 1972.

————, ed. *Transcaucasia: Nationalism and Social Change.* Ann Arbor, 1983.

Svetachev, N. *Imperialisticheskaia interventsiia v sibiri i na dal'nem vostoke (1918–1922 gg.).* Novosibirsk, 1983.

Talbert, Roy. *Negative Intelligence: The Army and the American Left, 1917–1941.* Jackson, Mich., 1991.

Tate, Michael L. "Pershing's Punitive Expedition: Pursuer of Bandits or Presidential Panacea?" *The Americas* 32, no. 1 (July 1975): 46–71.

Terebov, O. V. "Kongress SShA i nachalo amerikanskoi interventsii v Sovetskoi Rossii (1917–1918gg.)." *Vestnik Moskovskogo Universiteta,* Ser. 8, Istoriia (1989), no. 6, 71–76.

Thelen, David P. *Robert M. LaFollette and the Insurgent Spirit.* Boston, 1976.

Thompson, Arthur W. "American Socialists and the Russian Revolution of 1905–1906." In *Freedom and Reform: Essays in Honor of Henry Steele Commager,* edited by H. M. Hyman and L. W. Levy. New York, 1967.

Thompson, Arthur W., and Robert A. Hart. *The Uncertain Crusade: America and the Russian Revolution of 1905.* Boston, 1970.

Thompson, John M. "Allied and American Intervention in Russia, 1918–1921." In *Rewriting Russian History,* edited by C. Black. New York, 1962.

————. "Lenin's Analysis of Intervention." *American Slavic and East European Review* 17, no. 2 (April 1958): 151–60.

————. *Russia, Bolshevism, and the Versailles Peace.* Princeton, 1967.

Thorsen, Niels Aage. *The Political Thought of Woodrow Wilson, 1875–1910.* Princeton, 1988.

Tishkov, A. V. *Shchit i mech revoliutsii (Iz istorii VChK).* Moscow, 1979.

Torrey, Glenn, ed. *General Henri Berthelot and Romania: Mémoires et Correspondence 1916–1919.* New York, 1987.

Toulouse, Mark G. *The Transformation of John Foster Dulles.* Macon, Ga., 1985.

Trani, Eugene P. "Woodrow Wilson and the Decision to Intervene in Russia: A Reconsideration." *Journal of Modern History* 48 (September 1976): 440–61.

Trask, David F. *The United States in the Supreme War Council: American War Aims and Inter-Allied Strategy, 1917–1918.* Middletown, Conn., 1961.

Travis, Frederick F. *George Kennan and the American-Russian Relationship 1865–1924.* Athens, Ohio, 1990.

Trow, Clifford. "Woodrow Wilson and the Mexican Interventionist Movement of 1919."

Journal of American History 58, no. 1 (June 1971): 46–72.

Troy, Thomas F. *Donovan and the CIA: A History of the Establishment of the Central Intelligence Agency.* Frederick, Md., 1981.

Trush, M. I. *Mezhdunarodnaia Deiatel'nost' V. I. Lenina: Zashita zavoevanii sotsialisticheskoi revoliutsii 1919–1920.* Moscow, 1988.

Tuve, Jeanette E. "Changing Directions in Russian-American Economic Relations, 1912–1917." *Slavic Review* 31, no. 1 (March 1972): 52–70.

Ulam, Adam. *Expansion and Coexistence: The History of Soviet Foreign Policy, 1917–1967.* New York, 1968.

Uldricks, Teddy J. *Diplomacy and Ideology: The Origins of Soviet Foreign Relations, 1917–1930.* Beverly Hills, Calif., 1979.

———. "Russia and Europe: Diplomacy, Revolution, and Economic Development in the 1920s." *International History Review* 1 (June 1979).

Ullman, Richard H. *Anglo-Soviet Relations, 1917–1920.* 3 vols. Princeton, 1961–68.

Unfug, Douglas. "German Policy in the Baltic States, 1918–1919." Ph.D. dissertation, Yale University, 1960.

Unterberger, Betty M. *America's Siberian Expedition, 1918–1920: A Study of National Policy.* Durham, N.C., 1956.

———. *Intervention Against Communism: Did the United States Try to Overthrow the Soviet Government, 1918–1920?* College Station, Tex., 1987.

———. *The United States, Revolutionary Russia, and the Rise of Czechoslovakia.* Chapel Hill, N.C., 1989.

———. "Woodrow Wilson and the Bolsheviks: The 'Acid Test' of Soviet-American Relations." *Diplomatic History* 11, no. 2 (Spring 1987): 71–90.

———. "Woodrow Wilson and the Russian Revolution." In *Woodrow Wilson and a Revolutionary World,* edited by Arthur S. Link. Chapel Hill, N.C., 1982.

Utkin, A. I. *Diplomatiia Vudro Vil'sona.* Moscow, 1989.

Van Der Rhoer, Edward. *Master Spy: A True Story of Allied Espionage in Bolshevik Russia.* New York, 1981.

Virmavirta, Ia. "Karl Gustav Emil' Mannergeim." *Voprosy Istorii,* no. 1 (1994): 56–74.

Volkogonov, Dmitri. *Lenin: A New Biography.* New York, 1994.

Von Laue, Theodore H. "Soviet Diplomacy: G. V. Chicherin, People's Commissar for Foreign Affairs, 1918–1930." In *The Diplomats, 1919–1939,* edited by Gordon Craig and Felix Gilbert. 1953. Reprint, New York, 1971.

Wade, Rex A. *The Russian Search for Peace, February-October 1917.* Stanford, Calif., 1969.

Waite, Robert G. L. *Vanguard of Nazism: The Free Corps Movement in Postwar Germany, 1918–1923.* New York, 1952.

Walsh, William J. "Secretary of State Robert Lansing and the Russian Revolutions of 1917." Ph.D. dissertation, Georgetown University, 1986.

Walworth, Arthur. *America's Moment: 1918.* New York, 1977.

———. *Wilson and His Peacemakers: American Diplomacy at the Paris Peace Conference, 1919.* New York, 1986.

———. *Woodrow Wilson.* New York, 1978.

Warth, Robert D. *The Allies and the Russian Revolution: From the Fall of the Monarchy to the Peace of Brest-Litovsk.* Durham, N.C., 1954.

Weeks, Charles J. Jr. *An American Naval Diplomat in Revolutionary Russia: The Life and Times of Vice Admiral Newton A. McCully.* Annapolis, Md., 1993.

Weeks, Charles J. Jr., and Joseph O. Baylen. "Admiral Kolchak's Mission to the United States, 10 September–9 November 1917." *Military Affairs* 40, no. 2 (April 1976): 63–67.

Weinstein, Edwin A. *Woodrow Wilson: A Medical and Psychological Biography.* Princeton, 1981.

Weinstein, Edwin A., James William Anderson, and Arthur S. Link. "Woodrow Wilson's Political Personality: A Reappraisal." *Political Science Quarterly* 93, no. 4 (Winter 1978): 585–98.

Weissman, Benjamin M. *Herbert Hoover and Famine Relief to Soviet Russia: 1921–23.* Stanford, Calif., 1974.

White, Christine A. *British and American Commercial Relations with Soviet Russia, 1918–1924.* Chapel Hill, N.C., 1992.

———. "'Riches Have Wings': The Use of Russian Gold in Soviet Foreign Trade, 1918–1922." In *Contact or Isolation? Soviet-Western Relations in the Interwar Period,* edited by John Hiden and Aleksander Loit. Uppsala, Sweden, 1991.

White, John A. *The Siberian Intervention.* New York, 1950.

Williams, Warren E. "Die Politik der Alliierten gegenüber den Freikorps im Baltikum 1918–1919." *Vierteljahrshefte für Zeitgeschichte* 12 (April *1964*): 147–69.

Williams, William A. *America Confronts a Revolutionary World: 1776–1976.* New York, 1976.

———. "American Intervention in Russia, 1917–1920." *Studies on the Left* 3, no. 4 (Fall 1963): 24–48; 4, no. 1 (Winter 1964): 39–57.

———. *American-Russian Relations, 1781–1947.* New York, 1952.

———. "The Frontier Thesis and American Foreign Policy." *Pacific Historical Review* 24 (November 1955): 379–95.

Wilson, Joan Hoff. *Ideology and Economics: U.S. Relations with the Soviet Union, 1918–1933.* Columbia, Mo., 1974.

Wolper, Gregg. "The Origins of Public Diplomacy: Woodrow Wilson, George Creel, and the Committee on Public Information." Ph.D. dissertation, University of Chicago, 1991.

———. "Woodrow Wilson's New Diplomacy: Vira Whitehouse in Switzerland, 1918." *Prologue* 24, no. 3 (Fall 1992): 227–39.

Woodward, David R. "The British Government and Japanese Intervention in Russia during World War I." *Journal of Modern History* 46 (December 1974): 663–85.

———. *Trial by Friendship: Anglo-American Relations 1917–1918.* Lexington, Ky., 1993.

Wriston, Henry M. *Executive Agents in American Foreign Relations.* Gloucester, Mass., 1967.

Yardley, Herbert. *The American Black Chamber.* Indianapolis, 1931.

Zhugzhda, Robertas. "Imperialisticheskaia interventsiia protiv Sovetskoi Rossii i Pribaltika." *Kommunist* no. 6 (June 1987): 36–42.

Zolotukhin, V. P., and V. L. Mal'kov. "Oktiabrskaia revoliutsiia i vnutripoliticheskaia bor'ba v SShA." *Voprosy Istorii* no. 10 (October 1957): 143–66.

INDEX

Page numbers in italic refer to illustrations.

for Russian debt, 59, 64; for aid to anti-Bolsheviks, 60, 62–63, 86; advises not denouncing Bolsheviks, 64; on rumors about recognition, 66; assures Wilson Russia pro-Ally, 67; fires Lomonosov, 67; on U.S. fear of Russian reaction, 68; at Paris Peace Conference, 69; criticized by anti-Bolsheviks, 72; on need for secrecy in propaganda, 72; attacked by liberal, radical press, 73; on Japanese intervention, 148, 192; on Tomsk and Horvath movements, 152; for use of "help," not "intervention," 158; on anti-Americanism in Siberia, 184; on protests against Siberian force, 184; for U.S. intervention for political end, 192–93, 203; disavows recognition of Estonia, 261; urges ultimatum to Baltic states, 261–62; on financing Russian forces in Baltic region, 262–63; for releasing arms to Iudenich, 263–64; requests flour for Iudenich, 265, 267

Bakhmeteff, G., 52, 54

Balfour, Arthur, 82; says Russia must be helped, 191; on intervention in north, 205–6, 208; on cooperation with Germans, 256

Baltic region, 128, 231–71 passim

Baltimore, 287

Baltimore Sun, 197

Balts, 246

Barclay, Colville, 213

Barrows, David Prescott: "Puritan" anti-Bolshevism, 43–44, 45; favorable reports on Semenov, 153; mission to Manchuria, 153–54

Bavaria, 243

Benes, Eduard, 161

Berle, Adolf A., 128–29, 181

Bermondt-Avalov, P. M., 257, 269, 340 (n. 90)

Bertron, Samuel R.: backs Bakhmeteff on aid to Russia, 63; on demand for action in Russia, 165

Bismarck, Prince Otto von, 26

Bliss, Tasker H.: on Japanese occupation of eastern Siberia, 146–47; on intervention in north Russia, 197–98, 206–9, 214–15, 218, 219–20; on maintaining anti-Bolshevik front in Baltic region,

262; on financing aid to Russian forces in Baltic states, 263; on transfer of arms from Germany, 264; on public opinion, 334 (n. 131)

Blockade: of Mexico, 17; of Soviet Russia, 6, 232, 248–52, 269–70, 278, 286, 287

Bochkareva, Maria, 162

Bolsheviks: publish Allies' secret treaties, 2; peace proposals, 2, 35, 36, 64, 145; disperse Constituent Assembly, 4; overthrow Provisional Government, 4; sign Brest-Litovsk peace treaty, 4; nationalize foreign assets, 4, 45, 177; repudiate foreign loans, 4, 45, 177, 178, 280; peace negotiations, 24, 37, 66; seize power, 33, 35, 56; alleged German agents, 36, 58, 62, 112, *133, 134*, 171, 191, 195–96, 198; propaganda, 39, 42; alleged to nationalize women, 43, 283; and election returns, 85, 152, 233; and invitation of intervention, 190

Bolshevism: Wilson's views of, 1, 24–25, 38–39; menace to America, 5, 23, 38, 66, 226; American images of, 24–46, *136–38*; composite of domestic challenges, 25; negation of Americanism, 25, 45; and atheism, 43; and immorality, 44, 227; as scapegoat, 44; menace in Baltic region, 234

Borah, William, 297

Borodin, Mikhail, 276–77

Breshko-Breshkovskaia, E. K., 108–10

Brest-Litovsk, Treaty of, 46, 66, 112, 146, 155, 164, 191, 254, 275, 283

Brusilov, A. A., 86–87, 88

Bryan, William Jennings, 17

Bublikov, A. A., 72

Buckler, William, 279, 285

Bukharin, Nikolai, 276

Bullard, Arthur, 108

Bullitt, William C., 321 (n. 90), 345 (n. 39); mission to Russia, 69–70, 283–84, 285; opposes Japanese intervention, 148; doubts Wilson can resist pressure, 165; for withdrawal from Archangel, 227–28; calls famine parent of Bolshevism, 235; views relief as path to accommodation with Bolsheviks, 243; protests one-sided cease-fire, 244; for lifting blockade of Russia, 248

Bureau of Investigation, 21
Burke, Edmund, 28, 229
Burleson, Albert S., 103, 157, 197

Caldwell, John K., 151, 158
Carranza, Venustiano, 18, 20
Carson, Edward, 80
Cecil, Robert, 81, 91–92, 97–98, 100
Central Intelligence Agency, 9–10, 126–29, 296
Central Powers, 4, 24, 45, 79, 104, 160, 278
Chaikovskii, N. V., 212–13, 225
Cheka, 107, 118–20, 122–23, 125, 223
Chicago Tribune, 228
Chicherin, G. V., 44, 74, 123, 194, 286; on cooperation with U.S., 123, 223; on intervention in north Russia, 201; and Hoover-Nansen proposal, 244; background and personality, 275; differentiates America from Allies, 276; on anti-intervention movement in U.S., 276, 280, 287; attacks U.S. support for Whites, 277; appeals for negotiations, 279, 280, 287; rebukes Russian critics of Martens, 282; meets Bullitt, 284; on trade and recognition, 288; puzzled by U.S. policy, 290
Chinese Eastern Railway, 151, 157
Churchill, Winston, 229
Civil War (American), 12, 25, 88
Class Struggle, 282
Clemenceau, Georges, 244, 247, 257, 284, 285
Clerk, George, 98, 100
Cleveland, Grover, 13
Cobb, Frank, 50, 259
Colby, Bainbridge, 288, 291
Colby Note, 291
Colcord, Lincoln, 86
Cold War, 7, 9, 126–29, 296, 298
Cole, Felix, 201; on anti-Bolsheviks at Archangel, 114; warns Russians will not fight, 204; on response to Allies at Archangel, 225
Columbus, New Mexico, 20
Comintern. *See* Communist International
Committee on Civic Education, 108–10
Committee on Public Information, 37, 56, 195, 196, 276
Communist International, 278, 282, 283

Communist Labor Party, 287, 289
Communist Party (U.S.A.), 282, 286–87, 289
Congress, 84, 296; administration not frank with, 5–6, 297; criticism of Theodore Roosevelt, 14; and Wilson on Mexico, 17, 20; and war against Germany, 34; on Soviet nationalization of women, 43; and Russian embassy spending, 61, 70, 75; administration avoids requesting funds from, 71, criticism of War Trade Board, 71; strained relations with Wilson, 71, 237; investigation of Russian propaganda, 72; inquiries on Russian embassy status, 74; restrictions on foreign loans, 79, 89, 90, 105; constrains spending on propaganda, 107, 110, 317 (n. 14); and inhibition of intervention, 129; and expedition to Siberia, 164–65, 180, 182, 183–84, 186, 187; on intervention in north Russia, 225–28; and policy toward Baltic area, 232, 234; debate on ARA appropriation, 237–39; expected to criticize blockade, 251; restrictions on transfer of arms, 263; and lack of funds for Whites in Baltic states, 267, 269; Soviet views of, 280, 281; criticism of use of funds in Poland, 336 (n. 26)
Congress of Soviets, 66–67, 192
Constituent Assembly, 4, 48, 174, 192, 233
Constitutional Democratic Party. *See* Kadet Party
Constitutionalists, 17, 18, 19, 20
Coolidge, Archibald Cary: suggests using Czech army in Siberia, 155; on response to Allies at Archangel, 225
Cossacks, 61, 78, 81–92 passim, 151, 179, 181, 184, 185
Council of Foreign Ministers: approves arms to Baltic states, 247; allows coal for Germans fighting Bolsheviks, 256; agrees Germans should remain in Latvia and Lithuania, 257
Council of Four, 243; on blockade of Bolshevik Russia, 249, 250; allows provisions to Germans in Latvia, 255; for German evacuation of Latvia, 257
Council of Ten: on protecting Baltic area, 247

Crane, Charles R., 157; declines to be
ambassador to Russia, 50; enthusiasm
for Provisional Government, 50; praises
Bakhmeteff, 52; disillusionment with
Provisional Government, 83; dismisses
Soviet "pantomime" government, 84;
influence on Wilson, 94–95, 103–4,
294; on Czech-Americans to Russia,
108; lionizes Masaryk, 156; predicts
Russians will fight for Wilson's program, 163; reports Siberian army excellent, 176
Crane, Richard T.: on Jewish-Bolshevik
conspiracy, 41; on Russian war effort,
51; urges consultation with Masaryk,
156
Creel, George: hopes Kerensky will defeat
Bolsheviks, 56–57; conveys Bakhmeteff
message to Wilson, 58–59; urges pledge
of aid to anti-Bolsheviks, 65, 95–96;
on propaganda in Russia, 109–10; on
Sisson Documents, 196; Borodin on,
276–77
Crimea, 291
Crissman, John, 189
Crosby, Oscar T., 88, 90, 92, 93–95, 99,
102, 103
Cuba, 13–14, 83
Czech-Americans: and propaganda in Russia, 108
Czechoslovakian legionnaires: clash with
Bolsheviks, 116, 117, 123–24; as anti-
Bolshevik "nucleus," 155–64; "rescue"
of, 160, 166, 295; threats to positions in
Russia, 166–67; crush Bolshevik resistance, 168; declining morale of, 179;
hand over Kolchak at Irkutsk, 184; and
north Russian expedition, 205, 210–11,
214–15, 217

Daniels, Josephus, 61, 89, 99, 222, 252
"Dark people," 90, 163, 181
Davison, Henry P., 241
Debs, Eugene, 38, 122
Decree on Peace, 35
Democratic National Committee, 293, 295
Denikin, A. I., 75, *142*, 266
Derber, Peter, 151–52
Des Moines, 1, 9, 183
Dial, 228

Díaz, Porfirio, 15
Directorate, 173, 176, 179
Dominican Republic: U.S. military occupation of, 3, 11
Donovan, William J., 127
Dukes, Paul, 125
Dulles, Allen W.: on Wilson legacy, 9–10,
128–29, 296; for intervention in Lithuania, 234; urges supporting anti-Bolsheviks before resisting Germans, 257–58;
for encouraging Baltic nationalism
against Bolshevism, 258; on intervention in Hungary, 321 (n. 89)
Dulles, John Foster: on role of Russian
embassy, 71; on propaganda and covert
action, 127–28; on Kolchak as White
Hope, 181; and War Trade Board, 239;
on blocking trade with Bolsheviks, 251;
and Wilson legacy, 296
Duma, 48, 49
Dvina River, 212, 214
Dzerzhinskii, F. E., 119

Eastman, Crystal, 282
Eastman, Max, 23, 282, 312 (n. 95)
Ellis, William T.: stresses sympathy for
Russian revolutionary spirit, 174; warns
intervention will strengthen Bolsheviks,
222
Embargo: Wilsonian tool, 4, 12; against
Soviet Russia, 5, 127, 291; and Mexico,
17, 18, 19, 20
Entente. *See* Allies
Espionage Act, 38
Estonia, 231, 236, 239, 240, 243, 267; in
war and revolution, 232–33, advance on
Petrograd, 245, 246, 247; and German
soldiers, 254, 257; autonomy and recog-
nition questions, 258–62; and disband-
ing of Iudenich forces, 268
Estonian Workers' Commune, 233

Federal Reserve Board, 248
Filipinos, 16
Finland, 231, 233, 239, 240, 241, 247, 261,
267; White Guards menace Murmansk,
193, 201; Hoover desire to aid, 236, 243,
253; proposals to capture Petrograd,
252–54, 339 (n. 76)
Finnish Information Bureau, 275

Foch, Ferdinand, 207, 215
Foreign Commissariat. *See* People's Commissariat for Foreign Affairs
Foster, John Watson, 29
Fourteen Points. *See* Wilson, Woodrow
Fox, Albert, 58
France, 46, 49, 55, 62, 66; aid to anti-Bolsheviks in south Russia, 76–77, 79, 92–95, 99–101; cooperation with U.S. intelligence, 114, 117–21, 123–24; for inter-Allied civilian board in Siberia, 167; military governor of Archangel, 212–13; and Hoover-Nansen proposal, 244; and U.S. military supplies, 263–64; and Prinkipo proposal, 280
Francis, David R., 150; urges eradication of Bolshevism, 39, 295; on menace of Bolshevism, 42–43, 211, 226; on revolution of March 1917, 49; praises Bakhmeteff, 52; on conditions for loans to Russia, 53, 60; lionized, 89; interest in anti-Bolsheviks, 111–14; suggests sending troops to Russia, 191; reports majority of Russians will welcome Allied intervention, 196; on rising opposition to Bolsheviks, 197; on Bolsheviks as German agents, 198; for ignoring proposal of Soviet representative to U.S., 200; for speeding troops to Archangel, 202; on anti-Soviet coup at Archangel, 211; on use of U.S. troops inside Russia, 211–14, 219; opposes military coup at Archangel, 213; for U.S. financing of Russian legion, 217; notes U.S. cannot declare war on Russia, 219; directed to keep quiet, 226; urges larger military intervention, 226; Breckinridge Long on, 227; for sending troops and food to Petrograd, 235
Free love, 42
Freikorps, 255, 257
French Revolution, 27, 29, 30, 31, 38, 40, 59, 229
Friede, Aleksandr V., 120, 122
Friede, Marie, 120
Frontier, 9, 14

Gade, John A.: on Jews and Bolshevism, 41; on intelligence and propaganda, 127; on Estonian fight against Bolshevism,

245; supports Iudenich forces in Estonia, 268; on failure of Whites in Baltic area, 269; on intervention and blockade in propaganda of Bolsheviks, 269–70; on Bermondt and Iudenich, 340 (n. 90)
Garrison, Lindley, 20
Geddes, Sir Eric, 208
Germany, 37, 40, 50, 51, 52, 76, 101; intelligence and subversion, 3, 129; domination and exploitation of Russia, 4, 8, 47, 48, 63, 65, 77, 103, 104, 112, 164, 293; "intrigue" in Russia, 35, 36; monopoly of trade with Russia, 111; transfer of troops from east to west, 143, 146, 164, 191; POWs in Siberia, 159–60, 324 (n. 58); greatest threat to Bolshevik rule, 194; demands Soviet resistance to Allies, 201; defeat certain, 218; soldiers in Baltic region, 232, 233, 234, 247, 254–58, 269, 270; revolution in, 254, 278
Goltz, Rüdiger von der, 257, 339 (n. 87)
Gompers, Samuel, 35, 36–37, 66, 286
Gough, Sir Hubert, 257
Graves, William S., 69–70; on supporting Czechs from Omsk, 172; reports Kolchak would be overthrown without Allied support, 179; strict construction of *aide-mémoire*, 180; holds up rifles for Kolchak, 184
Great Britain, 49, 55, 62, 74; Wilson fear of war with, 13; involvement in Mexico, 16; aid to anti-Bolsheviks in south Russia, 76–77, 79, 80–82, 87, 90–94, 97–104; cooperation with U.S. intelligence, 108, 110, 114, 117–25; support for Semenov, 153; and agitation for intervention, 162, 165; marines at Murmansk, 193–94; plans to link north Russia and Siberia, 205–17; attempts to manipulate Wilson, 209; War Office, 210, 219; resistance to relaxing blockade, 249; economic competition with Americans, 249, 256, 270, 315 (n. 64); trade agreement with Soviet Russia, 291
Greene, Warwick: urges food for areas freed from Bolshevism, 245; on Latvian struggle against Bolshevism, 246; on German action against Bolsheviks, 255; against immediate departure of Ger-

mans from Latvia, 256, 257; urges aid to anti-Bolshevik Russians, 262; for sending an army to Baltic states, 267

Grenard, Fernand, 117, 119, 120

Grishin-Almazov, A. N., 176

Groome, John C., 265

Haiti: U.S. occupation of, 3, 11

Hale, Robert, 261

Halsey, Jesse, 225

Hapgood, Norman, 295

Harbin, 146, 147, 151, 172, 175

Hard, William, 289

Harding, Warren G., 287

Hardwick, Thomas, 239

Harper, Samuel N.: interprets Russian Revolution, 49–50; against use of "intervention," 158; on German POWs in Siberia, 324 (n. 58)

Harris, Ernest L.: urges removal of Grishin-Almazov, 176; worries socialists will foment strife, 177; advises against recognizing Omsk, 178; claims SRs practically Bolshevik, 178; on radicalism worse than reaction, 185

Hawaiian Islands, 13, 106

Hawkins, William, 291

Hays, Rev. Walter G., 43

Henderson, Loy, 241

Hermonius, E., 231, 264

Herter, Christian A., 242, 321 (n. 90)

Hitchcock, Gilbert, 228

Hoover, Herbert, *141*, 229–30; on Jews and Communism, 41; on food to Russians in Baltic area, 231–32; views of Bolshevism, 232, 236; portrays relief as apolitical, 232, 241–43; against invasion of Russia, 234, 335 (n. 9); on Americans against policing Europe, 235; experiences before 1917, 236; for U.S. Army feeding Russian POWs, 239; on expiration of ARA appropriation, 240; alleged sabotage of relief plan, 243; for quarantine of Bolshevism, 243; sees foreign food as counter to Bolshevik use of rations, 244; argues Estonians must support anti-Bolshevik Russians, 245; directed to feed "nonbolshevist areas," 245; urges military and naval protection of food to Riga, 246; for aid to and

recognition of Finland, 253; urges German occupation of Riga, 256–57, 339 (n. 87); says Baltic peoples lack experience in self-government, 261; agrees to supply food to Russians on credit, 264; glad food reached Russian army, 265; insists ARA fed only civilians, 265; urges special support of Iudenich, 266

Hoover-Nansen proposal, 242–44, 285

Hope, George, 247

Horodyski, Count, 81

Horvath, D. L., 151–52, 153, 175

House, Edward M., 29, 34, 36, 53, 62; suggests silence better than lying, 2; tolerance of Bolshevism, 4, 31; on Mexico, 15, 16, 17, 19, 20; on socialism and revolution, 30–31, 37; for recognizing Bolsheviks, 37, 66; for recognizing Provisional Government, 49; sympathy with Bakhmeteff, 54; for no more advances to Russia, 60; consults Bakhmeteff on address, 64; praises cleverly worded message, 67; on aid to anti-Bolsheviks in south Russia, 80–83, 90, 93–94; recommends secrecy, 81–83; on public opinion, 82, 148, 194; for dividing Russia, 93, 258, 259; on propaganda, 107–8, 317 (n. 14); on expedition to Siberia unpopular, 145; stresses projecting idealistic aims, 145; agrees with Bakhmeteff on Japanese intervention, 148; on anti-Japanese feeling in U.S., 148–49; supports relief mission to Siberia, 158; disagrees with Wilson handling of Russia, 172; on Soviet consent to intervention, 194–95; advises withdrawal from north Russia, 227; opposes Churchill proposal for anti-Bolshevik crusade, 229; says food is remedy for Bolshevism, 235; views relief as way to *modus vivendi* with Bolsheviks, 243; tries to use fear of Bolshevism to press for peace, 244; fears German evacuation will allow spread of Bolshevism, 254; supports Bullitt on Soviet peace terms, 284; against intervention, for relief, 293

House of Representatives: Committee on Appropriations, 237

Huerta, Victoriano, 15, 16, 17, 18, 19, 20, 21, 22, 58, 202, 280

Hungary, 128, 243, 250, 283, 285, 321 (n. 89)

Hunt, Frazier, 228

Huntington, W. Chapin, 94–95, 112, 235

Hurban, Vladimir, 164

Imbrie, Robert W., 124–25; on Finnish attack on Petrograd, 252–53

Immigration, 25; and radicalism, 37, 38, 41, 283

Industrial Workers of the World (IWW), 35, 36, 38

Intelligence services: unleashing of in Great War, 3, 129; in Soviet Russia, 5, 6, 107–29

International Harvester Company, 50, 235

International law, 14, 21, 22

Interparty League for the Restoration of Free Russia, 254

Intervention: 3–4, 13; definition of, 7–8, 302 (n. 38); avoidance of use of word, 158, 225

Irkutsk, 112, 146, 155, 157, 176, 184

Ironside, Edmund, 219

Ishii, Kikujiro, 161

Isolation, 14, 22

Isolationism, 5, 235, 237, 289

Iudenich, N. N., 75, 125, *142*, 241, 248, 251; negotiations with Mannerheim, 253; and recognition of Estonia, 261; and offensive against Petrograd, 261–69; valuation of U.S. support, 268; failings of, 268–69

Izvestiia, 110

Janin, Charles Maurice, 171

Japan, 4, 38, 190, 194; intervention in Siberia, 144–45, 146–51, 152–86 passim, 325 (n. 84); increases forces in Siberia, 166, 180; chases Reds from Vladivostok area, 168; friction with U.S. seen by Soviet leaders, 274, 275, 276, 279, 287

Jenkins, Douglas, 111, 116

Jewish-Bolshevik conspiracy, 33, 41–42

Jewish Daily Forward, 164

Jewish immigrants in U.S., 32, 41, 44, 275

Jews in Russia, 33, 41

Johnson, Hiram W.: denounces expedition to Siberia, 183; on expedition to north

Russia, 226–28; suspects U.S. bayonets to prop up Baltic states, 239; attacks undeclared war in Siberia, 297

Judson, William V.: warns Kaledin front is chimerical, 84; compares Russians to Negroes, 90; on Red Cross and propaganda, 109; on Robins' secret service, 110; urges sending U.S. troops to Siberia, 147

Jusserand, Jean Jules, 38, 99, 165, 167, 174, 204, 207; against U.S. constraining Allies, 217–18; argues anti-Bolshevik Russians are for intervention, 195–96

Justice, Department of, 21, 67

Kadet Party, 51, 76, 85, 88, 113, 116, *139*, 152, 173, 174, 179; calls for intervention, 200

Kalamatiano, Xenophon D., 107, 114–26, *139*

Kaledin, A. M., 78, 79, 81–93, 96, 98–102, 104, *139*, 154

Kamchatka, 287

Karakhan, L. M., 221, 276

Kazan, 124, 170, 176, 216

Kelley, Robert F., 320–21 (n. 81)

Kennan, George (writer), 162; antipathy to Bolsheviks, 44; criticism of Provisional Government, 54; on Siberian welcome of U.S. troops, 163; on equipment for Siberian winter, 168; on sympathy for socialists in Siberia, 174; anger at passivity of U.S. in Siberia, 186; on Bolsheviks as German agents, 198

Kennan, George F. (historian), 63, 307 (n. 4)

Kennedy, Zinaida Mackenzie, 125

Kerensky, A. F., 48, 75, 83, 113, 152, 176, 178, 185; Lansing skeptical of, 54; and Kornilov revolt, 55; attempts to recover power, 56–57, 78; opposes support for Kolchak, 181; treated coolly by Americans, 224

Keynes, John Maynard, 91

Kharlamov, V. A., 101

Khrushchev, Nikita, 7

King, William, 239

Knight, Austin M., 151, 159, 174

Kolchak, A. V., 69, 70, 72, 74, 75, 127, *142*, 157, 263, 266, 280, 283, 286, 287;

becomes dictator at Omsk, 179;
promises to repay foreign loans, 179;
expected to capture Moscow, 180, 244;
retreat across Siberia, 183–84; defeat
and execution, 185; rejects Iudenich-
Mannerheim agreement, 253
Konovalov, A. I., 159
Kornilov, Lavr, 55, 83–84, 88, 99, 102, 154
Kotlas, 212, 214
Krasnaia Gorka, 269
Kuban, 102, 243
Ku Klux Klan, 31

LaFollette, Robert, 297
Landfield, Jerome B.: doubts popular government can form army, 177
Lane, Franklin, 83, 177
Lansing, Robert, 99; religious beliefs, 4, 30,
33, 43; relationship to Wilson, 4, 58, 93;
for aid to anti-Bolsheviks, 5, 63–64,
87–89; on humanitarian intervention,
14, 22; rigid opposition to Bolsheviks,
25, 37; family background of, 29; on
revolutions and socialism, 30, 40; views
Bolsheviks as German agents, 36; on
menaces to social order, 37, 41, 43, 98;
for condemnation of Bolshevism, 39;
for supporting Provisional Government, 49, 55; on war between democracy and absolutism, 50; for military
dictator in Russia, 54, 85, 87; against
recognition of Bolsheviks, 58, 62, 66,
84–85, 85, 295; meets Bakhmeteff, 59,
60; lauds Bakhmeteff's tact and discretion, 68; opposes division of Russia,
68, 80, 85, 258–62, 268; for recall of
Judson, 84; approves propaganda in
Russia, 108; seeks information on anti-
Bolsheviks, 111, 121, 147; uncle of Allen
Dulles, 128, 234; on obstacles to intervention in Siberia, 150, 154; on using
Czechs in Siberia, 156, 158, 160; on
"sentimental" presentation of intervention, 160; values Kennan's advice, 162–
63; advises Wilson on demands for aid
to Russia, 165; on need to enlarge expedition to Siberia, 165–66; contrasts
"intervention" to relief of Czechs, 167;
says Russians view British as imperialistic, 167; on need to send Czechs winter

clothing, 168; abhorrence of Red Terror,
171; refuses to promise aid to Omsk,
175; declares U.S. for Russian government that meets foreign obligations,
178; approves declaration on aid to
Kolchak, 179–80; rules against recognition of Kolchak, 184; on public and
congressional opposition to Siberia
expedition, 184, 186; on Kolchak's lack
of popular support, 185; prefers autocracy to disorder, 185; favors Japan containing Bolshevism, 186; faith in democratic spirit of Russians, 191; more
favorable to intervention in north Russia than in Siberia, 196; warns British on
political interference at Archangel, 213;
commends Francis's judgment, 214; on
U.S. not at war with Bolsheviks, 219;
against Kerensky visit to U.S., 224; on
food and arms to defeat Bolshevism,
236; thinks Congress might impeach
Wilson, 237; on difficulty sending aid to
Baltic states, 239; regrets inability to pay
troops in Latvia, 240; on political conditions for relief, 242; on opposing socialism only where undemocratic, 245; for
relaxing blockade of Baltic states, 249;
on Congress and blockade of Russia,
251; on Finnish attack on Petrograd,
253–54; sees Bolshevism as greater
menace than Absolutism, 255; says U.S.
and Allies are allies of Germany in
Baltic region, 256; anticipates freeing of
Russia from Bolshevism, 258–59, 260;
agrees with Bakhmeteff on integrity of
Russia, 261–62; decides not to urge
transfer of arms to Iudenich, 263–64;
for supplying food to Iudenich, 265,
268; on Bullitt trip to Russia, 283–84
Latvia, 231, 232, 233, 239, 240, 245, 246,
247, 270; and German troops, 254–57;
and recognition question, 258–62
Latvian Riflemen, 118–20, 233
Latvian Socialist Soviet Republic, 233, 246
League of Nations, 40, 45, 126, 183, 249,
285, 297
Leffingwell, Russell C., 56, 60, 61, 64, 79,
82
Lenin, V. I., 37, 41, 45, 64, 86, 98, 201;
Decree on Peace, 35; on Bakhmeteff

Printed in the United States
786500002B

9 780807 849583